The History of Government

VOLUME II

The
History of Government
From the Earliest Times

VOLUME II

THE INTERMEDIATE AGES

S. E. Finer

OXFORD UNIVERSITY PRESS

Oxford University Press, Great Clarendon Street, Oxford OX2 6DP
Oxford New York
Athens Auckland Bangkok Bogota Bombay Buenos Aires
Calcutta Cape Town Dar es Salaam Delhi
Florence Hong Kong Istanbul Karachi
Kuala Lumpur Madras Madrid Melbourne
Mexico City Nairobi Paris Singapore
Taipei Tokyo Toronto Warsaw
and associated companies in
Berlin Ibadan

Oxford is a trade mark of Oxford University Press

Published in the United States
by Oxford University Press Inc. New York

First published 1997

British Library Cataloguing in Publication Data
Data available

Library of Congress Cataloging in Publication Data
Data applied for

ISBN 0-19-820665-8

3 5 7 9 10 8 6 4 2

Printed in Great Britain
on acid-free paper by
Biddles Ltd., Guildford and King's Lynn

CONTENTS

Book III

Overview

1. THE INTERMEDIATE AGES

*I*t is conventional to divide European history into Classical Antiquity, Modernity, and a 'Middle Ages' in between. Roughly speaking, the intermediate period spans the millennium AD 450–1450. But while many historians might agree that this threefold periodization could be applied to, say, China or India and other places, the respective periods would fall between different dates in each different country. For instance, whereas the European Middle Ages conventionally run between AD 476 and 1453, the Middle Ages in China are usually placed in the 400 'Years of Disunity' from the crumbling of the Han in AD 190 to the coming of the Sui in AD 581.

For all that, in so far as the evolution of political forms is concerned, this millennium does in certain respects constitute a significant and distinctive stage, not just for Western Europe but globally. It saw three developments: the emergence in all civilized areas of what Bellah[1] calls the 'Historic' religions; the destruction of the old established state structures and the creation, after a time of troubles, of completely novel ones, in some areas; and—finally—the interruption of this same process of state-and-community building by wild incursions of uncivilized hordes from the Eurasian 'heartland'.

2. THE POLITICAL RELEVANCE OF THE 'HISTORIC' RELIGIONS

These religions—neo-Zoroastrianism in Iran, Christianity in the Roman Empire, Islam in the Middle East, and even Buddhism in India and then China, shared the view that they and they alone worshipped the 'true' God and/or professed the 'true way'. They were *exclusive*, and in Europe and the Middle East as far as the Jaxartes and north India, rulers enforced them on their subjects under more or less severe sanctions for the first time in history.

These historic religions are to greater or lesser degree *congregational*, that is to say, they are communities of believers in which every individual has his own personal stake in his redemption, as pressing and as valid as that of any

[1] R. N. Bellah, *Sociologists at Work: Essays on the Craft of Social Research* (Basic Books, New York, 1964).

of his co-religionists and, equally, of his rulers. The religion was not a mere cult whose rituals were performed by special persons for the benefit of the people, but a matter of direct personal participation in divine worship. The individuals who professed the common beliefs formed what the Jews called the *kahal*, Christians the *ecclesia*,[2] Muslims the *umma*, and (more restrictively here) Buddhists the *sangha*.

So, on the one hand, there had emerged mass communities of believers which, severally, maintained that outside their particular confession there was no salvation (*extra ecclesiam nulla salus*), and on the other, rulers who sought to impose those confessions on their subjects. This was something quite new. Not even the Jews had gone as far as that. (The Laws of Moses were obligations for the Jews alone, the gentiles could be saved by observing only the seven Laws of the Sons of Noah.) How severely rulers enforced the religion varied according to the religion and the times. The Sassanians revived Zoroastrianism and made it a highly organized and at times harshly persecuting Church. The Christian confession in Western Europe and the Byzantine Empire was fiercely and ubiquitously enforced. Islam, on the other hand (save at certain epochs), simply accorded Muslims social, civil, and fiscal privilege and inflicted corresponding disabilities on non-Muslim subjects. Chinese Buddhism and Taoism never attained to the status of state orthodoxies and in any case were protean enough to absorb and be absorbed into the more general religious beliefs of the country.

The political effects of what we can summarily call state-enforced religious orthodoxy were nothing short of revolutionary. To begin with, as in ancient Israel, the believers felt a direct involvement in how their rulers conformed to the principles of their religion. Even their secular policies could be perceived as inconsistent with those principles, and cult practices and observances were obviously so. To the extent that the congregants felt strongly and deeply about such things, the religious community now became concerned with the governance of the state: very strongly in Christendom and in Islam, less so among the subjects of the Sassanians of Iran, and least of all among China's Buddhists because of their monastic structure. By the same token, these religions (again excepting Chinese Buddhism) played a prime role in legitimizing or delegitimizing rulers. The Arian Visigoth and Vandal kings in Gaul and Spain were not legitimate in the eyes of their Catholic subjects, a Sunni caliph was illegitimate in the eyes of many Shiite sectarians, and so forth. Relatedly, mass religion now provided a popular base and ideology for loyalty inside a political boundary and/or across it;

---

[2] 'Church', or 'Kirk' (Scottish), derive from the Greek adjective *kyriakos*, as in *kyriakon doma* (the Lord's house).

western Christian states found a common bond in antipathy to Greek Orthodox Christianity in the Byzantine Empire, which in its turn could rely on its subjects' orthodoxy to conduct its unceasing struggle against Muslim neighbours who, in their turn, reacted with fury on the Crusaders and Byzantines who threatened their religion. But the mass religion was perhaps more politically important as a divisive force than as one making for solidarity. By enforcing a religion or a particular version of it that his subjects found repugnant, a ruler could alienate them and, at worst, could drive them into open rebellion. We meet any number of similar examples when we come to explore the Byzantine Empire and the Caliphate. State-enforced orthodoxy implies state-persecuted heresy. The heretics were unlikely to forgive their persecutors, so states could be torn apart by theological controversy with alien invaders at their very gates.

Yet another political effect of state-enforced orthodoxy was to give a new stimulus to colonization, or domination, and as a by-product, the 'domestication' of outer peoples. Peaceable evangelization was matched by forced conversion by conquest—one thinks of Charlemagne's mass baptism of the conquered Saxons, the rule of the Teutonic Knights in East Prussia and Lithuania, or the Crusades; and the Muslims, much less inclined to convert non-believers by force, nevertheless believed it their sacred duty to carry *jihad* from the Dar-Al-Islam to the Dar-al-Harb.

We may conclude by noting three epiphenomena of the historic religions and the enforcement of state-orthodoxies. The first is that governments, under the sway of religious zeal or picked on by those who were over-zealous, began for the first time in history to deprive, or humiliate, or mulct, or torment or mutilate, stab, and burn to death not only those of their subjects who rebelled against them, and not only those who did not outwardly conform to the prescribed rituals, but even those who simply held different religious opinions from their own. This odious practice sprang from the historic religions' view, unlike that of their predecessors, that worldly life was merely a transient probation for the real—and eternal—life to come, and to their unshakeable conviction that only by right thinking, not just good conduct, could the human soul be saved from eternal torment hereafter. The persecution of heretics was a feature of Sassanid Zoroastrianism but, especially, of Christianity. For this it has to thank St Augustine of Hippo.[3]

Another feature is the re-emergence of the organized professional priesthoods as a check on the lay ruler. Known to us in the Archaic Age in the Middle East and in Egypt, but insignificant in the Graeco-Roman world

---

[3] P. Brown, *Augustine and Hippcratus* (Fodor, 1967), 234–8; and 240 'the first theorist of the Inquisition'.

and in China, these now reappear, but vastly more autonomous and power-ful than before. In some societies they were a body of 'learned men', not a formal or hierarchical corporation, but none the less highly influential because of their command over the masses: the *ulema* who form what is spoken of as not 'the Muslim priesthood' but as merely the 'religious institution' was of this kind. The Brahmins of the various states into which India was divided were similar. The Buddhist *sangha*, however, consisting of monks and coalitions of their monasteries, could play—as in Japan—a foremost political role. The most organized of all these religious establish-ments were undoubtedly the Greek Orthodox Church in the Byzantine Empire and, even more independent and destined almost to become the master of the secular authorities, the Catholic Church as organized by the Papacy. In every one of the states we shall be examining these religious establishments or organized churches introduced a new element into the political structures and processes. And even in China, where, as we shall see, Buddhism failed to sustain its early promise as a countervailing power to the emperorship, a reinvigorated Confucianism became a (laic) functional equivalent of Christianity and Islam not least in respect to the third of the epiphenomena—culture. As belief systems, Christianity, Islam, Bud-dhism, Hinduism, and Neo-Confucianism came to mould popular outlooks and life-styles into distinctive and diverse culture-worlds. They created a social thought-frame which nourished but also constrained the various forms taken by the exercise of political power.

3. NEW STATES FOR OLD

Early in the third century the major political structures began to collapse one after the other. The Han dynasty was extinguished early in that century and China thenceforward experienced some 400 years of political fragmen-tation. In the fifth century the Western Roman Empire slowly disintegrated and at roughly the same time the Gupta Empire of northern India was invaded and destroyed by Eurasian nomad hordes. The two great states that still survived—the East Roman Empire and its rival and neighbour, Sassa-nian Persia—were at each other's throats when both were overwhelmed from an unexpected quarter. The Arabs had arrived. Persia, the Levant, and North Africa fell to them. By then the only one of the ancient states to survive was a (shrunken) Byzantium in Anatolia and the Balkans.

There was to be no successor to the Gupta Empire in India, which was destined to remain a congeries of rival kingdoms. The truncated East Roman Empire turned definitively into the Greek-speaking, Orthodox Christian, bureaucratized autocracy which we call the Byzantine Empire.

However, elsewhere there was territorial integration, not disintegration. Thus, just before the Arab assaults began, the ferocious Sui dynasty (589–618) and the T'ang (618–907) had reunited China on traditional lines and presided over its great classical flowering.

But elsewhere the collision between barbarian invaders and the classical structures led neither to destruction (the Gupta) nor reconstitution (Byzantium, old China), but to wholly new forms of polity. The Arabs first ruled, as predatory overlords, by the administrative techniques they found in place. But as they consolidated their hold, their own tribal organization transformed itself along autocratic lines. However, what made the Caliphate different from any precedent bureaucratic autocratic empire was its religious component. Islam supposed a theocracy. A tension arose between religion and *raison d'état* not dissimilar from that which had plagued ancient Israel. This tension and the subsequent symbiosis that flowed from it made the Caliphate different from previous forms of state in that region.

Different too from the Late Roman Empire were its successors in Western Europe. Here tribal kingships settled into the place of the imperial administrations, inaugurating a long, barbarous interlude in which literacy almost perished and political authority was atomized. Not till the middle of the tenth century did it begin to reintegrate itself, and when it did so it was in an unprecedented way, in what—to use a contested term—is described as feudalism. By the thirteenth century England, the Kingdom of the Franks, and Sicily, for instance, were feudal monarchies. Out of the feudal kingdoms in England and France were to emerge, around 1450 or 1500, the 'national state'. This was yet another novel form.

As these *regna* began to irradiate the uncivilized tribesmen on their borders the latter, ruled by kinglets or war-leaders, acquired traces of their culture, and were induced—or forced—to become Christian. So, to resist this aggression they organized themselves politically along similar lines to the *regna*. Slav states in Bohemia and Poland and Hungary emerged. In the Scandinavian lands powerful nobles subdued their rivals to emerge as kings of, respectively, Denmark, Norway, and Sweden and were evangelized to become Christians during this process. While Christian states were being formed like this in the north and east of Europe, the Spanish kingdoms of northern Spain finally broke the Arab power to their south, conquering it as far as the Kingdom of Granada by 1248. Meanwhile, from 1095 the variously styled rulers of the *regna* and the great principalities had been carrying fire, sword, and the Cross into the Levant to form the crusading feudal kingdoms there.

All the foregoing had been the work of Latin, that is, Roman Catholic, Christendom, but the Orthodox Church of Byzantium had not been backward. Its missionaries evangelized the South Slavs of the Balkans and penetrated into Rus. These Slav territories took the empire as their political model, particularly as concerned the relationship of Church and sovereign. So arose primitive kingdoms in Bulgaria and Serbia, and various principalities inside Russia. This great area of Byzantine irradiation has been aptly called 'the Byzantine Commonwealth'. But as a result of the Fourth Crusade's sack of Constantinople in 1204 the empire became too weak to resist new Muslim assaults. This time the challenge no longer came from the Arabs but from a new race whom the Arabs had converted to Islam. They were the Turks.

In the eleventh century the Seljuk Turks had conquered Persia, ejected other (and Shi'ite) Turks from Baghdad, and taken their place as the protectors of the caliph. These Seljuks revived the military power of Islam. At Manzikert (1071) they destroyed the Byzantine army and seized half Anatolia. They inflicted the decisive defeat a century later at Myriocephalon (1176). Thenceforward it was the Turks who ruled the Middle East. They extinguished the Crusader kingdoms, and it was they too who established a new military dynasty in Egypt, the Mamluks, which soon became the mainstay of Muslim power in the region. In Anatolia, however, the Seljuks were destroyed by the Mongols in 1243. Then, as this Mongol suzerainty waned, local power passed to another group of Turks already installed there. These were the Ottoman Turks, and it was they who extinguished the Byzantine Empire and then, passing on to conquer the Arab lands, Mamluk Egypt, and North Africa, created the powerful Ottoman Empire that was to last some 500 years.

Long before all this was happening, and on the other side of the world, the reconstituted Chinese empire of Sui and T'ang (589–975) had meanwhile reached hitherto unsurpassed heights in military power and the civilized arts. Itself the recipient of Indian Buddhism, it became its transmitter. China exported its art, and above all, its script and its literature to its neighbours and provided them with a political model. All these were carried by its armies and its colonists into its deep south. Around this great power primitive states formed themselves in defensive reaction, among the Tibetans eastwards and the Turkic and Mongolian tribes north of the Wall. Its influence was most significant, however, in Korea and Japan. While Buddhist missionaries evangelized Korea, its three kingdoms emulated Chinese models, and their court language, literature, and script were Chinese. Korea acted as the bridge between China and Japan. These islands enter very late into the world history. Until the third century Japan was semi-tribal, with imperial authority residing in one of the clans. The Chinese script and Buddhism were introduced before the formation of a Japanese state in any meaningful sense. This did not begin until 604 at the earliest, but is better dated at 646. This saw the imperial court initiate the 'Taika Reform', a grandiose measure designed to establish a centralized and bureaucratized imperial monarchy, exactly like the T'ang. But the political and social reality was one of bitterly hostile warring clans and the new political order became more and more nominal. When the Japanese reality caught up with mere form, in the eleventh century, its polity became quite unlike China's and much more like Western Europe: it was *feudal.*

4. MIGRATIONS AND INVASIONS

The same thing that had crippled or destroyed the civilized empires of the Classical Age went on to obliterate or at least retard the formation of their successor states. That thing was the irruption of waves of uncivilized tribesmen, mostly from what the geopolitician Mackinder called 'the heartland', the centre of the great Eurasian land-mass. From there they could fan south, east, and west, like so many fingers of barbarism, into the outer (and civilized) fringe of the continent: into China, India, Persia, the Middle East, and Europe.

In the eleventh century the kingdoms of northern and western Europe and the statelets inside the Holy Roman Empire were beginning to settle down, Islam was being pushed back in Spain, eastern Europe was being Christianized and soon to form kingdoms of its own. But the movements of Asian peoples did not cease. In the Far East the Jürchen, a mongoloid people, wrested control of north China from the Sung dynasty and set up a powerful state of its own. And as we have already noted, the various Turkish tribes had fragmented the Caliphate and occupied most of the Anatolian plateau where they established a well-organized Seljuk state, just as in Egypt they established the exotic slave-soldier state of the Mamluks.

Then, as all those states were settling down—including nascent ones in south Russia—there came another of those devastations from the steppes. A Mongol, Temujin, united all the clans under his supreme rule as Chinghiz Khan ('most mighty Khan'), and under his rule and that of his sons China was conquered and the Sung dynasty extinguished. Persia fell, to be ruled in future by the Mongol ilkhans. They pressed westwards through conquered Persia to sack Baghdad and execute the caliph (1258). They smashed the Seljuk state of Anatolia and put its rulers under tribute. They were turned back only in Syria where the Baybar, the Mamluk, beat them in 1206 at Ain Jalui. Mongol armies also penetrated into Europe. They occupied southern and central Russia where, on the Volga, they organized their state as the Golden Horde. They smashed the armies of Poland and Hungary and of the

Germans (at Liegnitz, 1241) and only withdrew because of succession problems after Chinghiz's death.

These conquests aborted the political evolution of south Russia, ended the Caliphate, broke up the Seljuk state in Anatolia, and threw state-building into confusion in south-eastern and eastern Europe. In China, after the not-unconstructive reign of the Mongol Kubla Khan, they reduced the state to confusion and finally to open revolt. The Chinese, led by a ferocious adventurer Chu Yüan-Chang, drove the Mongols far beyond the Wall and founded the aggressive Ming dynasty (1368). In Anatolia the Turkish marcher lords made war on the Byzantine Empire and by 1393 had created an empire in Anatolia and the Balkans, where Bayazid brought Serbia, Bosnia, and Bulgaria under his yoke when once again—and for the last time—the Asian nomads launched another assault. Timur (Tamerlaine) overran Eastern Persia, defeated the Golden Horde, took Baghdad (1393), and in 1402 defeated Sultan Bayazid at Ankara. But except in Central Asia his conquests did not survive his death. All they did, as far as the development of the new states is concerned, was delay the consolidation of the Ottoman Empire for half-a-century and, by shattering the Golden Horde, strengthen the nascent Duchy of Muscovy.

5. THE STATE SYSTEM AT THE CLOSE OF THE MIDDLE AGE

If we start in, say, the eighth century, we find the following. *China*: the powerful expansionist T'ang Empire, stretching into Central Asia. The *Caliphate*: from the area where T'ang influence ended all the way to the Atlantic coasts of North Africa and Spain, an over-extended bureaucratic autocracy limited by its religious establishment and heretical dissidents, and hamstrung by its vast distances. The *Byzantine* Empire: Orthodox and Christian, confined to the Balkans and Anatolia (and toeholds in Italy), a bureaucratic caesaropapist autocracy, struggling for survival against Slavs and Bulgars and Arabs. The European West is in its darkest age. It is covered by ephemeral German kingships. Its Scandinavian north is still pagan and tribalized, and so are its eastern borders beyond the Elbe. Not till the eleventh century will durable polities arise here, and then on the basis of a quite novel principle: feudalism.

By 1453, the date when Constantinople fell to the Turks, the situation is far different. China is a united, wealthy, and enormously vigourous empire under the Ming. Japan has cast off its imitativeness and is a warlike feudal state, but racked by terrible internal conflicts. India is still a congeries of petty states. In Central Asia the Timurids still rule, but west of them is now a great Muslim state stretching up to the borders of Hungary and the

Adriatic Sea—the durable, militaristic Ottoman Empire which still has two centuries of aggression before it. In furthest eastern Europe the Duchy of Muscovy is on the attack against the Golden Horde and shortly to conquer the Ukraine and form the beginnings of a Russian national state, caesaro-papist like Byzantium. Powerful kingdoms have been formed in Poland, Bohemia, and Hungary. However, in the middle zone of Europe, from the Baltic to the Mediterranean, there is no consolidated territorial state but only principalities and city-states, among which Venice, perhaps, is supreme in power and empire. In the West the feudal polity is in its last throes. Here, unlike in China, where the successor states to the Han Empire were reconstituted into a unitary state—that is, where the empire was success-fully revived—western and northern Europe were divided into what by now are national states, and so they would remain.

PART I

Eastern Europe and the Middle East

I

The Byzantine Empire (*c.*1000)

We talk of Byzantium and the Byzantine Empire, but their inhabitants never did. They called themselves *Romaioi*, and if they called the empire anything at all they called it Romania. Byzantium had been the site of Constantine's new capital in the east—Constantinople—or, making better sense for our present concern, New Rome. At first it was the alternative capital of the one and sole emperor; then the capital of one of the two co-emperors. Although after AD 476 there were no more co-emperors at Rome, this was not unprecedented; all it meant was that one sole emperor was governing from Constantinople. The great difference from 376 or 276 was that North Africa, Iberia, Gaul, and Britain were now lost to rude barbarian kings. But all the provinces east of a line drawn from the Danube through the Adriatic to the gulf of Sirte survived intact, subject to the same regime, governed by the same laws and in the same way as in the past. In brief: the Roman Empire had shrunk—but it was still there. And it comprised the richer, more populous and highly urbanized provinces of its former self.

The period when the institutions of this empire were most characteristically 'Byzantine' lies between 610 and 1204. During this long period of six centuries, although some institutions palpably altered and the imperial diadem might change hands very rapidly, the essential nature of the regime—almost the purest type of Palace polity we are likely to encounter—did not change at all.

1. CHRONOLOGY

The initial phase, in which it was still the Roman Empire, culminated in the reign of JUSTINIAN (527–65). Nephew of an illiterate soldier-usurper, Justinian sums up the aspirations of this epoch. He still spoke Latin, unlike most of his subjects, who spoke Greek. Rigidly Orthodox, he forced this doctrine on the Monophysite Syrians and Egyptians, who responded with hatred. To contemporaries, his greatness lay no doubt in his foreign policy. Holding off the Persians to the east, he not only repelled the newly come Slav invaders on the Danube but reconquered Italy, North Africa, and the southern part of Spain. But his enduring monument was the codification of Roman law undertaken at his command. His Codes were the vehicle by which a unique element in Roman government was preserved, transmitted to medieval Western Europe, and finally became the basis for most of Western Europe's legal codes up to and including the present day.

For the rest, his work fell to pieces. The Slavs and other barbarians renewed their pressure to the north, the newly arrived Lombards recovered half Italy, and finally the imperial succession itself collapsed in a welter of murders and usurpations. The empire was on the point of succumbing to Persia when HERACLIUS (610–41), son of the governor (*exarch*) of Africa, seized the throne and defeated Persia decisively. But at the very moment of this great victory both Persia and the empire alike were assailed by a horde of barbarians from the one area where neither had ever questioned military security—the south. The Arabs attacked, and without let or pause took all Persia up to Oxus and Indus, while from the empire they snatched Spain, the entire south Mediterranean littoral, Egypt, and Syria. The Arabs even pressed on every year between 673 and 677 to besiege Constantinople itself. They were repulsed but the empire now consisted of only the Anatolian heartland, the Balkans between the Danube and the Adriatic, and some fragments of Italy . With this débâcle the old East Roman Empire fades out and the distinctively Byzantine phase of the polity's history commences.

In foreign affairs, that history consists of literally never-ending warfare against Islam in the east, the south, and the great Mediterranean islands, and successive waves of barbarous Bulgars, Magyars, Serbs, Russians, Petchenegs, and the like in the north. As if this were not enough, these foes were joined in the eleventh century by a third force, from the West: the Normans, the Genoese and Venetians, and the Crusaders.

The final Arab siege of Constantinople in 717–18 was raised by LEO III (717–41) the Isaurian, who was able to found a brief dynasty. But success abroad was ruined by religious division at home, which so weakened the state that the Bulgarians were able to defeat the empire in the Balkans while the Arabs established command of the seas. For this is the period of the Iconoclast controversy, between those who rejected the cult of icons and those who supported it; very much a battle between the forces of the court and superior ranks of the army against the monks and the common people. It lasted an entire century (and ended with the victory of the image-worshippers, the Iconodules). It was not the only source of weakness, for the economy was in very bad shape. Plague ravaged the cities for the next two centuries and they fell into steep decline. An Arabian geographer, writing in the ninth century, observed that Anatolia contained only five cities—Ephesus, Nicaea, Amorium, Ancyra, and Samala.[1]

Leo's dynasty was extinguished with the deposition of the Empress IRENE (797–802). The empire lost command of the seas to the Arabs and suffered severe defeats from the Bulgarians. But in the tenth century the imperial armies of the Macedonian dynasty (867–1057) took the offensive on all fronts. The great emperors were BASIL I (867–86), ROMANUS LECA-PENUS (919–44), BASIL II (976–1025), called *Bulgaroctonos* (the 'Bulgar slayer') because of the terrible defeat he inflicted on that people, NICEPHORUS PHOCAS (963–69), and his assassin, JOHN I TZIMISCES (969–76), the great victor over the Arabs. Antioch was recovered along with Crete and Cyprus. The christianization of the Balkans and Russia went on apace. At home the Justinian code was again revised as the Basilika code (887–93), so as to be more accessible to the common people. Trade and commerce experienced a massive revival. By the eleventh century, when there were no cities worth the name in the West, little commerce or currency, and the state had all but disintegrated, Constantinople's population was some 200,000 or more, and the city was the best-administered, the most powerful, and the wealthiest place in that world and its unrivalled commercial and financial capital.[2]

But after John I's death, when the emperorship devolved on the nieces of Basil II and their successive consorts, the armies and fleets were run down. And although the Caliphate was now in full decay, it was being replaced by another formidable menace—the Turkish tribesmen steadily advancing into eastern Anatolia. So far the empire had regarded them as a nuisance rather than a threat, but in 1071 ROMANUS IV DIOGENES (1067–71) was totally defeated at Manzikert. Half Anatolia passed to the Turks and with it the great recruiting grounds of the Byzantine armies.

Manzikert is the decisive date in the decline of the empire. Yet we say this only with hindsight. For, despite the continued menace of the Turks, of

---

[1] Quoted in C. Mango, *Byzantium: The Empire of New Rome* (Weidenfeld and Nicolson, London, 1980), 73.

[2] S. Runciman, *The Emperor Romanos Lecapenus and his Reign* (CUP, Cambridge, 1963), 21–2; *Cambridge Medieval History* [hereafter referred to as *CMH*], ed. J. M. Hussey (CUP, Cambridge, 1966), iv.2, p. 79.

the newly formed Slav kingdoms, and finally of the Normans of south Italy, it was held together and staged a remarkable military recovery under the gallant and resourceful ALEXIUS I COMNENUS (1081–1118), his capable son JOHN II (1118–43) and grandson MANUEL (1143–80). But the institutions of the empire were subtly changing and so was the social structure. In the interior of Anatolia the local notables had now blossomed into 'Great Families', and these were rapidly absorbing the yeoman farmers on whom the imperial armies had depended. This military-minded aristocracy found itself increasingly at odds with the civil service aristocrats of the capital, and indeed the Comneni themselves were its representatives.

The age of the Comneni shows the immense recuperative powers of the empire. But the hundred years' revival after Manzikert ended as it began when in 1176 Manuel was utterly routed by the Turks at Myriocephalon. When he died in 1180, to be succeeded by an infant, the accustomed wars for the succession broke out again. It was on this state, weakened by insurgency, by the secession of local magnates, by Norman aggression, Bulgarian insurrection, and the Third Crusade, that there fell the predators of the Fourth Crusade. They did not get near Jerusalem but instead they attacked Christian Constantinople in 1204. Having captured it in one of the worst orgies of destruction, rape, and looting in history, they then partitioned the empire between them.[3]

The year 1204 marks the end of an era. True, the Latins were driven out and the empire reconstituted—but it was not the same empire as before. Smaller, poorer, dependent on the goodwill of local magnates for its armed forces, impoverished by the loss of its trade routes, and, always, threatened by the Turks, it lost province after province, then became the vassal of the Turkish Empire, until it was reduced simply to the city and its purlieus. In 1453 the Turkish army invested it. The newly perfected cannon brought down the obsolete curtain walls that had resisted so many enemies for so long, and the last remnant of a once great political community disappeared from history.

Before moving on to consider the nature of this Byzantine state, it is important to note three geographical factors that underlay all its history and help to explain both its greatness and its downfall. To begin with, Constantinople formed a crossroads; it held the sea-lanes from east to west and the land-bridge from north to south. Hence it became a vast entrepôt. After the silkworm had been smuggled in from China, it became a great textile manufacturing centre as well. Though the Arab conquest temporarily

---

[3] S. Runciman, *A History of the Crusades*, 3 vols. (CUP, Cambridge, 1951; reissued Peregrine, 1978), iii. 123, for a vivid description.

interrupted the eastern trade, it also destroyed the Syrian merchant marine so that, though the empire lost, Constantinople gained. Gradually the eastern trade resumed, coming to the city via Anatolia or through the Black Sea port of Trebizond. Meanwhile a northern trade was developing also. The Chazars brought slaves and dried fish to Cherson from the steppes, while the Russians brought them in down the Dnieper. From the Baltic and central Europe metals and amber flowed down to Thessalonika. The political significance of all this is that it permitted the authorities to raise vast sums from transit dues (the only easy method of indirect taxation open to these primitively agrarian states), and what is more, to collect these sums in cash. Constantinople was full of gold, and because of this gold the government was able to maintain its formidable armies and back up its wily diplomacy among the barbarian peoples at a time when Europe was a primitive, poverty-stricken natural economy, where even silver was scarce, let alone a golden bezant. But just as the mercantile and manufacturing basis of Constantinople provided the sinews of war and diplomacy up to the eleventh century, so the subsequent alteration in the trade routes and the rise of the Italian merchant marines denatured them. The Seljuk Turks blocked the ways to Trebizond and Asia Minor, so that the Eastern trade was diverted southward towards Syria, whence it was carried directly to the West by the Genoese and Venetians. When the Comneni had to raise ready money quickly to pay their mercenaries, their concessions to these Italian traders undermined the empire's fiscal base. They paid only 4 per cent in customs duties whereas everybody else—including the subjects of the Empire—paid 10 per cent.

But the location of the city was of vital *military* significance, also. The Arabs had seized the chief urbanized provinces of the empire, so that now its only two sizable cities were Thessalonika and the capital. With its more than 200,000 people, Constantinople was at once the great entrepôt, the centre of administration, the focus of the political process, and the Holy City of 300 churches and innumerable sacred relics. Whoever possessed Constantinople possessed the empire. Now the straits protected her from the Arab land armies; and they are so narrow that they were easy to hold against blockade. And in the only other direction from which the city could be assaulted, landwards to the west, Constantine and successive emperors built vast walls; in fact there were three sets of such walls, so that the fortifications were some 190 to 207 feet deep as well as 100 feet high. Again and again enemies broke through from Adrianople but were thrown back at these walls; so that after a time the enemy hosts—Avars (626), Arabs (673–77 and 717–18), Bulgarians (813, 913)—had no choice but to retire. Then, from this unvanquished centre of population and wealth, the emperors would once again tighten the reins of government, re-equip the armies, and renew the battle.

Finally, though the fate of the empire depended on the inviolability of the city, the city's fate depended on its hinterland in Asia Minor. It was here that the eastern trade-roads ran; it was here that the bulk of the land tax was collected; and above all, it was from here that came the manpower of the imperial armies. When the Turks overran it at Manzikert they cut off all three. The subsequent Turkish victory at Myriocephalon, a century later, made the loss irretrievable, and from that time the shorn and parcelled empire slid into vassalage.

2. THE NATURE OF THE BYZANTINE POLITY

Unlike many other polities described in this book, the Byzantine Empire made no inventions in the art of government. It was an almost pure type of Palace polity, akin to the Late Roman Empire from which it was sprung, and to the Chinese Empire, its contemporary. It is included here for three reasons. First, it really would be absurd to leave it out, for it maintained the same political community and essentially the same regime for nearly 1,000 years (counting up to 1204), and in somewhat altered form for another two centuries. Polities of this durability are rare in the history of government and deserve study for this alone. Secondly, it is almost the paradigm case of the Palace type of polity. And finally, it stood out so strikingly from its contemporary neighbours that it throws light on the nature of their polities as well as its own.

The heyday of the empire, in the tenth–eleventh centuries, was contemporaneous with the emergence of Western Europe from the Dark Ages. It was ending just as William was taking England, when France was hardly more than a place-name, and when the popes and the emperors were just embarking on the war of the Investitures. Bréhier is worth quoting here:

The originality of Byzantium in medieval Europe lies in the fact that until the thirteenth century it and it alone presented a centralized type of state where the volition of the central government reached the most distant provinces and was capable of imposing one single purpose on populations and races who spoke different languages and sometimes had divergent interests.

The Byzantine state differed from the ancient Sassanid Empire, which was decentralized, with its great feudalistic dominions and even from the Muslim states with their theocratic basis, although these borrowed a good deal from it. Byzantium differed above all from the western countries, where the notion of the state, of the 'Public Thing', had disappeared, stifled by the development of the man-to-man relationship, and was to be recovered with such labour only because Byzantium had preserved Roman imperial law. Thus it was that only in Byzantium and to some extent in the Muslim states 'did there continue to exist officials who exercised a portion of the authority of the State and were accountable to it . . . This notion of the State was confounded with that of Palatine status which, in theory, bound the officials to the Emperor more closely than if they had simply been officers of the state. But as servants of the Basileus they were *ipso facto* slaves of the public interest, *douloi tou koinou*.'[4]

This Byzantine state greatly resembles the Late Roman and the Chinese empires. It is a Palace-type government with a highly structured standing army and bureaucracy. As time went by, however, two elements that were either absent or subordinate to the palace at the outset began to develop a modest degree of independence. One was the Orthodox Church, although to the very end the emperor remained preponderant. The other was a landed nobility in the interior, which, non-existent at the outset, grew up in the ninth and tenth centuries and, reflecting military priorities, challenged the palatine bureaucracy.

The organized Church and the presence of the landed class could act as some intermittent and weakly kinds of curb on the emperors. More importantly—and here the empire simply continues Late Rome, while it contrasts with the Chinese Empire—Byzantium was law-bound. Justinian's codes were revived and reformulated; unlike the T'ang code of China (see below), which confined itself to criminal and administrative matters and contained almost no civil law, the Byzantine codes did. Thereby they brought contract and property within the purview of the judicial system; and although the emperor, *qua* living law and subject to absolutely no legal restraints whatsoever, could change the law whenever he found it conveni-ent, it was nevertheless the convention that he would be bound by the laws in force.

Since there were no institutional outlets for popular discontent, the governments of all three empires frequently encountered popular riot or even rebellion. In China this took the form of great peasant risings, some on a national scale. Herein it differed from both Imperial Rome and the Byzantine Empire. The risings which took place there were got up by some pretender to the diadem, or were religious revolts like the Paulicians'. But whereas such risings were comparatively rare, riot and rebellion in the capital was very common indeed, and it was something every emperor had to watch out for with the greatest care.

---

[4] L. Bréhier, *Les Institutions de l'Empire Byzantin* (Albin Michel, Paris, 1949), 128–9.

Let me now summarize the nature of this polity according to the criteria laid down in our typology.[5]

It is a Palace-type polity. The ruler's legitimacy is of supernatural origin; he is *Isapostolos* ('Equal to the Apostles'). True, he is 'elected by acclamation', but this is an epiphany, not an act of choosing.

The political process is characteristic of the pure Palace type—a matter of routines on the one hand and conspiracies on the other—all within the confines of the palace. The emperor's relationship to such institutions as might restrain him—Church, army, the street—find their political focus and power inside the palace.

The palace is served by two sophisticated sets of decision-implementers—the standing army and the complex and professional bureaucracy. These will come to have different viewpoints and interests in the eleventh century and the palace politics of those years will revolve around the clash.

There are no procedural constraints on the emperor, either at the central level or from the localities, where both substantively and procedurally the local authorities have very limited discretion. The emperor is, however, subject—but only by convention—to certain substantive constraints: there are limits to how far he can push the cult and the Church, and he is supposed to observe the laws—particularly the civil laws—in force. This offers security in matters of life, contract, and property.

3. THE TERRITORIAL FRAMEWORK

Circa 1000 the empire consisted, broadly speaking, of Asia Minor, the Balkans from Adriatic to Aegean up to the Danube, some areas in south Italy, and the islands of Cyprus and Crete. Altogether, its population might have reached 20 million—a very large number of subjects by the standards of that day, and all the more significant in that they formed a single political unit, unlike the fragmented early-feudal *regna* in the West. For the central political fact is that from his palace in Constantinople the emperor governed the empire directly without intermediaries. But this required imperial agents in the localities. These were the *strategoi*, and their jurisdictions were called 'themes'. This theme organization is said to have been initiated by Heraclius. But this is controversial. It seems it just crept in and was then systematized.

The reason lay in the military consequences of the Persian wars and then the Arab conquests. For want of wealth the empire had to replace the paid standing armies of the previous era with indigenous troops, while to

---

[5] 'The Conceptual Prologue', ss. 2 and 3.1.

accommodate the disastrous effects of the loss of the Egyptian grain supply it developed and maintained peasant smallholdings. The vital element in the new arrangement lay in the settlement of farmer-soldiers in the themes: indeed, a *thema* originally meant simply a division of troops. The government made hereditary grants of land (*stratiotika ktemata*) to families on condition that they gave hereditary military service, and at first there were but four very large themes, all in Asia Minor. But by the end of the tenth century they numbered twenty-six, and became still more numerous later. One reason for this was the expansion of the empire under the Macedonian dynasty; the other was that the emperors subdivided existing themes because they rightly feared over-large concentrations of power in the hands of a *strategos*. The themes continued to function as a military resource until the fall of Constantinople in 1204. Their military aspect will be discussed later. At this point we consider them *qua* units of local government.

The *strategos* combined the military and the civil functions. He was served by an *officium* consisting of a military staff together with civil officials. But the theme also housed central government officials who were directly responsible to the central authorities, such as the *chartularius*, who kept the military roll and supervised soldiers' pay. Again, judges (*praetors* or *kritai*) were answerable, on appeal, to the courts in the capital.

The tax administration stood apart. It is described later and for now it is enough to note only that both assessment and collection were carried out by central government officials (or government-licensed tax-farmers).[6]

The way the *strategoi* received their salaries provides a most striking illustration of their dependency on the central government. In the western, less important themes the *strategoi* were paid from their local revenues but not so in the militarily and politically critical Asian ones. Once every year their *strategoi* filed in their order of precedence past a long table covered with sacks of gold coins, and took their salary from the emperor's very own hands.[7]

4. THE CENTRAL GOVERNMENT

4.1. *The Emperor: Dignity and Powers*

The powers of the emperors were as vast as their tenure was precarious. Here I deal with the powers; the next section, on the political process, will serve to explain the precariousness.

---

[6] Bréhier, *Les Institutions*, 214.   [7] Ibid. 134–5.

The state was completely identified with the emperor and his administrative and military machine.

The Emperor is chosen of God, and under the protection of the Divine Provi-
dence. He is entire master of the government of the Empire, the commander-in-
chief of the army, supreme judge and sole law-giver, protector of the Church and
guardian of the true faith. With him rest decisions of war and peace, his judicial
sentence is final and irrevocable, his laws are considered to be inspired by God. It is
true that he has to observe the existing law, but it is in his power to promulgate
new laws and revoke old ones, and in doing so he is bound only to obey the
common demands of justice. As master of the state the Emperor has in practice
unrestricted power, qualified only by moral precept and tradition. Only in religious
affairs does the absolutism of the Emperors find itself genuinely limited.[8]

'In the Byzantine Empire the conception of the supremacy of monarchical power was more deeply rooted and less contested than anywhere else in
medieval Europe.'[9] He was *basileus*, the Byzantine equivalent of the Roman
imperator; he was, *autokrator*, a synonym that went on to express the plenitude
of his despotic power; he was, till the fourteenth century, also *despotes*;
likewise, *kosmokrator*, overlord of the universe, since there was only one
emperor in the world, and it was he. God and the Kingdom of Heaven
were visualized as the imperial court writ large, and the emperor as *isapostolos*
('equal to the Apostles', hence superhuman and sanctified); he is *theios* (the
equivalent of the pagan Roman *divus*); he is *hagios* (holy), and his palace is
'sacred'. 'In the rhythm and order of the Imperial power', wrote the emperor
Constantine Porphyrogenitus, 'is seen the image of the harmony of the
creation and the government of all things by their Creator.'[10] It was a
dogma, it was an axiom, that the emperor's authority came directly from
God, and it was by this facile route that the Byzantines reconciled the
supreme authority of the emperors with the frequency of their overthrow. It
was the fact that God chose each and every emperor which explains why
there were no human rules for choosing him. The emperor might be evil, for
God in His wisdom might choose to send a bad one. If an emperor was
deposed, this meant that the Grace of God had departed from him; by the
same token, the failure of the pretender proved that he had opposed God's
will. The circularity of the reasoning is identical to that lampooned in the
old verse:

> Treason doth never prosper; what's the reason?
> Why, if it prosper, 'tis no longer treason.[11]

[8] G. Ostrogorsky, *History of the Byzantine State*, trans. J. M. Hussey (Blackwell, Oxford, 1956), 218.
[9] *CMH*, iv.2, p. 1. [10] Quoted ibid., iv.2, p. 7.
[11] The author was Sir John Harington (1561–1612).

For all its supernatural trappings, the doctrine is pure pragmatism: to become emperor proves that one is entitled to be emperor. Possession confirms the right. It is an exact parallel to the Chinese Mandate of Heaven doctrine.[12] It is a very destabilizing doctrine, since it invites anybody to try to seize the throne. Irrespective of how he had won it, once he was recognized the emperor was the sole repository of sovereign power.

But how was he 'recognized'? Here the Byzantine Empire was far worse off under this pragmatic doctrine than Imperial China, where the hereditary principle prevailed and brought about long-lived dynasties. But it was late in the day and even then only in a weak form that the Byzantines recognized hereditary descent as constituting a title to the throne. Instead, it had inherited the Roman Empire's purported elective principle. The Byzantine Empire still possessed a Senate, which supposedly elected the emperor. This Senate now consisted of the great ministers and palace officials, all of them appointed by the emperor. It had lost its original legislative functions but was very important as the emperor's advisory body; and indeed, his inner council of advisers and administrators was a kind of committee of the Senate. But political independence it had none, so that its 'election' of a new emperor was a formality. It had become traditional that the emperor-elect should be crowned by the patriarch but here the patriarch was acting as an 'elector', not as the head of the Church as such; and not till the twelfth century was it obligatory for the emperor to be anointed. Two practices brought some stability to the imperial succession. As in the Roman Empire, an emperor might designate a co-emperor. Secondly, where the emperor was a minor or an incompetent, the dowager-empress, his mother, could bring in a co-emperor to rule alongside him and so preserve his heritage. Two of Byzantium's most famous and successful warrior-emperors acceded in this way—Romanus Lecapenus and Nicephorus Phocas.

When one couples the loose and indefinite rules of the succession with that self-fulfilling formula of the 'divine mandate' which *ex post facto* legitimized even the most outrageous hijack of the throne, it becomes evident that the commonest mode of justifying a claim to rule—by reference to the *source* from which it derives—was a feeble and unreliable one. It lasted only as long as—as it lasted! It positively invited perennial challenge. So, to continue to wear the imperial purple an emperor had to justify his reign by results.

To retain his throne an emperor had to be a successful warrior-diplomat. After Heraclius (610–41) it is unusual to find an emperor who did not lead out his troops just as it is usual to find the unsuccessful ones deposed.

[12] Already described, above, at Bk. II, Ch. 5.

Finlay says that in the 150 years following the accession of Leo III, 'not one of the Emperors failed to appear at the head of the army',[13] and while this is not quite true—the Empress Irene did not, for instance—he could have gone on and extended his list to, at least, the death of Basil II in 1025. The tradition was resumed by the warrior Comneni in 1081 and was to continue with them for the next 100 years. By the same token, the army was critical in the struggles between the incumbent emperor and his challengers. The acclamation of the troops raised many great emperors to the purple: Heraclius, Leo III, Nicephorus Phocas, Alexius Comnenus; it also tempted many ambitious pretenders like George Maniaces, Bardas Phocas, and Bardas Scleros into attempting the throne, only to be defeated by loyal regiments.

An emperor would be wise, also, to be on terms with the Church. He was head of that Church, certainly, but he was not a priest (although some emperors claimed that they were), so that there were limits beyond which he could not push it. The situation was quite unlike what was developing in the West, where the Roman Church was monocratic and was parallel to the lay power, not subordinated to it. The collision between the two was denounced and deplored by the 'imperialists' like Dante or Marsilius of Padua, and indeed by many modern historians. But a Byzantine emperor was in the paradoxical situation that, precisely *because* he had greater control over the appointment of the patriarch and the definition of doctrine than any Western sovereign, he was at much greater political risk than they were, and not less as one might have expected. For the subjects of the Byzantine empire were passionate *aficionados* of theology. For them salvation lay not just in holding the right creed, but in the route by which one reached it and the rites with which it was performed; any deviation from one or the other brought damnation. When the emperor chose to lay down dogma, he put himself in the firing line of all those who happened or cared to disagree with it. In such cases, an emperor could find himself facing massive and often lethal political dissent.

The task of the emperor was, really, only to safeguard the existing creed. He was a layman. He appointed the patriarch, but only with the consent of the clergy, and similarly with dismissals—but it was usually not difficult for him to override their dissent. He could neither revoke nor alter decisions by a Church council, either. This was the highest court of appeal in the Church and only it could formulate the correct decisions on matters of faith; but here again, the emperor could and often did exercise irresistible pressure.

[13] G. Finlay, *History of the Byzantine Empire*, 716–1057 (1854; Everyman edn., Dent, London, 1906), 190.

The problem was that he did so at his peril. Leo III, the Isaurian, a great soldier who restored the fortunes of the empire, wrote to the pope saying 'I am Emperor and Priest',[14] and on the strength of this initiated the struggle against the adoration of icons, the Iconoclastic controversy. By way of consequence he and his successors had to contend with patriarchs, popes, fanatical monks, and the common folk of Constantinople who erupted in street riots. The dispute continued until 843 when the widow of the Emperor Theophilus finally restored image veneration. What the controversy demonstrates, in the present context, is that the emperor could get his way on doctrine if he tried hard enough, but that he had to count on resistance from the Church congregation; also, that in the end its prejudices proved to be the stronger. Two final examples will underline this conclusion. After Alexius IV (1204) had made the clergy submit to the Latin rite, the population rebelled and deposed him. Again, after John VIII had agreed to the Union of the Two Churches at the Council of Florence (1439), he found he could not implement it. In 1452, though the Turks were just about to besiege Constantinople, Constantine XI paid the West's price for assistance by submission to the Latin rite, only to have the population reject it. They preferred infidel rule to abandoning the Orthodox rite.

In addition to successfully defending the realm and Orthodoxy, the emperor who wished to retain his diadem would be wise to cultivate what the Byzantines called *philanthropeia*. He had to be 'man-loving'—to wit, generous, lenient, but firm in enforcing the laws. We get a good idea of what this meant in practice from the comments of Michael Psellus on Constantine IX (1042–55).

Constantine had no very clear conception of the nature of monarchy. He failed to realize that it entailed responsibility for the well-being of his subjects, and that an emperor must always watch over the administration of his realm and ensure its development on sound lines. To him the exercise of power meant rest from his labours, fulfilment of desire, relaxation from strife . . . As for the administration of public affairs, and the privilege of dispensing justice, and the superintendence of the armed forces, they were delegated to others. Only a fraction of these duties was reserved for himself.[15]

But none of these characteristics, singly or together, *guaranteed* that an emperor would keep his throne. To take but one instance: Michael III was murdered in his bed by the bosom companion of his ferocious drinking

---

[14] Quoted in A. A. Vasiliev, *History of the Byzantine Empire*, 2nd Eng. edn. (Blackwell, Oxford, 1952), 257.

[15] M. Psellus, *Fourteen Byzantine Rules (The Chronographia)*, trans. E. R. A. Sewter (Penguin, Harmondsworth, 1982), 179.

bouts, the low-born Basil, who thereupon ascended the throne in his place. There was always treachery at court. This brings us to the political process, which explains it, and how it operated.

4.2. The Emperor and the Political Process

All roads led to New Rome. Wherever disaffection or revolt flared up in the empire, this was where its fate was sealed and in many cases this is where it had begun. But when we talk of the political process we ought to distinguish between the process by which the emperor arrived at his decisions, and the process which decided who the emperor should be. The latter is the stuff of the histories and chronicles. The former, routine-ridden as it often was, is largely concealed from us by the misfortune that practically all the archives of the administration have disappeared.

Decisions as to who should be emperor were usually reached in the way that is typical of Palace-type polities. Finlay explains the long reign of the usurper Basil I by saying that he 'prevented the factions of the court, the parties in the church, the feelings in the army and the prejudices of the people from ever uniting in opposition to his personal authority'.[16] I do not know of any comparable great polity in which the throne was so precarious: I count sixty-five emperors between 518 and 1204, and of these no fewer than twenty-eight had usurped the throne.[17] 'Of the 107 sovereigns that occupied the throne between 395 and 1453, only 34 died in their beds, and 9 in war or by accident; the rest either abdicated—willingly or unwillingly—or died violent deaths by poison, smothering, strangulation, stabbing, or mutilation. In the space of those 1,058 years we can count, therefore, 65 revolutions in palace, streets, or barracks.'[18]

The emperor was supposed to be the source of all major policy decisions and much more often than not, he was. I have quoted Michael Psellus reproaching Constantine IX for idleness. Let me now quote his account of the routine day of a Byzantine emperor. We must imagine him in his gorgeous robes and his purple boots; in a vast and ornate hall; surrounded by his court, all dressed in their bright-coloured uniforms of office. Here Psellus is describing the court of the joint-empresses Zoe and Theodora, in 1042.

Court procedure, in the case of the sisters, was made to conform exactly to the

---

[16] Finlay, *History of the Byzantine Empire*, 2.

[17] Derived from Bréhier, *Les Institutions*, 587–9.

[18] C. Diehl, *Byzantium: Greatness and Decline*, trans. N. N. J. Watford, 2nd French edn. (1926) (Rutgers UP, Rutgers, 1957), 128.

usual observance of the sovereigns who had ruled before them. Both of them sat in front of the royal tribunal, so aligned that Theodora was slightly behind her sister. Near them were the Rods and Sword-Bearers and the officials armed with the *rhomphaia*. Inside this circle were the special favourites and court officials, while around them, on the outside of the circle, was the second rank of the personal bodyguard, all with eyes fixed on the ground in an attitude of respect. Behind them came the Senate and the privileged class, the persons of the second class and the tribes, all in ranks and drawn up at proper intervals. When all was ready, the other business was carried on. There were lawsuits to be settled, questions of public interest, or contributions of money, audiences with foreign ambassadors, controversies or agreements, and all the other duties that go to fill up an emperor's time. Most of the talking was done by the officials concerned, but sometimes, when it was necessary, the empresses also gave their instructions, in a calm voice, or making their replies, sometimes being prompted and taking their cue from the experts, sometimes using their own discretion.[19]

Further consideration of the policy-making dimension of the imperial office is continued within the discussion of the bureaucracy, later in this chapter. Here, I turn to the pathology of palace politics, the devious and/or violent ways in which emperors attained their office or were deposed. As we noted earlier, the emperor could face danger from the generals, the Church, the courtiers, and the street, and most incidents involved two or more of these elements acting together. The examples are so numerous that the slightest attempt to summarize them here would be tantamount to writing the empire's political history. The best way to try to give some idea of the style and atmosphere of palace politics in this short compass is to outline the rise and fall of the great warrior-emperor Nicephorus Phocas.

Nicephorus was the son of the old general Bardas Phocas, and succeeded him as 'Domestic'. The emperor was Romanus II. His wife was the extremely beautiful Theophano. Some chroniclers maintained that she was nobly born, the others that she was nothing but a barmaid. Romanus II was a debauchee who had enough discrimination to appoint able ministers. He got rid of his late father's *parakoimomenos*, a very able but unscrupulous bastard son of a former emperor, now a eunuch, namely, Basil the Bird; and in his place he appointed as his *parakoimomenos* one Joseph Bringas, who had had a brilliant career, first as the 'Grand Treasurer' (*logothete*) and then as the 'Grand Admiral' (*drungarius*) of the fleet. These two were, therefore, deadly rivals.

Romanus died in 963, leaving two male children. He had made Theophano the regent but specified that Bringas was to continue to run the empire. Theophano loathed him. To get rid of him, she turned to Nice-

---

[19] Psellus, *Fourteen Byzantine Rulers*, 156.

phorus Phocas who had just retaken Crete from the Arabs. Bringas tried to get his two ablest lieutenants—John Tzimisces and Romanus Curcuas—to conspire against him. Instead, they revealed the plot and promptly got their troops to proclaim him emperor. Nicephorus marched on the city, where his supporters rioted. Bringas's attempt to capture Bardas, the father of Nicephorus, was foiled by yet another riot. At this point, the former *parakoimomenos*, Basil the Bird, threw his 3,000 retainers into the street and after three days of rioting and fighting Nicephorus entered the city and was crowned emperor.

Five weeks later Theophano had married him! Again the chroniclers differ as to her motives. Some say she did it to protect her two sons. Others say that she liked being an empress. Nobody says that she did it for love, because there was a thirty-year gap between Nicephorus and herself, aged 20. This last judgment has obviously been made by eremites who do not understand how very taken and flattered a beautiful young woman can be by a much older man, particularly a highly distinguished soldier.

As emperor, Nicephorus waged extremely successful campaigns against all enemies, and particularly the Muslims of Syria. But these campaigns were costly and his devotion to maintaining the strength of the army by harsh fiscal policies cost him the support of the Church and infuriated the street. Riots broke out which he suppressed with extreme ferocity. A gloomy, mystical man at the best of times, Nicephorus became paranoid. To stop his enemies getting at him, he fortified the Boucoleon Palace and shut himself up there, alone. By this time Theophano had come to hate him and had given herself to General John Tzimisces. Theophano arranged to have her husband murdered—some say, in the expectation that John Tzimisces would marry her and that she would continue to be empress. At all events she and her women let down a basket from the ramparts of the palace and admitted John and his fellow-conspirators to the antechamber beyond which, door unlocked, the emperor lay sleeping on the floor of his monkish cell. They fell upon him and when he was dead Theophano had his corpse flung from the window on to the snow beneath—so that everyone could see that their emperor was dead! John Tzimisces was acclaimed emperor in his place.

It may be added that in the sequel the patriarch forbade John to marry Theophano and she was packed off kicking and screaming to a nunnery for the rest of his reign, while Basil the Bird returned to the new emperor John's side as *parakoimomenos*.

4.3. The Bureaucracy

4.3.1. ORGANIZATION AND FUNCTIONS

'Byzantine' has become a household expression for anything that is conspiratorial, hard to fathom, and very complicated: thus, 'Byzantine diplomacy', 'Byzantine intrigue', and 'Byzantine bureaucracy'. How labyrinthine the administration was in reality we simply do not know. As the *Cambridge Medieval History* admits, 'We still lack an over-all picture of the machinery of government in the late Byzantine period'.[20]

It was probably less labyrinthine than we have been led to believe, but it certainly appears very complicated because the honorific order of precedence is different from the functional ranking order. Another reason is that new honorific titles with marvellous, long-sounding names were being created without cease. And a third is that the 'law of the inflation of titles'[21] operated very strongly, so that at any time we care to consider the service is littered with magniloquently named posts whose functions are disappearing and humbly named posts whose importance is immense.

Many of the old Latin titles survived from the Late Roman Empire, but the structure of the bureaucracy was no longer pyramidal, one layer of higher officials overlaying and overseeing a lesser one down the hierarchy. Instead, every major office (and they numbered about sixty) worked directly to the emperor, as did the *strategoi* of the themes.

Everything of importance was decided in the palace. The emperor represented the concentration of all power in a single hand, and the centre of government was where he lived, his palace. This was 'at once the private dwelling of the emperor, his family and his household (the *cubiculum*)—and also the centre of administration. It is there that political councils are held, that the emperor dispenses justice and that bureaux organized according to Roman imperial tradition despatch orders and correspondence, receive and examine petitions.'[22] What Bréhier calls the 'originality' and the 'complexity' of Byzantine institutions lay, for him, precisely in that 'the palace dominated the entire administrative organization'.[23] Strictly speaking there were no 'public' officials, only the *douloi* (servants) of the emperor.

The *axiae* ('dignities') were of two kinds, the purely honorary and the functional. The former arranged the imperial officers into eighteen classes, the four highest being reserved for the imperial family. Side by side with the

---

[20] iv.2, p. 32.

[21] 'A continuous tendency by which the titles of offices are inflated in proportion as their influence is diminished.' See above, pp. 490–1, 573–4.

[22] Bréhier, *Les Institutions*, p. 80.   [23] Ibid.

list of fourteen ranks of commoners went another—confined to eunuchs. About these and their part in the central administration there is much more to be said later, but here it is to be firmly noted that these eunuchs not only were *not* inferior to the masculate officials, but the reverse: the eunuch who held the title of a *patricius* took precedence over a masculate *patricius!* Eunuchs played a central and recognized role in government, as will be seen.

This central administration comprised only the civil offices; the military commanders were quite separate. Since there were some sixty different civil departments it is not possible to describe them systematically, as it would be for a hierarchically ordered administration. The most important units, however, were the various bureaux, and most of these were concerned with finance, of course. For by now we should surely have come to expect that in these old agrarian polities the two chief governmental preoccupations, apart from administering justice and maintaining order, neither of which cost a lot—indeed, justice could actually be profitable—were the army and the money to pay for it.

The top officials in these financial bureaux were the *logothetes*, the lesser were the *chartularii*. A *logothete tou genikou* was responsible for the land tax and controlled the divisions which assessed and collected the taxes. The *logothete tou stratiotikou* was the paymaster-general of the armed forces. The chief financial officer, supervising all these financial bureaux, was the *Sakellários*, sometimes called the *megas* (grand) *Sakellarios*, and at the end of the eleventh century, the *megas logariastes* or grand accountant. Among these bureaux-chiefs we meet a *logothete tou dromou*, in charge of the imperial postal service. This office involved handling gifts to foreign embassies as well as intelligence duties, and it gradually became a kind of Foreign Ministry.

The existence of sixty separate departments whose duties overlapped must have required a great deal of cross-referrals and filing. This was provided by the Chancery, headed by the *protoasekretis*. Associated with him was the 'Custodian of the Imperial Inkstand' who had to hold the pen and the ink whenever the emperor was signing a document. This post sounds comic but it was in fact very senior and very important because, effectively, it gave the official the duty to countersign, since in his absence no document could be issued. Also, by the same token he was constantly in personal touch with the emperor. It is not surprising, therefore, that this post was filled by the well born. During the minority of Michael III, for instance, it was held by Theoktistos, who was also the *logothete tou dromou*, that is, foreign minister, and in consequence was all-powerful. After his murder in 856 the post was held by the emperor's uncle, Bardas.

Having met the more important *dramatis personae*—with the exception of the ubiquitous and exceedingly influential eunuch officials—we are in a better position to consider the routine techniques of decision-making. In principle the emperor governed by himself alone; there was no official vizier or chief minister to whom the duty was devolved. In practice he took counsel, and one of his counsellors would achieve such influence over him as to become an effective chief minister, although he would be holding some humble title or even no official title at all. This, as we shall see, is where the eunuch establishment enters the picture we are about to draw.

The emperor would take no decisions until he had studied the matter and called the Chancery to provide reports. He then took counsel in his private quarters, the *koiton* or 'bedchamber'. After coming to his decision, he either drew up the orders himself or had them drafted in his presence by a private secretary, the *grammatetes hypographeus* (which could be the starting-point of a great career, as in the case of Michael Psellus). These orders then went to the Chancery. This central department contained, *inter alia*, the bureaux of the Custodian of the Imperial Inkstand and of the Master of Petitions, which itself contained other specialized bureaux. All the acts of the emperor had to be countersigned by the head of Chancery—the *protoasekretis*—to guarantee their validity. They were then sent to each relevant office to be registered there.

On publication these imperial acts acquired the status of law for all. Though the emperor was acknowledged to be 'living law', he could not necessarily commit arbitrary actions. He was, as the Code said, *legibus alligatus*: 'For our authority depends on the authority of the law, and indeed the subordination of sovereignty under the law is a greater thing than the imperial power itself', runs a passage of Justinian's Code.[24] His exercise of power was dominated by two notions, first, that it had to have legal authority, and next, that he must govern with *philanthropeia*, that is, for the good of his subjects.

I now come to what to many will appear the most singular feature of the Byzantine administration—the central role played in it by eunuchs and the outstanding fact that throughout the entire period up to 1204 the chief minister, whose word directed all affairs under the emperor alone, was with only one exception a eunuch. The great and remarkable difference between this and the situation in China is that there, at all times, the eunuchs were an intrusion between the emperor and his regular officials, the Mandarinate. Never accepted, never institutionalized, they were *anti-institutional*, for between them and the Mandarinate there was a lethal hatred. In Byzantium, by contrast, the eunuchs were fully incorporated into the regular governmental structure, entitled to hold certain high posts and also certain high

24 Quoted from *Cod. Just.* I, 14, 4. in *CMH*, iv.2, p. 14.

honorific titles. They were unique because, although eunuchs had free access
to high posts in, say, Assyria or Persia, only in Byzantium were they elevated
into an official and highly dignified order.

It has long been the custom [comments Runciman] to talk of eunuchs as always
having a demoralizing influence all round, and historians that seem otherwise sane
talk Gibbonesque cant about the intrigues and cowardice rampant in a life so full
of eunuchs and women . . . Such generalizations are a disgrace to the historians
who make them. You cannot interpret history if you create three inelastic types,
man, woman, and eunuch.[25]

Their rise was coeval with the genesis of the empire. In the sixth century the
great general Narses, the conqueror of Italy, was a eunuch. By the tenth
century, by which time eunuchs took precedence over the non-eunuchs of
similar rank, many of the most prominent laymen, not to speak of churchmen, were eunuchs. As in China, parents would even have their sons
castrated to open the way to advancement in the government.

But no eunuch could attain the Purple, and this was the chief reason why
emperors chose to give them high office. There were additional reasons. It
was unusual for a eunuch to come from a powerful family (exceptionally,
Basil the Bird, Constantine VII's *parakoimomenos*, was the bastard of the
Emperor Romanus Lecapenus), and so they were easily broken without
raising any great disturbances at court. Again, they could not found families
either, so there was no risk of a post becoming hereditary as in the feudal
polities of Western Europe. And finally, quite contrary to Gibbon's derisive
comments,[26] many of them were highly energetic and excellent administrators.

The eunuchs made quite formidable men of war both on land and sea.
Between the sixth and the twelfth centuries one can count well over forty
eunuch generals and admirals, mostly victorious. Emperors used them in the
field or as *strategoi* of the themes because, unlike masculate generals, they
could never rise to the throne by raising a military revolt.

The role of the eunuchs in civil affairs was even greater.

Surrounded by a powerful aristocracy every member of which thought himself
worthy of the throne if the occasion arose, the emperors were accustomed to see a
pretender in every man whose talents or duties made him conspicuous. To the
contrary they felt quite secure alongside eunuchs who, however high they had risen

---

[25] Runciman, *The Emperor Romanos Lecapenus*, 31.

[26] E. Gibbon, *Decline and Fall*, ch. 19, remarks, *inter alia*, that they were almost incapable 'of
conceiving any generous sentiment, or of performing any worthy action'. The entire passage is worth
reading.

in honours and in power could never dream of the Purple . . . above all if they came from humble backgrounds, which was frequently the case.[27]

The three senior posts most frequently held by eunuchs were, in ascending order, the *protovestiarius*, the *sakellarios*, and the *parakoimomenos*. The first of these was what we might call the First Clerk of the Wardrobe; as in the Western feudal monarchies, the Wardrobe was an office where enormous sums in jewels, cash, and bullion were kept for the emperor to use at need. In the ninth and tenth century this post was held exclusively by eunuchs. But though a *protovestiarius* met the emperor frequently, the office did not as such have any political role, unlike that of the *sakellarios*, the 'Grand Treasurer'.

But *parakoimomenos* was the very highest post in the entire Empire: the grand administrator or chief executive under the emperor alone. This post descended from the 'Prefect of the Sacred Bedchamber' in the Late Roman Empire, and the Greek term means the person who sleeps near to the emperor—which, in fact, he did, as well as setting a eunuch guard around him. The post was unofficial; it was given to the confidant whom the emperor most trusted. Many of these *parakoimomenoi* were of the utmost ability—one thinks of Joseph Bringas and his arch-rival, Basil the Bird, for instance. With one exception—when Michael III gave the post to his favourite, Basil—it was always held by a eunuch. (That exception proved fatal since, as we mentioned earlier, it enabled Basil to penetrate Michael's bedchamber, murder him, and then assume the throne.) One can see, now, why Runciman summed up the eunuchs' role as 'practically, the government of the Empire'.[28]

4.3.2. PERSONNEL

The qualifications never varied: what was demanded was literary or juristic skill and a good general education. After the literary revival of the ninth century, a Greek education became the chief passport to promotion in the service. By contrast, the military notables of the interior—with whom the civil service aristocracy were to engage in a disastrous clash—were 'often unable to write a sentence even in the simplest Greek without some grammatical or orthographical blunder'.[29] Nearly all the highest positions were held by the literati. The efforts of numerous emperors to reorganize liberal and juristic studies and the foundation of the University of Constantinople were all aimed at turning out civil servants. The Byzantine approach was not systematic, regular, and exacting like the open competitive

[27] R. Guilland, 'Les eunuches dans l'Empire Byzantin', *Études byzantins*, 2 (1944), 185 ff.; 3 (1945), 179 ff., at 215.   [28] Runciman, *The Emperor Romanos Lecapenus*.
[29] *CMH*, iv.2, p. 81.

examination system being contemporaneously perfected in the Chinese Empire,[30] but it formed a singular contrast to most neighbouring states. In principle the recruitment was open: many were the humble provincials who attained high office. But in the period we are discussing, and connected with late ninth-century changes in legislation to be outlined later, nepotism and family tradition were transforming the higher civil service into an increasingly closed service aristocracy.

It will be recalled that in the Later Roman Empire it became common to obtain an office by offering a *suffragium*, effectively a purchase price. Efforts to suppress this in Byzantium proved vain, so that in the end Leo VI (886–912) laid down a fixed tariff for buying posts at prices proportional to the salary they carried. This is rather like the *paulette* under the *ancien régime* in France:[31] effectively, the government was receiving a public loan, and the purchaser was investing his capital, although at a low rate of return.

Officials were paid an annual salary, called a *roga*, the same as for a soldier's pay, deriving from an expression signifying something supplicated for and given by grace and favour. They were usually entitled to other payments also—fees or rations, and periodic gifts of rich robes and the like. All these were handed them personally by the emperor, as we have already mentioned. (Of course this only applied to those living in Constantinople. *Strategoi* of the western themes, for example, received no salary but levied a special tax in lieu.)

The service was enormously prestigious. It was uniformed, and like the Chinese mandarin, the official was entitled to ceremonial robes—which were truly magnificent among the higher officials—according to the orders of precedence. The emperors strove very mightily to prevent it abusing its power. From Justinian's day the officials had to swear on the Gospel to administer without 'guile or fraud'. They were forbidden to accept any presents whatsoever. They had to remain for at least fifty days in their locality at the end of their mission there. They were forbidden to marry any of their relatives among the natives of that locality. And, still in order to prevent them striking local roots, they were forbidden to build houses while serving, except with higher permission. It was Leo VI's *repeal* of this provision that was to have the disastrous effects, for over time the higher officials began to acquire houses and property, and so became landed proprietors. In this way a service aristocracy of great landowners came into existence. In the eleventh century they gained the ascendancy in the affairs of the empire. They opposed expansionism and ran down the army and navy, fatally weakening the empire. Their policy brought them into

---

[30] See below, Bk. III, Ch. 3.   [31] See below, Bk. III, Ch. 6.

open conflict with the traditional warrior aristocracy which had always despised them anyway, and the struggle between the two groups hastened the empire's destruction.

5. THE SERVICES

5.1. *Defence: The Armed Forces and Diplomacy*

5.1.1. THE ARMY

The Byzantine army was the most efficient military machine in Europe until at least the middle of the eleventh century. It was the very corner-stone of the state, which did not begin to perish until the army was in steep decline. To simplify somewhat, the military establishment consisted of three components. The first was made up of the metropolitan troops, the *tagmata*. Of its four regiments the most important was the *scholae* whose *domesticus* (i.e. commander-in-chief) commanded all the other forces in the capital, too. In the tenth century he took command of the entire field army in the absence of the emperor. Among the other metropolitan troops were an infantry regiment (the *numeri*) and, particularly important, the emperor's personal bodyguard, the *hetaireia* (literally 'the retinue'), composed mainly of foreign mercenaries—at this time, mostly Norsemen and Anglo-Saxons. All these units went into battle alongside the emperor or his deputy. They can be regarded as the strategic—and highly mobile—reserve.

The bulk of the army consisted of the *themata*, units stationed in each theme and commanded by the *strategos*. The modal size of a theme army corps was in the order of 4,000 men and was organized more like a modern army than any European army right up to the seventeenth century. The commonest estimate of the number of *themata* troops in the tenth century is some 120,000,[32] but this relates to the total effectives, for no more than 30,000 could take the field at any one moment, and in fact most field armies were half or one-third of this size, depending on the enemy and the nature of the attack.

Recruitment to the *themata* is one of the most original features of the Byzantine army, and it survived until after the disaster of Manzikert and the destruction of the theme system in Anatolia. Families held substantial farms under the hereditary obligation to supply a fully armed heavy-cavalryman, with his horse and weapons, whenever summoned. So, socially, it was made up of substantial yeoman farmers, closely attached to their soil. The serving soldier received a stipend also, but this was small. (Officers, on the other hand, were richly rewarded.) Certain policies followed by successive emperors

---

[32] *CMH*, iv.2. p. 39.

only become intelligible in the light of this theme system of recruitment. One is their effort to prevent big landowners from buying up the peasant farms. Another is the resettlement of devastated areas by peoples from other parts of the Empire and indeed, by prisoners of war.

The third component of the army was that of the *akritai*, best translated as frontier-guards on the disputed borderlands where the emperors had set up special districts called the *kleisurae*. They contained chains of forts from which these irregular *akritic* forces carried out raid and counter-raid against the enemy, rather as Turkish *bashi-bozouks* were to do later.

These three components of the armed forces co-operated in a single strategic design. Beacons and other visual signals warned of invaders. If they got past the *akritai* and their frontier-forts, local infantry levies came in behind them to cut their retreat and light cavalry harassed them to give time for the *strategos* to call up the main body of the theme army. Meanwhile the surrounding themes had been alerted and their armies would join in the defence and counter-attack. The metropolitan troops under the emperor or his deputy acted as the strategic reserve.

The élite forces were heavy armoured cavalry, armed with lance and bow. Light cavalry were, effectively, mounted bowmen. The infantry fought with spears and battle-axes. They had large baggage trains filled with the military impedimenta for entrenchment, cooking, and the like. They might be accompanied too by artillery trains of catapults that fired stone shot or arrows—or even Greek fire—at the enemy. Their siege equipment was excellent. And the armies contained specialized medical units whose members received a reward for each soldier they recovered from the battlefield.

The Byzantine approach to war was completely different from that of the feudal warriors of the west. The empire was, basically, defensive not expansionist. It did not like fighting for fighting's sake and would do anything possible to avoid battle: diplomacy, marriage alliances, and huge money payments were all pressed into play. Generals were told never to engage unless in superior numbers and position. There was no nonsense about chivalry: every means of deception—ruse, feigned flight, the breaking of solemn promises—was permissible. The emperors Maurice, Leo VI, and Nicephorus Phocas each wrote important manuals of military science, specifying how the tactics were to be adapted to the characteristics of the many different kinds of foes.

The theme army, as outlined above, had its greatest successes under Basil II at the very time that, deep down, it was beginning to decay. The *dynatoi* were buying up the farmers and turning them into dependents,[33] and with

---

[33] See p. 659 below.

Manzikert the Turks took over Anatolia. Consequently later emperors turned to mercenary troops and greatly extended the *pronoia* system. In this, in return for the revocable and short-term grant of landed estates, the proprietor undertook to produce a given quota of armed soldiers when required. The system is similar to the *iqta*, used in the Muslim lands and particularly in Mamluk Egypt, but in the Byzantine case the proprietor exercised local jurisdiction over his tenants.

5.1.2. THE NAVY

It was pre-eminently the navy that broke up the Arab assaults on Constantinople. Its high period runs between 649, when Mu'awiya, the Arab governor of Syria, took to the sea and attacked Constantinople, and 960, the year when the Byzantines recaptured Crete and established undisputed command of the eastern Mediterranean.

Around 1000 the naval forces consisted of the metropolitan fleet and the theme fleets. The latter comprised the Cybyrrheot theme on the south coast of Anatolia, and the Aegean theme. They were maintained by the local *strategos* or *drungarius* out of local funds. The metropolitan fleet was maintained from central government funds and was always much larger than the others put together. Its task was to patrol, and it had naval stations at Durazzo and the Dalmatian coast, in the purlieus of Sicily, and above all, in the Straits. It was commanded by the *drungarius*, and divided into three-to-five squadrons each commanded by a *navarch*. The theme fleets were equipped with the same type of vessels—the *dromons*, which were two-banked heavier ships, and the lighter *pamphyli*—and their task was to maintain patrols and repel enemy raids. The Cybyrrheot theme was by far the most important one, partly because the area was traditionally renowned for the quantity and quality of its seamen, and partly because it lay on the frontier with the Emirates of Tarsus and Adana.

The navy was recruited from these Cybyrrheots, from certain groups of aliens who had been resettled inside the empire like the Mardaites of Mount Lebanon, and from mercenaries, such as the Russians. In 910 the imperial fleet consisted of sixty *dromons* and forty *pamphyli*, while the theme fleets, altogether, comprised forty-two *dromons* and thirty-five *pamphyli*. A *dromon* carried 230 oarsmen and some 60 men-at-arms; the complement of the *pamphyli* was 160 men all told. In all, the naval forces comprised 35,340 men, including the oarsmen.

Success in a sea battle is notoriously unpredictable (witness the protracted and indecisive engagements between the Genoese and Venetians in the Middle Ages). Leo VI, author of the *Tactica*, had advice for his naval commanders as well as his generals. Like the latter, the admirals were adjured never to engage unless necessary and then only when they were in superior strength. But the greatest advantage of the Byzantine navy over its enemies was tactical; it and it alone possessed the secret of *Greek fire*. The secret was so well guarded that we do not know to this day the nature of this substance. It was some highly combustible liquid, composed of sulphur, naphtha, and saltpetre. It was hurled in grenades which immediately deto-nated and burst into flames, or was ejected through metal tubes on the prow of the warships by a propulsive mechanism of which we are ignorant. In brief, it was used either like petrol-bombs or flame-throwers at the present day, and its effects could be devastating. It was Greek fire more than anything else that destroyed the Arab fleets besieging Constantinople and was responsible for the similar destruction of a Russian fleet of 200 vessels in 860.

5.1.3. DIPLOMACY

Encircled as they were by wave after wave of enemies—many of them inchoate tribal hordes, as well as by the organized and formidable forces of the emirs and the Normans—the Byzantines, like the Chinese, preferred to negotiate rather than to fight. They were adept at dividing their enemies. They analysed with care the intelligence brought back by traders, mission-aries, and the frontier commanders. Constantine VII's treatise *De administrando imperio* contains highly exact characterizations of the main neighbours of the empire. Byzantine inquisitiveness and knowledge con-cerning these went far beyond anything in the Roman Empire.

Every resource was used to further its diplomacy. Gold was the most important. For very special reasons some kind of marriage alliance was sometimes arranged such as, for instance, between Princess Theophano and the Holy Roman Emperor Otto I. The pomp and ceremonial of an ambassador's official reception was particularly potent for swaying uncouth and illiterate barbarian chieftains.

The foreigner was led into the audience Hall of the palace through rows of imperial bodyguards with glittering arms and past the assembled throng of high dignitaries in rich vesture. One final curtain was drawn aside to expose the Emperor clad in his robes of state and seated on his throne. Golden roaring lions watched beside the imperial throne and mechanical birds sang in a gilded tree. And while the envoy made the three prescribed prostrations, the throne was raised aloft to mark the unapproachability of the now yet more richly bedecked monarch.[34]

---

[34] *CMH*, iv.2, pp. 51–2. The same kind of thing was practised in the imperial court of China. Indeed it is a standard practice: the *miranda* of power.

5.2. *Justice and Security*

5.2.1. POLICE

There was no single police force. Every government department had its own units, the most important being, as one might expect, the ones attached to the judicial and administrative authorities like the *strategi* of the themes, and the *logothete tou dromou*, who controlled the imperial postal service, whose employees all doubled up as police officers. Constantinople had its own force controlled by the Eparch, to be described later.

Our information as to how this policing was carried on is scanty. In the ninth century the police of a theme came under its *strategus*, while there is evidence of a kind of mobile rural constabulary that pursued robbers, recaptured runaway serfs, and arrested spies. Surveillance was particularly sharp on the frontiers where the lack of a passport could lead to instant imprisonment and brutal interrogation. When the future stylite monk Luke was crossing the frontier in order to retire to a monastery, he was arrested by a troop of soldiers who asked him who he was, where he came from, and why he was travelling. When he piously replied that he was 'the slave of Christ' the soldiers took this to mean that he was a fugitive serf and, after beating him up, flung him into prison.[35]

The *logothete tou dromou*, meanwhile, had a corps of agents who inspected and reported back from the frontier provinces and the imperial domains. And the emperors all maintained a secret service for sniffing out conspiracies.

5.2.2. THE JUDICIAL SYSTEM

It was Byzantium that gave us Roman Law, the Justinian codes. It was the continuator of the Roman legal tradition and it retained that law-bound character which, we have seen, was a unique feature of the old Rome.[36] Justinian's codes were written in Latin. Later they were condensed, and issued in Greek. Thereafter the code called the *Ecloga* replaced Justinian's codes, departing from them in many respects; but the tenth-century emperors, Basil I and Leo VI, abrogated it and returned to the Justinian tradition. A handbook of extracts from those codes was published, which in turn was followed by a collection of all the laws of the empire and published as the *Basilica*. This was the foundation of all law in the empire thereafter.

These Macedonian emperors also reorganized the judicial system which had fallen into disarray. Basil I paid high salaries to the judges to make them

---

[35] Bréhier, *Les Institutions*, 202. The entire passage in the text is based on Bréhier's brief account.
[36] See above, Bk. II, Ch. 7.

independent, and their qualifications included being able to recite by heart all forty sections of the code. He also organized a kind of legal aid bureau in the capital to give financial assistance to poor suitors who had come to bring actions against magnates or officials. Leo VI was equally solicitous. Judges had to swear an oath to prefer truth to falsehood at the commencement of each case, and their verdicts had to be written and signed by hand.

The emperor was the supreme judge and at times he might judge in person. But usually it was the *eparch* who presided in his court, the *basilikon kriterion*. This was the supreme court of appeal for the entire empire, and the court of first instance in cases of treason. Side by side with it, the quaestor also held a court to deal with wills, testaments, and matrimonial affairs. There were two other specialized courts also—later fused—which adjudicated disputes over rank and precedence, and disputes between palace officials.

Leo VI and his successors established a university at Constantinople, and a law school, though whether this was independent or part of the university is obscure. But neither lasted very long. Legal education was highly technical, like the teaching of English common law today, and it lay in the hands of the two guilds of the lawyers and of the notaries. These regulated the criteria for admission. For instance, the notaries' guild comprised twenty-four individuals and to be admitted one had to furnish proofs of respectability, to have good handwriting, a good general education, the power of eloquence, and in addition, to know by heart all forty sections of the code. These two guilds provided the avenues for the future jurist: he was inducted either by apprenticeship under a practising lawyer, or else by following a course of studies under a professor.

Whereas the civil law generally followed Justinian's code, the penal law did not. Though the death penalty could now only be carried out by the sword (so getting rid of crucifixion and similar methods) it was usual to replace it by ghastly mutilations: cutting off the nose, ears, tongue, or hands and gouging out the eyes. Purportedly, the intention was to spare life. But Bréhier thinks that it simply reflected the barbarizing influence of the Turks, Arabs, Persians, and Syrians who had been accustomed to such practices since remote antiquity. He remarks that that most mild-mannered and bookish Emperor Constantine VII, acclaimed for his humanity, nevertheless put out the eyes of any individuals he mistrusted. Bréhier also cites examples of the highest officials being flogged at the emperor's orders (the same kind of thing took place in the imperial court of China). Internment in a monastery could be pronounced for the simplest of common-law crimes. The only correctives to this harsh penal regime were the mercy of the emperor, and the right of asylum in a church. This right the patriarchs defended with the greatest tenacity and with success.

5.3. *Taxation*

Taxation was heavy, harsh, extensive, and complicated. We have already glanced at the agencies for administering it. Under the control of the *sakellarios*, the *logothete tou genikou* controlled a dozen or so bureaux, with one of his officers—the *chartularii*—in each. Among the more important bureaux were those whose officers inspected the treasuries in the themes and those that supplied and controlled the inspectors of taxes there, and, under them, the *dioiketai* or collectors. We must remember, however, that this referred only to the 'public sector'. The pay and personnel of the armed forces came under a separate bureau of the *logothete* of the army, while the private-imperial sector was handled by no less than three separate bureaux, the *sakellion*, the *vestiarium* (Wardrobe), and the *eidikon*. It should be remarked straight away that the distinction between the 'public' and 'private' sectors was not very firm, because the emperors used their private treasuries for public purposes. The most striking example is the huge Cretan expedition of Nicephorus Phocas (949), which was financed entirely from the *vestiarium*.

5.3.1. DIRECT TAXATION

The *synone* was a land tax that only affected landholders. The *kapnikon*, however, was a hearth tax, so that peasants could escape it by running off. Townsfolk paid 'urban taxes' in a variety of ways, on funerals, for instance, but also on incomes (which must have been very crudely assessed). The land tax was assessed according to quality and crop—vines or olives or pasture. To minimize tax evasion—for instance, by a peasant abandoning his farm—a system of collective guarantee was in force, known as the *allelengyon*. The territory was divided by the assessors into groups of communes, each group being taxed at a certain rate. All the inhabitants were collectively liable for payment, and abandoned lands reverted to the state. Those farmers who could not pay their taxes were recruited into the army at the expense of their neighbours, who gave them a set sum of money and paid their debts to the taxman.

In addition, the population had to supply certain corvée services. For example, those adjoining the postal routes had to furnish horses and mules and offer food and drink to users. The population also had to billet troops and officials, and give up a dime of their cereal crop to feed them. These services could all be commuted for cash.

The system of land taxation necessitated a general cadaster, and this was compiled from the theme cadasters, which were very detailed. They showed all the goods that were liable for tax, the nature of each holding, its location, area, and population, what each farmer was liable for, his family circumstances, the number of his beasts, and so on. Those not liable to tax were listed on a separate register. These theme cadasters were periodically revised by the *epoptai* or inspectors, one per theme, each with a staff in every fiscal district who were responsible for its assessment. The most important officer in these staffs was the *anagrapheus*, whose task it was to adjust the area of the fiscal units to the number of its taxpayers. Collection had long since passed from the hands of the local councils, the *curiales*. Now it was some-times handled by a paid official, the *dioiketes*, and sometimes by tax-farmers.

5.3.2. INDIRECT TAXATION

This apparatus of specialized officials and its elaborate cadaster should not delude us into thinking that its results were anything but crude, cumber-some, and unjust. The reasons are the same as for all pre-modern land-tax systems, including, for instance, inherent difficulties in assessing lands by crops and cattle, and political and bureaucratic reluctance to review the cadaster regularly.[37] Luckily, the empire had a parallel source of revenue equalled only in the lands of Islam and almost totally lacking in Dark Age and early medieval Europe. Because Constantinople was a vast emporium it was possible to levy customs duties, and taxes on the merchant ships. The dues they levied (the *komerkion*, later known as the *dekateia*) were an *ad valorem* tax on the cargoes, supplemented by additional taxes such as the fees that went directly to the customs officers. These imposts were virtually inescap-able: there were customs officers at every port in the empire.

5.4. *The Government of Constantinople*

To Byzantines, Constantinople was 'The City'. Its population of some 200,000 (*c*.950) embraced, at one extreme, slums and *vicoli*, full of beggars, harlots, and *lazzaroni*, and at the other the gorgeous palaces of noblemen and merchant princes. The palace was the greatest of its merchant firms and a centre of manufacture, too. It contained the mint and had a monopoly of bullion. Most of the city's silk cloth was manufactured in its gynaecaeum. It bought foodstuffs wholesale and then sold them cheaply to the tradesmen's guilds. Among these, particular importance attached to those handling food supplies, a necessity given such a huge population to be fed. Other guilds

[37] See 'The Conceptual Prologue', 6.3 ('Taxation–Extortion'), partly based on the work of G. Ardant, *Histoire de l'impôt* (Fayard, Paris, 1971).

specialized in silk-manufacture; and even notaries, money-changers, and goldsmiths were organized in such *collegia*. But these corporations were expected to carry out any functions the government chose to devolve on them, and their entire activity was controlled by the *eparch*. In the vital matter of food supplies, for instance, he regulated the amounts to be bought, supervised the quality, fixed the buying and selling prices, and exercised a tight control over exports while taking every step to encourage imports.

The *eparch* was also the police chief. He saw to the licensing of shops, to weights and measures, Sunday observance and fire precautions. He was responsible for public order, and this was no easy task since riots erupted frequently and with great violence, for the inhabitants of the poorer end of the city lived in dreadful conditions. The destitute were estimated (around the tenth century) to number 30,000, and there were probably an equal number of thieves and criminals, not to mention great swarms of prosti-tutes. To keep the population quiet food prices were subsidized. These poorer folk lived in veritable shanty towns; filth and dung littered the streets and alleys everywhere. A perpetual flotsam of incomers washed through them—city-beggars, discharged soldiers, runaway peasants—who slept where they could, often out of doors. Enteric fever and smallpox were rife. Small wonder, then, that extensive precautions were taken for main-taining order. A civic watch, accompanied by a strong body of imperial guardsmen patrolled the streets; a curfew was imposed at an early hour and anybody found breaking it received a terrible flogging.

This misery was partly alleviated, however, by the practice of charity. Consequently, begging was a recognized institution and the professionals jealously defended their pitches. The imperial family and other wealthy citizens provided hospitals, orphanages, and old-age homes. The greatest of the providers was, as one might expect, the Church—which not only possessed enormous wealth but was bound by its faith to give alms. From time to time there were special distributions of food and money to the poor. Sometimes these were prompted by an acute crisis—an especially cold winter, a scarcity of food—but some distributions took place regularly. The chief of these was at the games which commemorated the founding of the city. Then, loaves and vegetables were piled up in the Hippodrome and fresh fish was distributed among the crowds.

6. APPRAISAL

6.1. *Defence*

The extravagant praise meted out by military historians to the Byzantine army strikes me as rather overblown. It is true that it successfully defended the borders of the empire, but only after having lost Syria, Egypt, Africa, Italy, and (for a time) Sicily and Crete, and yielding the Danube line to the Slavs and Bulgars. The empire which the armed forces successfully defended consisted in fact only of Asia Minor and the southern Balkans. Even here, the army seems to have lost as many great battles as it won.

Sometimes this was due to bad generalship, for example, the Bulgarians' defeat of Nicephorus I (811) or the failed Sicilian expedition of 965. Sometimes it was due to treachery on the field; there is more than a suspicion that this was what lost the day at Manzikert. But the underlying cause seems to be the poor discipline and low morale of the troops. Sometimes they fled the battlefield. They murdered the Emperor Maurice because of grievances over pay. Repeatedly, throughout the empire's history, some soldiers somewhere could be sure to rise in support of their leader's attempt on the throne.

This low morale was to some extent due to the fact that the troops were really only part-time soldiers who returned to the plough after the campaign, so that their fighting skills were not all that high and they lacked the unthinking, ingrained discipline of regulars. Furthermore, they lacked any such patriotic sentiment as the ancient Romans had when they faced Hannibal. By now the population was largely a mixture of peoples resettled from distant parts. Perhaps the one sentiment common to the soldiers was their Orthodox faith. They went into battle singing the Trisagion, and accompanied by holy icons. This buoyed them up against Muslims and Franks, but the only emperor who wanted to make the war against the Caliphate into a Crusade—Nicephorus Phocas—was rebuffed by the Church. In any case, the piety of the more-recently settled populations did not run very deep. For all these reasons, victory depended on the personality of the individual commander.

Nevertheless, it is undoubted that the armed forces did indeed keep the rump of the empire intact for some 600 years, and that is a long, long time to remain inviolate. Furthermore, it would be unfair not to emphasize the magnitude of their task, for military pressure was, literally, ceaseless, and came from the north, the south, the east and finally—with the Crusaders— from the west as well. The Byzantine army was a somewhat brittle and unpredictable fighting force, but despite many a setback it fulfilled its task until the fatal day of Manzikert. Even then, it was the subsequent civil war and anarchy that made the defeat decisive.

6.2. *Security and Stability*

The greatest flaw in the Byzantine polity was its chronic predisposition to military insurrection, even civil war,[38] partly because there were no fixed rules for succession, partly because ambitious generals could find ill-disciplined troops to follow them, and finally because the mere winning of the throne proved, in itself, that one had a divine title to it. Yet was it more torn than most other polities in the western hemisphere at that time? The number of emperors deposed or murdered certainly much exceeds that in Western Europe, where hereditary succession had early established itself and was hardening into the rule of primogeniture. But the deposition of an emperor did not imply a civil war, and civil war of one kind or another was not noticeably more common in the empire than it was in the loose-knit feudal polities of the West. And anyway, civil wars or no civil wars, the empire was a vastly more stable, unitary, and cohesive polity than any western monarchies save—with a big 'perhaps'—England and Sicily; certainly more so than the Regnum Francorum and Charlemagne's empire, let alone its faltering successor states.

The contrast between those western countries and the empire becomes even more striking when one distinguishes—as one must—between the stability of the throne and the stability of the regime. Western Europe experienced a set of perceptible institutional changes—the first witness to that marked fluidity that has characterized Western Europe in distinction from everywhere else. In the Byzantine Empire, throughout all the riots, palace assassinations, military usurpations, and civil wars, all that was ever at stake was who was to be emperor. Never at any time, not even in the faintest whisper, can one discern any intention to alter the imperial autocracy as such. Through all changes of throne and all vicissitudes, the regime continued unchanged till the very end. The only comparable polity in this respect was the Chinese Empire. That was more stable than Byzantium in one sense, less so in another. There the dynastic principle was entrenched, so that the throne was stable. On the other hand the country was swept again and again by vast popular risings which have no parallel in the Byzantine Empire. My conclusion would be that as far as the security of life and limb from self-inflicted wars is concerned, the Byzantine Empire,

---

[38] e.g. Bardas Phocas, 971; Basil II v. Bardas Skleros, 976; Constantine IX v. Maniakes, 1043; Nicephorus and his rivals, almost continually, 1078–1118.

for one or the other of the reasons given above, was better off than either Western Europe or Eastern Asia.

6.3. The Bureaucracy and Public Administration

While the territorial integrity of the empire was due, as we saw, to its armed forces, its enduring political cohesion was due to its numerous, professional, and highly differentiated bureaucracy. It is easy enough today to point up the flaws in the central administration: the multiplicity of independent bureaux, the collection and distribution of state finance through several autonomous departments, the aggregation of several offices at once by individual civil servants, their rapid transfer from one important post to another. Without doubt it worked slowly and multifariously. But such were the general faults of its time, and it was immensely superior to the primitive administration of the early feudal monarchies of Western Europe, more regular and law-bound than that in the Muslim countries, and comparable only to the Chinese Mandarinate, which was even larger, more intricate, and equally slow and cumbersome.

Unhappily, the bureaucracy shared other characteristics with the states of its day—corruptibility and greed—and the lawcourts were filled with cases arising from malpractice which was proverbial. But then, in the year 1000, where else in the world was it possible to proceed at all against the state officials in a duly appointed court of law?

6.4. Legality and the Courts

There can be no doubt at all that the empire was a law-bound state: the emperor, though himself the fountain of law, was by powerful convention *alligatus legibus*, private concerns were regulated by a sophisticated code of civil law, it was possible to proceed via this law against the agents of the government, and finally there existed, as in Greek and Roman times, recognized professional advocates and notaries. In all this it was altogether superior to the primitive Western European polities which had not yet developed even feudal law, let alone rediscovered the Roman law; and from Imperial China where the only civil law was simply customary law and where the T'ang code confined itself to administrative and criminal matters, and it was impossible to proceed against a government official. In the empire the flaw did not lie in the absence of law or the corruption of the courts, but in the very elaboration of the law and the chicanery of the trained professionals who practised it. By the eleventh century, it becomes clear, the entire judicial system was clogged up and court proceedings very, very slow. The imperial court could not cope with the burden of cases and in the theme courts the lawyers were adept at protracting the proceedings: they would challenge the form of documents presented, or delay correspondence, or challenge the jurisdiction of one court so as to have the case transferred to another and then repeat the manœuvre there. One such case is well reported: the dispute between Ann, niece to the defunct archbishop of Nicodemia and Stephen, the archbishop of Caesarea, who both claimed the right to inherit. This case was fought through four different courts, one after another, and in the end had to be settled in the imperial court itself.[39]

We have already described the horrors of the penal code. We have to remember, however, that punishments were even crueller in China, and that the Caliphate's penal code was in certain respects—as will be shown—unspeakably bad. Indeed we might wonder if there was a great deal of difference between cutting off the criminal's nose or hands and letting him live, and hanging the condemned by the neck till he was half-dead, then cutting out his living entrails and burning them in front of him before cutting his head off and, finally, chopping his body in four pieces. This last was the penalty for treason in England! The truth is that until the Europe of the eighteenth century practically every people showed an indifference towards suffering and death to a degree that is incomprehensible to the cocooned city-dwellers of today.

One final point is that Byzantium was like all other polities up to quite recent times in applying what might be called a law of exception to cases of suspected treason. As elsewhere, the presumption of guilt was all but overwhelming and the normal processes of interrogation were overridden. Not merely that, but the penalties—like the English hanging, drawing, and quartering we have just mentioned—were more than usually cruel. Given the conspicuously cruel tone of the Byzantine code we should not be surprised to find that it surpassed itself in the treatment of condemned rebels and traitors. Anna Comnena has left a horrible picture of how an aristocrat named Michael who had plotted to murder the emperor was treated after his arrest.

[Michael] Anemas and the other prominent rebels, after having their heads completely shaved and their beards cut, were paraded on the Emperor's orders through the Agora. Then their eyes were to be gouged. The persons in charge of the show laid hands on them, clothed them in sackcloth, decorated their heads with ox and sheep entrails (to imitate crowns) put them on oxen (not astride but riding sideways) and drove them on through the palace court. In front of them rod-

[39] Bréhier, *Les Institutions*, 189.

bearers charged, bawling a comic ditty with alternate refrains suited to the occasion . . . People of all ages hurried to see the show.[40]

6.5. *Taxation and Public Finance*

Tax default was one of the three crimes for which sanctuary in a church was not admitted. As in Roman times, the tax-collectors came to the villages every year accompanied by a posse of soldiers. Turning deaf ears to pleas in mitigation, they would flog defaulters on the spot and distrain their goods. Some defaulters were imprisoned *en masse* and beaten and tortured in custody. A case is attested in Cyprus where the tax-collectors set savage dogs on the defaulters. Things were far worse when the government employed tax-farmers instead of its own agents, since the farmers stood to keep everything between what the taxpayers owed the central treasury and the sums they actually collected.

This dreadful harshness brought the money in, and that money defended the empire. Herein lies the most fundamental difference between the administration of the empire and the western feudal regimes. In the latter, the ruler was not fiscally absolute. Apart from the revenue from his own estates, the only way he got military service was by paying for it in land-grants. Over time the recipients—the knights and barons—managed both to reduce their services and get hereditary possession of the land. Once the time arrived when the monarch's stock of land had run out, the only way to augment it was to confiscate the magnates' fiefs, which was militarily impossible since they provided his forces, or to conquer new lands abroad, where the process would simply repeat itself. So, no feudal monarchy was in a position to maintain a standing army or navy. It could fight brief campaigns, but to fight wars both sides would negotiate truces in which to raise money. But in the Byzantine money economy where magnates and officials were paid in coin by the emperor himself, this manner of remu-neration required no contraction of the imperial domain lands. A standing army and navy became feasible and the military effort could be sustained on a continuous and highly protracted basis, not spasmodically as in the feudal West. Until after the partition of the empire in 1204, the territorial noble-men of Anatolia were never in a position to emulate the semi-independence of their feudal counterparts. This is why the empire was and remained centralized and cohesive for so long.

---

[40] A. Comnena, *The Alexiad*, trans. E. R. A. Sewter (Penguin, Harmondsworth, 1969), 385. In the event he was spared at Anna's intercession.

6.6. *The Condition of the People*

There was a sharp distinction between the social conditions in Constantinople and in the provinces. The highest class in the capital consisted largely of the literate and well-educated service aristocracy that we have already described. The merchant and artisan classes were politically and economically feeble, because the government minutely regulated all their transactions through their guilds and corporations. Below them came the mass of the population—workmen of various kinds—and at the bottom that 5 per cent or so of human detritus, perpetually renewed from outside, as in the shanty towns in Latin American conurbations today.

In the Byzantine countryside, however, until the tenth century, conditions were better. Free smallholders, congregated in hamlets and towns of between fifty to 500 inhabitants and farming the adjacent countryside, lived hard lives but were far better off than the poorer class in Constantinople. All this began to change as early as the ninth century when social differentiation between rich landowner and yeoman farmer began to widen. A number of factors contributed to this. One was the new legislation which permitted officials in post to buy up local lands. Another was the process which occurs inexorably in every early agrarian economy: the erosion of the free peasantry by the combination of poor harvests and inflexible taxation, and the consequent forced sale of his landholding in return for the right to farm it as a dependant. We have seen this process at work in early Greece, the early Roman Republic, and also in China. In Byzantium the purchasers were the so-called *dynatoi* (the powerful) and their victims the *ptochoi* or *penetes* (the poor). Since this development eroded the basis of army recruitment, successive emperors enacted laws designed to protect the smallholder, but in vain. These dependents were effectively like the *coloni* of the Later Roman Empire. They were tied to the soil and this condition was hereditary.

The heavy taxation began to produce the same effects as in the Roman and Chinese empires. Peasants began to flee their farms, escaping to the cities or even going abroad. This of course increased the burden on those farmers who remained, and it will be remembered that they were collectively responsible for the shortfall. So a vicious cycle of deprivation was created.

6.7. *Freedom and Orthodoxy.*

There were slaves in the empire, but we do not know how many. They were employed almost exclusively in the cities where they helped depress the wages of independent labourers, but not on *latifundia* as in the old Roman Empire of the West. The dependent tenant farmers, that new generation of *coloni* mentioned above, were only theoretically free; the government admitted that there was little to choose between them and slaves. Apart from these slaves and serfs, the emperor's subjects were equal before the law, for the line between *nobiliores* and *humiliores* had disappeared. It is hard to make a trustworthy comparison between the degree of freedom of the generality of the common folk in the empire and those of neighbouring polities, but in the eleventh century—the period we are considering—it would seem that they were considerably better off. Serfdom was very much more widespread in the feudal monarchies, and their self-governing towns were still a long way off in the future. And there could be no comparison between the condition of the Byzantine rural population and that of the peasantry in some lands of the Caliphate.[41]

There was one respect, however, in which the population of the empire was less free than in most and perhaps all contemporary polities and that is in thought and expression. I do not refer here to the right of political dissent—this was sternly sought out and repressed everywhere—but to all religious, artistic, and philosophical freedom. This was stifled by the suffocating and all-pervading presence of the Greek Orthodox Church. Religion enjoyed 'a supremacy unequalled in history . . . it is impossible to insist too much on the dominion of religion over Byzantium'.[42] The empire swarmed with priests and monks. In the eleventh century John of Antioch reckoned that half the total land in the Empire belonged to the Church.[43]

'Religion entered into every aspect of Byzantine life. The Byzantine's holidays were religious festivals; the races which he attended in the Circus began with the singing of hymns; his trade contracts invoked the Trinity and were marked by the sign of the Cross.'[44] In an age which was universally suffused by religions, Greek Orthodoxy stands out as the most bigoted, intolerant, conservative, and obscurantist. 'One God, one Empire, one Religion', was the watchword. But Orthodoxy entailed not only that all the empire's subjects were to be Christian but that they were also 'to subscribe to a single and highly abstruse doctrine defining the nature and relationship of the three persons of the Trinity, for even the slightest deviation therefrom was considered to be heresy'.[45]

Whatever may be thought about the uplifting religious qualities of this Orthodoxy, it had only the most baneful political and intellectual conse-

---

[41] E. Ashtor, *A Social and Economic History of the Near East in the Middle Ages* (Collins, London, 1976), 157–9; 169–73.　　　[42] Runciman, *The Emperor Romanos Lecapenus*, 25, 27.

[43] Ostrogorsky, *History of the Byzantine State*, 122.

[44] T. Ware, *The Orthodox Church* (Penguin, Harmondsworth 1980), 43.

[45] Mango, *Byzantium*, 88–9.

quences for the empire. It was the zeal for 'One God, one Empire, one Religion' that embroiled the rump of the empire in the self-destructive Iconoclastic Controversy, that fatally alienated the armed support of the West, and drove heretical sects like the Paulicians and the Bogomils into active collaboration with the empire's enemies. It was the foe of humanism and intellect. It regarded the teachings and the literature of Greek paganism—readily accessible and indeed part of the schooling of any educated Byzantine—as akin to heresy. The accession of Leo III, wrote a classical Byzantinist, 'gave nearly five centuries of despotic power to a system hostile to the development of the human intellect'.[46]

It may be retorted that religious bigotry and persecution were universal in this age, but this is simply untrue. There was no religious persecution in the great empire of China. Islam tolerated other—and hostile—religions, reluctantly perhaps and by necessity perhaps, provided that their adherents accepted second-class-citizen status. Notably, the Ottoman successor state to Byzantium found no difficulty whatsoever in permitting each and every sect within its borders to worship in its own way. And although in Western Europe the Roman Catholic Church did indeed promote itself and persecute its opponents as zealously as Greek Orthodoxy, it was a broader church, able to tolerate, adopt, adapt, and finally incorporate a wide variety of the new religious movements that were always welling up inside it: the monasteries, the friars, the military, charitable, and teaching orders.

'We do not change the boundaries marked out by our fathers: we keep the tradition we have received . . . We beseech therefore, the people of God, the faithful flock, to hold fast to the ecclesiastical traditions. The gradual taking away of what has been handed down to us would be undermining the foundation stones, and would in no short time overthrow the whole structure.'[47] This is what explains the peculiar and repellent barrenness of Byzantine intellectual achievement at the very time when the Roman Church was engendering Scholasticism, when Islam was fostering poetry, science, mathematics, and when, under the Sung, the Chinese were experiencing the great reinterpretation and efflorescence of the Confucian persuasion. Above all, art in Byzantium was the 'Handmaid of Religion'.

---

[46] Finlay, *History of the Byzantine Empire*, 183.
[47] St John Damascene (675–749), quoted in N. H. Baynes, *The Byzantine Empire* (OUP, Oxford, 1925), 75.

7. CONCLUSION: THE SIGNIFICANCE AND LEGACY OF THE BYZANTINE POLITY

The Byzantine Empire provided the Grand Dukes of Muscovy with a splendorous vision and inherent justification of unmitigated autocracy. Also, in the shape of the Greek Orthodox Church and its servility to the lay power, it transmitted a vital support for just such a regime. But the idea that there was a direct link as exemplified, for instance, in the title of 'Tsar', the device of the two-headed eagle, and even Philotheus' doctrine that 'two Romes have fallen, the third stands, and a fourth there will not be' has been discounted.[48] On the other hand there does seem to be a direct link between the administrative arrangements of the empire and those of its Ottoman succession-state.[49] But it is neither for these reasons nor for any innovations in the theory and practice of government that the empire rates in this *History*. It does that for the reason stated at the outset of this chapter—that it is virtually the archetype of the Palace polity as we have conceived it. It is more archetypal than Imperial China in that the Byzantine emperors, with few exceptions, were both expected to be and were highly active in war and civil policy, whereas this is true only of a few Chinese emperors (notably the early Manchus). The majority of them were subject to the Confucian doctrine of the passive emperorship, and its consequential neutralization by the Mandarinate.[50]

The long duration of this undiluted autocracy drew from J. B. Bury the observation that: 'There is virtually no constitutional history in the proper sense of the term in [Byzantium], for there was neither evolution nor revolution. The monarchical system remained in all its essential points unchanged, and presents a remarkable picture of an autocracy of immense duration *which perfectly satisfied the ideas of its subjects.*'[51] The numerous revolts and conspiracies were directed at changing the monarch, not the system. This is not to say that they reflected nothing but private ambition. From the death of Basil II (1025) the unending court intrigues conceal what is essentially the clash of the civil and the military aristocracy, but the form this struggle took was not to challenge or even try to persuade the autocrat of the day, but to depose and replace him.

For a thousand years this empire was the most important European centre of culture and learning. It had an excellent legal system, a highly sophisticated and differentiated civil service, and an equally well-trained and

---

[48] D. Obolensky, *The Byzantine Commonwealth* (Cardinal edn., 1974; Weidenfeld & Nicolson, London, 1971), 468–73.   [49] Diehl, *Byzantium*, 290–1.

[50] See esp. Bk. III, Ch. 3, below.

[51] My italics; J. B. Bury, 'Roman Empire, Later', *Encyclopaedia Britannica* (11th edn.; 1910–11), xxiii. 519.

organized standing army. Its economy and financial system was well developed, and its gold bezant acted as an international currency. (Over its entire lifetime the empire, unlike the feudal and later-medieval states, never stopped payment on its debts.) In its core areas it provided its population with a high level of security, protected their property rights, observed and enforced a predictable rule of law, and promoted a tolerable, even if poor, standard of living. The emperor, hub and motor of the entire state, was far more often than not a man who worked hard, felt responsible, and lived up to such responsibility. In every one of these respects the empire was on an altogether higher plane than its contemporary states *c.*1000; and indeed, as far as Europe is concerned, one can hardly speak of states existing there at all.

One great criticism levelled against the regime is the harshness of its fiscal policy, but this was no harsher than that suffered by the serf populations of Europe, or the people of China and the Muslim lands, and it gave much better value for money. It was the necessary price paid for the defence of the core areas, and what the failure of that defence meant in practice is luridly illustrated by what took place when the Arabs captured Thessalonica in 904 and the Crusaders sacked, stole, raped, and murdered their way through Constantinople in 1204. A recent work argues that the reason why past empires declined and fell was that they assumed over-ambitious foreign commitments that eventually ruined their economies.[52] That does not fit the Byzantine case at all. It did not collapse because it was economically bankrupt but because it lost its frontiers, and consequently its chief source of military manpower. It was not the expansion but the very *contraction* of its territories that fatally weakened it.

The truly lethal flaw in the Byzantine state was not economic but political. It lay in the openness of the succession and the self-defeating political formula which, effectively, maintained that *whoever* held the throne did so by just and indeed divine title. In China the similar doctrine of the Mandate of Heaven was vastly mitigated by the hereditary principle, but in Byzantium it provoked the most damaging civil wars and treachery on the battlefield. It was rivalry for the throne that bedevilled the Byzantine army at Manzikert and led to its defeat. That great authority, Bury, maintained that the Byzantine tradition of mingling what he calls 'the two principles, the dynastic and the elective', secured the state the best of two worlds. 'There were far fewer incapable sovereigns than if the dynastic succession

---

[52] P. Kennedy, *The Rise and Fall of the Great Powers: Economic Change and Military Conflict*, 1500–2000 (Unwin Hyman, London, 1988). But to be fair, Kennedy does not argue his case for the pre-1500 polities.

had been exclusively valid, and fewer struggles for power than if every change of ruler had meant an election.'[53] It is difficult, indeed impossible, to see how anybody could substantiate such a reckless counter-factual. For us, that sorry recital of depositions, murders, and civil wars constitutes a persuasive refutation.

[53] H. Temperley (ed.), *Selected Essays of J. B. Bury* (CUP, Cambridge, 1930), 106.

2

The Empire of the Caliphate (*c*.900)

The empire of the Caliphate[1] was the Muslim state established by the successors ('caliphs') of Muhammad (d. 632). It is quite proper to call it an 'empire', since it fulfilled the two conditions that define that kind of polity.[2] In the first place its populations were subjected to particularist domination, first by a tiny group of ethnic and Muslim Arabs, and later—at the time we are concerned with—by the Muslim minority as such. Secondly, it was immense. It aggregated what had formerly been Visigothic Spain, Byzantine North Africa, Egypt and Syria, all Sassanian Iraq and Iran, and even the lands beyond it up to Samarkand and the Hindu Kush. Such vastness, along with great wealth and populousness and a life-span of some 230 years, would in themselves justify inclusion in this *History*, but there are other and weightier grounds for doing so. Although the Caliphate is patently one of the Palace-type polities, it manifested profound differences from all those considered so far except, curiously, the two ancient Jewish kingdoms. These do indeed offer an analogy, but the enormous difference in scale and the fact that the Caliphate was a conquest state make it significantly different from those diminutive and impoverished statelets. But its great originality and distinctive character lies in the fact that it was *Islamic*.

It is significant for two other reasons also. One is that it left an enduring political legacy in that the extensive common culture area it had established engendered, in the shape of Mamluk Egypt and the Ottoman Empire, succession states which were equally Islamic but of greater vigour and durability. Another is that, throughout the busy coming-and-going of individual rulers or entire dynasties and even political communities, two things persisted both in the Caliphate and the succession states as well. Respectively, they were the culture and civilization of the society which had been engendered in the original Arab-Islamic conquest state and the Palace-type of polity. These two stood unshaken among the debris of particular

[1] In this chapter the word 'Caliphate' sometimes refers to the empire, which is also sometimes called the 'Caliphal' empire or (as above) 'The empire of the Caliphate', and sometimes it refers to the institution of caliph. The context makes clear which is which.

[2] See the definition given in the 'The Conceptual Prologue', pp. 8–9.

states and dynasties because one buttressed the other; indeed, each was the outgrowth of the other.

It is impossible to proceed further than this point without considering Islam, which is central and integral. A great volume could scarcely do justice to the character of this religion.[3] The rudimentary notes that follow are presented apologetically, but without something like them the rest of this chapter would be unintelligible.

Islam is the religion communicated by God to His Prophet Muhammad. It is embodied in the 6,000 verses of a scripture—the Quran—and was spread not by military might and conquest but, certainly, on the back of it. This last is important. Whereas the Christian paradigm is that of the suffering Godhead, for the Muslim it is the Armed Prophet.

It is a salvation religion, a religion of personal piety, a religion in which each and every member of the religious community participates on equal terms in his access to God, through His revelation to the Prophet. This religious community is the *umma*. The first political act of Muhammad, in the course of receiving his revelation, was precisely to bind his believers into a mutual pact and covenant, the *umma*. So Islam, like Judaism and Christianity, is pre-eminently what we have been calling a *kahal*-type religion.

The Quran opens with these words:

> In the Name of God, the Merciful, the Compassionate
> Praise belongs to God, the Lord of all Being,
> The All-merciful, the All-compassionate,
> The Master of the Day of Doom.
> Thee only we serve; to thee alone we pray for succour.[4]

Its monotheism is stark and uncompromising:

> God, there is no god but He,
> The Living, the Everlasting.
> Slumber seizes him not, neither sleep;
> To Him belongs
> All that is in the heavens and the earth.[5]

God—Allah—is ineffable, incorporeal, transcendent. The Muslim was forbidden to make any image of Him. There is a sense in which Allah is even more of the one unique transcendent essence than the God of the Jews, for Jews often address God not just as *Adonai Elohanu* ('The Lord, our God')

---

[3] Among the most successful brief introductions, see Alfred Guillaume's short but cogent *Islam* (Penguin, Harmondsworth, 1954) and the longer—and very instructive—*Islam in the World* by Malise Ruthven (Penguin, Harmondsworth, 1984).

[4] Translations here and elsewhere are from *The Koran Interpreted*, trans. A. J. Arberry (Oxford, 1964).

[5] Ibid., ll. 271 ff.

but also as *Ovenu Malkanu* ('Our Father, our King'). They manage in this way to combine the abstract and remote nature of the divinity with the comforting feeling of a personal presence.

God's revelation to Muhammad is final. God had sent messages before, through His prophets Moses and Jesus and others. But the Jews and then the Christians had muddled them all up. This time God had found the Prophet who could understand and communicate them accurately in their pure and pristine form. Muhammad was the Seal of the Prophets. The finality of the message was to be reinforced in the ninth century in the orthodox pronouncement that the Quran was uncreated, hence coeval and co-eternal and co-immutable with God himself.

To be a fully practising Muslim is very exacting, for, as we shall see, the prescriptions to be obeyed are manifold. But to become a Muslim and be received as a member of the *umma* is easy. All the individual has to do is to repeat before witnesses the *shahada* ('testimony'): 'I testify that there is no God but Allah, and I testify that Muhammad is the Prophet [sometimes translated as the 'Messenger' or the 'Apostle'] of Allah.' This *shahada* is the first of Islam's so-called 'Five Pillars'. The second is *salat* (prayer) to be performed five times a day, bowed in the direction of Mecca, Islam's holiest city. The next is obligatory almsgiving—the *zakat*—which is effectively a tax for charitable purposes. The *sawm* or annual fast in the month of Ramadan is the fourth of the five pillars, and the final one is the obligation (exempting those too poor or disabled from performing it) of making the *hajj*, the pilgrimage to Mecca.

These may be regarded as the minimal obligations of the practising Muslim. But to be fully observant he would have to fulfil a voluminous compendium of the most minutely detailed prescriptions for his daily conduct, even down to its most intimate minutiae. This *corpus* has been built up on the verses of the Quran itself, then on the attested sayings and doings of the Prophet—the *hadith*—and finally on the rescensions and elaborations of all these as made by the learned—the *ulema*—in the ninth and tenth centuries. The result is the *sharia* law. Nothing in Christian civilization corresponds to this, since Christianity does not prescribe moment-by-moment rules of personal activity. But Judaism does. It closely parallels Islam in regulating daily conduct by a vast network of rules based on the Pentateuch, the Prophets, and then on the centuries-long accumulation of rabbinical judgments which make up the *halakha* (the oral tradition) and the Talmud. So great and encompassing is the volume of these latter regulations that in the sixteenth century an abridgement was prepared for the use of housewives: this is the *Shulhan Aruch* (the 'spread table'), and the pious use it to govern their conduct to this very day.

The theological differences between Christianity, Judaism, and Islam do not concern us, fortunately, but their political implications do; and here Christianity stands on one side and Judaism with Islam on the other. The political implications of the two latter resemble one another in three main ways. First, each religion constitutes a total life-style, what has been called a 'blue-print of a social order . . . a set of rules, eternal, divinely ordained, and independent of the will of men, which defines the proper ordering of society'.[6] Secondly, this set of divine rules, written down as it is, is equally accessible to all believers. They may well be aided by the unusually pious and learned, but these do not constitute a privileged class which is nearer to God, let alone being the intermediary between God and man. Their learning and piety are works of supererogation. Consequently, neither Islam nor Judaism (since the destruction of the Temple) has any specialized clergy or church organization. Thirdly, and as a corollary of these two features, Muslim political society fell into the same dilemma as the old Jewish kingdoms, described in Book I, Chapter 5, above. Since the divine laws governed all aspects of life, a political ruler was a redundancy—except, perhaps, to defend the cult and administer its rules. Or, if the mind rebelled at this conclusion, then the only legitimate political ruler must be the immediate vehicle of God on earth, a charismatic ruler. This implied *caesaropapism*. Or—and this is the nub—there was a third way. For, as occurred in the ancient Jewish kingdoms, supreme authority could be *bisected*, one entire segment of authority being withdrawn from the ruler, who, for his part, was left to exercise his own portion in however despotic or arbitrary a manner as he liked and his subjects would tolerate. As we shall see, the Muslem *umma* found itself facing these three alternatives in the very first half-century of its existence.

I. THE RISE AND DECLINE OF THE EMPIRE OF THE CALIPHS

CHRONOLOGY

Muhammad, c.570–632

*c.*570/580	Birth of Muhammad
*c.*612	Beginning of Muhammad's mission
622	The flight (*hijra*) of Muhammad and his followers (the Companions) to Medina
630	Muhammad and the Companions return in triumph to Mecca
632	Death of Muhammad

[6] E. Gellner, *Muslim Society* (CUP, Cambridge, 1981), 1.

The Four 'Rightfully Guided' Caliphs, 632–661

632	Abu Bakr
634	Umar
644	Uthman
656	Ali
	Foundation of the Empire: the Arabs overrun and hold Syria and Mespotamia, Iran, Egypt, and Cyrenaica
657	Battle of Siffin between Muawiya (governor of Syria) and Ali. The Kharijite secession
661	Defeat and death of Ali. Accession of Muawiya, so founding the Umayyad dynasty

The Umayyad Dynasty, 661–750

680	Battle of Kerbela—defeat and execution of Husein, son of Ali. The beginnings of the Shia ('the party' [of Ali])
705–714	From the capital at Damascus, further imperial expansion: Bukhara and Samarkand, Transoxania and Indus valley, North Africa, and Spain
c. 700	Rise of a 'religious opposition' to the Umayyads, stigmatized as impious and tyrannical
743–750	Anti-Umayyad revolts. Activities of Abu Muslim
750	Umayyads overthrown. Election of Abu'l-Abbas, the first caliph

The Earlier Abbasids, 750–861

750–842	From capital at Baghdad, the empire at its height. The great caliphs:
	754–75 al-Mansur
	786–809 Harun
	813–33 al-Mamun
	833–42 al-Mutasim
750–855	Flowering of Sharia jurisprudence
	Abu-Hanifa (d. 767), Malik (d. 795), al-Shafii (d. 820), on Hanbal (d. 855)
833	al-Mutasim builds capital at Samarra to house his Turkish slave corps. Beginnings of the Turkish slave army
756 onwards	Progressive crumbling of Caliphal authority at the periphery:
	756 independent Amirate (later Caliphate) of Cordova under a surviving Umayyad
	789 Idrisid amirs in Morocco; (800) Aghlabid amirs in Tunisia; (821) Tahirid governors in Khorasan

The Later Abbasids, 861–1258

861	Turkish soldiery murder al-Mutawakkil and proclaim al-Muntasir
861–70	Five successive caliphs enthroned and dethroned by Turkish amirs'

military coups

869–83	The Zanj black-slave revolt in south Iraq
891–906	The Qarmatian uprisings
867–969	*Disintegration of the empire:*
	867 Saffarid governors in South Iran
	868 Tulunid governors in Egypt
	875 Samanid governors in Transoxania and Khorasan
	909 Fatimids take Tunisia and in 969 establish their counter-empire and counter-Caliphate with its capital at Cairo
	945 Buyids (Shiite and barbarian) enter Baghdad, reduce caliphs to puppet status
1055	Buyids defeated and replaced by the Seljuk Turks. Their leader takes the title of sultan
1258	Mongols, led by Hulagu Khan, raze Baghdad, massacre its inhabitants, execute the caliph and his family, *and extinguish the Abbasid Caliphate of Baghdad*

2. SOME STRENGTHS AND WEAKNESSES OF THE EMPIRE

2.1. *Strengths*

The empire's first asset was wealth. It formed a gigantic common market. Hence trade expanded greatly and its merchants penetrated to India, the East Indies, and even Canton. Gold flowed in from the confiscated treasuries of churches and palaces, and from the mines of Africa. Silver came in also, from the mines of Afghanistan and eastern Iran. Initially there was a great rise in population. Several of the towns, some of them new foundations, were immense compared with their impoverished and shrunken counterparts in contemporary Europe. In the ninth century Fustat, the capital of Egypt, is thought to have had 100,000 inhabitants, Kufa about 150,000, Basra some 200,000, while estimates for Baghdad range between 300,000 and 560,000.[7]

Another asset was military power. How, in the course of the initial conquests, those bands of wild horsemen could have overthrown battle-hardened armies of superior size continues to baffle as well as amaze historians.[8]

---

[7] E. Ashtor, *A Social and Economic History of the Near East in the Middle Ages* (Collins, London, 1976), 90–1. He estimates the population of what is now Iraq at 10 million, of Syria at 3–3.5 million, and Egypt at some 4–4.5 million. All these estimates, we must emphasize, are highly conjectural.

[8] For a critical account of no less than eleven theories on this matter see F. M. Donner, *The Early Islamic Conquests* (Princeton University Press, Princeton, 1981), and, of course, the entirety of that work itself. Cf. also F. Gabrieli, *Muhammed and the Conquests of Islam* (Weidenfeld & Nicolson, London, 1968) and G. E. von Grünebaum, 'The Sources of Islamic Civilisation' in *Cambridge History of Islam*, vol. II, ed. P. M. Holt, A. K. S. Lambton, and B. Lewis (CUP, Cambridge, 1970), 469–510.

Thereafter the going was easier, since up to the tenth century the only great power the Caliphate had to face was Byzantium which, as we saw earlier, tended to stand on the defensive. As for Europe, the feudal shock-cavalry was still in its first making, while in Central Asia the Caliphate had only tribesmen to contend with.

A third strength of the empire was that it did not have to create an administrative apparatus. Instead it inherited, or rather, overlaid the highly sophisticated Byzantine and Sassanian bureaucracies even to the extent of employing the same personnel. In respect to its administrative apparatus, therefore, it was incomparably superior to, indeed in quite a different league from, the ephemeral empire of Charlemagne or the Ottonian Holy Roman Empire.

Another source of strength imponderably important, was the creation of a new society and a new cultural *oikumene*. 'Islamic civilization is the outcome of a barbarian conquest of lands of very ancient cultural traditions. As such it is unique in history.'[9] For the Arab tribesmen neither disintegrated nor assimilated to the native culture, as the northern nomads did in China (see Chapters 3 and 4 below) but, instead, Arabized and Islamized the native inhabitants. The process was extraordinarily rapid. The Arabs who overran the ancient empires in the Conquest period probably numbered only 100,000–200,000,[10] and (in 684) only 3–4 per cent of the population of the Caliphate was Muslim. But by 820 half the population of Iran is estimated to have converted, and by the eleventh century, which closes our period, the Islamization of Iran, Mesopotamia, and to a large extent Syria was almost complete. (In Egypt the Copts proved more resistant, and most Spaniards remained true to their creed and also to their language.)

Along with Islam the Arabic language was the other great force in the process of creating this new Islamic civilization. The invaders considered Arabic as sacred—it was the language in which God had chosen to give the Arabs a testament all of their own. (This is why the Quran was not translated for a long time, even in the Muslim lands that did not take up Arabic). Iraq and Syria adopted Arabic very soon, since their populations already spoke cognate languages, but most Egyptians spoke Coptic till the thirteenth century, when the language was suddenly abandoned. In Iran, on the other hand, a Persian vernacular resurfaced in the ninth century, and burgeoned in the verses of Rudaki (d. 940), Firdausi (940–1020), and Omar Khayyam (d. *c.*1123). Arabic lived on, however, as the language of religion and to some extent of philosophy also.

---

[9] P. Crone and M. Cook, *Hagarism: The Making of the Islamic World* (CUP, Cambridge, 1977), 73.

[10] C. Cahen, *Les Peuples musulmanes dans l'histoire médiévale* (Damascus, Syria, 1977), 175.

Finally, binding all these elements together was the common law, the *sharia*, which dictated even the minutest details of the daily domestic lives of every Muslim and by extension controlled that of all non-Muslims. In brief, four elements in combination contributed to the eminence of the Caliphate: wealth, soldiers, and bureaucrats, all sustained by this new but deep, rich, and fecund civilization.

There was another strength too, the steady reinforcement of the governing classes. The penetrative power of Islam created a vast cultural *oecumene* but at the same time—and wholly unforeseen by the invaders—it reinvolved the élite of the conquered peoples in the administration of their own countries. At first the Arab tribesman acted simply as an exploitative ruling caste, using the native administrators to extract resources for them. But once the Abbasids gave the swelling numbers of non-Arab Muslims parity with their Arab fellow-Muslims, the Iranian aristocrats and country-squires and the almost hereditary civil-service families began to participate once again in the business of government. This process strengthened the governing echelons of the empire by what Pareto called the 'circulation of élites'. The ruling stratum creamed off the most active and able level of the immediate substratum, so reinforcing itself and simultaneously enfeebling the other.[11]

2.2. *Weaknesses*

Despite these apparently formidable strengths, the empire collapsed within about 300 years. For, from the very beginning, it also suffered from three crippling weaknesses. The most obvious factor is its over-extension—from Central Asia to the Pyrenees—in an age when the fastest means of land-communication was the horse. The immensity of the territory to be ruled is reflected in the crude mode of governing it through provincial plenipotentiaries. Responsible for the peace and the defence of the province and for the collection and transmission of the taxes to the capital, the governors were therefore the linchpins of the empire. If a governor defected, then his province was lost to the government along with its army and revenue. Such a loss further weakened the central government's ability to compel obedience. But in any case, its armies would be very slow in coming. It is reported that a courier covered the distance from Rayy (Teheran) to Merv—750 miles— in only three days![12] And we are told that a journey accomplished in only

---

[11] V. Pareto, *A Treatise on General Sociology*, trans. Bongiorno and Livingston, as *The Mind and Society* (New York, 1963), paras. 2053–2059.

[12] This was in 811. M. J. Goeje, 'The Caliphate', *Encyclopaedia Britannica* (11th edn., 1910), v. 5. 46.

four days by relays of the fastest horses, took ten days by racing camel and no less than sixty days for an army on the march.[13] On this showing, mounted infantry would have marched about twenty-five miles a day so that an army would have taken about 200 days to get from one end of the empire to the other.

There were three ways in which caliphs could secure obedience from their governors: through their respect for caliphal authority, through mutual wheeling-and-dealing, and through force of arms. The period ending with the death of al-Walid I (715) is one of the unquestioned authority of the caliph. The years between 715 to the reign of al-Mamun (813–33) see both transactional accommodations, or, alternatively, caliphal repression of rebel governors. The third period, from the accession of al-Mutawakkil (847) or perhaps the Zanj revolt (868–83), sees the central government unable to repress the self-assertion of the governors or of rebels like al-Saffar who make themselves such, and in consequence sees the breakup of the empire into independent states with the caliph (as far as secular government is concerned) a purely nominal figure.

The reason lies in the second of the empire's great weaknesses—its heterogeneity. The Caliphate was in ceaseless turmoil from the outset to the end. In comparison, the Byzantine Empire appears rock-solid. From the beginnings until the end of the Umayyads, for instance, it was plagued by the inter-tribal feuds the Arab overlords had brought with them from Arabia. Now that the spoils were so much richer the rivalry among the tribes grew sharper. 'Everywhere in the caliphal territory the Rabia and the Azd held together against the Tamim and the Bakr. This hostility developed in time into hostility between north and south Arabs, between the Qais and the Kalb, and it was conducted with a bitterness we now find hard to understand.'[14]

These inter-tribal struggles disappeared with the eclipse of the Arabs under the Abbasids, but not so the sectarian strife which had invaded the Caliphate almost from its beginnings. Religious revolt, which was endemic, often reflected rifts and fissures in society: the Ismaili Qarmatians, for instance (an extreme sect of the Shia which awaited the coming of the 'concealed' Imam of the line of Ali, and who terrorized Arabia, Syria, and lower Mesopotamia in the ninth century) believed, like early Christians, in a communistic society and even set up a republic along these lines. In 833 a man called Babak appeared as a leader of a heretical sect, and carried all Azerbaijan before being defeated. And so one could go on. It is very difficult

---

[13] Tabari, *Chroniques: L'Age d'or des Abbasides*, trans. H. Zotenberg (Sinahad, Paris, 1983), 183.
[14] Grünebaum, *Sources of Islamic Civilisation*, 69–70.

to separate what was religious, what political, and what economic and social; usually all three are found rolled up together. The Qarmatians, for instance, can be taken as Ismaili fanatics, communistic millenarians, or Bedouin tribesmen in opposition to the townsfolk: and in fact they were all three. Social and economic oppression seems by far the most obvious motivation for the Zanj revolt of the black slaves of lower Iraq but all the same its leader, Ali ibn Muhammad, was another of those who claimed to be the Mahdi.[15] It took fourteen hard years to suppress the Zanj, but this revolt was only the most spectacular of numerous economic and social uprisings: tax rebellions were too frequent and widespread to record here.[16]

All these sectarian, political, social, and economic motivations interacted with and nourished one another, but what gave them such very free rein was the third of the Caliphate's great weaknesses: the lack of any firm and clear tradition of caliphal legitimacy. *What* was a caliph? How could he be recognized? Who was entitled to recognize him? This confusion is one of the chief matters explored when, later, we come to discuss the central authorities of the empire.

3. THE NATURE OF THE POLITY: COMPARISONS AND CONTRASTS

First and foremost the Caliphate is a Palace-type polity. It belongs to the great family represented by the Chinese, the later Roman, and the Byzantine Empires but it is not identical with any of these.

It had no affinities with the West European feudal polities. Its landlords were not identical with its ruling class and vice versa. The *iqta* extensively developed in the late tenth and the eleventh centuries was a benefice, not a fief: the dues of an estate which went to its landlord (the *muqta*), who had to provide military service in return. It was revocable and, indeed, often revoked. Nor did the *muqta* exercise jurisdiction over its inhabitants. In these respects it differs completely from European feudalism.[17] A second distinguishing characteristic is that neither the Caliphate nor (with the two exceptions below) its succession states became territorial national states.

[15] But much controversy surrounds Ali and his beliefs. See H. Laoust, *Les schismes dans l'Islam* (Payot, Paris, 1977), 95–6. A great many details are related by Ashtor, *Social and Economic History*, 116–18, but must be treated with caution.

[16] For a short list of the more important ones, see Ashtor 68–9.

[17] The most complete work on the *iqta* is that of C. Cahen, 'L'évolution de l'iqta du IXe au XIIIe siècle' (first published in *Annales* (1953), 25–52, and reprinted in his *Les Peuples musulmanes* (n. 10 above), 232–69). Later, in the 13th and 14th cents., some *muqtas* did come to acquire hereditary possession, and also jurisdiction, thus much more closely resembling European feudalism—ironically, just at the time this was dissolving in Europe.

The concept of the Muslim *umma*, the universality of Arabic, and the overarching authority of the *sharia* law militated against that. Of the lands conquered by the Arabs, only two were to become national states before the advent of nineteenth-century ideas of nationalism: Spain and Iran. In each country the people spoke their own non-Arabic tongue and professed their particular brand of religion (Shiism in the case of Iran). The basis for the emergence of national states in these parts was the same linguistic-cum-religious one that was to generate the European state-system under the Treaty of Westphalia.[18]

The Caliphate, then, is uncompromisingly a Palace polity. The Abbasids extruded the Arab nobility and replaced them by a service aristocracy, so that, given their attendant paid professional bureaucracy and the newly created standing army, 'the State', in Wellhausen's striking phrase, 'shrank to the dimensions of the Court . . .'[19] There was no hereditary landowning aristocracy to serve as a counterweight to the palace, and the religious institution, though very influential indeed, was not organized into a church. As the centre of decision-making the palace stood on its own.

But there are a number of profound differences between it and the other empires mentioned above. In the first place, it was a 'conquest' empire. By this I mean that for much of the period considered here its government was simply a military occupation. It was a government by tribal Arab chieftains superimposing themselves as an exclusive racial/religious military caste on the pre-existing administration and living as parasites on the population. This Arab hegemony lasted for more than 100 years before native converts to Islam secured equality with the Arab Muslims, a development which took place after 750 and the Abbasid triumph (though the Arabs retained their superior social status long after they had lost their political supremacy).

The second special feature follows from the above: it was a more than commonly exploitative empire, where 'exploitative' means taking in from subjects far more than is handed back to them. The principal motivation of the Arab tribesmen in following leaders (who themselves, certainly, were religious zealots), was booty, and this was immense. Next, the taxation system they introduced was deliberately designed to keep the Arab extractors apart from the subjects, the providers. The subjects worked for them, while for their part they formed a *rentier* class. Little of this taxation came back to the subjects in the way of public works. In Iraq the caliphs certainly continued the canal-building and irrigation projects of the Sassanids, but

---

[18] But Spain is not on a par with Iran since unlike the latter it was not a national state in Islam and only became one after it stopped being Muslim.

[19] J. Wellhausen, *Das Arabische Reich und sein Sturz* (Berlin 1902; repr. Calcutta, 1927), 348–50.

they also overtaxed the soil. In northern Mesopotamia, and particularly Syria, they neglected to maintain the hillside terraces that channelled the rains. The net effect of their work for agriculture was a partial decline in yields and cultivated area at the outset which then accelerated and became intense by the eleventh century.[20]

It was not as Arabs but as Muslims (at first the two had been identical) that the new rulers discriminated against their subjects, fiscally, socially, and of course, politically. Subjects were permitted to practise their religion under their own religious leaders and to continue with their economic avocations in security, as *dhimmis* ('protected people'), but they paid a fiscal price for this. Whereas the Muslim paid only *zakat*, a fairly light charity tax, the *dhimmi* paid land tax (*kharaj*) and the poll tax (*jizya*). The latter entailed deep personal indignity: for a *dhimmi* traveller had to wear a receipt for the payment of the tax round his neck or wrist—otherwise he could find himself in jail. A second price paid was exclusion from political and administrative office, though in practice this prohibition was often disregarded. A third handicap was judicial—the *dhimmi* was unequal before the law in that every case involving him with a Muslim was judged according to Islamic law; nor was a *dhimmi* permitted to give evidence against a Muslim. In many parts of the empire the *dhimmis* were required to wear distinctive dress, to serve Muslim customers from a lowly stooping position, to step aside for Muslims. It is not at all surprising that large numbers, and finally the great majority, of the subjected population preferred to join the *umma*, but the point here is that at this period these Muslims were still a distinct minority of the population.[21] So that although the Abbasids ended the exclusively *Arab* hegemony, the Muslims continued to discriminate against the majority till the end of our period.[22]

A third characteristic that distinguishes the Caliphate from some other Palace polities—the Roman Empire would be an excellent example—is a feature already commented on: the absence of a hereditary, territorially autonomous nobility. Instead, the Abbasids' service nobility came to replace the Arab sheikhs. Over time, however, many of the posts they held became hereditary, or effectively so.[23] But they were not 'free-standing' like the

[20] Ashtor, *Social and Economic History*, 45–66. A. Hourani, *Islam in European Thought* (CUP, Cambridge, Mass., 1991), 103.

[21] It seems that nobody knows the exact proportions, but Bulliet calculates that in 820 only half the Iranians were Muslims and perhaps one-quarter of the Egyptians. Cf. R. W. Bulliet, *Conversion to Islam in the Medieval Period* (Harvard UP, Cambridge, Mass., 1979), 44, 83, 97, 109.

[22] *Dhimmi* status persisted in Muslim states into the 19th cent. and in one or two cases, the 20th cent.

[23] Despite previous asseverations to the contrary. These have been overwhelmed by a formidable piece of prosopography by Patricia Crone: see *Slaves on Horses: The Evolution of the Islamic Polity* (CUP, Cambridge, 1980), app. V. ('The Abbasid Servants, 750–813'), 173–96.

former tribal leaders. What could happen when a family of such service nobles became overconfident in its hold on the administration is illustrated by Harun's massacre of the Barmecides.

A fourth characteristic of the Caliphate sets it apart from all the other Palace polities except, to repeat ourselves, the diminutive and short-lived kingdoms of Israel and Judah. This characteristic derives from what is often called 'the religious institution'. This deliberately nebulous term is used for want of anything better to designate a critical ambiguity—that in the Empire of the Caliphate *there was no organized church, but there was no religious class either*. To explain: some men are learned and pious enough to instruct others in the faith. These are the *ulema* (from the root *ilm*, meaning 'knowledge'). The *ulema* lead the less knowledgeable—but only by the latters' free consent. They are just like the rabbis in post-Temple Judaism, or like the prophets in the still earlier days. Where all life is organized by and around a religion, as in Islam, the *ulema*, who instruct the Faithful in this religion, obviously exert a powerful influence over their opinions and actions; but they do not form a class, a caste, or a college; they are simply a category. Even if they arrive at a consensus there is no institutional or constitutional channel by which this is expressed. And, in any case, there is no institutional or constitutional or even conventional mode of guaranteeing that they *will* arrive at any consensus: each *alim* can arrive at his own conclusion, and there is no sanction to constrain him to the viewpoint of his fellow *ulema*. In short, though there may be an 'orthodoxy', this is simply existential, not official.

Because of their great influence over opinion and action a consensus among the *ulema* helped legitimize a caliph. The trouble was that it could also de-legitimize him. The fall of the Umayyads demonstrated this dramatically. Dissentient *ulema* could and did provide religious legitimation for rebellion against 'the false caliph in the capital'. The bitterly opposing sects which sprang up from the beginning were, sooner or later, to rebel, and a number successfully established their own schismatic states. For their part the caliphs, unlike the kings or the emperors of Europe or Byzantium, did not have an organized hierarchy to confront or to compromise with, but an amorphous polyarchy, fitfully but poisonously active through one or more of its myriad hydra heads. Consequently, although the 'religious institution'— unlike the Christian Catholic or even Orthodox Church—did not operate as an unremitting institutional constraint on the caliphs, it could and did give religious sanction to spasms of volcanic violence. The collision between the individuals' two roles as subject and as believer consequently expressed itself not in any regularized or constitutionalized dialogue with the government but in incessant religiously inspired riots, rebellions, and revolutions.

This recourse to religio-political violence was reinforced by that aspect of the nature of Islam already mentioned: that in principle the divine law was all-sufficient for the conduct of wordly affairs, and all that was needed was correct interpretation. This thrust the Caliphate into the same dilemmas that attended the Jewish polity: either nomocracy or caesaropapism, or as in the ancient Jewish polity, bisected sovereignty, leaving one segment to the *ulema* and the other—the segment we should call the strictly political one—to the absolute discretion of the ruler. This last position, which was the one the Jewish kingdoms arrived at, was also the Muslim solution, though in a somewhat different way and by a different route.

A final and quite vital difference between the empire of the Caliphate and Rome, Byzantium, and even contemporary Europe, relates to the legal code. In all those polities the monarch was held to be *alligatus legibus*. Furthermore, the laws to which he was bound distinguished between private and public actions, and because these states possessed the concept of a legal—as opposed to a natural—person, they all permitted subjects, by various devices, to sue and be sued by the public authorities in a court of law. There the sovereign and the subject engage in a *lis inter partes* on, as it were, equal terms.

But unlike Christianity, Islam did not grow up inside a pre-existing legal code of this sophisticated kind, but outside any kind at all except the pre-conquest Arabic tribal law and—inevitably—the Quran, and it failed to generate the concept of 'the state'. If the caliph *was* indeed 'bound to the law' it was in a profoundly different sense from that prevailing in the polities we have just named: *in his own segment of authority* the ruler was not *alligatus legibus* but made up his judgements as he went along, and the subject's rights against him were extremely precarious.[24]

3.1. *Summary: The Nature of the Polity*

This is a good place to pause to follow our uniform practice and set out the main features of the caliphal polity, as already noted and/or to be elaborated later.

1. It is a Palace-type polity, but subject to many more qualifications than in the Byzantine case. The authority of the caliph is 'divine' or supernatural only in the sense that it is conferred by Allah and that he is the

---

[24] See p. 693 below.

Representative of Allah,[25] or as one of his styles puts it, 'the shadow of Allah on earth'. But much ambiguity surrounds his authority and how it is recognized.

2. It is a Palace polity too, in that it is in the palace that ultimate policy decisions are taken, while the population at large are non-participating subjects whose function is to obey. For the Abbasid rulers have no territorial aristocracy to deal with, but are served instead by the courtiers they themselves have created. But the political process differs from that in the Byzantine Empire. The great decisions are indeed made inside the palace by the caliph, but the decisions as to who shall make these decisions, that is, who is to be caliph, are not, as in Byzantium, palace-centred. On the contrary, they are decided outside, in territorial/religious uprisings.

3. The caliph is served by two sets of professional decision-implementers. The bureaucracy—the *diwan*—is effectively inherited from the Byzantines and Sassanids and the army becomes a standing regular force after 750.

4. At his palace, the caliph suffers from *no* sort of *procedural* restraints whatsoever. His word is law. But he allows his provincial governors all-but-complete procedural discretion and wide substantive discretion, also. The empire, therefore, is highly decentralized, very unlike the Byzantine polity. Substantively, moreover, the caliph is limited. This reflects the bisection of authority already noted. Since there are no procedural constraints upon him on his side of this bisected authority, the caliph is therefore so absolute within this sphere as to be styled despotic. But despotic as he is, his authority is constrained in two ways. The first is common to all pre-modern societies—the need for the co-operation of a stratum of 'notables' at grass-roots level, while the second is peculiar to Islamic societies. It is the highly *persuasive* authority of the *sharia* even in the area where it is the caliphal writ that runs.

4. THE TERRITORIAL FRAMEWORK

4.1. *The Formal Organization*

The Caliphate was organized in Governorates whose governors exercised plenipotentiary powers, utilizing the former Byzantine and Sassanid administrations which were still in place. It is a primitive way of governing an empire. Of all the empires so far discussed, it resembles most Achaemenid

---

[25] P. Crone and M. Hinds, *God's Caliph: Religious Authority in the First Centuries of Islam* (CUP, Cambridge, 1986).

Persia with its satrapies. The empire was, really, a sort of confederation of
Governorates and subunits that nested inside them. All pre-modern empires
were to some extent like this, but the Caliphal Empire was considerably
looser-knit than the late Roman, Byzantine, or the Chinese empires—
especially the last. Its makeshift character, though justified by the speed
with which the empire (from Cyrenaica to Merv) had been assembled in a
mere twenty years, was nevertheless retained in permanence with only the
few refinements noticed below.

In the beginning, there were a small number of great Governorates with
lesser territorial units nesting inside them. Syria, comprising the area from
the Taurus Mountains to Gaza, was subdivided into four (later five) military
districts (*ajnad*), Palestine, Jordan, Damascus, and Hims (to which Qinnasrin
was later added); this area was governed by the caliph himself, with sub-
governors appointed by him. Iraq was divided into Kufa and dependencies
(Mesopotamia and north-western Iran) and Basra and dependencies (the
rest of Iran as well as Transoxania, roughly Soviet Uzbekistan and south
Kazakhstan, and Sind). Kufa and Basra were sometimes assigned to separate
governors and sometimes awarded together, and the governor who received
both would control the whole of the former Sassanian Empire, or indeed
more. The Maghrib comprised Egypt, North Africa, and Spain. Finally
there was the Governorate of Arabia, subdivided into Mecca and Medina,
Oman, Yemen, and so forth. Outside Syria the caliph appointed the
governor, who in turn appointed the sub-governors.

As the empire was consolidated these great Governorates were broken
down into smaller ones, and the local administration strengthened and
regularized as follows. The governor was the *amir* or general. Alongside
him the caliph appointed an *amil or* 'agent' to collect the tribute. The
relationship between *amir* and *amil* fluctuated over time. Sometimes there
were two individuals, sometimes the two offices were held by one and the
same man. Under the Umayyads, governors' terms in office seem to have
been brief, with many abrupt dismissals, but in the distant provinces things
were not always that simple. There, the governor was virtually independent
until dismissed and a successor appointed, so that the latter might even find
himself resisted by the official in post (as in the well-attested case of Abu'l-
Khattar in Spain, 743).

Except for the centrally appointed *amil*, governors made all local appointments themselves. The most important of these were the chief of police and
the judge (*quadi*). Below the level of the Governorate and the province, the
territorial arrangements differed. Towns were represented by some 'head'
whose title varies from place to place, and divided into precincts, each of
which would elect its elder. Villages would be represented by their 'local

headman' (known as *mazut* in Egypt).[26] In the numerous nomadic zones the governor would deal with the tribesmen through their sheikh.

In the course of time military and political power shifted from the centre of the empire to the east, a shift reflected in the location of the imperial capital. At first it was Medina but after the conquests it was moved to the more central city of Damascus, and then, after the Iranian lands had provided the backing for the Abbasids, it was settled in Iraq, at Baghdad (and for a time at Samarra). Indeed, only a violent revolt in Baghdad prevented the great Caliph Mamun from setting up his capital in distant Merv on the easternmost rim of the empire.

4.2. The Human Geography

Before passing on to other matters, three features in the human geography of the empire demand attention. The first is the relationship between town and desert.

Although nomads played an important (if controversial) role in the conquest of the empire, Islam had been founded by town-dwellers, and it presupposed urban ways and conditions; witness such institutions as the communal Friday prayer, the muezzin's call from the minaret, and the recuperative nights of the fast of Ramadan. It was the town that formed the focus of Islamization and Arabization and the creation of the new Islamic civilization: the *hammams*, the markets, the mosques and minarets. It is not insignificant that the merchant tended to be regarded as superior to the peasant, and it should certainly be underlined that the bedouin, who appear romantic to the West, were universally detested as the very worst offscourings of society. As the conquests succeeded and large numbers of Arab tribesmen fanned out across the empire a curious demographic paradox arose: nomadization in the arid zones alongside the multiplication of towns and the development of urban life. It goes without saying that the nomads and the sedentary population were antipathetic, incompatible, and mutually hostile. Ibn Khaldun[27] saw this antagonism between nomadic desert tribesmen and townsmen and cultivators as the basic dynamic of the political process. He argued that a cycle begins, consisting of desert rebellion, then the tribal conquest of the towns, then the seduction of the tribesmen by the towns, hence a fresh desert rebellion, opening a new cycle. This theory has been espoused and elaborated by Gellner, who accepts that

[26] R. Levy, *The Social Structure of Islam*, 2nd edn. (CUP, Cambridge, 1957), 34.

[27] Ibn Khaldun (1332–1406), *The Muqaddimah* (*An Introduction to History*), ed. N. J. Dawood, trans. F. Rosenthal (Pantheon Books, New York, 1967). In this text all references are to the abridgement of N. J. Dawood, (Routledge, London, 1967).

it did not apply to Mamluk Egypt or the Ottoman Empire. Other Islamicists maintain that it only applies fully in North Africa.[28]

Another feature of the human geography—no surprise after what we have said about the Achaemenid Empire (see above, pp. 287–8)—was the unevenness of its landscape and population. The Caliphal Empire embraced vast deserts like the Dasht-i-Kavir, where no life can exist at all, and the arid or semi-arid zones dotted with the flocks and the black tents of the wandering bedouin. Elsewhere great mountains provided strongholds for dissidents and rebels. Hence there were many areas impenetrable by public authority. In these, the local squires and chieftains became Muslims and, for the rest, continued to govern as before.

It is within such a human geography that the caliphal authority was exercised.

4.3. The Informal Organization

Contrary to our own assertion at page 672 above, it has been averred that 'the Provinces were ruled by Governors sent by the Caliph and their authority was absolute until they were dismissed by their master. If any of the local people were so misguided as to attempt a rebellion, the units of the great Khurasani army . . . could be drafted in to chastise them. The system was, in short, an absolute military dictatorship.'[29] This 'Hobbist' vision of the polity also seems supported, moreover, by the abject quietism advocated by the eleventh-century jurist al-Ghazali.[30]

This was not how it was, nor was it ever so in any of the pre-modern polities, especially the extensive and usually highly heterogeneous ones we call empires. The brutal fact is that the central government's full-time officials were too thin on the ground to exercise that continuous and relentless pressure that characterizes government today. In all cases—even in today's bureaucratic polities—the government was obliged to call in, at some lower administrative level or other, the co-operation of local laypersons. In the sharply inegalitarian societies of those times these were, inevitably, those individuals who, because of their superior learning, piety, lineage, or wealth, were regarded by the population as their 'natural' leaders. Such people—as we have seen—went under the name of 'gentry' in China, decurions or perhaps *nobiliores* in the Roman Empire, *dynatoi* in the Byzantine

---

[28] Gellner, *Muslim Society*, 1–87.

[29] H. Kennedy, 'Central Government and Provincial Élites in the Early Abbasid Empire', *Bulletin of the Journal of African and Oriental Studies*, 44 (1981), 26.   [30] See p. 693 below.

Empire, and were to become known as *buzones*, gentry, squires, and the like in England. For the Caliphal Empire, Islamicists call them the 'notables'.

The qualifications for being a notable differed from one place and one time to another. In medieval Nishapur the *ulema* and the scholars enjoyed especial esteem, so much so that wealthy men who aspired to local leadership would trade wealth for religious prestige, a little like the way the local moderate-income gentry in Ch'ing China qualified for leadership of their communities by passing one of the state civil service examinations. Elsewhere it might be a wealthy landowner with many retainers at his command. Elsewhere again it could be (as at Damascus) the *ashraf* or descendants of the Prophet (who were also wealthy, to boot). In some places—Mosul is one—local sheikhs with their tribal followings exerted political influence.[31]

It was on such as these that the governors of provinces or important cities had to rely. It is axiomatic in the literature on public administration that, unless the officials can win a measure of popular acceptance, they must use coercion and threats; and that to do this unremittingly over a long time is highly expensive, time-consuming, distracting, and ultimately self-defeating. There were other and more specific reasons, however, for this reliance on the notables. Most governors served for short terms of one to three years and were nearly always strangers to the locality.[32] And most caliphal governors suffered another handicap as well in that the regular army garrisons were small, if they existed at all, and it was uncommon for units of the central (the Iraqi) field army to be sent to the provinces. (The exceptions seem to have been Ifriqiya and Khurasan.) Consequently, when the governors wanted to exact taxes from tribesmen or repel raiders or suppress tax revolts they had to rely on the militia. Militias could run to a fair size: at Mosul they numbered some 2,000 men, and in Egypt 5,000.[33] In highly stratified societies such popular militias are invariably officered by the local notables. (The English army was a popular militia for 1,000 years and one could identify the make-up of the local notabilities in any century by simply observing who commanded the shire levies.) The Caliphate was no exception. For instance, in Egypt the *sahib al-shurtah*, the commandant of the militia, was chosen (by the governor) from among the local notables, the *wujuh*;[34] so that, since the force on which the governor had to rely was captained by the local notables, he had no alternative but to court them. We hear of an extremely harsh and unpopular governor of Egypt who collected the taxes so pitilessly that the population revolted. Unluckily for him, he

[31] The literature is cited in Kennedy, 'Central Government' and in B. Shoshan, *The Politics of Notables in Medieval Islam* (Asian and African Studies, Haifa, 1986).

[32] As in China and with the same consequences—see p. 766 ff. below.

[33] Kennedy, 'Central Government', 31–5.   [34] Ibid. 35. *Wujuh* means 'faces'.

had also alienated the notables. They officered the militia, so that when the governor led it out to meet the rebels he found himself deserted.[35]

We do not have equivalent information as to how things were managed at village level, but the same kind of relationships applied. For instance, as recounted elsewhere in this chapter, in some places a great landowner was made responsible for tax collection. At all echelons, from the caliphal downwards to the hamlet, some degree of co-operation was demanded of the local notables—not very grand personages, no doubt, at the level of the hamlet—and to the extent that this was so, the superior echelon had to bend itself in some measure to the locals' velleities.

This had critical implications for the government's field officials at every level of interface with the lay-notables. A governor or a mayor who provokes tax revolts or riots is not much use to his superiors and they will remove him. Hence these officials have to 'get on with' the local population. But if the only way to do this is by espousing its interests, this too is a reason for the government getting rid of them. And the obverse is true. If the governor is left in place long enough to get to know his locality well he tends to 'go native' and champion it against the central power. Yet if the government tries to prevent this close assimilation by rotating the governors and/or making sure that they were strangers to their province—as the caliphs did—they will be so ignorant of the local power structures, and indeed often of the local language, that they will be forced to depend on the local bigwigs and fixers.

The upshot of all this is that in the Caliphate, as in all other pre-modern states of any size and particularly the empires, control was patchy and there was much wheeling-and-dealing at the interface where officials and local populations met.

It does not follow that the caliph was no despot or that the polity should not be described as despotic. Despotism consists of the autocrat's 'capacity, in practice and not just in theory, to take at his personal will the life, the limb, the liberty, and the property of any of his subjects without due process of law'.[36] This does not mean that in the pre-modern state the autocrat's freedom to act, as just defined, was exercised all the time on all the population in all classes of matter. A despotic government of that kind would be better termed 'totalitarian'. But the material pre-conditions for this latter kind of polity did not exist until well into the present century. Jean Dunbabin, in her study of early medieval France, has put the point very

---

[35] Kennedy, 'Central Government', 34. This governor was Musa, the same man who had earned a reputation for fiscal ferocity in the Jezira and whose operations there, as described by the Christian Denis of Tell-Mahré, are recounted below at pp. 722–3. Readers may be happy to know that this brute received his come-uppance.   [36] Cf. 'Conceptual Prologue', pp. 66–70.

well: 'What distinguishes government from personal control is its unremitting character. To be governed is to be subjected to the regular pressure of an authority operating according to fixed rules. In the full sense of the word, it is arguable that nobody was governed before the later nineteenth century.'[37]

5. THE CALIPH

5.1. *The Caliphate*

Muhammad is the veritable archetype of the 'charismatic' ruler, and this is why the nature and role of his successors, the caliphs, were so exceedingly problematical. Muhammad's unlimited authority simply ran wherever he chose to exert it and its legitimation was itself.

So, now he was dead, who was to succeed him, by what title, and with what powers? In principle, the Islamic community ought to be no more than a nomocracy—a government of (divine) laws and not of men. But this was clearly too simplistic. Since the divine *nomos* does not talk, it fell to some human to say precisely just what it said; and, again, some human had to give effect to it. Were these two functions to be entrusted to a single person (like Muhammad himself) or to reside in two different persons or colleges?

The entire matter has been given theoretical expression by Max Weber. 'In its pure form', he says, 'charismatic authority may be said to exist only in *natu nascendi*.' Once the charismatic individual has disappeared his authority, if it is to persist at all, is either 'traditionalized' or 'routinized', or both; and Weber then goes on to list the various modes by which this condition is brought about. In the Caliphate the practice followed one or more of three modes of deciding on the successor. In one, the charismatic leader himself designates his successor, as Moses (it is said) designated Joshua. An alternative is for the entourage of the dead leader to designate. Weber instances the original mode of choosing and crowning a bishop of the Church, and in the Caliphate this mode of transmission was usually pursued by committees of six senior advisers (Companions of the Prophet)—a *shura*. The final option is hereditary transmission.[38] In the event the caliphal succession came to be based on a mixture of all three methods. But this did not come about by any premeditation: on the contrary, the sudden and unexpected death of the Prophet left his entourage in total confusion and the succession (of Abu Bakr) was the outcome of a quarrelling, self-appointed committee

[37] J. Dunbabin, *France in the Making, 843–1180* (OUP, Oxford, 1985), 277.
[38] *Max Weber: Selection in Translation*, ed. W. G. Runciman, trans. E. Matthews (CUP, Cambridge, 1978), 246–8.

of notables, hastily meeting in secret. Only after it had reached a conclusion was the nomination announced—to popular acclamation.

This odd and idiosyncratic series of events set three precedents for those who would later be called the Sunni and represent mainstream Islam. They were: a caliph must be a Qurashi because this was the Prophet's own tribe; the office was elective; and the privilege of nominating the new caliph lay with the leading notables, those who 'had power to release and bind', with the public ratifying their designation. A fourth precedent was set when the dying Abu Bakr successfully urged the Companions to elect Umar as caliph; with this the designation of the successor by a reigning caliph was accepted.

At this point an even more unwholesome element intruded. After Umar's assassination the *shura* appointed as caliph one of the Prophet's sons-in-law—Uthman—and passed over the claim of Muhammad's cousin and son-in-law, Ali. But Uthman was assassinated in his turn so that Ali finally succeeded. In the eyes of the ambitious governor of Syria, Muawiya, who came from the same Umayyad clan as the murdered Uthman, Ali was less than zealous in pursuing the murderers. Muawiya challenged Ali's title, and in the event deposed him and took the throne. His accession, which seems pure usurpation to us, was not necessarily so regarded at that time, for it could be held to conform in part to the precedents enumerated above. The avenging of a blood debt was fully legitimate in Arab eyes but, more to the point, Muawiya had acceeded by a sort of *shura* council, and had duly received the popular acclamation in Jerusalem and then elsewhere.

From this date (661) the chief mode of choosing the caliph came to be designation by the ruling caliph in the context of hereditary principle: Muawiya and his successors kept the Caliphate in their own family for ninety years. But the element of electivity was preserved in so far as a ruling caliph had to get the agreement of the generals and the like to his choice, and also to have the approval of the *ulema*.

The controversial methods of selecting the patriarchal caliphs—especially the dispute between the Umayyads and the Alids—drove many Muslims back to first principles, and by the inherent nature of that faith every political attitude was promoted by some religious sect and every religious sect promoted some political attitude. Given the nature of Islam, it was inevitable that these sects should split along one or other of its three fault-lines already mentioned—nomocracy, caesaropapism, or bisected sovereignty.

The first of these is the *Kharijite* position. Its essence is that the community itself is charismatic, that the divine law of Islam is transcendent, and that therefore the ruler is but a temporary instrument of the Faithful. He is there only to see that the Law is duly observed. Ultra-pious and violently fanatical, Kharijites held that the impious had ceased to be Muslims *ipso facto* and must be killed. The mere recitation of the *shahada* did not in itself make a person a Muslim; good deeds were also necessary and it was by these that worthiness was to be judged. From this it followed that the only criterion of caliph-worthiness was piety. It did not matter whether the caliph was black or white, noble or base-born. These views set the Kharijites against any hereditary transmission of the Caliphate and, particularly, the notion that the caliph must be a Qurashi. They demanded an elective Caliphate, where the sole criterion was piety. This doctrine, coupled with a belief that *jihad* (holy war) was a sixth 'pillar of Islam' (cf. pp. 698–9 below), turned them into fanatical rebels against Alids, Umayyads, and Abbasids alike, and their uprisings were frequent, bloody, and widespread.

In direct contrast are the views of those sects whose ideal ruler was a charismatic autocrat in instant touch with the divinity. To them the caliph was the very vehicle of Allah, the divinely inspired and hence infallible interpreter of the Quran. Their ideal, then, was caesaropapist: the true ruler combined supreme temporal and spiritual authority in his own person.[39] This view was common to all the many sects which are collectively called the Shia.

This term stands for *Shiat Ali*—the 'party of Ali'. Once again it is necessary to return to the Umayyad–Alid conflict. Ali's defeated supporters convinced themselves that special charismatic virtue resided in the Alid line of the Quraish—and nowhere else. With Ali dead, they transferred their faith to his two sons. One of these—Husain—took up arms only to be defeated and executed on the battlefield of Karbala, in 680. This Husain became a martyr figure, and to this very day the Shiites commemorate his death with ritual self-flagellation in the streets. But not even Husain's death ended the matter, for the Shia transferred their allegiance to his descendants; and with this they became far more numerous and dangerous, for events took a turn that conducted them into messianism. Like the Sunnis, they called the messiah (which is Hebrew for 'the anointed one') the *Mahdi* ('the divinely guided one').

This messianism was due to the Shiites regarding the descendants of Ali, through the successive generations, as the genuine imams—the true spiritual-cum-temporal leaders of the *umma*. In 765 some Shiites recognized Ismail, one of the sons of the sixth imam, as his successor, hence the seventh imam. This was emphatically not the view of the majority of the Shiites, who recognized his brother as the true successor. The former group came to believe that Ismail's son would return as the Mahdi. Hence they were sometimes called the 'Seveners' or Ismailis. Some of their sects were to

---

[39] Crone and Hinds, *God's Caliph*.

be uncompromisingly bent on a universal and fundamental reordering of Islamic society, honeycombing the Caliphate with their secret societies. Over time the Ismaili sect split further. One group has given rise to the Druzes of today. Another branch, the Nizaris, gave birth to the notorious Assassins. Another and far more destabilizing Ismaili sect was the Qarmatians (see below, p. 701).

Ismail's brother, the man to whom most of the Shiites had given their allegiance, continued his line until the eleventh generation of descendants. His son was a mere child and in 874 he disappeared and was never found again. The Faithful would not credit his death and insisted that he would eventually reappear, and so became known as the Twelvers (as contrasted with the 'Seveners'). So began the so-called 'great concealment', the notion of the 'Hidden Imam', who was to come again as the Mahdi but was in the meantime represented on earth by the *mujtahidun* ('the strivers [after learning]') who guide his flock. (This is the state orthodoxy of Iran.)

Thus Kharijism represents the triumph of the divine law by the redundancy of the ruler, and Shiism its triumph in the person of the ruler. But the vast majority of Muslims are *Sunnis*.

Sunna means the beaten path, the *mos maiorum*. Its beliefs and practices are derived from the *hadith* or the words and deeds of the Prophet as collected and interpreted by the learned, the *ulema*, on the basis of *ijma*, consensus. This Sunni majority doctrine in due course came to accept the *de facto* bisection of authority between the *ulema* and the caliph. The way this position was reached and its momentous political consequences will be considered later on.

I have spent so much time on these sectaries because, as the sequel will show, they kept the Caliphate in a constant turmoil of usurpations, uprisings, civil wars, and secessions.

5.2. *Absolutism and Constraints*

5.2.1. THE FIRMAMENT OF LAW

Why authority came to be bisected can only be appreciated inside the context of Islamic sacred law, the *sharia*. The *sharia* goes far beyond what lay opinion in the West considers as law properly so called, that is to say a set of rules which permit or forbid, and carry sanctions for disobedience. The *sharia* is nothing less than the revealed will of God, and as such 'an all-embracing body of religious duties, the totality of Allah's commands that regulate the life of every Muslim in all its aspects'.[40] It is as much concerned

---

[40] J. Schacht, *Introduction to Islamic Law* (OUP, Oxford, 1982), 1.

with religious rites and worship and with intimate everyday behaviour as with what the West considers as 'legal' subject-matter. Furthermore, unlike Western systems which dichotomize actions into those that are permitted and those that are prohibited, it ranges them through the spectrum of obligatory/recommended/indifferent/reprehensible/forbidden. Since it is God's commandments, the *sharia* was not the creation of the Caliphate but preceded it. It was not, in principle, shaped by Muslim societies but the reverse—it shaped them—shaped them in every jot and tittle of personal behaviour and stamped on them a stratification and a set of values which gave them the distinctive character we instantly recognize as 'Islamic' or 'Muslim' today. And being the revealed will of God, it could be interpreted but never altered.

Law was the command of God, and Muslim *fiqh* (jurisprudence) consisted of the discovery of its terms. The most obvious—and incontrovertible— source was the Quran, but for the most part its verses could only provide guide-lines. Yet in a short space of time the new rulers fitted materials from highly diverse sources into them: pre-conquest Arab tribal elements, local customary law, Romano-Byzantine law, Jewish law, as well as the adminis- trative practices of the Umayyads, though these themselves were not infre- quently based on some of the elements listed above.[41] In addition to this and of enormous importance were the actions and sayings attributed to the Prophet himself and authoritative early jurists—the *hadith*, the 'oral tradi- tion'—which parallels the *halakha* in Jewish law.

The *ulema*—laymen-scholars—interpreted and expounded the Quran, but the traditions that they accepted differed widely from one area to another, so that what was held to be the law differed in different areas or among different 'schools' of *ulema*. It was at this stage that certain particularly erudite and specialized *ulema* began to try to systematize all these elements, and of all these jurists the most influential was Shafii.

Shafii (767–820) took hold of existing elements in juristic thinking and systematized and restructured them in a new way. He did it by clearly identifying the sources of the law and their relationship to one another. The sources were the so-called 'four roots' of the law. The first was obviously the Quran. Next came the *hadith* or sayings and doings attributed to the Prophet. Where these two sources were insufficient in themselves to apply to a particular case the third source, *qiyas*, that is, analogical reasoning, came

---

[41] The matter is highly controversial. For a long time the classical text was J. Schacht, *The Origins of Muhammadan Jurisprudence* (OUP, Oxford, 1950). The most recent work is P. Crone's *Roman, Provincial and Islamic Law* (CUP, Cambridge, 1987), whose first chapter (entitled 'The State of the Field') is an admirable critical history of the study of the topic, and, parenthetically, contains a withering critique of Schacht.

into play. And where, even after all this, there was still controversy over the outcome, the matter was to be settled by *ijma*, consensus—the consensus of the *ulema* in particular. In the course of time this last source came to play a much more prominent part in Muslim jurisprudence than that assigned to it in Shafii's *Risalah*.

Shafii's work did not ensure uniformity in the law. There are still four great 'schools' of Muslim law, but they differ on details within the juris-prudential criteria that Shafii had laid down. We might well add, paren-thetically, that since this seamless web of *sharia* is the supreme integrative agent in Muslim life, his unifying work was far more significant for the Caliphate (and its successors) than anything done by, for instance—to choose just two names of the few who are familiar to the West—Harun al-Rashid or Saladin.

By these routes the learned were able to spin out of the sparse and exiguous injunctions in the Quran a most intricate and fine-woven web of detailed provisions covering all the conceivable predicaments of mankind, however improbable.[42] But these routes are quite different from those by which the West had arrived at its laws. There, law had grown out of the practice of the courts or the remedies they could offer, but the *sharia* was not a corpus of positive law. It was an abstract theoretical and deductive exercise—an extreme case of a 'jurists law',[43] one where the law is not the creation of the state as legislator but is the product of legal science and is to be found in its scholarly textbooks.

During the jurists' heyday (*c.*750–850) the application of the law to particular cases was being pursued creatively. The activity, the striving for the solution, is *ijtihad*. It is often rendered as 'the power of independent judgment'. But after this high period, as various points of disagreement between jurists were narrowed down, *ijtihad* withered: it was still needed for the application of the law, so juristic thinking continued. But no new schools of law were formed and it was agreed that nobody might form new ones, while the bulk of jurists, the uncreative ones, fell back on 'imitation' (*taqlid*) by which every jurist was bound to accept and follow the doctrines already propounded.[44]

As the law rigidified, the gap between its theory and the practice in the real world widened and its normative (as opposed to positivistic) character became more salient than ever. Jurisprudence had arrived at what has been

[42] See e.g. the examples, in N. J. Coulson, *A History of Islamic Law* (Edinburgh UP, Edinburgh, 1964), 81–2. For example, at what precise moment does succession open to the estate of a person turned into stone by the devil?   [43] Schacht, *Introduction*, 209.

[44] W. B. Hallaq, 'Was the Gate of Ijtihad Closed?', *International Journal of Middle East Studies*, 16 (1984).

called 'doctrinaire isolationism': 'divorced from actual legal practice, [it] had become an introspective science.'[45]

So the situation amounted to this: 'The *sharia* is . . . divinely given . . . it cannot be altered by human legislation. The only human control of the *sharia* is through interpretation, and interpretation is taken to include the application . . . to novel circumstances. The only authorized interpreters of the *sharia* are the *ulema* . . .'[46]

The caliphs duly set up *sharia* courts, conducted by trained specialists, the *qadis*, but because so much of *sharia* law was unsuited or unaccommodated to the running of a state, the caliphs had also established their own court whose principal duty had been to deal with complaints against and between their officials. It was an 'administrative court' of complaints, the *mazalim*. To remedy the *sharia* courts' inadequacy for administering the empire, they attracted into these *mazalim* courts entire classes of business relating to statecraft. It was by these steps that the empire came to have one law—the *sharia*—but two separate jurisdictions: a *sharia* jurisdiction and a non-*sharia* (not a contra-*sharia*) jurisdiction, that is, the caliphal one, not unacceptable to the *ulema* who had always recognized that he had the right to define the jurisidiction of the *sharia* courts. So, while the latter handled religious, family, and most civil matters, items like police, taxation, criminal justice, and military affairs fell within the caliphal jurisdiction. (The fact that the separation was not entirely clear-cut will be referred to below.)

The *ulema* reconciled the theory of the transcendent and all-embracing authority of the *sharia* with this second and caliphal jurisdiction by conflating two propositions: one, that as the imam, the caliph was, of all Muslims, bound to observe the *sharia*, and two, that he had 'the wider and supreme duty of . . . the protection of the public interest . . . [and] hence overriding discretion to determine according to time and circumstance how the purposes of God for the Islamic community might best be effected'.[47] So they glossed the *sharia* to give *ex-post facto* legalization to caliphal activities, and to this end devised the theory of *siyasa shariyya*. This doctrine affirms that the caliph possesses complete discretion to 'apply and complete the sacred law' as long as the *sharia* 'sets him no bounds'.[48] But, as Grünebaum instantly adds, 'this was an ambiguity [the Abbasids] never managed to master'. For in principle, where does the *sharia* not set

[45] Coulson, *History of Islamic Law,* 82.
[46] W. M. Watt, *Islamic Political Thought* (Edinburgh UP, Edinburgh, 1964; paperback edn., 1980), 94.
[47] Coulson, *History of Islamic Law,* 129–30.
[48] So, Grünebaum, 'Sources of Islamic Civilisation', 85.

bounds?[49] How can there be 'whole areas of law . . . where the *sharia* did not apply . . .'[50] The most economical explanation is that: 'The jurists made the best of a bad job by maintaining the fiction that the sovereign when giving judgment in the mazalim courts was exercising his authority, within the limits permitted by the *sharia*.'[51]

It would appear, then, that the basic law gave the ruler total, definite, and permanent discretion to do what he pleased, when he pleased, in matters to do with government. Differently put, as far as government is concerned, the *sharia* is comparable to those constitutions which contain clauses to the effect that they may be suspended by the decree of the ruler, and that the decree is issued at his absolute discretion.

So—was the caliph a *despot*, not bound by the laws, and if so in what respects? Since the caliph could apparently do what he liked within his own sphere, I have presented the situation as a *bisection* of authority between *ulema* and caliph, each supreme within his own sphere. An opposing view is that since 'the Sunni solution deprived the caliph of a say in the definition of the law all the while insisting that he abide by this law, it *could* be said that the scholars succeeded in turning an absolutist monarch into a constitutional one'.[52] The authors of this view see the problem as a matter of theory versus practice—that although the *sharia* controlled the actions of the caliph in principle, there was no machinery to effect this.[53] But the mere promulgation of a constitution does not in itself imply or entail constitutionalism. The *saria* certainly was a constitution, but if it was a dead letter, how can the caliph be said to be bound to it?

The contention that the fault lies in the absence of a machinery to safeguard the constitution cannot stand. For what prevented the caliph from invading or taking over the law in the *qadi* courts—why was he not as absolute there as he was in his *mazalim* courts and his palace? The answer has nothing to do with a 'machinery' to protect them. The *qadi* courts were protected by public opinion. Throughout history there are multitudes of 'absolute' monarchs who are subject to similar limitations, though there is no machinery to enforce these. Convention, tradition, or religious conviction sufficed.

---

[49] The ways in which Islamicists have expressed the problem, let alone offered a solution, differ quite remarkably. For instance, while some say that the *sharia* was seamless and applied to the caliphal authority as much as to the *qadi* courts, others state quite baldly that it did not. For instance, the caliph's 'courts were not bound by the *sharia*': Watt, *Islamic Political Thought*, 94.

[50] R. M. Savory, *Introduction to Islamic Civilization* (1976).

[51] Ibid. 58; Watt, *Islamic Political Thought*, 96.

[52] Crone and Hinds, *God's Caliph*, 108 ff. Emphasis in the original.   [53] Ibid. 109.

As to the second contention, that the caliph was a 'constitutional' monarch, we shall simply have to invent a new term to describe Queen Victoria.

There is a third defence of the contention, which is this: although caliphs exercise absolute discretion within their own jurisdiction, that jurisdiction is 'constitutionalized' because the *sharia* has authorized it. This is tantamount to saying that if a ruler enacts or inherits a constitution which grants him unlimited powers, that makes him a constitutional monarch.

Caliphs only rarely interfered with the *qadi* courts, and to this extent could fairly be described as *alligatus legibus*. That is emphatically not the case in respect of the caliph's ordinances and decrees (which had the full force of law but might not be called by that dread word since the one and only law was the *sharia*, and it was immutable). As regards these decrees and so on the caliph was not bound at all. He could at his whim take the life, limb, liberty, or property of any of his subjects and he did so as the need or fancy took him (see below at pp. 719–20). This is so obvious that Islamicists unhesitatingly use the terms 'absolutism'[54] and 'absolute despotism'.[55] 'The spirit of absolutism', writes Hodgson, 'remained profoundly contrary to that of the *sharia*. By the side of the great monarch stood his executioner, to behead a man at a word from the caliph. Here was no question of mufti and qadi or of the *sunnah* of Muhammad.'[56]

Inside his jurisdiction this caliphal power was so absolute and the position of the subject so precarious that it amounts to *despotism*, the utterly unbridled exercise of personal power. 'Might in fact was right and this was eventually recognized by the scholars in their denunciation of civil disobedience even when political authority was in no sense properly constituted . . .'[57] In 'abject surrender [they maintained] that obedience was due to the political power whatever its nature . . . even the most impious and tyrannical regime was preferable to civil strife . . .'[58] 'Sixty years of tyranny are better than an hour of civil strife.'[59] The great apologists for this view came much later than our period, but they were simply rationalizing *ex post facto* the political reality: 'An evil-doing and barbarous sultan, so long as he is supported by military force, so that he can only with difficulty be deposed and that the attempt to depose him would create unendurable civil strife, must of necessity be left in possession and obedience must be rendered to him, exactly as obedience is required to be rendered to those who are placed

[54] M. G. S. Hodgson, *The Venture of Islam*, vol. I, *The Classical Age of Islam* (University of Chicago Press, Chicago, 1974), 347. H. A. R. Gibb, 'Constitutional Organisation', in Khadduri and Liebesny (eds.), *Law in the Middle East*, vol. I (Washington, 1955), 19.   [55] Schacht, *Introduction*, 49.
[56] Hodgson, *Venture of Islam*, i. 347.   [57] Coulson, *History of Islamic Law*, 83.
[58] Ibid. 133.   [59] Gibb, 'Constitutional Organisation', 15.

in command.'[60] This does not mean that the caliphs were not subject to certain *practical* restraints, and to these we must now turn.

5.2.2. DESPOTISM AND CONSTRAINTS

Majesty and Might

Inside his own jurisdiction, which embraced most of the field of public policy, the caliph's discretion, then, was total and complete. Like the Byzantine emperor, the *isapostolos*, his office was wrapped in sanctity. It was he or the person deputizing for him who led the congregation in prayer, and he for whom prayer was said in the mosques. He was God's Deputy, the Shadow of God on Earth, the Commander of the Faithful, the Redresser of Wrong. It is difficult to convey an adequate idea of the overwhelmingness of caliphal power. To suggest reading *The Arabian Nights* seems outrageously frivolous, yet, curiously, the impression it leaves is much more right than wrong. The most direct way to sketch the vast dimension of the caliphal power is by describing its seat—the palace.

The palace was the centre into which the vast tax revenues and booty of the opulent empire flowed, and out of which political power radiated. An Arabic text[61] describes the Byzantine ambassadors' audience with Muqtadir (917). Having entered via the Grand Stables they proceed to the zoo and on to the New Palace which lies in a garden where a pool of mercury shimmers amid 400 date-palms; then on to the Palace of Paradise, thence to another eleven palaces one after the other until they come to the Court of Ninety, adjoining the Pavilion of Salvation. Here they are at last permitted to sink down on divans and take cool drinks of sherbets. The chronicler also describes the marvellous adornments of these diverse palaces: here the walls are hung with 38,000 tapestries and 22,000 carpets are spread underfoot; while yonder there there are running brooks and fountains. Finally, the audience takes place. The location is the Palace of the Diadem. Here the caliph sits between two strings of nine collars of the most precious stones. After the ambassadors have kissed the ground in obeisance, some automatic device indicates where they should stand. Suddenly the caliph makes a signal, and lo! from out of the ground there springs a tree which fills the cupola and, with mechanical birds twittering on its metal branches, spurts out jets of musk and rosewater.[62]

This enormous complex, the supreme expression of all that was materi-

---

[60] Quoted from al-Mawardi, in Gibb, 'Constitutional Organisation', 19. Cf. P. J. Vatikiotis, *Islam and the State* (Routledge, London, 1987), 34.

[61] Quoted and summarized in D. and J. Sourdel, *La civilisation de l'Islam classique* (Artaud, Damascus, 1968), 335–42.   [62] Ibid. 342.

ally and intellectually most precious in the empire, served three main purposes. It comprised, first of all, the halls and audience chambers for the caliph's public duties, along with the lodgings for their numerous attendants. It also contained guardhouses and the guards to man them. And it contained, finally, the private quarters of the caliph and his harem. The latter was immense. One source says that al-Mutawakkil's harem contained 12,000 women. However, another version puts the figure at 4,000, and—alas for exactitude!—one manuscript reads only 400![63]

These wide acres of buildings and ornamental space swarmed with the multitudinous and motley members of the caliph's household. A palace budget of 918–19 lists specialist artisans, slaves, and freedmen; the multitude of eunuchs; the great court officials, notably the chamberlain (the *hajib*), the treasurer, the commander-in-chief, the 'Grand *Qadi*', and, most important of all, the vizier. Though brief, the catalogue shows how the high official and public posts melted by degrees into the ranks of the most frivolous or the most humble of the caliph's slaves and servants. For there were also the:

Watchmen and others of like station, such as gate-keepers; white provincial and foreign mercenaries; negroes (mostly slaves bought in Egypt, Mecca, etc.); freedmen of the Caliphs (they acted as chamberlains at the palace and as escort on journeys); private body-guards—foot and mounted; seventeen classes of officials employed about the *Dar* and including messengers, Quran readers, muezzins, astrologers, cupbearers, jesters, etc. . . . water-carriers for the palace, bakeries, etc.; private servants; craftsmen and artisans (tailors, fullers, shoe-makers, furriers, etc.); courtiers, physicians, huntsmen, etc.[64]

The Regular Political Process: The Caliph's Day

In the ninth century the caliphs usually worked together with a vizier, though the powers of this officer were still episodic.[65] The vizier was the 'caliph's man', and this meant that he was there not just to apply the law in financial matters and resolve technical administrative problems, which were things that all 'men of the pen' were expected to do, but had in addition to carry out the personal wishes and decisions of the caliph. These related to police and repressive justice, all fiscal and money matters, including rates of pay and pensions, fines and confiscations, and all the administrative and private suits attracted to his *mazalim* court. The caliph was the head of military operations and diplomacy. It was he who appointed and dismissed all

[63] A. Mez, *The Renaissance of Islam*, trans. S. Baksh and D. Margoliouth (Jubilee Printing and Publishing House, Patna, India, 1937), 142.   [64] Levy, *Social Structure of Islam*, 324, n. 3.

[65] D. Sourdel, *Le Vizirat abbasside de 749–936* (Damascus, Syria, 1959–60), 630–1.

agents, amirs, provincial officers of the police, posts, and finance, and also the *qadis*,[66] and it was a cardinal principle that nobody, anywhere in the empire, exercised any authority except by delegation from the caliph. In all these matters the caliph worked with his vizier, whereas the Umayyad caliphs had operated by taking counsel with various groups of notables.

We get some idea of the working day of a conscientious caliph in al-Tabari's (doubtless somewhat idealized) picture.

Al-Mansur was occupied, in the middle of the day, with ordaining and forbidding, with appointing and dismissing, with assuring the protection of the marches and the safety of the roads, with examining the problem of the land-tax, and the expenditure therefrom, with procuring the subsistence of the populace so as to lighten their poverty and induce them, by benevolence, to stay calm and tranquil. Then, after the evening prayer, he examined the letters from the marches, confines and provinces and on these he questioned his confidant of the day on the subjects he knew about until the first one-third of the night had passed,—the hour of his bed-time when his confidant left him . . .[67]

In the mid-ninth century the vizier was still attending the palace every day together with the other secretaries, and would meet the caliph in council together with them. He would present the caliph with the relevant files, and receive and note his instructions for passing on to the departments concerned. During the whole of such sessions he remained standing, even carrying his own inkstand.[68] But towards the end of the ninth century he had become the sole intermediary between the caliph and the administration. It was symbolic of this high status that he now took precedence over the commander-in-chief of the army. He worked from his own magnificent official residence in the city and only went to the palace on the official audience-days, for on the most important affairs of state he consulted the caliph informally. But the more expanded the vizier's administrative role, the more precarious his tenure. A caliph who had abdicated day-to-day control of affairs to his chief minister could only alter their course by dismissing him and appointing someone else. This was something that viziers anticipated. Whenever the caliph summoned his vizier to his presence, the vizier would reply by asking: 'Am I to attend in official dress or in every-day clothes?'[69] The most famous expression of a strong caliph's power to remove his vizier must be Harun's destruction of the Barmecides (Barma-

---

[66] Not always nor in all Governorates. Sometimes the governors appointed, as stated at p. 680 above. See Levy, *Social Structure of Islam*, 339.

[67] Sourdel, *Le Vizirat abbasside*, quoting al-Tabari (III), 402.

[68] Sourdel, *La civilisation*, 367.   [69] Ibid. 369.

kids), so famous—or notorious—that it passed into Arab folklore and can be followed (suitably embellished) in *The Arabian Nights*.[70]

The dismissal of viziers became a commonplace. The usual fate of a disgraced vizier was some enormous fine and/or the confiscation of his goods. He might, however, end his days in prison or be tortured or even executed. It is not at all surprising, therefore, that viziers took steps to strengthen their position by playing palace-politics, the by-now familiar collusion with the harem or the generals or both to secure the accession of one candidate, if necessary by removing the ruling caliph himself. And this brings us to consider the pathological political processes of the Caliphate. These differ significantly from those in the Byzantine Empire: in the Caliphate there is usually little or no connection (as there was in Byzantium) between the internal intrigues of the court and the ever-recurring revolts against caliphal authority in the provinces.

5.3. *The Pathology of the Political Process*

5.3.1. THE FLAWED TITLE TO THE CALIPHATE

In practice the office of caliph was hereditary. The caliph designated a member of his family, usually a son, as heir apparent; if he had not done this before his death, however, a self-appointed clique of court notables made the nomination from members of his family. In either case the nomination had to be 'recognized'.

When a caliph designated his successor, he took steps—historians like al-Tabari narrate many vivid examples—to get the binding assent of the most influential governors and other generals and officials, and it was absolutely necessary that he should also get the approbation of the *ulema*. But both of these were problematical. In the first place, the reigning caliph might—indeed was almost bound to—prefer one of his sons to the others, and this could end in palace conspiracy or civil war. In the second place, which of the numerous *ulema*, scattered all over the Caliphate, were entitled to confer approval? The Sunni jurists finally worked out a complex set of rules, but the only significant one was that the caliph must be of the Qurashi clan.[71] All the rest was just *ex post facto* rationalization. What happened in fact was that the caliph, after designating his successor and

---

[70] *The Book of a Thousand Nights and One Night* (rendered into English from the literal and complete French translation of Dr J. C. Mardrus, transl. P. Mathers (Routledge, London, 1947), iv. 707–23. ('The End of Jafar and the Barmakids').

[71] From al-Mawardi, al-Akham al-Sultaniyya, quoted in *Islam: From the Prophet Muhammad to the Capture of Constantinople: Excerpts from Muslim Writers: The Documentary History of Western Civilization*, ed. B. Lewis, 2 vols. (Macmillan, London, 1974), i. 173–7.

securing the approval of the notables, would get the *ulema* of the capital to do the same—a foregone conclusion among the *jamai-sunnis*.[72] So, in fact, the entire process was not legally determined at all, but simply *ad hoc*.

Where the ruling caliph had *not* designated a successor, the jurists wrote that 'The Imamate is conferred . . . by the choice of the electors' (literally, 'those competent to bind and to loosen'), and they then specified the qualifications of these electors. But this entire exercise was just as futile as that relating to the qualifications of the candidate. In practice the designation was effected by whichever group of dignitaries could get in first.

In either of the two cases much the same group of people would be involved—members of the ruling family, the highest dignitaries, and the chief military commanders. Sometimes it was the vizier, sometimes the Grand *Qadi*, sometimes the commander-in-chief who exercised the strongest influence over the choice. Once agreement was reached each 'elector' would advance and give the *bayah*—the token of allegiance—in the form of a handshake. To do this was to take an oath to which both the caliph-designate and the 'electors' were contractually bound. So much so, in fact, that no caliph-designate, having received the *bayah*, could be divested of the designation except by his own consent.

Once this small group had pledged their allegiance it was required that the *umma* give its consent. This had now become a ritual: the caliph went to the Great Mosque for his first formal audience and would sit on the *minbar*, wearing the insignia of his office: the mantle, the staff, and the signet ring of the Prophet. Then he would address the congregation, giving public thanks to Allah, and receiving formally the pledges of his notables to which was now added that of the congregation as a whole.

These rules were the ones the Sunnis accepted. But any group of sectaries who rejected these rules, such as Karijites or Shiites, could, together with their own *ulema*, anywhere and at any time claim that their own candidate was the true caliph while the ruling caliph was an impious usurper, an anti-caliph in fact. Here, for instance, is a Kharidjite summons to rebellion against Marwan II, the last of the Umayyads:

We met your men . . . and summoned them to obedience of the Merciful and the judgment of the Quran, and they summoned us to the obedience of the Devil and the judgment of Marwan and the house of Marwan. By God! what a difference between Good and Evil! . . . Is he not a polytheist idol-worshipper, a polytheist of

---

[72] e.g. the orthodox, middle of the road, 'communitarian' Sunni, who took an absolutely quietist position *vis-à vis* authority. (See the reference to al-Ghazali, for instance, above). *Jamai-sunnis* is a term of art used by Hodgson (*Venture of Islam*, vol. i; see its Index).

the People of the Book, or a tyrannical Imam, O men of Medina? He is an enemy against whom we must make war.[73]

So, endlessly, caliph after caliph tended to come under armed challenge from some group or groups somewhere or other in the empire, as we shall describe shortly.

5.3.2. THE PATHOLOGY OF THE POLITICAL PROCESS: INSIDE THE COURT.

As we have already stated, with the Abbasids the Caliphate became a pure Palace-type polity. The pathology of the political process took two forms which, with the brief exception noted below, are separate—not just distinguishable but distinct. They may be described as the politics *inside* the court and politics *against* the court. Almost the only time that these may be said to have interconnected was during that brief period 813–47, when the caliphs tried to impose a Mutazilite doctrine via an inquisition court. (That brief and unsuccessful episode resembles, in Byzantium, Heraclius' vain attempt to impose monotheletism, and the efforts of the Isaurians to enforce iconoclasm.)[74]

At the outset, the politics reflect personal intrigues as to who should succeed. A good example is the feud between al-Hadi (785–6) and his mother, who resented her exclusion from power. Al-Hadi tried to poison her but failed, and she retaliated by presenting him with two delicious slave-girls who, at the opportune time, smothered him to death with cushions.

Then viziers begin to be involved. We have already noted Harun's destruction of the Barmakid viziers. In the next reign, it was the vizier of Caliph al-Amin who persuaded him to cut his brother al-Mamun out of the succession. Hence the great civil war, 810–13, which ended in al-Amin's execution and the accession of al-Mamun.

It is not long before a new set of characters enter. These are the amirs (the 'commanders' or 'generals') of the Turkish slave troops (to be described below), who now made up the army. The Grand *Qadi* also begins to play a role at this time. The strands can be seen woven together in the matter of the succession to al-Wathiq (842–7). Al-Wathiq had not designated a successor, so that it fell to the self-appointed 'electors' (see above p. 698) to select a candidate. The Vizier pressed the claim of al-Watiq's infant

---

[73] 'A rebel sermon of 747–748', quoted, Lewis, *Excerpts from Muslim Writers*, ii, 59.

[74] Bk. III, Ch. 1, pp. 634–5. 'Mutazilitism' was for a time the dominant philosophy under the Abbasids. It stood for 'a position between the two positions' (i.e. between Sunni and Shiite), for nationalism, the belief in free will, and hence in 'the created Quran'. *Concise Encyclopedia of Islam*, ed. C. Glassé (Stacey Int., New York, 1989), 291–3.

son, but was opposed by the Grand *Qadi* and the Turkish amirs, who secured
the succession for al-Watiq's brother al-Mutawakkil. The latter's immediate
act was to confiscate the goods of the defeated vizier and have him tortured
to death. Al-Mutawakkil likewise procured the assassination of the commander-in-chief of the amirs. He met his fate when, finally, he tried to
murder his heir-apparent (al-Muntasir) in order to change the succession.
Al-Muntasir struck first, and the Caliph was cut down in his cups by
Turkish officers.[75] This ushered in the forty-year hegemony of the Turkish
amirs who made and unmade caliphs at their will.

But by the reign of al-Muqtadir (908–32) still more *dramatis personae* had
arrived, while the political manoeuvres transcended mere personal struggles
for power and money and reflected policy options. These new actors were
the chief secretaries in the administration. The reign was dominated by the
veritable blood-feud between the families of the two chief secretaries, Ali
ben Isa and Ibn al-Furat, the former insisting on retrenchment, the latter on
expenditures—and the former representing the Sunnis, while the latter—
vizier three times over but ultimately executed—represented the Shiites.
Though the two were at odds over religion, politics, and finances and
cordially hated one another, both wholeheartedly opposed the amirs and
particulary Munis, the formidable eunuch commandant of the Baghdad
police. But in the end, in 927, Ibn al-Furat was left with no choice but
to seek Munis's help; otherwise Baghdad would fall to imminent capture by
the ferocious Qarmatian sectaries. (See below.) From that time on it was
Munis who made and unmade viziers, and the dynasty became the puppets
of the Turkish *Amir al-Umara* (Emir of Emirs), who was later, under the
Seljuk Turkish domination, to be called the '*sultan*'.

5.3.3. THE PATHOLOGY OF THE POLITICAL PROCESS: AGAINST THE COURT.

The political process inside the court as described above was not unaffected
by movements outside the court, of course. Indeed, the court was always
trying to repress the innumerable revolts that keep breaking out everywhere,
so that the fortunes of a general like Munis, for instance, might depend on
how well he handled such matters. But those movements of dissidence and
revolt were never incubated from within the court. In the Caliphate the
revolts are extraneous affairs directed *against* the palace. It is in this respect
that this set of pathological political processes differs from the Byzantine.

The sheer profusion of the rebellions and their diverse nature defy

---

[75] Al-Tabari's dramatic account of these events is reprinted in Lewis, *Excerpts from Muslim Writers*, i.
30–4.

describing them *seriatim*, and statistics would not convey anything of the passions involved. The following tries to do a little of both.

In some rebellions the inspiration was (1) simple personal ambition and in others (2) dynastic ambition. In some it was (3) regional particularism, frequently provoked by excessive and arbitrary taxation. At least one case is (4) pure social revolt. A large number are (5) inspired by fanatical, often millenarian, sectarianism. And a number are (6) straightforwardly military mutinies. The difficulty about categorizing them thus is that rarely does one find a case in which two or even more of these inspirations is not found commingled. In *every* case, without any exceptions at all, however, a religious motive was invoked—as inevitably it had to be for reasons already explained. But in many cases this was no mere pretext but intense religious conviction, and this could often embody a demand for radical social reconstruction.

Among the saliently sectarian revolts are those, for instance, of al-Muqanna, 'the veiled one' (776–9) and Babak (816–37). They were in the 'Abu-muslimiyya' tradition—called after the arch-conspirator who had masterminded the Abbasid revolution and whom al-Mansur had had murdered. Some people looked to his return as the Mahdi (above, pp. 687–8). The Arab historians accuse these sectaries of being antinomians and libertines who refused to recognize any of the prohibitions of the Prophet.[76]

Arguably *the* most serious of all of the sectarian revolts also carried an enormous political and social charge. This was the Qarmatian revolt. The Qarmatians were Ismailis. The sect arose (probably) in Iraq but was directed from Syria, spreading from Kufa to Bahrain. Its uprisings began in 897 and were no sooner quelled in one quarter (e.g. Iraq, 897–901) than they flared up elsewhere (e.g. in Syria-Palestine, 902–6). It failed in the central heartlands of the empire, but one of its leaders succeeded in founding a state in Bahrein. From this base the Qarmatians raided into Iraq and western Arabia: they took Basra, sacked Kufa, cut the pilgrim route to Mecca and in 930 seized Mecca itself in a sack that lasted eight days, and carried off the Black Stone of the Kaaba. This Qarmatian state of Bahrain, which lasted to the end of the eleventh century, was extraordinary. The state owned 30,000 black slaves who did all the work while the Qarmatian over-class lived a semi-communistic life, paying no taxes, receiving loans if in need, and having their houses or mills repaired and their grain ground free of charge.

---

[76] For a useful summary of these doctrines and the revolts that sprang from them, see Laoust, *Les schismes*. The text is primarily based on this book, but additional sources have also been used.

The Saffarids of Seistan exemplify a social-cum-particularist movement. Here one Yaqub ben Laith, a coppersmith turned brigand, roused the rural proletariat against the Tahirid governors. He extended his borders as far west as Fars and as far north as Khurasan. Although he himself was defeated when invading Iraq (876), his brother Amr continued the independent dynasty in Seistan which Yaqub had founded, where it lasted into the tenth century.

Finally one turns to the Zanj uprising, the most incontestable example of a social revolt, but also coupled with sectarian messianism. It arose among the black slaves who toiled among the swamps of southern Iraq, groups of fifty to 500 men, barricaded in barracks at night, and by day subjected to the unremitting lash of the taskmasters. Their leader, a certain Ali ben Muhammad from Rayy (Teheran), had a history of failed sectarian revolt. Professing Kharijite beliefs, he too was one of those who veiled their face and claimed to be the Mahdi. The slaves seized weapons from their opponents, taxed the villages that sided with the caliphal troops, built their own capital near Basra (which they seized and sacked in 871), and pushed into the centre of Mesopotamia before the caliphal armies checked them. They failed principally because, as slaves, they could not win over any other classes to join them. As Sunnis, those classes took against the Zanj's religious creed. Also, they nourished a racial prejudice against blacks. Furthermore, the Zanj had received a certain amount of assistance from some Bedouin clans, objects of loathing and fear among the townsfolk and villagers.[77]

If the 'stability' of a polity is reckoned by the speed with which the throne changes hands irregularly, the Caliphate was much more stable than the Byzantine Empire. Between 632 and 944, some 300 years, only six caliphs (out of sixty-five) were deposed and/or killed. Out of the 107 Byzantine emperors between 395 and 1453 (i.e. 1,058 years), the comparable number was no less than sixty-four. In other terms, only one in ten caliphs was deposed and/or killed against six out of ten Byzantine emperors. These figures are partly reflected in, and partly explained by the hereditary principle in the Caliphate. With one exception only (the Abbassid revolution), every one of the fifty-one caliphs (661–1242) was a blood relative, usually a son, of his predecessor; whereas of the fifty-two Byzantine emperors (641–1204), only twenty-seven were blood-related to their predecessors.

But if one reckons stability by the number and frequency of violent internal conflicts the picture alters dramatically. Compared with the Caliphate the Byzantine Empire, for all its strong propensity to civil war (remarked on above, p. 624), appears as a veritable paragon of stability.

<hr />

[77] These details are derived from Ashtor, *Social and Economic History*, 113–21.

TABLE 3.2.1. *Conflict in Byzantium and the Caliphate*

	Byzantium, 602–1204		The Caliphate, 632–944
Total revolts, etc.	36		42
Mutinies (no serious campaigning)	13+/−3	(36.0%)	4 (9.5%)
Territorial revolts	8	(22.0%)	
(i) Tax issues	—	(10.0%)	—
(ii) Religious	—	(17.0%)	—
Civil war	15	(41.0%)	11 (26.0%)

Unfortunately, it is extremely hard to express this in precise quantitative terms, because there would first have to be agreement on what constituted a 'violent conflict'. It does seem possible and worthwhile, however, to present the following statistics, because they do at least convey some idea of the relative orders of magnitude. Thus, turning to a record of the violent incidents in the two empires as reported in a well-known historical encyclopaedia and hence (one assumes) selected on similar principles, the total number of violent conflicts between 602 and 1204 in the Byzantine Empire is reported as thirty-six, while the total for 632 and 944 in the Caliphate amounts to forty-two. Thus, on average, Byzantium suffered a violent incident every 16.7 years while the Caliphate did so every 7.4 years—*at more than double the rate.*[78]

I have already pointed out the difficulties in classifying such civil conflicts as religious, social, and so on. But on the basis of my own personal classification, for whatever it is worth (and at least it applies an equal judgment to both polities), the incidence of the types of conflict, and their respective proportions of the total are as shown in Table 3.2.1.

However, Muir's *Caliphate*, an old-fashioned work, presents much more detail and yields sixty-four incidents.[79] This catalogue suggests that the rate of disturbances in the Caliphate was not two (as we have just reported) but *three* times the incidence in Byzantium—one in every five years on the average. Muir's list breaks down into the categories shown in Table 3.2.2.

The Caliphate, in short, was rarely free from violent turmoil, and it is not at all surprising that whereas the Byzantine Empire kept itself together until the seizure of Constantinople in 1204, the Caliphate had fallen apart long before. A glance at the Chronology (above, pp. 668–70) shows how it

[78] Derived from Langer, *Encyclopaedia of World History* (5th edn., 1972).
[79] W. Muir, *The Caliphate: Its Rise, Decline and Fall* (Religious Tract Society, London, 1892).

TABLE 3.2.2. *Conflict in the Caliphate*

Type of conflict	Number	%
Regional particularist	24	39.3
Personal ambition	5	8.0
Sectarian	20	33.0
Dynastic (excluding Alid claims)	4	6.5
Social (including Qarmatians)	2	3.3
Military mutinies and coups	6	10.0

Source: W. Muir, *The Caliphate* (1892).

decayed from its outer edges. That is exactly what one would expect given its immense outreach and slow communications.

By 945 when the Buyid tribesmen (of Iranian extraction) seized Baghdad and as amirs to the caliphs became the rulers of the empire, this had shrunk to no more than what today is Iraq and the western half of Iran.

6. THE CENTRAL GOVERNMENT

The tasks the central government set itself were the usual limited list common to the pre-industrial empires: defence and security, a courier and intelligence service, the dispensation of justice, and above all, levying taxation—to which we might add the defence and promulgation of the Faith. The role of the imperial administration was architectonic. Yet, despite its limited tasks, the central administration became increasingly elaborate just as the empire was falling apart. The reason is almost certainly the financial crisis of the late ninth and the tenth centuries which demanded more careful management than previously.

6.1. *The Civil Administration*

6.1.1. THE HOUSEHOLD

We have already given some idea of the huge numbers and miscellaneous avocations of the members of the household. The eunuchs are particularly important, as well as certain high officers, whose chief duties were respectively to regulate and restrict access to the caliph and to supply him with money. The rest—harem and bodyguards, jesters and astrologers—do not concern us.

The eunuchs were valued for the same reason as in China and the Byzantine Empire—they were faithful, because they could not found families and were supremely dependent on the good graces of their sovereign. Though they must have conformed to some strictly enforced hierarchy, no record has survived and the best indication we have comes from a late Mamluk (Egyptian) source describing the Fatimids' palace. If that is anything to go by, the eunuch staff would have been headed by the Grand Eunuch, and comprise, *inter alia*, the Intendant of the Palace staff, the butler, and in addition, the politically significant posts of the Master of the Audience Chamber, the Director of the Privy Purse Office, and the Bearer of the Inkstand.[80]

The head of the entire palace establishment was the *hajib*. This title is significant. It is cognate with the word *hijab*, which meant the curtain that separated the sovereign and his assistants during audiences; in short, much the same sort of idea as the European *cancellus*—whence Chancellor.[81] Often humbly born, he was usually one of the caliph's *mawlas* (a freedman, hence client, and hence pledged to him) and, quite often, a eunuch. He was not required to have had any special education. He was simply the caliph's own choice of supreme confidant and *aide*. His principal duty was always to attend at the sessions of the caliph and his high officers. By our period—the mid-ninth century—the office of *hajib* doubled with that of the head of the palace guard, which signifies, *inter alia*, that he was one of the Turkish amirs. By the close of our period, in the troubled early tenth century, the *hajib*, Turkish chief of the guard, was high up in palace politics. He often advised the caliph on the choice of ministers and was in a position to decide the outcome of palace plots. (For instance, it was the *hajib* who crushed the conspiracy that threatened to depose al-Muqtadir.) His role recalls that of the Byzantine *paracoemomenus*, but what made it significantly different was that it was in competition with the vizier. Although he could advise the caliph to depose his vizier, he could not do the vizier's job. It was a sort of dyarchy, and it illustrates the patrimonial nature of the administration: for the relative influence of the two officers depended on the caliph. This is why the contemporary historian Maiskawayhi reports that the vizier must consult with the *hajib*.[82]

The *hajib* had no financial responsibilities. These were a matter for the Treasurer of the Privy Purse, which was not so much a treasury-office as an Arab equivalent of the western European and Byzantine 'Wardrobe', that is, a repository of bullion, precious stones, costly robes, and the like. The post was usually entrusted to a financier (of whom Baghdad had many). There

---

[80] For its Byzantine equivalent, see above at Bk. III, Ch. 1, pp. 639–43.

[81] See pp. 641 above, 912 below.

[82] D. Margoliouth and H. Amedroz (eds.), *The Eclipse of the Abbasid Caliphate (being the 'History' of Ibn-Maiskawayhi [930–1030]*), 6 vols. (Blackwells, Oxford, 1921), iv. p. 52.

was also a Secretary for the Domain Lands. But these treasurers and yet others who are sometimes mentioned had ill-defined responsibilities.

6.1.2. THE DEPARTMENTS

The main features at this time were as follows. First, the management of the administrative structure, differently from Byzantium, was centralized, with the vizier in supreme charge. The way he exerted his control is best described after a glance at departmental organization. Known as *diwan*, the departments were subdivided into sections, or *majles*. A *diwan* contained at least three main *majleses* which respectively handled the correspondence, the general administration, and the programmes for action. They also contained two control departments called *diwan al-usul* and *diwan al-zimam*.

The *Chancery*—renowned for literary grace and calligraphy—[83] contained three sub-departments which suggest its role and *modus operandi*. One was for incoming correspondence. A second was named 'Decisions', that is, it handled the minutes of decisions taken in various committees and meetings, the most important being those between the vizier and the caliph, already described (p. 696). The last was the 'Seal', i.e. the official stamp on the outgoing correspondence resulting from the foregoing operations.

No complete list of the *diwans* survives and some mentioned by the chroniclers were clearly temporary.[84] The simplest way to describe them is to set aside the departments of the Chancery and the palace for the moment, and think of the remainder as three groups, concerned respectively with spending, raising, and handling the public revenues.

The largest spending department was the Army Office, the *diwan al-jaysh*, which kept particularly meticulous accounts.[85] Another, *diwan al-nafaqat*, paid for the civil servants and lesser palace officials and distributed certain classes of pensions. It is to be distinguished from the privy purse. Just after our period two other departments were created for the upkeep of the Holy Cities and for public works (dykes, bridges, etc).

These spending departments drew their funds from the public treasury— the *bayt al-mal*, which was where most of the revenue was paid in. It was responsible for balancing expenditures against income. If it ran out of cash it could be helped out by the privy purse (a common expedient, as in China, Rome, and Byzantium). The department was more or less coeval with the arrival of the Abbasids—it dates from *c*.754. It became very important from the time of al-Mutadid (892), because it was not only receiving income from

---

[83] Cf. *Hamlet* (v.ii): 'I once did hold it, as our statists do, | A baseness to write fair'!

[84] But see Margoliouth and Amedroz, *The Eclipse of the Abbasid Caliphate*, iv. 170, where Miskawayh lists eleven departments, of which one is clearly temporary, one relates to the palace, one to the army, one to the signet and seal, and all the rest are fiscal.   [85] For some idea, see ibid. 172.

the domain lands, but also from most of the fines and confiscations which were multiplying at this time, as well as a considerable proportion of the provincial revenue.[86]

The collecting departments underwent considerable modification. There were two possible principles of organization: according to the nature of the tax and/or the area of collection. At around 900 the picture had resolved itself in the following way. The collection of the main land tax, the *kharaj*, was controlled from three 'geographical' departments, for the Sawad (the richest part of Iraq), the East, and the West.[87] The other main tax, the *ushr* or tithe, was controlled from the *diwan al-diya*, the Department of Domain Lands. But by 920 this was itself subdivided into a Department which looked after the public domain—the *amma*—which supplied the public treasury (as described above), and a department handling the caliph's private estate—the *khassa*—which supplied his private purse. Other revenue departments were set up from time to time, mostly after 920. They included a Bureau of Confiscated Goods and another, a Bureau of Rebels; also a department to supervise the money-changers who played a vital—and extortionate—part in tax-collection. Another bureau collected the revenues of the state factories.

Outside these three groups one department remains, and that is the *barid*. It was probably a direct copy of the Roman and Byzantine courier-cum-spy agency, since the name is the Arab version of the Latin *veredus*—a post-horse. Its basic function was providing a courier service for government business. Caravanserais and staging-posts were established along the main routes, notably the great Khurasan highway and the Yemen–Mecca–Baghdad road. Messages went by mule or—commonly in Iran—by runner. (There was also a pigeon-post.) Not just messengers but, in emergencies, bodies of troops also might travel by *barid*. But as in Byzantium, the courier was a priceless news-gatherer in an empire starved of information, and as in Rome and Byzantium the local *barid* offices became intelligence-centres from which reports flowed to the *sahib al-barid* in the capital, who in turn made a digest of them and presented it to the caliph.[88] It was but a short step from this to using the *barid* as a secret intelligence agency.

The affairs of these diverse departments were centralized in and regulated by the vizier. The routine was as follows. Caliphal and/or vizieral orders concerning appointments went to the Chancery, those for cash payments to the *bayt al-mal*, and for other payments to the appropriate departments. There they were checked by the department of *zimam* and then passed to the

[86] Sourdel, *Le Vizirat abbasside*, 595.   [87] So Levy, *Social Structure of Islam*, 326.
[88] Ibid. 301, n. 3

Seal Office of the Chancery, which sent them off. The vizier was *ex officio* the head of the Chancery, so that all documents, diplomas, and letters were addressed 'as from the caliph' but 'on the responsibility of the vizier'. The Seal Office in the Chancery could only apply the seal and dispatch the documents after the vizier had satisfied himself that they were correctly drawn up—and control of the seal was another *ex officio* duty of the vizier. Finally, the vizier supervised the financial departments. He watched out for falsified documents, examined the accounts, reviewed the modes of collection and, above all, of assessment. It was he who demanded bond from officials during their course of duty and, equally, fixed the fines on officials who had been dismissed. He was kept informed on the balances in the Treasury and advised the caliph accordingly.[89]

It should be noted that these central departments were supervisory, not executive: the details of execution, particularly the way taxes were collected, varied from one place to another according to what the Arabs had found in place and taken over. As to the layout of the departments, this is quite unoriginal. Apart from the Vizierate, totally absent in Byzantium, it followed similar organizational principles to there. Most historians, however, insist that the model was Sassanid. As we know next to nothing about Sassanid administration it is hard, to say the least, to provide evidence.

6.1.3. THE PERSONNEL

The senior personnel are known as 'secretaries' (*kuttab*). Their character changed between c.850 and 950. At the outset of this period many were still non-Muslims. Even so, they were thoroughly Arabized and indeed wrote the most beautiful Arab prose. Their education—when they were not accountants as many were—was highly literary, not scientific, and it was emphatically not religious. Hence the *ulema* were at loggerheads with them, reproaching them with impiety and levity. They were also extremely arrogant, another thing that irritated the *ulema*. One of them sneers that the moment a man becomes a secretary he thinks he is all-wise and immensely superior, and shows off by adopting a wide-flowing robe, and a peculiar coiffure, whereby the sidelocks are braided over the cheeks and the forelocks are cut into a 'V'-shape. As the Iranians converted to Islam, however, they

---

[89] The account in the text is largely based on Sourdel, *Le Vizirat abbasside*, esp. 605–13. One gets a splendid idea of the office of vizier, and how to do everything wrong (and so, by the same token, how to do it right) in Miskawayh's account of the vizier Ibn Isa's cross-examination of his predecessor, the incompetent and dishonest Khasibi (in Margoliouth and Amedroz, *The Eclipse of the Abbasid Caliphate*, iv. 171–4). Ibn Isa was a highly accomplished administrator and an inveterate economizer of candleends—one of the very few caliphal officials whom one can come to respect.

became increasingly caught up in the great Shia–Sunni controversy and formed two rival camps whose leaders contended for the Vizierate.

The influence and social standing of the senior ranks of the *kuttab* was immense. Many belonged to families which had held administrative posts for several generations, even from Sassanid times. One might almost call them a hereditary class. Those families were well-to-do or even very rich. The salaries they recieved reflect their social standing as much as their administrative indispensability. A clerk, on 6 dinars a month, was earning about six times the income of a skilled workman, such as a carpenter. The higher ranks could receive up to about 20 dinars a month. But viziers and the various treasurers and heads of departments received immense emoluments.

The largely hereditary nature of the *kuttab* was matched by their cliquishness, in which they closely resemble the Chinese Mandarinate. They formed 'old-boy nets' with friends and relatives in the other departments. One consequence was that certain posts remained in the possession of a handful of families for generations. For instance, it has been calculated that between 870 and 940, out of thirty-seven vizierships, thirty were occupied by only sixteen viziers, and these derived from only four families.[90]

6.2. *The Army*

6.2.1. PERSONNEL AND RECRUITMENT

In the two centuries following the conquests the caliphal armies underwent an amazing transformation, from being composed of the most independent of freeborn warriors anywhere, to one made up largely of slaves and ex-slaves. Since 750 the army had come to consist entirely of the paid Khurasani regulars, now settled in the new capital, Baghdad, where they came to be known as the *abna*.

When he was heir-apparent al-Mutasim had built up a 3,000-strong bodyguard of Turkish ex-slaves, then known as *ghilman*, but better known by their later appellation, *Mamluks*. (Al-Tabari tells us that 'al-Mutassim liked' Turks.) After his accession in 833 he expanded this force to (we are told) 70,000. The Khurasani *abna* of Baghdad and the city population rioted against these alien cavalrymen in their streets, so that al-Mutassim built a completely new city to house them, at Samarra, where they lived under the strictest non-fraternization orders from the caliph, a race apart. As for the Khurasanis, they gradually fade from history.

The terms *Mamluk* and 'slave-troops' are open to serious misunderstanding. Mamluks—or Mamelukes as they are Anglicized—are usually thought

[90] Ashtor, *Social and Economic History*, 139–40.

of as simply a Muslim Egyptian dynasty, while 'slave-troops' suggests that such soldiers served, *qua* slaves, without pay. In fact, 'slave' or its equivalent, *mamluk*, means a male *of slave origins*, in this particular context a male purchased as a slave (usually at the age of puberty) who was given military training and might then be manumitted by his master, though this was becoming less common and most of these *ghilman* troops were slaves until they died. Towards their master they bore—or at least, were supposed to bear—a duty of lifelong fidelity. These 'slave' troops served for pay. That indeed was the reason for their incessant discontents, mutinies, and ultimately, usurpations. (In theory no such mutinies, should have occurred, given the convention of freedman loyalty.)[91]

6.2.2. MILITARY FORMATION, TACTICS, AND ORDER OF BATTLE.

The army referred to here is the army of the central government, sometimes called the 'Iraqi army'. There were also the provincial troops under the command of the governors. These could be sizeable—in the civil war of 909–13 al-Mamun was able to raise an army of 20,000.[92] Precise figures for the size of this central army do not seem to have survived, but it may have been about 80,000 men.[93]

The army was organized in multiples of ten. Each ten came under its *arif*. A battalion of ten *irafa* was captained by a *qaid*, ten such battalions formed a regiment, and the entire army formation was called the *tabiya*, commanded by an amir. The recognized order of battle consisted of five regiments, making up a vanguard, rearguard, centre, and two flanks. The artillery

---

[91] The question of why the Mamluks of Egypt continued to obey their Sultans while the *ghilman* troops of the Caliphate revolted and finally reduced the caliphs to puppets does not seem to have been widely addressed. In principle, these caliphal Mamluks should have remained ever-faithful and obedient. Patricia Crone (*Slaves on Horses*, 82–4), attributes it to the unwarlike character of al-Mutasim's successors. I think that the explanation is probably to be found in the relationship between a ruler and the Mamluks of his predecessor. Ayalon says that the relationship was cold and often envenomed, the previous ruler's Mamluks resentful of the new ruler's favouritism showed to his own troops (see D. Ayalon, *Studies on the Mamluks of Egypt (1250–1517)* (Variorum Reprints, 1975), ch. 1, p. 28). Now in Baghdad the new caliph had relatively few *ghilman* of his own when he acceded, so that he took over an army recruited by his predecessors and owing him no particular loyalty. This was sometimes the case in Egypt but the difference there was that a sultan was, almost by definition, the amir with the largest troop of personal Mamluks before his accession—which was often due exclusively to this superior strength. Any disaffection on the part of the previous rulers' Mamluks would not have been very serious in these circumstances.

[92] Levy, *Social Structure of Islam*, 416.

[93] We are told that the peacetime upkeep of this army was (908–22) 1 million dinars per annum (Ashtor, *Social and Economic History*, 132) and also that the average pay per soldier was 13.5 dinars a month (ibid.)—which yields a figure of 62,000; and we are also told that al-Muhtadi lamented that he had 100,000 troops on his payroll. (Levy, *Social Structure of Islam*, 419. The estimate given at p. 323 is nonsense.)

travelled with the rearguard, while light-armed troops and scouts, not part of the formation, hovered all around.[94]

In battle the same fivefold formation was maintained but the units were combined in different ways as the tactics seemed to demand. The army was almost exclusively a cavalry force in which speed and mobility were at a premium. The favoured weapon was the bow, but the full equipment ran to javelin, lance, and sword, and, for protection, shield and helmet, with cuirass or chain-mail. The Muslim cavalry were always more lightly armed than the Byzantine cataphracts—as their horses were not big enough to carry the Byzantines' weight of armour.[95]

The troops fought in ranks, usually three, though in some battles they were deployed in a deep formation of thirteen ranks. The front rank consisted of archers and the second of spearmen. These were mounted infantry. The cavalry formed the rear rank. The idea was that the archers would break up the enemy charge from long distance, then such enemy as got through would be dealt with by the spearmen, whereupon the cavalry would swing into action, charging the enemy in their turn. The foot encounter followed by the cavalry charge was executed by each army in turn until one broke and fled.[96]

The defence of the frontiers was effected by the equivalent of the Byzantine *clisurae*, that is, fortresses and strong-points which were garrisoned by local tribemen or foreign mercenaries and supported by strong-points in their rear, known as *al-awasim*. The most important frontier was the Byzantine one, of course, but Harun al-Rashid also protected the sea-coasts of Syria and Ifrikiya with forts known as *ribat*—hence the place-name Rabat, for instance. These forts were connected by a network of lookouts and signal stations.

7. THE SERVICES

7.1. *Defence*[97]

The army was organized in four corps, plus the palace guards. These guards were under the caliph's personal control. He paid them as part of his household and supplied their mounts and arms. They lived inside the

[94] Ibid. 412, 426, 432. V. J. Parry and M. G. Yapp (eds.), *War Technology and Society in the Middle East: Essays* (OUP, Oxford, 1975), 829–30.

[95] Levy, *Social Structure of Islam*, 427–9, 434. V. J. Parry, 'Warfare', in *Cambridge History of Islam*, vol. 2 (CUP, Cambridge, 1970), 829–30.   [96] Parry and Yapp, *War Technology*, 828–30.

[97] The entire section on defence and the *ard* (review) is based on Levy, *Social Structure of Islam*, and in particular on Bosworth, in Parry and Yapp, *War Technology*, esp. 62–3 and 69–74.

palace precincts and indeed at some periods they actually lived inside the palace itself, hence their name, *hujariyya*, from *hujar*—a 'chamber'. Caliphs were so fearful of being betrayed by these guards that they placed them under the continuous surveillance of their palace eunuchs; for instance, they could not leave the palace and ride outside except in the eunuchs' presence.

The army proper—the *jaysh*—was administered by the *diwan al-jaysh*. Its director, the *sahib diwan al-jaysh*, was at once the paymaster-general, quarter-master-general, and muster-master. The duties appertaining to this last role were designed to maintain the efficiency and integrity of the troops and to allocate soldiers between the four corps. He exercised these functions in the review or *ard*. Periodically units of the army were paraded on the Lesser Square of Baghdad for inspection in the presence of the palace guards. The sahib presided, attended by the secretaries of the department. One set of these secretaries tested the military proficiency of the troops. Another set of secretaries advanced and checked the features of each trooper against his description in the nominal roll, so as to detect spies and subversives, but it also served to prevent defalcations. At the close of the review troopers were posted to one or other of the four corps. Those rated 'excellent' were called the caliph's personal army, and in fact formed the main field army. Those rated as 'fair' came under the command of the prefect of the Baghdad police, and were sent to patrol the Bagdad–Khorasan route and garrison strategic points in Iraq and western Iran. The third-call troops were posted to the provinces to assist the local police and the tax-collectors. Finally, there was a *corps d'élite* consisting of men picked out as the bravest in their regiment.

The army kept the Byzantine frontier but could not contain dissident governors, since once they acquired the caliph's tax revenues they could build their own Mamluk army. So, the more independence a rebel governor asserted, the stronger he became.

7.2 *Law and Order*

We have described the existence of two separate jurisdictions each with its own set of courts, the *qadi* and the caliphal ones. (More exactly, there were three jurisdictions, because in civil and religious matters the *dhimmis* were tried in their own courts under their own law). The *qadi* courts are often called the 'religious' courts because the law they administered was the *sharia*. These courts developed an extensive jurisprudence, arrived at in the way already described,[98] and which came to present an ideal remote from the

---

[98] See p. 688 ff. above.

realities of everyday life, a goal to strive for, albeit unattainable. The custodians of the *sharia*—the learned and pious scholars or the *ulema*—set this ideal so high that they 'walked on the other side' when confronted with such things as torture or the personal executioner who stood at the caliph's side, which they knew to be wrong but would not openly condemn.[99]

The *qadis* were appointed by the caliph or his delegate who, in this period was the Grand *Qadi*, one of the caliph's most influential advisers. The *qadis'* role was essentially local. The courts in the Caliphate were not arranged in an orderly hierarchy, nor was there a regularized system of appeals. Once appointed, the *qadi* was supposedly independent, and to the extent that he ran his own court through his own clerk, and delivered his own verdict, he was. But he could do no more than articulate it; only the caliph's administrators could enforce it. Furthermore, the caliph could and from time to time did step in to overturn a verdict that displeased him. So the independence was for all practical purposes nominal.

All the same, the caliph was unlikely to take an active interest in the bulk of the matters that came the *qadi*'s way for these were mostly connected with religion, public worship, marriage and divorce, inheritance, and religious mortmains (the *waqfs*). But some matters also came under his jurisdiction, for instance, the six specific *hadd* offences mentioned in the Quran, and—possibly—the payment of the *zakat* tax since this was supposedly 'alms' and regulated by the Quran. But the *qadis* accepted the caliph's right to define their jurisdiction and applied the concept of *siyasa* (literally 'policy'), so that they admitted the ruler's right to adopt any criminal or fiscal measures he liked—always providing that they did not openly violate an express and explicit prohibition of the *sharia*. The *qadi* courts lost such matters to the ruler all the more easily because, as we shall note, their procedure was radically defective. The net upshot was that pretty well all matters of public policy flowed into courts run by the administration and dispensing 'ruler's law', that is, the *mazalim* or 'complaints' courts, the police courts, and the ministrations of the officer called *muhtasib*.

The *mazalim* court came to perform two functions. It was the court of appeal from the *qadi* courts and any other kind of inferior tribunal and a court of first instance in suits brought by subjects against officials' malfeasance as well as in the caliph's own suits against folk like heretics, or the very highest of officials such as generals or viziers in what were effectively state trials. The *mazalim* courts were presided over by the caliph himself or the vizier, and by his deputies in the various quarters of the capital and in the provincial cities. They could initiate actions relating to official acts of

[99] Schacht, *Introduction*, 567. Hodgson, *Venture of Islam*, i. 347.

oppression, the unjust levying of taxes, or malfeasance by government clerks. They could entertain complaints by such clerks in respect of their salaries and likewise those of subjects against the wrongful seizure of their property. They came in to enforce the judgments of qadis or muhtasibs. And, finally, they had a concurrent jurisdiction with the qadi courts, being able to hear cases where qadi rules of procedure would otherwise prevail. Effectively all matters of public policy—land law, criminal law, fiscal law, military law, as well as the misconduct of officials—came within the scope of these courts.

Next, there were the police courts. The police-force was called the shurta, the Arab version of the Roman/Byzantine cohors, suggesting a Byzantine inspiration. In the capital city the shurta was a very large force indeed, and was responsible for the protection of the caliph as well as policing the town. Munis, al-Muqtadir's eunuch prefect of police, disposed of 9,000 men.[100] There were similar forces in every city where a governor or some other high official resided. The commandant of such a force was the sahib al-shurta, and it was his responsibility to forestall, investigate, and punish crime. To these ends he disposed of a court procedure that was flexible to a fault. Like the contemporary magistrates in T'ang China, the judge considered circumstantial evidence, and could, unlike qadi court procedure, admit witnesses of bad character and cross-examine them under oath. And he could, where he felt it necessary, extort confessions by beatings and the like, a procedure that became routine. Some police commandants were notorious for their savagery.[101]

Finally we come to the most ubiquitous and intrusive of all the quasi-judicial subordinate officials, the muhtasib. Originally his primary function was identical with that of the Byzantine agoranomos or 'inspector of markets'. As such, he did indeed control weights and measures, and prevent counterfeits and fraud. In such matters, however, he could only try the case summarily where the facts were undisputed; otherwise it had to go to the qadi. But in addition he had the discretion to order the townsfolk to repair walls, purify wells and streams, prevent non-Muslim houses overlooking those of the Faithful, halt the obstruction of streets and alleys by protruding houses or shops, tell householders to get rid of projecting rain-spouts and open drains, and by the same token to give permission for buildings, canals, and latrines to be constructed. Lastly and most Islamically, the muhtasib acted as the enforcer of Muslim faith and morals in so far as they were expressed in public view (he was not permitted to enter private

---

[100] This is why he ended up as the hegemon over the caliph. See p. 700 above.

[101] See e.g. the description of Abd al-Rahman b. Ubayd, by a contemporary, in Levy, *Social Structure of Islam*, 333–4.

houses). He had to see that prayers at the mosque were conducted properly, to check for persons who ate during Ramadan or men publicly consorting with women; to stamp out wine-selling, repress drunkenness, and see that the non-Muslims wore their distinguishing yellow badges (the *ghiyar*).

7.3. *Taxation*

Apart from a wide variety of taxes on townsfolk and merchants, the taxes fell into three generic types. In practice, however, there was no uniformity in either the way they were assessed or collected, and in most of the Caliphate, for most of the time, the taxes were farmed.

The first type of tax was the poll tax, the *jizya*, which fell exclusively on the *dhimmis*. The second was the *zakat*, or alms tax, which *ex origine* fell only on Muslims. It was (nominally) a tithe, levied mostly on land but also on beasts and movables. Finally, and the most important, comes the land tax, called *kharaj*. In the beginning this was levied exclusively upon the *dhimmis*. But as their numbers contracted and the number of converted Muslims— the *mawali*—expanded, the revenue began to dry up, so it was imposed on Muslims as well. Thus at this period everybody paid *kharaj* and *zakat*, while *only* the *dhimmis* paid the poll tax as well. (I have greatly simplified this exposition.)

The methods of assessment of the *kharaj* differed widely in different regions and different epochs. All, however, were very complicated, for the usual technical reasons.[102] In such and such a place the assessment was based on the area of the land, but elsewhere it was based on just the cultivated area, and took into account the quality of the soil, the mode of irrigation, and the nature of the crops. In other localities it was based on the average return from the land, taking into account, of course, the mode of cultivation but making no variation between one year and another, whereas in yet other places the direct contrary prevailed and the assessment varied every year. The modes of collection varied likewise, but it would seem as though one principle was well-nigh standard—the tax would be collected as a global sum. In each Governorate or, possibly, province or even sub-province there was either an *amil* (tax-collector) and his staff, or else a tax-farmer. Sometimes, however, the big landowner of the neighbourhood was made responsible for the collection. Tax-farming was becoming the norm, except in Mesopotamia and especially the Sawad, but it was resorted to even there when the government found itself exceptionally short of ready cash. To illustrate the general principle from roughly contemporary Egyptian

---

[102] See 'The Conceputal Prologue', p. 81 ff.

practice, where the taxes had long been farmed out on standard four-year contracts: the tax-farmer was allowed 'deductable expenses' for any improvements he made such as dykes, canals, and the like. In return he was under bond to pay a fixed sum to the Treasury.[103]

Tax-collection was beset with technical problems. If the payments were in kind, the collectors had to arrange the share-out, the transportation, and the subsequent sale. What is more, they might have to come on three separate occasions where, as in Upper Mesopotamia, the tax was paid after each of the three harvests.[104] If the tax was paid in coin, the bimetallic standard made it necessary to utilize professional money-changers—salaried officials appointed by the central government. And there was always the danger of violent resistance, so that the collectors were always accompanied by squads of soldiers.

As in virtually all the technologically primitive tax systems of these agrarian economies, the methods of assessment and of collection alike lent themselves to extensive and persistent corruption and extortion. The government and its agents did not care how the money was raised, so long as it flowed in.

8. APPRAISAL

8.1. *Defence and Internal Tranquillity*

The army's failure to keep the empire together cannot be ascribed to poor fighting qualities. It is true that some 80,000 caliphal troops were once put to flight by—so it is said—a mere 3,000 fanatical Qarmatians, but the victories of Munis or the gallant Saif ad-Dawlah were more typical. The latter instance is particularly striking in that Saif ad-Dawlah levelled with the entire Byzantine Empire, although he had only the resources of Syria to draw on. Until the late ninth and early tenth centuries the army did, in the end, manage to suppress all the numerous socio-religious revolts.

The disintegration of the empire was due to the compounding together of three deep causes, instantly recognizable from what has been said before. The first was the widespread scepticism about the legitimacy of the caliphal dynasties, whether Umayyad or Abbasid. The second was the plenipotentiary power devolved on the provincial governors, and the third was the governors' remoteness from the metropolitan forces (see above, p. 679 ff.). Indeed, it is most remarkable that the Umayyads were not only willing but able to send one army after another to try to hold Morocco and even more

---

[103] Levy, *Social Structure of Islam*, 316.   [104] Cahen, *Les Peuples musulmanes*, 412–13.

surprising that they were temporarily successful. In Abbasid times the more usual course of events was for a powerful governor to achieve *de facto* autonomy but acknowledge his vassal status and continue to pay the provincial tribute to the imperial treasury. This arrangement would last until, one day, this now autonomous Governorate would be overrun by outside forces (e.g. the Fatimid conquest of Aghlabid Ifriqiyya [Tunisia]), or overthrown by internal rebels. In either case, the new rulers severed the province's connection with the imperial capital, except, perhaps, on a purely nominal basis. The fate of Khurasan provides one example. Khurasan had become autonomous under the Tahirids, allowing Transoxania, which was part of their jurisdiction, to be ruled by Samanid sub-governors. The Tahirids succumbed to the social revolt of the Saffar family (see p. 702 above) These Saffarids were in their turn overthrown by their Samanid sub-governors in Transoxania, who annexed Khorasan as well, so establishing a great and wealthy state which they ruled with absolute authority, whose vassaldom to the caliph was wholly nominal.

Provinces to the west of Baghdad—Spain, North Africa, and Egypt—also broke away, and though the date and the circumstances differ in each case, all demonstrate the intermingling of the three elements mentioned at the outset: distance, the plenipotentiary power of governors, and the continual revolts led by religious sectaries. Against all this, even the greatest military efforts of the caliphs and the valour of their troops could never in the long run avail.

What is more, these breakaways culminated in the creation of a lethally vicious circle. When the empire ceased to expand in the eighth century, the flow of booty ceased and, in the latter part of the ninth century, even the war-indemnities exacted from the Byzantines came to an end. These losses occurred just at the time when the economy of the central provinces was running down. The result was the contraction of the tax-base. On top of all this, the Zanj revolt (869–83) absorbed all the efforts of the Baghdadi armies for fourteen years. Ashtor regards this revolt as a 'decisive phase', where the 'disruptive forces became so strong that they brought about [the Empire's] decomposition'.[105] In reality it stimulated a vigorous revival of caliphal power under the regent al-Muwaffaq, but the huge military expenditures, the opportunity for certain governors (like Tulun in Egypt) to reduce or withhold the provincial tribute to the capital, disorders and brigandage in the disturbed conditions[106] took their toll, and with the

---

[105] Ashtor, *Social and Economic History*, 121. Cf. 115–32, *passim*.

[106] Ibid. 121–3. Examples are Abdul Aziz in west-central Iran, Muhammad b. Harun in Rayy (Tehran). Also according to Ashtor, there was a general recrudescence of Bedouin brigandage.

accession of al-Muqtadir (908) the central government was in deep financial crisis. It had no money to pay its troops, who mutinied. The mutinies came to destabilize the central administration itself, the amirs took power from the caliphs who became mere figureheads, while the once world-spanning 'empire' had shrunk to little more than Mesopotamia.

8.2. *Justice*

We start by recalling the two jurisdictions, *sharia* courts and *mazalim* courts. In so far as we concern ourselves with the *sharia* jurisdiction here, it is to clear up some misconceptions. For instance, the four great 'schools' of law which persist in Sunni Islam differ from one another on sometimes highly material detail, and it might be thought that this caused confusion or inequity. Common sense prevailed, however, and the individual would be judged by the law of his own school or by the one agreed in the contract. Again, much is made of the undoubted fact that neither the *qadis* nor the *mazalim* judges were independent; all could be removed, and the decisions of the former could also be reviewed by the latter. But how far this affected civil actions we do not know and, at a guess, given the enormous area and complexity of the empire, it is highly unlikely that the caliph and the central bureaucracy would have interfered in such matters. The lack of independence was significant only in the *mazalim* courts, but subject to reservations expressed later on.

Other examples of apparent flaws are the various ways of evading the prohibition of usury (*riba*). But an example that is more pertinent to our interest is the apparently absurd institution of the 'professional' witnesses. Conviction in the *sharia* courts required the testimony of witnesses (usually two); it had to be oral, no other kind of evidence being admissible; and cross-examination was not permitted. So the entire outcome of the trial turned on the credibility of the witnesses, and if they swore that the statement of one of the two litigants was true the judgment followed automatically. To make quite sure that the witnesses were reliable, the *qadis* took to initiating intimate inquiries into their character, and this necessitated hiring a staff of investigators and then, having banned the 'bad' witnesses, establishing a roster of the trustworthy ones. Only these might attest in the court and so they had become 'professional witnesses', and this institution lasted into the nineteenth century. Now this sounds quite absurd. But in the tenth century it was turned to a most useful purpose. Documentary evidence was obviously indispensable in commercial transactions and yet could not be invoked in the *sharia* court. The litigants, therefore, took their documents to a professional witness to get him to swear to the truth of their claims in court. In this way the professional witness ended up as a public notary, in the tenth century a member of a permanent corps of judicial officials.[107]

A final illustration of an apparent flaw much mitigated in practice relates to the 'legal personality'. Muslim law never developed this concept, so that it would never recognize corporations, for example, municipalities, and this could make it difficult for the city authorities to make people remove obstructions or clean out their gutters. But in practice the authorities, that is, the judges of the *mazalim* courts or the commandant of police, could act *proprio motu* against persons accused by their agents of offences against public order and the like.

But this is not to say that the failure to develop the concept of legal personality was not important. It was *vitally* important, because it loaded the dice against the individual *vis-à-vis* the authorities. The latter comprise the judges of *mazalim* courts,[108] the commandants of police (*sahib as-shurta*), and the *muhtasibs*. The two former could initiate proceedings against a suspect on any grounds, such as finding stolen goods or burglar's tools or offensive weapons in his house or about his person, and on hearsay and gossip as well the result of investigations.[109] The *muhtasib* was intended to 'reach the parts the other judges and officials could not reach': the 'surveillance over moral imperatives in every field that escaped the competence of other authorities'.[110] Though the matters his court handled were small beer, they were innumerable and highly restrictive. The *muhtasib* was the licensed arch-snooper of the town. So, altogether, the repressive apparatus of the Caliphate was very considerable indeed.

But the reverse situation, the ability of the subject to challenge the public authorities, did not obtain at all. In Rome, since the days of the Republic itself, the rights of the state had been conceived as vesting in a legal person so that—as we saw—in civil affairs the citizen's complaint against the authorities (or the other way round) was settled in court as a *lis inter partes*. But Islam did not really possess a concept of the state in the aforementioned sense and the best the subject could do was to *supplicate* the caliph or the caliph-by-delegation, namely, the presiding officer in one or other of these

---

[107] Mez, *Renaissance*, 228. This bizarre work is replete with the most curious miscellaneous information but is particularly interesting on this point. See 227–30. *Inter alia*, Mez points out that the office of *qadi* often became hereditary in one family and cites a number of such judicial dynasties (p. 230).

[108] As if to underline his administrative status, he was not called a 'judge' but the *sahib almazalim*, or the *wali al-mazalim* or *nazir* (Master) *al-mazalim*: E. Tyan, *Histoire de l'organisation judiciare en pays d'Islam* (Brill, Leiden, 1960), 445.

[109] Ibid. 443, 445, 572–3, 604.

[110] Ibid. 621.

administrative tribunals, so that the administrator was being asked to judge in his own cause.

This one-sided arrangement put at risk the subjects' life, limb, liberty, and property. We can and indeed ought to reject most of the wild anti-Umayyad charges of the Kharijite rebel Abu Hamza, but we ought certainly to note that they are not just about impiety but the violation of individual rights. One caliph 'made servants of God slaves'; others 'shed forbidden blood and devoured forbidden property'; yet another 'abraded faces, put out eyes, and cut off hands and feet'. 'These Banu Umayya [i.e. the Umayyads] arrest on suspicion, make decrees capriciously, kill in anger, and judge by passing over crimes without punishment. They take the alms tax from the incorrect source and make it over to the wrong people . . .'[111] We know how extremist the Kharidjites were and can discount the rhetoric, but not, it seems to me, the general thrust of the indictment.[112] Such 'shedding of blood' is attested by the brutal treatment of the Iraquis by al-Hajjaj and other governors, and there are notorious Abbasid examples too, such as the treacherous murder of Abu Muslim by the Caliph al-Mansur, and Harun's massacre of the Barmakids. As for the violation of property rights, from very early on it became routine, a 'fixed institution', for the caliph to confiscate the property of rich burghers, merchants, and high officials under the name of 'contributions' (musadara). In short, for all the lurid language, there is some fire beneath Abu Hamza's smoke.

This was not the only flaw in the administration of justice if we are to believe the accounts of judicial corruption. It was charged that the 'professional witnesses' took bribes, while 'neither the investigator of [their] morals nor the qadi himself were insensitive to the material advantages which flowed to them from the choice of particular candidates'.[113] The court records are sparse and the cases the historians bring to our attention are likely to have been the pathological ones, but authoritative Islamicists are quite explicit that there were such violations. 'Islamic law'

did not remain immune from malpractices within its own sphere of application, such as bribing of qadis and witnesses, and high-handed acts of governments and individuals with which the qadi was powerless to deal. The degree to which this happened depended on the character and the strength of the government, and the most unblemished period in this respect probably coincided with the prime of the Ottoman Empire. The early Abbasid period, on the other hand, was distinguished by frequent acts of usurpation (ghasb), misappropriation of private property.[114]

---

[111] These splendidly purple passages are taken from Crone and Hinds, God's Caliph, app. 3, pp. 130–2.
[112] See pp. 686–7, 698 above.   [113] Sourdel, La Civilisation, 242.
[114] Schacht, Introduction, 200.

As Schacht spent his entire life in the study of Islamic law and presumably went through all records that touch on such matters, there is good reason to rely on him, until at least further research proves the contrary.

Nor, according to the Sourdels, could the subject hope for redress in the *mazalim* court. They warn us not to be deluded into thinking that the state was very rigorous in investigating and controlling its officials. The procedures for appeals, which depended closely on the caliph, always remained somewhat fluid, while the representatives of the authorities, whether they were administrators, police, or generals, had ways of applying presssure against which the subjects were as a rule helpless.[115] (Nowhere is this better exemplified than in the matter of taxation, the subject of the next section.)

The Muslim subject had duties to God but rights against his neighbours, and among the latter he had rights to life, limb, property, and freedom of domicile. When these were infringed by his fellow subjects he could litigate with them on equal terms. But towards Allah, in complete contrast, the subject was, obviously, in no way on level terms but very, very much the reverse: total obedience to Allah was his first, his last, his only duty in life. Whatever rights in principle subjects might have against the caliph, inside his own jurisdiction the caliphal power over the subject was absolute and there was no legal remedy the subject could activate. Whether, as received opinion has it, concepts regarding individual civil rights were unknown to Islam, is neither here nor there: the point is, the caliph's unquestionable capacity to exercise unbridled personal power is properly described as *despotism* (above, p. 692). But this despotic power of the sovereign did not exist simply because the law lacked remedies against the ruler, but worse: because the law came actually to insist that the subject had a *positive duty never to resist the* sovereign, even when he was wrong. In Gibb's telling phrase, the law 'consecrated a theory of absolutism'.[116] Al-Mawardi (d. 1058) and al-Ghazzali, the great apologists for this view, wrote much later than our period, but were rationalizing, *ex post facto*, the political reality of those times. We must recall again the words quoted above: 'An evil-doing and barbarous sultan, so long as he is supported by military force . . . must of necessity be left in possession and obedience must be rendered to him, exactly as obedience is required to be rendered to those who are placed in command.'

---

[115] Sourdel, *La Civilisation*, 245.   [116] Gibb, 'Constitutional Organisation', 16.

8.3. *Taxing and Spending*

In the years 772–5, when the Caliphate is deemed to have been most glorious, a host of tax-agents descended on Upper Mesopotamia to raise revenue to pay for a campaign against Byzantium. What happened is described in a work attributed to the Monophysite patriarch, Denys of Tell-Mahré.

The agents, he tells us, were 'numberless'.[117] Each came accompanied by a small posse of soldiers. There was a separate tax-collector for each different kind of tax. And finally, all these collectors appeared *three* times each year. The first burden on the villagers was to feed and lodge all these mouths at their own expense. Next, in cases where the taxpayers were obliged to pay their taxes in the town, it was they who had to pay the costs of transportation. Some taxes had to be paid in silver coin. To acquire it the peasants had to sell their produce immediately. The tax-collectors were in league with the chandlers, and what took place was effectively a forced sale at knockdown prices—between one-third and two-fifths of the market price for grain, one-half for beasts. Then there were the illegal supplements: for instance, making the peasants supply the foodstuffs and also supply the paper used in the transactions; exacting a fee for the use of the scales; declaring the coin to be debased or clipped and insisting that the shortfall be made good.[118]

Consequently peasants were always late in payment, and the tax-collectors resorted to the same kind of brutalities familiar to us from China and Rome and Byzantium. Denys describes how on one occasion the collectors locked the peasants up for three whole days in a church. On other occasions they would tie defaulters up in the burning sun, or apply the garotte.[119] As in the Chinese and the Roman empires, peasants fled the land. The authorities countered by posting police along the roads, laying ambushes, and attacking passers-by as though they were brigands (while the real brigands took advantage of this by passing themselves off as policemen), and by carrying out identity checks in the towns. The *dhimmis* were subjected to the indignity of being tattooed or having to wear collars, like dog-tags, which carried their names and addresses.

Denys goes on to say that every village had its 'boss', who was the principal landowner, and the government often made them responsible for collecting the tax. Hand-in-glove with the government's own agents, they would impose the kind of forced sales we have noticed already, and

---

[117] Cahen, *Les Peuples musulmanes*, 407. This article is Cahen's summary and commentary on the chronicle of Denys, and I have followed it in the text above (unless additional authority is cited).
[118] These particulars from Levy, *Social Structure of Islam*, 308.   [119] Ibid. 308.

make short-term loans to the peasants on the security of their land or their beasts: with results we can already anticipate in the light of what happened everywhere else in these primitive agrarian societies in such circumstances, and to which I shall return below.

So much for the extortion that went on at the grass roots. But the wealthy were not necessarily spared either. In the disaster-struck period in the 900s the government began making a capital levy on the wealthy under the name of 'fines'. Known as the al-musadara, the practice became a permanent institution, not only in the Caliphate but in its succession states as well. The importance of these fines can be gauged by the fact that in 923–4 they are believed to have formed no less than 48 per cent of the total revenue![120] Another abuse was the sale of offices, or exacting fees from officials as a price for keeping their jobs. And when in 917 the vizier (Ibn al-Furat) established a separate 'department of secret profits'[121] to receive part of the bribes which officials had taken, we can say that bribery was institutionalized. More evidence on this will be given below.

But not only private citizens suffered; the very topmost officals were similarly afflicted. To supplement their privy purse the caliphs began to make a regular practice of letting the vizier and other top officials accumulate private wealth, then accusing them of extortion or corruption, investigating them, finding them guilty, and ending up by confiscating (for the caliph's own personal advantage) vast amounts of wealth from them. The practice is attested from Umayyad times.[122] By the end of the ninth century this had become a regular practice.

What we see, in fact, is quite extraordinary. It is not just a thoroughly corrupt fiscal system, for that is quite common in a large number of Third World states today. What Miskawayh's history of al-Muqtadir's reign demonstrates[123] amounts in effect to a *privatization of public administration* based on *systematized* corruption.[124]

My understanding of Miskawayh is this. The caliph takes tenders for the office of vizier. The successful bidder promises by note of hand to provide a specified sum to the caliph's privy purse. There is much competition for this post among rival candidates, each bidding up the amount they will 'offer' the caliph though, as now, it is not always the highest tender that is accepted.

[120] Ashtor, *Social and Economic History*, 135.   [121] Ibid. 136.

[122] Crone, *Slaves on Horses*, 227, n. 239, for this and other examples.

[123] Margoliouth and Amedroz, *Eclipse of the Abbasid Caliphate*, iv. *passim*.

[124] There can be no comparison—such as has been suggested to me—with the privatization of public power in the West. These were Europe's Dark Ages, in which the state as the Romans had known it had dissolved at the time the Caliphate had come to inherit the sophisticated administrative apparatus of the Byzantine and Sassanian empires. The tragedy is that whereas the Europeans slowly built up the state anew, the caliphs were busily dismantling it.

The vizier in his turn strikes bargains with individuals, some already in official posts and others whom he intends to appoint, to farm the taxes of particular districts. Some of these officials take the tax-farm of the *kharaj*. Others are appointed to such posts as prayer-leaders, generals, governors. They receive *iqta*. (There is a land-grant called by the same name and generically related, but distinguished by the jurists from this present form.) What this means is that they give their own note-of-hand or bills of exchange for a set agreed sum to be paid into the public treasury, in return for the tax-farm or the official posting.

The striking feature of these arrangements is the privatization of the public administration. This is turned into a self-serving network of dyadic contacts between the vizier and these individuals. Agreed, the bureaux they direct do keep very careful accounts and files. But there is no sense of public *purpose*, no sense of state, let alone sense of empire. Most viziers—Ibn Isa seems to be highly exceptional—were in it for the money.

Hiring and firing viziers becomes frequent and regularized. The incoming vizier dismisses and or arrests the ex-vizier and all his appointees, and fines them quite enormous sums, which he then pays into the public treasury *and* also the privy purse. This money is extracted from the defeated faction under threat and even torture. The implication is this: every official has made illicit gains—hence torture him and get it back. But usually, once he had paid he would be appointed to another lucrative position. In short, the entire fiscal system consisted of mutual arrangements reaching down from one echelon to another, permitting and encouraging each official to make an illicit surplus for himself, provided part of this came in as extra revenue to the government! The fiscal system was, in short, operated like one of today's crime syndicates.

One question remains, however. Perhaps these devices of deceit and extortion were required, were *necessary* for defence and security, or public works? Not so. The sums reported by the chroniclers are doubtless exaggerated, but even after deflating them several-fold they point in one direction only—fraud and extravagance. For one thing, the cost of raising the revenue was enormous since a vast amount of the taxes exacted from the population was diverted into the tax-farmers' pockets before any reached the central government at all. But even when it got there it certainly did not all go on the objects we have suggested earlier. Far from it! It is calculated that the total revenue of the central government in 918–19 was some 15.5 million dinars. I calculate that at least 10.5 millions went on the caliphal household, and from a catalogue of the items of its expenditure for 918–19,[125] it is

[125] Levy, *Social Structure of Islam*, 323–4.

safe to say that most of it was spent on the most wild and outlandish extravagance.

9. CONCLUSION: THE NATURE AND LIMITATIONS OF THE CALIPHAL EMPIRE

Throughout this *History* I have emphasized the distinction between 'social' culture and 'political' culture, between the state of the arts and crafts and the arts and crafts of the state.[126] Nowhere is that contrast more vivid than in the Caliphate. The new and Islamic civilization that was emerging at this time from an amalgam of Islam and the already-rooted cultures of the conquered societies was intellectually, artistically, and religiously as rich and sophisticated and, above all, durable as any the world has ever seen. But the way it was ruled was inferior.

The great historic accompishments of the Caliphate were that, first, it acted as a kind of factory for converting its subjects and also the eastern pagan barbarians—notably the Turks—to Islam. Next, it maintained an immense common market, which, moreover, controlled the Golden Road to Central Asia and distant Cathay. Finally, inside this area it stamped a common social structure and way of life on its subjects and created a cultural universe where, as in medieval Europe, scholars and pilgrims could wander and root themselves freely anywhere between Atlantic Oxus and Indus, within a common idiom in arts, learning, and literature. The Caliphate was in these respects a momentous and irreversible turning-point in world history, and all the more stupendous for being so unexpected and immediate. But in respect to any advances in governmental practice, or political thought, or individual liberties, or the prosperity of the peasantry, or finally in the sheer, simple power to survive, the Caliphate was a conspicuous failure.

The yardstick must not be the contemporary Dark Ages in Europe, in which the linkage between the fleeting barbarian kingdoms and the Roman imperial practices had been severed. In contrast, the Caliphate carried on the political practices and even the bureaucracies themselves of the Byzantine and Sassanid empires, so that the only appropriate comparisons must be with the empires of Rome, T'ang China, or Byzantium—particularly Byzantium: for, sharing few of that empire's virtues, the Caliphate exaggerated its excesses.

It is no reproach to the Caliphate that it was a slave society, for so were

---

[126] The difference between what I have called the *political culture* and culture in the sense of the intellectual and artistic level of a civilization: Finer, *Man on Horseback*, 78.

the United States and Brazil into the nineteenth century; nor that it discriminated against the religious minorities, for it treated them far better than Christian Europe treated Jews or nonconforming Christians or heretics. Although we have not talked about its 'public provision' for the people, this is not because it did not exist but simply because it was mostly provided by pious benefactors. Schools and centres of learning, hospitals, public baths, and other amenities were made available in this way, with the caliphs themselves often being great benefactors.

The Caliphate was not more brutal than surrounding empires, and as a matter of fact the tariff of penalties laid down in the *sharia* is remarkably mild for that age and is even gentle compared with the ferocity of China's. Again, though we have drawn attention to the extensiveness of the Caliphate's repressive power, repression was the order of the day in every state anywhere at that time. Nor was the empire uncommon in that its learned doctors preached passive obedience and condemned rebellion for any cause. But what did lack in the Caliphate but was present in Byzantium (and would later emerge in Europe) was legal defence against offical oppression, for enforcement was violent. 'I see many heads rolling; let each man see that his own head stays upon his shoulders!' cried one governor.[127] 'By God, O people of Iraq', shouted another, '. . . By God, I shall strip you like bark, I shall truss you like a bundle of twigs, I shall beat you like stray camels.'[128]

In autocracies, where, definitionally, the individual has no political control over his government, all that stands between the people and oppression is the law. This legal protection did exist in Byzantium, but in the Caliphate it did not. Against the authorities nobody's life, limb, property, or freedom was guaranteed, which precipitated frenzied alternations of abject submission and murderous, religion-inspired uprisings. This legitimacy-vacuum was the empire's essential vice of origin. Islam was incompatible with anything but a theocratic ruler or college. So, reacting to the surliness or active hostility of parts of the population, the caliphs responded by putting it under something not far removed from a military occupation. What mitigated and softened its impact (always with an eye to the interests of the powerful) was the governorment's need to acquire the co-operation of the local influentials. The Caliphate was in no way totalitarian but it *was* despotic. The state 'was . . . something which sat on top of society, not something that was rooted in it'.[129]

---

[127] Quoted, Grünebaum, *Sources of Islamic Civilisation*, 71–2.
[128] Quoted, Lewis, *Excerpts from Muslim Writers*, i. 23–4.
[129] Crone and Hinds, *God's Caliph*, 109.

One devastating outcome of this condition was the sequence of local riots, regional uprisings, religious revolts, military mutinies, and civil wars to which I have drawn attention. A second, and lethal, one was the collapse of the empire. It may be argued that the breakup was inevitable because of the long distances and poor communications; but the Ottoman successor state (admittedly less extended than the Caliphate) maintained itself for some 600 years, and the Roman Imperial Republic and Empire was in continuous existence from, say, 150 BC to AD 476 before losing its western provinces to the Germans. Others might plead that Islam's propensity to proliferate sects was bound to lead to secessions. Certainly it encouraged and nurtured them—but Mamluk Egypt and the Ottoman Empire were equally Muslim yet enjoyed long and stable life-spans.

The Caliphate shows up particularly badly against the Byzantine Empire. It was much larger, much wealthier, and apart from the Byzantines themselves, had no particularly worrisome enemies trying to overrun it. The Byzantines for their part were encircled by deadly foes who attacked them unremittingly. Yet the Caliphate fell apart in some 300 years while the Byzantine Empire held together for some 900.

Judged by the standards of most of the preceding and contemporaneous polities (Dark Age Europe clearly does not qualify), the Caliphate must rank low. As an imperial structure it was ramshackle, cobbled-up, unintegrated, improvised. It fell to bits the moment it stopped expanding. As a despotic form of government, many of its caliphs and the majority of its administrators both high and low, and reputedly many of its judges, seem self-serving and lacking a sense of empire. It is remarkable that so brilliant and creative a society and culture could give rise to so impoverished a system of government.

A Note on Mamluk Egypt (1250–1517)

1. SIGNIFICANCE AND NATURE OF THE MAMLUK POLITY

The nature and political role of the Mamluks in the Caliphate were described in the preceding chapter. There, their rule was exercised covertly and intermittently and was very obviously a usurpation. The particularity, perhaps the uniqueness, of Mamluk rule in Egypt was that it was open, institutionalized, and legitimized. Its Mamluks were a self-recruiting and self-reproducing army which, through its amirs and its chief amir—the sultan—openly ruled the state.

Although no such regime is to be found anywhere else, some individual characteristics are be found in other polities. For instance, its mode of recruitment and self-perpetuation resembles the Ottoman 'Janissaries'. It may well occasion surprise, however, to suggest that the relationship between sultan and amirs is not so very dissimilar from what could be found in, say, parts of nineteenth-century Latin America. Both conform to the common pattern—described in the Conceptual Prologue[1]—of a number of notables disposing of armed dependants, all of whom are rivals for an authority which is so supreme as to be despotic. In Mamluk Egypt these notables are the amirs and their followings of Mamluk troops while in Latin America they would have been the *jefes militares*. The amirs had their dependent Mamluks, the *jefes* their *gente*. In both cases the political process is a contest between these roughly equal military notables for succession to the supreme power: in the Egyptian case the Sultanate, in Latin America the Presidency. Once established the sultan, or president, finds it hard to retain power, and several rulers are successively overthrown until one day a contender establishes an undisputable supremacy over all the others, after which a period of stability ensues. A good analogy to the Mamluk political process in Egypt would be, for example, the civil wars that preceded the triumph of Porfirio Diaz in Mexico in 1876 and the long continuity of his rule thereafter.

The most salient characteristics of this Egyptian Mamluk polity are these. First, the social and political solidarity of the Mamluk army and its establishment which formed a ruling caste entirely separate from and

---

[1] See 'Conceptual Prologue' above, 3.3 and 4.1.2.

superior to the population. Next, a dramatically unstable tenure of the throne, evinced by long stretches of despotic and apparently secure rule punctuated by wild, staccato bursts of fighting. Finally, in contrast to this volatile tenure of the throne, the just-as-dramatic stability of the regime itself—a Palace-type form, which was never subject to any collegiate limitations, only open to military challenge.

2. MAMLUKS: GENERALLY

2.1. *Why Mamluks?*[2]

The Mamluk, miscalled the 'slave'-soldier, is rarely, if ever, found outside the Islamic lands, but within these became well-nigh universal. It is very hard to see why. It could not have been simply a result of military competition—because the caliphal Mamluk army was not superior to, say, Byzantine troops. One key element was undoubtedly the shortage of Arab military; another was the fidelity to be expected of the freed slave.

2.2. *Who were Mamluks?*

There is a fascinating parallel between the characteristics of the eunuchs at the Byzantine court and the Abbasid 'slave-soldiers'[3] (though at their court, unlike the Egyptian one, eunuch and Mamluk were not mutually exclusive— a good example would be the famous Amir Munis under the Caliph Muqtadir). The parallel consists in this: that both eunuchs and Mamluks were bought young, from outside[4] the empires, and were initially (in principle at least) of a different religion from the host country's. Further-more, just as in Byzantium the eunuch officials outranked their masculate counterparts, so in the Caliphate these freed slaves, these Mamluks, were regarded as superior to their opposite numbers. If we were comparing only the Mamluks of Egypt with the Byzantine palace-eunuchs, a further parallel presents itself—each category was one-generational, since neither could pass on their privileges to descendants.

---

[2] For a list of which see D. Pipes, *Slave Soldiers and Islam* (Yale UP, New Haven, Conn., 1981), 159–61.

[3] Known there as *shulam*, for *shilman* = 'boys'.

[4] There were always some 'home-made' eunuchs in Byzantium as in China, but they were exceptions.

3. EGYPT

This note is about the Mamluk institution, not Egypt as such, but some background is necessary to understand how they came to seize power.

The Arab conquerors, 639–45, started out by simply imposing themselves on the Byzantine political, administrative, and economic substructures. Indeed, even 700 years later the Copts were still in charge of 'book-keeping and tax-collection' because (Ibn Khaldun tells us) 'they have been familiar with these matters since ancient times'.[5] The Arabs stayed apart from the native population—socially, religiously, and also topologically, for they lived in the newly founded garrison town of Fustat near where Cairo stands today. They left the land system undisturbed but taxed it very heavily. The Copts launched widespread tax revolts in the eighth century, but these all failed and the Copts learned they must live under the yoke.

The Arabs rotated their Egyptian governors to lessen the risk of their bidding for autonomy, so that in 230 years (639–868) there were no less than 100 different governors![6] Harun al-Rashid himself appointed twenty-four governors in his twenty-three-year reign.

In 868 Ibn Tulun, a Turk, was sent as governor. He annexed Syria and made himself autonomous. Though a caliphal army was able to reconquer Egypt for the Abbasids, 905–32, a later governor emulated Ibn Tulun by annexing Syria, making himself autonomous, and so founding the line of the Ikhshidids (935). But this dynasty was deposed by the Fatimids, who invaded and conquered Egypt from their homeland in North Africa. The Fatimids were so called because they claimed they were direct descendants from Fatima, the Prophet's daughter. They therefore maintained that the Abbasids were usurping anti-caliphs. Consequently these Fatimids (969–1171), whose empire embraced North Africa, Egypt, and part of Syria, were not merely independent of but at war with the Caliphate. Their rule ushered in Egypt's rebirth as an independent state, and a period of glory and prosperity.

We have now reached the time of the Crusades and the Latin kingdoms of the Levant. Egypt was critical to them and their rivals, the Turkish amirs of Syria. It was one of the latter who triumphed and his nephew Salaah al-din (Saladin) who became the governor of Egypt. He and the Ayyubid dynasty he had founded were highly successful in warfare, relying on a strong component of Mamluk troops. In 1250, when Louis of France's Crusaders landed at Damietta, it was their regiments that carried the day

[5] Ibn Khaldun, *Muqaddimah* (ed. Dawood), 198.

[6] Calculated from D. S. Margoliouth, 'Egypt, History (Mahommedan Period)', *Encyclopaedia Britannica*, 11th edn. (1910), ix. 91–2, which gives a list of the governors.

at the Battle of Mansura. This victory happened to coincide with a profound succession crisis in the dynasty. The Mamluk amirs exploited this by deposing the sultan and proclaiming his estranged stepmother as queen. They rectified this anomalous (for a Muslim state) situation when a few weeks later the queen married the commander-in-chief of the Mamluk amirs. So was inaugurated the Mamluk dynasty.

4. MAMLUK RULE

4.1. *The Polity*

The form of the Mamluk polity need not detain us long for it is a pure Palace type, where the sultan wielded absolute power outside the *sharia* sphere of jurisdiction, and maintained it by a cunning mixture of military strength and successful management of his amirs. He had no reason to court the population, which was treated as an inert mass to be taxed and pushed about—and acted like one. Nevertheless, two particular points must be noted. The first relates to the legitimation of these sultans. Eight years after the Mamluks had seized power in Egypt, Hulagu destroyed Baghdad and slew the caliph (1258). The Mamluk Sultan Baybars thereupon invited a survivor of the Abbasid family to Cairo and recognized him as caliph. This provided the Mamluk sultans with a relationship *vis-à-vis* a caliph like that which had legitimated the Baghdadi sultans. The second point to notice is that Egypt which (as we saw) had been highly centralized and bureaucratized under the pharaohs and continued to be under the Ptolemies, the Romans, and the Byzantines, remained so with the Byzantine administrative arrangements virtually unchanged, under the Muslims.

We have here, then, a characteristic Palace polity of the Muslim type, that is, of bifurcated religious/secular authority. The advent of the Mamluks did nothing to alter this at all. What it did indeed alter, and what makes it significant, was the character and provenance of its ruling class. From 1250 onwards political control resided exclusively—we must repeat, *exclusively*—in the Mamluk military establishment.

4.2. *The Mamluk Establishment*

The army was now the ruling body in Egypt and Egypt's ruling body was now the army. This army was a one-generational military aristocracy of 10,000 men. The great aristocrats were the amirs, and the greatest of them all, the sultan. The least significant aristocrats were the Mamluk rank-and-file who provided each amir, and the sultan above all, with his military following. Two points need underlining here. The first is the single-generational characteristic of this aristocracy—one might even call it an order. *This* is what makes it so strikingly unusual. The order reproduced itself by recruiting new boy slaves, and training them as soldiers. Once trained the soldier was manumitted—he was now free. Consequently his sons could not also become Mamluks—since they were not slaves, but free by virtue of being the sons of free men. The second point is that this order lived, worked, dressed, and spoke its own language in total isolation from Egyptian society.[7]

The slaves had to be young lads of non-Muslim origin and born outside the Mamluk state, preferably in the Kipchak steppe or—later—in the Caucasus. The amir responsible for purchasing the sultan's slaves acted as *tajir al-mamalik*, 'Merchant of the Mamluks'. The *tajir* made his purchases and brought the boys to the slave market in Cairo. Those bought for the sultan were paid for out of the *bayt-al-mal*, the palace treasury. On the death of a sultan those of his slaves who were still in training were solemnly purchased by his successor.

The young slaves were sent to special schools (of which there were twelve, each capable of lodging 1,000 pupils)[8] where they learned to read and write, and were instructed in the Muslim religion and the *sharia*. As they approached adulthood they began military training. These schools were staffed exclusively by eunuchs, in the hope of preventing homosexual relationships between cadets and adult Mamluks, who were very partial to homosexuality. Such homosexual relationships, it was argued, would destroy discipline.

As long as the cadet (*kuttabi*) was at school he had no right to pay, and possessed neither arms, horse, nor *iqta* of his own. He had to pass the training before receiving these. Passing-out parades were held for some 200–300 cadets at a time. At the end of the ceremony each cadet received his *itaqa* (a diploma) signifying both that he was now a fully trained soldier and also a free man—a Mamluk, in fact.

All the amirs, that is, the senior Mamluk officers, as well as the sultan were in the market for boy slaves. To the master who had freed him and only to him the Mamluk was attached by the tightest of bonds and owed fidelity to his last breath. Disloyalty was regarded as unspeakably vile. But the enfranchised Mamluk was also expected to be faithful to his colleagues in servitude and manumission, his *khushdashiya*, and to act in concert with them. The followings of the amirs busied themselves with getting their ex-owner proclaimed sultan, and if they succeeded did their utmost to consolidate his

---

[7] In what follows I have relied very heavily on Ayalon, *Studies on the Mamluks*, i.   [8] Ibid II.

power. For his part that ex-owner gave them office in place of rival amirs and their followings. This is the root of what passed for the political process in Mamluk Egypt: on the one side the intense in-group solidarity of the *entire* Mamluk establishment and its studied self-seclusion from Egyptian society which it ruled absolutely, on the other intense and often lethal conflicts between rival amirs and their followings, to become sultan.

4.3. *The Mamluk Army*

The most important corps in the army consisted of the Royal Mamluks. These included the Mamluks of the preceding sultan, those of the reigning sultan, the sultan's personal bodyguard, and Mamluks of various amirs who had been seconded to the sultan's service. This corps was much more numerous than any amir's personal contingent. There was also a third and less important component, not part of the ruling Mamluk establishment, which was made up of the sons of amirs and of local recruits. The amirs were rank-ordered: amirs of ten, of forty, and of one hundred. Only Mamluks could become amirs and only those Mamluks who were freedmen of the reigning sultan could claim the succession.

This army rarely exceeded 10,000 men, which was a sizeable military force for the time but is an astonishingly small number to serve as a ruling caste so effectively and for so long. It fought as a mounted archery, but every man carried lance, sword, and mace as well. The Mamluks' military prowess was their chief asset in securing the obedience of their subjects. They destroyed Louis of France at Mansura in 1250, they defeated the Mongols in general battles, and by taking Acre in 1302 they wiped out the last trace of the Crusaders in the Middle East. These victories won them the reputation of invincibility.

Most Mamluks received wages in cash or kind, but the pay of all the senior officers (and some junior ones too) came mainly from the revenues of their *iqta*. To recapitulate briefly, the *iqta* was a source of revenue, usually landed estates, that was temporarily assigned to an officer so as to bring him an income corresponding to his grade on condition that he brought to the field a certain number of men-at-arms. That revenue was, effectively, the land tax (the *kharaj*) due from these parcels of land (for it was rare for the *iqta* to consist of continuous territory). It was not a 'fief' in the European sense but a 'benefice', a fiscal device. The *muqta* neither resided on these estates nor exercised jurisdiction within them. The sultans strove mightily and successfully to prevent the *iqta* becoming hereditary. In Cairo a numerous Coptic bureaucracy in the 'Office of the Army' (also known as office of the *iqta*) plus a network of branch offices in all large towns or provinces maintained the cadaster on all these lands, calculated their yields, kept the register of all *iqta* holders, and oversaw the periodical reallocations of the *iqta* after an incumbent's death.

The sultan allocated to himself ten twenty-fourths of the income-yielding land of Egypt but this proportion gradually sank until it was no more than four twenty-fourths.[9] It is hazardous to work out the incomes of the various ranks, but one estimate, made in 1957, calculated that in 1316 a private of the Royal Mamluks received only 24–52 dinars. The amir of a hundred, however received 109,000–126,000 dinars—an indication of the wealth and high rank of the amirs.

4.4. *The Political Process*

We remarked earlier that the Mamluks closed ranks entirely to all outsiders, while maintaining ferocious rivalry among themselves, and these statements can now be expanded. As to the first point: the vast majority of the Mamluks lived in Cairo, where they paraded their exclusivity with no lack of ostentation. For instance, they and only they were entitled to— and indeed were obliged to have—Turkish first names; they spoke Turkish, not Arabic; they usually married slave-girls of their own homeland or the daughters of other Mamluks. Only they might purchase Mamluk slaves, while their subjects were limited to black slaves. They wore distinctive dress and were the only individuals (apart from the rarest of exceptions) who were permitted to ride on horseback. They were the better able to sustain this exclusivity by being quartered inside the vast citadel of Cairo, the *Qal'at al-Jabal* ('Fortress of the Mountain'). This established a barrier against the city population, which they terrorized.

Yet this exclusive Establishment was riven by the endless struggles of the amirs for the Sultanate and, consequentially, the rapid deposition of one sultan after another. There was no accepted rule or procedure for settling the succession. The first of the two Mamluk dynasties, the *Bahri* Mamluks, did try with some success to introduce the hereditary principle, but the Circassian Mamluks who succeeded them explicitly rejected this.[10] The average length of reigns is only five-and-a-half years, compared with the seventeen in the Caliphate (632–1258) and the twelve-year spans in the Byzantine Empire. The modal tenure was far shorter. Among the twenty-four Bahri sultans, for instance, eleven reigned for one year or less; nineteen, three years or less; and twenty-one, five years or less. There were three very

[9] *Cambridge History of Africa* [hereafter referred to as *CHA*], eds. J. D. Fage and R. Oliver, 8 vols. (CUP, Cambridge, 1975–85), 47–8.   [10] Ayalon, *Studies on the Mamluks*, 244.

long reigns (though the longest of these was punctuated by two depositions) of, respectively seventeen, fourteen, and forty-one years.

One consequence of the Black Death (1341–2) was to depopulate the
recruiting grounds of the Kipchak steppes, and the amirs turned instead to
Circassia. Meanwhile the Bahri dynasty was falling into decay: a succession
of twelve sultans, some mere children, occupied the throne, helpless against
a handful of quarrelling amirs. Amidst this confusion a Circassian amir
seized power in 1382, so initiating the 'dynasty' of Circassian Mamluks
('dynasty' being something of a misnomer in that the Circassians rejected
hereditary succession and their amirs aimed at making the sultan a mere
primus inter pares).

The followings of the sultan and the greatest amirs constituted so many
separate politico-military parties, each bound together by that solidarity we
have already noticed. The amir who aspired to the throne could not succeed
except by forming a coalition of these factions in his support; but when he
succeeded he usually found he had little control over them. If he managed to
hold on long enough to die in his bed, the amirs would elect his son—but
only in order to win the time in which to settle their mutual rivalries and
select a chosen successor. When this was accomplished the latter deposed
the sultan and took his place; and so on, *da capo*. It comes as no surprise to
learn, therefore, that of the twenty-three Circassian sultans, the reigns of
fourteen do not add up to more than fourteen years. But from time to time
some great personality emerged. Barquq, Bars-bey, and Qait-bey, men of
immense physique and powerful personality, reigned for respectively twenty-
one, sixteen, and twenty-nine years.

5. THE BALANCE-SHEET OF MAMLUK RULE

During this entire Mamluk period Egypt was not just the Nile Valley but
the centre of a large and powerful empire that stretched from Cyrenaica to
Mesopotamia. It was highly prosperous, not just on account of its prover-
bially rich cereal harvests and its manufactures—notably textiles—but
because by this date Egypt had become the entrepôt of the eastern trade
which now passed via the Red Sea to Cairo and thence to the Italian city
republics. Nor did the arts or literature or learning languish. The sultans,
whatever their private vices and however extortionate their tax officials,
lavished money on mosques and *madrasa*s and charitable foundations. Yet the
way this country was governed was quite barbarous. The rulers, for all their
encouragement of charity, religion, and the arts, were rude and uncultivated
soldiers, completely alien, living a hermetic life of their own and not even
speaking the native language. Their wild and uncouth troopers terrorized

the streets of the capital: women could not venture out, peasants would not bring their cattle to market in case the troops or the palace officials seized them for their own use, while tumults and street-fights between the rival groups created havoc. But these were family quarrels: to the outer world they presented a united front manifesting a remarkable instinct for collective self-preservation. There is a tag about political parties being kept together by 'the cohesive force of public plunder'—and this perfectly applies to the entire Mamluk establishment. Unlike so many ruling groups, none of its factions ever thought of inviting foreigners or elements of their own subject population to join them in their internecine struggles.

Historians concur that decline set in after the Black Death—which took a terrible toll—but they do so on the strength of considerable hindsight. For the Circassian Mamluk armies were able to stand up to Timur and to capture Cyprus, as well as repressing (amidst horrible tortures) the great Bedouin uprising in Upper Egypt. But the seeds of decay were indeed there. The signs are manifold. Administration became laxer. The strict rules that had regulated the training-schools lapsed and instruction in Islam was dropped as unnecessary. Vacancies in the ranks were now filled by adults as well as by boys. Evidence of governmental corruption multiplies: governorships and other official posts began to be sold openly to the highest bidder, and judicial verdicts were delivered in return for bribes. (In one case an unpopular vizier was flogged, tortured, and executed without trial by his enemies at the price of a 75,000 dinars gift to the sultan.)[11]

One reason for this growth of bribery and corruption was to supplement the state revenue which had now become insufficient to meet the ever-more serious pressure of the Ottoman Empire, also with an army of slave origin, the Janissaries.[12] The prodigious costs of warfare in Syria and the Jezira fell on an Egypt weakened by the effects of the Black Death and experiencing a secular decline in its economy. The sultans responded by manipulating or debasing the currency and establishing state monopolies in sugar and pepper (and to some extent in cereals and meat); but these measures only made matters worse, so that a vicious cycle set in.

Although the Egyptian economy was in full decay by 1500, defects in the army were what proved the regime's undoing. For one thing the Mamluks were land animals and neglected their navy—and this at a time when navies had become critical to Mediterranean supremacy. But much more importantly, the very military virtues of the Mamluks turned into vices. Immensely proud of their successes as a force of swift mounted archers, they fell

[11] S. Lane-Poole, *A History of Egypt in the Middle Ages* (Methuen, London, 1901), 329.
[12] See Bk. IV, Ch. 3 below.

into the same trap as other proudly self-confident military establishments elsewhere, notably the Japanese Samurai and Europe's feudal shock-cavalry. Like them, the Mamluks declined to handle firearms and relegated them to their inferior, non-Mamluk units. The Ottomans, on the other hand, were arguably the best cannoneers in the entire Mediterranean theatre. In 1517 Selim I met and defeated the Mamluks and incorporated Egypt as a province of the Ottoman Empire.

Not that the Mamluks disappeared! On the contrary, they remained in being and, as the Ottoman central government weakened in the seventeenth century, so their amirs—now called *begs*—effectively substituted themselves for the Turkish officials, until by the eighteenth century they were once again ruling the country. It was they who met—but were defeated by—Napoleon at the Battle of the Pyramids in 1798. Even this did not get rid of them. That did not come about until the Turkish Empire sent a new governor to Egypt—Mehemet Ali. In 1811 he disposed of them for ever by the drastic expedient of having them all massacred.

5.1. *Appraisal*

The Mamluk polity is full of paradox. The cultivation of the arts, sciences, and literature goes side by side with the barbarous terrorization of the population. A small group of 10,000 utter foreigners seizes complete control of a vast and populous country, exploits it for its own advantage, brings signal economic advantages to the population—as by a side wind, but nevertheless does do so—and persists in power even beyond the time-span of the empire (267 years), up to 1798. The murderous internecine struggles of the rival Mamluk followings coexists with unshakeable collective solidarity against all outsiders. The collective welfare of the entire Egyptian community goes hand in hand with the servitude, abasement, and insecurity of the private individual.

All in all this polity was a success in terms of its age. It guaranteed the territorial integrity of the empire, it permitted a high degree of economic prosperity, and although the incumbency of the throne changed feverishly, the regime as such was completely stable. The polity was bound to come under strain as its external foes grew more united and powerful and the trade-routes shifted to the Atlantic sea-lanes. True, the Mamluks, as we have seen, made matters worse for themselves ultimately by their economic and military measures; but by 1600 the entire geopolitical and economic pattern of the world had so changed that no manner of Egypt was going to able to exert the same military and commercial hegemony it attained to in the fourteenth century.

PART II

3
The T'ang Empire

1. INTRODUCTORY: FROM HAN TO SUI

The demise of the Han Dynasty in AD 220 ushered in some 350 years of disunion. The destruction of that great empire inevitably provokes comparison with the collapse of the Roman empire in the West. In both cases, barbarians from the north took over half the empire; a salvationist religion—Buddhism and Christianity respectively—acquired a mass following; and finally, both reverted to a natural economy. But the outcomes were profoundly different at least in two respects. First, in Western Europe Christianity was the carrier of Roman political tradition. But in China Buddhism was an alien religion, profoundly antithetical to Chinese Confucian political tradition, with which, finally, it had to come to terms. The second fundamental difference of outcome is that the succession states to the Roman Empire in the West established an entirely new form of government, namely feudalism, and then went on to consolidate themselves into disparate sovereign units. The Roman imperial tradition had been shattered and was finally abandoned. In China, by contrast, the empire was reconstituted in a superior version of the Han.

1.1. *The Successor State: Chronology*

The expiring Han Empire broke into 'the Three Kingdoms'. The metropolitan area, containing the capital (Chang-an) and Loyang, called itself Wei: Szechuan called itself by the ancient name of Shu. The entire area south of the Yangtse formed the kingdom of Wu. They fought incessantly, in this way tempting the northern horse-nomads to invade. So opened the period the Chinese call the 'Five *Hu*'—the 'Five Barbarians'—the first, the partly Sinicized Hsiung-nu (Huns?) sacked Loyang in 311 and in 316 took the capital and extinguished the dynasty. The Fifth 'Hu' were Turkic people from Eastern Siberia and in 386 one of their tribes, the Toba, formed a durable empire (the Northern or Toba Wei), which controlled all China north of the Huai River. Its dynasty provides a classic illustration of the rapidity and completeness with which such barbarian clans adopted Chinese civilization. By its end, in 529, it was in effect a Chinese dynasty and a Chinese state. This, indeed, was the reason for its downfall. A court faction, supported by the tribesmen, resisted the Sinicization and it broke into two. In 577, however, the western state (Chou) reunited all the territory north of the Yangtse. Then in 580 its most prominent general, Yang, murdered the ruler and all his clan and assumed the throne himself. Finally, in 589, calling himself 'Emperor of the *Sui*', he annexed the kingdom (now called Ch'en) of south China and, taking the throne-name of Sui Wen-ti (581–604), he became emperor of all China. His reign and that of his son, Sui Yang-ti (604–18), created the reunified state which the T'ang dynasty was to usurp and then to rule from 618 to 907.

CHRONOLOGY

577	Northern Chou conquer Northern Ch'i. All North China united
581	YANG CHIEN (WEN-TI), general and chief minister of Chou, usurps throne and founds the Sui dynasty. Capital at Chang-an, 583
589	Yang conquers Southern Ch'en. REUNIFICATION OF EMPIRE
605	YANG-TI. Eastern capital at Loyang. Massive public works, three failed campaigns against Korea, hence:
617	Mass risings. LI YÜAN rebels, captures Loyang
618	Yang-Ti murdered
618	Li Yüan usurps throne as emperor of T'ANG DYNASTY

The T'ang, 618–907

618–26	Li Yüan (posthumously T'ang Kao-tsu)
626–49	T'AI-TSUNG. Eastern and Western Turkic states destroyed; expansion into Central Asia
649–83	KAO-TSUNG. Sick man, dominated by his second empress, Wu Chao. China expands west up to Ferghana
683–4	CHUNG-TSUNG, deposed by Wu
684–90	JUI-TSUNG, deposed by Wu
690–705	Wu takes throne in own right as the EMPRESS WU
688	Rebellion of T'ang princes crushed. Reign of terror

705	Empress Wu persuaded to abdicate
705–10	Chung-tsung (restored)
710–13	Jui-tsung (restored)
713–56	HSÜAN-TSUNG
735–52	Chief Ministership of Li Lin-fu
751	Battle of Talas (Turkestan); Arabs halt westward expansion
755	An Lu-shan rebellion. Loyang captured
756	Rebels capture Chang-an. Emperor flees to Szechuan, made to abdicate in favour of heir SU-TSUNG
762–79	TAI-TSUNG
763	Tibetans sack Chang-an. Final defeat of the rebellion
780–805	TE-TSUNG
805–6	SHUN-TSUNG
806–20	HSIEN-TSUNG. Dynamic autocrat, re-establishes firm central control. Murdered
820 onwards	The continuous advance of eunuch power
820–4	MU-TSUNG
824–7	CHING-TSUNG
827–40	WEN-TSUNG Feeble creature, put on throne by eunuchs. Tries to defeat them, hence:
835	The 'Sweet Dew' plot. Its failure strengthens eunuch influence
840–6	WU-TSUNG. Fanatical Taoist. Proscription and despoliation of Buddhism
846–59	HSUAN-TSUNG
859–73	I-TSUNG
873–88	HSI-TSUNG
875	Huang Ch'ao raises rebellion
880	Huang captures Chang-an
883	Huang driven out of Chang-an
884	Huang killed, end of the rebellion, rise of local war-lords, breakdown of central control
888–904	CHAO-TSUNG. Increasingly anarchic conditions
904–7	N-TI
907	*End of the T'ang Dynasty*

1.2. Change and Continuity

Momentous new developments occurred in the three-and-a-half centuries of division but, with hindsight, we can see that the continuities were much more important.

One of the new characteristics of the age was the division between the two Chinas, north and south of the Yangtse. The South had been colonized originally by Chinese latifundists who reduced the natives to dependency and constituted a kind of plutocracy. These southern clans regarded themselves as the true, indeed, the unique, repositories of traditional Chinese culture and despised the Sinicized barbarian lineages of the North. But though the luxurious court-culture, the local brand of Buddhism, and the latifundist economy differed from the northern kingdom's, both North and South shared a single Chinese culture and also, for all the rivalry, their contacts became more and more commercial than military.

A second great development was the mass-adoption of Taoism and Buddhism. As well as philosophical Taoism, there also developed a popular religion of mystic practices, multifarious cults, and the quest of physical immortality through contemplation, breathing, and exotic diets. Later, many T'ang emperors were to become addicts of this cult which was a serious and embittered rival to Buddhism. The latter became a mass religion of personal salvation. It required, and to a greater extent engendered, a genuine personal piety. From the fourth century its monasteries and temples began to span all China. Buddhism became one of the bonds uniting the two halves of the land, all the more so when, in the 6th century, the divergent northern and southern doctrines were syncretized. Buddhism proved highly appealing to the barbarian dynasties in the north: many of the emperors espoused its doctrines and protected and indeed nurtured its organizations. It may be they did so in order to avoid giving themselves up to Confucianism—for to do that was to make a total surrender to the Chinese way of life and its rituals, its observances and its social code, as embodied in the 'Five Relationships' and all their political implications. To the masses, however, Buddhism provided the answer to their despair and hopelessness amidst the carnage, arson, and devastation, the deracination and the impoverishment caused by the ceaseless mutinies, rebellions, and wars.

There was one development of profound political consequence which occurred *especially* in the North, because it was a consequence of the barbarian invasions and it was destined to persist into and through the T'ang: the emergence for the first time since the very early Han, of a genuine aristocracy, i.e. an aristocracy of birth. The rise and overthrow of the many northern dynasties represented the rise and overthrow of one clan by another. Just as it had been on the steppe, so now whether the chief were called king or emperor he was not much more than a *primus inter pares*, the leader and manager of the other clan chieftains. A *noblesse de sang* was officially recognized, graded into nine degrees, each supposed to marry only within its own degree. The state required proofs of nobility, so genealogical trees and almanacs proliferated. These great families were as rich as they were noble. As occurred in late Rome, many of the smallholders fled to them for protection—against the taxman as much as against ban-

dits—and they turned their vast estates into fortified, self-sufficient hacien-
das, filled with dependants and retainers of every variety.

These aristocrats were strengthened by another consequence of the civil
wars and invasions: the educational system, such as it was, collapsed, and
with it the method of selecting civil servants. From 220 this was supplanted
by a nomination system. The commandery (*chün*) inspectors (mostly civil
servants from the capital) drew up lists of candidates for civil service posts
classified in nine grades. The names were then vetted by higher officials for
approval by the ministers, and since these were the influential clan aristocrats they accepted only their own relatives. Thus the public service fell into
their hands also.

Though these changes were very considerable, the continuities were the
more important. In the first place, Chinese society remained a two-class
system. The upper stratum was the landed aristocratic and ruling class.
They were the *liang*—the wealthy. Below them were the *yi-men*—the unpri-
vileged mass, sometimes simply called *ting*, 'adults'. Although a free peasantry still survived, most agricultural workers had yielded themselves or
been reduced to dependent status on the aristocratic estates. Next, the law
codes (little of which survive) followed the same spirit of administrative
repression as under the Han. Justice continued to vest in the administrators
and not an independent judiciary, and the punishments were equally if not
more severe than in the empire. Civil administration—in so far as not
overridden (in the North) by governors or 'Grand Administrators' with
troops at their command—was not nominally much altered, either. The
chung-shu-ling, the Secretariat, which was the key policy department of the
central government under the Later Han, lost its authority and became
purely executory, and its policy passed to six bureaux (which later developed
into the T'ang 'Six Ministries').

But above all there was a continuity in the style and tradition of
government and indeed, to a large extent, in its personnel. Either the
nomads must exterminate their Chinese subjects so as to turn their farms
into cattle-runs, or they had to rule them, and only the skilled and literate
Chinese knew how this had been done; and that was the Confucian way.
Among these same Chinese advisers and officials Buddhism made no
impact, for it had no significantly political philosophy. The new rulers
were shown that if they wanted to fill the role of a Chinese emperor they
had to carry out the great seasonal sacrifices and court rituals, and all these
were Confucian. These gestures, they learned, were their legitimation.
Certainly by this time Confucianism had run out of new ideas and Buddhism and Taoism were the intellectual innovators, but the Confucian
Classics, quintessentially *Chinese*, were still the basis of the Chinese gentle-

man's education. And, of course, they formed a perfect ideological kit for authoritarian rule. Hence these Classics and their traditionalism and hierarchical temper continued to dictate the style and outlook of government.

So, sooner or later, and sooner rather than later, the Turkic or Tungus tribal aristocracy not only governed in the Chinese style but ate, dressed, and spoke Chinese. A classic case is the great Toba state of North Wei, already mentioned. Its Emperor Yao-wen (471–98) decided to adopt in their entirety the traditional Chinese institutions of the South. Among other things he suppressed the 1,200 sanctuaries of the Toba cult and instituted the Chinese imperial cult in its stead; adopted the Chinese system of robes and costumes; introduced the cult of Confucius; moved his capital to Loyang; forbade the use of the native Toba language at court; and adopted Chinese family names, even to the point of calling his imperial house the Yuan.[1]

1.3. The T'ang Empire

The T'ang is widely seen as the high point of classical Chinese civilization in every respect—power, government, religion, art, and literature.

Buddhism and neo-Taoism produced a new intellectual ferment to which a tired and jaded Confucianism was at last—in the tenth century—forced to respond, heralding the great Neo-Confucianist revival. The T'ang was the golden age of classical poetry, the time when Buddhist sculpture reached its pinnacle, and where the canons of classical painting for all future time were laid down. Abroad, the regime was powerful, expanding for a time right across Central Asia as far as Persia, conquering Korea, and colonizing north Indo-China. The wealthy South now united with the North, enlarged the tax-base, and provided a vast stimulus to commerce, finance, and the concomitant growth of cities based on them. The structure of government, based on the tradition of the Han, was more sophisticated and complex. This system, which like Chinese culture was widely admired and emulated throughout Asia, was to prove the prototype of all subsequent imperial government.

Like the Han Empire this great T'ang construction collapsed in blood and rapine after lasting some 300 years. In what at first sight seems a perfect replay, both the T'ang and the Han were preceded by short-lived dynasties

---

[1] H. Maspero and E. Balazs, *Histoire et institutions de la Chine ancienne* (revised edn., Demi-ville, Paris; Presses Universitaires de France, Paris, 1967), 120, n. 1. The many diverse ways in which the nomads addressed the question of how to handle their new Chinese subjects (who of course *vastly* outnumbered them) is brilliantly analysed in W. Eberhard, *Conquerors and Rulers: Social Forces in Medieval China* (Brill, Leiden, 1952).

which had already completed the unification to which they were simply heirs: in the Han case, the Chin dynasty of Shih Huang-ti, in the T'ang case the Sui dynasty (581–618). Each was punctuated by a civil war after which the dynasty was restored—but with significant differences; in the Han case, the usurpation of Wang Mang, in the T'ang case the revolt of An Lu-shan. Each staged an imperial revival and each collapsed in the midst of widespread popular insurrection, militarism, and court intrigue. The parallel reaches even to some important details of central government, to wit: the suppression of the regular administration by the Inner Court, and the control of the Inner Court by the eunuchs. And the collapse of each of the great imperial structures ushered in the similar dismal periods of disunion, carnage, warlordism, and court dissension, followed by the predictable barbarian invasion and conquest.

1.4. *The Sui Legacy*

The true unifiers of China were the two emperors of the Sui dynasty. The T'ang built on their secure foundations. In 581 Yang Chien—a vengeful, hyperactive, domineering soldier who belonged to one of the great aristocratic clans—seized the throne, calling his dynasty Sui and taking the throne-name of Wen-ti. His accession must have appeared as simply another palace coup, and indeed the dynasty lasted only thirty-seven years before being usurped by the T'ang. In that time, however, Wen-ti (581–604) and his son Yang-ti (604–18) transformed China. In the first place, Wen-ti conquered and annexed the southern state of Ch'en, so reunifying all China north and south of the Yangtse, and Yang-ti made the unification a reality by forcing (it is said) $3\frac{1}{2}$ million men and their families—$5\frac{1}{2}$ million persons in all—to put in their due twenty days of duty-labour to construct a series of canals.[2] These canals linked the Yellow River system (which served the capital Chang-an and the eastern capital, Loyang) with what are now Beijing, and Hangchow, so joining the Yangtse basin to the historic heartland of China. Furthermore, reacting against the laxity and diversification of the era of disunion, the administration of this new empire was ruthlessly systematized and strengthened: the currency was reformed and the penal laws recodified more concisely and clearly, the system of the commanderies (the *chün*) was made more uniform, a new census brought another million-and-a-half families into the tax net, and arrangements were made to cope with local famines by means of state and village-granaries throughout the country.

[2] *Cambridge History of China* [hereafter referred to as *CHC*], iii. 1 (CUP, Cambridge, 1979), 133–5.

The nemesis of the Sui emperors was the same familiar gigantism that possessed the great pyramid-building pharaohs of the IIIrd and IVth Egyptian dynasties or, to return to China, Shih Huang-ti, the First Emperor. Wen-ti conscripted labour on an enormous scale to repair the Great Wall, dig the Kuang-t'ung chü canal near the capital, build his new palace: and, finally, to engage in a disastrous campaign (598) to conquer Korea. His son, Sui Yang-ti went much further. The chronicles portray him as a megalomaniac who wasted his people's lives for his own pleasure amidst insensate sensualism. Most of this is simply Confucianist legend. His wars and his promotion of commerce by means of the great canal system ran counter to their antipathy to an emperor's personal power, and to their physiocratic economic outlook also. But there is no doubt about his contempt for human life, however posterity can justify (as it can) its economic and political rationale. His arguments for rebuilding the eastern capital, Loyang, are amply justifiable, and for constructing the great north–south canal he has justly been dubbed 'the second founder of the Chinese Empire'.[3] But millions of Chinese and their dependants were mobilized to execute these projects. To crown all, Yang-ti resumed the unsuccessful war against Korea in which thousands died. His third campaign in 614 touched off a general uprising throughout the entire empire and more than 200 rebel organizations were in arms by the time Li Yuan, duke of T'ang and one of the Sui's most powerful generals, seized Loyang and proclaimed himself emperor.[4]

1.5. *The T'ang Empire, 618–907*

The 300-year duration of the T'ang empire makes for a problem of presentation. The governmental system at the end of the dynasty was not identical to the one at its beginning. So, to select a particular year or reign as representative of the entire dynastic span would be misleading.

It is universally agreed that the rebellion of An Lu-shan in 755 represents a watershed. But the second half of the dynastic span was also punctuated by the great rebellion of Huang Ch'ao in 875, and though finally suppressed, it proved a death-blow to the dynasty. Accordingly, I propose to present T'ang government at three points in time: from the foundation to An Lu-shan's revolt; between the suppression of that revolt; and finally the rebellion of Huang-Ch'ao and the terminal agonies. I shall style these three periods. Early T'ang, Later T'ang, and the Final T'ang.

[3] Maspero and Balazs, *Histoire et institutions*, 165.   [4] *CHC*, iii. 1, pp. 160–1.

2. THE EARLY T'ANG (618—755)

2.1. *The Central Government: Overview*

In completely uninterrupted tradition, government resided in the emperor, the Son of Heaven, absolute and supreme. The emperor however acted upon advice and in principle anybody whatever in the empire could memorialize him. But face-to-face advice to the emperor was proffered though a council of *tsai-hsiang*, 'Grand Ministers' (the expression is a designation, not an office) made up from the chiefs of various departments which always included the Chancellery and the Secretariat. This Council of Ministers might contain as few as those two ministers or as many as twelve. In practice, it tended to be dominated by one or a couple of the ministers influential at a particular time.

The departmental structure of the administration was very much more developed and differentiated than that of the Han and served as the prototype for all successive dynasties to the very downfall of the imperial regime in 1912. The core of the administration consisted of the Secretariat, the Chancellery, and the Ministry of State Affairs, the last being the executive proper. As such it controlled the so-called 'Hundred Officials', distributed in the six great departments of state, each in turn subdivided into four bureaux. These six departments were the Ministry of Civil Servants, of Finance, of Rites, of the Armed Forces, of Justice, and of Public Works. There were, additionally, the departments which ran the Imperial Palace—for example, the Management Department of the Inner Palace—consisting only of eunuchs, and the harem, whose denizens were ranked in official grades and classes corresponding to those of the civil service, just as in the days of the Han.

Related to and dependent on these central departments were two groups of offices. The first was the survival of the Han's 'Nine Ministries', now called the *Nine Courts*: these comprised the courts of Sacrifices, Imperial Banquets, Imperial Insignia, the Imperial Clan, and the Imperial Equipage, but they also included four other departments of more public significance: the Supreme Court of Justice, the 'court' of Agriculture, the Imperial (i.e. personal) Treasury, and the 'Equitable Balance' office. The second group of offices consisted of five technological directorates: the University for the Children of the State, the Imperial Workshops, the Imperial Works and Building Office, the Office of Armaments, and the Office of Water Control.

Alongside, but set apart from and in opposition to, all the supervisory and executive departments so far mentioned stood an organ the like of which had never previously existed in China or indeed anywhere else in the world. It is one of the unique innovations and inventions of the Chinese polity. This organ is always translated as the 'Censorate': it would be better, perhaps, nowadays to translate it as 'Procuracy', for its function strongly resembled that of the Procurator's Office in the now-defunct USSR. In brief, it was a branch of the bureaucracy with the duty of observing, scrutinizing, and investigating the actions and processes of all and any civil servant, high or low, and where it found irregularities, to denounce those to the emperor and have the offender brought to trial. The Censorate was headed by a staff office, made up of a president and two vice-presidents. They controlled three courts. The Great Court (*t'ai yüan*) or Court of General Business consisted of six censors whose duty was to investigate and denounce administrative irregularities. The Court of the Palace, with nine members, exercised similar powers over court etiquette. The third court, of External Investigations, had wide powers indeed. It investigated the administrators in the provinces, but it also exercised jurisdiction over lawsuits, the office of armaments, the Imperial Treasury, Buddhist temples, and the Ministry of Currency; in short, over the behaviour of the 'Nine Courts' which were the vestiges of the 'Nine Ministries' of Han times mentioned earlier. Additionally they investigated the levy of tax and corvée, military colonies, and from the eighth century, the postal service. But many of these powers passed, in that same century, to *ad hoc* special commissioners.[5]

The Censorate was not the only organ of surveillance and control. There existed another group of thirty-two officials known as the *chien-kuan* or 'remonstrating officials', half of them in the Secretariat and half in the Chancellery, made up thus: eight 'Grand Remonstrators', twelve comissioners, and twelve 'Reminders'. Their duties were roughly the same: to wait on the emperor and give him advice, however unwelcome.

The personnel who manned this great and complex governmental organization fell into two groups, superior and inferior, those 'within the stream' and those 'outside the stream' (of affairs). The former are those we refer to in the West as 'mandarins', a Portuguese term of uncertain etymology, but which seems to have meant, simply, 'those who command'.[6] They seem to have numbered about 19,000. The 'outsiders'—petty officials, clerks, office-boys, storekeepers, and the like—numbered some 30,000 to 40,000. These civil servants were graded, as under the Han, into nine grades made up of thirty classes. The petty official structure replicated this.

The significant change from Han practice lay in the mode of recruitment and promotion. Nothing like this was to be seen anywhere else in the world

---

[5] See p. 759 below.   [6] Cf. 'Mandarin' in *OED*.

until at least the eighteenth (though I would prefer the nineteenth) century in Europe. In T'ang China the aristocratic clans retained their hold on high office and most entrants to the Mandarinate continued to come in by recommendation, it is true, but a fresh start was made on an examination qualification for entry, and this became more and more significant throughout the dynasty.

The first mention of a written examination occurs in 595, under the Sui. Originally there were three types of examination. In 681 one of these was dropped, leaving only the *chin-shih* and *ming-ching* examination. The latter demanded a textual knowledge of the Confucian Classics. (Later, knowledge of the Taoist 'scripture', i.e. the *Tao-te ching*, was also required.) The *chin-shih* required knowledge of the Classics, but also demanded literary compositions and a dissertation on some political or philosophical theme. The *chin-shih* became the more prestigious of these exams. But to pass it did not automatically guarantee a post. For that a further selection examination— the *hsüan*—was required, its rules being codified in 669.[7] There was always a surplus of qualified candidates: in 657 it was estimated only one in three was successful in obtaining a post.[8] The unsuccessful went on to careers in education or in the local administration.[9]

Such examinations were not the only ones used. Some emperors set up palace examinations which they themselves superintended—the Empress Wu (690–705) found this particularly useful in extending her control over officialdom—and the device became more and more common as the dynasty went on. It must not be supposed at all that these examinations were a 'soft option' or a device for exercising favouritism; just the reverse, they were conducted with an extraordinary rigour.

It will be noted that the subject-matter of the *chin-shih* and *ming-ching* examinations was the Confucian canon (the *Tao-te ching* was inserted as a sop to the resurgence of Taoism, which many emperors espoused). Thus the traditional ideology of the Chinese upper classes which had maintained itself at court despite four centuries of barbarian rule in North China and in the teeth of the Buddhist and Taoist challenges was now once again institutionalized as the necessary and central ideology of the state.

Arrangements for the subaltern civil servants were different. To gain probationer status, the candidate sat the *first* minor examination in calligraphy, arithmetic, and current affairs. Then, only after passing three merit-reviews, might he sit the second minor examination.[10] The annual merit-

---

[7] *CHC*, iii. 1, p. 276.   [8] Ibid. 330.   [9] Ibid.
[10] *Traité des fonctionnaires et traité de l'armée*, trans. R. des Rotours, from the *Hsui Ou Yang*, 'New History of the T'ang', chs. 46–50 (Brill, Leiden, 1974), 49–50, 51 ff.

review for these subaltern officials is itself a startling innovation and does not seem to have been adopted anywhere outside China until the nineteenth century. Officials were annually graded on a check-list of desirable attributes. There were nine grades, and the check-list included such qualities as their virtue, justice, integrity, fairness, diligence, and so on. Additionally, the official received a grading for his attainments in exercising what was considered the quintessential requirement of his particular post; for example, for those in charge of corvée labour, 'that the works are completed, and the labourers and artisans do not complain'. Or, for a magistrate, 'when he investigates a criminal matter he gets to the bottom of it: he judges and sentences with equity and sincerity'. There were twenty-seven such *desiderata*—called in usual flowery Chinese style the 'Twenty-seven Perfections'.

The empire's population is estimated at some 50 million. How many civil servants were there? Balazs[11] calculated conservatively that there were about 150,000 to 160,000 officials of all types, including employees, of whom some 10,000 worked in the court and central government offices in the capital. Counting five persons to a family yields a figure of about 1 million persons making their living from officialdom—some 2 per cent of the population: as he says 'a tiny minority grafted on to the enormous peasant majority of the population'.

Contemporary calculation gives these figures: *Sui* dynasty: 2,581 officials in the capital, 9,095 in the provinces, a total of 12,576; *T'ang* dynasty, 2,620 in the capital, 16,185 in the provinces, a total of 18,805. However, these totals do not include employees, only superior grades. Working from the *T'ang liu-tien*, composed in 739, Balazs arrives at the estimates for officials *and* employees shown in Table 3.3.1, to which must be added sundry persons in the General Protectorates and others dependent on the imperial commissioners. This compares with the figure for the Han dynasty, in 1 BC, of 130,285 officials and employees.[12]

2.2. *Local Government*

In the early T'ang period the local government system was—in effect—restored to something like it was in Han times: the former commanderies (*chün*) were now *chou* (prefectures), and below them the perennial sub-prefectures or counties, the *hsien*. But the T'ang created a (still rather tenuous) unit embracing several *chou*: a *tao*. This word means path or road, and in this case, a 'circuit'. Finally, the frontier areas to north and

---

[11] Maspero and Balazs, *Histoire et institutions*, 193–4 and 193, n. 2.   [12] Ibid. 193, n. 2.

TABLE 3.3.1. *Government officials in the T'ang dynasty*

	Number of units	Officials and employees
The *hsien* (counties, sub-prefectures)	15,000	90,000
The *chou* (prefectures)	350	35,000
The governorates-general	50	8,000
Central government and court:		10,000
TOTAL		143,000

north-west were treated exceptionally. A word or two on the *tao* and on frontier zones seems desirable before outlining the normal structure.

Over time the T'ang experienced the same difficulties as the Han both in respect to keeping an effective watch over the *chou*, and also in respect to problems affecting wide areas embracing several of these units. At first they tried to meet these difficulties by sending censors into the countryside from time to time, each being allocated a *tao*, or circuit, sometimes ten in number, at other dates fifteen. In due course the censors were replaced by inspecting commissioners—rather like the Han *mu* ('shepherds').[13] From 734 fifteen *tao* were created, each served by inspecting commissioners. Their duties were advisory: on regional problems of famine relief, migrant families, and land distribution. They were simply an inspectorate, with neither executive nor judicial powers. They must *not*, therefore, 'be thought of as constituting an additional, provincial, layer of government'.[14]

The imperative at the frontiers was to reply immediately and in force to nomad incursions. By the early 720s the north and west frontiers were organized in nine major command zones in which the military governor had his own large HQ staff and army as well as exercising complete military jurisdiction over all other troops in his zone. Logistical problems—always severe for these frontier areas—led these military governors along the same path that the Prussian local army commands were to tread in the seventeenth century: to take over a more and more civil function. In 725 this new role was formally recognized when they were empowered to undertake major financial transactions. At this date the governors were civilians—mandarins on temporary secondment from the capital. After 737, however, the frontier armies were reorganized as fully professional standing forces and in its train, military governors were professional generals. This, as will be seen, was to spell disaster for the Emperor Hsüan-tsung.[15]

---

[13] See p. 500 above, in Bk. II, Ch. 6.   [14] *CHC*, iii. 1, p. 404.   [15] Ibid. 366–9.

The standard local government arrangement was, briefly: fifteen *tao* (circuits) of the imperial inspectorate; some 350 *chou* or prefectures; some 1,500 *hsien*, sometimes translated as sub-prefectures or counties; and some 16,000 *hsiang* or cantons, embracing varying numbers of villages or *li*.

A *li*, consisting in theory of 100 hearths, was headed by a headman (*li-ch'eng*), and he would certainly be one of the rich men of the community. His duty was to draw up the register of families, collect the taxes, and apportion the corvée. The 'canton' or *hsiang* theoretically comprised five *li*. At its head was its *shi* or the elder: his duties covered the same ground as the village headman's but, unlike him, the *shi* was appointed by the sub-prefect of the hsien. His chief duty was the collation of the triennial census.

As always, the *hsien* was the maid-of-all-work, the veritable building-block in the entire system, and starting from this level leading officials were all members of the imperial bureaucracy proper. The chief official was the *hsien-ling*, variously translated as county magistrate or sub-prefect. His duties were multifarious—public order, tax-collections, the allocation of the corvées, the administration of justice—quite apart from carrying out all and any orders from superior authority. Something is gleaned from his personnel establishment: an assistant, a clerk of the registers, one or two clerks of the court, a finance office and a judicial office each with numerous clerks, a dozen or so prison officers and warders, a director of markets, a granary-keeper, and one or two schoolteachers.[16] Even more can be got from van Gulik's imaginary reconstruction of the cases of the celebrated T'ang magistrate 'Judge Dee' (Ti)[17] (although this relates to the late imperial period).

Next come the *chou*, or prefectures. The prefects (*t'zu-shih*) had the same range of duties as their subordinate *hsien-ling*, but at a higher level and with a larger and better staff. These prefectures fell into three classes according to their population. Every year the *t'zu shih* had to take the tax revenue to the capital and report on his administration to his superiors. Finally, as already stated, the prefectures were checked by the *tao* inspectorate.

---

[16] Maspero and Balazs, *Histoire et institutions*, 191.

[17] See e.g. R. van Gulik, *The Chinese Lake Murders* (University of Chicago Press, Chicago, 1977), being one example of van Gulik's 'Judge Dee murder mysteries'.

2.3. *The Practice of Government*

2.3.1. THE CENTRAL GOVERNMENT:

Emperor and Court

Outwardly, the form of the central government was the same as the Han, a Palace-type system: an autocrat within his court buttressed by his army on the one hand and his bureaucracy on the other. In practice, however, the style was significantly different. For one thing, the early T'ang emperors were less trammelled by their immediate families, and particularly by their 'in-laws', the notorious 'outer relations'. Secondly, though aristocratic lineages contended for office—which, on the whole, they successfully monopolized—the clan cohesion was much weaker than under the Han; the obscure relatives of a distinguished family could expect little support.[18] Court factionalism was based partly on regional rivalry—the north-western clans (from which the T'ang derived) *versus* the disdainful endogenous clans of the north-east—partly on rivalry between the aristocratic ministers as a whole and the professional bureaucrats—a mere meritocracy—but most of all, on a pure and simple desire for power. Power was instrumental: each great family could benefit from a son in the inner circle who could protect the interests of the family estates. Furthermore, there were always more eligibles than there were places for them, and factionalism was an expression of this competition for position. Thirdly (the Empress Wu apart), government was based on the emperor's consultation with ministers and was more open than under the Han. Let us pick up these themes in more detail.

First, as regards the imperial family: imperial princes were usually numerous and their temptation to conspire too often irresistible, but cases of rebellion were rare, almost non-existent except, it seems, under the Empress Wu. Such plots as there were concerned the succession, the weak spot in all monarchies not adhering strictly to the rule of primogeniture. 'I have already appointed my eldest son Crown Prince', said Tai-tsung (642), 'but'—he added—'the fact that his brothers and the sons of my concubines number almost forty is a constant source of worry to me.'[19] Indeed, throughout the early T'ang the succession was irregular. Yet these intrigues did not lead to civil war or impair the stability of the dynasty, nor did they significantly constrain the political choices of the emperors. Only the enfeebled sons of Kao-tsung and Empress Wu were intimidatable. All the others, and particularly the Empress Wu, were their own masters.

[18] Cf. *CHC*, iii., p. 706.
[19] A. F. Wright and D. C. Twitchett (eds.), *Perspectives on the T'ang* (Yale UP, New Haven, Conn., 1973), 249.

As with sons, so with in-laws. There was no return to the dominance of an empress's relatives as under the Han. The reign of the Empress Wu is not only not an exception: it powerfully supports the rule. The Empress Wu did notoriously help her relatives—notably her rascally nephew—but only up to a point, and that point was where they encroached on her personal power. In Han times her clan would have taken over the entire court. The Empress Wu conducted a balancing act, keeping the opposing forces in play, systematically resisting her family's ambitions.[20]

In short, unlike Han emperors, the early T'ang emperors' political choices were not constrained by family or by their wives' clansmen. They *were* constrained, however, by the ministers and the higher civil service— what we may call the *Outer Court*. It is this that distinguishes early T'ang 'style' from the Han. The background to this—and it provides most of the explanation—is that in the early reigns of the dynasty the merit system was only just beginning, and ministers came from among these powerful clans so that the hidebound conservatism, the deadly bureaucratic routine, the almost caste-like solidarity of the Mandarinate was yet to come. Furthermore, the emperors were men of action. The Empress Wu, who took over from her sickly husband Kao-tsung, was a woman of indomitable will and energy who broke all opposition to her. In short, at this stage emperors were virile (none more so than Empress Wu), officialdom was not yet fully reconstituted, and the aristocratic clans who provided most of the ministers lay between these two poles. In working with them, emperors neither retreated into helplessness nor advanced into confrontation, but tended, like successful medieval monarchs in Western Europe, to practise 'baron-management' and consultation, as we shall describe shortly.

T'ai-tsung (627–49) was later regarded as a model of (Confucian-style) enlightened rule, a harmony of emperor and his great officials. 'His chief officials slept in shifts in the Chancellery and Secretariat so that he could summon and question them at any time, night or day, about the affairs of the empire. When memorials became numerous, he had them posted on the walls of his bed-chamber so that he could examine and consider them well into the night.'[21]

In subsequent reigns the relationship was not without tension, either because the monarch could find no one minister or group of ministers in whom to confide completely, or the chief ministers quarrelled among themselves (a tendency exaggerated by the lack of a defined command structure in the administration, as will be seen later). In either case the

[20] C. P. Fitzgerald, *The Empress Wu* (University of British Columbia Press, Vancouver, 1968).
[21] *CHC*, iii. 1, p. 190.

sovereign's reaction was the same—to change ministers—if necessary again and again until, perhaps, he found someone in whom he could put complete confidence. The self-willed—and innovative—Empress Wu governed by perpetually changing ministers. In T'ai-tsung's reign the average term of a *tsai-hsiang* (chief minister, see below) was seven years, but under Empress Wu it was only two.[22] T'ai-tsung disgraced and dismissed one in three of his *tsai-hsiang*; the Empress Wu demoted or exiled or even executed four out of every five.[23] Whereas she acted because of policy differences, Hsüan-tsung's (712–56) motive was to stop bickering among his chief ministers. He characteristically met this kind of challenge by employing only a very small group of chief ministers, usually two or three men, and making one of them predominant. From 736 onwards, for the next sixteen years, he confided in the aristocrat Li Lin-fu, who was so supreme that western historians refer to his tenure as his 'dictatorship'.[24]

The interface between the emperor, his chief ministers, and officialdom was a series of councils, ranging from tiny and confidential cabinet councils at one end, to the open court at the other.

Two streams of advice had their sources in the administrative structure itself. One consisted in the right of *any* official to memorialize or remonstrate with the emperor and the duty of the thirty-two *chien kuan* or 'remonstrating officials' to do so. The latter were in theory and in actual practice the establishment's own licensed critics. The second source sprang from the organization of the bureaucracy which sometimes by inadvertence and sometimes by deliberate design created numerous areas of friction and contestation. In such inter-ministerial or interdepartmental contestations, each contender had to memorialize his own point of view and at the end of the day the emperor would have to decide.

The widest of such councils was the Special Audience, twice monthly, where all officials above the ninth grade—in short the entire metropolitan Mandarinate—were present. But this was far too large for anything but ceremonial matters; it was followed by a private meeting in an adjoining chamber, the *shang-ko*, between the emperor, his chief ministers, and others specially authorized to attend. Less wide than the Special Audience was the audience that took place daily and, subsequently every third day, of the really senior officials, those of grade 5 and above. These, together with the 'remonstrating officials' whose grade was inferior to grade 5, used to meet in the *liang-i* hall. These meetings, in the *shang-ko* and *liang-i* halls were genuine

---

[22] *CHC*, iii. 1, 309–10.   [23] Ibid.

[24] E. G. Pulleyblank, *The Background of the Rebellion of An Lu-shan* (OUP, London, 1955). He was himself succeeded by (disastrous choice) Yang Kuo-chung.

forums of debate. The most important of such councils—or cabinets— however, was the one that met in the so-called Hall of Government Affairs—the *Cheng-shih T'ang*. We shall see that the two major departments of state, the Chancellery and the Secretariat, could veto one another. To avoid this—or alternatively, to resolve the difficulties—the chancellor, the secretary, and their deputies, along with others specially invited, met there under the presidency of the emperor and acted effectively as the cabinet of the empire; so much so that in 723 it was institutionalized with its own secretariat (as will be described later).[25] It met daily, and, as described above, those attending were styled *tsai-hsiang*, 'Grand Ministers'.

In any of these cabinet councils most of the business would be generated from inside the bureaucracy but some at least would originate from the *chien kuan*, the 'remonstrating officials'. Those were always liable to meet the emperor's displeasure, even forfeit their lives if they overstepped the mark, and yet they could be amazingly forthright. Wei Cheng, Tai-tsung's critic, wrote no less than 200 memorials along the usual morose Confucianist lines. Absolutely fearless, often plain insulting, he was the emperor's gad-fly—but, also his confidant.[26] For instance, when the emperor inquired as to how his reign compared nowadays with his earlier years, Wei replied: 'Long ago before the Empire was pacified you always made righteousness and virtue your central concern. Now, thinking that the Empire is without troubles you have gradually become increasingly arrogant, wasteful and self-satisfied.'[27] Another—unnamed—official rebuked the emperor in open court! 'Yü, the Great Emperor did not brag, yet none in the world could compare with him. Your Majesty has swept away disorder and returned the Empire to rectitude. Your myriad officials truly are not up to contemplating such pure brilliance. But you need not come to Court to brag about it!'[28]

This is not to reckon with the right of the Secretariat officials to amend or even reject decrees of the emperor either by refusing to draft them or by changing the wording—as T'ai-tsung's secretary Li Fan did by deleting the name of the man the emperor had designated as chancellor! T'ai-tsung at least always told his ministers that he did not want yes-men who would do nothing but correct verbal forms; he wanted men to correct him and reject his decrees when necessary.[29] Not so the fierce Empress Wu. Many ministers and lesser officials paid for their temerity in crossing her. The most

---

[25] H. J. Wechsler, *Mirror to the Son of Heaven: Wei-ching at the Court of T'ang Tai-tsung* (Yale UP, New Haven, Conn., 1974), 95–7; Mu Ch'ien, *Traditional Government in Imperial China* (Hong Kong, 1982), 38–41; *CHC*, iii. 1, p. 350. [26] Cf. Wechsler.

[27] *CHC*, iii. 1, p. 197. [28] Wright and Twitchett, *Perspectives on the T'ang*, 250.

[29] C. O. Hucker, *Chinese Government in Ming Times*, seven studies (Columbia UP, New York, 1969), 242–3.

famous case, perhaps, is when an official of the Secretariat called Liu Wei-Chih scoffed at the empress's personal edict and rejected it as illegal because it had not been countersigned in the Secretariat and Chancellery: he paid for this with his life.[30] But neither this nor her infamous reign of terror in 684–91 ought to be taken as a norm. There are many instances where, warned or lectured by ministers, she acted on their advice. Indeed, one Chinese historian under the Ch'ing dynasty (Chao I) actually praised her for her receptivity to remonstrances and criticism.[31] And the institutionally imposed limits of imperial despotism even under so incalculable, imperious, and ruthless a ruler as she are, perhaps, best appreciated by considering the following anecdote. In 705 the censors finally succeeded in impeaching her favourite, Chang Ch'ang-tsung, on a charge of treason. One of the three judges, called Sung, refused to acquit Chang of the charge. In order to replace Sung by someone more compliant, the empress ordered him into the provinces 'to investigate corruption and malpractice'. In reply—I quote—

he pointed out that according to the regulations, when officials holding the posts of Prefect or District Magistrates were accused, they were then investigated by Censors of the Court of General Affairs if of high rank; by Censors of the Court of Exterior Affairs, if of low rank. The Vice-Presidents of the Left and Right Boards [Sung was a Vice-President] were only sent to the Provinces if the matter was of great importance affecting the security of the Empire, or military necessity. As the cases to which he had been assigned did not come within this category, he could not dare infringe the regulation by taking up the appointment. This argument was found to be irrefutable and Sung Ching did not leave the capital.[32]

All in all, there is every reason to accept Wechsler's view that in the early T'ang there was probably more official freedom to criticize and more official participation in policy-making than at most other periods in Chinese history.[33]

The Bureaucracy

What, above all, makes Chinese palace-style government distinctively different from most of the many other varieties of this format, is its bureaucracy. In the course of this history, we have met with bureaucracy from the very dawn of recorded government down to the Roman Empire and Byzantium. We have spoken too, of the origins of the Chinese bureaucracy at the time of the Han. This had somehow survived the four centuries of disunion up to the coming of the Sui but the bureaucracy of T'ang times was a reconstitution in the sense that the solidarity, the *esprit de corps*, the

[30] *CHC*, iii., p. 298.   [31] Ibid. 310.   [32] Fitzgerald, *The Empress Wu*, 186.
[33] Wechsler, *Mirror to the Son of Heaven*, 4.

marriage of ruling servants with an ideology of state, were revived. T'ang bureaucracy, though no more than a beginning, was, for scope, complexity, size, training, and recruitment quite without parallel in any other parts of the globe at that time. If the Byzantine and Arab Empires matched it in one or even two of these respects—which in itself is doubtful—they came nowhere near matching the combination of all of them together; and it is this cumulation of characteristics which makes the T'ang bureaucracy a genuine innovation in the history of government.

Earlier pages have outlined its general structure. Here I propose to comment on some of its peculiar features and their implications.

Its Structure and Function

Its most striking aspect was specialization. Each specific function was serviced by specific officials, every official had his specific function, and all—both functions and personnel—were integrated in a grid whose axes were set, laterally, by specified and distinct departments and vertically by the nine grade–thirty class hierarchy. So much is simply bare fact. The astonishing completeness and symmetry of the administrative system can only be sensed by poring through des Rotours' translation of the *Treatise on Officials and on the Army*.[34] There in page after page are detailed each department and its duties, every official and his duties; rather like a cross between the U.S. Government Manual and a telephone directory. Only then can the logic, ingenuity, and neatness of this magnificent triumph of organization and design be grasped. On a vast scale, every function had its official, every official had his function. Specialization and differentiation are its hallmarks.

Remarkably, at the summit there was no corresponding integration. The training, the mode of recruitment, the full-time professional status, the hierarchy of civil servants, impels many commentators to look on this bureaucracy in Weberian terms. They see it as a great pyramid of authority tapering to a summit. It does *not* taper to a summit at all. It tapers, yes, but to a number of peaks. Some are higher and some lower than others, but they are separated.

The truth is that, partly by accident or partly by design, the system at its higher levels was collegiate. The scheme did not—yet—envisage a single supreme official as the emperor's sole adviser but just the reverse. These many advisers all had to have the same access to the emperor and so, by parity of reasoning, none might override the rest. Hence it appears to modern eyes as a system of internal checks and balances. The most important of these were:

[34] *Traité des fonctionnaires.*

(a) the right of the two premier staff departments, the Chancellery and the Secretariat, to block one another;

(b) the power of the six executive ministries to block one another on any matter crossing departmental jurisdiction;

(c) the right and duty of the Tribunal of Censors to denounce and impeach any members of the active administration whatsoever;

(d) the right and duty of any of the 'remonstrating officials' to memorialize and denounce any official decision, including that of the Tribunal of Censors to the emperor; and even to criticize the emperor himself.

(a) *The Imperial Chancellery* is the western translation for *Men-hsin sheng*, literally 'Gates Descending' Department. It was headed by two presidents, who were second-grade, first-class mandarins. Their duties were to *transmit* the orders of the emperor and to make sure they were executed and to direct matters pertaining to rites and the 'proprieties'.

The Grand Secretariat is a western translation of *Chung-shu sheng*, literally 'Central Writings Department'. Its two presidents were to 'assist the Son of Heaven in the direction of high affairs of state'. They published and signed all government orders, made them known a second time to the emperor, and then had them applied.[35]

Its Secretaries drafted edicts and other documents such as the emperor's answer to petitions. A number of alternative drafts were made and the assistant secretary-general chose among them. Assuming that the document then received the emperor's signature, it next went to the Chancellery. This might have no comments, but it was entitled to make them and ask for alternative options from its previewing officers, who were very senior, grade 3 mandarins. If it opposed the original form of the decree, it went back to the Secretariat with suggestions for revision. Disagreements were brought to the daily meeting of the two departments' principals in the Hall of Government Affairs in the presence of the emperor.

(b) *The Six Ministries* formed part of the Department of Government Affairs (*shang-shu sheng*). At the beginning of the dynasty it was headed by the emperor himself. His successors did not follow suit and the department quickly ceased to be a policy-advisory body equal to the Chancellery and the Secretariat and became purely executive. Its personnel was often styled 'The 100 officials'. Each of the six departments was independent of the others. It is worth noting that matters affecting more than one department were not settled by a simple lateral reference by one official to his opposite number in another department. As in many bureaucracies today, the lateral commu-

---

[35] *Traité des fonctionnaires*, 130, 174, 176.

nication was transmitted formally by a chit duly stamped and dated from the official in question up to his headquarters—the Department of Government Affairs itself—and thence downwards again.[36] It can be imagined how time-consuming this was. For matters affecting more than one department, the six ministers therefore met together in council.

(c) The *Censorate* was independent of all the other government agencies. Censors did not act collegially. Each censor presented his own memorials to the emperor via the president and vice-presidents; then, even if they approved, it was processed in the usual way via the Chancellery and the Secretariat.[37] The institution, for all that, enjoyed great autonomy. But individual censors might well be influenced by fear of retaliation or the jeopardizing of their career prospects (since censors were drawn from the general run of officials and moved back to join them after their spell of office) or, above all, by fear of the emperor's displeasure. It was considered improper for the emperor to punish a censor for his criticism but it could and did happen. Nobody could predict the reaction of an irate emperor.

The Censorate, the *yü shih t'ai*, was presided over by a president and two vice-presidents. Its duty was 'to utilize the penal laws and regulations so as to seek out and correct the crimes and errors of civil servants'.[38] Beneath the three senior officials, there were three courts (or boards, the word *yüan* serves for both). One was concerned only with the Inner Palace. Another, the *Court of General Affairs*, comprised six censors of fairly low grade—(sixth grade, second class)—charged with denouncing reputedly delinquent civil servants; attending the Imperial Audience and receiving the emperor's orders; and acquainting themselves with which matters they should examine as a judicial body and would denounce to the throne.[39] When they did denounce a civil servant's irregularities, their president and vice-president signed an Address to the Throne. The third court, of Exterior Affairs, did much the same for irregularities in the prefectural and sub-prefectural administration.

Some scholars have idealized this organ as a democratic institution, a surrogate for public opinion. Others have seen it as the opposite, an instrument through which the emperor could intimidate the line administration and make it subservient to him. Neither view is acceptable. The general administration and the Censorate had far, far more in common than either had with the vulgar populace. The line of political cleavage in Imperial China ran between the ruler-administrators on the one side and

---

[36] Ibid. 25.
[37] C. O. Hucker, *The Censorial System of Ming China* (Stanford UP, Stanford, 1966), 21.
[38] *Traité des fonctionnaires*, 280.   [39] Ibid. 296.

the populace on the other. As to the other view, while it is true that an emperor could, like the Empress Wu, turn the Censorate to his own political advantage against the officials he wanted to disgrace, it is perhaps more common—and unquestionably more striking—to find the Censorate being used by the line-administrators to crush the emperor's personal entourage in the Inner Court, as in the last years of the Ming (c.1620–44). Kublai Khan said, 'the Secretariat is my left hand, the Bureau of Military Affairs is my right hand, and the Censorate is the means for my keeping both hands healthy'.[40] The service frequently deviated from this ideal. A self-willed emperor could abuse the service to strike down recalcitrant officials, a weak emperor could leave a power vacuum that the censors rushed to fill with partisan criticisms that fragmented the court still further.[41]

With a competent emperor as moderator to the governmental system, the Censorate approximated to its ideal role. That role was indispensable to the well-being of both the administrators and the administered. For there was no other organ or process by which maladministration and corruption could be detected and prevented: no media to identify grievances and mobilize public opinion, no parliament to control the administrators, and above all, no tribunals in which one could sue officialdom. Government and administration were, as far as the subject was concerned, a self-contained universe: no forces and few controls existed outside it, or at least, no constitutional ones, only revolts and mass rebellions. An analogy exists in the defunct USSR. Its ruling Communist Party realized that, since for its own health as well as what was due to its subjects it needed criticism, and since also it admitted no political agencies outside itself, it had to provide for one part of the machine to criticize the rest: in Soviet terms 'self-criticism'.

Neither then nor now did the Chinese system permit the subject to sue the government. That recourse is specifically European, its beginnings lying in Roman and feudal institutions. When medieval pluralism was overtaken by absolutist bureaucracy in post-1600 Europe some states independently invented a somewhat similar self-policing mechanism to the Chinese Censorate (in the Napoleonic *Conseil d'État*, for instance, and the early-nineteenth-century Swedish Ombudsman) but these did their work in an atmosphere of widespread and relatively free public discussion. They never attained the completeness of the Censorate because these bureaucratic systems were only part of the political process. By contrast, the Chinese bureaucracy and the Chinese state were virtually identical.

[40] Hucker, *Censorial System*, 6.   [41] Cf. ibid. 300–1.

Finally, it is proper to underline that no equivalent institution existed in the states contemporary with the T'ang, neither the Later Roman Empire or the Byzantine Empire or the Caliphate. The Censorate is a striking Chinese innovation in the practice of government.

It must be re-emphasized that in the earliest T'ang reigns *every* official had the right to remonstrate and the supervising secretaries could block draft edicts and decrees being prepared.[42] But Wechsler[43] states this privilege was later withdrawn (probably after the death of T'ai-tsung).

(d) The so-called 'remonstrating officials' (the *chien kuan*)[44] also, like the censors, had a duty to criticize. Their functional equivalents elsewhere, if they existed at all, were clerics from outside the governmental system: priests and monks in Christian Europe and Byzantium, *ulema* in the Caliphate. In China, like everything else relating to government, including the emperors' numerous harems, the function was bureaucratized. In all, some forty officials had the duty to remonstrate. Under the T'ang they comprised four Grand Counsellors of grade 3, another eight of grade 4, and four Grand Secretaries of grade 5. In addition, there were two classes, each of twelve officials, the first called 'Reminders', the second called 'Omissioners'. These were of seventh and eighth grades. The former drew the emperor's attention to matters he had overlooked, the latter to arguments or considerations he had omitted in taking his decision. To judge by two memorable 'remonstrating officials', Wei Cheng (under T'ai-tsung) and the master-poet Po Chü-i (under Hsien-tsung, 805–20), these duties were fully executed, even at the risk of personal danger.[45]

Developing Trends in the Central Bureaucracy, 618–755

The checks and balances of the early T'ang administration system imposed a severe burden on the emperor because they presupposed him as the active co-ordinator. If the emperor took this function seriously, he either tried to run the bureaucracy as his own chief minister, like T'ai-tsung; or, if he retreated into the role of mediator and moderator among the conflicting agencies, he had to have a loyal and competent personal staff. Conversely, if he wished to opt out of either role, and confide in a particular chief minister, he merely pushed the same problem of co-ordination and direction on to that minister, who, in his turn, had to seek ways to direct and co-ordinate the various agencies. So attempts were made to put the administration under a single administrative head.

---

[42] Hucker, *Censorial System*, 19; Hucker, *Chinese Government*, 242–3.

[43] Wechsler, *Mirror to the Son of Heaven*, 108. It was called the power of *feng-po*, i.e. 'blocking and annulling'.   [44] See p. 754 above.

[45] See p. 755 above.

The movement towards creating a 'single-seated' apex to the administration began in 711 when the Department of State Affairs became purely executive. This left the Chancellery and Secretariat meeting alone with the Emperor in the Hall of Government Affairs,[46] which turned this into the administrative apex, responsible for formulating and drafting policy documents and reviewing their outcomes. In 723 the two departments were combined as the 'Secretariat-Chancellery' (*chung-shu-men-hsia*). As their respective duties became more and more intertwined, they coalesced as the administrative apex and became a fully institutionalized body when it acquired its own secretariat, organized into five chambers. These (the *wu fang*) were respectively responsible for civil service matters, political affairs, and military, financial, and judicial business. Much of the drafting and reviewing of documents came to be undertaken by men seconded from the various literary Academies. Perhaps the most important of these was the *chi-hsien yüan*, attached to the Secretariat. It was composed of especially gifted officials holding offices in the administration but concurrently at the disposal of the chief ministers and emperor as draftsmen and scholarly advisers.[47]

This was as far as 'single-seatedness' got under the early T'ang. For a further development we should have to leap ahead to the reign of Wu-tsung, a century later, who entrusted a chief minister, Li Te-yü (840–6), with the right to make the most important decisions on his own. He ordered that government directives should all 'issue forth from a single gate', a chief minister's office. Li instituted minuting the sessions of the Council of Ministers, writing them himself as the chief minister, and making his colleagues co-sign them as a correct record.[48] But this remarkable development ended with Li himself and no further moves in this direction were ever made again.

The second main line of development under the early T'ang stemmed from the emperor's role as supreme co-ordinator in this still pre-eminently conciliar structure of government. To fulfil the task, he needed his own secretaries and his own sources of advice. An early symptom is to be found in the reign of the Empress Wu. Even before the death of her husband, the empress had collected around herself a group of scholars to work on projects designed for her own political purposes. These soon became a secret Secretariat, called the 'Scholars of the Northern Gate'. She used them to draft memorials to the throne embodying, naturally, the changes she proposed the emperor should make.[49] It was this secretariat that enabled

---

[46] See p. 758 above.   [47] *CHC*, iii. 1, pp. 377–8.   [48] Ibid. 659–63.
[49] Ibid. 263.

her to pursue her unwavering quest for power against the emperor's Council of Chief Ministers.[50] Once empress, she used the scholars to carry out her political decisions whenever the chief ministers blocked them.[51] The Emperor Hsüan-tsung created a palace organization, for himself alone. This *han-lin yüan* was a collection of writers, poets, calligraphers, and Buddhist and Taoist clergy, all at his personal disposal. In 738 he formed a new section of this body, called the 'Academy of Scholars'—the *hsüeh-shih yüan*—as a confidential secretariat. Hsüan-tsung also began to rely on eunuchs as confidential messengers and advisers. Indeed, his most trusted servant was the loyal eunuch, Kao-Li-Shih, who served him for fifty years and shared with him his final humiliating tribulations, as he fled into the mountains from An Lu-shan, the rebel general. But neither the emperor's private secretariat nor the eunuchs had anything like the power they were to attain in the second stage of the dynasty, after that revolt had been crushed. It is precisely this development of the Inner Court, that is, the palace as the centre of policy, that is the most significant development in the later T'ang central government.[52]

The Social and Political Significance of the Bureaucracy

It was not necessary for the son of a mandarin to pass the *chin-shih* examination to secure entry to the Imperial Service, and up to 733 few mandarins were products of the examination system. Even the 10 per cent who did enter by this process were aristocrats, albeit from minor families. In short, the entire Establishment preserved its upper-class tone.

Nevertheless the introduction of the examination system did have a political and social impact. This was due to the immense social prestige attached to passing the *chin-shih*. To the very end of the dynasty, there were haughty aristocratic chief ministers who detested the examination system and memorialized the emperor to abolish it. They claimed—like their late-nineteenth-century British counterparts—that not book-learning but breeding and the habit of authority were the best, indeed the only, preparation for government. Yet so prestigious was book-learning in China that even those whose father's status guaranteed them the immediate right to a selection board chose to sit the examination. Of Hsüan-tsung's thirty-one chief ministers, eleven were *chin-shih*. Under Hsien-tsung (806–20) fifteen out of twenty-five were *chin-shih*. In this slow and subtle way the claim to high office began once again to shift from lineage and territorial wealth to merit, from aristocracy to merit-bureaucracy. Under the early T'ang, however, the process was only just beginning; it was not completed until the time of

---

[50] *CHC*, iii. 1, 269–70.   [51] Ibid. 310–11.   [52] Ibid. 450.

their successor dynasty, the Sung.[53] In the short run—especially in the later T'ang—the examination system had a destabilizing effect. Not only did aristocratic clans contend against the *chin-shih* graduates for the chief ministership, but whenever the latter triumphed they split into factions based on their 'filial' ties with their examiner and the other candidates he had admitted, a relationship akin to that of master–disciple. In this way examiners acquired political followings and in consequence factions contended for the right to appoint examiners.[54]

The T'ang's paramount contribution was to create the definitive hierarchical organization of the bureaucracy (from now on referred to as the Mandarinate), for this served as the model down to the very end of the imperial regime 1,200 years later, and its political and social consequences were determinative. This cannot be over-emphasized. Balazs, the great interpreter of Chinese bureaucratic institutions, puts it this way: 'The nucleus of T'ang institutions, or, rather the frame, the key-stone of all these institutions is 'officialism'—the definitive constitution of, and the hierarchic organization of the Mandarinate.' By this Balazs meant 'not just that henceforth the class of the lettered and bureaucrats took over the uncontested direction of Chinese society but that the comportment, ideas and habits of the civil service dominate every phenomenon of public and private life—their spirit if not their persons, being ever-present whether it be a matter of government, the army, or trade, or literature, or religion'. Increasingly, 'the nobility of the pen', says Balazs, 'extruded the nobility of blood'.[55] Why, even the hereditary princes were classified, as *ex officio* officials (*kuan* or mandarins)! The Mandarinate became the frame of reference for the entire society.

The examination system imparted its own flavour to this ruling corporation because, as against the older values of the warrior-aristocracy, it reintroduced the Confucian ethic. The Buddhist or Taoist inclination of a T'ang emperor had not the slightest effect on this; nor even the introduction of the Taoist classic, the *Tao-te Ching*, alongside the Confucian Classics in the *chin-shih* examination. This Confucian official ideology dominated political, social, and economic life. Here again we quote Balazs. These Confucian literati, he writes, were

Always trying to soften the rigours of the public works programme: in theory at least, they never ceased proclaiming themselves the disinterested directors of the public interest in general and the peasants in particular, ready to defend the latter's

---

[53] I. Miyazaki, *The Administration of Justice during the Sung Dynasty: Essays on China's Legal Tradition*, ed. J. Cohen, R. Edwards, and F.-M. Cha (Princeton UP, Princeton, 1980), 112–13.

[54] Ibid. 114.   [55] Maspero and Balazs, *Histoire et institutions*, 172–3.

interests against the exactions of an absolute monarch. In reality the literati-bureaucrats never decided to leap to defend the people except at the moment their own self-interests were involved. Each time some Emperor of exceptional enterprise threatened to exercise autocratic power and thus deprive them of the initiatives in despotic measures, they cried down tyranny in order to preserve their own prerogative of tyranny.

They would denounce luxury and debauch and equally the positive measures in which they themselves were full participants: and then, provided the next Emperor was more docile, once more apply these very same measures. They hated having their hand forced. The sovereign must never overstep his prescribed rôle of a representative symbol, enclosed within the rituals of 'non-activism'. If an Emperor did so, he lost his prestige and his sacral character and *ipso facto* became 'a mere tyrant, doomed to the just punishment of Heaven and the execration of mankind'.[56]

'Never lose sight', cautions Balazs, 'of the real profit that the indirect, camouflaged, and paternalistic tyranny of the literati-bureaucrats knew how to extract from the melancholy yet productive efforts of the open tyranny of the Emperors whom they featured as the personification of evil.'[57]

2.3.2 THE LOCAL GOVERNMENT

To recall: the regular local government system was the traditional two-tier arrangement of prefectures (now called *chou*) and sub-prefectures or counties, the *hsien*. Each unit in the system down to the *li* replicates the duties of the higher unit and every lower unit is responsible to the higher unit.

Their subordinate officials were the central government's 'all-purpose' authorities, with the general duty of maintaining peace and security, administering justice, and enforcing the complicated statutes relating to the taxes and for the rest, carrying out any further instructions from the central government. Ennin's travel diary of 838–45[58] (to be quoted below) demonstrates the constant reference upwards, the absence of local initiatives, and the pedantically strict adherence to regulations.

What was to prevent a prefect from establishing his independence? This happened not once but twice in the dynasty's history. Yet both lapses were exceptional; they were brought about by the collapse of the central government's power to intervene locally after it had succumbed to armed force.

There were three chief reasons for the very firm central control. The first

---

[56] Maspero and Balazs, 171.   [57] Ibid.

[58] E. O. Reischauer, *Ennin's Diary: The Record of a Pilgrimage to T'ang in Search of the Law* (Ronald Press, New York, 1955).

was the nature of the T'ang Mandarinate. The Mandarinate consisted of *all* higher local officials, whether in the localities or the metropolis. They were transferable units within one single unitary service. Thus they were the cement which bound the localities to one another and to the centre. Once the country had been fully pacified, successive emperors set out to weld the metropolitans and local officials into a single corporate body. Officials naturally preferred to reside in the capital and did everything they could to avoid provincial service.[59] So, many local officials were promoted to metropolitan duties and metropolitan officials were, reluctantly, made to serve in the localities[60]—or were relegated there after displeasing the emperor in some way or another.

In any event, the local prefects and county magistrates (the *tz'u-shih* and the *ling*) were mandarins, with an ordained place in the Mandarinate hierarchy. Thus, a prefect of the upper division was a grade 3, class 2 mandarin, ranking him just below six ministers and the vice-presidents of the Secretariat and Chancellery and on a par with the presidents of the Nine Courts, and no prefects of any division ranked lower than grade 5. Now all mandarin grades of 5 and above were the senior civil servants of T'ang China, the super-privileged élite, with the right to present their sons to the official selection board without their having to pass the *chin-shih* examination. Those sub-prefects (*hsien* magistrates) of 'first-class rank' were grade 6 mandarins and even they were the equivalent of the censors at the capital.

A further reason for the prefect and sub-prefects' lack of autonomy was that they were rotated from one district to another every three years: a reflection of the unitary nature of the Mandarinate. And the final reason was that these local officials had no standing military forces at their command. The provincial forces (the *fu*) were militias which were directly responsible to the court. In any event the forces mobilizable in a single prefecture were too small to be of any military significance when acting alone.

Thus the provincial officials were disarmed and, at the same time, part of a greater, nationwide civilian corporation subordinated, in grades and ranks, to the highest officials in the capital. Their techniques and quality was too poor and their numbers too few to carry out the very complicated regulations prescribed by the early T'ang taxation system. But this local administrative system was completely successful in posing no political threats of rebellion or secession. For one-and-a-half centuries there was domestic tranquillity, union, and order. That this was broken was due not to defects in the regular provincial administration but to those in the marcher pro-

---

[59] *CHC*, iii., pp. 352, 379.　　　　[60] Ibid. 379.

vinces in the north and north-west, and is more appropriately dealt with as an aspect of the T'ang military institutions below.

For all the tight central control, the prefectures enjoyed some measure of autonomy because they had local revenues which could be spent at discretion and could also draw on a pool of unpaid or largely unpaid 'special duty' labour for a multitude of minor official duties. This will all be discussed later.

Furthermore, by subsequent standards supervision by higher authority was lax.[61] But by contemporary standards T'ang China seems centralized: the laws and regulations reached down to and legal accountability reached up from the very lowest levels of local authority and the imperial orders were everywhere obeyed. It is unlikely that this was so in the remoter rural areas of the Byzantine Empire, and it was certainly not so in the Abbasid Caliphate which had to concede substantial and ultimately total autonomy to its furthest provinces. What mitigated 'centralization' in the Celestial Empire was what tempered it everywhere in the agrarian empires: the need to rely on local notables to secure enforcement and the consequent 'bending' of laws and regulations to suit their interests. For the minor officials in prefectures and counties came exclusively from the localities themselves and all manner of petty evasions and distortions then came into play.

Scholars have laid great stress on the background and the role of this sub-bureaucracy under later dynasties, for example, the Sung, when greater efforts were made to regulate its activities. It seems to me that, despite scanty evidence, its role under the T'ang should be given more attention. The men who performed these somewhat humble duty-labour services were not nobodies by any means; the annalists often style them 'the wealthier classes'. They played an important role in keeping the peace and a pre-eminent one in compiling and maintaining the tax-assessment register and in the statutory redistribution of land. Especially at the *hsien* level, the mandarin officials, who were always incomers and statutorily posted away from their birthplaces, were entirely dependent on these notables. Their role in the administration of the empire was similar, therefore, to that of the *decuriones* in the Roman Empire or the 'notables' in the Caliphate. As long as they were meticulously supervised, they greatly enhanced the quality of T'ang administration. In the early T'ang they were too subordinate to pursue their own devices too openly, and their interests coincided broadly with the government's. When they were no longer so carefully supervised

---

[61] D. C. Twitchett, 'Local Financial Administration in Early T'ang Times', *Asia Major*, 15 (1969), 82–143

and, at the same time, their interests diverged from the government, it bred
trouble and this duly arrived under the last of the T'ang.

The best way to form a general impression is by looking at the administration of the more important individual services concerning, notably,
taxation, the economy, law and order, and defence.

2.3.3. THE PUBLIC SERVICES

As usual in every pre-industrial empire, so in the T'ang: the public services
revolved around the axis of defence and taxation. The soldiers and gen-
darmes enforced the payment of the taxes which paid them, and all other
services were either modifications of these primary ones or were entailed by
them. For instance, justice was part of maintaining the peace. The distribution of land to the peasants was to provide them with the means of paying
their taxes. Public works and the road and canal systems served the same
main end: enriching the tax-base. In the course of this large-scale recycling
of taxes into public services, vast resources stuck to the fingers of the
intermediaries, which is to say the palace, the court, and the bureaucracy,
all of them tax-exempt by law.

The Taxation System

Like their barbarian predecessors, the T'ang emperors found deserts instead
of homesteads and, like them, saw the solution in a resettlement and land-
distribution programme. Since the money economy of the Han had long
since disappeared—although coin still circulated—most transactions were
now in kind, and taxation was the largest transaction of all. Thus the land
system and the tax system were two sides of the same coin.

Some 90 per cent or more of the revenue came from the basic land tax,
the remainder from certain miscellaneous taxes. The latter presupposed
households differing in wealth and hence ability to pay, the former did not.

This basic tax was a fixed one for every registered household because,
quite simply, it presupposed that each of these had received a fixed entitlement of land. Each adult peasant received, in principle, 80 mou (=13 acres)
of land on a *life*-tenure. This was his *personal* allocation and it was inalienable. Additionally, he received 20 mou (=3⅔ acres) of garden-land as his
hereditary allocation, *plus* one more mou for every three persons in his
household. The *personal* allocation returned to the village community on
the cultivator reaching the age of 60 or, alternatively, on his death. Every
three years the sub-prefect (i.e. county magistrate) was to assemble the
peasants and re-allocate these lots of 'personal' land so that all once more
had the legal quota. On this basis—everybody being legally provided with a
sufficiency of land—the fixed land tax called *t'sung-yung-tiao* was imposed. It

comprised three basic liabilities: payment in grain (*tsu*), in cloth (*tiao*), and in unpaid compulsory labour (corvée) for a fixed term, this liability being usually commuted by the taxpayer. So here was a system where, administratively, it was very easy to calculate the tax-liability (in fact it did not have to be calculated at all, it was a constant), but very complicated to re-allocate the land.

The miscellaneous taxes were quite light (which did not prevent widespread and successful evasion) and varied with the presumed wealth of a household. These taxes, called *ch'ai-ko*, comprised special obligatory labour duties and a household levy, in cash, from which nobody, not even the nobility, were exempted and, later, a land levy which began as a device to make peasants store grain in anticipation of scarcities but ended as just another exaction. To calculate liability, the local authorities were supposed to classify the households into nine categories according to their wealth, property, and size. Here, then, much administration was required both to classify and to calculate the liability and, since the administrators were the well-to-do, they had an incentive to underestimate their own liability. For how were these land-allocation-cum-taxation systems carried out? The process started, every year, in each village. Every head of family there was obliged to make an annual written declaration of his family members, his entitlement to land and the amount of land he had received. The headman (*li-cheng*) was obliged to conflate these returns into a list for the whole village. Then every third year the sub-prefect (the *hsien* magistrate) stepped into the picture. On the basis of the returns he divided the village households into their nine categories (most of course fell into classes 8 and 9, at the low end). He then conflated all this information into the *census*, and this provided the national basis for all land-allocation and tax-liability as well as the local basis for land re-allocation. He assembled the villagers at the year's end and transferred the land from those in surplus to those in deficit.[62]

It used to be thought that so complex a system was, like its predecessors under the barbarian dynasties, unworkable and hence a dead letter, for no documentary evidence had survived. At the turn of this century, however, a hoard of archives was found at a remote Buddhist monastery in Tun-huang on the edge of Kansu and Sinkiang provinces, not far east of Lop Nor and the Gobi Desert. One would have thought that the land allocations were less respected there than anywhere else. In fact they were respected, though the statutory land-grants fell short, owing to local conditions. The inference is that though the statutory land-grants were not necessarily made in

---

[62] Maspero and Balazs, *Histoire et institutions*, 200.

full, registration of households and the triennial allocations were faithfully executed elsewhere too.[63]

Though it seems highly equitable, the system was in practice unequal and regressive. A geographer of the early ninth century observed, 'it takes three peasants to support seven idle mouths'.[64] One reason lay in the growth of the *latifundia*. Mandarins invested their savings on retirement to purchase new landed property, run, usually, by stewards, and rented out to farmers or more frequently to the 'vagrants', the great swarms of peasants who fled the land to evade taxation. Their settling on the *latifundia* made matters worse. On the one hand, the fact that they paid no tax on their former holdings increased the burden on the rest of the community. On the other, when they settled on the *latifundia* they went unregistered and so they paid no taxes there either. The ubiquitous proliferation of Buddhist and Taoist monasteries produced similar effects because they were tax-exempt, so that many small farmers threw up their farms and went to work for them for this reason. In their turn big landholders made fraudulent donations of land to the monasteries to avoid taxation. Meanwhile the imperial clan, the ancient nobility, all officials, and those of honorific official rank were all tax-exempt.

Furthermore, although peasants were legally prohibited from selling their personal and perpetual lands (save in certain exceptional cases) they evaded the legislation. The inherent vicissitudes of the agricultural basis of society, which we have noted in all societies so far, continued necessarily to operate in China. Even if the fixed level of taxes was light, a bad crop, floods, and other natural disasters would force peasants to get into debt to pay their taxes, or force them to mortgage their lands and at the end of the day persuade them that they were better off working as tenants or sharecroppers on a big estate. These pressures were made more severe by the intractability of the land-allocation system: it could only apply in full where land was freely available. In densely populated areas like those around the capital the areas allocated were reduced to a mere half. Nor did the system cope with the question of the quality of the soil. Yet, whatever land the peasant had and of whatever quality, he was deemed to have his legal quota and had to pay the fixed tax. So, the poorer he was, the higher the proportion of income he paid in taxes. For all this, it seems that the T'ang were able to finance the empire up to the 750s without undue hardship to the peasantry as a whole and this despite mammoth evasion; since in 754/5, it is calculated, only about 17 per cent of the households in the empire appeared on the tax register. This was not just due to the drift from the farms but also to

[63] Maspero and Balazs, *Histoire et institutions*, 201; Twitchett, 'Local Financial Administration'.

[64] Maspero and Balazs, *Histoire et institutions*, 205.

the sheer administrative incapacity to keep the registers up to date, and this is the chief *political* interest of the topic. It illustrates, as usual, the sheer *technical* obstacles to efficient and equitable taxation in pre-industrial or, rather, agrarian societies.

Three features in the local administration of this highly complex fiscal system are noteworthy: strict accountability to the central government, an inherent degree of discretion to the prefectures, and—the feature that accounts for the failure to keep accurate registers—the sorts of personnel employed at the local levels.

The degree of central regulation is astounding but wholly typical of Chinese 'bureaucracy run mad'. Until 736 the calculations relating to six different taxes were each performed separately and written up annually. The taxes went to different central offices, involved all 300-odd prefectures, and all sub-prefectures. A chief minister estimated that the calculations took up 'more than half a million sheets of paper and the trouble involved in assigning them to various government departments for copying was extremely complicated'. The procedure took so long it was hard to complete the calculations in time, and since revenue and taxation were always changing, all kinds of abuses crept in.[65] Tax-returns had to be kept on file for fifteen years in the prefectures and sub-prefectures and no less than twenty-seven years in the central Board of Finance. These arrangements were finally scrapped and replaced by a permanently applicable directive; in effect this established tax-quotas and expenditure levels for the prefectures.

Every stage of fiscal administration was subject to detailed scrutiny. The commissioners of each *tao* periodically inspected the prefectures. The prefects made annual inspections of the *hsien*. The prefectures had to maintain daily accounts, based on the official record of the transactions which at the year's end were totalled together and signed by a responsible official. These annual accounts were then sent for audit to the Department of Judicial Control (*pi-pu*, part of the Board of Justice) at the capital. The chain of accountability reached down to the sub-bureaucracy in the *hsien* and beyond to the *li-cheng* (the village headman), and the Turfan documents we noted above suggest that this system of accountability was *real*.

However, as we noticed briefly before, the prefectures enjoyed a certain freedom to spend because they legally disposed of various purely local revenues. The household levy, for instance, was designed to provide for the *local* military and postal services. The salaries of these local officials were funded by the income of lands 'settled' on each office. In addition, certain

---

[65] Twitchett, 'Local Financial Administration', 91, quoting the Memorial of Chief Minister Li Lin-fu.

official duties offered local opportunities for making official profits, for example, the buying and selling of grain for the 'ever-normal granary' service,[66] the fixing of prices in official markets, and administering the official state loans. Finally, the prefect could summon ordinary individuals to work for his senior officials. These 'special duty-men', like jurymen in Britain or the United States, owed 'liturgical' service to the state, usually two months per annum. As we have already stressed, they formed the entire sub-bureaucracy at the village and hamlet levels and provided the minor staff at the hsien and chou levels. (We have no evidence as to whether or how those who had to work full-time, e.g. clerical staff, were paid or not.) Only the better-off were pressed into service. They could commute this if they preferred exemption, but to be pressed brought considerable benefits, since duty-men were exempt from the general corvée contribution of twenty days service per annum and also from military service. In any event, however, all this staff could be employed ad lib by a prefect at little or perhaps no cost.[67]

There were just not enough prefects and sub-prefects. These officials were maids-of-all-work. Dispensing justice took up at least half their time: in addition they were personally responsible for maintaining order, organizing pressed labour, and seeing to flood prevention or grain supplies. Under the early T'ang there were 328 prefectures and 1,573 sub-prefectures, for an estimated population of 56 million and an area of some 13,000,000 square miles. At a rough estimate, therefore, each sub-prefect cared for some 36,000 persons, each prefect for about 171,000. They were sparsely distributed over wide areas of marshes, forests, and mountains ill-served by roads. An average sub-prefecture would have measured about 100 miles by 100 miles; an average prefecture double that: 214 miles by 214 miles. This is why prefects and sub-prefects had to rely on the unpaid duty-workers at the village levels, i.e. the parochial notables, what we might visualize as squires, often owning a manor and maintaining a band of retainers. Such persons were leaders of local society and up to their eyes in its domestic involvements (often shady, to judge by the character of Chao Gai, for instance, in the fourteenth-century novel *Outlaws of the Marsh*).[68] It is easy to imagine

---

[66] See p. 773 below.   [67] See Twitchett, 'Local Financial Administration', 98–112.

[68] *Outlaws of the Marsh*, composed in the 14th cent., is based on materials of the Sung dynasty, c.1100. But the rural society depicted there was not substantially different from that of the T'ang period. As for local finagling, the author's personal experiences in a rural area of North Wales have given him a happy insight into how and what things can happen in tightly knit communities even in late 20th-cent. Britain. Shih Nai-an and Lo Kuan-chung are the names traditionally associated with the creation of *Outlaws of the Marshes*, trans. S. Shapiro (Foreign Languages Press, Beijing, 1980). For the character of Chao Gai see e.g. i. 20 ff. *Outlaws of the Marsh* is the title of this particular translation—a more common translation is *The Water Margin*, while the American writer, Pearl S. Buck, has translated it as *All Men are Brothers*.

how much finagling and fraudulence were allowed to enter the family registration and the triennial allocation of land.

Public Works and Enterprises

As paternalists, the mandarins were happy to interfere with the economy; as Confucianists, they favoured peasants and disapproved of commerce and free enterprise.

Intervention Relating to the Peasants and Agriculture

Undoubtedly the greatest of the government's interventions in respect to the peasant was the land-allocation programme. Relatedly, there were frequent but usually unsuccessful attempts to set up agricultural colonies to resettle the landless. But otherwise, like the Han, the T'ang engaged in the two related fields of flood prevention and famine relief. It created a Bureau of Water Affairs (the *shiu-pu*), responsible for 'everything concerning quays, barges, boats, rivers and bridges, dykes and barrages, ditches and irrigation canals, fishing, grain transportation, and grain-mills'.[69] This bureau controlled a local Bureau of Works in each prefecture, which worked to a similar bureau in the sub-prefecture. These bodies enjoyed a discretion in how they went about their work and drew up their own local rules of procedure. Furthermore, as in fiscal administration, the subordinate executive work of supervising the distribution of water, maintaining the canals and dykes, and levying the corvée for these purposes, was largely carried out by the non-ranking subordinate duty-men.[70]

The corollary of flood prevention was famine relief and the T'ang revived the ancient Han device of 'The Equal Balance' (otherwise, 'the ever-normal granary').[71] They also developed a Sui dynasty innovation, the 'relief granaries' or *i-tsang*. As we saw,[72] prefects levied a special grain tax, the *ti-shui*: this grain was stored in local granaries which they threw open during famines. This system was highly successful in countering the succession of natural disasters in the 730s and 740s.[73]

The greatest handicap to famine relief was the wretched state of communication. Bulk transfer including tax-payments (in kind) had to rely almost wholly on navigable waterways. Some figures relating to relative costs and speeds of transfer make this vividly clear. To move 100 lbs weight of goods on horseback cost 100 cash for 100 li (a li = one-third of a mile). By cart it cost six times that sum. But by boat it cost only 15 cash upstream and

[69] *Traité des fonctionnaires*, 129. [70] Twitchett, 'Local Financial Administration'.
[71] See above, Bk. II, Ch. 6, pp. 514–15 for a description. [72] See p. 744 above.
[73] *CHC*, iii. 1, p. 358.

5 cash downstream. Nor was horse-travel necessarily much faster. The horse could travel 70 li in a day, a man or an ass 50, a cart only 30; a boat, however, could move 30–45 li upstream and as much as 80 li downstream. Hence the Sui emperors' obsessional efforts to construct their great network of canals.[74]

This network proved entirely inadequate to provision the capital Chang-an, which by 750 was much the largest city in the entire world, with a population approaching 2 million. As in the Roman and Byzantine empires, provisioning great cities and especially a capital city had supreme political significance. Now, Chang-an was very inaccessible indeed. Foodstuffs had to move along the Yellow River (Huang Ho), and then join the local river system at the formidable rapids of San-men ('Three Gates'). The Yellow River was prone to dry up and the sluices and dams at San-men required constant attention and were never wholly satisfactory. Thus, famines frequently threatened the capital, and whenever this happened the entire court had to uproot itself and make the twenty-four-day journey to the Eastern Capital of Loyang. In twenty years (717–37) the court had to make ten such journeys! The problem was finally solved by a youthful aristocrat whom Hsüan-tsung placed at the head of an entirely new agency outside the normal bureaucratic organization. This was the Commission for Transportation. It had its own large staff, granaries, and fleets of barges. The aristocrat P'ei Yau-ch'ing (681–743) sectionalized the water route from Yangchow (on the Yangtse) to Chang-an; each section had its own granaries and its own local boatmen. The bulk grain was first delivered into a granary complex at Ho-Yin, then in stages, from one granary to the next; as soon as conditions were ripe the local boats set off for the next granary. In this way twice as much grain was shipped as before and much more cheaply.[75] The Commission became a vast commercial and financial organization and the virtual master of the entire economy of southern China.

Intervention in Commerce and the Towns

During this period many of the 'vagrant' or 'settler' families migrated south of the Yangtse, although even at the end of the dynasty only one-quarter of the total population were to be found there. The opening up of the southlands by the canal network, the acceleration of maritime trade by coastal shipping there, the construction of seven arterial roadways radiating in all directions from the capital, and the general pacification of the interior stimulated commerce and the growth of towns and markets. The bureau-

---

[74] Maspero and Balazs, *Histoire et institutions*, 221.
[75] *CHC*, iii. 1, pp. 399–400; Maspero and Balazs, *Histoire et institutions*, 220–3.

cracy despised trade and merchants and, like its Byzantine counterparts, did nothing to promote, only to regulate them.

China had more and larger towns than contemporary Western Europe. As noted, Chang-an contained 1–2 million inhabitants, Loyang seems to have contained some 400,000, and many others[76] were around the 100,000 mark. No more than in the Caliphate or Ottoman Empire were these towns like Western cities. There was no trace of municipal franchises, charters, or other privileges. A Chinese town was usually not commercially driven but an administrative base, pre-eminently the seat of the imperial prefect and the Mandarinate, who treated the towns as service centres. The commercial laws of the T'ang, such as they were, addressed themselves to regulation of weights and measures, quality standards, contracts of sale, and breaking-up price-rings. As in today's oriental cities, still, the various tradesmen, established in specific streets (*hang*), soon became, effectively, so many corporations, and the street headman (nominated by the government, in all likelihood) was responsible for keeping order inside it, and acted as its representative and spokesman *vis-à-vis* the authorities. 'Official' taxation was very light—possibly only a 3.3 per cent tax—because of the Mandarinate's obsession with agriculture and agricultural taxes which, therefore, had to provide over 90 per cent of all revenue. On the other hand, the local officials (who came from the landowning classes) were prompt to milk the merchants through all manner of unofficial extraordinary taxes. All the merchants could do was to shut up shop by way of a demonstration.[77]

The early T'ang also tried to invigilate trade right across the empire. They did this by setting up official markets in the two capital cities and all towns that were the seats of a prefecture or sub-prefecture. In the capitals the central Court of Treasury fixed prices and qualities of goods and the market director (of high bureaucratic rank) policed the market, opening and closing it at the due hours, and patrolling it night and day. It was he who fixed prices for every commodity and named a cash price for each of three qualities. The significance of this went beyond simply local transactions, for the director's lists were circulated to the local authorities and became the standard 'rate of exchange' when these had to pay for goods they bought or requisitioned.[78] The prefectural and sub-prefectural markets were all organized along similar lines to the metropolitan ones with this notable detail: that except in the very highest grade of prefecture (a population of some 200,000+), the director was an unpaid duty-man, selected by the prefect. Such duty-men had to serve four annual turns of duty. They were chosen

[76] Ibid. 225.   [77] Ibid. 228–30.
[78] D. C. Twitchett, 'The T'ang Market System', *Asia Major*, 12 (1966), 213.

either from honorific officials (retired soldiers of fifth rank or above) or from among the minor officials.[79]

The official regulations concerning markets were carefully enforced, then began to show signs of lapse towards the end of the dynasty, and totally disappeared with the fall of the T'ang. The boom in trade and urban prosperity that followed the establishment of the Sung dynasty made any return to the system impossible. The Sung period marked the high point of the pre-industrial commercialization of the Chinese economy.

Law and Order

Of all the glories of the T'ang, the law code is arguably the greatest. It is to China and the Orient what Justinian's code was to the West. It served as a model for Japan and Korea, and later for Vietnam. In China it remained in force, with only minor modifications, for another 600 years, until the accession of the Ming (1368). And even under the Ch'ing (1644–1911), that is, up to modern times, some 30 to 40 per cent of the criminal code consisted of articles taken over, unchanged from the T'ang code.[80]

The code originated in 624, in the reign of the founder of the T'ang, Kao-tsu. It was largely a recension of the code of the preceding Sui dynasty, which itself was made up of elements of the previous dynasties' codes. The 624 code was entirely recast under the Emperor T'ai-tsung (626–49), by his brother-in-law, the Chief Minister Ch'ang-sun Wu-chi (?–659). Each succeeding reign saw further updating and recodification, culminating in the revision by the Hsüan-tsung's great minister, Li Lin-fu, in 737.[81]

The code is divided into 'General Principles', comprising one-third of the volume, and 'Specific Articles', making 502 Articles in all. It was supplemented by the *Statutes*, the *Regulations*, and the *Ordinances*. *Regulations* were supplements to the code and *Statutes* and *Ordinances* the administrative rules for specific occasions.

The code is in the full tradition of Chinese law, that is, it is primarily concerned with crime, against the state or against the person. Other forms of conflict were left to be resolved by private means—by mediation, by guild law, and the like. It is remarkable in two respects. It is an attempt, seemingly successful in practice, to bureaucratize law; to specify in advance every possible offence and every extenuating circumstance, and then attach a fixed penalty to each. The magistrate had absolutely no discretion. If ever the ideal of 'penny-in-the-slot-machine' justice was approached in actual

---

[79] D. C. Twitchett, 218–26.

[80] W. Johnson, *The T'ang Code*, vol. 1, *General Principles* (Princeton UP, Princeton 1979), 9.

[81] *CHC*, iii. 1, pp. 178, 206, 207, 273–4, 354–5, 414.

practice, it was here. Secondly, it is an attempt to enforce by harsh criminal sanction the Confucianist pattern of the social order. It is inegalitarian, root and branch. The crimes include not only offences against the political order or even the social order but the moral order too, for instance, striking a parent or failing to observe the period of mourning. And the punishments, by the same token, are unequal: lightest and most easily escapable for the superior ranks of society, heavier and inescapable for the common folk, and ferocious for the 'inferior' classes, which included slaves.

For these characteristics it has been very severely judged by some Western scholars. Balazs[82] wrote, for instance:

the spirit of Chinese justice, if justice is the right term, did not change much: its objective, as always, was intimidation and repression, by way of harsh penalties, of every slightest wish to transgress the social order . . . To speak precisely, we ought not talk of 'law' in the Western sense. It was a body of laws that was solely *penal,* and whose ancient principle 'the laws do not apply to the nobles' was re-affirmed and announced in 94 AD in its definitive form by a celebrated jurist of the later Han: 'What does not fall in the sphere of the Rites (=Li) comes within the domain of punishment (*hsing*)[83] . . . The concept of *law* does not even skim the Chinese legislator. For him it is simply a matter of finding the flexible and effective rules to administer by, and prevent the populace from committing crimes that would endanger the established order by means of harsh punishments.[84]

This is true, but not the whole truth. It overlooks the humanity of its penal code as compared to earlier codes (and for that matter even to Justinian), and its procedural safeguards. The penalties were much less severe than those in the Han code.[85] In the T'ang code they were: bastinado—of varying degrees; penal servitude or life exile—also of varying degrees; and execution, either by strangulation or decapitation.[86] The sub-prefect could impose nothing heavier than bastinado; penal-servitude sentences had to be approved by the prefect, life exile by the central Board of Punishments, and capital sentences by the emperor himself. When a magistrate of no matter what level pronounced sentence, he had to cite the exact provision of the code, statutes, regulations, or ordinances. Failure led to his suffering thirty strokes with the light baton.[87] He was punished too if he applied the incorrect sentence for a cited crime. If the sentence were penal servitude or

[82] Maspero and Balazs, *Histoire et institutions,* 124.

[83] Ibid. 127, attributes this statement to Chin-shu. It rejects, of course, the famous statement of Confucius: 'The Rites (*Li*) do not extend down to the common people, punishments do not reach up to the officials.' (*The Li Ki,* 2 vols. Hsien Hsien, trans S. Couvreur (imprimerie de la Mission Catholique, 1913), 109.)   [84] Maspero and Balazs, *Histoire et institutions,* 127.

[85] See Bk. II, Ch. 6 above.   [86] Johnson, *T'ang Code,* 55–61, being *Code,* Arts. 1–6.

[87] Ibid. 36.

worse, he had to persuade the prisoner and his family to accept the punishment; if they refused, he had to hear the case again.[88] And, as in the Han code, the magistrate could secure a conviction only on the basis of the prisoner's confession. It was here that abuse crept in because the accused could be—and usually was—beaten until he signed one.[89]

To all this, however, there was one major exception—crimes against the state. Here the procedural safeguards were flimsy and the punishments extended, as of old, to all the criminal's family. Here rank did not provide mitigation. Rebellion (that is, plotting to endanger ruler or state) and grand sedition (destroying the ancestral temples, tombs, or palaces of the dynasty) entailed decapitation of principals and accessories alike, plus strangulation of the fathers and sons of the criminals, plus slave-status for large numbers of their collateral kin[90] and life-exile for others. Plotting treason—betraying the imperial house or a city or surrendering territory to rebels—also carried the sentence of decapitation, but fewer of the relatives were punished. Another highly serious offence which carried the penalty of strangulation was the making or keeping of *ku* poison which was associated with magic spells and sorcery. Furthermore, the emperor's person was specially protected. A man who deliberately criticized the emperor, or resisted his messengers, or indeed merely mislabelled his medicine or stole his possessions, was also considered to have plotted rebellion as above and was sentenced accordingly.[91]

These crimes form part of a special category in the Code entitled the 'Ten Heinous Crimes' where the normal procedural safeguards did not apply and the punishments were especially severe. Many remaining 'heinous crimes' relate to the Confucian social code. The most serious included plotting to kill a parent or paternal grandparents (decapitation and life exile respectively) and striking a parent or godparent (decapitation). An official below the fifth grade who struck one of the third-grade or higher suffered a year of penal servitude. And harsh penalties awaited persons who did not observe mourning on learning of the death of parents or paternal grandparents.

The official dynastic histories are filled with accounts of execution or exile of ministers convicted—often on the flimsiest evidence—of rebellion and the like. But, as we have said again and again, state trials can give a false picture of the way justice was generally administered. In the T'ang case my impression is that, though the law was harsh and punishments unequal, it

---

[88] Johnson, *T'ang Code.*   [89] See p. 779 below.   [90] Johnson, *T'ang Code,* 18.
[91] Ibid. 21.

was fixed, impersonal, and complete: and it was observed, with rectitude if not with mercy, down to the lowest levels.[92]

Something of this can be seen in the standard procedure in a criminal case. (Here, for lack of detailed evidence on the T'ang, I draw on the Sung period, some sixty years later. The Sung retained most of the T'ang code, as we have seen, and there was only marginal change in the procedures.) The sub-prefect—the magistrate of the *hsien*—held his court (*ya-men*) throughout the year except at the farming season. Any individual could bring a criminal complaint and the police and military likewise could arrest on suspicion. In the former case, the litigant had to present a written complaint (scriveners were available if he was illiterate). This went to the 'Punishment Section' of the court and was put into a complaint box there. The section decided whether there was a prima-facie case; if so it handed it to the sub-prefect who summoned all persons concerned in the case. The accused might be locked up if it looked as if they might run away.

The trial had two phases, investigation and the application of the code, and the magistrate handled both. He questioned the prisoner and his object was to get a confession. Without that the accused could not be adjudged guilty even though all the evidence was against him. So, where the evidence seemed convincing and the prisoner refused to confess, the magistrate issued a writ ordering a bastinado and had it countersigned by his assistant-magistrate and his record-keeper. The beating was carried out in their presence. The accused could deny a charge, the complainant would contradict him, and the magistrate acted impartially for both. When, finally, the accused admitted the crime, his confession was taken down verbatim, read over to him, and he signed it in writing or by finger-imprint. Once attested, the facts were taken to have been established.

At this point the magistrate had to apply the law, which meant establishing the relevant Article of the code and consulting all available precedents. On this basis he wrote out his judgment, consisting of an outline of the case and the reasons for his decision. The due punishment was then carried out.

At prefectoral level the prefect's draft sentence was put to his law-officers and they could decline to sign it. The prefect could override them, but only at his own peril if higher authority thought him wrong. Note, too, that if an official successfully cleared an accused of a serious charge he was given a reward and public acclamation.

Only the Supreme Court in the capital could impose the death sentence, and before the execution actually took place its recommendation of capital

---

[92] Cf. Wright and Twitchett, *Perspectives on the T'ang*, 29–30.

punishment had to be made three consecutive times to the emperor and receive his assent on each occasion.[93]

This may not be what Balazs refers to as law 'in the Western sense',[94] but it is unmistakably law. A determinate series of offences is matched by an equally determinate series of dire penalties and the task of the judicial authorities is exhausted once the offence is identified and then proven. After that the penalty is automatic. Whatever may be said about the system, arbitrary or capricious or even discretionary it is *not*.[95] It is the precise opposite—a monument to fixity, regularity, and predictability. Compare it, then, with the T'ang handling of *civil* cases, for it is pre-eminently in this field that Roman law excelled, and in which it established a jurisprudence. Here the litigants could not appeal to the central and supreme authority, nor could any lower court give a *final* decision. If plaintiff or defendant were dissatisfied with a verdict they could ask the superior court to review it, but this court could do no more than review the documents and hand the case back to the lower court with instructions that the prefect perform his duty impartially. So, if the litigants were obstinate, cases might pass up and down for years![96] For in civil cases the principle was conciliation not enforcement.

Alongside this body of, largely, repressive law, the T'ang established impressive and, as far as I can find it, highly effective policing arrangements. For rural areas what follows is gleaned from near-contemporary literature— specifically, *Outlaws of the Marsh*[97]—so this account should be treated with due caution. The extensive references to current police procedures in *Outlaws of the Marsh* are thrown in as so much background, as something that was common knowledge. The court procedure previously outlined is confirmed in every respect, with one exception,[98] namely the beating of suspects. The court was entitled to beat a suspect where he refused to confess though the material evidence pointed clearly to his guilt. This is what happend to Bai Sheng, suspected of being an accomplice in a mammoth gang robbery: the police found his share of the loot buried in his house. Notwithstanding this, he repeatedly denied the charge, upon which 'they beat him three or four times till his skin split and blood was flowing from his wounds'.[99] On the other hand, when one Yang unintentionally slays a man and goes and openly confesses this to the court, the prefect says 'Since he has come forward voluntarily, let him be spared the preliminary beating'.[100] This does suggest that, as under the Han, the interrogation normally *began* with a routine beating.

---

[93] Miyazaki, *Administration of Justice*, 59–67.   [94] See p. 777 above.

[95] The same point is made in Bodde and Morris, *Law in Imperial China*, cited in Bk. IV, Ch. 2, p. 1155 below in respect to the Ch'ing 700 years later.   [96] Miyazaki, *Administration of Justice*, 66.

[97] Otherwise known as *The Water Margin*. See n. 68 above.   [98] *Outlaws*, i. 55–8.

[99] Ibid. 269.   [100] Ibid. 191.

The novel also gives us information about the local police-force. The prefect had an official, here translated as his sheriff, who controlled two constables. One, the 'Infantry Constable' had a force of twenty pikemen and twenty foot-soldiers, the other, the 'Cavalry Constable', twenty mounted archers and twenty foot-soldiers.[101] When the prefect had to mount a large police operation he tells his two constables to ride to the local garrison and pick up a force of soldiers.[102]

Towns, especially the two capitals with their vast populations, represented a special risk and this was met by a massive security apparatus. The prefectures' head towns followed the general pattern of the capital, albeit on a much reduced scale. Like the capital, most were laid out on a rectangular gridiron pattern, thus creating a number of rectangular wards, and these, like the city itself, were surrounded with walls. Each wall had a gate and a strict curfew was enforced in every such walled ward. In the capital there were regularly spaced drum-towers which announced the impending closure of all the gates in the city walls and the wards, so that citizens were completely penned into them. At night nobody was allowed on the main streets which separated the wards except for emergencies, in which case one had to get an official pass from the sub-prefectural officials, or from the headman of the ward. This curfew was enforced in the capital by patrols of guardsmen in police posts at the main crossroads, and in the larger guard-houses at the city gates.[103]

All in all, this was surely one of the most impressive performances in the history of government up to the industrial age. This vast empire, as large as the United States, containing enormous cities and, equally, huge tracts of desert or marshland with sparse or non-existent populations, was clamped together from one centre by 'a system of uniform rules and procedures . . . embodied in a centrally codified corpus of statute law applicable throughout the empire'.[104] And these laws, as we have seen, were no dead letter. They were actively enforced, backed by an efficient and uniformly organized rural constabulary and military police.

2.3.4. DEFENCE AND THE MILITARY ESTABLISHMENT

The empire had foes to the north, the east, and the west. To the north roamed the nomadic Eastern and Western Turks, to the east the expanding Kingdom of Koguryo (Korea), and on the west lay the wild Tibetan tribesmen. China's problem was therefore—like that of Imperial Rome—

[101] *Outlaws*, 204.   [102] Ibid. 278.
[103] Twitchett, 'The T'ang Market System', 211–12. Cf. similar arrangements in the Caliphate (Bk. III, Ch. 2) and in Tokugawa Japan (Bk. IV, Ch. 1, below).   [104] *CHC*, iii. 1, p. 19.

the control of frontiers. The infrastructure of the military system was the T'ang road network and the Imperial Post, as well as the seven great commercial roads that radiated to each point of the compass from the capital. The post, like the Roman Imperial Post, was strictly reserved for official communications and personnel. Supervised by the Central Bureau of Military Equipment, it consisted of 1,297 land relay stations, 260 river stations, and eighty-six mixed stations, spaced out at distances of roughly ten miles. Each post was equipped with remounts, carriages, and the like. A small hostelry, serving each station, was run by some wealthy local notable franchised by the government.[105]

Up to 737 the army organization was based on the principle of brigading conscripted units with metropolitan regular cadre troops. On the frontiers the T'ang deployed a force of some 600,000 conscript troops, purportedly serving for one entire year, in practice serving three. Balazs surmises that many, perhaps most, were convicts.[106] The forces of the interior comprised two elements, the first being the regulars. These were stationed around the capital. They comprised the 'Southern Barracks' of sixteen guard units: the Guards of the Left and the Guards of the Right were specially recruited from the mandarins or sons of mandarins. Each comprised 500 officers and it was these cadres which commanded, together, the 120 conscript militia units to be described below. The other guard units were regular volunteer infantry and specialized corps, like the Police Guards, the Guards of the City Gates, and the Bodyguard. In addition to these sixteen guard units of the Southern Garrison, the troops of the Northern Garrison were a kind of Praetorian Guard, formed from veterans and persons from the privileged classes.

These two metropolitan concentrations directly controlled the local militia forces. At the system's height they numbered 633 in units of 800, 1,000, or 1,200 men conscripted from among the better-off peasants, and were officered by the regulars. Training took place in the dead season of the agricultural year. The commander was of quite high rank and his forces included cavalry and mounted archers as well as infantry. The conscripts provided and maintained their personal weapons and equipment, heavier equipment and body armour being stored in the armoury. These militias (fu-ping) were concentrated around the metropolitan area and the ones closest by were those brigaded under those guard units mentioned above.

This system served the T'ang very well. Not only was the interior pacified, it was civilianized. The cost was low, while on the frontiers the Eastern Turks and then the Western Turks were crushed and, after long

---

[105] Maspero and Balazs, *Histoire et institutions*, 218.   [106] Ibid.

struggles, subjugated. As to the west, the Tibetans were checked so that the Kansu corridor was reopened and the T'ang moved into the immense spaces of Central Asia, along the Silk Road to the borders of Iran, and halted only when their remote forces were defeated by the rising Arab Caliphate and its Uighur allies at Talasin (751). The T'ang state had become the T'ang Empire, and it is from this point that the development on the frontiers and in the interior began to diverge so signally and disastrously.

The military problem was how to counter nomadic cavalry raiders. This required immediate and flexible counter-attack, plus very large concentrations, since every able-bodied barbarian tribesman was a warrior, so that their armies ran to five figures. The centrally controlled T'ang frontier garrison, with the local prefect in control, was no match for anything but a small raid. To meet large-scale invasions, the government had to raise armies *ad hoc*.

Initially the government responded by putting quite large standing forces on the frontier, the long-term (three years) assignment of militiamen, plus professional long-service troops already mentioned. But these were still not large or strong enough to withstand major invasions. This string of fixed forces along the frontier was supposed to act as a screen or trip-wire, its function being to hold the enemy while a field force was hastily raised *ad hoc* in the metropolitan region and led by commanders-in-chief who acted side by side with their military governors and their permanent commands. In 737 this strategy was replaced by an entirely new one. The frontier forces were henceforth composed of long-service regulars. The hitherto civilian governors were replaced by professional soldiers who served up to three years in their region before going on to another. The government fixed establishments for each of the regions.[107]

All existing frontier guardsmen were offered permanent engagements, their allowances were raised, and they were permitted to bring their families with them and (like Roman *limitanei*) to settle. In 738 conscription for the frontier forces was ended. These forces totalled 490,000, including 80,000 cavalry. When the local militias are counted in, the number standing to arms in the empire was 574,711—1 per cent of the population. The costs proved formidable: between 714 and 741 they quintupled, to rise by another 40–50 per cent between 742 and 755.

While these military governorates were arising, like the marcher lordships of medieval Europe, the interior provinces enjoyed a self-indulgent peace.

---

[107] Cf. here the Late Roman experience: first the reinforcing of the frontier forces by Diocletian—the concept of static defence; then, with Constantine, *limitanei* as the trip-wires on the frontiers, and a mobile cavalry field army in the interior. Bk. II, Ch. 8, pp. 586 above. For further comparison of frontier policing, see chapters on Byzantium, Bk. III, Ch. 1, p. 646, and the Caliphate, Bk. III, Ch. 2, p. 712.

The local militias were not abolished but with the frontiers patrolled by standing armies their *raison d'être* disappeared and they became mere paper units. All that remained were local defence militias called the *t'uan-lien* or *tuan-chieh*, made up of part-time soldiers and farmers, under the control of the prefect.

The general aura of peace settled on the standing forces at the capital, also. But as Hsüan-tsung's reign, that golden era, ran on, with shattering successes on the frontiers and prosperity and peace in the interior, these troops too were neglected and by the 750s the metropolitan army was a sham. So, by the 750s the emperor and his ministers had no military forces at their direct disposal, whereas on the frontiers there were professional generals with huge forces of trained professionals under their command. The disequilibrium brought ruin to the empire.

3. THE LATER T'ANG (755–874)

3.1. *An Lu-shan's Rebellion*

Regrettably, we have no space to recount the extraordinary and disastrous rebellion of An Lu-shan,[108] but briefly, here is what happened. He was a barbarian soldier who, after a somewhat precarious start to his career, rose rapidly and became one of the new brand of professional military governors in the north-east sector. He became a great favourite at court and by 752 had received the command of no less than three frontier provinces and was easily the most powerful general in the empire. The year 752 was the one when the masterful chief minister, Li Lin-fu, died and his replacement—Yang Kuo-chung—engaged in a deadly rivalry with An. In 755 An resolved to end it by marching on the capital. He took Loyang, where he proclaimed himself emperor, and finally the western capital Chang-an. The emperor fled into the Tibetan marches. Although An Lu-shan was murdered in 757, the fighting continued and the rebellion was not finally quelled till 763. These seven years of internal strife marked a watershed in the history of the T'ang institutions. Though the dynasty was restored, things were never the same again.

3.2. *The Post-Rebellion Settlement*

The new emperor, Su-tsung (756–762), and his immediate successors (Tai-tsung, 762–79 and Te-tsung, 779–805) faced two critical problems, one military, one fiscal.

---

[108] The whole matter is fully explored in Pulleyblank, *The Background*.

In the course of the war, the court had had to create militarized provinces whose governors had concurrent civil authority as prefects in the city where they had their headquarters. There were some thirty-four such provinces at the close of the rebellion and most were ruled by generals whose armies ranged from a few thousand to as many as 100,000. The total numbers they commanded was 850,000, whereas the court did not have one effective army under its direct control.[109] The other problem was that the court had little money to buy new troops. In the wars millions of peasants had been uprooted and the tax records had become obsolete and useless, if indeed they had not been burned or dispersed. So the old fiscal structure had collapsed.

Yet it did not take the court more than thirty years to restore its authority throughout the state, with the exception of Hopei Province. The foundation of its recovery was its control of four key areas. They were: the metropolitan district around the capital (now Kuanchung); the north-west frontier zone, which was under attack by the Tibetans and whose troops, lacking a local resource base, depended on the court for their pay; the Yangtse–Huai basin, which had escaped much fighting and was rapidly becoming the most prosperous part of the state; and finally, the canal zone through which the revenue from the Yangtse–Huai area and the south had to pass.

In the second place, in a desperate search for revenue during the rebellion the court had reverted to one of the most ancient fiscal institutions in Chinese history: it revived the Han's Salt and Iron Commission.[110] Established in 785 and with access to the rich Yangtse area and even to certain provinces where the military governors were acquiescent (since it did not prevent them levying direct taxes), the salt monopoly, within ten to fifteen years of its first establishment, was supplying no less than half the government's revenue.[111]

Control of the four key regions and its ability to raise revenue for troops established a narrow but solid platform from which the court could push patiently towards eliminating the local war-lords. The proportion of provinces with military governors, which was 75 per cent at the end of the rebellion, had fallen to some 33 per cent fifty years later, and by the end of the T'ang dynasty all had disappeared except in the frontier zones and the indomitably recalcitrant Hopei area.[112]

With imperial unity and civil law and order restored the T'ang state,

---

[109] CHC, iii. 1, pp. 487–9.

[110] That is, it established a monopoly of the salt supply. There was no attempt to monopolize iron—the word was an empty part of the antique title.   [111] CHC, iii. 1, p. 495.

[112] Ibid. 543.

though it had lost the Central Asian protectorates, Kansu, and authority over Hopei, stood where it always had. But the processes of government were different in three important respects. First, at the capital the Inner Court prevailed over the regular administration with a concomitant political emergence of the palatine eunuchs. Next, there was a much looser, decentralized relationship between the central government and the localities where, parenthetically, *permanent* provinces were now set up. Thirdly and finally, an entirely new fiscal system was introduced which ended the Confucianists' ideal of land allocation, as well as pointing a new strategy towards towns and commerce. Since these could not be repressed, then they should, at least, be exploited.

3.3. *The New Practice of Government*

3.3.1. THE PALACE SUPERSEDES THE MANDARINATE

One effect of the rebellion was to undermine the organizational and moral cohesion of the regular bureaucracy. Many offices became nominal and others functionless sinecures, and the situation was always in flux.[113] The bureaucracy, especially for an entire forty-year span beginning in 821, broke into venomous, mutually destructive factions (*tang*) lacking in any particular ideological or organizational characteristics. They were loose 'affinities'[114] based on personal relationships, what in modern China is called *kuan-hsi*. Recent attempts to relate these factions to social differences have run into the sand.[115] It was a simple case of 'ins' versus 'outs'. The perpetual power-struggle disrupted the administration and made it difficult for any emperor to rule 'through ministers' as in the early T'ang.

Moreover, the regular bureaucracy found itself diminished by new specialist agencies which not only robbed it of very important responsibilities but—oh, horror!—introduced government officials who were neither literati nor aristocrats, being men of specialist skills but dubious antecedents. The most important were the new breed of financial specialists. Under the salt monopoly (in effect a *gabelle* or salt-tax), salt had to be sold to regional offices, which in turn resold it at a huge profit to the distributors. The system was administered by the Commission for Salt and Iron. Once the rebellion was deemed over, in 765, the government set up two financial zones. The Salt and Iron Commission was responsible for central China and the Yangtse valley, and the Public Revenue Department of the Board of

---

[113] *CHC*, iii. 1, 19.

[114] This was the expression which served in England in the late 13th cent.

[115] Ibid. 20.

Finance looked after the capital, the north, and Szechuan. Between them they raised more than half the entire imperial revenue and consequently dominated the fiscal system. They employed huge numbers of petty officials whom they recruited directly and not through the regular procedures of the central Board of Civil Office. It is easy to imagine how vastly the new agencies and their skills had extruded the regular bureaucracy.

Developments of this kind, however, were as nothing compared with a third that was truly decisive, since it entirely altered the way policy decisions were arrived at. Briefly, power shifted from the emperor's mandarins to the emperor's eunuchs. This is a critical change which makes the character of the later T'ang regime quite different from the pre-rebellion one.

Eunuchs traditionally used to staff the *nei-shih sheng*, the Administrative Department of the Inner Palace, notably its harem. At the beginning of the dynasty the department numbered less than 100, but it had expanded to some 3,000 by 706 to 4,000 under Hsüan-tsung, and in 820 is estimated at 4,618.[116] (The rise in numbers is probably accounted for by the proliferation of subsidiary establishments for royal princes and princesses, and the growth in the number of 'wives' in the imperial harems, which later reached the ridiculous total of 40,000.)[117]

Eunuchs were supplied to the court by the local officials in Kwangtung, Min, and especially Fukien, who seemed to have acquired them from slave-markets selling captives from the aboriginal tribes and from parents who voluntarily mutilated their children and sold them to the authorities.[118] (In the later T'ang the governors of the *taos* were required to send an annual quota of *castrati* to the capital.) They were illiterates and so remained, except for especially intelligent ones who were sent to a special palace school, and it is clear that these were competent enough, by 741, to staff a palace 'College of Literary Studies' for the instruction of the harem ladies. The chroniclers said that they were not very literary—eunuch verses that have survived being of poor quality—but all this means, really, is that unlike the Mandarinate they had not been reared from childhood in the study and literary emulation of the Classics. Indeed, the nature of the administrative and political duties they subsequently undertook makes it quite impossible to believe that they were not fully literate and numerate.[119]

It is clear, though, that under Hsüan-tsung the eunuchs were simply a subordinate palace staff, and eunuch participation in government was limited to a few isolated incidents and specially gifted individuals like

[116] J. K. Rideout, 'The Rise of the Eunuchs During the T'ang Dynasty', Part I (618–705): *Asia Major*, 1 (1949), 53–72; Part II: *Asia Major*, 3 (1953), 42–58, part II, p. 57. [117] Ibid.
[118] Ibid. 55. [119] Cf. ibid. 56, 68.

Hsüan-tsung's gifted and omnipotent minister Kao Li-shih; but after the rebellion the eunuchs suddenly appear as an *institution* and at the very centre of policy and administration. The initial reason lay in the perilous circumstances of the emperors during and immediately after the rebellion. Their ministers could not be trusted, their field commanders were far away and not necessarily to be trusted either. Furthermore, when the capital fell into rebel hands, the court and administration had to be improvised from whatever persons were at hand.

In these circumstances, the emperors could look for loyal service to one source and one alone—their eunuchs.[120] For eunuchs were absolutely and unconditionally loyal to the emperors. This indeed is true, not only for the Chinese Empire but for all the others that used the services of eunuchs—Persia, late Rome, Byzantium. Eunuchs had neither lands nor fortunes nor families to fall back upon. To the generals they were half-men, to the mandarins guttersnipes with neither the breeding nor the education of a gentleman. The Emperor, therefore, was their sole support and they lived or died, rose or fell, entirely by his favour. Often, however, there was much more in the relationship than cupboard love. Crown princes were reared by eunuchs and educated by them: in most cases they responded with personal warmth and affection when they acceded to the throne. Indeed, some emperors like Su-tsung (756–62), who reigned during most of the rebellion, and his son Tai-tsung (762–779) owed their thrones, even their lives, to their chief eunuchs, while Tai-tsung's successor, Te-tsung (779–805), had specially good reason to feel grateful for eunuch fidelity. Driven from his capital in 783 by a military uprising and popular rebellion, he escaped capture and death only by virtue of a small band of men under the command of two of his palace eunuchs.[121]

What with incidents like this, bickering civil servants, untrustworthy chief ministers, and rebellious generals, successive emperors from Su-tsung to Hsien-tsung learned that their eunuchs alone were docile and perfectly obedient. From one reign to another the confidence placed in them increased. Tai-tsung used them routinely as army supervisors, to report on each provincial and frontier administration. Te-tsung pushed further. He made these eunuch supervisors the key link between him and the provinces and their reports were definitive when new governors were to be appointed. Above all, in gratitude to the two eunuchs who had counter-attacked the rebels to rescue him, he made them the supervisors of the two 'Divine

---

[120] Cf. the functional equivalents of eunuchs at other points in this history: notably *ghulam* and *mamluks* in the Caliphate and in Mamluk Egypt (Bk. III, Ch. 2, and Add. 2a); the *kapikulu* in the Ottoman Empire (Bk IV, Ch. 3, pp. 1183–4, 1194), and the palace bond-servants under the Ch'ing in China (Bk. IV, Ch. 2, p. 1135).   [121] *CHC*, iii. 1, pp. 586–7.

Strategy (Palace) Armies' that served as his personal troops. From that time (783) forward, these armies were never led by any other than eunuchs, and this was to be the basis of their power.

By now eunuchs were formed into a regular establishment with an official hierarchy of nine grades.[122] The final development, in that it provided the coping-stone to the entire edifice, occurred under the able and vigorous Hsien-tsung (806–20), for in his reign emerges an officer similar in function to the Han 'Masters of Writing Office'.[123] This was the *shu mi shih*, variously translated as Commissioner of Privy Affairs or Commissioner of Secret Documents. He is first mentioned as existing as early as 765, when his function was the elementary one of conveying the emperor's wishes outside the Inner Palace.[124] Shortly there were two commissioners who headed an office called the *shu mi yüan* or Board of Privy Affairs (or Secret Documents). This soon linked up with the two eunuch supervisors of the Divine Strategy armies. With this the eunuch organization was complete. A linked imperial secretariat and supreme army command, both staffed exclusively by eunuchs, existed solely to serve the emperor in person.

This eunuch apparatus was not—or not always—the usurpation of the emperor's power which the Confucianist historians have persistently maintained. Most of their references to eunuchs, wherever these occur, are quite misleading. The eunuch apparatus was a flexible and completely docile instrument in the hands of strong-willed and self-confident emperors. It was a self-perpetuating and self-interested power structure only where the emperors were weak, or minors.

Tai-tsung, Te-tsung, Hsien-tsung, and Hsüan-tsung (846–59) were all masterful emperors. For example, Te-tsung only turned to the eunuchs (and for that matter to Han-lin academicians) when he felt his regular ministers had failed him. 'Te-tsung remained the supreme ruler. Eunuchs never harmed him, nor those whom he protected . . . Their gains in the 790s were realized under an Emperor who was no fool. No court figure and no eunuch was ever powerful enough to challenge him.'[125] Much the same verdict has been reached for the truly formidable emperor, Hsien-tsung: '[The eunuchs] remained no more than instruments, and Hsien-tsung had every confidence in his ability to control them.'[126] As for Hsüan-tsung, this

---

[122] Cf. Byzantium, where there was a graded eunuch hierarchy running in parallel (and senior) to the regular hierarchy (Bk. III, Ch. 1, pp. 641–3).   [123] See Bk. II, Ch. 8, p. 492 above.

[124] G. Wang, *The Structure of Power in North China During the Five Dynasties* (Stanford UP, Stanford, 1963), p. 89, n. 9.   [125] *CHC*, iii. 1, pp. 600–1.

[126] C. A. Peterson, 'The Restoration Completed: Emperor Hsian-tsung and the Provinces', in Wright and Twitchett, *Perspectives on the T'ang*, 189. It must be noted, though, that Hsien-tsung's sudden and early death, in his forties, is attributed by two traditional histories to assassination by a eunuch

unpredictable personality, embittered by the humiliations inflicted on him as a child and a young man, was so savage that his ministers would tremble and sweat with fear whenever he cross-examined them.

But matters were far otherwise under emperors of weak will and personality, which, for practical purposes means Mu-tsung (820–4) and his three sons, Ching-tsung (824–7), Wen-tsung (827–840) and—possibly—Wu-tsung (840–6). During this entire span the eunuchs decided the succession; for since there were alternative choices as emperor, the eunuchs, as unique custodians of the private quarters of the palace, were in an unchallengeable position to announce the choice. In one case they even forged the late emperor's decree.[127] Mu-tsung was such a poor creature that many scholar officials simply declined to serve him.[128] When he died after a mere four years on the throne, the eunuchs' choice to succeed him, Ching-tsung, who was only 15, turned out to be so debauched and drunken that, in the end, the highest-placed eunuchs decided he must go—and had him murdered in his cups.[129] Their next choice, not unanimous, was his half-brother, the 17-year-old Wen-tsung. Very unlike the murdered emperor, he was humane, frugal, and scholarly; alas, he was also grotesquely irresolute. He was no match, therefore, for the chief eunuch Wang Shou-ch'eng (dominant since Mu-tsung's death).

On his death the new emperor, whose throne name became Wu-tsung (840–6), turned out to be dangerous. He was a fanatical Taoist and dabbled with their elixirs of immortality (and indeed one of these killed him after only six years on the throne). Far from being weak-willed, he gives the impression of a hyperactive dementia. Wu-tsung reverted to the pattern of Hsüan-tsung. He picked a chief minister he felt he could trust and gave him plenary power. But the Divine Strategy armies still remained under eunuch command and as long as this was so the palace eunuchs were safe. Sure enough, when Wu-tsung had poisoned himself to death at the age of 33, it was the eunuchs who once more decided the succession. This time there was no contest. The choice fell on Hsüan-tsung, the hitherto despised and humiliated half-brother of Mu-tsung. As we have seen, Hsüan-tsung was a

---

named Ch'en Hung-chih. The charge is reviewed by Dalby, in *CHC*, iii. 1, p. 634. Dalby is sceptical, as he well might be. What possible motives could the eunuchs have had in getting rid of an emperor who had so favoured them? (Ibid. 634). I, personally, would raise another objection. Hsüan-tsung (ruled 846–59), a son of Hsien-tsung who came to the throne late and after many unhappy experiences, was obsessed throughout his life with the mystery surrounding a father he adored, and spent endless hours trying to track down his murderer. Is it not most improbable that he would have continued to rely (as he certainly did) on the eunuch establishment if he had thought them in any way connected with his father's death?

[127] See p. 798 below.   [128] *CHC*, iii. 1, p. 639.

[129] As far as I know, this instance of the eunuchs laying violent hands on an emperor is unique.

masterful character. In his initial years he dismissed one minister after another—only one of seven survived more than a year—and he stamped out the endemic factionalism of the court. With him the central government regained its stability, both ministers and eunuchs serving firmly under his authority.

The steady growth of eunuch power in the ninth century was due to two opposite causes. In the first place, and obviously, it was due to the deliberate policy of the 'strong' emperors who saw in it a ready means of enforcing their personal authority. But paradoxically, it was also due to the efforts of the 'weak' emperors to break free from it and destroy it; because at each unsuccessful attempt the eunuchs gained a fresh accession of strength, while the emperor and his mandarin allies were correspondingly enfeebled. Let one—highly colourful—example suffice: the tremulous Wen-tsung's second anti-eunuch plot (the first is too ignominious a failure to record here). This second and very audacious attempt in 835 is known as 'the Sweet Dew plot'. The Emperor's instruments were an eminent (and eunuch) court physician and a Han-lin scholar. Wen-tsung appointed these two as his chief ministers. Their plan was to play on the rivalries in the eunuch leadership. They allied themselves with Ch'iu, one of the two eunuch leaders, to have his rival murdered, intending after that to dispose of Ch'iu in his turn. By various petty ruses they cobbled together a posse of soldiers. On the appointed day, as the emperor opened his dawn audience, a chamberlain (in the plot) kowtowed and announced that a most auspicious omen had been observed in the outer courtyard: 'sweet dew' had descended on a pomegranate tree! This was the pre-arranged cue for the emperor to send the dedicated victim, Ch'iu, along with other eunuchs, to proceed to the garden and verify this fantastically marvellous news. Unluckily for him, just as Ch'iu reached the courtyard a gust of wind blew a tent-flap open and he saw the soldiers inside. Ch'iu and his colleagues dashed back to the Inner Palace and got in just as the gates were closing against them, then bundled the emperor into his harem and sent runners to summon the Divine Strategy armies. Once these had arrived Ch'iu and his colleagues had a thousand courtiers massacred, rounded up their families and connections, and brought the entire affair to its bloody end by publicly executing three chief ministers. The emperor's spirit was quite broken. He dragged out the rest of his reign a tearful drunkard, obsessed with the poor figure he was bound to cut in the official dynastic history.

That event marked the apogee of eunuch power for, as we have noted, Hsüan-tsung stamped his personal authority on not only the Outer Court but on the Inner Palace, that is, the eunuch establishment alike. But it is as well to summarize the eunuch structure in the palace at this moment.

They not only cared for the emperor's palaces, gardens and estates, but supervised the postal service, the Imperial guest houses, and the Buddhist establishment at the capital. More importantly they had acquired deliberative responsibilities as Imperial Secretaries (Commissioners of Privy affairs: *shu-mi shih*) in the palace, and control of the emperor's Privy purse. They acted as Supervisors to the provincial armies, and as a channel of communication between the emperor and his provincial governors. But their supreme power was control of the *Shen-t'se* (Divine Strategy) armies, which were not only the emperor's personal troops, but also the main force at the disposal of the central government.[130]

3.3.2. THE NEW PATTERN IN THE LOCALITIES

Apart from Hopei (which, however, contained one-quarter of the entire population), central control of the interior was completed within fifty years of the end of the rebellion. In 763 over half the country was ruled by military governors who combined civil functions with their army commands and, between them, disposed of about half-a-million paid troops. But by Hsien-tsung's time (806) the central government had re-acquired complete control of local appointments. In perhaps six provinces—those with direct military responsibilities—generals were still appointed as governors; elsewhere all were career bureaucrats. All had limited tenure, six years being the absolute maximum before transfer elsewhere. They were entitled, like Roman governors, to bring their personal entourage with them, but as time went on the numbers in such teams were strictly regulated and they had to be broken up at each new posting.

We mentioned that they were controlled by the emperor's eunuchs but this demands elaboration. Attached to each governor and reporting directly to the emperor, the eunuchs' duties (to make an independent report on the governor's activities) expanded into powers to intervene in his administration, to negotiate with recalcitrant officials and garrisons, and to take over temporarily at a governor's death. After 820 the eunuchs possessed their own personal staff and a military escort which could—exceptionally—run into thousands. In fact their interference in routine administration became so common that in 855 they were made co-responsible with the governor for serious shortcomings. Clearly this edict was intended to make their personal responsibility commensurate with their power, but of course it also confirmed them in their usurped right to interfere.[131] The increasing volume of complaints about their activities shows that their power was a real one. The military governors in particular came to detest them, with dire results for the dynasty, as will be seen.

During the troubles governors had acquired military and financial lever-

---

[130] *CHC*, iii. 1, p. 703.   [131] Ibid. 544.

age over the prefects and, below these, the sub-prefects. They had usurped the authority to post garrison commanders throughout the prefectures and the *hsien* who were responsible to themselves. Furthermore, the direct taxes of the province, which came from the prefectures and were in theory divided between them, the provinces, and the central government, could be and were retained by the governor to pay the troops. Effectively, this put the prefects under financial pressure from the governor.

The central government met both these problems in the same way, by confining the financial and the military authority of the governor solely to the prefecture which was his seat. Thus the prefectures were to retain taxes for their own upkeep and pay *all* the surplus to the central government, that is, none to the governor; while the governor, although he no longer had to pay anything to the central government, was now entitled only to the revenues from his home prefecture. This was also true of the military establishment. The governor's military authority now extended only to his home prefecture. The prefects were for the first time given explicit military powers to command the forces within their prefectures. Thus the often formidable troop concentrations at the disposal of a governor were fragmented into smaller units, unlikely to combine and incapable by themselves of posing a military threat to the government.

In principle, these decrees cut the governor down to being the fiscal and military administrator of just one prefecture, the one his capital was situated in. But in practice, governors of provinces still retained great powers. Indeed the *first* main difference between pre-rebellion and post-rebellion local administration lies precisely in this, that the system was no longer the traditional two-tier prefecture/sub-prefecture one, but one with three tiers: the province interposing between the central government and the prefectures and *hsien*. Though the latter had been restored as the basic maids-of-all-work, they were now subordinated to the governor in a number of ways. For instance, by establishing a military need a governor could extract tax-revenue from the prefectures; he still commanded the largest force in the area; he was responsible—as supervisor—for evaluating local officials who correspondingly would tend to toady to him; and he was entitled to punish them for infractions and maladministration. Above all, he was responsible for security: local security, the repression of rebellion, and even, where necessary, raising troops for expeditionary forces.

In the second great change in the local administrative system, the stringently detailed fiscal regulations that had accompanied the old three-tax system and the concomitant land-redistribution service were totally abandoned. They had proved difficult and often anomalous to administer at the best of times and now the elaborate paperwork on which their complexities depended had been destroyed or dispersed during the civil wars. The new tax system introduced in 779–80[132] simply told each province the fixed amount it had to deliver to the central government, and did not inquire too deeply into the precise ways this revenue was raised, extortionately or otherwise, by extraordinary exactions and the like. Henceforward the central government abandoned the ideal of uniformity. Tax rates varied from one province to another. 'It is no longer possible to speak of a "Chinese" level of taxation', and indeed, it never would be again.[133]

3.4. Services: Defence, Taxation, Security

In the 830s the Uighur empire collapsed and the Tibetan state entered a period of anarchy. This removed the northern and eastern menace, but the military governors of the Hopei area remained unsubdued, though the government fought repeated and very costly campaigns against them. Furthermore it waged prolonged but fruitless war in the deep south to try to acquire and colonize the Yunnan area.

Government strategy was to maintain the frontier establishment and the palace (Divine Strategy) armies—large numbers of the latter serving on the north-west frontier—while reducing the swollen establishments in the interior. This was no easy matter. Governors resisted their loss of power and the men their loss of livelihood. The governments therefore relied on natural wastage, and although the statistics bequeathed to us are contradictory it does seem that some reduction did occur. In fact, it might even be that the reduction went too far; we cannot tell, because governors often inflated the pay rolls of their armies by large numbers of imaginary soldiers. The effects will be noticed in due course, as we analyse the situation under the last of the T'ang emperors.

However that may be, these large forces, amounting in all to perhaps 800 or even 900 thousand men—about 1 per cent of the total population—constituted a vast permanent drain on the resources of the state. The old T'ang three-tax system had, as noted already, collapsed in the wars and revenues brought in by the salt monopoly were not adequate. Given the overwhelmingly agricultural basis of the economy, land-taxation was also essential. In 779–80—only thirteen years after the suppression of the rebellion—an entirely new agricultural tax called the double tax was introduced. The basic flaw in the old system—like the late Roman one—was that it assumed an indissoluble link between taxpayer and land. If a man had no land, then he paid no tax. Worse, if he did cultivate land as a squatter it

---

[132] See below.   [133] *CHC*, iii. 1, p. 18.

was not registered and therefore he paid no tax either. Conversely, if the government insisted on a tax, it had to provide the taxpayer with the land necessary to generate it.

The Double Tax did away with all that. It combined two taxable bases. The first was the household: universally, irrespective of whether he was a registered resident or a squatter, every householder paid a poll tax (*hu-shui*), according to the duly assessed size and property-value of his household. The second was the land: every piece of land under cultivation paid a tax based as its extent, crops, quality, and so on—this was the *ti-shui*. All the miscellaneous taxes were abolished along with land redistribution. This new arrangement was to have profound economic and social consequences as it turned out, but administratively and fiscally it represented a considerable rationalization. It was much simpler to administer than the old system. The taxes were collected, all together, at two specified times in the year. Tax commissioners, after consultation with the governors and prefects of each province, set a tax quota for the year and thereafter let these local officials get on with raising the agreed sums—a widely decentralizing measure, as we noted above. Inside the provinces the revenue was divided in this way: each prefecture raised its tax quota, retained what was needful to cover its own expenses, and divided the remainder giving a proportion to the provincial governor (to help maintain the armies) and the central government. The home-prefecture of the governor likewise levied its quota, retained what was necessary for its own upkeep, and sent the remainder to the central government. The land-levy was usually assessed in grain but the household tax was assessed in coin. (This was to create immense problems in the middle of the ninth century when the state ran out of copper coins, but this matter properly belongs to the analysis of the *collapse* of the T'ang.)

Finally, the policing of the country showed no material change. We can form an excellent picture of its effectiveness from the travel diary of Ennin, a Japanese Buddhist monk who landed in China in 835. This was the year of the Sweet Dew plot, already mentioned, and the efficacy of the policing in the provinces strikes a remarkable contrast to the turmoils of the court. Ennin was one of a party of visiting Japanese officials and his own private desire was to visit the monastery at Mount T'ien-t'ai in the south, in today's province of Che-kiang, while the main body proceeded to the capital. But, caught by storms, the entire party made their landfall in a desolate wilderness near the mouth of the Yangtse. There they ran into an officer of the local Salt Bureau who directed them to the local garrison HQ. Resting there, they were soon approached by the official, accompanied by eight soldiers, to put them on their way to the prefectural capital. First, they were escorted to the head town of the *hsien* and brought before its seven principal officials. These arranged to have them escorted to the prefect himself and, having met, he instructed Ennin to petition the emperor for permission to go south to Mount T'ien-t'ai. Several days elapsed before the capital replied, the governor declining to allow Ennin to proceed to the capital on his own initiative, since (he said) his writ ran only to the border of his own province and could in no way bind his neighbours. The monk, he insisted, could receive permission from nobody but the emperor. Finally a letter from the capital did arrive and it informed Ennin he was *not* permitted to go to Mount T'ien-t'ai. Since the other members of his party would already have left for Japan, leaving him stranded, Ennin and a partner decided to hide up in the mountains and make their own way to Mount T'ien-t'ai and then to Chang-an. Found by locals as they wandered, lost, on an icy hillside, they pretended at first to be Koreans, but the elder of the village where they had been led for shelter not only saw through their ruse but told them that the prefecture was already on their tracks—and at that very moment three military police arrived and confronted them. This time they admitted they were Japanese but said that while they were sick, ashore, the rest of their party had sailed away. They had to write all this down for the sub-prefect and the prefect. The authorities meanwhile went looking for the Japanese ships, while the monks spent their days at the guard-officer's post, where they were later interrogated by the main officials of the sub-prefecture. Finally, the authorities succeeded in finding one of the Japanese ships which had been turned back by the weather. Even so the monks were not allowed to board until the prefect himself had seen them. They were then escorted on board while the movements of the ship northwards were carefully monitored. When they ultimately made a landfall further north it was to find that the sub-prefecture had been apprised beforehand and held a full dossier on them. The prefect and the harbourmaster were duly informed of their arrival and so on and so on, until they left China at last.[134]

4. THE END OF THE T'ANG (874–907)

China is a huge country and quite different events and processes may be taking place in different parts at the same time. Even as Ennin was receiving the impression of an orderly peaceable countryside, so, far away from his route, bandits and salt-smugglers were raiding the Yangtse river barges and spreading havoc. From the middle of the ninth century, there were local outbreaks of disorders and banditry. Garrisons mutinied and sacked towns,

[134] Reischauer, *Ennin's Diary*, 1–144.

with wide popular support. In 875 a popular rebellion of immense proportions broke out which quickly embraced all classes of provincial society. At
the root of all this unrest lay the perennial problem of a beleaguered
agrarian society: how to defend the soil from ever-repeatable waves of
nomad attack when the cost of static defence outstripped what could be
wrung from that soil. All agrarian societies found this problem difficult to
solve over the long term, but it is impossible to reject the view that
misgovernment made the débâcle certain. The last three decades of the
T'ang are a case-study in the pathology of political institutions.

At one level, the failure lay in the 'perils of success'. Hsien-tsung's
successful 'civilianization' of the provinces left too many of them with
forces too dispersed, too few, and too ill-exercised to suppress their local
uprisings. But at another level it lay in the fateful decision of 780 to fix tax
quotas for the provinces and leave the local officials very much to their own
devices as to how they raised them. In one sense again the fault lay in the
central government itself; demoralized by factions, by the eunuch—minister
feud, and by incompetent emperors, it did not exert itself like the early
T'ang to search out and penalize administrative laxity. But in another sense
the trouble originated at the local level, in garrisons made mutinous at
reductions of pay or over-strict discipline, and also in the local 'wealthier
classes' who staffed the prefectures and the hsien at subordinate level as
'duty-men', many of whom gave leadership to the importunate landless
migrants and saw advantages in teaming up with bandit-gangs.

But one thing lay at the bottom of every problem and every symptom:
taxation. Notwithstanding the new 'Double Tax', the salt taxes, and tea
taxes, revenue was only three-quarters of the expenditure.[135] The Double
Tax system was abused from the start. Governors and prefects imposed
extra-legal taxes. The former ingratiated themselves by extracting additional
sums in the form of 'tributes' for the emperor's personal treasury, 'tributes'
which became an essential resource of the central authority. Just as in the
Roman Republic, individuals paid a vast bribe to become a provincial
governor; one official is known to have paid 2 million strings of cash in
ready money. Most would borrow the money, and it was worth it, for it was
reckoned that the bribe could be recouped three times over in the course of
a single provincial tenure.[136]

Finally, it will come as no surprise to find that tax administration was
technologically incompetent. As usual, the triennial assessments were not
kept and families were often assessed on the higher valuation fixed twenty
years before. Officials—and it must be remembered that these were the

[135] *CHC*, iii. 1, p. 684.   [136] Ibid. 545.

local rich—failed to keep track of changes in ownership, so that the original owner had to pay and the purchaser paid no tax at all. Taxes were usually paid in kind but were assessed in cash, and deflation had increased the real burden on the peasants. As usual, these rich men/tax officials fiddled the 'rate of exchange' between goods and cash to their own advantage. In brief, the local notables were shifting the burden of taxation even more on to the peasantry and away from themselves. And finally, even apart from maladministration, the very ground-plan of the Double Tax was flawed.[137]

The social effects were widespread, profound, and terrible. An immense flight from the land occurred. Caught by poor harvests, individual peasants dropped out and became migrants, vagrants, 'marginalized' people; or if they fell foul of the authorities, took to the hills and marshes to become bandits. The pool of disaffected and marginalized persons expanded. Not only the uprooted peasant, the village toughs, and others for any number of reasons fled the authorities, but members of the squirearchy and the 'wealthier classes' of the localities, involved in shady deals or in connivance with smugglers, resented the interference of the local governor.

The central government knew all this yet lacked ability and will. At provincial level many governors had no particular reason to serve it with overmuch dedication, since most were only in the provinces as victims of yet another see-saw in the factional struggles at court; they were too often ex-ministers condemned to an honourable exile. The chief ministers were mediocrities almost as a matter of policy. Even the line-bureaucracy was crumbling. 'Offices split apart, orderly relationships were lost, and as some offices changed their function . . . others disappeared except in name. Moreover, such important basic functions as the selection of officials and the drafting of edicts no longer belonged to any specific office but were more commonly entrusted to individual officials on a temporary basis.'[138] The court was paralysed and convulsed by turns in the struggle between the ministers and the eunuchs. The latter were now at the height of their pretensions, near indeed to becoming an integral part of the imperial institutions as, by this time, they had become in the Byzantine Empire. By the early 860s they were actually claiming recognition for a due share in ministerial authority. Indeed, the chief eunuchs were now calling themselves the *ting-ts'e kuo-lao*, 'the policy-making elder statesmen'; while the two Secret Documents officials (the *shu-mi shih*) together with the two chiefs of the Imperial Household (the *hsüan-hui shih*) had now received the title of 'the Four Ministers' (*su hsiang*), suggesting that they were the equals of the Outer

---

[137] Twitchett, 'Local Financial Administration', 44 ff.   [138] *CHC*, iii. 1, p. 711.

Court where the number of chief ministers had now stabilized at four.[139] Powerful as their position was, it became even stronger when the boy-emperor, Hsi-tsung, succeeded (another eunuch choice) in 873, for this child looked on T'ien Ling-t'zu, the chief eunuch, as his foster-father. Top eunuchs like T'ien were by no means ignorant upstarts. T'ien was well educated and very clever, and through his influence with the emperor, who left everything to him, the appointments of the high eunuchs to posts in the court and the provinces were thenceforth made in those solemn forms hitherto reserved for the chief ministers.[140] The eunuch Yang Ku-fing (incidentally, T'ien's enemy) had a pedigree and a career pattern similar to that of any normal court official; members of the eunuch 'family' which had adopted him had served in the Divine Strategy Army for the past century. His cousin, Yang Fu-kuan, like himself well-educated and a man of great integrity and resolve, was a soldier who rendered vital services to the dynasty during the Huang Ch'ao rebellion.[141] Eunuchs such as these were the adopted sons of eunuch predecessors, and they themselves adopted sons and placed them in high positions. For instance, Yang Fu-kuan alone had more than ten such as prefects and provincial generals and even higher.[142] Though at times the ministers agreed to co-operate with them—as they finally did when the eunuchs manipulated the succession to bring I-tsung to the throne—they did so only because they had no option. For most of the time they spared no effort to try to rid the palace of them and regain their monopoly of influence with the emperor.

Modern historians see a growing and cumulative pattern of lawlessness and rebellion from the mid-ninth century.[143] Stated thus, the buildup appears inexorable and the outcome inevitable, and the wonder becomes why the court did not realize it. Peasant uprisings were endemic (it is reckoned there was about one every year) and military mutinies were common too. But it is easy to underestimate the commonplace. So there was little disposition to inquire into causes. Instead, the authorities dealt with each outbreak as a particular event and in the time-honoured way: by repression, and, if that took too long, buying off the leaders by government employment.[144]

---

[139] Ibid. 704–5.   [140] Ibid. 716.   [141] Ibid. 717.
[142] Ibid.   [143] Ibid. 682.

[144] In 874 a Han-lin scholar, Lu Hsi, did indeed memorialize the throne showing how a desperate situation had been building up since the 860s. Despite drought and famine, the extraordinary taxes were collected remorselessly and peasants were selling their children into slavery to meet them. He urged the government to stop collecting taxes at once. The court accordingly issued an edict to that effect; but officials found it was impossible to carry out (ibid. 720). In the following year an Act of Grace analysed carefully many of the pressing problems and laid down a programme for reform. But

From numerous examples in Chinese imperial history, Eberhard has evolved a 'model' for the evolution of the bandit gang. This begins with village youths having time on their hands. In their desperate economic circumstances, the village elders sometimes tolerated these youths and sometimes even encouraged them when they harassed local officials, tax-collectors, or landlords. In return, the latter organized local forces and drove the youths away. They fled to mountain or marshes but kept in touch with the village which sent them food and supplies. Over time the gang attracted more members and so to maintain itself had to extend its area of depredation. This brought it into collision with neighbouring gangs. The victorious gang incorporated the conquered group. The local landlords resist the enlarged gang stoutly. In so far as they succeeded, the gang had to look elsewhere for its livelihood and launched attacks on the nearest large town. Once this was done the government troops were involved. Battles were fought. If the troops were not quickly victorious the bandit gang swelled. Now the local squires were in a cleft stick: if they resisted they would be defeated, if they joined they would have become rebels. Some did join the gangs and take leading positions. By this time the rebellion would be widespread and the bandit army might finally capture a city. At this point the government would move in troops on a large scale, while the gang leaders would co-opt the local squires. If, in the end, they defeated the government, these squires would become the élite of the new dynasty. (In only three cases did this happen—the founding of the Han dynasty, of the Later Liang dynasty, and of the Ming dynasty).[145]

Such is Eberhard's 'model', and in most respects the bandit gangs of the last T'ang dynasts conform to it. The name for the bandits is *wang-ming*, literally, 'those who have abandoned their lot', marginalized individuals. The bandit gangs as such were *not* the working peasants who, indeed, often formed vigilante groups to beat off both government troops and bandits alike. The main basis of banditry lay in the *ex*-peasants, the landless, the dispossessed, and the migrants. Once these joined a bandit gang, bandits are what they became. Rural riots were endemic in China but afterwards the farmers went back to farming. Not so in the bandit rebellions—Hsien-chih and Huang Ch'ao, the two leaders of the great 875 rebellion, never led any spontaneous peasant risings, were never accepted as peasant heroes, and never sought to advance the lot of the peasantry. Bandit armies, in so far as

before any of this could be enacted banditry was so widespread that the government had no recourse but confrontation and repression (*CHC*, iii. 1, 721).

[145] Eberhard, *Conquerors and Rulers*, 89, 91–103.

their organization is known, also conform to the Eberhard model: great confederations of individual bandit gangs.[146]

Like the popular uprisings, the military rebellions also were seated in the marginalized classes, for soldiers were the lowest of the low, serving for pay and just as likely to turn on local civilians as on the loyalist troops opposing them. There were very many mutinies and rebellions. Undoubtedly the most serious was that led by T'ang Hsün in 868–9; its immediate cause was the authorities' decision to keep a time-expired unit for a further tour of duty in the extremely arduous and unpopular war in Nan-chao (in the deep south). Like all its predecessors, this rising too was crushed; the government generals and troops had proved effective. Thus, when two more bandit leaders raised an insurrection in 875—Wang Hsien-chih and Huang Ch'ao—it seemed mere repetition. It was not. To the military difficulty of defeating ferocious mobile bandit armies, a new factor was superadded. A number of disaffected generals decided to play both sides against the middle, calculating that if the bandit leader became emperor after all, they could come in behind him as supporters. So began a vicious circle: the inactivity of a general protracted the rebellion and the longer this lasted and the more problematical became the survival of the dynasty, the more did generals look to themselves and build up their own military base, either to compete for the throne themselves or to rush to the aid of the winning side. Instead of recognizing this, a frivolous and faction-racked court seemed intent on showing its successful and loyal generals how ungrateful it could be. For instance, General Liu Chü-jung defeated and could have dispersed the rebel army at the Yangtse, but to the contrary he let them proceed northwards. 'The T'ang', he reportedly said, 'exploit people. In times of danger it gives generals rewards but when peace comes, so do the punishments. The best plan is to let the bandits go and wait for later good fortune.'[147]

Similarly, as Huang Ch'ao and his bandits drove straight at Loyang and Chang-an, General Kao stood completely idle. Controversy still rages over his reasons, but Japanese and American scholars, who have tried to justify Kao's inaction in military terms,[148] are refuted by Wang Gungwu.[149] In his words, Kao, like the other generals, was for 'leaving the bandits there as an investment',[150] and certainly all his subsequent actions speak uniformly and plainly for his treacherous intentions.[151] The rebel Huang Ch'ao was allowed to go on to seize the capital and proclaim himself emperor before the court called in Turk troops and finally crushed him. But for all this, the

---

[146] *CHC*, iii. 1, 723–5.   [147] Ibid. 741.   [148] Ibid. 743–4.
[149] Wang, *The Structure of Power*, 23, n. 27.   [150] Ibid. 18.   [151] Ibid. 23, n. 27.

regime was doomed. It was now quite obvious that the famous 'Mandate of Heaven' was in doubt. A power-vacuum had been exposed.

Just as in the last days of the Han, military commanders began taking over their provinces. Wang Gungwu has shown that in 883 only thirteen of the thirty-three provinces were ruled by governors chosen by the court; six were governed by persons whom the court had no choice but to confirm and nine by self-appointed governors. The government lost control of the prefects and of the local armies, since the former simply put themselves at the disposal of the military governors and the militia officers lacked any power to back up their authority and, indeed, helped the governors to trim their sails to the latest change of wind at court. For there the eunuchs and ministers continued their perennial battle, but with this lethal difference: each side and every faction within each side now made calculations and alliances with the war-lords in the provinces.

On the death of the emperor in 888 the eunuchs arranged the succession for the very last time and chose Chao-tsung. Alarmed at the presence of army commanders in his capital, this new emperor moved against one of them with a hastily recruited army. Easily beaten, he was forced to execute his chief minister and four leading eunuchs. The situation thereafter was one in which three governors squared up to one another other to seize the person of the emperor. The emperor's eunuchs sought help from one governor and, in reaction, the bureaucrats, led by Chief Minister Tsui Wen, sought the support of a rival governor. It was the latter who won and, like the military governors before him at the end of the Han, he massacred every eunuch at court and made the emperor order all governors to kill their eunuch supervisors. He went on by having Chief Minister Tsui Wen, the very man who had called him in, put to death. Then he took the emperor to Loyang, where he had him murdered (904) in favour of the emperor's 12-year-old son. In habitual fashion, he soon deposed the boy and, proclaiming himself emperor, announced a new dynasty, the Liang.

So collapsed the entire imperial structure: emperor, chief ministers, and eunuchs at the top, and the entire civilian structure of provincial and prefectural rule in the localities. So collapsed, too, the Mandate of Heaven, for the deposition of 907 heralded no reunification but continued division and civil war as the *Wu Tai*—the Five Dynasties—succeeded each other in the North, and the Ten Kingdoms sprang up in the South. The T'ang dynasty had lasted nearly all of 300 years, but for the last fifty it had lived on borrowed time. The court, whether eunuch-led or minister-led, had distanced itself from the people and, when they rose up, turned to its generals who had no time for it. It was a very different scene from the suppression of the An Lu-shan revolt 150 years before. Then it had been a great general who revolted, but the provinces and most of the people had rallied to the dynasty. This time neither generals nor populace rallied to it. And, one may well surmise—even had the generals not opened the front for the bandits, even if they had suppressed them in the first year—that would not have been the end of the affair. The military imperatives and the tax exactions it entailed would have become no less; the laxity in the fiscal administration no less either; and the inability of the fractured court and central administration to resolve the underlying social problems would have been equally marked.

5. CONCLUSION

During the T'ang period, three major problems emerged and it can be said that none were satisfactorily solved.

The first was the problem of absolutism: in principle, the governmental structure had an apex and that apex was the emperor. This permitted three variations. In the first, the emperor acted as arbitrator between conflicting agencies. This was the Confucianist ideal, and the original structure of T'ang government presupposed it by the way agencies, the Censorate, and the 'Remonstrating Officials' could check and balance one another. The principal difficulty here was that it also presupposed an ideal emperor. K'ao-tsu and T'ai-tsung were able to fill the role, partly because they were clear-minded persons of strong character but partly because the tasks of government and, for that matter, its machinery, were so much less complicated than later on. In the absence of such an ideal emperor the agencies cancelled one another's initiatives so that, at the worst, government initiatives halted and, at best, came in fits and starts.

The second variation was for the emperor to entrust a minister with overriding authority—as Hsüan-tsung entrusted Li Lin-fu, or Wu-tsung entrusted Li Te-yü. But this solution only pushed the problem one stage further down, for how was the chief minister to impose his authority on this self-cancelling structure? Hence the perceptible but slow and incomplete moves towards single-seatedness already noted but never completed.[152]

The third variation was to leave the routine to the department but take *policy* out of their hands by creating an extraordinary, overriding institution. This was the palace or Inner Court, as opposed to the Outer Court. The fact that it was made up of eunuchs is idiosyncratic. It could have been composed of any class of persons totally obedient to the emperor, like

[152] See p. 762 above.

freedmen in the early Roman Empire. But this institution was never a complete substitute for the bureaucracy, and simply provoked discord.

All of these variations were tried, none were persisted with for long, and in practice they were usually not clear-cut alternatives but each contained elements of the others. These T'ang alternatives turn up throughout Chinese imperial history. The Sung dynasty as a whole used the emperor–moderator variant and the Ming the Inner Court variant (with a massive reliance on eunuchs, and terror).

The second intractable problem was civil–military relations. Here the dynasty seems trapped in a no-win situation because by the mid-eighth century it concentrated military power on the frontiers, leaving itself no troops. This led to the possibility of military rebellion and the difficulty in suppressing it. In the mid-ninth century it stripped the interior of troops, but surrounded itself with the *Shen-ts'e* (Divine strategy, i.e. palace) armies (above pp. 788–9). Hence the spread of banditry, with which these armies were not large enough to cope. Hence a new militarization was developed in the interior provinces to cope with the bandits and, once again, the government fell into a confrontation, this time fatal, with its own generals.

The third unsolved problem was the condition of the peasantry. Defence of frontiers by regular troops required heavy taxation, which led the peasants into either dependency or into flight from the land and still heavier burdens on those who remained; hence banditry, hence the need for more defence and more taxes. This was the familiar coercion–extraction–coercion cycle. It was a *vicious* cycle, however, because the subsistence-agricultural economy could not maintain the necessary armed forces without destroying the free peasantry in the process and so making the fiscal deficit.

Though the T'ang failed to solve these problems, neither did its destruction. The three problems recurred under the Sung and the Ming and they failed to solve them either.

On the credit side, the T'ang presents itself as one of the more remarkable of the world's exercises in large-scale government. In its scale—a country the size of the USA; in its duration—300 years; and in the regularity of its laws and administration until the final convulsion it is an outstanding achievement. For much of the period it was both peaceful, and by contemporary valuation, prosperous.

Finally, in the perspective of the great historic forms of government it produced three outstanding innovations. The first was the creation of a rational bureaucracy, wholly secular in outlook, solidary in ethos, and self-directed by a comprehensive ideology that was self-consistently social and ethical as well as political. A bureaucracy, furthermore, whose structure, like that of modern bureaucracies, was framed in two dimensions: the vertical dimension of hierarchical grades, and the horizontal dimension of specia-lized agencies and departments. The second innovation was the mode of recruitment and promotion—a merit system based on competitive exam-ination. The third was the institutionalization of auto-criticism by means of the surveillance ('censorial') and the 'remonstrating' officials. What was not merely unique to China but destined to remain so till the abolition of the entire imperial system in 1912 was the establishment of this Order of Scholars as the ruling, the cultural, and the social élite on whose values, mores, and mode of conduct the entire society had to pattern itself: something that struck Voltaire and the *encyclopédistes* as altogether wondrous when they encountered it in the eighteenth century.

4

Government Under the Ming, 1368–1644

*P*atriotic Chinese hail the Ming dynasty as the last native one on Chinese soil before the alien Manchus (Ch'ing) took over in 1644 and ruled the country up to the close of the entire imperial regime in 1911. Such a dynastic dichotomy does violence to the institutional history, for the Ming governmental system persisted through the Ch'ing: effectively, the same form of government prevailed in China for the entire 1368–1911 period, 543 years.

If the criterion of an effective governmental system is the ability to maintain the state's sovereignty, territorial integrity, and domestic tranquillity, then the Ming must be reckoned one of the most effective in history. Unlike the Han and T'ang empires, its span was not punctuated by massive popular revolts. Unlike the Sung, it did not have to give up half its territory. On the contrary, the Ming Empire remained united and pacified for an unbroken 278 years.[1] No contemporary state approached this record. Even the Ottoman Empire, its nearest competitor in size (but with at least one-third less of population) faced civil wars, military mutinies, and manifold civil disturbances over that same span of time.[2] As to the troubled war- and rebellion-ridden states of Europe, they only point up the contrast with the peace and security of the 70 (rising to some 130) million subjects of the vast Chinese realm.

One can go even further if one chooses to consider the entire Ming/Ch'ing period as the same continuum, as today most Western scholars do. In that event, the terminal period of the Ming from, say, 1636 to the definitive establishment of the Ch'ing in 1681 constitutes a 'time of trouble' parallel to that between the Wars of Religion and the Fronde in France, or the Commonwealth and Protectorate in England, the Thirty Years War in Germany, and so forth. In this light, it would be a mere forty-five-year interruption in a political system that was to guarantee a degree of peace and security, and a measure even of prosperity, to a population that would rise to

---

[1] Cf. the record of Tokugawa Japan, 1600–1868 (see Bk. IV, Ch. 1 below).

[2] The Ottoman population was never more than 28 million—less than half the Ming and destined to shrink still further. The Moghul Empire was more comparable in size of population, but far more troubled by internal interest. Its effective life was 1526–1707.

more than 350 million in an empire twice the area of the Ming until at least the 1840s.

Furthermore, if the criterion of effective government is enlarged so as to include 'good' government, meaning one that guaranteed well-being to the population, then the Ming/Ch'ing system still does not come out too badly. The condition of the peasants under the Ming was not, apparently, worse than in previous dynasties, and arguably it was better, though they were more numerous. In the Ch'ing period up to 1800 their condition was much superior. Furthermore, the Ming state provided many more facilities for the population than did Europe, notably an empire-wide educational system.

If, however, the criterion be modified yet again, to mean *efficient* government, that is, government that most economically applied means to ends, then even the most charitable verdict would have to be 'could do (much) better'. The system 'got by'. In all major respects it was effective only in spite of itself. This is true whether one looks at the commitment of its emperors, the organization and outlook of the civil service, the mobilization of financial and military resources, the taxation system, the organization and training of the armed forces, or at the corruption that pervaded every process of public administration. Given all these defects; given also bored emperors, a strife-torn bureaucracy, and a decrepit army, the wonder is not that it did as well as it did but that it survived at all. Their Manchu successors made good two of these cardinal defects. Their first four monarchs (1644–1796) were highly energetic and capable and so were their military forces, the Manchu bannermen. For all that they were alien— and exploitative—the Manchu usurpers gave the Ming system new life.

1. MING SOCIETY AND ECONOMY

1.1. *The Economy*

In the West the advent of gunpowder and the printing press mark the transition from the feudal-agrarian society to the 'modern age'. Those inventions had come to China some 200 to 400 years before reaching Europe, and in the Ming era Chinese society and its economy were highly advanced.

The basis for this remarkable development occurred just as the T'ang state was collapsing through the inability of a primarily subsistence agriculture to generate the grain surpluses needed to support an enormous standing army. The ability of the T'angs none-too-able successor, the Sung dynasty (960–1279), to maintain even larger standing armies as well as to support grossly inflated government establishments was due to economic developments so rapid and far-reaching as to merit the expression: 'the medieval economic revolution'.[3]

Agriculture provided the launching-pad. In the Yangtse area and South China, the Champa rice-strain introduced in 1012 made two harvests possible and the Sung government systematically distributed its seeds, while the Ming introduced newer and improved varieties, as well as new varieties of hemp, cotton, and tea. These agricultural improvements furnished the basis for the development of inter-regional trade and the commercialization of agricultural production. They permitted a huge increase in population, which doubled between the tenth and thirteenth centuries from 53 million to 100 million.[4] Big towns arose, the centres of specialized craftsmen. The new agriculture stimulated a range of new agricultural machines such as seeders and water-lifting devices. The design of these machines and the best ways of sowing and planting were disseminated everywhere by government-sponsored handbooks. Metallurgy developed more strongly than ever as coal was pressed into service for fuel and the hydraulic bellows was invented, so that cast-iron production (in which China had always led Europe) now surged ahead. In 1078 China produced 114,000 tonnes, whereas England was producing only 68,000 tonnes as late as 1788! Ceramics developed too, with the invention of porcelain in the twelfth century.

As a further consequence, inter-regional trade expanded so much that, under the Sung, the volume of private trade for the first time exceeded the volume of grain and textiles transported by the state as taxes-in-kind. In the eleventh and twelfth centuries the revenues from commerce equalled the agrarian tax-income; indeed, in the South Sung Empire (1127–1271) it actually exceeded it.

The wide dissemination of handbooks about the new agricultural techniques had been made possible on so wide a scale because of the invention of printing. Paper had been in general use since the end of the second century (not to be manufactured in Italy until the thirteenth century!). The practice of taking rubbings from stone or bronze stelae had followed, so the invention of carved wood-block printing at the end of the eighth century was a natural development. The first full 'book' to be printed in this was the Diamond Sutra text in 868, and by the year 900 printing was in general use. The Nine Classics were printed by imperial command at the capital, 932–52. Movable type was invented in 1068, but for the Chinese language, composed of perhaps 30,000 separate ideograms, it is not as serviceable as it is for the

[3] M. Elvin, *Pattern of the Chinese Past* (Eyre-Methuen, London, 1973), 112 ff.

[4] J. Gernet, *A History of Chinese Civilization*, trans. R. J. Foster (CUP, Cambridge, 1982), 319.

alphabetic scripts of the West. Woodblock printing, therefore, remained the principal technique.

Just as printing is deemed one of the two hallmarks of approaching 'modernity' in Europe, so is gunpowder. The first mention of a formula (coal, sulphur, saltpetre) is found in a Chinese text of 1044; in Europe, not until 1285. By that latter date the Chinese had perfected incendiary and explosive grenades and special catapaults to hurl them. By 1280 the Sung were using bronze and iron mortars against the Mongols.

Under the Ming silver ingots began to circulate as currency, and this greatly accelerated social mobility. Capital moved from land into commercial and craft enterprises, the poorest agricultural labourers drifted to find employment in the towns, where silk- and cotton-weaving, iron and steel production, ceramic and porcelain manufacture began to assume an industrial character. There were new agricultural machines for turning the soil, for irrigation, and for sowing seed, and new food crops—groundnuts, the sweet potato, and maize. The population continued to increase, therefore, from some 70 millions on the establishment of the dynasty to 130 million at its demise in 1644. From 1560 China was a very prosperous country. Its economy, moreover, was recognizably 'modern' in the Western sense, in that it comprised a proletariat, an urban middle-class, merchants, and businessmen.

It was, however, still a basically agrarian society, and even at the close of the dynasty most of its tax revenue was still collected in kind. During this dynastic span the social structure in the countryside underwent a great transformation which had profound political consequences, as we shall describe later. Initially, the founding emperor's expropriations served to re-create a nation of smallholders (although, in 1397, 14,341 households still retained 120 acres of land or more), but from the beginning of the fifteenth century the peasant proprietors began to disappear. Some abandoned the land and found employment in the towns, the mines, or the army and a large number became *déclassés*—wanderers, drop-outs, or bandits. But most became not so much tenants as bondsmen. This is the theme of Elvin's chapter on 'manorialism without feudalism'. Not merely were there immense *latifundia* worked by tenant-farmers but often this status implied personal subordination.[5] This was true, in many cases, of hired labourers also.[6] The risings that destroyed the Ming in 1644 were often revolts by serfs, and also by tenants revolting against their dependency.[7] This is not to say that there was no independent peasantry left, but that 'the manorial order with serfdom and a serf-like tenancy continued to *dominate* [my italics]

---

[5] Elvin, *Pattern of the Chinese Past*, 236–7.   [6] Ibid. 238–44.   [7] Ibid. 246–7.

the countryside—though [Elvin adds] with diminishing vigour as time passed by'. (It was due to disappear only in the eighteenth century when, as Elvin puts it, 'The landlord and the pawnbroker took the place of the manorial lord and financial relationships displaced those of status'.[8]

1.2. *Literacy, Ideology, and Society*

Confucianism had never ceased to be a force—indeed, one might more correctly say *the* force—at a Chinese court, but it had had little appeal outside the court and officialdom until the coming of the Sung. The Sung emperors were without exception Confucianist, and their personal commitment set up developments which enabled Confucianism to irradiate a far wider circle than ever before. For one thing, the Sung perfected the civil service examination system and in an act of supreme (and expensive) supererogation, not only expanded the number of the competitions but paid stipends to all successful candidates for whom no positions could be found. For another, in their genuine zeal for arts and letters they established a great central college, created schools through the empire, set up a state publishing house, and patronized the mushrooming private academies. They both responded to and fostered two great innovations that thenceforth linked hands: the invention of block printing, already mentioned, and the revival of Confucian philosophy. The latter, so-called Neo-Confucianism, advanced just as the great Buddhist philosophical schools were stagnating in the eleventh century, probably because the middle T'ang's great proscription of 845 had stripped its monasteries—which were also its seminaries—of their copper, land, and serfs. Drawing metaphysical and cosmological ideas from those Buddhist schools, Confucianist scholars went back to the Classics, particularly what came to be known as the Four Books (the *I Ching*, the *Analects*, *Mencius*, and the *Book of Rites*). Their views were synthesized by the scholar Chu Hsi, who substituted his philosophical commentary for the philological exegesis that had previously served as explication. Chu Hsi's interpretations were to become the orthodoxy of the Ming period, and indeed of the Ch'ing after it.[9]

This new and burgeoning dimension of Confucianism made it (to non-Westerners) an enormously potent synthesis of morals, cosmology, and metaphysics, and it proved irresistible to the literate classes at the very time when the invention of printing put the Classics and the commentaries into the hands of a reading class that was being enlarged all the time by the expansion of the urban middle classes. The Mongol Yüan dynasty failed to

---

[8] Elvin, *Pattern of the Chinese Past*, 235.   [9] Likewise Tokugawa Japan. Cf. Bk. IV, Ch. 1.

sustain its initial hostility to Confucianism. By 1340 the political factions at court were having to couch their differences, formulate their arguments, and justify their activities in Confucianist language.[10] The Ming found Confucianism the working ideology of the entire (and now widely expanded) literate and wealthy class; indeed, of virtually everybody outside the founding Hung-wu Emperor himself (though he took pains to bone up on it), and the circle of uncouth generals who had assisted him in his path to power. Hitherto it had been possible to speak of Confucian government in China, but not of a Confucian state because the sub-officials at the county *yamen* and in the villages had not been completely Confucianized. Now this Confucian state was coming into being as these locals were swept into the net, and with it there also dawned the Confucian *society*, as townsfolk and villages were in their turn indoctrinated by the local officials, the scholar-gentry, and the schoolmasters. They did not comprehend philosophical Confucianism but they were taught to recognize its symbols and its rites. And while they maintained their popular Buddhism and Taoism, and went on worshipping their local deities and indulged in magic and witchcraft, they were gripped by the central tenets of Confucianism—patriarchy and ancestor worship. To them these were not metaphysical. They were immemorial practice. Confucianism's axiomatic assumptions that human relationships were asymmetrical, as reflected in the Five Relationships, their embodiment in a meticulously elaborated code of social rituals which were enforced by the strictest paragraphs of a harsh penal code, were not, therefore, unwelcome. In this Ming period, itself a stepping-stone to its fulfilment in the Ch'ing, Confucianism can no longer be regarded as a mere official ideology. It would be quite improper, of course, to define it as a religion, but it was the functional equivalent of, say, Islam or Christianity in so far as it provided society and indeed *pervaded* society with a code of social, moral, and civic norms, a pattern to conform to, a metaphysic and a cosmology. It was a synthesized and complete world outlook. And whereas Chinese society conformed to it, the Confucianist ideologues *internalized* it. Many acted it out in gestures of political defiance as devout, as stubborn, and as suicidal as any Christian martyr. The political processes of the Ming dynasty are not comprehensible unless one thinks of Confucianism as a powerful lay religion, trapping emperors and civil servants alike, and simultaneously setting them at one another and confining them within the same limited circle of options. Of this more will be said when we come to the nature of the Ming civil service, the very nucleus of militant Confucianism.

[10] J. W. Dardess, *Conquerors and Confucians: Aspects of Political Change in Late Yüan China* (Columbia UP, New York, 1973), 93.

2. THE TRANSIT OF THE MING

The Ming dynasty was founded on the ruins of the Mongol (Yüan) dynasty. Initially it was openly exploitative of the Chinese, then ineffectually Sinicized. Like all its predecessors it failed to remove the causes or suppress the consequences of peasant distress. On the contrary, Mongol depredations added to it. Chinese xenophobia contributed to the numerous peasant revolts that undermined its rule, until by the 1350s China was again overrun by local war-lords and bandit chieftains. Among the latter an ugly, imperious man of poor parentage, at one time a Buddhist novitiate and then mendicant monk, rose to pre-eminence on the Yangtse. Defeating and incorporating the troops of his rivals, he drove the Mongols from their capital, Ta-tu (Peking) and became emperor. His name was Chu Yüan-chang. His temple name was, as customary, T'ai-tsu. The regnal name was Hung-wu—hence he is known as the Hung-wu Emperor. Contemptuous and indeed hostile to officialdom, he ruled his court with an iron hand and his ground-rules for the dynasty and institutional arrangements were to set the pattern of government to its end. His grandson, Hui-ti, succeeded in 1398 while still a youth, only to be dispossessed after four years of fighting by his uncle (the founding emperor's son). This was Ch'eng-tsu, the Yung-lo Emperor (1402–24). He was as imperious as his father and, like him, imposed a lasting pattern of the forms and institutions of government.

The Hung-wu and Yung-lo emperors, and the two who followed (Jen-tsung, the Hung-hsi Emperor (1425), and Hsüan-tsung, the Hsuan-te Emperor (1425–35), all pursued a vigorous foreign policy. The Mongols were driven far north to their steppe capital at Karakorum. Maritime expeditions under the Muslim eunuch Cheng-ho showed the flag in southern waters and received tribute from more than twenty states which included Sumatra, Borneo, Siam, Cambodia, and Vietnam, while Ming prowess in the north secured similar recognition from Korea and Japan. But this expansionist drive faltered when Annam, a tributary, secured full independence from China in 1431, and the Cheng-t'ung Emperor (1435–49 and 1457–64) was captured in a sortie against the Mongols in 1449. After that, for reasons that are still obscure to us, Ming China adopted a defensive posture and the great naval expeditions ceased.

The middle period of the dynasty, from the mid-fifteenth to the mid-sixteenth century, saw no decisive events. Concerned with the vulnerability of the long sea-coast to foreign intrusion—the Japanese and the newly arrived Portuguese—the court closed down foreign trade, so provoking attacks by frustrated Japanese traders-turned-pirates whose successes demonstrated how pacific—and stagnant—the imperial government had become. But, belatedly, the dragon awoke once more, the armies were (temporarily) refurbished, the attacks were turned back. So were renewed Mongol attacks in the north. Meanwhile, in the capital, a line of emperors made their historical reputation only by withdrawing from their principal ministers (the Grand Secretaries) and conducting imperial affairs through eunuch messengers from the interior of their private quarters. The short 'principal ministership' of the Grand Secretary Chang Chü-cheng, who governed during the minority of the Wan-li Emperor (1572–1620), provided a too-short interlude of vigorous administrative reform. On his death the all-blanketing bureaucratic reaction set in, and from that point the dynasty went into terminal decline.

In the north a tribe of Jürchen, inhabiting the area north-east of Peking—and calling themselves the Manchus—seized the Mukden region from the empire. From 1636 they proclaimed an imperial dynasty, the Ta Ch'ing, at Mukden and pressed down on the Great Wall. In the Chinese interior bandit gangs roamed the countryside exerting further strain on the imperial government. The old and mild fiscal apparatus proved quite unequal to raising the huge sums so suddenly required to fight the interior and external threats simultaneously. The court itself was not so much supine as convulsed in a bitter ideological faction fight between ex-civil servants of the Tung-lin Academy and their supporters, versus the incumbents of power, and notably (familiar story) the eunuchs. In 1644 the rebel leader Li Tzu-ch'eng was able to lead his forces into, and capture, Peking, and the Ch'ung-chen Emperor, who had acceded in 1627, hanged himself with a silk scarf on Coal Hill in the Forbidden City. The Ming generals were certainly not going to accept the bandit leader as their sovereign, and the most redoubtable, Wu San-kuei, opened the Great Wall to the Manchu bannermen. The latter decisively defeated Li but did not hand back sovereignty to the dynasty, as the Chinese generals had, perhaps naïvely, expected. Instead they entered Peking and proclaimed their own dynasty—the Ch'ing—as the sovereign of China.

CHRONOLOGY

1328	Birth of Hung-wu. As ex-monk and wanderer, he will lead rebels against the Mongol dynasty (Yüan)
1368	Last Mongol ruler expelled
1368	HUNG-WU proclaims himself emperor of the Ming dynasty
1387	All China liberated. General land register of the empire
1398–1402	The CHIEN-WEN EMPEROR. Deposed by his uncle

1402–24	The YUNG-LO EMPEROR. Overseas expansion in Pacific and South East Asia
1421	Capital moved to Peking
1425–35	The HSÜAN-TE EMPEROR
1435–49	The CHENG-T'UNG EMPEROR. Captured in battle by Mongols, deposed
1449–57	The CHING-T'AI EMPEROR
1457–64	The CHENG-T'UNG EMPEROR (restored) as the T'IEN-SHUN EMPEROR
1464–87	The CH'ENG-HUA EMPEROR
1487–1505	The HUNG-CHIH EMPEROR
1505–21	The CHENG-TE EMPEROR
1521–66	The CHIA-CHING EMPEROR. Resumption of Japanese piracy on the coast
1566–72	The LUNG-CH'ING EMPEROR
1572–1620	The WAN-LI EMPEROR, 1593, Chinese defeat Japanese in Korea. Conflict between eunuch party and the Tung-lin scholars (1615–27)
1620	The T'AI-CHANG EMPEROR
1620–7	The T'IEN-CHI EMPEROR
1621	The Jürchen take Mukden
1624–7	Supremacy of the eunuch Wei Chung-Hsian
1625	Fearsome persecution of the Tung-lin scholars
1627	Death of Nurhaci, founder of the Jürchen-Manchu power
1627–44	The CH'UNG-CH'EN EMPEROR
1635	The Jürchen start to call themselves Manchus
1644	Rebel leader Li Tzu-Ch'eng enters Peking. The Chung-ch'en Emperor commits suicide. Manchus drive out Li and proclaim the MANCHU dynasty

3. THE STRUCTURE OF GOVERNMENT

As always, supreme authority rested with the emperor: in theory absolute and autocratic, in practice, of course, dependent on a military establishment which at its peak numbered 100,000 officers and some 4 million troops; and on the civil service, which averaged about 15,000 mandarin-class officials and 100,000 lesser functionaries.

The capital was now Peking. The conquering Mongols had made their capital at Ta-tu, and the founder of the Ming, Chu Yüan-chang (the Hung-wu Emperor), had launched his campaigns against the Mongols from a power-base at Chiang-ning, on the Yangtse. As the Emperor T'ai-tsu of the new Ming dynasty, he made Ta-tu his northern and principal capital, with

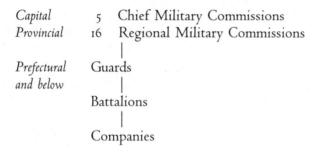

Capital	5	Chief Military Commissions
Provincial	16	Regional Military Commissions
Prefectural and below		Guards
		Battalions
		Companies

FIG. 3.4.1. *The organization of military services under the Ming*

the 'skeleton' capital at Chiang-ning. Hence the new names of these towns: Peking (northern capital) and Nanking (southern capital).[11]

By now there was a regular military service, side by side with the civil service. In 1380, after the emperor detected, so he thought, a plot to usurp his throne, he replaced his chief military commission at Peking with *five* chief military commissions, of equal rank, each looking after a designated group of regional military commissions. Thus, the completed system was as shown in Fig. 3.4.1.

The civil organization, still not a single, hierarchical, monocratic organization, comprised four clusters: the ceremonial branch, the educational branch, the main-line civil administration proper, and a group of 'service' agencies.

The *educational cluster* was concerned with the state-supported schools throughout the empire, while at the capital it included the Imperial University and the Han-lin Academy. The former admitted pupils from the state schools, and gave them final training either for the civil service entrance examination or for direct entry into the service. The Han-lin Academy we have met before. It was staffed by the best of all the scholars of the civil service and its members were available, by secondment, for all manner of assignments.

The *ceremonial agencies*, subordinate to the main civil administration, were the survivors from the 'Nine Ministries' of the Han and the 'Nine Courts' of the T'ang.[12]

The *main administration* was headed, at the outset, by a unitary Secretariat which controlled the by now traditional Six Ministries, and headed by a member who fulfilled the role of prime minister. The then-prime minister

---

[11] It is worth noting that this divorced the maritime and trading centres of the empire from the far North which was preoccupied with guarding the northern border.

[12] See Bk. II, Ch. 6, pp. 506–7 and Bk. III, Ch. 3, p. 746 above.

was allegedly the prime mover in the plot to dethrone the emperor in 1380. Not only were he and his supposed collaborators executed in an immense and bloody purge, but the emperor abolished the office itself and laid down the house-rule that anyone proposing its re-establishment must be executed. Nobody dared, and so from 1380 the top position in the administration was nominally the emperor himself working to the Six Ministries. In a short time he found the services of Han-lin scholars necessary to cope with the huge volume of paperwork and by the middle of the fifteenth century the informal body of Han-lin secretaries became, in practice, the Grand Secretariat, similar in function to the old Secretariat and capable, like it, of throwing up powerful personalities who functioned, effectively, as 'prime minister'. By the 1450s, the central administration was controlled by the Grand Secretariat. Below this lay the six Executive Ministries: Personnel, Revenue, Rites, Justice, War, Works.

This central apparatus worked to the thirteen provincial administrations, and to the *chou* and *hsien*. But at the most senior level authority was trifurcated between the Regional Military Commission, the Provincial Surveillance Commission of the Censorate, and the Provincial Administration Office. The resulting confusion necessitated 'Grand Co-ordinators' (latterly governors) plus 'Supreme Commanders' whose authority encompassed two or more provinces.

Below the provincial level the pattern was the traditional one of prefectures and counties (*hsien*), with this modification that there were now new authorities, more important than the counties but still subordinate (like them) to the prefectures. The prefectures were now called *fu*; the counties were still the *hsien*; those new subordinate authorities were called *chou*, and they themselves held authority over a number of *hsien*.

All three branches of the administration—the educational, the military, and the general administration branch—were subject to the surveillance and inspection of the fourth branch, the *censorial* one—again following the now traditional pattern. Relating to the civil service as a whole it was small—some 400—for a corps of 15,000 mandarin-level officials.[13]

The censorial officers operated at both central and local level. The Censorate proper resided in the capital. It was now called the *tu-ch'a yüan*, the Chief Surveillance Office. It was headed by a chief censor, two vice-censors-in-chief, and four assistant censors-in-chief, aided by 110 investigating censors. While on routine duty in the capital, they spent their years going over all judicial records from the Provincial Surveillance offices and inspecting and auditing the records of every central administrative agency.

[13] Hucker, *Censorial System*, 66.

But investigating censors also went on special missions as regional inspectors. The tenure was one year, and during this period each visited every government area within a particular province. They had a complete run of every record, and carried out a review of every aspect of the administration. Since they could also impeach on the basis of individuals' memorials sent directly to the throne, they possessed enormous power and prestige and were so greatly feared that the local officials consulted them in advance on all big issues. In addition to the all-purpose regional inspector, other investigating censors visited provinces as 'troop-purifying' inspectors and 'record-checkers': the first reviewing the state of the military organization and the second checking all files.

Whereas censors corrected maladministration after the event, the Offices of Scrutiny prevented it. In six separate offices monitoring each of the Six Ministries, a chief secretary, two vice-secretaries, and four to eight secretaries exercised editorial and substantive control over all the documents flowing in and out of their relevant ministry. This was the power of *feng-po*, veto power over a document: for if they objected to phrasing or, more significantly, to substance, they were empowered to return it for reconsideration. These officials were so important that they attended imperial audiences and could submit remonstrances to the throne.

Meanwhile each province possessed its own Surveillance Offices, autonomous of but working in close conjunction with the Chief Surveillance Office at the capital. They were known collectively as the 'Outer Censorate'. Headed by a vice-commissioner, each office was made up of so many assistant commissioners, each in charge of a prescribed geographical—or functional—jurisdiction, called a circuit (or *tao*).

The censorial establishment, therefore, was keyed in at both central and local level with the organization of the educational, military, and general administrative branches and their specialized agencies. The organization was much more complex and differentiated than at its origin under the T'ang, and in theory no act of delinquency by vice of form or error of substance, or of omission or commission should have escaped its attention. But although no such thoroughgoing and elaborate control organization existed anywhere else before or at that time, we shall be demonstrating how and why most Ming administrative practice was poor, to put it at its mildest.

4. THE CHINESE CONSTITUTION

In the Ming period the censors are said to be 'the custodians of *Feng* and *Hsien*'. *Feng* means customs and usages. *Hsien* means fundamental laws or polity. The censors are therefore spoken of as 'the custodians of the customs and fundamental laws'. In just such a way the Paris *Parlement* of the *ancien régime* and the English common lawyers under the early Stuarts claimed to be the watchdogs of the fundamental laws and liberties of the country. A long train of precedent, custom, and convention had crystallized into a self-conscious tradition of how government should be conducted. This tradition was held to bind even the autocrat himself. Absolutism—as against despotism—implies *limits*.

Neither Louis XIV nor Charles I of England saw it that way. The latter was defeated by the opposition, Louis XIV was victorious over them, but Ming China witnessed no such final decision. The custodians of the constitution in China were, as always, the Confucianist literati. All mandarins were literati. Imbricated with the state and with landowner families, these men were the 'scholar officials', an aristocracy of the brush. The problem was that emperors often refused to govern with them, but could not govern without them.

This, it may be said, is twice-told—for Han times and for the T'ang. But under the Ming it is told with a difference and that difference is due to the perfection, since the Sung, of a dedicatedly neo-Confucianist civil service and the associated creation of a far wider neo-Confucianist literati class. The most ideological among the scholar-officials claimed that the emperor was constitutionally bound never to act except on advice. As Confucianist scholars, whose doctorate attested their possession of the transcendent and absolute truths, that advice could constitutionally and morally come only from them; and as these truths were as binding on the emperor as on themselves, they were the partners, not the servants of the emperor in a joint enterprise of 'bringing peace to the empire'. They claimed a role which popes and prelates claimed over kings and emperors in the West: the right to limit options in accordance with their religiously held opinions. Or one might alternatively suggest that their self-perceived role approximated to that of the lay nobility in medieval Western courts, in that they felt they were the 'natural' counsellors of the monarch. But the former analogy is the more exact, because they were not primarily moved by considerations of practicality or utility but, rather, by morality. Just as the medieval Catholic Church in Europe judged 'usury' not on practical grounds but on moral ones, so these Confucian scholar-officials fought activities they disliked by turning them into questions of morality—Confucian morality, of course.

From Han times there had always been some Confucian scholar-officials who expressed similar views but their present numbers, sophistication, and authority stemmed from the policies of the Sung dynasty. The Sung emperors were Confucianists who truly believed in learning and accordingly made the open competitive examination the main mode of entrance to the civil service.[14] The examinations were systematized on a state-wide basis in three successive competitions—at prefectural, provincial, and metropolitan (and, possibly, palace) levels. Candidates could opt to take examination in a range of subjects, but the *chin-shih*—the literary doctorate—soon out-topped all others in prestige. The competition was ferociously selective: less than one in ten succeeded at the prefectural level, and less than one in ten at the further, provincial level. The success at metropolitan level was therefore much less than 1 per cent of the total original candidates.[15] Their number, greater at this time than ever subsequently, averaged 239 per annum in the twelfth century.[16]

In Ming times this system had become more elaborate still. For one thing, preliminary qualifying tests had to be passed even to sit each level of the examination. The first stage was examination at prefectural level. The candidates at prefectural examinations came from the local schools or from the National University, but increasing numbers were private indi-viduals. Those who passed were called *hsiu-ts'ai*, Bachelors, and qualified for the provincial examination. The successful candidates were styled Licentiates (*chü-jen*) and could go on to the metropolitan examination, and if they passed, entered the palace examination. Those who passed were called Doctors—*chin-shih*—and were certain of civil service careers. The Licentiates were sometimes assigned low-rank offices and sometimes they entered the National University for further study and became eligible for appointment after concluding them. But by the middle Ming virtually every civil servant of high rank was a *chin-shih*:[17] some ninety men fell into this category each year (the examinations, however, were held only every three years).[18]

Success in the examinations was quite enormously prestigious. In fact the only analogy that comes to mind is the way an ancient Greek city fêted a son returning victorious in the Games. (The contrast is equally instructive; the Chinese intelligentsia loathed physical games and prowess!) Even for the qualifying prefectural examination, heralds ran to the successful candidate's house shouting 'Congratulations' and fixing to his door a great red poster inscribed:

---

[14] But see E. A. Kracke, *The Civil Service in Early Sung China, 960–1067* (Harvard UP, Cambridge, Mass., 1953), 75 for an estimate that perhaps one-half still came in as children of civil servants by their *yin* (nomination) privilege.   [15] Ibid. 65–7.

[16] Ibid. 59.

[17] Cf. the T'ang when only 10 per cent were *chin-shih* (see Bk. III, Ch. 3, pp. 763–4 above).

[18] C. O. Hucker, 'Government and Organisation of the Ming Dynasty', *Harvard Journal of Asiatic Studies*, 21 (1958), 14.

VICTORY ANNOUNCEMENT
This school gives notice—May he come in
first for three Degrees in a Row.[19]

Moreover, although the *hsiu-ts'ai* (Bachelor) status did not qualify the candidate for anything except permission to sit the provincial examination, it instantaneously put him into the superior class, completely apart from and above the common people. As a *sheng-yüan*, a 'graduate', he was immediately received on terms of ritual equality by the local magistracy as well as all other *sheng-yüan*. In brief, he was a member of the literati. See, for instance, Wu Ching-tzu's *The Scholars*—a satirical novel of the early Ch'ing dynasty—for a description of how the poverty-stricken Fan-Chin, who has just passed, is instantly visited by the wealthy ex-magistrate Chang Ch'in-chai.[20] Huge numbers aspired to this status, some thirty failures for every success.[21] When all levels of examinations are taken into account, the system involved 1 million aspirants for official positions: 'virtually all the empire's literary talent.'[22] The successful, irrespective of whether they came from wealthy families or became wealthy by being a *sheng-yüan*, formed the so-called 'gentry-class' and they became what passed for 'the public' in the 'public opinion' of the Ming Empire. Their level of information about public affairs was very high, perhaps higher than among the élite of any contemporary state;[23] and it was to them that their peers in the civil service could appeal when they fell out with the emperor or among themselves.

To our world, which ascribes status and commits political power to the wealthy, the soldiers, the businessmen, the hereditary aristocracy, there is something magnificent in a system where rank and political power went exclusively to those clever enough to earn an academic degree; it is also somewhat absurd. This is not just because the system excluded all skills other than the literary ones and all qualities other than a certain type of cleverness, which are the usual criticisms. Even more, it is because of the values embodied in the texts they had to memorize. Many successful candidates did, no doubt, pay mere lip-service to these values, but a sufficient number to set the tone for the civil service and the wider literary constituency in the localities internalized them: and these operated against orderly and effective government.

Confucianism believed in good men, not in laws; in personal ties of

---

[19] That is, the provincial, metropolitan, and palace examinations.

[20] C.-T. Wu, *The Scholars* (Foreign Languages Press, Beijing, 1973), 38–9.

[21] F. Wakeman and C. Grant (eds.), *Conflict and Control in Late Imperial China: Essays* (University of California Press, Berkeley, 1978), 3.

[22] R. Huang, *1587: A Year of No Significance* (Yale UP, New Haven, Conn. 1981), 55.

[23] Hucker, *Censorial System*, 67.

loyalty and reciprocity, not in abstract, universalistic rules and regulations. The family was more important than the state, the person more important than the rule. For one thing, this turned a good deal of high decision-making into an exercise in man-management. For instance, instead of invoking hierarchy, laws, and regulations, a Grand Secretary would quietly and patiently shift this official here, another one there, square a third and reward a fourth, until he had enough of them in line to secure support for his policy. For another, it served to fractionalize the civil service into dozens of cliques. Officials who had passed the same *chin-shih* examination—the 'class of 1580', for instance—considered themselves lifelong brothers who owed loyalty to one another. They felt allegiance, likewise, to the officials who had examined them. They backed their own minister against the officials of another one. Officials from one region likewise formed cliques against those of another. Not merely were these private loyalties not considered improper—as they certainly would be in any modern Western bureaucracy—but not to adhere to them was regarded as vaguely unfilial![24]

Again, though a large number of the bureaucracy doubtless came in for material rewards, the more ideological Confucianists disregarded office. To them office was, as the Classics taught, a duty thrust on them in their quality as scholars, a work of supererogation. The Confucian persuasion, now so dominant and all-pervasive that its infallibility was taken for granted, resembled ancient Judaism, Christianity, and Islam in this, that it articulated standards to which the ruler must conform. But whereas the Jewish prophets, the Christian Church, and Islam had come into existence outside the state form (indeed, *against* the state), and claimed a supernatural sanction, the Confucian establishment had been called into being by the state itself, and its doctrines were man-made things. In the former cases, the entire people were congregants and witnesses to the verities; if the ruler breached them it was they who formed the opposition, and as the people were thus sucked into politics rulers found themselves having to cultivate popular opinion. Whereas in China the *sheng-yüan* played that role. One million Chinese men had entered the examination contests—though not more than between 30,000 and 60,000 passed at the lowest, prefectural, level under the Ming,[25] and of these only some 15,000–20,000 were mandarins, that is, grades 1–9 in the civil service. Whether the figure be taken at the million mark or the 15,000–20,000 mark, either was a tiny fraction of the 100–130 million population of the empire. It was this stratum alone and not the people at large that was trying to enforce its quasi-theological certain-

[24] Hucker, *Censorial System*, 161.   [25] Wakeman and Grant (eds.), *Conflict and Control*, 3, n. 5.

ties. When the people rebelled it was not in support of the *sheng-yüan*. It was against them.

Thus the Chinese constitution was a contested concept capable of setting the emperor against the civil service. The mutual tension generated irregular and informal procedures in the transaction of government business, which in turn generated still more tension.

What, according to the 'custodians of *Feng* and *Hsien*', was this constitution? It all centred on the emperor, the Son of Heaven, what he must and what he must not do. The emperor must carry out all the necessary rituals and these were numerous indeed. He must make annual sacrifice to Heaven and to Earth, plough the first furrow, celebrate New Year's Day; he must sacrifice in the imperial tombs and the clan temple, observe the birthdays and the death-dates of all preceding emperors and empresses; he must report all important events to his ancestors in the temple of the clan, proclaim the annual calendar, grant princely rank, authorize the weddings of members of the imperial clan, receive foreign ambassadors, bid farewell to departing officials, review the troops, and dispose of prisoners of war. He must hold daily audiences with the entire court, one that had to be completed before dawn, another at noon, another in the evening. The morning audience was sacrosanct; never postponed for bad weather; stiffly formalist, a terrible burden to the emperor, who had to sit quite motionless while listening to reports and giving (well-prepared) instructions.[26]

The Confucians did not expect the emperor to leave the palace compound, that walled complex we call the Forbidden City, not even to make an excursion into the walled Imperial City which, with its parks and gardens and the government pavilions, surrounded it. He was required to stay at the palace, where he lived as the only male, among women and eunuchs, so as to be able to perform the rituals that balanced the *Yin* and the *Yang* and brought earth into harmony with Heaven, and in order, too, that he could authorize actions proposed by his officials. Under the constitution the emperor was Authority: only he could validate decrees, but he was a neutral. He must never be personally involved in a decision; he must be strictly impartial. He was never expected to initiate policy. His role was to make choices between the alternative draft-rescripts presented to him by the officials, but not to write his own. He could dismiss officials, but not appoint his own. He ought not to lead his army.[27] Some decisions were so important that the dynasty's own regulations had laid down that they must be made in a court conference. This brought together the heads of the Six Ministries, the Censorate, the Transmission

[26] Huang, 1587, 4–7.   [27] Ibid. 93–4.

Office,[28] the Grand Court of Revisions, and the Offices of Scrutiny.[29] Each participant seems to have had an equal voice and voted by submitting a formal written opinion. A unanimous decision was by convention held to be binding on the emperor.[30]

The emperor's decisions were issued as edicts. Ideally, they emerged from a complex procedure. A simplified flow-chart (Fig. 3.4.2) conveys its nature. Most initiatives emerged from memorials and reports from the lesser offices to the Six Ministries. They went to the Transmission Office, effectively the central registry of the entire administration. Some, uncommonly marked *Secret and Urgent*, went straight to the emperor. The great bulk were sorted either into the routine reports which went straight to the appropriate ministry or into those addressed to the throne. The latter passed to the appropriate Office of Scrutiny and thence to the Grand Secretariat.[31] This body drafted a set of alternative rescripts which were sent to the emperor for his decision. It could be that the decision was for further consultations. However if the emperor decided there and then, he minuted it in vermilion ink and it went back to the Office of Scrutiny. If the officials there approved it, they would send one copy for action to the appropriate ministry and another, for the record, to the Transmission Office. However, the Office of Scrutiny was not bound to approve. If it objected, it duly noted the draft rescript and sent it back to the palace.[32]

Such, then, broadly speaking, was the constitution as the officials saw it. The actual practice of policy-making was for the most part very different. The emperors declined the role the officials assigned them. The Ming emperors fell into two broad categories. Some carried out smash-and-grab raids on the constitution and the others went on strike against it: the former at the beginning of the dynasty, the latter from 1450 to 1627, by which time it was too late for the last emperor (the Ch'ung-ch'en Emperor, 1627–44) to retrieve the critical situation into which the empire had fallen.

It was the dynasty's founder, Hung-wu, and his eldest son, the Yung-lo Emperor, who breached the Confucianist constitution from the very beginning and set the guide-lines for the rest of the dynasty. Hung-wu was a violent and totally ruthless man who had seized the throne by the sword and had, from direct observation during his poverty-stricken and

[28] See below and pp. 827–8.

[29] J.-P. Lo, 'Policy Formulation and Decision-Making', in Hucker, *Chinese Government*, 49.

[30] Hucker, *Censorial System*, 41–2.   [31] See p. 825 ff. below.

[32] Hucker, *Censorial System*, 100–2. For a more complete account of the procedures, however, see U. H.-R. Mammitzsch, 'Wei Chung-Hsien (1568–1628): A Reappraisal of the Eunuch and Factional Strife at the Late Ming Court' (unpublished Ph.D. thesis, University of Hawaii, 1968), 43–51.

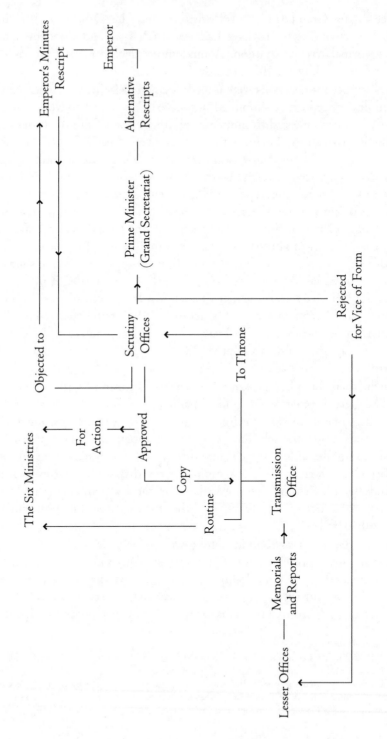

FIG. 3.4.2. *The decision-making routine: Ming Dynasty*

rootless youth, conceived a mistrust, indeed a hatred, for the scholar-official class.[33] He knew he had to employ them but he intended to be their absolute master. It was he who not only had offending officials flogged publicly in open court but, to make the humiliation even worse, at the hands of eunuchs, and such beatings were a notorious feature throughout the rest of the dynasty. His very person at court audiences terrified the officials, and with good reason. In the alleged treason plots of 1380 (the Hu Wei-yung case) and of 1390 (the Lan Yu case) he executed some 45,000 relatives and associates of the accused.[34] His bodyguard unit, the Brocaded Uniform Garrison (*chin-i-wei*) was a secret-police agency, with its own prison and powers of arbitrary arrest, and it, too, continued to function throughout the dynasty. Yet, under the law code which he promulgated, no scholar might decline office on pain of death![35] Indeed, the emperor openly acknowledged that he was acting beyond the law, claiming that the reign of terror was only temporary and that his successors must never depart from his Great Code.[36] His son, the Yung-lo Emperor (1402–24), was another violent character who usurped the throne from his nephew in a four-year military campaign. The youthful Ch'ien-wen Emperor whom he dispossessed had been given a thorough Confucian indoctrination so that in the civil wars the scholar-officials stood by him. In contrast, the court eunuchs, whom the former had begun to persecute, fled to the rebel prince. Thus any sympathy the new Yung-lo Emperor might have had for the scholar-officials was quite dissipated and his trust in eunuch officials correspondingly strengthened.

These two emperors along with the Hsüan-te Emperor (1425–35), defied the 'constitution' and the institutional changes they introduced were to bedevil the conduct of government business to the end of the dynasty. We have already noted how the first innovation was the founder Hung-wu Emperor's abolition of the 'prime ministership'. Its immediate effect was to swamp him with paperwork (a much-quoted passage relates that he had to decide on 1,660 documents relating to 3,391 separate matters written in a single ten-day period).[37] This led to the use of Han-lin scholars, who from 1420 onwards, as 'Grand Secretaries', began to play the dominant role in the administration. Their number ranged from three to six. They were housed in pavilions in the south-east corner of the imperial palace compound and from the 1480s they were formally entitled the *nei-k'o*. This means, simply, the *Inner Chamber*, but Western Sinologists choose to translate it as *the Grand*

---

[33] His given names were Chu Yuan-chang, his honorific name was T'ai-tsu ('Great Founder'), and his throne name was Hung-wu. Mote paints a vivid picture of his character (see F. W. Mote, 'The Growth of Chinese Despotism', *Oriens Extremus*, Year 8 (1961), 20–6).   [34] Ibid. 28.

[35] Ibid. 36.   [36] Ibid. 34.   [37] Ibid. 28.

Secretariat. From 1424 they were given substantive posts in regular agencies so as to outrank senior departmental officials, and from the 1430s the Grand Secretariat processed the memorials addressed to the emperor and drafted the alternative rescripts for him to decide on, in the way shown in the flow-chart (Fig. 3.4.2).

In this way the Ming emperors, just like their predecessors in the T'ang and in the Han, obtained their own private secretariat, with equally pre-dictable consequences among the scholar-officials of the Outer Court. The fact that the secretaries were not only Confucianist scholars, but the very best of them, meant nothing. To the Outer Court officials they were an unconstitutional and highly unwelcome intrusion between themselves, the emperor's 'natural counsellors', and the emperor's person. Their resentment was rationalized by the Confucianist scholar and philosopher Huang Tsung-hsi (1610–95) in his *A Plan for the Prince* written after the fall of the Ming, in 1662, and his argument was reiterated by Confucianist historians ever afterwards. He argued that the restoration of the office of prime minister was essential because it symbolized that the ruling power did not reside solely in the emperor but had to be shared with others; that a prime-ministership was based on merit, whereas the hereditary principle might well produce an heir-apparent who was an incompetent, and that, since in any case the emperor had to seek help in discharging the burden of office, if this help was not provided by the prime minister it would be provided by irregular means or persons.[38]

Since Outer Court officialdom deemed the Grand Secretariat irregular, it became just that. Its status was always ambiguous. From time to time senior Grand Secretaries dominated the political scene but this was a function of their personalities, not an institutionalized feature of the office. At other times the Grand Secretariat was overshadowed by other court influences— the eunuchs, perhaps, or the emperor himself. Its status was uncertain. As Huang puts it, 'it was not so clear whether [it] was a Liaison Office between the civil service and the throne, a command post over the ministries, merely an advisory agency, or even an arbitrating agency'.[39]

But what was unprecedented under the Ming was not a private secretar-iat, so to speak, but the development of an 'inner secretariat' within it! This body would come to be styled the *wen-shu fang* (the Civil Documentation Bureau), and it consisted of the emperor's *eunuchs*. Its establishment reflects

[38] W. T. de Bary, 'Chinese Despotism and the Confucian Ideal: A Seventeenth-Century View', in J. Fairbank (ed.), *Chinese Thought and Institutions* (University of Chicago Press, Chicago, 1957), 175. Note the 'inarticulate major premises'—only an Outer court official was 'regular', i.e. constitutional, and the ruler must share power with him.   [39] Huang, *1587*, 45.

the emperors' continued distrust of scholar-officials, even in their own Grand Secretariat.

The Ming witnessed the zenith of eunuch influence in the entire history of Chinese imperial government. It grew in three overlapping developments. The first was the institutionalization of the eunuch establishment inside the palace. The founding Hung-wu Emperor kept no more than perhaps 100 eunuchs in his palace, mostly for messenger duty and menial tasks. His son, the Yung-lo Emperor, well-served by eunuchs in his usurpation of power, vastly increased their numbers. They continued to increase until the end of the dynasty, when one source says they numbered 70,000, surely an exaggeration. How could so many people—half the present-day population of Oxford, for instance—have been housed in the Forbidden City? The number was more likely to have been 20,000 or so. They constituted the Directorate of Palace Attendants, the *nei-shih-chien*, whose complexity increased with their numbers. In its final form it contained twelve director-ates, four offices, and eight bureaux, organized like the bureaucracy proper and similarly graded, the senior eunuchs being grade 4, class 2, for instance. The head of this organization, who controlled all personal placements and assignments, was the Chief Director of Ceremonial. This is an office to be noted and remembered. It was to be of key political importance.

The first stage in the development of eunuch influence, then, came as they were institutionalized in this way. Most had mere menial tasks, for the Forbidden City and the outer Imperial City were self-sufficient in supplies and their factories and workshops of all kinds all came within their purview. Additionally, even at the early stages they looked after the emperors' personal treasury, destined to became prodigiously large as the dynasty wore on.

Overlapping this phase, a second stage put the eunuchs in charge of state security alongside the *chin-i-wei*, the secret-service-cum-bodyguard organization of the Brocaded Uniform Garrison.[40] This came about because in 1420 the Yung-lo Emperor discovered that its commander was contemplating a coup[41] (and he was also concerned about plots in the provinces). This exclusively eunuch secret service was located in the palace compound's Eastern Depot. Everyone in the empire was subject to its investigation. Since these eunuchs were given the right to memorialize the emperor directly (and regardless of time of day the memorials had to be delivered immediately), they acted in total secrecy from the Grand Secretariat and the Office of Transmission. (Later in the dynasty a second eunuch spy-centre

---

[40] See pp. 825 above and 848 below.

[41] R. B. Crawford, 'Eunuch Power in the Ming Dynasty' (*T'oung Pao*, 49; 1961–2), 131.

was set up to keep watch, so it would seem, on the existing one. This was the Western Depot (1477; then abolished but re-established in 1506).[42] These two agencies collaborated but also quarrelled for influence, predominance going sometimes to one, sometimes to the other.

The third stage arrived when the Hsüan-te Emperor ignored the founder's instructions and opened a palace school for the eunuchs. From the moment the eunuchs became fully literate their role as simple messengers was discarded and they intervened in the policy process. For a long time now the palace memorials had been routed from the Grand Secretariat to the eunuch Director of Ceremonial, as Keeper of the Imperial Seal,[43] for transmission to the emperor. The huge flow of business this entailed led to the establishment of a special office staffed by ten eunuchs, the wen-shu fang, already mentioned. It registered the inflowing documents, including the rescripts prepared by the Grand Secretariat, and likewise the outflowing imperial comments or instructions. In the last case it was the Director of Ceremonial who minuted the emperor's oral instruction, which he then passed on to the Grand Secretariat to consider.

In theory this wen-shu fang office simply transmitted, inwards and outwards, without change, like the Office of Transmission in the Outer Court. In practice, from about 1435 onwards its eunuch staff interpolated their own ideas into the rescripts which they passed along from the Grand Secretariat. This is a very summary description of what actually took place.[44] They could likewise modify the emperor's oral instructions in the course of transmitting them to the Grand Secretariat. In some cases the emperor would promulgate an edict directly through them without any intermediation by the Grand Secretariat or the ministries at all. It must not be assumed that these processes were done behind the emperor's back or in a haphazard way. It was all most systematic. The inflowing documents came into the

---

[42] R. B. Crawford, 132.   [43] Ibid. 134.

[44] The detail is described by Mammitzsch, 'Wei Chung-Hsien (1568–1628)', ch. 3. According to him (and even the following description is abbreviated), all memorials, etc., after passing the Transmission Office, came to the wen-shu fang, most of which (i.e. except the most important documents which went straight to the Director of Ceremonies) went to the Grand Secretariat. They returned from there—presumably with the usual alternative rescripts attached—and thence went to the chief secretaries of the wen-shu fang (the ping-pi) who had a host of clerks at their disposal. These might make various recommendations. The said documents now returned to the wen-shu fang headquarters staff who passed them up to the Director of Ceremonies. Some of these not requiring the emperor's attention he signed by himself in vermilion ink. They could now be acted on. In respect of those which required the emperor's decision, he convened all the ping-pi. They conferred and, once agreed, were ready to meet the emperor with the documents and the recommendations. The emperor's decisions were then conveyed both to the wen-shu fang and the Grand Secretariat. It will be noted that this left the latter in a very subordinate position.

wen-shu fang throughout the day and had to be processed all through the night so as to be ready for the emperor very early next morning.

These three developments—the elaborate palace organization of the eunuchs, their hold on espionage and the secret service, and their powerful if not predominant involvement in the formulation of imperial policy— made the senior eunuchs extremely influential, and some, over short periods of time, effectively controlled the government—the so-called eunuch dicta- tors.[45] On the other hand, at times, it was a Grand Secretary who controlled the government. The fact is that, at best the *wen-shu fang* was a private secretariat, it was not the bureaucracy, and the eunuchs were a (detested) influence, not a counter-government.

The Grand Secretariat was riven by dissensions; so too (pre-eminently) was the regular bureaucracy and so, also, was the eunuch establishment. Supreme power did not rest with any of these three groupings. It did not even fluctuate between one or the other; there was a set of temporary amalgamations and accommodations between them, with one or other predominating.

But the regular bureaucracy was indispensable. The emperor could have his officials flogged or tortured or executed; he could act on private advice rather than theirs; but he could not rule without them. It was from them that the memorials and reports emanated in the first instance, it was they who regulated his ritual appearances, it was through them that he adminis- tered. Their delays, arguments, and protests were ubiquitous and never- ceasing. The virile and imperious early emperors had their way with them. The turning-point came in 1449, in the notorious T'u-mu incident. The emperor, insistent on leading his army against the Oriats, was ambushed and was taken prisoner. Thenceforward, it seems, emperors (with one notable exception) became passive. They not only retreated into the Inner Palace, they refused—for years at a time—to meet their Grand Secretaries. They simply sent messages by their eunuchs over the thousand yards that separated the Secretariat's Pavilion of Literary Profundity from their private quarters. Emperors held no audiences with their ministers during the periods 1465–88, 1488–1506, 1506–22, 1589–1602 (punctuated by one solitary exception); in short, for an aggregate of seventy years out of 137!

It has been inferred that these emperors neglected the affairs of state. The historians and annalists—all of them Confucianist scholar-officials, of course—not merely imply that they left decisions to their eunuchs, but also that they were ne'er-do-wells who allowed the eunuchs to take decisions for them while they indulged their private pleasures. But Professor Ray Huang,

---

[45] Hucker, 'Government and Organisation', 11, Crawford, *Eunuch Power*, 120–3 for brief biographies.

starting from the known fact that after the imperial capture at Tu-mu in 1449 the bureaucracy had successfully resisted all attempts by emperors to leave the Forbidden City, claimed that the emperors' withdrawal from audiences and their indulgence in private pleasures might be due to sheer boredom.[46]

The martial early emperors had indeed broken out by brutal arrogance. Their successors were stopped by the dedicated passive resistance of the bureaucracy. The paradigm case is that of the young, ardent, and martial Cheng-te Emperor (1505–21). The Confucian historian portrays him as a playboy, pretending to be a soldier. In fact he thrice led his troops in person to engagements at the frontier. But at all points he was met with nothing but massive reprobation from his officials. When he returned in triumph from driving off the Mongols from a threatened frontier post, the scholar-officials of the Han-lin Academy pointedly refused to congratulate him and some of the Scrutiny Office officials actually resigned.[47] When, in 1518, he ordered the Grand Secretaries to issue him the commission to inspect the northern frontier, all of them, humbly kow-towing the while, flatly refused. He flung off regardless for a full nine months, during which time literally hundreds of officials in the capital sent in their remonstrances. The next year, 1519, as he set off on yet another tour, all the censorial and surveillance officials in the capital joined in two joint-petitions to call off the trip. The emperor simply disdained to answer, so they all collected together before the Meridian Gate where they knelt in line requesting a reply, while others from the educational literary branch (which included the Han-lin Academy) circulated a petition requesting him not to go. This time the emperor lost his patience. He had 146 of the demonstrators flogged, with thirty strokes apiece of the split baton; eleven died of the flogging. All the Grand Secretaries tendered their resignations but he refused to accept them.[48] Yet from the death of this emperor in 1521 no other tried to leave the tiny enclave of the Forbidden City. Boredom rather than vice seems a better explanation of their withdrawal.

Alienation also played a part. This is the case that Huang makes for the notorious inactivity of the Wan-li Emperor. He desired to set aside his first son as the crown prince in favour of his third son, by his beloved concubine, but the entire court establishment ceaselessly assailed the proposal. The provincial officials were not slow to come in on this totally Confucianist question of morality, and so too did the Confucianist intelligentsia of the

[46] Huang, 1587, 12. The entire Imperial City which surrounded the Forbidden City covered less than 3 sq. mls.   [47] Ibid. 97.
[48] Ibid. 97–9.

private academies which had mushroomed with the cult of letters. Beaten, the emperor gave way, but nourished a deadly hatred for the establishment. To spite them, he refused to fill official positions as they fell vacant. The remonstrating officials filled his post-bag with their criticisms and complaints, as was their right, and according to the 'constitution' he should have appended a rescript to their remonstrances. Since the latter went through the official transmission routines, they would have received publicity in the *Peking Gazette* (which circulated important rescripts throughout officialdom). To deny them the publicity they eagerly sought, the emperor simply pigeonholed the remonstrances. Likewise with the resignations which officials tendered; to answer them courted publication, so the emperor simply ignored them. Some quit without authorization. To have proceeded would, again, have courted publicity, so the emperor just let them go.

From the mid-fifteenth century the Chinese Empire was not run under the 'constitution', and it was not run against it either. It simply was not run at all. It was, so to speak, put on automatic pilot, on a care-and-maintenance basis, except that these terms, misleadingly, imply some precision and decisiveness. There was none. The imperial regime as such was entirely premissed on active inputs from the emperors, but the emperor went on strike. Likewise the entire imperial administrative system was premissed on a self-correcting mechanism, the Censorate, but censors proved more apt to criticize the immorality of emperors than to correct the bureaucracy for its increasingly manifest shortcomings. Only an emperor—like an American president today—could give unity of direction, while the Chinese bureaucracy—like the American Congress today—sought to deny him the requisite power. But in the absence of imperial direction, the bureaucracy—again like the American Congress today—was incapable of providing this by itself. It was too self-cancelling and too divided into cliques, factions, and personal rivalries. It could generate no coherent policy. All this came out with terrible force in the years of the Tung-lin movement in the Tien-chi reign (1620–7). The ins-and-outs of this fearsome story are far too intricate to be recounted here.[49] Suffice it to say that from 1620 (on the death of the 'striking' Wan-li Emperor), a group of what are best described as ultra-puritanical Confucianist scholars and ex-officials, loosely linked via the private Tung-lin literary academy, infiltrated the central bureaucracy with a view to taking it over and imposing their programme of reforms. Their chief target was the young emperor's favourite, the illiterate, clever,

[49] They are brilliantly analysed in C. O. Hucker, 'The Tung-lin Movement of the Late Ming Period', in J. K. Fairbank (ed.), *Chinese Thought and Institutions* (University of Chicago Press, Chicago, 1957). But for a different interpretation focusing on the role of the eunuch Wei, see Mammitzsch, 'Wei Chung-Hsien (1568–1628)'.

and ruthless eunuch Wei Chung-hsien. Overreaching themselves in 1624, just as they seemed successful, they provoked a counter-attack from Wei who, until the emperor died in 1627, launched one of the most notorious reigns of terror China has ever known, several of the Tung-lin 'partisans' (to be styled the Tung-lin martyrs) perishing after slow, repeated, and horrible tortures.[50] The point here, however, is the incoherence of both the Tung-lin partisans *and* their court opponents. The former only managed to effect their entrance through the friendly services of a eunuch faction opposed to Wei, and this eunuch was as much manipulated by regular court officials as he was their master.[51] Both sides split into factions and in the general mêlée the entire court was totally paralysed.

In short, if left to itself the civil service was quite incapable of providing that which it refused to allow the emperor to provide for it—clear central direction.

5. PAPERWORK AND PARALYSIS

The tasks undertaken by government were wide, the regulations that pre-scribed them were highly detailed, the number of senior commissioned officials was probably less than 20,000 (for a population that finally reached 160 million). It took six weeks for a message from Yunnan to reach the capital, and the emperor and the court received all their information by written reports.

A number of these were undoubtedly eyewitnesss reports, almost all of them from officials in the Censorate. The most immediate seem to be those from special investigations into extraordinary events such as floods and other natural disasters or the military conditions in a threatened area. Other reports came from those inspectorates that were specially charged with narrowly specified assignments, such as the patrols on the Peking Canal, the inspectors of the four salt-producing areas, and the provincial education intendants who had to visit schools and examine pupils. But the keystone of the Censorate's inspectorial system was regional visitation. There were twenty-one jurisdictions, to each of which an inspector was assigned every year for a one-year term. In this jurisdiction they were expected to visit every locality,[52] inspect every single branch of official activity, impeach any delinquent, and even to inflict bodily punishment on low-ranking mandarins as well as the lesser functionaries. The full list of their duties, which is extremely wide, parenthetically illustrates the great

[50] Hucker, *Censorial System*, 284–5 for the details.
[51] Mammitzsch, 'Wei Chung-Hsien (1568–1628)'.
[52] Hucker, *Censorial System*, 87.

range of governmental activity. They had to review local criminal cases, inspect local ritual sites, inquire into the care of the orphans, widows, and the old, inventory the local granaries, examine students in the local schools. They had to observe

the levying of corvée task, the condition of irrigation and flood-control installa-tions, the progress of wasteland reclamation, the condition of the postal services remounts and runner stations, the condition of bridges and roads, the adminis-tration of all taxes and the census, the requisitioning of military supplies, the administration of state manufactories, the standardization of units of measurement, the handling of litigations in the magistrates' courts, the requisitioning of local-government office personnel, the existence of notably filial sons and notably chaste wives, the functioning of village self-government institutions, the validity of all official seals and warrants, and the reputation left by the previous years' inspector. He had to make suitable interrogations to see that every official properly under-stood both the general laws and the particular regulations pertaining to his office. He was also required to prepare a detailed map of his jurisdiction and a personal file for every official in it.[53]

No inspector could ever have handled each of these tasks at first-hand. On a rough calculation, assuming a figure of 1,100 *hsien* c.1600, he had fifty-two *yamens* to visit, whose population (out of a national total of 160 million) would have been some 145,500 apiece. The region—or province itself— contained (on the average) a population of 7,600,000—bigger than that of modern-day Hong Kong and twice that of Norway! A highly conscientious inspector might have talked to all the prefects and the sub-prefects, and carried out spot-checks, but most of the information must have come in official returns and documents. Some of the duties clearly imply this: for instance, the checking of judicial records, the compilation of the map, the personnel files, the audit of local government records. The impression is confirmed by the *pro forma* he had to send to the capital. It consisted of sixteen items whose general tenor can be gleaned from the fact that each item starts with the words 'How many?': how many granaries and store-houses have been inventoried, how many orphans and aged persons had been given care, how many offenders had been tried and sentenced, etc., etc.[54] Reliance upon reports and not firsthand inspection must have been still heavier at the provincial level. The average staff for a Provincial Surveillance Office was only thirteen, some of them engaged only on record-checking. In short, little firsthand information reached the court. Most was based on reports from one level, which were based on reports from the lower level,

---

[53] Ibid. 88–9.   [54] Ibid. 89.

which in the last resort were what the local community leaders chose to report.

Since virtually every official act throughout the entire imperial administration had to be and was committed to writing, a further requirement for preventing maladministration imposed itself: checking the records. The Chinese seem to have put the most enormous faith in this device. Each Provincial Surveillance Office contained an established record-checking division. Record-checking came into the purview of the regional inspectors' duties, also. But the chief responsibility for record-checking lay with an agency specially designed for this purpose. This was the group of Scrutiny Offices, six in number, each working to one of the Six Ministries. One of their tasks was to make sure that imperial orders were actually carried out by those ministries. The Scrutiny Office registered the orders, copied them, and sent them to the ministry with a time-limit for compliance. When the ministry signalled this, they cancelled their registry entries. Should the ministry fail to comply, the supervising secretary in the Scrutiny Office lodged an impeachment with the emperor. (This sounds impressive but as time wore on the deadlines had to be extended, while the supervising secretaries for their part grew remiss in impeaching the ministries for failure to comply.)[55]

A similar procedure was used in checking the response to a ministry's instructions to its field agents; every such instruction was registered with a time-limit by the appropriate supervising secretaries. For instance, the tax quotas sent out by the Ministry of Revenue were subsequently compared, in the Scrutiny Offices, with the receipted invoices from the granaries and storehouse receiving the taxes. An ingenious counterfoil system ensured that a Scrutiny Office knew of all the correspondence of the ministry with its field agents.[56] The correspondence of these field agencies, in and out, was checked by the Provincial Surveillance Office, which read over the agencies' files. Each maintained a number of local branches engaged solely in this record-checking. The Provincial Surveillance Offices regularly reported their findings to the Censorate in the capital. Here its own metropolitan circuit checked the Central Ministries' records (already being checked, as noted above, by the six Scrutiny Offices!), and those of all administrative agencies.[57] There was a routine procedure by which files were endorsed according to whether or not, and in what way, a particular transaction had yet been completed.[58]

---

[55] Hucker, *Censorial System*, 103.   [56] For a description, see ibid. 104.
[57] Ibid. 105.   [58] Ibid. 106.

Professor Hucker, who has made the classic examination of the Ming censorial system, makes this comment:

When record-checking activities of such intensity are added to the checks that Supervising secretaries exercised over memorials and rescripts, and when all these types of document-control surveillance are added to the censorial receipt of routine reports and complaints and the direct censorial observation described above, the result becomes a truly formidable surveillance net stretched over the entire governmental apparatus.[59]

One can immediately agree. However, his observation prompts two queries: Why, after all, was such an elaborate system necessary? And was it 'cost-free'?

As to the first question, Professor Hucker himself provides the clue when he concludes his chapter with the remark: 'However deficient the public news media were, there seems to have been no reason for the Ming censorial system to lack information on which to base its efforts to "rectify administration".'[60] It was not, however, just the inadequacy of 'public news media' that conjured up this huge internal critical apparatus. It went far wider. It was the virtually total absence of any opportunities for the common people—the 'administered'—to express complaints or criticisms against perceived maladministration or injustices. In a modern democracy maladministration comes to the attention of ministers by a vast battery of extra-administrative, often extra-constitutional avenues. In cases of alleged illegality the citizen can appeal to the courts. In cases of perceived unfairness he can appeal to an ombudsman, to a parliamentary representative, or to his party. Cases of delay, inattention, stupidity, or abuse are challenged daily in the media, and by political parties and pressure groups. Ministers, sensitive as they must be to these expressions of disesteem, rely on their senior civil servants to keep them out of trouble. They, in turn, expect their juniors to avoid any action or omission that can be complained of. The vast bulk of public activity touching the citizen, such as social security benefits, are challengeable by easy procedures, through administrative tribunals. Consequently, the bureaucracy itself can confine its self-critical functions to a handful of inspectors, a system of financial audits, and possibly the surveillance of its activities by a committee of the elected legislature. The certain publicity attending malfeasance, non-feasance, and delay takes care of the rest. The Chinese censorial system and above all its documentation-checking certainly reflected the desire and intention to deal properly and fairly by the public, but it was necessary solely because the system recognized the people only as subjects—'objects' would be the better word—to be admi-

---

[59] For a description, see ibid. 107.   [60] Ibid.

nistered. Nobody in China—not even the higher mandarins—had *rights*. This was inherent in Confucianism, a system of graduated duties. In practice, China was a two-class society of the rulers and the ruled, a government *of* mandarins *by* mandarins. The intention of the record-checking was simply to try to prevent it becoming a government *for* mandarins, as well. As will be seen, it was not entirely successful.

It is true that there was a highly formalized avenue through which a subject could complain. The complainant would address the *yamen* of his county (*hsien*) and if dissatisfied must go 'through channels' to the prefect and so on up to the regional inspector. (In practice the local officials found easy ways of alleging that the complainant had not gone through the prescribed channels.) It may be imagined how likely it was that a humble smallholder or street-vendor would ever dare pursue his complaint—even at the local *yamen* level—and if he did, how far he would get. In principle, again, if the regional inspector failed him he could send a petition to the Transmission Office at the capital, who would pass it to the Censorate. Failure there left open only an appeal to the emperor. This could be done by a sealed memorial to the throne, but it was made clear that this was admissible only on an issue it was important for the emperor to know about; or, as the very last resort, by dropping the complaint into the famous Palace Drum.[61] If this last were done the censors were obliged to prepare a detailed report for the emperor, and this channel was in fact used—mostly, it seems, in cases of death sentences. In a dramatic case of 1426 it resulted in a reprieve for nine soldiers wrongly convicted of armed robbery.[62] But the tortuous and bureaucratic procedure 'through channels' and the dramatic last instance appeal via the Drum are reminders of how limited and circumscribed were the opportunities to publicize or to litigate against maladministration and, therefore, why the elaborate record-checking had to be instituted instead.

No doubt it resulted in greater regularity and probity than if it had not been instituted, though there is no way of measuring this. It did, however, generate administrative 'costs'. To begin with, it led to an enormous multiplication of paperwork. One report says that the censors in the capital investigated no less than 64,812 transactions over a four-year period, and found 19,742 violations for which 5,116 different persons were, in part, responsible.[63] Two things are noteworthy here. First, the number of files

---

[61] i.e. a bronze urn, first established under T'ang empress Wu in 686, with four openings for messages, as follows: 1) self-recommendations; 2) criticisms of the government; 3) complaints of injustice; 4) omens, prophecies, and secret plots. *Cambridge History of China*, vol. 3, ed. J. K. Fairbank and D. Twitchett (CUP, Cambridge, 1979), 297–8.   [62] Hucker, *Censorial System*, 100.

[63] Ibid. 107.

checked averaged forty-four a day, every day, for all of the four years. The second is the high proportion of violations—no less than 30 per cent! This figure may be interpreted to show both the effectiveness and the need for the record-checking. By the same token it suggests that the administrators were thoroughly slipshod. This conclusion is borne out, as will be seen, by other independent sources.

The second administrative cost was caution at all levels. It is well known that in systems which attach great penalties to breaches of the regulations officials take pains to adhere to them very literally; hence, at any cost to refrain from initiatives that might cause them trouble. Stability and a desire 'not to make waves' became the chief motivation of the official classes. However, if rules cannot be defied they may be evaded, particularly if there is a financial inducement to do so, and the mandarinate had every such inducement. By any standard of reckoning they were grossly underpaid in the Ming (and Ch'ing) period, and most had run up considerable debts in the lengthy course of preparing for and taking the examinations. Wherever rules were over-complicated or ambiguous—like the rule relating to local 'fees'—they resorted to extra-administrative short-cuts. The line between these and corruption was often difficult to draw (the prevalence of corruption or *blat* in the tightly regulated economies of Communist China and hitherto Eastern Europe reflects identical cause-and-effect in our own day). In some cases, too, the detailed regulations were unworkable or, owing to the insufficiency of officials, not enforceable.[64] Further confirmation on the point is unnecessary here, for it will appear even more pronouncedly in what is now to follow.

6. THE GOVERNMENT–NOTABLES ALLIANCE

The government relied on local men to carry out its regulations among the masses. These local agents were the richest and/or most prestigious men in the area. In China, their influence and relative independence from the central government varied over time. Thus, in early T'ang times they were not at first very salient. In the later T'ang, with weaker central control, the abandonment of the land-redistribution system, and the relaxation of detailed rules over tax-collection, the post of village headman—*li-cheng*—began to be filled by men of importance once again.[65] The Sung pressed the better-off into local service, and it is from then that the elaboration and systematization of their control over the rural population is developed. It

[64] Cf. Huang, 1587, 71 for the unsuccessful efforts of Chang Chü-cheng (1572–82) to tighten up the administration.   [65] See above, Bk. III, Ch. 3, pp. 767–8.

was based on two principles: the enforced *collective* responsibility of defined rural populations for, *inter alia*, taxes, duty-labour, and security, and the control of these collectivities by the local notables. The Sung period also saw another related development at the level of local government: the increased technical importance to prefects and sub-prefects of their subordinate civil service staff, whom we may call the *yamen* clerks. In Sung times many of those clerkships became virtually hereditary. They also became increasingly remunerative.

In Ming times these two related developments became highly visible, partly, no doubt, as an artefact of the rich documentary evidence but chiefly because, although the population had more than doubled since Sung times, the number of civil servants had remained the same: about 13,000 'within the current' mandarins and some 100,000 subordinate clerks and the like[66] (leading, parenthetically, to increased rivalry and factionalism among the numerous competitors). At the same time, society was more complex and the tasks of government wider. Because the service was under-manned it had to devolve executive duties on to the notables in the localities. Because it was complicated, the sub-prefects and even prefects had to rely more and more on their clerks. There thus grew up *two* sets of intermediaries between the sub-prefects and the people.

Since prefects and sub-prefects served (normally) for only three years before being posted to another locality and were forbidden to serve in their native spot, they came to places where they might not even understand the local dialect, and which had, in any case, their own customary law and local conventions on tax matters, so that for several months they were entirely dependent on the clerks, who were both permanent and native to the area. From 1424 these clerks were not permitted to take the *chin-shih* examination and were, therefore, regarded as 'low'. But it was they—not the mandarin magistrates—who processed all the business of the *yamen*, they who could speed up or delay, lessen criminal charges or increase them, extort or go easy

---

[66] Although the trend is quite unmistakeable and the disproportion was destined to grow much larger under the Ch'ing, the estimates vary. B. E. McKnight (*Village and Bureaucracy in Southern Sung China* (Chicago UP, Chicago, 1971, 8–9) for the 1160s suggests a population of 50–60 million, a 'within the current' Mandarinate of 12,000, of whom 8,000 were in the capital and 4,000 in some 170 prefectures and over 800 sub-prefectures. The latter, with average populations of 70,000, 'probably' employed 100–150 subordinate civil servants apiece. The total, therefore, was between 80,000 and 120,000. For the Ming, Hucker (*The Traditional Chinese State in the Ming Times* (1368–1644), University of Arizona Press, Tucson, Texas, 1961), estimates a population of over 100 million by the 17th cent. (p. 23); over 15,000 within-the-current civil servants by that time (p. 14); and over 100,000 subordinate civil servants (p. 17). Huang, however (1587), puts the Mandarinate at 20,000, of whom (he says) only 2,000 were in the capital. He counts 1,100 *hsien*, and says there would have been some six civil service officials in each plus a dozen locally recruited clerks (p. 50). He gives no estimate for the lower ranks.

in tax-collection and in duty labour. The popular view—reflected in novels like *The Scholars*—typecast them as shifty and self-serving rogues.

The Ming government openly allied itself with the local notables by conferring on them the (unpaid) responsibility of governing the rural population on its behalf. They did so through the systems of collective bonding called the *pao-chia* and the *li-chia*. The *li-chia* began to fade out in the late sixteenth century when monetization allowed the government to consolidate local taxes-in-kind into a commuted sum payable in silver. It was a crude system of enforcing payments-in-kind and labour services.[67] Notional 'villages' with a given tax quota to fill and called a *li*, were made up of 110 households apiece. The richest *ten* households became 'captains' (*li-chang*). The remaining 100 households were divided into ten *chia*, each of ten households. Each year in rotation one of the ten richer households provided the *li-chang*, the captain of the entire *li*; while, similarly in rotation, each one of the *chia* households became captain of his *chia*, the *chia-shou*.

The *chia* captains, working under the *li* captain, had four duties. Every ten years they were to compile the census of families in the 'Yellow Books'. They had to collect the tax quota for the *li* and were directly responsible for seeing that it was paid in full. Likewise they had to supply the *yamen* with its necessities—paper, ink, oil, and the like—and also the men to serve there as duty clerks, runners, sweepers, and so forth: for the *yamen* was supposed to be self-sufficient. Likewise they had to supply transportation for conveying the tax grain. Finally, they were responsible for maintaining good order, which was held to entail making the tax-allocation equitable.[68] Shortly after the *li-chia* was set up (1381), the arrangement was extended by establishing *chu* or 'divisions' comprising several *li*, and these were put under the command of the most powerful landlords in the capacity of 'tax captain' (1397). His duty was to collect and transfer the tax grain from each *li* in his jurisdiction and get it to the state granary: he also drew up the duty-labour roster. (The posts were originally assigned for a whole lifetime but were so burdensome that in the early sixteenth century they were collectively shared by several persons.)[69]

The *pao-chia*, similarly organized, was responsible for law and order and local policing. Each month the community was assembled to listen to the 'community agreement', a charter of duties based on a model drafted by the founding emperor.[70] There they bound themselves by oath to preserve the

---

[67] See pp. 843–5 below, under taxation.

[68] N. Tsurumi, 'Rural Control in the Ming Dynasty' in L. Grove and C. Daniels (eds.), *State and Society in China: Japanese Perspectives on Ming and Qing Social and Economic History* (Univ. of Tokyo Press, Tokyo, 1984), 258–61.   [69] Ibid. 261–2.

[70] Cf. similar practices in the Ching, and in Tokugawa Japan, Bk. IV, Chs. 1 and 2.

good customs of the *li* and to uphold the law; to deal with lawlessness themselves; to care for the poor; to assist communally with the expenses of weddings; to maintain a community altar and a community school. But above all each community as a whole (the *pao*) was held responsible for the conduct of all its members. As reformed at the end of the dynasty, the *pao* consisted of 1,000 households divided into tens, so that ten *p'ai* made the *chia* and ten *chia* made a *pao*. Each *chia* had its head, the *chia-chang*, and the *pao* itself was headed by a *pao-chang*, the *pao* captain. Every household hung lists of its members on its door. Individuals were obliged to watch out for crimes and report them to the captain, who reported to the magistrates. Failure to do so brought collective punishment.[71]

The *li-chia* and the *pao-chia* under the Ming represent something like ideal types, because the government experimented with variants of these systems and there must have been considerable overlap, the same people often wearing different hats. The consistent note in all of them is that landowners commanded non-landowning individuals and the wealthy the poor.

Who were these people? Any answer is bound up with the controversial term 'the gentry'. This authentically native English term should never have been used, and each Sinologist uses it in a somewhat different way. The problem turns on the relationship between landlordism-wealth, and literate status.[72] In practice, even in Ming times, the category of large-scale landlord and the graduate class largely coincided and, as Hucker has put it, 'so many opportunities for the acquisition of wealth came with degree-holding status that *literati* possibly begat landlords to a greater extent than landlords begat *literati*'.[73] However this may be, it was a category of these landlord-literati who were the local notables. They co-operated and intermarried and shared a consciousness of kind throughout the entire country. They were unquestionably a status group who thought of themselves as a charmed circle.[74] Their values were conservative, in favour of the social *status quo*, and in the great peasant rebellion at the end of the dynasty they stood by the throne, unlike many of their forbears during the T'ang rebellions.[75] The government did not interfere in the *status quo* in the villages, and the 'gentry' were both its agents in perpetuating this— and the beneficiaries of so doing.

---

[71] I. C. Y. Hsu, *Rise of Modern China*, 3rd edn (OUP, Oxford, 1983), 58–9. Cf. also Wakeman and Grant (eds.), *Conflict and Control*, 5, 7.   [72] Cf. Elvin, *Pattern of the Chinese Past*.

[73] Hucker, *Traditional Chinese State*, 36.

[74] See C. T. Wu, *The Scholars*, (Foreign Languages Press, Beijing 1973).

[75] See Bk. III, Ch. 3, pp. 767–8 and 800 above.

7. MALADMINISTRATION

The barbarous Hung-wu Emperor ordered that the skins of executed officials must be stuffed with straw and hung up outside the *yamen*. That was his way of suppressing corruption. His equally ferocious son, the Yung-lo Emperor, also terrified his officials. It was said that never had government been so uncorrupt as in his reign. But in the 1570s, nearly 200 years later, Chang Chü-cheng, in decreeing that local officials must clear their tax arrears and arrest all their bandits under pain of nothing more unpleasant than forfeiting promotion and transfer, 'made an enemy of the entire Empire'.[76] Chang was pulled down and his noxious decrees repealed. There, in short order, is the sordid history of Ming administrative practice. The first four emperors, war-lords and activists, stamped an institutional pattern on the empire. Their successors just let it run. The only significant changes away from the initial institutions were the introduction in *c*.1550–80 of the so-called Single Whip system of taxation, and the change-over, at about the same time, from a hereditary conscript soldier class to mercenaries. Both were reactions to the obvious deliquescence of the older arrangements and neither succeeded in its purpose. There was no thrust behind the government. The mandarins would not permit the emperor to exercise it and they themselves neither could nor would. Their aim was a quiet life. Stability, domestic tranquillity, was their ideal state. Of course, there were at all times some men among them with vision, one or two of great energy and others, like the Tung-lin 'partisans', who pursued their puritan ideals undeterred by torture and the threat of execution. The fact remains that, over a quite limited span of time, all these energizers were swamped—one might more justly say devoured—by their own fellow officials. The Mandarinate became like Peer Gynt's Boyg: '"*Roundabout*", said the Boyg.'

There were three reasons for the corruption, the maladministration, and ultimately the deliquescence of Ming administration—institutional, partly institutional, and personal. Starting with the last, mandarins were grossly *underpaid*. Gone were the lush years of T'ang and particularly Sung when they received princely salaries.[77] The founding emperor, as an ex-mendicant monk, believed in extraordinary frugality. The palace eunuch received no more than board and lodging. The very top mandarin salary, fixed in 1392 and unchanged in the entire course of the dynasty at 144 taels of silver, fell below what was required for a respectable standard of living in the late Ming.[78] The *average* pay for a civil official was a bare 10 taels, only five times

---

[76] Huang, *1587*, 71.   [77] Maspero and Balazs, *Histoire et institutions*.

[78] R. Huang, *Taxation and Governmental Finance in XVI-Century Ming China* (CUP, London, 1974), 276.

the pay of a mere private in the army.[79] True, these payments were supplemented by a grain allowance, but this rarely exceeded 133 lbs per month.[80] Few individuals came into the Mandarinate with private fortunes. Rather the reverse: most came in with huge debts, for the course of the examination was long as well as arduous, and it was usually necessary to make several tries at an examination before succeeding. Officials made ends meet and tried to meet the debt by accepting extra payments which were outside the law. Senior mandarins in Peking, for instance, received 'gifts' from their provincial subordinate officials.[81] They commuted the services of their personal attendants (provided free by the government) by letting them go home for the price of 12 taels silver per man, a practice that soon became general.[82] The magistrates in the provinces were in a grave plight because Hung-wu's notion of rustic simplicity led him to finance the expenses of the *yamen* by a system of payments in kind and labour service that might leave it—as in one notorious case at least—with no more than 100–200 taels a year to meet office expenses.[83] Prefects and sub-prefects made up their pittances by charging all manner of supplementary fees: 'meltage charges', where tax was paid in silver, transit taxes on salt shipments, fees for appointing a man as *li*-captain (in the *li-chia* system already described), and so forth.[84] The legal tax-rates consequently became purely nominal and varied from locality to locality.

Although censors still picked up individual cases of gross corruption, more and more illegalities of the kind mentioned came to be taken for granted. Not to have done so would have rocked the entire civil service, and the civil service was the government. But once such practices were connived at, where did equity stop and corruption begin? What was the 'fair' rate of extra-legal payments for the *hsien* magistrate, unable to raise his family on his statutory 27.5 taels of silver? If 300, why not 600? Or 3,000? So, in short order, and once free of the founding emperors' reigns of terror, corruption became endemic. One may go further: it was *functional* to the system. If the system worked poorly, without corruption it could not have worked at all.

Maladministration transcended purely personal greed, though to be sure there was plenty of that. It was inherent in the system. This is most obvious in the cases of the two greatest agencies, the fiscal service and the armed forces. Their administrative arrangements were laid down by the Hung-wu Emperor. Though seriously flawed they were persisted in with little but

---

[79] R. Huang, *Taxation and Governmental Finance in XVI-Century Ming China*, 275.
[80] Ibid. 276.   [81] Huang, *1587*, 3.   [82] Ibid. 48–9.
[83] Huang, *Taxation and Governmental Finance*, 185.   [84] Ibid.

incremental modification for well over 200 years, during which time the Ming population had soared and its complexity had also vastly increased.

7.1. *Taxation*

The Hung-wu Emperor translated his crude miserliness into his fiscal system. His basic conception was that all services should pay for themselves by unpaid duty service. Thus the villages should provide the fiscal administration and support the prefects and sub-prefects on a self-sufficient basis: the army, hereditary in some 2 million 'military families', should support itself on farming colonies. Most officials should receive no more than a bare household ration, and some—the palace eunuchs—simply bed and board. This wholesale use of unpaid service enabled the Hung-wu Emperor to lower taxes to one-fifth of the Sung level.[85] The amount of tax per annum was *fixed* at some 27.5 million piculs (=133 lbs) of unhusked grain or its equivalent a year, plus the proceeds of the salt monopoly (one-tenth of that figure) and custom duties. These fixed arrangements remained a strait-jacket until the mid-sixteenth century, after which some piecemeal alterations were made.

The chief source of revenue was the land tax (*hu*). Simplistically, the emperor fixed a standard tax per *mou*. He carried out a thoroughgoing census in the Yellow Books, in 1381. Then he allocated tax quotas for each province. This tax was therefore regressive—a flat rate per *mou*. In respect to labour services, however, households were classified into nine grades and the duties allocated accordingly, so that these taxes were progressive. This progressive element in the system disappeared after 1550 when the services were commuted to silver payments and combined with the land tax.[86] The level of taxation was light, as the emperor intended, but too much so. It led directly to the extra-legal and illegal fees and surtaxes merging into plain corruption, as we have just seen.

The village registers—the Yellow Books—were supposed to be revised every ten years. Some were, but most went without any substantial revision for over 200 years, some even longer! And during all this time the tax quotas for the provinces were adjusted only slightly.[87] The sophisticated Ministry of Revenue could have checked these registers by direct observation but, true to form, all they did was to check documents against other documents. They scrupulously checked the figures in the Yellow Books for internal consistency. If these did not add up they sent them back for correction by

---

[85] Ibid. , 24, 25, 38, 46.   [86] Ibid. 182–3.
[87] Ibid. 47.

the village officials. Once they had done their sums right, that ended the matter. In Ch'ing times some of these registers still contained the names of the householders of some 300 years ago![88] For *actual* tax allocation, the local officers compiled their own, realistic 'White Books'.[89] It goes without saying that the anachronistic Yellow Books and tax quotas generated gross injustices. Failure to readjust the provincial tax quotas meant that provinces which had become rich over time were lightly taxed whereas others which had become poor had to pay much more; and here the prefects were obliged to impose illegal exactions.

The uniform, standardized flat tax-rate per *mou* took no account whatsoever of the huge regional disparities and the vast variety of crops, the differential fertility of the soil, and so on throughout the empire. To have made true census returns reflecting these features was quite beyond the empire's technical competence; after all the Yellow Books were compiled by the local rustics![90] Furthermore, though it may seem a simple matter to assess the tax due at a fixed rate on so many 'standard *mou*' of land, it was so complex in practice that pages and pages were required to explain it[91] and, in any case, it varied from one locality to another. This was due to the incremental adjustments to make the revenue meet the tax quota by all manner of surcharges and surtaxes on the basic assessment, each of which had to be calculated separately; also to the complexities of striking appropriate 'rates of exchange' when payment in kind was commuted to payment in silver; and finally, to the ways various components of the revenue had to be attributed to different sectors of the public services.[92]

Those difficulties were intensified by the dynasty's misunderstanding of currency. A string of 1000 cash was the equivalent of 1 tael (roughly, an ounce) of silver. The Ming circulated little but unminted silver.[93] The tax due on a *mou* of land would usually come to two or three copper cash, that is, *thousandths*, of a silver tael. The frequent surcharges on the tax were, of course, mere fractions of it—maybe 5 per cent, maybe 1 per cent—so that these were fractions of fractions! Furthermore each one of these half-dozen surtaxes had to be calculated individually. Such was the terror of committing an arithmetical inexactitude that—unbelievable as this seems—tax-rates were calculated to twelve, even fourteen decimal points, and it took till 1685 (under the Ch'ing) to have this reduced even to five decimal points![94] And each individual calculation had to be duly itemized and logged! The consequence was increasing delays in tax-collection, and it was this Kafkaesque complicatedness of the bureaucratic machinery, not the

[88] Huang, *Taxation and Governmental Finance*, 61–3.   [89] Ibid. 63.   [90] Ibid. 313.
[91] Ibid. 82–140.   [92] Ibid.   [93] Ibid. 91.   [94] Ibid. 89–91.

peasants' inability to pay, which led to the financial crisis at the end of the dynasty which contributed so much to its downfall. In 1632 340 *hsien* (nearly one-third of the total) were in arrears of up to 50 per cent of their tax quotas, and of these 134 (one in eight of the total) had collected nothing at all.[95] (Admittedly there were other reasons for this failure to meet the quotas, the small surplus left to peasants after paying their rents and mortgage, etc. which drove the marginal ones down to near-subsistence level.)[96]

But throughout most of the dynasty taxes were collected in kind, and the Hung-wu Emperor's apparently ingenious solution of the logistical problem entailed by all such systems bedevilled the dynasty to its end, even when silver cash payments had become important. The problem was that the tax grain had to be got from the point of origin to where it was needed, and stored along the route as well as at the destination.[97] Amazingly—and amusingly—Hung-wu's solution was to reinvent the system of ancient Assyria![98] Each tax-point had to arrange to transport its grain, and so on, to where it was to be consumed—to this garrison here, to that customs post there—up to as many as twenty destinations. But meanwhile each such garrison, customs post, and so on, was receiving similar tax payments from perhaps twenty other tax-points. The entire empire was criss-crossed by tiny quantities of tax products moving in and out of the tax-collection centres and into tax-consumption ones. This certainly eliminated the difficulties attending the construction and maintenance of state granaries and warehouses, and the bulk transportation of produce over the waterways, but it caused the most enormous complications in accountancy, added to the already vast pyramids of paperwork, and made a national set of accounts impossible.[99]

It must be emphasized that throughout most of the dynasty taxation was light: the land tax amounted to only 10 per cent of total agricultural output.[100] But the complexities outlined above made the system inelastic and regressive, so that to raise additional revenue was a slow business, and overburdened the marginal smallholders, already forced down to subsistence level by landlord exploitation. The low tax-yield was adequate to the empire over most of its life, when it was not seriously threatened from outside and its military expenses were low. But it imperilled the empire in its last forty years when Manchu pressure—plus the fact that the army was now a paid standing force—required huge cash sums quickly. Ming China's resources

[95] Ibid. 308.   [96] Ibid. 309.
[97] Cf. above, Bk. III, Ch. 3, for the T'ang's Commission for Grain Transportation, p. 774.
[98] Bk. I, Ch. 4, p. 233.   [99] Huang, *Taxation and Governmental Finance*, 14.
[100] Ibid. 38.

were easily adequate to overwhelm its Manchu enemies, but it could not mobilize them fast enough. By attempting to do this, it provoked war on the internal front—peasant and bandit revolts—until, caught between two fires, it succumbed.

7.2. Military

We learned that the Hung-wu Emperor thought he could maintain up to 2 million troops at no expense by designating his demobilized troops, along with others, as hereditary soldiers, settled in agricultural colonies.[101] The idea was that a proportion of the troops worked the land—which was inalienable—to feed the soldiers in the line. The rotation of these troops into and out of farm-work soon ceased and in the end some 70 per cent of the troops were nothing but farmers. Again, despite visitations by the censors, officers grew rich by appropriating colony land or, failing that, the adjacent wastes and commons. Tied to the soil by their hereditary status, many common servicemen deserted, reducing many colonies by the 1550s to as little as 20 or 30 per cent of their paper strength.[102] Basically, this was due to these troops having no fighting to do. The system fell victim to the 'perils of success', just like the Samurai under the Tokugawa.[103]

Officers inherited their positions but had to pass a qualifying examination. Its basic components were archery and horsemanship. There was not the slightest pretension of teaching military science.[104] For this neglect of military affairs the Mandarinate was entirely responsible. Never had military prestige fallen so low.[105] The fastidious Confucianist scholar-officials despised the unlettered officers and, even more, the illiterate, brutish, uncivilized soldiery. They wanted no military adventures on the frontier, and in the interior looked on the troops as ancillaries to the civil arm in maintaining order. Despite the 'troop purification commissions' in the Provincial Surveillance Offices of the Censorate, their interest in efficiency and their competence to recognize it were negligible. The state of the military art and the standards of military equipment attest this. In the 1550s it was found that 'there were no military handbooks or field manuals, no schools that specialized in the martial arts, not even an effective ordnance department'.[106] As to equipment and supply, this had from the start been integrated with the civil administration, on the basis, already described, of the *hsien* distributing their taxes laterally to the consumption

---

[101] This device was common in the agrarian empire. Something like the system is to be found in Hellenistic armies, Roman *limitanei*, and Byzantine themes.   [102] Huang, 1587, 160.

[103] See Bk. IV, Ch. 1.   [104] Huang, 1587, 162.

[105] Cf. its prodigious prestige in contemporary Japan (Bk. IV, Ch. 1).   [106] Huang, 1587, 159.

centres. Since, as noted, a *hsien* might disburse to some twenty consumption centres which were receiving their supplies from some twenty other tax-points, the failure of any single one of these to supply disrupted the whole exercise and could generate a major shortage. Yet no higher logistical command-level existed. Moreover, armaments counted as a category of tax-payments and as such consisted of articles made in the villages. For instance, while the palace workshops in the capital were turning out chain-mail for the Imperial Bodyguard, the villages were supplying local garrisons with surcoats of quilted cotton, some stuffed with iron strips, others with mere waste-paper.[107]

The censors duly noted the decadence and the corruption in military circles but their reports did nothing to change matters. An Imperial Rescript of 1434 shows that abuse and corruption were prevalent even as early as this—only ten years after the passing of the warlike Yung-lo Emperor. The abuses, incidentally, were similar to those endemic in contemporary Europe. 'Where there are campaigns [the officers] send off the poor and sell exemptions to the rich: and when requisitions are levied, they pass along ten-fold demands. Some convert soldiers into their private attendants. Some make them "kick back" their monthly salaries. Some permit them to engage in trade. Some usurp their monthly rations. Some hold back the issuance of winter uniforms.'[108] And, again as in Europe, officers padded the ration-rolls to collect the excess rations for their own use.

Training was neglected. Forces were below battle-strength and matters did not improve when, at the end of the sixteenth century, the military colonies had decayed so far that the government had no alternative but to recruit soldiers for pay. These mercenaries were the veritable scourge of the population and they behaved like their European or Muslim counterparts. They were ever-ready to riot over grievances, particularly over arrears of pay, which became increasing frequent.[109] They received little or no military training, their discipline was poor, and they mutinied at attempts to drill them. Many deserted to become bandits. One censor, reporting on the Ching Ying army that protected the capital, claimed that of the 120,000 men on the rolls, half were no longer there and the remainder were riffraff.[110] They were as much feared by the population as the enemy were, for they requisitioned mercilessly, looted, and kidnapped women. But for all that,

[107] Ibid. 161.   [108] Quoted Hucker, *Censorial System*, 76.
[109] A. Chan, *The Glory and Fall of the Ming Dynasty* (University of Oklahoma Press, 1982), 201.
[110] Chan, *Glory and Fall*, 202.

and above all, they were no use! They were beaten by the Manchus again and again, and they failed to crush the domestic rebellion.

By and large the administration of the empire got by; in modern terms it 'satisficed'. What is clear is that the existence of a censorial department was unable to guarantee administrative efficiency. This was not entirely due to the excessive reliance on checking records rather than facts, as we have suggested. Censors did indeed report on the maladministration in the fiscal services and in the army but, for reasons explained, the most that happened was the disgrace of an offending individual, not the reform of an ineffective institution. The great lesson to be learned from Ming corruption and inefficiency is Napoleon's simple maxim: 'Nothing goes of itself.'

8. THE NATURE OF THE REGIME

Reduced to its bare essentials, the Chinese 'palace state' is an absolute monarch served by his bureaucracy and his army. But whether he commanded the bureaucracy or it commanded him is precisely what Chinese palace politics was about.

One common view[111] is that the Ming dynasty marks the point where the absolute *authority* of the monarch and his exercise of personal power coincided and consequently moved from *absolutism* to *despotism*, where I have defined *absolutism* as *juridically* unfettered authority to make all decisions and *despotism* as its effective exercise. Others, for example, Wolfram Eberhard,[112] regard the Ming as being only partly despotic, reserving this last expression for the Ch'ing. Mote's account is, really, an account only of the Hung-wu Emperor, not his successors. Having acceded by conquest, this emperor, with powerful armies at his beck and call, could do as he pleased—and did. He remoulded the government, and to such effect that, as we have seen, his innovations remained a strait-jacket on institutional development ever after. But Mote's characterization of the regime as despotism goes further by dwelling on two other aspects of this emperor's style of rule. The first is his personal secret police (the Brocaded Uniform Garrison) with its own prison and its extra-judicial and illegal practices.[113] The second relates to his use of mass proscriptions and executions in the purges of 1380 and 1393, and to his use of new and terrible tortures such as the 'death of a thousand cuts'[114] and a

[111] Cf. Mote, 'The Growth of Chinese Despotism'.

[112] W. Eberhard, *A History of China*, 4th edn. (Routledge & Kegan Paul, London, 1977; 1st edn., 1930), ch. 10.   [113] See pp. 825 and 827 above.

[114] Also known as the death 'by slicing'.

particularly horrible form of beating to death; and above all, to his flogging of officials in open court.[115]

These two features of Hung-wu's reign were indeed, as Mote says, perpetuated throughout the dynasty. To the *chin-i-wei* were superadded the Eastern and Western Depots; and all emperors continued the practice of having their officials flogged in open court, or forcing them to kneel in front of the palace for days on end. The question is whether these aspects exhaust the definition of imperial despotism, and the submission here is that they certainly do not. The power of a monarch, whether Shaka Zulu or Chinghiz Khan or the caliph or the sultan, to order punishment and execution without due process of law seems, in the West, to be the ultimate in supreme power and hence the essence of despotism. But if one is considering whether such unlimited—and capricious—exercises of personal power extended over all major aspects of the Ming polity—and at all times—then the answer must be that it did not. What is surprising about the not-infrequent use of these powers to punish at will is how ineffective they were, taking the dynasty as a whole, in imposing the emperor's will on the polity. One is almost tempted to say, 'the dog barks but the caravan passes on'.

When Father Ricci writes in 1609 about the government of China, he begins his account by describing the absolute authority of the emperor. Then, quite abruptly, he reverses himself and says that in truth the government is not conducted by the emperor personally, that really the country is 'governed by an *aristocracy*'; unique, to be sure, for it is the aristocracy of 'the *letterati*' (*sic*)—the lettered ones[116]—but an aristocracy nevertheless. The flaw in the 'despotism' interpretation is that it concentrates on the first sixty years of the dynasty, with active and ferocious war-leaders as emperors and before the Mandarinate had been fully reconstituted. From the 1450s the Mandarinate was in full fig and had successfully routinized the function of the emperor.

Another argument used to support the 'personal despotism' view is the process outlined previously by which the Inner Chamber (the *nei-ko*), the Grand Secretariat, replaced the line-bureaucracy as the policy-formulation unit and was later itself supplanted by the eunuch *Wen-shu-fang* headed by the Director of Ceremonies. Certainly, this put the ball in the emperor's court: and by the same token it gave the Han-lin secretaries (in the *nei-ko*) and the eunuchs (in the *wen-shu-fang*) privileged access to the emperor and, critically, control over the information he received. The traditional view in the *Ming-*

---

[115] Mote, 'The Growth of Chinese Despotism', 27–9.

[116] M. Ricci, *Della entrata della Compagnia di Giesu e Christianita nella Cina*, 3 vols. (1609), i. 156.

Shih (the annals of the Ming dynasty) and the chronicles is that the eunuchs, vile and insidious perverts, controlled the emperors' judgements and were therefore responsible for everything that went wrong. But this eunuch influence—which is of course a fact—is important in the shortcomings of the Ming only because it constituted an irritant and highly divisive element at court. This was of great importance towards the end of the dynasty when the court was tearing itself to pieces instead of concentrating its efforts on the fiscal crisis and the Manchu threat. But two points must be emphasized. First, the eunuch establishment was not an alternative government: whoever advised the emperor did so on the basis of memorials and reports that came up from the line agencies, and, also, the eunuchs had to assume that these agencies would carry out the imperial edicts. Secondly, eunuchs were only solidary when challenged *qua* eunuchs, just as the Mandarinate was only solidary when challenged as such, for example, by the emperor and his close servants. The usual condition of each and either of these rival establishments was *faction*. The efforts of Tung-lin 'partisans' to reform the Court are portrayed in the chronicles as 'good elements against bad elements' and mandarins against eunuchs; but in fact the partisans only infiltrated the government by the help and patronage of the Wang faction of eunuchs, and the subsequent dictatorship of Wang's rival, Wei, and his dreadful purge of the partisans during his reign of terror were actively assisted and even promoted (Mammitzsch says 'master-minded') by those mandarins who opposed the Tung-lin party. Thirdly, eunuchs as such never had a 'eunuch policy', the Grand Secretaries as such never had a specific policy, as opposed to the regular line bureaucracy. There were able eunuchs and able mandarins, wicked and extortionate eunuchs and wicked and extortionate mandarins. On the issue of 'despotism' the eunuchs are a supreme irrelevance.

Finally, the extent of personal decision-taking by the emperor or his eunuchs can be grossly overestimated. As in the Roman Republic and the Principate, the emperor was under a conventional obligation to consult, and so were individual ministers. The originals of the memorials and petitions from the ministries which finally landed up with the eunuch (or Grand Secretary) conferring with the emperor[117] were usually the product of *departmental* conferences (*pu-i*). Issues involving more than one ministry were discussed by them in *joint* conferences[118] and major issues of state were discussed in the *court* conferences (the *ting-i*).[119] Their importance fluctuated over the dynasty, for instance, they were frequent in the 1440s,

---

[117] See pp. 825 and 828 above.   [118] Lo, 'Policy Formulation and Decision-Making', 48.
[119] See pp. 822–3 above.

entirely absent in 1457–64. Where Grand Ministers were dominant at court—the reigns of Chia-Ching Emperor (1521–66) and the Wan-li Emperor (1572–1620)—only ranking officials spoke, the rest remaining silent. But in the last years of the dynasty the conferences were a pandemonium.

Jung-Pang Lo[120] summarized the results of his case-studies in foreign-policy formation[121] thus:

Even . . . when absolutism was at one of its heights in China, and when members of the bureaucracy were often brow-beaten, intimidated, and persecuted, the principle of consultation prevailed. Even the tyrannical early Emperors, T'ai-Tsu and Cheng-Tsu, made shows of consulting their ministers and strong-willed Hsüan-Tsung [1425–35] though personally committed to withdraw from Annam acted to withdraw only after encouraging his ministers to argue out the problem in his presence and giving careful consideration to differences of view between them. From Hsüan-Tsung's time onward, in an uneven development, the centre of decision-making power as regards major issues gradually shifted from the Emperor to the high-ranking ministers. Emperors might hint and threaten and court favourites might coerce and intimidate, but Court Conferences persisted as the focus in which important issues were resolved. And when rulers or their favourites planned unpopular courses of action, officialdom found it possible to block them by collective action.

Not only were many men thus involved in decisions about war and peace, their decisions were usually arrived at only after long deliberation in which proposals and their consequences were carefully studied and chances of success were carefully calculated.[122]

A third view about the nature of the polity is Marxist,[123] and stems from the People's Republic of China and neo-Marxist historians at Tokyo University. This view sees the regime as class exploitation of the peasantry and focuses on the role of landlords in dominating the rival populations by the li-chia and pao-chia systems. The state, qua Mandarinate, was the coercive and ideological framework which empowered the local rich to rule the countryside. It is proper to stress this aspect, but not to make it central. The Peking government had been retreating from its own direct control of the countryside since the collapse of the early T'ang. Its institutional expression was the freezing of the size of the Mandarinate in the face of the population explosion and, as noted, the deficit in numbers was made good by pushing responsibilities on to the local notables, so forging the bureaucracy–notables alliance already described. In this the Ming (and the Sung before them

---

[120] Lo, 'Policy Formulation and Decision-Making', 70.   [121] Ibid. 55–70.
[122] Ibid. 70.   [123] Tsurumi, 'Rural Control in the Ming Dynasty'.

and the Ch'ing after them) were following the commonest pattern of
government in the pre-industrial states: in Imperial Rome, in British India,
in Europe's feudal monarchies. The Ming Empire saw the national dominance of the Mandarinate, delegating control at rural level to the 'gentry'
and turning a completely blind eye to their exploitations.

9. THE STRENGTHS AND WEAKNESSES OF THE MING REGIME

The fall of the Ming dynasty in 1644, it turned out, signalled no more than
the displacement of one clan of rulers by another. The regime persisted. It is
essential to keep separate the dynastic and the institutional issues: to ask
why the dynasty persisted for 276 years and then collapsed invites a different
answer from each as regards the viability of the state.

The dynasty persisted because of the ground rule laid down by the
Hung-wu Emperor. The ground-rules of founder-emperors (the *tai tsus*)
bound their successors, and each successive founder looked very carefully
into the mirror of the past to discover what he thought were the mistakes
that had brought the last dynasty down and enabled him to win the throne.
The Hung-wu Emperor saw the threats to dynastic survival in any concentration of power outside his direct control, whether it was civil, military,
or familial. The Ming emperors wed only commoners, there was no provision for regencies, and the imperial sons, except for the heir-apparent, were
banished to the provinces. After the Yung-lo Emperor none of the emperors
were troubled by wives, in-laws, or dynastic revolts. The concentration of
civil power was destroyed when the Hung-wu Emperor abolished the chief
ministership in 1380. He truncated the military power by splitting the
Central Board into five coequal ones, and guarded against the field commanders' tendency to forge personal links with their troops by holding them
inactive until required. These measures guaranteed that the dynasty was
never supplanted by a chief minister or again threatened by an army revolt.
From a purely dynastic point of view they were entirely successful.

If, however, the question is why the state held up, and preserved its
territorial integrity without meeting more serious difficulties than endemic
and familiar peasant unrest and banditry in the interior, occasional nomad
raids in the north, and Japanese piracy on the coast, the answer is partly
institutional and partly fortuitous. Institutionally its success was due to its
practice (it was hardly conscious policy!) to do no more than establish rules
and regulations for the provinces, but let the local notables get on with
them without too many questions asked, providing quotas were met and
banditry was suppressed. A similar latitude was permitted to prefects and
hsien magistrates in interpreting the Great (Ming) Codes. Notionally,

administrative practice must strictly follow law; here the law legitimized administrative aberrances. What in Weber's strict 'legal-rational terms' were abused were more than tolerated, they were actively connived at. Not law, but instrumental pragmatism—expediency—was the order of the day. This regime would have seized up except for corruption; so corruption became endemic. In Ibsen's *Peer Gynt* what does the Boyg finally counsel? Not 'to thyself be true', by any means, but 'to thyself be *enough*'. It is characteristic of this 'get-by' mentality that the Ming Mandarinate failed to develop any monetary policy. It did no more in the way of transportation than to keep the Grand Canal open (there was no new road construction nor any road maintenance). The management of the salt monopoly and the arms factories was abysmal.[124]

But the Ming were also very lucky. For over 250 years they faced few foreign threats to test their thoroughly decrepit army, or which required large additional revenues from the inelastic and cumbersome fiscal system. At the same time the economy was flourishing, particularly in the sixteenth century, and the tax burden though uneven, was light and indeed on a number of occasions was actually reduced.

The reasons why the dynasty failed to surmount the crises of the 1600s are almost the mirror-image of the reasons for its success up to that date. The crisis was a compound of very serious Manchu pressure in the north and peasant and bandit rebellions in the interior, and a consequent acute shortage of ready money to pay for the troops who alone were capable of handling either. The Ming Mandarinate's supercilious policy of subordinating *wu* (warfare) to *wen* (civility) left the army thoroughly inefficient. Its alliance with the local notables, which permitted the latter to establish manors and reduce their tenants to virtual serfdom, either drove the tenants to abandon farming and then turn bandit, in open arms against the regime, or to become soldiers who—confronted by ex-peasant bandits or peasant rebels, were as prone to fraternize with them as to support the dynasty. The army was consequently just as useless in suppressing peasant and bandit uprising as it was in defeating the Manchu cavalrymen.

From the 1620s, when the crisis became acute, the government was headless, since the Wan-li Emperor had ignored all requests to fill vacancies and consequently the departments were barely able to function. At the same time, the fanatically Confucianist Tung-lin 'partisans' and their opponents, each side aided and abetted by its own eunuch faction, tore the court apart and consensus on policy proved impossible.

---

[124] Huang, *Taxation and Governmental Finance*, 320.

The terrible details of the last days of the dynasty do not concern us here.[125] It is enough to say that the 'one-eyed bandit' Li Tsu-cheng smashed through to the capital and occupied it, that the emperor thereupon hanged himself on Coal Hill in the Imperial City, and that some of the imperial commanders, notably General Wu, allowed the Manchus through the Great Wall to help them. Li went up to meet them but his troops were defeated and he himself was killed. Wu's plan then went awry for the Manchus had no intention of restoring the dynasty. To the contrary: they declared the Ming deposed and proclaimed their own monarch as the new emperor of China: the Ch'ing or the 'Pure' monarch of a new dynasty. The persistence of the Ch'ing dynasty till 1911 confirms the view that the Ming *system of government* was not to blame for the collapse, so much as a combination of failures to work it. For the Ch'ing supplied the two principal deficiencies of the Ming. In place of sulky or incompetent emperors it planted a line of three enormously vigorous, civilized, and dedicated ones, and modified Ming institutions so as to endow them with a despotic potential greater than ever before. The Ming had suffered a chronic military threat from around 1610–44 and failed to repel it. What had now happened was that this threatening military power had incorporated itself in the Chinese Empire and was at its disposal!

Meanwhile a third reason for Ch'ing success was fortuitous. The revolts of the 1630s and 1640s had shattered serfdoms, but not tenancy. The great estates began to fragment as each in its turn was divided between the children and then the grandchildren, and China became once again a country of smallholders.

---

[125] Cf. E. Backhouse and J. O. P. Bland, *Annals Memoirs of the Court of Peking* (Heinemann, London, 1914), 86–137.

PART III

5

The Feudal Background

1. THE DARK AGES

*F*or 500 long years after the last emperor of the Roman Empire in the West had been deposed its provinces slid deeper and deeper into anarchy and decay. Indeed, it is only with the benefit of hindsight that one can discern around the year 1000 the turning-point towards a new political and social order. That order was to be quite different from the Roman imperial system. In those 500 years the Roman law disappeared[1] and localized customary laws took its place. So did the entire constitutional and administrative structure. The towns shrank to insignificance (except as the seat of bishoprics) in all areas except Italy. The currency collapsed along with the Mediterranean trade, and Europe reverted to an agricultural natural economy. The various parts of the former empire began to grow apart along linguistic lines, the lands east of the Rhine speaking German, the lands inside the former *limes* (Gallia, Hispania, Italia) talking their own brands of vulgar Latin—the *lingua popolare*. Moreover, the definition of 'Europe' changed. Most of Spain was lost to the Arabs (as was Sicily until the eleventh century). In compensation, Germany up to the Elbe now became an eastward extension of the new Europe under the Carolingian dynasty. By the end of the millennium 'Europe' comprised principally the British Isles, the Scandinavian countries, France, Germany, Italy, and northern Spain, with shadowy fingers probing into what are now

---

[1] Except in one or two areas in Provence and Italy where it survived in vulgarized form.

Poland, Slovakia, the Czech Republic, and Hungary. This Europe, unlike the ancient empire, was land-bound and its poles of power were in the north, not the south.

On the ruins of the imperial order two structures emerged, one a continuation of it, the other a departure. The latter was the dominance of the Frankish monarchy. Originally situated in the lowland areas at the mouth of the Rhine, the Franks went on to conquer the remaining German tribes in Gaul and finally the Lombards of Italy as well. Charlemagne's empire thus included 'France' and 'Germany' and north Italy. The Carolingian Empire collapsed soon after Charlemagne's death. It simply did not have two essential prerequisites for survival: neither ready money nor a bureaucracy. But various Frankish dynasties persisted, and through them and their geographical reach introduced and exported two of the essential institutions of the nascent new Europe: the military technique of the armoured cavalry charge and the improvisations which were to evolve into feudalism.

The Franks had a mighty hand, too, in shoring up the one great structure that had survived the empire—the Church. By the time of Charlemagne England had been re-evangelized, while the Saxons, Norsemen, and Magyars had also joined the Christian ranks. Christianity, which was to be the all-powerful, all-pervading world-view of Western Europe, was greatly assisted by the Franks in establishing its self-identity as a specifically Latin form of both the faith and the Church hierarchy. The earliest German dynasts had been Arians, a feature that isolated them from their Romanized subjects, whose faith was defined for them by their bishops, who in turn recognized the primacy of the Bishop of Rome. The Franks, under Clovis, were the first of the Germans to convert to 'Catholic' and 'Roman' Christianity. Their conquests expunged the Gothic Arian kingdoms, carried Catholic Christianity into East Europe, and, at the Bishop of Rome's urgent plea, conquered the Lombards. The Frankish monarchy and the Bishop of Rome—the Pope—entered into the alliance which was symbolized in the papal coronation of Charlemagne as emperor of the Holy Roman Empire. As long as the emperors were strong, popes were dependants. But, in principle, at least, the Bishop of Rome was now recognized as the Supreme Pontiff in the West, and the stage was set for the papacy to centralize the Church hierarchy under itself and frame the remarkable international corporation which grew to challenge, and at moments to dominate, but at all times to constrain the behaviour of the secular power.

2. FORCES AND INSTITUTIONS IN THE HIGH MIDDLE AGES

The Middle Ages were regulated, shaped, and permeated by two great institutions: Christianity and Feudalism. But in this preface to the study of the medieval political systems we should not omit the highly significant phenomenon of the mailed knight and the new art of war. If the cathedral is the stone symbol of the Middle Ages, so, equally, is the castle. Feudalism and the feudality embraced them both.

2.1. *Christianity*

Medieval Europe was saturated in Christian values. It was wholly removed from the thought-world of secular values we inhabit today. The medieval Church was identified with the whole of organized society. With the rarest exceptions, of which the vilified and persecuted Jews were the great example, one became a member of the Church as an infant by way of baptism, and woe betide you if you ever tried to revoke it. In effect, the Church was a compulsory society, and with the quite marginal exceptions already noted, coextensive with the entire population. Until the thirteenth and perhaps the fourteenth centuries it was, as Lecky says,

perfectly in accordance with the intellectual wants of Europe. It was not a tyranny, for the intellectual latitude it permitted was fully commensurate with the wants of the people. It was not a sect or an isolated influence acting in the midst of Europe and forming one weight in the balance of power but rather an all-pervasive energy animating and vivifying the whole social system. A certain unity of type was then manifested which has never been restored. The corporations, the guilds, the feudal system, the monarchy, the social habits of the people, their laws, their studies, their very amusements, all grew out of ecclesiastical teaching, embodied ecclesiastical modes of thought, exhibited the same general tendencies and presented countless points of contact or of analogy. All of them were strictly congruous. The Church was the very heart of Christendom and the spirit that radiated from her penetrated into all the relations of life and coloured the institutions it did not create . . .'[2]

This thought has been carried further in R. W. Southern's masterpiece of clarity, charm, and understanding, *Western Society and the Church in the Middle Ages*:

The church was not only a state, it was *the* state: it was not only a society, it was *the* society—the human *societas perfecta*. Not only all political activities but all learning

---

[2] W. H. Lecky, *History of the Rise and Influence of the Spirit of Rationalism in Europe* (1st edn.; Longman, London, 1865; Green, 1910), ii, 28. Compare this with our account of Islam and of Islamic social structure and mores: Bk. III, Ch. 1 and Bk. IV, Ch. 3 below.

and thought were functions of the church . . . To all this it added the gift of salvation—the final and exclusive possession of its members. And so in its fullness it was the society of rational and redeemed mankind.

One of the greatest achievements of the Middle Ages was the detailed development of their idea of a universal human society as an integral part of a divinely ordered universe in time and in eternity, in nature and supernature, in practical politics and in the world of spiritual essence . . .[3]

More than any other of the great world religions, Christianity is a religion of the world to come. 'Outside the Church there is no salvation.' Its notion of an Original Sin visited by God on the human race whose punishment was inescapable except by baptism and the subsequent act of conscious faith—again unique among the world religions—was given the most literal of interpretations. By its means the Church achieved, for a long time, an extraordinary and almost total control over morals. Men had not ceased to be superstitious with the advent of Christianity. (Perhaps, indeed, the reverse!) All that had changed was the objects of superstition—wonder-working relics, sacred icons, miracles and portents of all descriptions—and the total absence of the sceptical, rationalist ruling class of the old Roman Empire. Princes and prelates, noblesse and commoners alike shared these beliefs, wore hair-shirts, did penance, and went on pilgrimages in order to obtain absolution. Christianity was not, in short, an instrumental creed for ensuring social control by the upper classes. They believed in its promise and in its punishments with the same fervour as the common folk, and this was precisely what made this creed so socially effective.

The central message—the resurrection of the body, the Last Judgment, and the sentence to Heaven, Purgatory, or Hell—was expressed in word, in letter, and above all in the innumerable frescos and paintings that decorate and decorated the walls of the churches and abbeys throughout Europe. The faithfuls' reward was eternal life among the saints. Here the 'Lord God had removed the tears from all Faces'. But the punishment of the faithless, the backslider, the heretic, and the wicked was an eternity of torment, and the ingenuity with which painters imagined this far outdoes their conception of Paradise. Everybody is familiar with the sadistic fantasies of Bosch, but his ingenuity is based on a tradition of countless anonymous church artists. The common form was to divide the panel into an upper half representing Christ in glory judging the dead and selecting the faithful to remain there among his elect, and a lower half showing the damned thrust into the fiery pit by fearsome horned devils and subjected to innumerable and repulsive torments. Michelangelo's great *Last Judgement* in the Sistine Chapel of course

---

[3] R. W. Southern, *Western Society and the Church in the Middle Ages* (Penguin, Harmondsworth, 1970), 22.

follows this tradition, but one suspects that by this time it had become more literary than literal (although, not long before, Savonarola had brought all Florence to a state of hysterical repentance by preaching the Last Judgement at them). The stark literalness of the message comes over best among the less well-known and less sophisticated painters of an earlier time; for instance, in the half-destroyed frescos of Santa Maria Novella in Florence or in the work of an unknown Bolognese painter in the Pinacoteca of Bologna. Here, in the under half of the panel, St Michael presides over the fate of the damned in Hell, his drawn sword cutting off all hope of escape. The centre foreground is taken up with the gigantic figure of Satan; he takes up more canvas than the three figures of God, Jesus, and Mary combined. He is black, hairy, and horned and he has two heads, one on his neck, the other on his belly. Around him, in pits guarded by brutal devils, are the damned men and women, naked and bound: and he is portrayed at the moment when he has half-devoured one man in his upper mouth, with another hanging head-down from his lower. But that is not all. In the right-hand background one devil is wrenching the head off a prostrate naked woman, others are flinging men and women into a well, still more are shooting their victims full of arrows. Among these scenes the painter depicts a bare tree from which a bound and naked figure is hanging by the neck. And this is merely the right-hand side of the picture. On the left the tortures continue. Devils are clubbing their victims there and, even more horrific, two naked bodies hang impaled on the sharp branches of a tree. Elsewhere the naked and defenceless malefactors are savaged by bears. The destruction affects *all* the wicked: there is a cardinal and a bishop present, as well as ordinary men and women.[4]

Lecky[5] describes this as 'religious terrorism'. It had diverse effects on different people at different times. To die with a penance uncompleted (and in the early Middle Ages the penances were exceedingly harsh, and 'were of all things on earth the most to be dreaded'[6]) consigned the unfortunate to eternal damnation. But, by way of compensation, the penitent could commute the penance for cash or pay somebody to do the penance for him.[7] Though for others only personal penance of the most mortifying kind could purge their consciences; so, for example, the hysterical outbursts of 1260 in Italy, where crowds of people thronged the towns beating themselves with whips for weeks on end, crying 'Have mercy O God and send peace,'[8]

---

[4] I forbear for reasons of space (anyway, the point has been made) to recapitulate similar or even worse torments in the voluminous literary sources. A brief sample can be found in W. H. Lecky, *The History of Morals from Constantine to Charlemagne* (Watt and Co., London, 1924), ii, 92–5 and cf. the bibliography cited there. [5] Lecky, *History of the Rise*, 15.
[6] Southern, *Western Society*, 227. [7] Ibid. [8] Ibid. 275.

or the religious fanaticism of the Beguines, condemned by the Church in 1312.[9] But most believers must have reacted, it seems to me, like Villon's mother, in the *Ballade* he made for her, where—praying to the Virgin—he has her say:

> Femme, je suis, povrette et ancienne,
> Ne riens ne scay: onques lettre ne leuz
> Au monstier voy dont suis paroissienne
> Paradis painct, où sont harpes et luz
> Et unq enfer où damnez sont boulluz:
> L'ung me faict paour, l'autre joye et liesse.
> La joye avoir fais-moy, hautte Déesse
> A qui pecheurs doivent tous recourir.[10]

By the time Villon wrote that—and Bosch depicted the torments of Hell— the Middle Ages had drawn to their close and with them the Church's monopoly, life-style, learning, and letters. Until the fourteenth century, however, that monopoly was unchallengeable.

The Church was the vehicle that carried into the barbarized, poverty-stricken, and (by now) totally illiterate northern Europe the traditions of a remote and an even more remote antiquity. But what little it transmitted it also transmuted. After the Merovingians, lay education all but ceased in Europe except in some Italian municipalities (notably Bologna). The courts of the Carolingians and their successors had perforce to use clerics,[11] and the Church—or rather the monasteries—maintained some connection with the Roman literary heritage. Study was part of the Benedictine Rule[12] and it was in its abbeys that the monks copied rare and precious manuscripts of their favoured Latin authors. By the late tenth and early eleventh centuries cathedrals and collegiate churches in the towns had their own schools where the pupils could go beyond a grounding in Latin, the liturgy, and church music, and pursue the 'Liberal Arts'.

But politically speaking the most significant developments took place in the lay school of the commune of Bologna, for it was there that the pupils

---

[9] Southern, *Western Society*, 330.

[10] François Villon (1431–63): 'I am a woman, poor, old, ignorant, who cannot read. But in my parish church I see pictured Paradise with harps and lutes, and a Hell where the damned are being boiled. One frightens me, the other gives me joy and solace. High Goddess, to whom all who sin must turn, I beg thee, give me the joy': Villon, *Ballades*, Allan Wingate, London, 1946. The sentiment expressed is very late compared with those I have cited. But so were the horrors depicted by the pessimistic and moralistic painter Hieronymous Bosch (*c*.1450–1516).

[11] This was cheap too. See p. 891 below.

[12] Founded in the 7th cent., the order was revivified from Cluny, 910.

began to study Roman law. Regarded suspiciously by the Church at first, this was soon seen to be of immense importance to it. Bologna became a university, to be followed by Paris, Oxford, Cambridge, and others. These universities were of course Church institutions as the affinity of *cleric, clericus, clerk* attests. Sponsoring the revival of the study of Roman law, the Church was preserving a second of Rome's great contributions, and it was explosive in its political significance. It served as a basis for reformulating and codifying the law of the Church (the Canon law), for arming the popes with the skills to handle the ever-proliferating disputes that were adjudicated at the Roman Curia, and for generating a line of reformist popes who had themselves been trained in Roman law. It served, too, to arm these popes with the political theory of the Church's supremacy over the secular arm and then, in return, produced a breed of imperial and royal Roman lawyers who returned the compliment. Let us pursue this political theory a little further.

In the middle of the twelfth century, 1141–50, a learned lawyer monk named Gratian compiled the oldest of the collections of Canon law that were embodied in the *Corpus* (1499–1502), and in its opening paragraphs the *Decretum Gratiani* abruptly marries the tradition of Rome with that of a far, far older civilization. We are back with the Jews.

Across from the railway station in Florence lies the great church of Santa Maria Novella. It is a Dominican church. The Dominican Order, founded in 1215, was particularly concerned with orthodoxy. It existed to smell out heretics. Its name—*Dominicanes*—in Latin makes a pun on *Domini canes*, 'the hounds of the Lord'. One of the church cloisters is known as the Green Cloister. That is because its four walls are covered by a continuous fresco in a greenish monochrome. This fresco, with contributions by such masters as Uccello and Masaccio, presents the history of mankind starting from Adam and Eve through to Jacob, but terminating (as we see it arranged today) with a huge representation of Christ. The point? This is a Dominican church, the church of persecutors of heresy, and here it has appropriated the entire span of *Jewish* history. For the Church, this history is *not* Jewish but Christian. Or, to put it another way, Jewish history as recounted in the Old Testament is Christian history. That is why it terminates with Jesus. If the Jews had been Christians they would have recognized Jesus as the Christ. But they were not and did not. They rejected him and arranged for the Romans to crucify him. The gentiles did recognize him. Thereby *they* became the *Verus Israel*. And Jewish history thereby became the part-history of the Christians.

Let us make no mistake. The Latin translation of the Bible—St Jerome's Vulgate—was the most widely read book of the Middle Ages. True, not many people were able to read. But everyone who was able to read, read the Bible. And this Bible comprised the Old Testament as well as the New. This Testament portrayed the empire of Divine Law over the King. It portrayed heroic Jewish kings who, by arms, upheld the Divine Law. It demonstrated the divine retribution on the backsliding kings. It showed the prophets rebuking them. Through and through, it made the single point: there was a Divine Order, a Divine Law, and kings were both its defenders and its subjects.

And so back to Gratian's first paragraph. It reads: 'Mankind is ruled by two laws: Natural Law and Custom. Natural Law is what is contained in the Scriptures [i.e. the Old Testament] and the Gospel.' With this the Roman concept of Natural Law and the Jewish concept of the Divine Law are brought together and equated.

With Natural Law we have for the moment no more concern except, perhaps, to say that even in Gratian it is equated with Reason, and that this aspect of it is expressed in its plenitude in St Thomas Aquinas's *Summa*. The point here is that it is equated with 'what is contained in the Scriptures and the Gospel'. In the Roman tradition Natural Law overrode positive laws. It was supreme. In the Jewish tradition it is the Divine Law, the Law of Moses, which overrode 'custom and constitution'. This was the very essence of the Jewish theocracy. The very concept, even in the Church Fathers, of kingly— and human—constraint under the Divine Law is found in the Jewish kingship. As we have seen, it is to be found nowhere else in the world before ancient Israel.

Now it may be remembered that when we were discussing the Jewish kingship we discerned two traditions. The underlying one, put with great persistence by the prophets from Samuel onwards, is highly theocratic, even to the point of sometimes being openly anti-monarchical. But there are also passages where the king is exalted as the embodiment of the faith, and others where he appears as a priest.[13] Psalm 110: 4 says of the king: 'Thou art a priest for ever, after the order of Melchizedek.'

It was this concept of monarchy that the Church adopted in the Dark Ages, when the Papacy required the Franks to protect and foster it. The Merovingians, and after them the Carolingians, were anointed like the kings of Judah and sacralized in the process. They cast themselves in the role of David. But, in return, the Church urged on these Frankish monarchs the constraints placed on David and his descendants as found in the Old

---

[13] 'I have set the crown upon one who is mighty. | I have exalted one chosen from the people. | I have found David my servant | With my holy oil I have anointed him': Ps. 89: 19, 20. (For similar references, see Ps. 2: 6.)

Testament: they must be just kings and never stray outside the Law of God. 'Always remember, my king, that you are the deputy of God, your king. You are set to guard and rule all His members and you must render an account of them for the Day of Judgement.'[14]

This exalted role of the emperor and the king disappeared with remarkable abruptness in the middle of the eleventh century, the key century in the transition from the Dark Ages to the Middle Ages. The monarch—quite suddenly—was seen to be a mere layman, not a sacred quasi-priest. The anointing with oil, which conferred (or recognized in him) this sacred nature, was demoted from being a sacrament to a sacramental.[15] Instead, the new line of reforming popes, beginning with Nicholas II (1058–61) and Gregory VII (1073–85), cut the monarchy down to mere human size and instead promoted the view that it was for the Church, as the repository of the Divine Law—and their own persons as the duly appointed successors of St Peter—to prescribe the metes and bounds of royal authority. They founded their claim on the New Testament passage, Matthew 16: 18–19. 'Thou art Peter and upon this rock will I build my church . . . I will give unto thee the keys of the Kingdom of heaven: and whatsoever thou shalt bind on earth shall be bound in heaven; and whatsoever thou shall loose on earth shall be loosed in heaven.'

But though the papal claim was supported by a New Testament text, the theory of monarchy which the papacy advanced derived from the Old. It was none other than the alternative theocratic and anti-monarchical view beloved of the prophets. Kingship was, at best, if not redundant, instrumental. It was there to defend the lives of the people and to dispense the law. It was God-given, not made by man at all. Christian monarchs were to be seen simply as chief executives circumscribed and regulated by (in Gratian's words) 'Natural Law (which) is contained in the Scriptures and in the Gospel'.

Lord Acton recognized the ancient Jewish kingships as the first example of limited monarchy, but then went to say: 'that early example of limited

---

[14] Quoted in Southern, *Western Society*, 32. The kings always had before them the history of Israel's various kings and it was to the history of Israel that they looked as a parallel—and yardstick—to their own reigns and problems. Thus the Franks were identified with Israel itself (J. M. Wallace-Hadrill, *Early Germanic Kingship in England and on the Continent* (Clarendon Press, Oxford, 1971), 49) and it became a commonplace from the reign of Chlotar II (613–23) that the Frankish kings were as King David (ibid. 48). But these and other kings were also exercised by the fate of the 'bad' Jewish kings, e.g. Ahab, Saul, etc. (ibid. 75 ff.): Louis the Pious (Charlemagne's son and successor) was particularly exercised by the fates of Ahab, Manasseh, and Jezebel, particularly since the Franks were the new Israel so that 'what could happen in the Old Israel could equally happen in its successor, the new Israel' (ibid. 125).

[15] W. Ullmann, *A History of Political Thought in the Middle Ages* (Penguin, Harmondsworth, 1965), 87.

monarchy and of the supremacy of law neither lasted nor spread.'[16] In this he was wrong. In throwing down its challenge to the secular power, the Papacy was turning its back on the Roman tradition of absolute emperor-ship and reverting instead to the tradition of the Jewish prophets. This launched it on a collision-course with the emperor, kings, and princes of the new Europe just at the time that *feudalism* was emerging as the new organizing principle of the political order. Each was to react upon the other, with profound consequences for the medieval political systems.

2.2. *Feudalism*

Certain medievalists will not use the concept 'feudalism', or 'feudal system'. They find the Middle Ages too protean, too full of exceptions and local idiosyncrasies to be captured in a formula. Instead, they follow Ranke's prescription of the historian's *métier*: 'To want simply to show what actually happened' (*wie es eigentlich gewesen*).

This approach is not open to me. I am not, like them, trying to write a history of an epoch nor even a history of the form of government in a particular epoch, but trying to present a history of successive and repetitive forms of government throughout the world, and this cannot proceed with-out constant comparison and contrast, and these in turn require formulae, constructs, and models to make similarities and differences plain. 'Feudal-ism' and 'feudal system' may be ill-chosen terms—most medievalists agree on that—but they have acquired a connotation which we still have to use because we can avoid it only at the cost of a tedious and, indeed, obfuscat-ing circumlocution. The fact is that in the West and central parts of Europe between the tenth and fourteenth centuries the form of polity was sharply different from any we have met with so far, and 'feudal' is the best name we can give it.

The polities we have met with were of two kinds, republics and auto-cracies. (The Jewish kingdom was the one great anomaly.) In the republics the citizen-body authorizes (in various ways) the appointment of magis-trates to govern it. These magistrates are the agents of the citizen-body, they act directly on it, they are accountable to and revocable by it. So, although a relatively large number of people are involved in the political process, there is a clear distinction between the magistrates and the people at large and between 'public' and 'private'. This is simply not the case in feudal government.

---

[16] Lord Acton, 'The History of Freedom in Antiquity', in *Essays in the Liberal Interpretation of History* (University of Chicago Press, Chicago, 1967), 246–7.

The contrast with the autocracies is, perhaps, even more revealing. In autocracies the ruler is absolute. The people are his subjects and he appoints officials to govern them. Their authority springs exclusively from the autocrat; they are his dependants. Here again, the line between public and private—state and subject—is clearly drawn.

The characteristic feudal polity does not fit either of these two categories. It is the *regnum*: literally, a kingdom. Here the king is not absolute at all. For one thing, there is a large complex of matters relating to the family and marriage, for instance, wherein neither he nor any lay person could intervene. They were matters for the Church to decide under its own Canon law. But let us leave this important restriction on lay rulership aside for the moment and concentrate simply on the secular matters, notably defence, law and order, taxation, justice, and general regulation of the community. Only on his own personal estates did the king exercise direct rule in respect of these through his own appointed and revocable agents (shire-reeves, *prevôts*, *ministeriales*, and the like). (There are notable exceptions, of course, in countries with adventitiously strong kingships like England and Sicily.) Elsewhere these matters lay in the hands of territorial magnates whose profession was that of arms. Government by a *consortium* of landholding warriors, each exercising wide jurisdiction over the people on his estates, is not uncommon in kingdoms we should not call 'feudal'. The peculiarity of the feudal *regnum* lies in the nature of this consortium and the relationship between its members and the king. They were not direct, revocable, and dependent appointees of the king. On the contrary, they were powerful in lands, fighters, and retainers by hereditary descent and their subordination to the king, such as it was, was defined in the landlord–tenant condition attached to the lands which they held from the king; conditions which included a powerful duty of giving general fealty and support as well as specific services. This personal loyalty and these specific undertakings went with the tenancy. They were, so to speak, 'a charge on the estate'. Though the estate was passed on from father to heir, the condition had to be renewed before the heir could legally take over. Furthermore, the conditions were not at all one-sided. The tenant owed certain duties *vis-à-vis* the king, but the king, equally, owed his tenant justice and protection in return.

Two remarkable differences from autocracy stand out at once. First, the distinction between 'public' and 'private' is effaced. In holding his lands, the tenant-vassal assumed 'vassal obligations', but he also acquired the rights to tax, regulate, keep order, and often do justice among his own tenants. Certainly a tenancy might carry with it the dignity and the responsibilities attaching to quondam royal offices, such as duke or count, which had once been direct agencies of the monarch, so one might argue that tenants like these were public (royal) officials. But this hardly altered the situation, since any fees or taxes a duke or count might notionally have derived from the royal office were indistinguishable, legally and financially, from those he derived from his domain. So, by virtue of (hereditary) tenancy, the vassal-tenant acquired a set of responsibilities which were regarded (and which previous states had certainly regarded) as public. His private right to his land entailed 'public' duties and by the same token, therefore, public duties were the consequence of private rights.

The second difference is the *conditionality* of the relationship. It is not unilateral, but what Ganshof[17] calls a *synallagmatic* contract, that is, one involving duties and responsibilities on both sides. Either side could denounce it. A vassal-tenant who thought the king had arbitrarily altered its terms and had failed to give him protection and support could, by due legal ceremony, terminate the relationship. This was known as the *diffidatio*, the casting-off of loyalty, that is, *defiance* (and, since this usually meant he had to support his action by revolt, we get the current meaning of the word 'defy'). A king who was dissatisfied with the vassal-tenant's compliance with the terms of the contract could, for his part, declare him in default and demand the forfeiture of his tenancy. This too was regulated by customary feudal law and usually involved summoning the vassal-tenant to the king's court (of which more later), consisting of fellow vassal-tenants of the presumed offender and executing their verdict. Though defiance and divestment were a matter of legal rights, it might (and often did) take military power to enforce the right.

The pivot on which the entire arrangement turns is the combination of vassaldom and fief, which is why Ganshof, for instance, uses the term 'feudo-vassalic' to denote the relationship of the 'men' or 'barons', to their 'lord'. Originally it was possible to become a vassal without receiving a fief and equally, the other way. The fief or fee (or *feu*), was a grant—usually of land—in return for certain services, mostly of a military kind. Fiefs were originally granted on a life-tenure. They became hereditary subject to the new fief-holder confirming the conditions on which his predecessor had held it. In fully developed feudalism, with uncommon exceptions, an individual became a vassal when and because he was granted his fief, and, equally, expected a fief if he agreed to become a vassal. This is why Maitland[18] could define feudalism in these words:

A state of society in which the main social bond is the relation between lord and man [i.e. *vassalage*], a relationship implying on the lord's part protection and

---

[17] F. L. Ganshof, *Qu'est-ce-que La Féodalité?*, 2nd edn. (de la Baconnière, Neuchâtel, 1947).
[18] F. W. Maitland, *The Constitutional History of England* (CUP, Cambridge, 1908), 143.

defence; on the man's part protection, service and reverence, the service including service in arms. This personal relation is inseparably involved in a proprietary relation, the tenure of land [i.e. the *fief*]—the man holds land of the lord, the man's service is a burden on the land, the lord has important rights in the land and (we may say) the full ownership of the land is split up between man and lord. The lord has jurisdiction over his men, holds courts for them, to which they owe suit. Jurisdiction is regarded as property, as a private right which the lord has over his land. The national organization is a system of these relationships: at the head there stands the king as lord of all, below him are his immediate vassals or tenants-in-chief, who again are lords of tenants, and so on, down to the lowest possessor of land. Lastly, as every other court consists of the king's tenants, so the king's court consists of his tenants-in-chief and so far as there is any constitutional control over the king it is exercised by the body of these tenants.

Once again let us return to the central point—the effacement of the distinction between public and private government.

The members of the feudal court met, not to fulfil a duty owed to the community, but a private obligation which they had assumed in return for the fiefs they held . . . the feudal state was one in which . . . private law had usurped the place of public law. Public duty had become private obligation. To understand the feudal state it is essential to make clear to one's mind that all sorts of services which men ordinarily owe to the public or to one another were translated into a form of rent paid for the use of land and defined and enforced by a private contract.[19]

In practice, in certain *regna*—and, one should add, in different centuries—a public sphere *was* preserved and gradually extended. The element in the *regnum* responsible for this was the kingship: not in its feudal aspect as *dominus*—the lord of lords—but in its ancient, primordial aspect as *rex*, the sacralized and originally near-absolute monarchy of the Merovingian and early Carolingian times. It was through the king's expansion of his primeval *regalia* at the expense of his barons who had usurped them that the feudal *regnum* would at last develop into the modern European state. Of this manifest or latent power in the kingship much will be said later on. For the moment it is enough to note that some feudal *regna*—Sicily and England stand out—were much more centralized than others which Maitland could describe as 'hardly more than a loose confederation of principalities'.[20]

The application of feudal principles gave political systems a highly peculiar texture: at once decentralized, polyarchical, and 'cellular'. Government was an activity shared between the king and his vassal-tenants, his 'barons'. The king did not—at least did not in many or even most

---

[19] G. B. Adams, 'Feudalism', in *Encyclopaedia Britannica*, 11th edn. (1910), x. 297–302.
[20] Maitland, *Constitutional History*, 144.

significant respects—govern his subjects directly, but through his barons, indirectly. In short, government was mediatized. Moreover, it was mediatized through a number of layers of barons, not just through his tenants-in-chief. For the tenant had the right to sub-infeudate, that is, to become himself the lord of a vassal by granting him a fief in return for homage and services. Thus authority became ever more local until the primary cell was reached: a knight and his dependent tenantry. They owed him labour services, and it was through these that he could maintain his dignity as a knight and bear the very considerable expense of equipping himself with war-horse and armour to fulfil to his own lord, in turn, the military service by which he held his fiefs. The total effect is a complex hierarchy of patron–client relationships. At each tier, starting with the king and tenants-in-chief, the former, as patron, owes loyalty, justice, and protection to his client, who owes loyalty, assistance, and specified services (usually military) to his patron the king. But he is himself the lord (patron) of his own vassal-tenants: and so on down. Thus the political system may be conceived as a number of cells. At the base is the primary cell of the knight and his dependent tenantry knit together by proximity, shared conditions, and symbiosis: protection and justice from above, labour services from below. Above this primary echelon, in turn, numbers of knights hold of a superior lord who owes them protection and the justice of his *curia* while they owe him fealty and military service in return. Thus the primary cells are grouped into secondary cells of greater extent and so on upwards, each echelon owing service to those above and receiving justice and protection from them in return. It is in this sense that the political system is 'cellular': it consists of followings, grouped into larger followings, and so on, upwards. But it is not anything like as regular as this suggests. For it was possible and not uncommon for a man to become the vassal-tenant of more than one lord and owe service to each of them. Likewise, it was possible and not uncommon for a lord with vassals of his own to become the vassal-tenant of another lord like himself, in respect of some particular territory. The most striking case is the status of a monarch like Edward I, who was king of England but also the vassal-tenant of the king of France in respect to Aquitaine. So the seemingly gradated hierarchy is complicated by these criss-crossing lines of fealty and dependence.

At the same time, because of the conditional and contractual nature of the lord–vassal, and even the lord–serf, relationship political authority resides nowhere in particular because it resides everywhere. Not one single person or even body of persons, not one single office or institution possesses complete and final authority. The feudal *regnum* is a *polyarchy*.

The word which sums up feudal concepts is *dominium* or lordship. Lordship was not sovereignty, though it gave the right to command; it was not ownership, though it gave the right to exploit. It may best be defined as the possession of incomplete and shared rights of government and ownership. No lord had complete control over his subjects or over his lands, his rights overlapped with those of other men. The king was the Lord King but he could issue direct commands only to his vassals; other men obeyed their immediate lords and not the monarch. The lord of an estate could not do as he pleased with the estate, for his superior also had rights of lordship there, rights which were recognized on occasion by heavy payments. Lordship usually implied the right to hold a court, but the jurisdiction of a feudal court was seldom complete. A petty lord might have a court which could try cases of simple assault and larceny; his overlord could punish men of the same district for robbery and mayhem: while only the count would be lord of a court which had jurisdiction in cases of murder and rape. This division of authority was inevitable, since feudal government was based on private relationships. Just as no contract today could give a private person a monopoly of economic power, so no feudal contract could give a lord a monopoly of political power'.[21]

One final and quite remarkable feature of the feudal political system follows from this. One may feel bewildered at how a complex network of relationships going up and down and sideways and across could ever acquire enough definition and predictability to constitute a 'system' at all. But this, in the end, it certainly did. Throughout, we and the authors we have quoted talk of 'rights'. Now we have drawn attention to the gulf between citizen-states, like the Greek *polis* and the Roman Republic and Empire, and the subject-states, like the ancient kingdoms and empires of the Middle East and China. The latter are not law-bound. The ruler issues commands to his officials and changes them at will. Those officials are themselves the judges in their own cause, and the ruler treats legal remedies against them as acts of grace which he can vary according to expediency or equity and his own discretion. They become, in other words, simple acts of administration.[22]

Now in the feudal *regnum* the king has in effect conceded part of his original jurisdiction to his vassals as a kind of property *right*. It is a contract between free men, conferring privileges on the one and demanding services in return. And this by sub- and cross-infeudation is generalized throughout the entire community of landholders. All have *rights* and all have corresponding duties. These rights and duties evolved from a variety of original sources, such as the *precarium* and *beneficium*. But the final result was the development of sets of land laws, varying from *regnum* to *regnum* and, more importantly, in the various regions of each *regnum*.

[21] J. Strayer and D. Munro, *The Middle Ages*, 395–1500 (Appleton-Century, New York, 1942), 110–11.
[22] See Bk. III, Ch. 3 ('The T'ang') and Ch. 4 ('The Ming'); and for Rome, Bk. II, Chs. 4, 7, and 8.

Carried to a logical conclusion there would have been no legal order, only, in Weber's words, 'a mere bundle of assorted privileges'.[23] But both lord and vassal-tenant were driven into disputes over the exact specification of what their respective undertakings meant. Each had 'rights'. Since these were contractual, they could not be determined by the say-so of the king or of his vassal either. They constituted a kind of *lis inter partes*. So arose the characteristic organ of feudal government, the lord's *curia*, his court formed of vassals and convened by their lord. In one way it was a council of vassals, its object being to counsel the lord. In another it was an assembly of the personages who actually governed the realm so, in this sense, a high administrative and legislative council. But finally it was a place where the lord and his vassals heard the king's complaint against a particular vassal or, alternatively, his complaint against the Lord King. In this way, the 'bundle of assorted privileges' were adjudicated and brought into relation with certain general principles. A 'feudal law' developed which was different in its particulars according to the district, but followed certain guide-lines. The reason why the complicated criss-crossing relationships became the framework of a stable political order lay in this emergence of law and a system of feudal courts to go with it. Thus, what had been command and administrative regulation in the autocracies was in the feudal *regnum* a *judicial* process. The Middle Ages were as law-bound as Rome, indeed more so, and the notion of individual rights re-emerged as far as freemen were concerned in an even more positive form than ever before.

Is feudalism as I have described it specific to Europe or is it a generic form, to be found in many different places throughout history? Certainly, the way it developed is time- and place-bound. The details here can be found in a number of admirable texts.[24] But its features—or some of them—are found elsewhere at various times. For in the course of this *History* we have come across the manorial system; dependent peasantry, that is, serfs; clienteles and followings; armoured knights as a ruling stratum; landholding as giving jurisdiction; royal officials becoming autonomous local rulers, and the like. And it can be shown that some, perhaps many, of these characteristics are to be found all over the world at different times.[25]

---

[23] Runciman, *Max Weber*, ii. 843.

[24] Notably, Ganshof, *Qu'est-ce-que La Féodalité?*; R. Boutruche, *Seigneurie et féodalité*, 2 vols. (Auber, Paris, 1968–1970); M. Bloch, *Feudal Society*, trans. L. Manyon, 2 vols. (Routledge & Kegan Paul, London, 1962; paperback edn., 1965). Cf. also Adams, 'Feudalism'.

[25] For a scathing and not altogether accurate summary see e.g. Boutruche, *Seigneurie et féodalité*, i. 240–321. Also the first 184 pages of R. Coulborn, *Feudalism in History* (Princeton UP, Princeton, 1956), i.e. the individual monographic constitutions. The synoptic, second part is highly misleading.

1. One such is the relationship of landlords and servile cultivators. Now this relationship is widespread throughout the pre-industrial world, persisting in some states, for example, parts of Central America, to the present day. The equation of such economic condition with 'feudalism' is a highly vulgar-Marxist notion, which compels Chinese Communist historians to describe their entire past from the First Emperor ('the triumph of land-lordism') to the nineteenth century as 'feudal'. But these conditions were common in late Roman Gaul, Hispania, and Africa (the *coloni*, and the villa system) and arguably in the ancient city-states and empires of the Middle East long before this time; and nobody would deem them feudal on that account.

2. Another and related definition singles out *clientela* or 'followings' as the key feature. But these are as widespread in space and time as a dependent tenantry. Indeed, it is often, though not always, an aspect of this. But clientelism (as 'dependent followings') existed in the very earliest days of the Roman Republic, and exists in some form in many modern polities (the Lebanon; parts of Latin America; the western Maghreb, etc.). One might see a characteristic variant in the 'boss and machine' politics of the United States and analogous polities elsewhere.[26] What this last demonstrates is that the client relationship is not necessarily bound up with land-tenure at all (it was not in Republican Rome nor in Tammany Hall, which are highly analogous).

3. A third definition, derived from the above, stresses the indirect, intermediate nature of feudal rule. The ruler does not have immediate access to his subjects: it is the vassal (i.e. his immediate dependant) who holds courts, levies taxes, keeps order. And the more sub-infeudation, the longer the chain of intermediaries between ruler and subject. If one adds this characteristic to the preceding ('clientelism') one finds a 'cellular' texture of government. But such features are—or were until recently—to be found in contemporary states (e.g. Brazil, till 1931).[27]

4. It follows from the preceding paragraph that the feudal regime is highly decentralized. But not all decentralized states are feudal!

5. Other definitions are more time-specific; they concentrate on the *land-grant* or the grant of the *usufruct* of lands as the essential feature. The

---

[26] See, for a general view, S. E. Finer, 'Patrons, Clients and the State in the Work of Pareto and at the Present Day', *Atti dei convegni Lincei*, (Accademia dei Lincei, Rome, 1973), 165–86, and the literature cited therein. Cf. also E. Gellner and J. Waterbury (eds.), *Patrons and Clients* (Duckworth, London, 1977) and J. Boissevain, *Friends of Friends* (Blackwell, Oxford, 1974). In the article cited above, I define the 'clientelist state' in the following words: 'it will be seen at once that though all feudal states were clientelist states, it will not follow that all clientelist states are feudal.'

[27] S. E. Finer, *Comparative Government* (Penguin, Harmondsworth, 1974), ch. 9, esp. 453–5.

tendency here has been to see the essence of feudalism in the grant of land in return for services, so that some have described the satrapies of ancient Persia or the *iqta* of the late Caliphate as 'feudal'. But there is a sharp analytical (and often empirical) distinction between the concession of lands or the revenues from lands in return for service (whether temporarily, or for life, or hereditarily) and the concession of lands entailing jurisdiction and government over their populations to the exclusion of the granting authority. The former are no more than fiscal devices. They are simply modes of paying salaries, not in cash, but its equivalent in the produce of a given amount of land. They are, in fact, *prebends*.[28] In the latter case, however, what is conceded is the devolution of the right to govern the ruler's subjects. In medieval Europe not all fiefs carried the right of jurisdiction and, likewise, such rights could be granted to a vassal over lands he did not hold; but most usually these coincided. The difference is very pronounced: the *prebendary* grant is consistent with a high degree of centralization and bureaucracy, and indeed autocracy to the point of despotism, as in Mamluk Egypt, for instance. The fief-cum-jurisdiction necessarily entails decentralization, localism, polyarchy, and implies the absence of a central bureaucracy on a large scale.[29]

6. We often find this distinction between the *prebend* and the fief crisscrossing with another, the *unilateral* land-grant *versus* the *contractual* land-grant. This distinction is even more fundamental to defining Western feudalism than the former.[30] In the former the ruler can revoke or alter his grant at will; in the case of the fief he cannot, for he as well as his vassal is bound by the contract. In the former the concessionary cannot change his overlord or choose between overlords; in the latter case he can. In the former, a superior makes a grant to a personal dependant and expects liturgical services; in the second, the concessionary has contractual freedom as well as owing personal fidelity and increasingly comes to promise the fidelity as a consequence and condition of holding his fief (whereas in the beginning the grant of the fief was a consequence of his being faithful, i.e. already being a vassal).

---

[28] That is, concessions by an owner to a personal dependant in the confidence that the latter will perform liturgical services in return.

[29] In one case uniquely all these characteristics are present, but subject to an overriding autocracy. This peculiar trick was accomplished by the Japanese Shogunate, 1600–1874. See Bk. IV, Ch. 1, p. 1090 below.

[30] Note that I write 'Western' feudalism. The reason Japanese feudalism could coexist with the autocracy of the Shogun, as noted above, is fundamentally due to the *unilateralism* of the land-grant in Japan, and the corresponding weakness of its contractuality. See Bk. IV, Ch. 1, p. 1090, below.

7. Now there is no doubt that this distinction—and the previous one between *prebend* and *fief*—can on occasion be purely analytical. For often patrimonial officials who held prebends could and did acquire hereditary title and could and did acquire local jurisdiction too. So in the 'intermediate' periods in ancient Egyptian history, when the nomarchs took over from the central power, so among certain satrapies of ancient Persia, and so too when the Caliphate broke up in the tenth century. These states then conducted themselves in ways similar to the European feudal *regna* but with one enormously significant difference: the cases are abnormal, pathological, and illegal; they are usurpations. In the feudal *regna* the condition is normal, regular, and *consecrated in law*. It is *de jure*, while the former is simply *de facto*, to be brought back to autocracy as soon as this can be managed. Western feudalism constitutes a network of bilateral political relationships defined and regulated by law. The elaborate *Coutumes de Beauvaisis* of Beaumanoir (1283) and the *Sachsenspiegel* of von Repkow (1230) so demonstrate.

So feudalism was a regular, legitimate, legally articulated system of government and those who choose to see 'feudalism' wherever they encounter dependency, clienteles, intermediated rule, and the cellular and decentralized nature of government must come to terms with this fact. For most of those conditions relate to *de facto* situations and not just that but to conditions that modify, distort, one could even say corrupt, the *de jure* constitution. For instance, in today's world one can find them everywhere distorting and falsifying 'popular' regimes where the choice of the ruler nominally rests on the votes of the citizen.[31] So, for example, in the Lebanon and the Brazilian backlands, they represent the oligarchic reality behind the democratic façade. If they are not illegal, they are certainly extralegal. What is arresting and profoundly original about medieval European feudalism is that the relationships of dependency and service which began as expedients should end up as a legal system of rights and duties, the framework of a lawful political order.

8. The medievalist sees Western feudalism as a consequence of the exigencies of the time and place: the insecurity of the times generates commendation from below, the necessity for making payments in kind, and not in currency, generates vassalage and the fief from above. Feudalism was a desperate improvisation reflecting the incapacity of the central power. But in its systematized juridical form feudalism attracts the attention of political scientists because some of its principles go beyond time and place and are of general application. Three of these are particularly important: *non-territoriality*, *federalism*, and *the privatization of public function*.

---

[31] For examples, Finer, *Comparative Government*, ch. 9, 'The Façade Democracy'.

2.2.1. NON-TERRITORIALITY

In principle, feudalism is a network of dyadic relationships based on homage and land-tenure and these relationships have nothing to do with what nowadays we call 'national frontiers'. The count of Champagne holds some of his lands there from the king of France and some from the Holy Roman Emperor in Germany and is a vassal of both. Transposed into modern or, to be precise, into future times, it is as if national frontiers have disappeared and the globe is in the hands of a dozen multinational corporations, which are conglomerates or 'holding companies' of dozens of smaller enterprises. A subject or a citizen belongs to one or other of these. It provides him with his job, his pension, and his protection in return for his loyal service. His home and work-place may be in Tashkent or Beijing, London or New York, it does not matter, because, if he is thrown out of his house or beaten up, his own multinational will seek redress for him against the offender. If the criminal is another of its employees it will *adjudicate*. If of another corporation, it will seek justice and amends from its officers and the two corporations will decide the dispute by arbitration or negotiation or retaliation or force. But *localities* will have nothing to do with the matter; only the employee–employer relationship will count.

Logically, therefore, feudalism had nothing to do with the territorial principle. If it had ever been 'pure' it would have dispensed with it entirely. But it was never pure, either in origin or application, and in practice placed great and increasing reliance on territoriality. For it had not emerged from a *tabula rasa* as a highly original way of organizing allegiance. It had started in *territorially defined* kingdoms, and it was, precisely, as the king of a *regnum* that the ruler had rights over his territory that he—and only he—could dispose of as fiefs to his subjects. The kings possessed the *regalia*: the rights to defend, judge, regulate, and keep the peace among the population inside the boundaries of his *regnum*. However, first in France, later in Germany and Italy, he was less and less able to exercise them. But his *right* to exercise them, like his right to grant fiefs, extended only so far as his *regnum*'s boundaries, *unless*, of course, he acquired lands and jurisdiction over the inhabitants inside the territory of another *regnum* by such means as marriage, inheritance, or treaty. But usually in such cases those lands would be carrying feudal obligations to the king of this second kingdom, so that the king who had just acquired the lands would have owed these obligations as fief-holder and vassal of the king of this second kingdom. The classic case is the king of England who is also the duke of Aquitaine, and in this respect (but only in this respect), vassal to the king of France.

Kings were on a par with other kings, as 'principals' with the authority to infeudate their lands. But by virtue of being *kings*, and not just *lords* (*domini*)—for they were both—they possessed primeval general rights over, and duties towards, *all* the subjects of their *regnum*. As soon as they began to recover these regalian rights—as they did in France in the twelfth century, for instance—they overrode the extraterritoriality of feudalism with a territorial jurisdiction. The constitutional history of France particularly, but *mutatis mutandis*, in England and the Spanish kingdoms also, is the history of the king's recovery of his regalian rights; in Germany and Italy, of his failure to do so.

2.2.2. FEDERALISM

In federal states, as we have seen,[32] the functions of governments are divided into those exercisable only by the central power, and those exercisable only by a number of juridically coequal local authorities, and that, strictly speaking (as in the USA) the central authority and the local ones are also juridically coequal, neither being empowered unilaterally to alter or abrogate the powers of the other. The pact embodying these stipulations is a written constitution and disputes under it are handled (except in Switzerland) by a supreme constitutional court.

In the feudal *regnum* the Lord King, the *rex et dominus*, divides power with the local *seigneurs* on a contractual basis. As *dominus*, the feudal lord of lords, disputes are settled in the royal court, made up of the tenants-in-chief and presided over by the king *dominus*. This functions as a sort of supreme constitutional court. As king, the *rex*, in the application of his regalian rights, may however claim certain rights over the population as a whole; in England, for instance, certain rights to tax and to draw into his own courts certain 'pleas of the Crown'. So a crude division of power operates, some exercised country-wide by the king, the other locally by the lords, his vassals.

The feudal *regnum* clearly shares with federal states the characteristics of decentralization and pluralism, but more than that, it approximates to the federal division of powers between juridically coequal, country-wide and local authorities. It is not surprising, therefore, that this feature attracted the attention of anti-state jurists like Duguit.[33] So, *a fortiori*, did another feature of the *regna*, although this one did not flow from the concepts of feudalism. This was the special autonomous position of the Church, with its own courts exercising jurisdiction over an entire range of cases from which the lay courts were excluded. Once the Church is taken into account, we find

---

[32] Bk. II, Ch. 3.
[33] Cf. L. Duguit, *Law in the Modern State* (Allen & Unwin, London, 1924).

not one central power but two. These divide functions between them on a juridically coequal basis but they are not split as between central and local authorities; instead they are divided between country-wide lay and clerical authorities, *ratione materiae* (according to their subject-matter). This is known as *functional federalism* and the notion proved immensely attractive to a number of early-twentieth-century would-be reformers like the guild-socialists.

2.2.3. PRIVATIZATION

The literature on feudalism that we have cited—in the work of F. W. Maitland, G. B. Adams, Strayer, and the like—is shot through, as we have seen, with the insistence that the distinction between 'public duties' and 'private rights' is effaced, and that the former become the latter. Two points are worth a comment.

The first is of general application. Simply, there is no 'natural' distinction between the matters carried out by the state and public official and those carried out by private individuals. The second point is that the very concept of 'public' right, duty, law is absent from the feudal relationship as such. In this, loyalty is due to one's lord, not to the community, and the obligations are undertaken as a private contract. The concept of the 'public' resides in only one point, institution, man in the entire *regnum*: not in the *dominus* but in the *rex*, the king. *He* is responsible for defence, justice, and his subject's security; and it is in that capacity, over time, that his high office reabsorbs the authority granted away to his vassals, and by so doing re-creates the public sphere.

2.3. *The Nobility of the Sword*

The feudal *regna* were all 'societies organized for war', and the connection between feudalism, the armoured knight, and the rule of a military aristocracy could hardly be more intimate. The three things all depend on one another and indeed might even be said to be extensions of one another.

2.3.1. THE NEW ART OF WAR

One hypothesis, indeed, goes so far as to say that feudalism was the direct outcome of a new technique of warfare. A hundred years ago Brunner, in an article entitled 'Knight Service and the Origins of Feudalism', claimed that feudalism was essentially military, a type of social organization designed to produce a support cavalry. This theory became the basis of an even more striking hypothesis by Lynn White,[34] who finds the reason for cavalry as

---

[34] L. White, *Medieval Technology and Social Change* (OUP, Oxford, 1962).

against infantary warfare in the introduction of the iron stirrup. From an ill-known provenance, this invention passed from Byzantium into Europe. It had far-reaching consequences. Not merely did it enable the rider to rear in his stirrups and wield his sword, mace, or axe from his full height and with all the weight of his body behind it, but he could use his lance in an entirely new way also. Since antiquity the lancer's thrust had been only as strong as his arm. Given stirrups, he could lay his lance in rest and strike his enemy with the entire momentum of the horse behind him. The shock cavalry charge—the central tactic of European medieval battle—had been born.

But, White went on, it came very expensive. The cavalryman had to wear protective armour as well as own a horse; more than one, for he would need remounts. In general, excluding remounts and auxiliaries, the military equipment for one man seems to have cost (he says) about twenty oxen: equal to the plough-teams of ten peasant families.[35] The cost never ceased to rise. By the time of the Third Crusade the cavalryman needed three remounts and two attendants as well as his own armour and weapons; and the suit of mail itself cost the value of a small farm. Later, as plate armour supplanted chain-mail and the steed had to be the heavy war-horse known as the *dextrarius*, the cost soared still higher. In short, the only men who could be heavy cavalry had to be rich—or made rich.

Subsequent studies have argued that both the stirrup and heavy cavalry came in much more slowly than White envisaged and were not standard until the late eleventh century.[36] But this does not alter the general thrust of his argument. The stirrup was decisive for the advent of the armoured mounted knight and the shock cavalry charge; the enthronement of this tactic was equally decisive for the creation of the knight's fee—the *servitium debitum*—and the spread of feudalism and, finally, for the installation of these fief-holders as the lords of the countryside, the new ruling class.

2.3.2. KNIGHTHOOD AND CHIVALRY

A common notion in the Middle Ages divided society into three orders: those who work, those who pray, and those who fight. The last were a new nobility. There had been a time when *nobilis* could mean simply any freeman, that is, any holder of allodial land; but by the eleventh century this usage became extinct along with most of that class. It was more and more exclusively confined to the most powerful and highly regarded of the royal vassals. In this way it came to denote a particular class of society. A noble

---

[35] L. White, *Medieval Technology and Social Change*, 29.
[36] P. Contamine, *War in the Middle Ages*, trans. M. Jones (Blackwell, Oxford, 1984), 179–84.

always lived off the work of others, which was as much as to say he was someone who lived off a manor. The manor indicated wealth and this was one of the two marks of the nobleman. The second was the profession of arms. Not all fighting men were noble by any means, only the best-armed and professional warriors among them; which means those who fought on horseback with the full equipment: lance, sword, battle-axe or mace, helmet and mail-shirt, greaves and gauntlets. The words used for such men varied. *Miles*—soldier—was a common term. In England the term that prevailed was *knight*, an Old English word for any boy, youth, or lord, but which in an obscure way acquired a singularly prestigious and honorific significance. The Old English word is cognate with the German *Knecht*, which still retains the original menial connotation. (Thus a sixteenth-century *Landsknecht* was a trooper—usually a mercenary.) Instead of *Knecht* the German noble warrior was called a *Ritter*—a horseman; and the same concept was applied in France (*chevalier*), in Italy (*cavaliere*), and in Spain (*caballero*). Such fully armed, professional mounted warriors, vassals, and fief-holders were the aristocracy and the ruling class. Some formed the retinue of a king or great lord— house-knights. But most lived on their fiefs in fortified manor-houses, which served to dominate the serfs of the manor but equally acted as their refuge and defence. Its lord was trained from childhood to follow nothing but the profession of arms and was interested—at first, anyway—in little else but that and the warlike diversions such as tourneys and hunting. He did not, and indeed was constrained not to, put his own hand to the plough, for that would have been deeply degrading. He did not even manage the estate—he left that to his steward. He held a manorial court for his tenants, but quite often would leave his bailiff to conduct it. On the other hand, he did have to attend and participate in the court of his feudal overlord. In the eleventh and twelfth century, particularly in France, the domestic life of the humbler knights was squalid, boring, and intensely parochial. It was also often very poor.[37]

But the overlords of such humble knights were wealthy men whose manor-houses were built of stone. They did justice among the lesser lords and they might form part of the court of the Lord Kings, not just to participate in justice, but—if rich and powerful enough—to give him counsel as part of his great *Consilium*: in brief, to participate in his conduct of affairs. It was such as these who were becoming literate in the twelfth century and in whose courts the knightly romances were to be welcomed and to give rise to the notion of courtly love.

---

[37] Nobody has pictured it better than Zoe Oldenbourg in her magnificent novels, *The World is Not Enough* (Gollancz, London, 1949) and *The Corner Stone* (Gollancz, London, 1954).

From 1100 onwards there developed special rules of behaviour for this knightly class, and it is no accident that the word for it is *courtoisie*, since it derived precisely from the wealthy baronial court or *curia*. Born in the courts of France, it was imitated in Italy, Germany, and England and it generated the code of the *chevaliers*, of 'chivalry'. We first hear of dubbing a knight in the mid-eleventh century: the young warrior, about to be acclaimed knight, knelt to his superior who gave him his sword—and a blow to the head. 'Knight' originally signified the status of the warrior who fought on horseback with full equipment; but within half a century, from 1100 on, it signified membership of an *order*, like the *ordines* of Rome. With this the ubiquitous Church entered into the ceremony by blessing the sword, and then influencing the moral code of *courtoisie*, sometimes by way of a sacred oath. The elaborated warriors' code soon found its way into the now prodigiously popular lay romances, like Chrétien de Troyes's (*c.*1165–80) *Lancelot*, *Yvain*, and *Perceval*, reaching its height in the English (anonymous) *Sir Gawayne and the Grene Knight* (*c.*1370). By the latter date kings had founded their orders of Knighthood (e.g. the Garter) consecrating the notion of knightly behaviour at the very moment that the knight *qua* mounted warrior was about to become obsolete. The code of chivalry lived on: pursuit of glory and contempt for fatigue, pain, and death; piety, and the defence of Holy Church; the protection of the widow, the orphan, and the poor; sparing the vanquished and keeping faith.

But just as for Confucius 'the rites do not go down to the common people', so the code of chivalric behaviour only applied to fellow-noblemen. To spare knightly captives in battle was chivalric but also profitable—they would bring a ransom. Ordinary prisoners of war were as often as not massacred. The knightly 'order' had nothing but contempt for the commoner. Froissart describes the marauding French peasants in the Jacquerie (1358) as 'small and dark, and poorly armed' and tells how the noblemen set on them and, 'in all, exterminated more than seven thousand Jacks that day'.[38] But by this time the knights had evolved into a hereditary nobility, which on the continent of Europe was a privileged legal order. And the notion that only knights had the right to fight fully armed (thus being distinct from 'sergeants', who were more lightly equipped), was hardening into a dogma. Lineage became much more important than initiation. *All* a knight's posterity was 'entitled to privileges rights and franchises which the nobles are accustomed to enjoy by virtue of the two lines of descent'.[39] Moreover, whereas a man had hitherto been 'noble' because he was a vassal,

[38] J. Froissart, *Chronicles*, abridged edn., trans. and edit. G. Brereton (Penguin, Harmondsworth, 1978), 154. [39] Bloch, *Feudal Society*, ii, 237

now the very *right* to be a vassal (i.e. to hold a fief) had become confined to those already noble! England was the great exception. Here the social and honorific privileges and dignity of the knight were transmitted only to the eldest son, not the entire progeny; and the category was too ill-defined to remain socially closed. The continental nobility were to go on to claim fiscal immunity and succeed. In England they paid up, along with the commoners. But this did not detract from their social dignity, particularly among the very great who, in the fourteenth century, began to model themselves on the self-defining exclusive 'peers' of France, and so separate themselves from the humbler 'knights of the shire'.

2.3.3. THE CONDUCT OF WAR

A great deal of the warfare during this period consisted of fairly small-scale campaigns to reduce defiant vassals. The king-emperors in Germany, however, were engaged in much large-scale fighting: defending and expanding the eastern marches in the eleventh century, embarking on expeditions to subdue northern Italy, and fighting widespread feudal rebellion at home.

Despite the omnipresence of the mail-clad shock cavalry, this warfare was paradoxically very static. Everywhere the armies encountered the castle, which became more and more elaborate as time went by, from the wooden motte and bailey of Anglo-Norman times to the massive stone fortifications of Richard I's Chateau-Gaillard or the Crusaders' Krak des Chevaliers in Syria. Siegecraft developed in rhythm with the castle's defensive capacity but, confined to mining, sapping, and battering down thick curtain-walls with stones cast from the new counter-weighted catapults, it was at best a slow business. So most warfare consisted of forays—*chevauchées*—to lay waste the enemy's lands, and the subsequent siege of his castles. The set-piece battle between feudal hosts was very rare, and indeed commanders were ordered to avoid them.

When they did take place the numbers involved were very small. The entire Norman army at Hastings numbered 6,000–8,000 at the most. The English had fewer knights at their disposal than the French kings of the thirteenth and fourteenth centuries. England maintained the Anglo-Saxon infantry tradition with a high infantry–cavalry ratio, and even the cavalry frequently fought dismounted. In France, from the end of the twelfth century, it became rare to call out the militia to the host, and the infantry was made up chiefly of specialist mercenaries like the Genoese crossbowmen. The average size of an army for all but the greatest emergency may be taken as some 10,000 or so until the fourteenth century, when numbers began to rise. Even so, at Crécy (1346) the English had only 4,000 men-at-arms and 10,000 archers, against the French army of 12,000 men-at-arms and numerous other forces.

Feudalism, as we noted, came into existence largely in order to 'fund' the heavy-cavalry army. Yet it is clear that the feudal array was a very inflexible formation and that the feudal arrangement was a most defective way of mobilizing an army.

To take the tactical matter first: it is pretty clear that even a handful of knights could scatter and destroy infantry, even light-armed cavalry, let alone packs of rebellious and ill-armed peasants. But pitched battle could be quite another matter. The terrain had to be suitable to the massed cavalry charge, the enemy had to lack missile weapons, and had to stand pat. In such circumstances the shock cavalry were irresistible. But they had to be well led and the enemy had to play their game. When both these conditions were lacking, the outcome was disastrous. They effectively lost the Holy Land at the Horns of Hattin (1187) and failed to beat the Mamluks at Mansourah (1250): in the former case because of despicable generalship—beleaguered on a waterless hill—in the latter case, entrapped in souks and alley-ways. The French cavalry was beaten by inferior English forces at Crécy (1346), Poitiers (1356), and Agincourt (1415) because they did not know how to react against the English combination of 'dug-in' armoured knights and superiority in missile weapons, the longbow in this case. They could not come to terms with the Kurdish-Turkish tactic of simply withdrawing before their cavalry charge until they were exhausted, then overwhelming them with missiles until the Turks' own cavalry finished them off, hence the calamitous defeat at Turkish hands at Nikopolis (1396). (This was another example of despicable generalship: no scouts or pickets were put out.) They could even be defeated by infantry, provided this was well marshalled: witness Legnano (1176), Lake Peipus (1242), and Courtrai (1302). Too much has been made of the role of the heavy Norman cavalry at Hastings in 1066, much too much. The English shield-wall held against repeated cavalry charges until part of it was drawn off by a feint; and even then only the death of Harold put an end to the now-pointless battle.

As a system of mobilization, feudalism was abysmal. For one thing, the *servitium debitum* was confined, usually, to two months or forty days. After that knights demanded pay, or went home. For another, the lord could not always count on the fidelity of the vassal, who might come with the minimum forces consistent with his pledge, or not even show at all; after all, he was in possession of his lands and what could his overlord do if defeated? At any time a number of fiefs might be vacant. Others might be held by mentors. The mobilization was slow. The knights might be absent from their fiefs. Sub-infeudation could, and indeed did, go so far that a single knight's fee became divided between a number of tenancies which had to club together to produce the said knight-in-arms. These and other factors always reduced the number of knights obeying the summons to far below the nominal tally. Furthermore, as time wore on many knights proved to be thoroughly out of practice. And what of castellans? A monarch or prince needed castle guard all the year round, not for forty days. Not only this, it was in the vassal's interest to whittle down his obligation as far as custom would permit, and in the overlord's interest to magnify it. As the sheer cost of horses and equipment increased—in England, at least between the eleventh and twelfth centuries, it went up threefold—the tussle between king and retainer increased. So by that time did the duration of campaigns. It comes as no surprise, therefore, that even in the eleventh century William Rufus of England preferred to take money from his English infantry contingents and use it to buy mercenaries, nor that Henry II should commute knight service extensively for 'scutage' to buy mercenaries for his wars in France. After 1307 the feudal array was summoned but once; thereafter all troops served for pay. In France the feudal array persisted longer, but even there *capitaines*, that is, military entrepreneurs, began to appear after 1350, to form the Grand Companies of *Routiers*. But not till after the defeat at Agincourt did the French feudal army disappear and paid professional companies take its place.

Shock cavalry still persisted elsewhere, paid or not. As ever it proved its rigid, bull-headed inadaptability when it encountered any novel enemy tactics. It was shattered by the Swiss peasant pikesmen at Grandson (1476) and Morat (1476), as well as by the Hussite war-wagons (1420–2). And if one asks why the clumsy, inadaptable formation had survived so long and so many disasters, the answer is patently clear. The formation was the exclusive possession of what, by way of that very possession, had become the noble class, the exclusive class, the wealthy class, and the ruling class. Their privilege was bound up with their knight service and knight service was bound up with being a mounted warrior. In the thirteenth century they had joined with the Church in condemning crossbows as inhuman; in the sixteenth century they would similarly condemn firearms. In the Middle Ages they were still the uncontested beneficiaries of a primitive mode of raising what, in its prime, had been the ultimate weapon.

3. STRUCTURES AND PROCESSES IN THE MEDIEVAL *REGNUM*

Wherever it had spread (and it by no means spread everywhere in Europe), feudalism, as we have described it, permeated the monarchy and the Church and subjected the still-exiguous class of townspeople. But the monarchy antedated feudalism, it was non-feudal, and it had its own logic and its own capabilities which were both anti-feudal. Likewise with the Church. And when towns began to revive along with the great population increase of the twelfth century, together with the growth of commerce and the return of cash currency, the townsfolk developed into an anti-feudal force too. The overwhelmingly feudal environment is a veritable sea, but a sea in which islands are visible. Are these islands rocks or sandcastles? *Autres pays, autre mœurs*: it depended on where one was—and in which century.

But these non-feudal and hence potentially anti-feudal elements, granitic or frangible as they might prove, were not on the same side. If the Church was non-feudal that did not put it into the same camp as the monarchy. As for the towns—well, they were for themselves and they sought allies where they could—but always against the feudal order.

No brief account can do justice to the feudal politics but long ones lose themselves in thickets. There are two outstanding reasons for this. The first is simple *fact*: what Marc Bloch describes as 'the infinite variety of local and regional customs'.[40] The second is complicated conceptualization: this age is one of quite different political traditions—from Judaea, Rome, Germania, *inter alia*—which are intellectually irreconcilable.[41] To quote Bloch again (and how many fellow-scholars will re-echo him): 'It is difficult to express with clarity conceptions which by their very nature are opposed to logic.'[42] So, in what follows let me simply assume feudal principles as a given and see how these three *non*-feudal institutions—monarchy, Church, and town communes—adjusted to it and to one another.

3.1. *Kingship*

Rarely is the conceptual confusion greater than in the matter of kingship. Medieval people seemingly held two mutually exclusive positions: that the king was the supreme legislator, *lex animata*, and that he was also (in Bracton's phrase) 'non sub homine sed sub Deo et lege' (not under man but under God and the law). As society grew more literate and more reflective, jurists, clerics, and ordinary laymen made numerous attempts to reconcile the two, while their modern glossators[43] try to reconcile their reconciliations. McIlwain, for instance, proposes to distinguish between the

---

[40] Bloch, *Feudal Society*, 371.   [41] See below, on the kingships, particularly.

[42] Bloch, *Feudal Society*, ii. 380.

[43] E. H. Kantorowicz, *The King's Two Bodies: A Study in Medieval Political Theology* (Princeton UP, Princeton, 1957; paperback edn., 1981); C. H. McIlwain, *The Growth of Political Thought in the West* (Macmillan, London, 1932); id., *Constitutionalism, Ancient and Modern* (Ithaca, 1940); W. Ullmann, *Principles of Governance and Politics in the Middle Ages* (London, 1961), for example.

king's *gubernatio*, where he is absolute, and the king's *jurisdictio* which draws the line around this.[44] Ullmann is more heroic. He supposes a so-called 'theocratic' monarch, drawing his power from on high and absolute, but adds that this presents the function of the theocratic king in its pure and uncontaminated state[45] and that it is 'only in conjunction with the feudal element in Kingship [that] the full mediaeval kingship emerges'.[46] Little would be served by pursuing such theoretical reconstruction. It is more to our purpose to recognize simply that by this time the cluster of beliefs about kingship derived from diverse sources: ancient Germanic traditions; Old Testament and New Testament tradition; the filtered, refracted memories of the great Charlemagne; the authority implicit in the coronation oaths; and, as time went on, increasingly loud echoes from the revived study of Roman law. This cluster of beliefs had a firm core but a hazy penumbra. In addition, it had to coexist with the new, feudal relationship in which the king was now enmeshed. Nothing is more natural than that the royal apologists should stress those strands of tradition and precedent favourable to the expansion of royal authority, while the apologists for the baronage or for the Church made the selection favourable to their own particular causes.

The essential point is that the kingship was 'a unique type of authority . . . not only superior theoretically to all others, but also of a genuinely different order'.[47] It was in the feudal order but not of it. Religious or magical ideas still clung to the king. Astonishingly, 'touching' for the 'King's Evil' (scrofula) persisted in England to the time of Queen Anne (who 'touched' the child Samuel Johnson in 1712) and to the 1789 Revolution in France; while even to this day the expression *Kaiserwetter* attests ancient belief that the king had magical powers over the weather.

This sacral character the Church itself recognized and consecrated in the coronation ceremonies. It was from the bishop that the king received his insignias and the crown. Above all, the bishop anointed him with the consecrated oil. All anointed kings thereby became new King Davids, consecrated by new Samuels. So the kings entered into the Old Testament tradition, and thus into both their authority and their constraints. The Old Testament taught that it was sacrilegious to touch the Lord's anointed; the royal psalms taught that he was the main participant in the ministry, though not really a priest (despite the references to the 'order of Melchezedek'). And certainly that was how Charlemagne expressed his role. But by the same token, the Church which anointed was surely superior to those it anointed? So the Church would argue from the mid-eleventh century

---

[44] McIlwain, *Constitutionalism.*   [45] Ullmann, *Principles of Governance,* 138.
[46] Ibid. 150.   [47] Bloch, *Feudal Society,* ii. 382.

onwards, claiming to be the surrogate of Samuel and the prophets in calling the king to respect the Divine Law. In conferring the unction the Church, in fact, stood between the king and his people (which meant his baronage), for though the king's person was inviolable the Church claimed the rights to release subjects from their allegiance to him.

The king, by ancient Germanic tradition and now sanctified by the Church, was the *thiudam*, the head of his people: and this means *all* the people. The essence of the feudal relationship is that it is *dyadic*: one to one; but the essence of the kingship is that it is *public*, which comes out in the various forms of the coronation oath. All of these promise, in one form or another, to protect and uphold the rights and privileges of the Church, to protect his subjects, and to do justice. So, for instance, Henry I of England (1100–35) promises to be 'three things': guardian of the Church, protector of the kingdom, and enforcer of its law and order and doer of right justice to all and everyone of his subjects. Note—*not* his vassals; Henry does not say that. He says his 'subjects', that is, 'the Christian people *subject* to me [*subditus mihi*]'.[48]

These attributes are quite clear as to principle. The problems lay in interpreting how far, deep, and wide they went in practice, and this is where king, baron, and Church pulled different ways according to their viewpoints and self-interest. As far as the Church is concerned, one might say that until the eleventh century kings assumed a Carolingian role of appointing its bishops and accepting responsibility for Church discipline. But from the reforms of Pope Gregory VII,[49] the Church tried, with great success, to form itself into a separate corporation, with sole responsibility for its own appointments, discipline, and laws. It was this challenge that provoked the famous Investitures dispute which in its turn led the Papacy to claim more than mere separate-but-equal status for the Church, and claim a status of ultimate superiority over the temporal power.[50]

The coronation oath implied that the royal jurisdiction (*arbitria*) was people-wide. That the king did justice between his tenants-in-chief was fully accordant with the practice of feudalism and raised no problems, but could he interfere in the judgements that his tenants-in-chief meted out to *their* tenants, and so on down the feudal line? The question was bound up with the concept of the king as *protector regni*, and the keeping of his *mund*—his peace. But before coming to that, one matter about the king as judge must be stressed, and indeed stressed repeatedly, for it contrasts most strikingly with the role of kings and emperors elsewhere. However accessible the

[48] W. Stubbs, *Select Charters*, 8th edn. (OUP, Oxford, 1900), 99. [49] See pp. 890–3 below.
[50] See p. 890 below.

medieval king made his justice, whoever he admitted to his courts or even his presence, he never tried a case and rendered a judgement as an individual, as Eastern monarchs often could and did. Neither a king nor, for that matter, a great baron judged a case except as a member of his *court*, composed of the chief personages of his entourage. The judgement was *collective*. In this way it differed not only from the one-man magistracies in China but from the courts of the Late Roman Empire. It is another illustration of the medieval attachment to not just 'law' (whatever that might be) but to 'due process', that is, to procedural safeguards.

Something of this attitude coloured the very vexed question as to whether and how far the king could make law, for as we have seen, in some quarters he was regarded as a *lex animata*. Charlemagne had certainly made laws—the *capitularies*—but we know that although some were expressly made in the presence and with the assent of great clerical and lay dignities, others, supposedly made in this way, were in fact his personal edicts. There was an ancient and powerful tradition that the law was tradition and custom, that kings and courts found it but did not make it; that the king could enact law which defined or particularized and even somewhat modified the good old law, but that he could not enact measures contradicting it without taking counsel of his great men. As long as the kingship was constrained by the power-relationship implied in feudalism, this remained a theoretical question, for the king could do nothing of any importance in any kind of matter without associating his magnates with him in advance. But as soon as a king began to challenge the feudal power-relationship, the theoretical question became immensely important and the issue, as we shall see, was decided very differently in France and in England.

Justice and lawmaking both merged conceptually into the king's central duty, the *protector regni*, the *tutor regni et ecclesiarum*. He was the war-leader. It was he and nobody else who summoned the host and called out the militia. It was he, again, who represented the *regnum vis-à-vis* other *regna*. And he was the ancient German *Mundbora*, the keeper of his *mund*, his 'peace'. Here his relationship to his subjects was a matter of their interests, not their desires; he stood towards them as a guardian to his ward. A disturbance of his peace was an offence against the king himself. It was also recognized that to protect the realm the king had the right to enact general emergency measures, pleading *publica utilitas*. Both the 'king's peace' and the 'public weal' were capable of indefinite theoretical expansion, to the point of absolutism indeed, but the practice was a very different matter, for no feudal monarch, whatever his title, was ever remotely what we could describe as absolute. Medieval kings made progress in extending the king's peace—in England, Sicily, and then in France (but not in Germany and Italy)—but that 'peace' was a tiny part of the parcelled sovereignties which still prevailed. We may note three constraints. One, the ecclesiastical jurisdictions, will be described later. The second was military constraint. He could impose his will on a recalcitrant magnate only by the goodwill of the others, except when he possessed a 'domain' rich enough to maintain a personal army big enough to quell all opposition. The royal power waned or waxed with the size of his domain.

The third constraint was the fiscal one, which runs parallel to the military one, in that unless the king was personally wealthy he could not even *buy* the military support he needed to impose his peace and measures of 'public weal'. In practice, *no medieval monarch was ever fiscally absolute.* Indeed, precisely the reverse. This is a central feature of the medieval kingship. That the pre-feudal German kinglets could and did levy general taxes for 'the public weal' is easily demonstrated.[51] Also, kings had ancient rights—so it seems—over traffic and hence over coming and going at sea and river-ports and bridges, and so on. These they still exercised in the feudal era (wherever they had not granted them away as fiefs). But by the eleventh century the king could not take the property of any freeman without his consent or, at least, the consent of great personages generally assumed to be able to speak for him. In short, the king had to carry out his duties as *protector regni* from his own resources. These were principally the revenues from his personal domain, where he, like any of the feudatories, was enlisted to 'tallage' (tax) the serfs on the manors. For the rest, they came from fines imposed in his courts, and the proceeds of dues arising from the obligations charged on his vassals' tenures. If the king wanted anything over and above those, he had to *ask* for it; he could not take it. And if he wanted to extend the taxation further, the same principle applied: the magnates were taken to speak for their inferiors.

The passion with which the sanctity of private property was affirmed is impressive. The early Bologna jurists, rediscovering Roman law, rejected imperial claims over subjects' property. Andrew of Isernia declared that a prince could not deprive a subject of his property against his will except for a crime, and John of Paris was dogmatic in asserting that neither pope nor lay ruler has any *dominium vel dispensationem* in any individual's property: it belongs to the individual, who has full power to dispose of it.[52] Not surprisingly, these beliefs were enthusiastically, indeed vehemently, endorsed

---

[51] H. R. Lyons, *Anglo-Saxon England and the Norman Conquest* (Longman, London, 1962), 303–14.

[52] R. W. and A. J. Carlyle, *The History of Medieval Political Theory in the West*, 6 vols., 5th edn. (Blackwood, Edinburgh, 1971), v. 102.

by all property-owners. From one end of Western Europe to the other, the cry went up: *N'impose qui ne veult.*

Yet throughout its period of material weakness, the sacredness and the public nature of the royal office as the ultimate source of justice, law, and order remained apart from and above the contractual ties of otherwise feudal society. If any institution were to recreate a public justice, a public law, a public order, a public utility—in short, to re-create a *state*—the only institution that could possibly do so was the kingship. If it failed, the *regnum* simply disintegrated. It did fail, and with just that result, in Germany and in Italy. In different ways it succeeded in England and in France.

But kingship did not have to cope simply with the feudatories. The Church stood in the way as well.

3.2. *The Church*

Immensely wealthy, literate in an illiterate age, the Church too was in the feudal order, but not of it. On the one hand, it was feudalized and its top administrators became royal officials. On the other, it exercised a wholly independent jurisdiction over a wide area of civil matters. Its members enjoyed immunity from the lay courts. It was subject to its own code of law and its own hierarchical discipline laid down in a distant country by the pope. And, from the late twelfth century, the pope with his own self-serving diplomacy swung the 'national' churches this way or that, for the king or against him, as the circumstances seemed to demand.

The material basis for its survival as an organized body throughout the collapse of the Roman imperial order and the vicissitudes of the repeated waves of barbarian invasions was its immense wealth. The Christian emperors had endowed it with the confiscated property of the pagan temples and exempted its land from imperial taxation. The Germanic dynasties honoured this immunity, and they and their great men endowed it afresh by innumerable pious bequests for the repose of the souls of themselves and their families. The re-foundation of the Benedictine order in the tenth century particularly prompted the private endowment of a great network of Benedictine abbeys. Rarely, if ever, did the Church alienate the lands it had received.

3.2.1. BEFORE GREGORY VII

Until the Gregorian reforms of the eleventh century the Papacy was unable and unwilling to control the bishops and archbishops, and these were the veritable pillars of the Church in the respective *regna* of Europe. In principle, the bishops and abbots were elected, by the clergy and people in the case of the former, the monks in the latter. With the emergence of feudalism, the appointments inexorably began to conform to a feudal pattern. There were some 500 bishops in Western Europe, most of them from well-born families, many of them administering estates whose vastness put them on a level with the greatest territorial magnates. It was inconceivable that kings, or the great dukes and counts who usurped their *regalia* (as in France, particularly), would allow such key resources to escape their control. At the very least they had to ensure the political neutrality of the bishops and abbots, at the best to extract resources—particularly military ones—from them. The power of kings and magnates to *fix* the elections in favour of their own nominees enabled them to impose knight service on the sees and abbeys. Once 'elected', the bishop had to enter into the property; so, whether we are talking of a humble priest taking charge of a parish, a bishop of his diocese, or the abbot his monastery, it was the lay ruler who carried out the ceremony of investiture. Thus, the king conferred the crozier and the episcopal ring on the bishop and expected vassalic fidelity in return. As feudalism and its forms advanced, the bishops and abbots came to do homage. Thus the offices of the Church became 'feudalized'. These bishops were great administrators and organizers and many were even warriors. Some sent knights to battle, in some cases led them. Essentially, the right to appoint the bishops and greater abbots was regalian, but where regalian rights broke down, as in the centre and south of France, for example, it was the great baron who appointed or, worse, openly sold the see.[53]

What was true of the mode of appointing bishops was also true of the parish priests. Here by ancient Germanic custom the church and its endowment actually belonged to the founder and donor—bishop, king, or landowner. The priest (mostly married at this time, Canon law notwithstanding) only entered his benefice on the lord's terms, that is, by payment of a part of its revenue, even of the spiritual fees. In a number of cases, too, the married priest was succeeded by his son.

To make matters worse, the very headship of the Church, the Papacy itself, had become the nominee of the Roman aristocracy in the latter half of the tenth century, and the courts of Tusculum in the first half of the eleventh. By then its moral and political authority had reached its nadir.

3.2.2. THE POST-GREGORIAN CHURCH

From this plight it was rescued by the emperor, Henry III, who appointed the first of a line of German pontiffs. Leo IX (1049–54) began the powerful impulse to cleanse and reform the Church and, under the influence of

---

[53] For the German case, Bk. III, Ch. 6, p. 941 below.

Cardinal Hildebrand, later to be elected pope as Gregory VII (1073–85), the Papacy embarked on a far-reaching programme of reforms, so sweeping as to be in certain respects visionary. These reforms, the new structure they imparted to the Church, and the Church's claims to supremacy over the lay power were to dominate the entire period up to the beginning of the fourteenth century, and inevitably to bring the Papacy and Church into collision with the lay power.

The chief elements of the programme were embodied in the *Dictatus Papae* of 1075. Among other things it claimed (1) that the pope was the sovereign head of the Church, establishing its laws, deposing and translating its bishops, and judging all its important cases, and (2) that he was the superior of the *emperor*[54] and kings, able to depose them and release their subjects from their oaths of allegiance. It maintained that bishops might not receive their office from any layman, nor might kings continue to appoint them. Gregory tried to establish the independent election of bishops, and suppress the inheritance of ecclesiastical offices and the sale of the same ('simony'). He began a process of centralizing authority in Rome: partly through bypassing the authority of the archbishops so as to make the appointment of the bishops tightly dependent on the Papacy, partly by acting through papal legates who took precedence over any member of the hierarchy in the land to which they were sent. From 1075, indeed, certain legates were permanent: 'Vicars of the Pope', they exercised full pontifical authority. These reforms coincided with Gratian's codification of the Canon law; and this, combined with the new centralization, drew more and more disputed cases to the Curia in Rome, vastly increasing the amount of papal business.

The programme, all the more for its abruptness and immediacy, appeared to the kings and the emperor to shear away a huge part of their power and authority, and their immediate reaction was to resist. The political effects in England were considerable, in Italy and, above all, Germany, disastrous. The way the quarrel led to the mutual ruin of both empire and Papacy will be described later. The immediate question is not the political and diplomatic repercussions of the Gregorian reforms but their effect on government.

The reforms had little effect at parish level, where the lords retained the right of nomination. As far as the great Church offices were concerned the most scandalous form of lay interference disappeared, but the electoral principle did not have quite the effect the Papacy had anticipated. For the rules of the electors confined the decision not to the majority but to the *maior et sanior pars*, that is to say, not to the unqualified majority but to 'the most sound'. This ambiguous formula permitted the monarch to

---

[54] See above, p. 885.

manipulate the elections. Furthermore, the post-Gregorian bishop or abbot was still master of vast manorial estates and continued to have to discharge the feudal obligations attached to them. Hence he still had to be and act as a vassal, even if he was no longer obliged to do homage. (In France, exceptionally, he continued to pay homage.)

While the Church remained locked into the governmental system by way of infeudation, at another level it was locked into the king's own household and its nascent officialdom. The time had gone by when the only literate persons a king could find at all were likely to be clerics, but it remained true that the brightest and best minds, the most experienced administrators, and the most knowledgeable bureau-chiefs were likely to be found most easily in the Church. The typical career structure was for a young man to take orders; go to the university and study, say, law; find a benefice; go on to help administer the estates of some abbey or bishopric; take a higher degree, and at the age of 40 or so have some bishopric or even archbishopric bestowed on him by the king. In short, he weaved in and out of an ecclesiastical and a 'lay' career or (like Thomas Becket) the other way round. This had quite enormous advantages for the royal court, for the king did not have to pay a penny for this service. All he had to do was to appoint his chosen man to some church benefice. In this way the Church was paying him! Utilizing the benefice to pay for royal officialdom was indeed the counterpart of making a benefice bear knight service; both were modes of siphoning the vast resources of the Church to the advantage of the royal power.

The introduction of the reforms, the degree of their success, and the net effect on the royal power have never been better expressed than by Richard Southern:

Kings and laymen lost their direct control of most ecclesiastical appointments; they lost their jurisdiction over ecclesiastical persons and causes; they lost their power to deprive incumbents of ecclesiastical offices; they could not defy the Pope for very long. All this was most dramatically displayed in a series of incidents which have caught the imagination of later generations—Henry IV of Germany at Canossa, Henry II of England in his shirt at Canterbury, King John a vassal of the Pope, the family of Frederick II destroyed, a papal nominee on the throne of Sicily. But these incidents do not tell the central truth that secular rulers had only to learn the rules of a complicated game in order to dispose of a larger reservoir of ecclesiastical wealth and talent than ever before.

The primitive rulers of Europe before the twelfth century had depended on their almost unrestricted control of ecclesiastical appointments for many advantages. This control had given them reliable agents in peace, troops and treasure in war, a regular replenishment of their income at every vacancy, a reserve of gold and silver in times of need, a variety of places to stay on their journeys. Naturally they viewed with apprehension the loss of these privileges. But by a slow process of adjustment they discovered that they had been unnecessarily alarmed. True, they could no longer simply appoint bishops or exact entrance fees for ecclesiastical office, they could no longer take ecclesiastical property or interfere with ecclesiastical law. But more than ever before they could use ecclesiastical wealth to finance the growing activity of secular government. Clerks in holy orders, though personally subject only to ecclesiastical jurisdiction, were the most effective agents of secular government in the twelfth and thirteenth centuries. They expected ecclesiastical promotion as the reward of their labours, and kings never found any difficulty in providing this. Ecclesiastical office was the main source of treasure from which secular rulers paid their ministers. Everyone from the Pope downwards acquiesced in this situation. Naturally therefore the army of royal officials grew by leaps and bounds. Papal dispensations made it possible for the most successful of them to accumulate very large revenues; and at the end they could expect a bishopric.

For all this a royal *fiat* was no longer enough. There were rules to be kept. Where there are rules, there must be experts; and where there are experts, there will be loop-holes. The clergy themselves provided the experts who showed the king how to use the ecclesiastical treasure according to the rules of ecclesiastical discipline. These experts, men like Henry of Susa, also expected ecclesiastical rewards from the secular ruler, but so long as the business was managed carefully there was no occasion for bitterness. The dramatic disputes arose either from clumsiness or ignorance or over-confidence or personal hatred. By keeping the rules and not going too far all unpleasantness could be avoided.[55]

This elegant quotation mentions how the monarch 'lost control over ecclesiastical persons and causes'. This is yet another of the (to our mind) odd peculiarities of feudal polity. We can—if painfully—take on board the notion of jurisdiction and government split between one country-wide authority and a number of local authorities, each being juridically equal. It is harder to accept the notion of an entire range of cases and individuals being exempt from the common law of the land and subject only to its own codes of practice. Such was the case. However, we have to distinguish two things here. The first is that from time immemorial certain matters were regarded as spiritual, and here the verdict of the Church was binding. The second, wholly different, was that all the personnel of the Church were immune from any discipline other than its own.

As to the first, neither baronial or royal courts had any right to deal with incest, adultery, bigamy, usury, or failure to perform oaths and vows. The latter grew to invade the sphere of contracts in general, so that the hand-clasp to seal a bargain was taken to imply a pledge of faith and hence justifiable only by the ecclesiastical court. All matrimonial cases came within

[55] Southern, *Western Society*, 130–1.

the Church jurisdiction also and this included all the impediments to marriage (an unbelievably comprehensive list) and the legitimacy of children. So wide was the potential ambit of ecclesiastical jurisdiction that conflicts between the Church courts and those of the lay power were bound to occur, and they did. Consequently, the list of purely ecclesiastical cases given above was modified in the different *regna* according to customs prevalent there and the degree of lay resistance. For all that, these courts excluded royal jurisdiction in a way unintelligible to a modern audience.[56]

Immunity of churchmen from lay jurisdiction was potentially more explosive, for it was novel. In the Anglo-Saxon kingdom, for instance, clerics who had breached the criminal law were tried in the hundred or shire courts as a matter of course. The Gregorians demanded an end to this. They insisted that the Church and only the Church could judge its ministers. As such, it could not execute but it could 'defrock'. After that, of course, the one-time 'criminous clerk' was like any ordinary subject. All the same, the claim meant at the least that the criminous clerk would have a second chance, and that the kings found repugnant.

Here they lost the battle, and nowhere worse than in England. It was precisely this issue which led to the assassination of Thomas Becket and Becket's murder forced Henry II to seek absolution and to abandon his case. The consequences came to be ludicrous. Arraigned before the criminal court—or after its sentence—the accused pleaded 'benefit of clergy'. The Church courts were then supposed to try him again, but usually acquitted and discharged him. Originally only ordained clerks, monks, and nuns could claim the privilege, but by 1350 it was extended to everybody who could read! And to satisfy themselves that the accused could do so, the judges required him to read (or recite!) Psalm 51![57]

To summarize: like the kingship, the Church anteceded feudalism, and like the kingship it was in the feudal system but not of it. Both of them were antibodies but strangely, as we have seen, it was the feudal arrangement which brought them into a symbiosis. Just as the baronage was at once the support of and the constraint on the monarchy, so too was the Church. Just as the baronage shared jurisdiction and power with the king on a territorial

[56] See Bk. III, Ch. 2 on the Caliphate for a similar division of jurisdiction in Islam. *Sharia* cases and *muzalim* (complaints) cases were handled by different sets of courts. But in principle *sharia* supposedly controlled the *muzalim* (secular) jurisdiction too. The *ulema* were never able to enforce this but never renounced it either. The *sharia*, the word of God, regulated everything. In Christianity, however, the Church recognized a due sphere for secular authority from its beginnings, on the basis of 'render to Caesar the things that are Caesar's and to God the things that are God's'. So although there is a dichotomization of authority in both cases, the grounds and the line of bifurcation are quite different.

[57] Admittedly, it is a very long psalm.

basis, so the Church shared it with both on a functional basis. It was one more (vast) immunity, a huge subtraction from an already parcellized central sovereignty.

It was not the last. To complicate the feudal polity still more, from the eleventh century groups entered on the scene who were not clerics but laymen, and yet neither vassals nor villeins. They were neither those who prayed, those who fought, nor those who supported both by labouring the fields. They were the *townsmen*.

3.3. *The Towns*

The towns are the third of the non-feudal elements lodged within feudal society. They have a later chapter solely devoted to themselves. The reason for this is that they were destined to play a role and exercise an influence in Western Europe such as they never did in the Middle East or the Orient. They are one of the forces—some have said the unique force—that turned it into something quite unlike the rest of the world; the springboard for its entire subsequent development, economic, social, and political. How far this claim is justified must be gauged by the rest of this *History*. What is clear at this point is that the towns were only able to develop in their peculiar way because their political environment was feudal. Though they could be and were slotted into a predominantly feudal polity, they were impelled by values and a dynamic that was not feudal and the political forms they evolved outlived feudalism.

Towns had survived into the Dark Ages, for the most part as either the administrative seat of the bishop or a fortified place—*bourg*—serving as an asylum for the country-folk and military headquarters for the lord. Exceptionally, a flicker of trade persisted in one or two places. Overwhelmingly, townsfolk were dependents of the ecclesiastical or seigneurial establishments, and their numbers were puny.

But by the late fourteenth century they were the most vital part of Western Europe's economic life and a quickening presence in its polities. Unlike their Dark Age prototypes, they were trading and manufacturing centres, their inhabitants were freemen, their governments were communal and conciliar, and their relationship to their traditional lords or kings ran the gamut from strictly controlled and chartered liberties to complete independence. The former types were incorporated into the feudal *regnum* via the country-wide assemblies the kings or princes were beginning to convene round about the last quarter of the thirteenth century. The independent cities revived an ancient form: they were republics.

By comparison with the great cities of the Middle East and the Orient, even the largest of these towns was tiny. At Marco Polo's death (1272) the population of his native Venice was 100,000, the same as Florence. The great towns of the Middle East and Orient vastly outstripped the largest and wealthiest of any European cities in every material respect. But these two groups of towns differed in kind. All those Eastern towns were the seats of an imperial governor and an army garrison to whom their populations were subject, and in many countries—China, Japan, the Arab lands—internal walls divided the town into so many quarters into which the population was literally locked for the night and patrolled by armed soldiers.[58] By contrast the European towns were communities of free citizens who, at the least, administered and controlled their own internal affairs by charter from their overlord or king and, at the most, owed allegiance to nobody at all except themselves.

They came to be like this because, in contrast to the cities of the Middle and Far East, they grew up in a feudal not an imperial environment. We noted how the feudal polity was a polyarchy, a loose articulation of localized power-points. Just like any castellany or marcher lordship, the towns could—and did—by dint of pushing, shoving, and even fighting, establish themselves as a 'liberty'; hence another autonomous power-point in the feudal network. They were restrained only by the counterforce of their local overlords or kings and if these were weak enough (e.g. as in Italy, Germany) they broke entirely free.

Their political race in the Middle Ages was necessarily an ambivalent one. They allied with any powers that could assist their drive to autonomy or independence, irrespective of whether these were local overlords against the king or vice versa, the lay power against the Church or vice versa, the foreigner against the fellow-countryman or vice versa. Thus, for instance, German kings—the Holy Roman Emperors—favoured the towns against the great ecclesiastical and lay princes, but were so weak they were ultimately forced to leave the cities to confront their local overlords by themselves. In Flanders and Italy the towns' diplomacy was complicated yet further by factual and economic cleavages among the townsfolk themselves, all evoking the aid of or resisting attack from outside powers. But as these complications and outcomes form the subject of a separate chapter, they need not be pursued any further at this point.

---

[58] See pp. 726, 775 above and p. 1109 below; also pp. 1224, 1244 re the Hindu polity in India.

6

The *Regna*

1. THE POLITICAL GEOGRAPHY OF WESTERN AND MIDDLE EUROPE

*T*he kingdoms were there first. They anteceded feudalism. A kingdom was, by definition, a territorial unit acknowledging a king as its supreme political authority. To the extent that it became the unique organizing principle in society, feudalism denatured the kingship, reducing it to the simpler role of overlordship. Left to itself, the highest integration feudalism could achieve was an equilibrium of polyarchic forces, usually unstable. Historically—perhaps logically too, but that is not important here—the non-feudal, pre-feudal attributes of the kingship were what provided feudally organized societies with their integrating principle. Where the kingship was powerful, a coherent political system emerged: the feudal *regna*, as in England, Sicily, and France. Where it was weak, the *regnum* dissolved into a congeries of petty principalities, free cities, and even city republics: such was the fate of 'Germany' and Italy.

The earliest of these *regna*, and the only ones we are concerned with for the moment, were succession states to the Roman Empire in the West. They were the kingdom of England; some petty kingdoms in the Iberian peninsula; the kingdoms of the West Franks, of the East Franks, and the 'Middle Kingdom' of 'Lotharingia'; and, finally, the kingdom of Italy.

In Britain, apart from the Celtic tribal principalities in Wales and the Scottish Highlands and the English-speaking proto-kingdom of Lothian in the Scottish Lowlands, the Anglo-Saxon *regnum* of England had been united under a Wessex dynasty with borders not very different from those of today. In the Iberian peninsula, the Arabs occupied four-fifths of the peninsula, confining the Gothic nobles to the north-west. A kingdom was formed in the Asturias in the tenth century with its capital at Leon and, as it expanded, it spawned the kingdom of Castile in 1031. In the mid-Pyrenees, meanwhile, a kingdom of Navarre arose *c.*900 and then, expanding in turn, spawned the kingdom of Aragon in 1037. North of the Ebro lay Christian territory that Charlemagne had fortified against the Arabs. This was the Spanish March, no kingdom but the County of Barcelona, which, until the mid-thirteenth century, was a fief of the kingdom of the (West) Franks.

This last kingdom was one of the three into which Charlemagne's empire had been divided by the three Carolingian heirs in 843 by the historical Treaty of Verdun. The western part, called Neustria, or West Francia, and later the Regnum Francorum, 'Kingdom of the Franks'—occupied four-fifths of the territory of modern France. Its eastern borders lay well west of the Rhine and the Rhône. The eastern part—East Francia at one time, but which anachronistically we will call Germany—ran from the Rhineland (the archbishoprics of Mainz, Rheims, and Speyer) and comprised all the lands which Charlemagne had conquered eastward to the Elbe. But in between lay the territory allocated to the third heir, Lothair, and most of that heterogeneous territory was destined to fall piecemeal to 'Germany' over the course of time.

Finally, there was the kingdom of Italy. This was, effectively, the successor to the earlier Lombard kingdoms, and covered the north and centre of the peninsula, down to the vicinity of Rome, with the exception of the Byzantine enclave of Venice.

These kingdoms varied greatly in size and population, as shown in Table 3.6.1.

Such were the succession kingdoms to the Western Roman Empire. The surprising thing about them is their durability. For despite all the tides of invasion, and in the face of the disintegration of political authority, their number varied remarkably little, and the singularity of kingship was so great that no local tyrant, however powerful, dared ever to usurp the title of king.

There remains to be mentioned that strange political entity, the Roman Empire, later (in 1157) called the Holy Roman Empire. Everyone is familiar with Voltaire's gibe that it was neither holy nor Roman nor an Empire, but this was not quite true. It was indeed an empire, for it embraced present-day

TABLE 3.6.1. *The sizes of the medieval kingdoms*

	Area	Population size	
		1000	1300
England (and Wales*)	0.15mkm^2	1.75m	3.75m
France	0.55mkm^2	6.5m	16.0m
Germany	0.36mkm^2	4.0m	9.0m
Spanish kingdoms (at			
Reconquista 1212)	—	N.A.	5.5m
North Italy	0.15mkm^2 (approx.)	N.A.	5.5m

Source: C. McEvedy and R. Jones, *Atlas of World Population History*.
Note: *Wales being less than 10% of the total.

Germany, the Lowlands, Switzerland, North Italy, and Croatia. It was Roman in that the would-be emperor had to be crowned in Rome. It was 'holy' (*sacrum*) in that it was envisaged as the secular arm of an indivisible Christian commonwealth of which the spiritual part was the Church, *quod semper, quod ubique, quod ab omnibus*. This high-flown theory of the empire was to lead to the struggle between the emperors and the popes whose shock-waves caused the political ruin of the kingdoms of Germany and Italy, and will be discussed in that context. Here it is enough to make only this brief comment. The coronation of Charlemagne as emperor by the pope in Rome in 800 seems to have been the pope's idea. Charlemagne, too, seems to have thought of the title as personal to himself, but for what are effectively family reasons he did pass it on to his successor Louis the Pious; by the Treaty of Verdun (843) it was to descend to the 'Middle Kingdom', that is, 'Lotharingia', running south from the North Sea and including the kingdom of Italy. That territorial unit turned out to be non-viable and the imperial title became nominal. The empire was re-founded by Otto I, the king of the Germans, and thenceforward it was always the German king who descended into Italy to be crowned king of Italy and then proceeded to Rome for coronation as emperor. The title and the office of king of the Germans was separate and distinct from that of the emperor, and the empire comprised, as noted, not only Germany but the Lowlands, the kingdom of Burgundy (soon absorbed into Germany)—not to be confused with the Duchy of Burgundy[1]—and north Italy. As will be seen, the empire as such never had a central bureaucracy, taxation system, or standing army. In fact its central institutions were non-existent. It was kept going only by the energy, resources, and diplomacy of the German kings.

The emperor did at certain times claim a jurisdiction over mere kings like those of England and France, a relation that was of course, consistent with the ancient Roman notion of the relationship between emperors and *reges*; but no French or English king took the claim seriously or indeed recognized it.

This little we have to say at this point, for the sorry history of the empire as a political system is part of the constitutional history of Germany and will be dealt with in that context.

2. THE DEVELOPMENT OF THE EUROPEAN *REGNA*

The fates of the kingdoms of Germany and Italy, France and England, between the tenth and the end of the thirteenth century were very diverse. The German kingdom in the tenth century was not feudal. Feudalism was

---

[1] Being that part of the original *regnum Burgundiae*, west of the Saône, which had been recovered by the French Carolingians, to remain part of the kingdom of France.

introduced there in the twelfth century. The kingdom started off with a powerful but primitive personal type of monarchy. By the fourteenth century this kingship was reduced almost to nullity and the kingdom itself was an almost nominal confederacy of independent units. The kingdom of the Franks, on the other hand, was in the tenth century in a similar condition to what Germany would come to be in the fourteenth, a largely nominal confederation of some half-dozen great territorial duchies and counties under a shadowy kingship; whereas by the thirteenth century it had been pulled together as the paradigm feudal kingdom, under a kingship which exploited to the full all the advantages it could extract from feudal law. England in the tenth century was non-feudal, like Germany, and it too possessed a powerful personalized kingship. Reinforced by the effect of the Norman Conquest, this kingship, a blend of Anglo-Saxon and feudal characteristics, ended up as the most effective and wide-reaching central government of the time,[2] but one whose activities were balanced and controlled by the equal and opposite growth of increasingly institutionalized restraints. From then on the constitutional development was to follow a recurrent rhythm in which every advance in the power of the executive was matched by a similar counter-advance in the restraining institutions, and every such advance of the latter provoked a corresponding advance in the former.

3. THE FEUDAL KINGDOM OF ENGLAND

3.1. *Development*

England was the smallest and least populous of the four great *regna*. Its area and its population was proportionately only about one-quarter that of the kingdom of the Franks. Also, its land frontiers were very short indeed compared with those of Germany or France, and in addition, the tribal principalities of Wales and the nascent Scottish kingdoms of Lothian and Strathclyde were weak neighbours, raiders rather than invaders. So the unification of England took place very early compared with the Continental kingdoms. By the death of Edgar in 975 England, in contrast to France, was recognized by its ruling strata—if not its population—as one indivisible *regnum*. Excepting the disputed area of Northumberland and Cumberland, its frontiers were much as we know them today. From that time onwards, aristocratic reaction to the Crown was to seek privileges or to rule the country, but not to return to the Heptarchy.[3] The two eleventh century-

---

[2] Norman Sicily is a possible exception.

[3] This consisted of the Seven Kingdoms that had emerged after the Teutonic conquest.

conquests—first the Danish (1013), then the Norman (1066)—only confirmed and strengthened the sense of a territorial unity.

This was a Germanic kingdom without the slightest debt to Rome, except for the Church. It was prosperous, with plenty of silver currency. More and more land was coming into the hands of a few great landed aristocrats, but fiscally, militarily, and judicially it was a freeholders' country ruled by monarchy and the aristocratic-Church establishment. Its army was the *fyrd*, a national levy around the professional core of the two or three thousand housecarls of the monarch, and similar but smaller establishments of the magnates. Its justice was the customary justice of 'folk-law', as determined in local courts attended by the freemen, and following the procedures of the compurgation and ordeal. Government was almost wholly a local affair, carried out in judicial form in defined territorial jurisdictions—the shires, the hundreds, and the vills—covering the country. But these were presided over by the king's officials: the bishop, the ealdorman (later called the earl), and the shire-reeve. These provided the links between king and locality. They were—in theory at least—removable by the king. For his part, his chief role was to defend the country. Any further activities, other than his privilege of putting a person or community under his protection (his *mund*) for limited periods of time, were 'dooms' (judgements) formulated in the presence and with the assent of his counsellors, the *witan*, that is, Church and lay magnates, called as and when he required. The king carried out day-to-day administration through his household officers, in 'patrimonial' style. By the eleventh century the chancellor's office had grown into an active department of clerks which issued a stream of royal charters and *writs*, these last being instructions, stamped with the royal seal.

The kingship lay within the royal house of Wessex, but descended not by primogeniture but by election—effectively a consensus of the great men of the kingdom. As an office it was universally respected, but its effectiveness depended entirely on the personality of the incumbent. The line of able kings ended with Edgar in 975. The government of the kingdom was in decadence on the eve of the Conquest.

The essential point about the Norman Conquest is precisely that it was a *conquest*. An army smashed all the English resistance and took the lands and the places of the Anglo-Saxon ruling class, and England was henceforth corseted by these 6,000 armoured knights. William declared the entire country royal property—*terrae regis*—and divided it accordingly: about one-sixth to himself alone, about two-fifths to his soldiers, and about one-quarter as Church lands; the remaining one-fifth stayed in the hands of the petty freemen. William treated his host as his army of occupation and he organized it along the lines he knew, that is, feudally. He apportioned the confiscated lands among about 180 tenants-in-chief in return for homage and knight service, along with all the accompanying feudal incidents (e.g. reliefs, wardships, marriage) and 'aids'. From then on the relationship between the king and the great men of his kingdom was to be the feudal vassalic contractual one.

But it was a feudal vassalic tie that differed in significant ways from its archetype in the kingdom of France[4]—and for that matter in William's own duchy of Normandy—and the reason is simply that in Normandy William's relationship to his barons was that of a duke, that is, he was a feudal *dominus* or 'lord', whereas in England he was their *king*. William entered fully into the tradition of the Anglo-Saxon kingship by coronation, unction, the coronation oath, and the subsequent acclamation of the notables—in short, by legitimation. Indeed, as victorious war-leader, disposer of the land, and himself much the richest of all landowners, William exploited every scrap of the authority of the Anglo-Saxon kingship.

1. He did not permit land-tenure to be the sole political bond with the king but, on the contrary, exacted an oath of fealty from all landholders and not just from his own tenants; all had to be faithful to him, even against their own lords. First exacted at Salisbury in 1086, the oath became part of the regular recurrent business of the local courts. Also, whenever a rear-vassal did homage for his land to a mesne lord he expressly reserved the fidelity he owed the king.

2. No right to conduct private war existed in Anglo-Saxon law and William (and on the whole his successors) successfully enforced the prohibition. We have to wait until the fifteenth century for such a rule to be finally enforced in France.[5]

3. The national, English military arm—the *fyrd*—was retained, and even called out by the Norman kings against their rebellious Norman barons. It was reorganized by Henry II in 1181 and Edward I in 1285.

4. For over a century the kings continued to levy national taxes in the Anglo-Saxon tradition on the entire free population (the 'geld', later called a 'carucage'.)

5. Finally, justice was only partially and temporarily feudalized. With some exceptions (e.g. the Palatinates), the shire courts and hundred courts persisted with their ancient Anglo-Saxon jurisdictions unchanged except that purely ecclesiastical matters were henceforward dealt with in ecclesiastical courts. Moreover, they continued to be linked to the Crown,

---

[4] See p. 921 below.   [5] See Bk. IV, Ch. 5, p. 1281 below.

being presided over by the king's personal representatives, the old 'shire-reeves' or sheriffs.

From this point on, the constitutional history of the kingdom is an ever-expanding royal jurisdiction at the expense of the feudatories, a corresponding professionalization and specialization in the king's *curia*, and a harsh exploitation of the Crown's feudal dues from its tenants; until, in the reign of John (1199–1216), a baronial revolt temporarily halts the advance and establishes a new line of development. Haltingly at first, confidently in the fourteenth century, a dialectic establishes itself between the king and his professional administrative officers in the (inner) council, and the wider circle of magnates supported by the lesser knights and then by the merchant class trying to control them.

The great leap forward in expanding royal justice at the expense of the feudatories took place under Henry II (1154–89). Henry, the heir to vast Angevin possessions throughout France and later, through his marriage to Eleanor of Aquitaine, the master of that huge territory also, ascended the throne after a bloody and protracted set of civil wars, fought on classically feudal lines and resulting in anarchy. Henry II was a great English monarch. The details of his works we shall pick up later when we describe the feudal kingdom at its apogee under Edward I, his grandson. But to sketch the main lines only: Henry did not merely restore the kingdom to its conditions under Henry I, his grandfather, but pushed the royal jurisdiction well beyond it.

Up to this time justice was either popular or feudal: that is to say, civil and criminal cases were dealt with either in the shire and hundred courts, or in the feudal and franchisal. In a series of measures spread throughout Henry's reign, he effected the most far-reaching changes in the judicial and administrative system. It must always be borne in mind that the two processes were not easily distinguishable in the Middle Ages, when what we should call administrative decisions were effected in a court by judicial processes. In the hope not to become entangled in the legal niceties, which take much space to describe accurately, we could summarize these innovations under three headings. In the first place, he brought a wide range of new cases into his own royal court. The criminal cases—breaches of the king's peace—may be regarded perhaps as inherent to his role as *rex*, but he broke completely new ground in civil cases relating to the dispossession of a tenant from his land by somebody else. By applying to his Chancery for a writ, the dispossessed plaintiff could, in effect, have the case heard before the royal justices. The most striking illustration is the writ called *Praecipe*. This writ was issued to the local sheriff, and it ordered the local lord to restore the land to the plaintiff forthwith or else appear in the royal court to answer for contempt of the royal authority.

In the second place, the 'royal court' was enormously extended. The royal court *as such* was the central *curia*. This was still largely undifferentiated, apart from the Chancery, its oldest specialized organ, which handled all the documentation and records, and the Exchequer, established as early as 1135, which handled the sheriff's accounts and had a division which functioned as a court for revenue matters. In 1178, however, we learn that two clerics and three laymen were appointed as judges to hear 'complaints of the people' and that they were not to depart from the *curia regis*. These judges were no longer interchangeable with the personnel of the Exchequer and they followed the king, as his *curia in banco*, wherever he held his court. (As we shall see, this court was the common ancestor of two courts, Common Pleas and King's Bench.)

In addition, from 1179 onwards the kingdom was divided into four circuits to be perambulated by five justices apiece. These justices held the king's court in each of the counties they visited. Now this court was not the traditional shire court, presided over by the sheriff. That continued as before. The justices' court was a *special meeting* of the shire court to which the sheriff had to summon all freeholders including the lay and clerical magnates, the reeve and four 'legal men' from every vill, and twelve 'legal' burgesses from every borough. (The magnates soon acquired the rights to be represented by attorney.) The justices then opened this court by taking the business before it and this was as much administrative as judicial: all pleas of the Crown held over from earlier courts, all private pleas for which suitors had obtained a royal writ, criminal offences, and the crown's feudal incidents (aids, wardships, and the like), the care of the royal manors, and so forth. (These were the 'Pleas of the Crown'.)

Finally, the procedure in these courts was very different from the archaic compurgation, ordeal, even trial by battle that obtained in the traditional popular (i.e. shire and hundred) courts, for the king permitted all freemen to establish their title to land by calling on a sworn inquest. It is in fact a *jury*. Knowing the facts, these neighbours could report right away on who last held such a piece of land, who last presented the incumbent to a particular church, and so forth. These juries found simply on facts: they were a little more than witnesses but less than judges. Here was the origin of the *petty* jury, what today we would call a *trial* jury.

But in addition Henry used the sworn inquest procedures to strike at crime. In the Assize of Clarendon (1166) he ordered twelve legal men from every hundred and four from every vill in a shire to appear before the sheriff and state on oath who they believed to be robbers, murderers, and thieves, or their harbourers. The individuals they indicted were to be tried only by the royal justices.[6] Here we have the origins of the presentment jury, or grand jury (still actively used in the USA).

Before turning to the crisis of John's reign, one point concerning this royal justice must be stressed. It did not come free. The plaintiff who requested a royal writ or elected to go to a royal court and have a jury of inquest empanelled for his case had to pay for these privileges. The presiding judges took fees for the cases coming before them and in criminal cases the fines and forfeitures went to the Crown. 'Justice', it was said, 'is a great source of income.' On the other hand, civil suits in the royal courts were in no way forced upon individuals, but they soon learned to prefer their procedure to the traditional popular courts and paid willingly for the privilege. Because royal justice was relatively attractive, it supplanted the alternatives.

In *all* feudal *regna* without exception the political process boils down to a struggle between king and feudatories, and is marked by what are tritely referred to as periods of royal 'expansion' and feudal 'reaction'. The reign of John is famously the period of 'feudal reaction'. It culminates in Magna Carta. But the significance of this 'feudal reaction' is that it did *not* seek to put back the clock to before Henry II's reforms. It accepted those reforms. What it did was to try and fix their metes and bounds in written form, *not* to revert to 'pure' feudalism. John abused his position as *rex* in so far as he self-servingly exploited the profits of royal justice and, indeed, began to deny it to some of the more refractory barons; and he abused his position as feudal *dominus* even more; but the thrust of the Great Charter of 1215 was to accept the strengthened Crown and its expanded jurisdiction, yet to try to eliminate the caprices of the individual monarch.

The Charter contains all manner of topical provision—fish-weirs, debts owed to Jews, and suchlike—and naturally (since the ecclesiastics played a large part in drafting it) provisions to guarantee the free election of the bishops and abbots of the churches in England. It also contains one or two large provisions of such generality as to leave modern commentary some- what at a loss: like the one, for instance, that constrains the king not to 'sell or delay or deny justice'. Commentaries, from the seventeenth-century common lawyers through Blackstone and Bishop Stubbs to the present day, have been legion, but as far as the present argument is concerned I wish to make only three points.

---

[6] The verdict always was still arrived at by compurgation and ordeal. The Lateran Council withdrew Church assent to the ordeal in 1215 leaving the authorities nonplussed if the accused refused to accept the verdict of a petty jury. From 1275 onwards they were imprisoned, later tortured, to make them accept it.

The first relates to the very often quoted and eminently quotable clause that runs: 'No freeman shall be arrested, or detained in prison, or deprived of his freehold, or outlawed, or banished or in any way molested; and we will not set forth against him, nor send against him, unless by the lawful judgment of his peers or by the law of the land' (Clause 39). There has been endless controversy over the 'judgment of his peers' and the distinction (if any) between this and 'the law of the land'. I do not intend to enter into this in any way, simply to draw attention to the significance of the clause as a whole in the light of every political culture (Greece, Rome, and Byzantium excepted) encountered in this book so far. The significance lies in that the barons who drafted it are not demanding independence or even partial immunities from the central government. They accept that the government has the right (and duty?) to punish them. What they want, however, is a *fair trial*. They want *due process of law* and *the application of nothing but the law*. Where at that time shall we find any such presumption on the part of subjects, or even the very *notion* of abstract legality? In Byzantium, perhaps, but not in the lands of Islam, nor in India, nor in China. And where have we ever found such a claim in the past? In the Greek city-states and the Roman Republic, but these had no connection at all, direct or indirect, with the sanctity of law in the European Middle Ages. This insistence on legality was without doubt powerfully strengthened by the tradition of the Old Testament, then by the Canon law of the Church, and then by the revival of Roman law in the twelfth century, but it did not begin with them. It was peculiar to the European Middle Ages. Nor let it be thought that the *fact* that the barons took up arms against their king rebuts their claim to be upholding law against caprice. For that rebellion was perfectly lawful. The barons renounced their allegiance by the formal *diffidatio* as, under feudal law, they had every right to do.

The second and third points can be dealt with more briefly. The Charter limits the Crown as *dominus* but upholds it as *rex*. It contains many provisions designed to define feudatories' rights and obligations and reasserts them against the Crown's recent abusive manipulation, but it also contains provisions which uphold the recent extension of the king's justice. The former can be read as a catalogue of John's abuses: they fix the amount an heir must pay by way of relief; protect wards and widows from extortionate fees; give widows the right to remain celibate; limit military service to what was hitherto due; and so forth. Such clauses embody and illustrate the contractual nature of lordship/vassalage. On the other hand the clauses relating to royal justice (which, it must be remembered, includes administration), while limiting excessive fines and punishment, are anxious to make this justice even more accessible and to entrust it to only the most reputable officials. So suitors should not have to follow the *curia* around to have their cases heard; these suits should be heard at a fixed place. (From this point, therefore, the Court of Common Pleas is held at Westminster but the court that still follows the king is called King's Bench.) Again, the king's three 'possessory assizes' (those dealing with ejection from one's lands) are to be taken *much more often*! Certainly, the Charter shows deep distrust of the sheriffs and limits their powers, but there was nothing new in this. Henry II had conducted a vast purge of sheriffs in 1166. What appears in the Charter is that, though the barons constrain and downgrade the office of sheriff, they are happy to accept the king's itinerant justices. Article 36 shows the popularity of judgment by sworn inquest (i.e. the jury), for it lays down that in cases involving life and limb this writ is to be granted *gratis* and not to be denied. Only one clause in the Charter appears to seek to restrict the scope of the new royal justice. It is Article 34, which limits the issue of the writ *Praecipe*.[7] This writ was resented because it transferred a case from a lord's court to the king's court and so deprived that lord of the feudal right to try a subtenant. But the meaning of the article is controversial, some saying that it *is* restrictive and others arguing that it relates only marginally to certain technical details; in practice, anyhow, the law was to develop in ways that made this clause inoperative.

Although the Church and the magnates were not the only beneficiaries of the Charter (London merchants and so forth also get some satisfaction), they were the chief protagonists and beneficiaries, so that it may seem surprising that in Clause 15 the barons promise to their own tenants the same limitations on the feudal aids and incidents they had wrung from the king. But the explanation is simple. The tenures were so various—a man might be lord in one hundred, subject in a royal hundred, a tenant by barony, a tenant by knight service, and many other kinds of tenure—that the tenants-in-chief simply had to generalize the concessions to all freemen. In this way the provisions of the Charter apply generally to the entire free population.

There remains one final point concerning the Charter of 1215. Its Clause 41 is an 'execution' clause. The original promoters of the rebellion (mostly petty barons from the north) were so distrustful of the king that a committee of twenty-five barons was to be set up with the right to seize the king's property and lands and seek justice in whatever way possible, saving only the persons of the king, the queen, and their children. In brief, it was a licence to make war and it is not surprising that the 'twenty-five' are largely the original promoters mentioned above. The course of subsequent

---

[7] See pp. 902–3 above.

events made this clause inoperative, but it represents a milestone. In, admittedly, the crudest of ways, it sets up a committee purporting to represent the general baronage to control the activities of the Crown. This device is due to be repeated in more and more modulated forms until, a century or so later, it becomes institutionalized. The next step in this direction occurred at the end of the reign of John's son, Henry III. During his long reign the royal judicial and administrative structures were strengthened and deepened, but all that we have space to refer to here is the re-emergence of feudatory constraint upon the personal government of the king.

Henry III was a miserable failure. During his first sixteen years he was a minor and the government was run by a baronial council. He himself was a pious ninny. When he assumed his majority in 1232 he got himself into the hands of Continental favourites and distanced himself from the older Anglo-Norman aristocracy. He made a hash of everything he attempted, whether war or foreign policy, but he did, continually, re-confirm the Great Charter.

From 1232, when Henry decided to dismiss the council of regency and govern in his own right, the issue, as the barons saw it, was of a king locking himself away with his household officials and submitting to the advice of (regrettably foreign) personal favourites. From the king's point of view, of course, he was emancipating himself from a suffocating tutelage by magnates who had engrossed the great offices of state, the treasurer of the Exchequer and the Chancery especially. The Exchequer, the most ancient specialized branch of government, pursued excessively hidebound accounting routines. The chancellor kept the Great Seal which authorized all other branches of the government to take action, and they included demands for money from the Exchequer. John himself, faced with the financial emergencies of war, had begun to use another and more intimate officer, the man who controlled his chamber wherein lay the royal treasure. Henry developed his own private secretariat in his *Wardrobe*; its officers used his private seal—the 'Privy Seal'—to order the chancellor to affix the Great Seal to Henry's order, and soon great sums of money were being ordered out of the Exchequer, or diverted from it into the Wardrobe, for the king's personal uses.[8]

Conflict with the barons came about after twenty-five years of conspicuously unsuccessful personal government—humiliating military defeats in

[8] What we are observing here is exactly what we saw occurring in the Han Empire—and indeed (as will be seen) throughout the Chinese imperial history. See Bk. II, Ch. 6, pp. 490–1; Bk. III, Chs. 3 and 4, pp. 762–3, 826–7; and Bk. IV, Ch. 2, pp. 1138–9.

France, the swamping of bishoprics and benefices by Italian clerics directly appointed by the pope and a consequent drain of enormous sums to Rome, perpetual indebtedness due to lavish church-building and military adventures—with the quite ludicrous and (to the barons) totally irrelevant claim of Henry's brother to the throne of Sicily. In 1258 the pope threatened to excommunicate Henry if he failed to pay the papal debt for this Sicilian adventure. He could raise the sum only if the baronage granted him an extraordinary aid. He convened them and the upshot was the plan embodied in what is known as 'the Provision of Oxford'. It assumes—or rather it recognizes from past experience with a shifty and feckless monarch—that as long as he is left in personal charge of the departments of state, that is, his inner *curia*, he will evade any promises he might be forced to make to his feudatories. Their solution was, basically, to make these departments answerable to the baronage themselves. It was done by a 'Council of Fifteen', appointed jointly by the king and his barons, to which the principal officers of the Crown were made accountable.

The arrangements were very short-lived. Hostilities broke out between the king's supporters and the barons, and the latters' victory at Lewes (1264) was turned into a disastrous and decisive defeat when the Prince Edward defeated the baronial army at Evesham and Simon de Montfort, its leader, met his death (1265). Yet, with hindsight one sees that the experiment marked the turning-point in the constitutional evolution of the feudal monarchy. Under the restoration the kingship regained its traditional control over the appointment and direction of the great officers of state and their departments, which indeed became more specialized, professional, and active than ever before. What the king could achieve with this mechanism was, just as evidently, circumscribed by what had once been called the King's Great Council and now—its membership widely extended beyond the great magnates alone—was more and more frequently to be called a 'Parliament'. The Crown goes its own way, with its inner council; the *commune consilium* ceases to be curial, it becomes parliamentary, and that will be the paradigm of the constitutional development of England in the future. But that pattern was not institutionalized until the next century. The reign of Edward I (1272–1307) is at once the apogee of the feudal monarchy and the moment of its decline.

3.2. *Government Under Edward I*

Let us recall that the governmental system of William I represented a substantial modification of the paradigm feudal system. The upshot of the preceding paragraphs is simply that, in addition to the powerful non-

and supra-feudal powers which the Norman kings had taken over from the Anglo-Saxon monarchy, their Angevin successors had extended their justice so as to push out both the popular courts and those of his magnates; and inside his feudal court there grew up a core of professional officials who were ever-more frequently styled the *curia*, the council, as opposed to the traditional outer ring of ecclesiastical and lay magnates who are the *magnum concilium*, now becoming known variously as *colloquium* and even *parliamentum*. In short, even the modified feudalism of William I has become eroded, and the first question to ask here is, what precisely remained of it; in what sense is Edward I's England still 'feudal'?

Sayles lays down four criteria of 'feudalism': (1) the man-to-man basis of political allegiance, symbolized by homage, the feudal contract, and the right of *diffidatio*; (2) service owed based on the (various and specialized) tenure of land; (3) government exercised by landlords, so that the lords rule their own tenants as governors of domains that are miniatures of the kingdom as a whole; and (4) a military organization based on the land tenures.[9]

The element conspicuously diminished is the third, the intermediated, private jurisdiction by the feudal lords. Certainly, all over England the lords hold their manor courts for their villeins. These dealt as a matter of course with actions affecting the land of the manor, and they had a petty civil jurisdiction which came to be fixed at cases not exceeding the value of 40 shillings.[10] Many had acquired a criminal jurisdiction, too, but how far this went depended on its royal charter or long-established practice. These latter were the 'franchise courts'. For in certain cases the lord's court had acquired the right, normally exercised by the king's sheriff, to review the collective police-units known as tithings,[11] and such courts were called Courts Leet. But the greatest of the franchise courts were those of the Palatinates, of which at this moment the most important was Durham, with the bishop as its lord. In a Palatinate the lord was a viceroy, so that the king's writ did not run there, nor were his justices admitted except by the lord's consent. There were also lordships on the Welsh marches whose lords successfully excluded the king's writ and, indeed, exercised despotic sway. It was in these great franchises, particularly on the Welsh and Scottish borders, that English government came closest to the feudal paradigm of government intermediated by the great landholders. (Significantly, it was from these areas that the threat to royal authority was launched, successfully, in the reigns of

[9] G. O. Sayles, *The Medieval Foundations of England*, 2nd edn. (Methuen, London, 1950), 205–56.

[10] Before Britain decimalized its currency, this was expressed in £.s.d., that is to say pounds (*libra*), shillings (*solidi*), and pence (*denarii*). The shilling (at 20 to the pound) has now disappeared.

[11] See p. 916 below.

Edward II and Richard II and under the Lancastrians.) But only in these
limited areas did feudal jurisdiction exclude the king's; elsewhere this had
been or was still being extended. In 1290 Edward I issued his writ *Quo
Warranto*, which called on every lord to show title for the 'liberties' he was
claiming. Faced with fierce opposition he conceded that continuous exercise
from before 1189 would provide an acceptable answer. (The year is the date
of Richard I's accession and is still in English law the date from which 'time
runneth not back'). The statute did, however, prevent further encroach-
ments.[12]

But apart from this royal justice, the other three elements mentioned by
Sayles still constituted the mainframe of the governing class and regulated
its relationships: the baron still did homage for his fief and acted on the
rights and obligations that flowed from it.

First, he remained in a freely contracted relationship. Well known is the
violent quarrel between King Edward I, who wanted his marshal and
constable to lead his southern army in Gascony while he personally led
the northern one in Flanders, and their refusal on the grounds that they
either served with the king or did not serve, and in any case were not by
custom obliged to serve overseas at all![13]

Secondly, the baron and his knights still formed the main part of the
army's striking force, the heavy cavalry. The importance of this army was on
the brink of decline, and more urgently, its feudal form had become a
debilitating handicap. The traditional forty days' service took no account of
permanent castle guard or protracted campaigns. Barons complained about
overseas service, as we have just seen. Also, their numbers were paltry to the
point of being grotesque. In principle there were 6,000 'knights' fees'; hence,
one would infer, 6,000 knights. Not a bit! Half the holders of these knights'
fees had rentals of £20 per annum and only half of these were actually *knights*!
And of these knights a mere 500 or so could take the field at any one
time. Edward tried to force all those with over £20 per annum to accept
knighthood, but passive resistance defeated him. Edward himself provided
one-quarter of the total cavalry force—his household knights and their
men-at-arms—a force of 500 cavalry in all.[14] In the event, on most
campaigns some magnates came *qua* feudal vassals, others served for pay,
and curiously, very often some simply served at their own expense.[15] But
three feudal features of the host remained prominent. Throughout his reign,
irrespective of the final shape of his forces, Edward continued to summon

[12] See M. Prestwich, *War, Politics and Finance under Edward I* (Faber and Faber, London, 1972), 224–35.
[13] Ibid. p. 77 ff.
[14] Sometimes less, sometimes nearly 1,000; in 1303 there were 588. Ibid. 52.
[15] Ibid. 67–91.

his barons in feudal *form*. Next, the major component in the cavalry arm consisted of the retinues of the great barons who refused pay for themselves or their men. Some retinues were large. One earl put 130 men-at-arms into the field in 1297–8, and the smallest was thirty.[16] Here we see the beginnings of those great private followings that were to challenge the Crown in the fifteenth century. But, finally, notwithstanding by whom or how the cavalry was raised, it was the feudatories who commanded it. The point is simply that the king, at this stage, had only a very limited force of soldiers under his own immediate command. It was his magnates who raised and commanded the bulk of his army.

To continue with Sayles's third criterion: apart from their military obligations, the tenants-in-chief—mostly big men—still owed and paid the 'incidents' of their tenure, involving wardship and marriage, as well as the three customary aids. These, together with the tallages on his own domain lands, escheats, fines from justice, and sundry miscellaneous customary sources, made up the 'ordinary' income of the Crown, and it was not much—some £20,000 per annum. It is estimated that in his thirty-five-year reign Edward spent just over 1 million sterling on war (including the cost of his castles), and that this amounted to two-thirds of his total expenditure, that is, £1,500,000. So that his '*ordinary*' revenue was a $(35 \times 20,000 = £700,000)$ mere *half* of what he actually spent. The magnates whose personal revenues could run to some £6,000 without any royal responsibilities (e.g. Lancaster's) nevertheless held absolutely to their side of the feudal bargain: that the king 'lived off his own'. Therefore, to carry on the king had to ask them and the ecclesiastical tenants as well for *extra*-ordinary aids. The Crown was not fiscally sovereign; and as we have underlined,[17] no matter how poor, all freemen tenaciously believed *n'impose qui ne veult*. Taxation without their consent was simply robbery and they would not have it. So both military *and* financial resources lay in the hands of the feudal magnates.

In short, the Crown could no longer run the country without extra-ordinary, that is, non-feudal sources of revenue. This strengthened the other aspects of the barons' feudal relationship to the king—the duty to give him counsel and to appear at his court. What was happening was that what were supposedly feudal *obligations* supportive of the monarch were being turned into feudal *rights* that constricted him. Because the baron had done homage, he could 'defy' his king. Because he had to give military service, he insisted on the feudal summons and rejected service for pay. Because he was liable for the feudal incidents and aids, he felt entitled not to pay anything else.

---

[16] Ibid. 64.   [17] See Ch. 5, pp. 887–8 above.

And now, on top of all this, he no longer saw counsel or court-service as onerous obligations; he insisted on them *qua* 'natural' counsellor of the king. Hence his jealousy of the king's (inner) council, the self-assertiveness of the *colloquia* or *parliamentia*, and under Edward I's successors, repeated attempts to control the royal ministers.

Such were the feudal elements that still underpinned the governance of the country. How, briefly, was this organized at the beginning of the fourteenth century?

The central government is centred on the monarchy and this has now become hereditary, by primogeniture, in the line of Plantagenet, though this does not exclude deposition (Edward II), usurpation (by Henry IV), and disputed succession (under Henry VI). The court is in constant movement and government is where the king is unless he is abroad; but the Exchequer and the Bench which is now called Common Pleas both have a fixed seat in Westminster. The nucleus of the royal court, wherever it might be, is a body of king's clerks. Over the reign, those who were entrusted with important processes and were well off numbered 135.[18] They were recruited in various ways: some were already officials of the royal domain, others of the house-holds of ecclesiastical or lay magnates, some had been to the university, others—significantly—were lawyers, who were being trained in the Inns of Court. Many—the high-flyers—followed that alternating *cursus* of which we have already spoken, from clerical to lay appointment and vice versa, or both together. Thus, seven of the bishops of the reign had been king's clerks and five of the fifteen judges of the King's Bench, likewise.

The king governs: he is supreme judge, head of the executive, and commander-in-chief, *but* he governs with and through his council, the former 'inner' *curia*. He decides its composition, which is changeable but always contains the judges, the great ministers, certain magnates, plus 'others of the council who should be called', and hence always the treasurer, the chancellor, the keeper of the Wardrobe, and the like, along with trusted clerks (called *secretarii* for this reason). By this time there are clearly demar-cated departments with their own staffs and their own routines. Two of these have gone 'out of court', that is, they are routine administrative agencies: these are the Exchequer, primarily an accounting office for the sheriffs' finances but with a division acting as a court in fiscal cases, and the Chancery, which under the Great Seal issues letters in accordance with royal instructions given elsewhere and expressed either by the king in person or by a letter under his Privy Seal. The great central department which in these times responds directly to the personal decision of the monarch is the

---

[18] Sir M. Powicke, *The Thirteenth Century, 1216–1307* (OUP, Oxford, 1962), 340, n. 1.

Wardrobe, which has become a new kind of Treasury and a new kind of Chancery too. Most extraordinary revenue, notably the subsidies which the parliamentary assemblies[19] had granted, passed to the Wardrobe and not the Exchequer and were paid out in its own and more flexible way. The Wardrobe attained this importance through the imperatives of war-finance, which demanded a speed and decisiveness of which the ultra-conservative, hidebound Exchequer was incapable. The decisions the king took were drawn up there, and only then, as authenticated by the king's private seal, went to the Exchequer or the Chancery for action.

By now the judicial business of the *curia* had divided between the Exchequer court and two others. Since 1215 one Bench had had to sit permanently at Westminster,[20] but the King still continued to do justice on his manifold peregrinations, and hence *coram rege* ('in the presence of the king'). By now the former—the fixed—Bench took on pleas between individuals and was styled the Court of Common Pleas, while the peregrinating court—the King's Bench—dealt with the cases in which the Crown was involved.

Although the departments and the courts were specialized and worked to their own routines, this was not true of the great ministers and the judges individually. Outside their office-chambers they still resemble the old 'patrimonial' household officers of earlier times. They are, above all else, the king's great servants and undertake all manner of special duties. The chancellor was, till the last years of the reign (when the treasurer took over the role) a sort of deputy to the king in matters of administration, a general expediter of government business. The judges of the King's Bench might be called on to act as tax-collectors, commissioners of array, or diplomats. And all these great officials were also members of the king's council and therefore involved in political administration and judicial decisions at the highest level.

The king-in-council was the official core of those wider assemblies which went under such various names as *colloquia* or *parliamentia*. These could be quite small or quite large, but even at their largest they comprise fewer people than we might imagine; the 'knights of the shire' numbered only seventy-four and were but rarely convoked. The number of barons could vary: forty-one (1295) or thirty-seven (1296), to as many as ninety-eight (1300).[21] Assemblies of one size and another and (to anticipate) for diverse purposes were surprisingly frequent: sixteen or seventeen between 1265 and 1272, nearly every year between 1274 and 1286, two per year between 1290 and

---

[19] See p. 911 above.   [20] See p. 906 above.
[21] W. Stubbs, *The Constitutional History of England*, 3 vols. (OUP, Oxford, 1880), ii. 221.

1294.[22] The origin and nature of the particular kind of assembly called a *Parliament* is still a matter of quite impassioned controversy. The two extremes are those which see Parliament as an extension of the council's judicial business, hence a high court, a court of courts as it were, and others who see it as the representative of the 'community of the realm'. The former view is reflected in the very large and increasing number of petitions for judgment or for grace which came up to Parliament; so much so that Edward, impatient to get on with financial or diplomatic business there, cast about for ways of siphoning them off. The latter view is borne out by the high politics of some of the assemblies where the king wanted to sound out his magnates and such others as he deemed appropriate on great matters of foreign policy: how Philip of France had cheated him in the matter of Gascony, for instance; or resistance to the fiscal veto of Pope Boniface VIII; or—as we have already noted—to agree to taxation, which would never be forthcoming without assent; or, finally, to get acceptance of some measures which altered the traditional law of the land or reinterpreted it in a radical way. When the law was restated thus in a Parliament, it was coming to be called a statute. This was not as sharply distinguished as in our day from the common law, the distinction being blurred by the doctrine that, once enacted, the new law became part of the common law of the land.

Between the two extreme views of origins mentioned above it seems sensible to pursue a middle course, especially since that age drew no clear-cut distinction between judging, lawmaking, and administering. But the recognition of two polar types of business is essential, for it accounts for the divergence between the English parliaments and the French *parlement* in the fourteenth century. The latter was nothing but a High Court, but the English Parliament combined the characteristics of the High Court of Parliament with that of the representative Assembly of the Community. At the close of Edward I's reign this outcome was still aleatory and another such aleatory outcome was who should participate. Magna Carta had distinguished between the great barons who were to be summoned individually and the lesser 'knights of the shire', summoned via the sheriff in the shire court. Again, how were the ecclesiastics to be summoned and who among them? In 1295, in the so-called Model Parliament, the great barons, the knights of the shire, and the town burgesses are all present, but it was still open as to whether this pattern was to become normal and whether these categories would deliberate together or separately.

The view mentioned above, that Parliament originated as a *judicial* session as witnessed by the flow of petitions, reminds us of the vast

---

[22] Powicke, *Thirteenth Century*, 341.

expansion of royal jurisdiction, both civil and criminal. We have already described the real property actions initiated by the royal writ.[23] One effect of these was increasingly to overlay local custom by uniform principles and determinations; in short, by the common law, and though local differences still survived,[24] they continued to decline. Another effect was to shrivel the jurisdiction of the communal (i.e. the hundred and the shire courts). After 1278 no action for more than 40 shillings would be taken without a royal writ to the sheriff, and since this issued from the king's court it was as cheap to have the action tried in the king's court; so that by the end of the reign the local courts, seigneurial as well as communal, had in respect of civil actions become trivialized. This was also the case with criminal actions. We have partly recounted this story. What the Anglo-Saxons called *mundbryce*, the breach of the peace, undergoes a huge extension under Henry II. Secondly, Henry, as we saw, sent his justices through the land to take the indictments of all suspected criminals by the new juries of presentment (the Grand Juries), and the justices to try the accused. But a further expansion of the royal jurisdiction goes on at the same time, as the king's judges extend the meaning of a 'felony'. In Henry II's time this was one crime amongst many. But since, *inter alia*, a felon's property escheated to the Crown, it was in the king's interests to bring as many crimes as possible under this heading. In this way all grave crimes became felonies. But by Edward's time 'the king's peace' became even more widely interpreted: it comes to apply to what are, in effect, not crimes at all, but civil wrongs (torts). A plaintiff was able to claim that a wrongful entry on his land was made *vi et armis* (by force and arms) 'against the peace of our lord king'. So arose the writs of *trespass*.

The net effect of all these changes was that, by Edward's reign, 'all serious obstacles to the royal jurisdiction had been removed. The royal courts had in one way and another become courts of first instance for almost all litigants.[25]

This royal jurisdiction was backed up by defence and local security arrangements that were, by contrast, of pre-feudal and pure Anglo-Saxon origin. This was of a piece with the Angevins' general policy to build up the non-feudal, communal institutions, particularly where these were of Anglo-Saxon origin and hence traditional. The most notable was the shire levy (as the ancient *fyrd* was now known). By the Statute of Winchester (1285), every

---

[23] See pp. 902–3 above.

[24] See N. Neilson, 'The Early Pattern of the Common Law', *American Historical Review*, 49 (1944), 199–212.   [25] Maitland, *Constitutional History*, 114.

man aged between 15 and 60 had to maintain weapons and armour according to his wealth. Twice a year two constables in every hundred or franchise came to make the view of armour and report to the justices. The shire levy was commanded by the county sheriff. In practice only a limited number of men were called up (and then only in counties near the scene of fighting), and these, as in pre-Norman times, were financially supported by those who stayed at home. The selection for active service was made by very senior royal officials—justices as it might be—who acted under 'commissions of array'. Edward used such militia forces for his infantry arm in his Welsh and Scottish wars (what stands out, as one might well expect, is the high desertion rate[26]). This policy of the Angevins forms a complete contrast with that of their French contemporaries, who had long ceased to call out the 'ban' and relied entirely on paid foreign mercenaries for their (small) infantry component.

Closely associated with the shire levies were the police and security arrangements. The Statute of Winchester, in fact, devotes far more space to these than to the former. For instance, it details that city gates are to be closed for the night, that all strangers must be answered for by their hosts and inquired into by the bailiffs, that each town or borough must maintain a watch who, *inter alia*, also must check all strangers. But the most interesting aspect of these security arrangements is the notion of collective penalties. For instance, the Statute says that if felons escape arrest the local community or communities where the crimes were committed are collectively answerable for them. More interesting still is the *tithing*, for it resembles Chinese practice from the earliest times.[27] From Anglo-Saxon times villagers had been grouped in units of ten (*tithings*) headed by a *tithings-man*. Its members were mutually responsible for one another's offences and had to produce the offender. The sheriff was responsible for compliance and twice a year held his 'tourn' in the hundred court, a process called 'view of frankpledge'. Many lords of franchises had acquired the rights to take this 'view'. (Where they did so, their court was called the Court Leet.)

Finally, we should notice the increasing use of local knights and other freemen, including the burgesses of towns and the reeves of vills, to carry out public duties, such as the empanelling of the juries or assessing individuals' wealth in 'movables' for tax purposes.

The expansion of royal jurisdiction and the increased use of non-feudal communal institutions were the two routes by which the span of royal

---

[26] Prestwich, *War, Politics and Finance*, 92–113.

[27] See above, Bk. II, Ch. 6, for the Han; Bk. III, Ch. 4 for the Ming, and Bk. IV, Ch. 2 for the Ch'ing. Also Bk. IV, Ch. 1 for Tokugawa Japan.

authority had become so greatly enlarged. They were brought together via the itinerant justices, the justices sent from the central courts into the shire courts. We must insist again that the shire courts were merely the *venue*, for once the justices were there they became royal courts and the justices who came there did so under one or more major commissions. The greatest of these was the General Eyre (*Iter,*) a commission to examine *omnia placita*, all the pleas in a shire. Every matter pending before the king comes before these itinerant justices, but these justices also inquire into those matters like escheats or various sorts of crimes that qualify as 'pleas of the Crown'. The entire county (shire) is summoned to meet them. These great inquests remind one of the commissioners whom kings of France were sending out from time to time under various names, but the English practice was regular, not *ad hoc* as in France; the General Eyre was supposed to take place every seventh year (though this period was not strictly observed). These Eyres, turning up every stone and fining delinquents for every infringement, petty or great, were, naturally, vastly unpopular and were discontinued from the mid-fourteenth century. More truly significant for linking central and local government were the central justices acting under commissions of assize who visited each county once a year. These were highly popular. In 1285 Edward gave these justices much more work under his Statute of Westminster II. By an arrangement called *nisi prius* ('unless before'), suitors in cases pending at Westminster were told the date on which the trial would be heard there *unless before* that date the justices of assize were sitting in the suitor's county, in which case the trial would be heard locally. By the same statute, these assizes were to be held three times a year (in practice, it became twice). The general effect was that more and more work was done by these circuit judges at the shire court.

These justices did not handle judicial business only, but also what we should call administrative business, and the shire court itself also became an administrative centre. It was the place of tax assessment and collection, the draft of the shire levy, police and security, the empanelling of juries. Officially the court consisted of all the freemen who held land in the county. But as we have seen, the great barons were busy enough at court or running their own honour-courts not to be present in person, so that the many duties imposed by the Crown were discharged by the lesser land-holders, and particularly by the most honorific ones (usually the most substantial), which is to say, the knights. Among these knights a category appears which we know as *buzones*, what we might call 'operators'. They take a real interest in all this county business and local politics. They, *par excellence*, are the persons entrusted with the king's local business. Meanwhile the 'county' (the *comitatus* as such) is treated by the monarch as a collective entity since it is easier to deal with a unit which is alleged to stand for a number of individuals than to deal with these separately. So 'the county' begins to acquire a sense of identity and community. It is 'the county' which is said to appear before the justices, gives judgment, is collectively amerced (fined) for malfeasance. The word *comitatus* stands for a geographical area, but also for the assembly in the shire court and, in the end, for all the inhabitants of the area.

It is unsurprising, then, that when the king wants to take counsel in the widest possible way—and this is especially when he seeks some extraordinary 'aid', that is, money—he should summon to his *parliamentum*[28] men who lead in the public affairs of their shires. The 1215 version of Magna Carta speaks of the 'common counsel of the realm' as consisting of the great barons who are summoned individually, and the rest who receive a general summons via the sheriff. By Edward I's time it is well established when *parliamentia* are convened. It is common form for the shire court to learn from its sheriff that the county is to 'elect' (we do not know how) two knights of the shire to go to Westminster as spokesmen for the *entire* community.

In this way the governmental cycle is completed: the assize justices bring the king's government into the shires, the knights of the shire bring these up into the king's government. Indeed, this involvement of the localities in the counsels of the government goes much further, for we have not mentioned the growing importance of towns, nor the complicated path by which the Church in England acquires a sentiment of solidarity with the community of the realm as opposed to the papacy; a matter emphasized by Edward's successful defiance when Pope Boniface VIII tried to veto the taxation of the English clergy, and destined to grow very strongly in the next century. These matters are not pursued any further at this point because they are to be treated in the later chapter on 'Representation'.

This sketch may give the impression of a well-ordered and highly organized kingdom, and indeed it is commonly regarded as the best in Europe at the time. Taxation was noisily resented by the well-to-do in Parliament but there does not seem to be any great protest or resistance among the villein class from whom, in the last resort, the baronial and knightly class had to raise the tax; a very different situation from France. Again, the peasants appear to have offered no resistance to being drafted to active service in the shire levy (though the desertion rate was enormous).[29] But while the government was not oppressive in intent, nor appreciably seen

---

[28] For this term, and its designation in this context, see pp. 913–14 above in this chapter.

[29] See n. 26 above.

to be so, it was by any modern standard quite appallingly incoherent, clumsy, crime-ridden, and corrupt. In 1289 Edward prosecuted many of his judges for bribery, corruption, and submission to influence. Sworn confederacies had arisen to bring pressure on the courts, so much so that a special writ of 'conspiracy' had to be introduced in 1293 to give sufferers a remedy. Justices found that juries had no indictments to present to them. The Statute of Winchester addresses this problem by imposing penalties for concealment, but this did not dispose of the problem. For instance, the justices at York in 1305 complain that the reason why no indictments had been brought was the existence of a sworn confederacy, a sort of mafia which had come to control the city. Violence was endemic: small private wars, the destruction of manor-houses, the breaking of enclosures and rustling of livestock, as well as the crop of 'robberies, murders, burnings and thefts' mentioned in the Statute of Winchester.[30]

Matters were far worse in France, as we shall see,[31] and much worse in Germany and parts of Italy. The reason for drawing attention to the poor state of affairs in England is not to condemn its governmental system for failing to meet the standards of the twentieth century, which would be unhistorical folly, but to show how far even what passed as the best of its kind for that era had to go to reach even the minimal standards of justice, fairness, and security we should consider tolerable today. In a history of government such a caveat is essential.

4. FRANCE: THE CLASSICAL FEUDAL KINGDOM

4.1. *Development*

To go by the grand tradition of French historiography there was always a France, but it broke up and was then reconstructed by kings. These romantic nationalists seemed to have a vision of today's 'Hexagon' existing sempiter-nally, and wrote their histories as a kind of teleology in which the original 'idea' was progressively realized over time to reach the frontiers and the national community of today. In fact there was no France to begin with, only a Regnum Francorum, that is to say, the western third of Charlemagne's empire as defined in the Treaty of Verdun of 843; and in 987 (when the first Capetian was elected as its king) it was no more than a nominal confedera-tion of great principalities, most of which, themselves, had fluid boundaries and were composed of scores of independent castellanies. Not only was the

---

[30] Cf. Prestwich, *War, Politics and Finance*, 287–9.

[31] Cf. C. Petit-Dutaillis, *La Monarchie féodale en France et en Angleterre, X–XII siècle* (Renaissance du Livre, Paris, 1933), 322.

formation of today's French state not pre-ordained, but in 987 and for over 200 years after that it would have appeared wildly implausible. It might have gone the same way as the East Franks—'Germany'—and wound up as a number of independent states. It might have ended as a unitary state but with significantly different frontiers from those of today. In 987 the former must have seemed much the likelier outcome. The forces of disorder and disintegration were at their full, while the authority, let alone the effective power of the monarchy, was at its nadir. This is the country where the fragmentation of political authority went to its most extreme, as a result of civil war, foreign war, invasions, and the ruthless *libido dominandi* of warlike primitives. It was out of this very confusion and insecurity that Western feudalism was born. It was there it achieved its classical expression. It was there that its rules were elaborated and refined into the 'Customaries' like de Beaumanoir's *Coutumes de Beauvaisis*. But it was there too that the kings, by shrewd manipulation of these same feudal rules, aggregated the great principalities together into a kingdom structured on classically feudal principles.

So the French monarchy started in 987 from a far weaker position than that of William the Conqueror in England, and it had different problems, proceeded by different routes, and reached a different conclusion in constructing the kingdom. In 975 England was a small but single political unit. The kingdom of the Franks, nominally covering four-fifths of the present-day area of France, was three times larger. Moreover, inhabitants of this wide area spoke diverse tongues: German in the extreme north-east, Celtic in western Brittany, Basque in the south-east, while the two main branches of the *lingua popolare*—French and Occitan—were mutually unintelligible. The law of the areas differed, too; especially in that a vulgarized Roman *droit ecrit* prevailed in the south as against the customary Frankish laws of the north. Central power was non-existent. Nor was it much stronger in the half-dozen or so great counties or duchies which covered most of the kingdom: effective power lay for the most part with the castellanies, fiercely recalcitrant to their overlords. Castles set up by royal dukes and counts as defences against the invasions now become hereditary in certain families and were used simply to dominate the countryside.

In tens and hundreds, principalities of every size became centres of independent military systems, including, in addition to specific means of attack and defence, the right and power to declare, pursue, and terminate war. From this sprang that multitude of skirmishes, sieges, raids, burning, encounter and battles, often on a very small scale, whose recital constitutes the daily fare of contemporary annalists and chronicles.[32]

---

[32] Contamine, *War in the Middle Ages*, 31.

'The Middle Ages', says another authority,

was an era of brutality. The nobility thought war was the normal condition of existence for a gentleman, peace as a *pis aller* for which you consoled yourself by bloody tournaments or ferocious hunting parties. Men fought to avenge an insult, to seize an inheritance or a woman, to pillage, to give oneself pleasure, or to help in the quarrels of one's overlord or one's vassal.[33]

A proto-feudalism, initiated under the Carolingians, came to be a desperate expedient to curb the anarchy which spread at the end of that dynasty. It differed in vital respects from the modified version which William imposed on England. In France fidelity was owed only to the immediate overlord. Consequently, though a suzerain (be he king, duke, or count) could expect fidelity from his immediate tenants (his tenants-in-chief), he could rely on the rear-vassals only via their duty to that tenant-in-chief; and so on down the feudal hierarchy. The mesne lord stood between the overlord and the rear-vassals, according to the rule: *vassallus vassalli mei non est meus vassallus* ('My vassal's vassal is not my vassal').[34] In England, every man was bound by law never to fight against the king and every freeman had taken an oath of allegiance to him. In France, however, if a vassal 'defied' the king and levied war, his vassals had to follow him, even against the king. By the same logic, the French overlord could not take over the jurisdiction or cut into the courts of his vassals. Thirdly, the ancient communal courts were abandoned and all courts and justice were feudalized. Again, in France private war was legal. Maitland wrote: '[English] public law does not become feudal . . . the public rights, the public duties of the Englishman are not conceived and cannot be conceived as the mere outcome of feudal compacts between man and lord',[35] but in France during this period they could be and they were.

The role and authority of the French king in 987 has to be described in the context of the six great 'principalities' which comprised the kingdom of France (Aquitaine, Flanders, Gascony, Normandy, Toulouse, and France). But note that two great areas were, legally, outside the kingdom of the Franks: Brittany had asserted its independence in the ninth century and in the next century its ruler assumed the title of count; and the duchy of Burgundy had once been part of the kingdom of Burgundy. South of the Loire, too, Provence was not part of the Regnum Francorum and in the eleventh century passed to the Empire.

These units we sometimes describe as 'principalities', a term of art, but a

---

[33] Petit-Dutaillis, *La Monarchie féodale*, 322.
[34] A. Luchaire, *Histoire des institutions monarchiques de la France sous les premiers Capétiens* (Paris, 1892), 224.
[35] Maitland, *Constitutional History*, 164.

useful one, providing we understand that at this point, the end of the tenth century, they were all more or less anarchical. In the next century Normandy and Flanders, and then Anjou, were to become organized feudal statelets where the prince exerted a firm control over his vassals. On the other hand, Aquitaine, particularly the area which had previously been Gascony, was to remain insubordinate for centuries.

The Capetians were 'princes' like the rulers of these various provinces. An early Capet had claimed that some Carolingian monarch had created him 'duke of the Franks'.[36] Hugh Capet was the duke of a shadowy area once called 'Francia' but, more significantly, he was the count of Paris, for this was where his domain lands lay.

In 987, when the throne was vacant, the Church, through the archbishop of Rheims, persuaded the great counts and dukes to elect Hugh Capet as king of the Regnum; a decision made possible, it would seem, because of the modesty of his resources. The Archbishop crowned and anointed the new monarch with the especially sacred oil that had been brought down from heaven by a dove in the remote days of Clovis. This certainly set him apart from the territorial princes. It sacralized his person. But in practical terms little distinguished him from the princes. He issued few charters, his prerogative of high justice was hardly recognized, only local personages attended his court, and though the great princes continued to promise fidelity they did not do homage, and the great southern counts and those of Brittany stayed away.[37]

Nor were his material resources considerable. His domain was an area around Paris and Orleans which amounts to about two of modern France's ninety-six *départements*. And even this was insecure.[38] But the northern prelates resumed the traditional alliance with the Frankish monarchy and encouraged the king to resume the regalian right and duty of protector of the Church. The abbeys and bishops' palaces provided him and his court with the *gites* which allowed him to peregrinate; and, above all, the Church lands owed him military service. Only the control of these ecclesiastical resources saved the Capetian dynasty from foundering in the century following Hugh's accession.

The king of the Franks was not relatively more powerful in 1087 than he was in 987, and even less so in 1187. By then the king of England (Henry II) was not only the duke of Normandy, but count of Anjou and of Maine and duke of Aquitaine, altogether an immense empire, which in practice was far more powerful than the diminutive domain of the French Crown. But when we jump to 1287 the entire scene has changed: two-thirds of the population

---

[36] Dunbabin, *France*, 47–8.   [37] Ibid. 137–40.   [38] Ibid. 163–4.

of the French kingdom live on the royal domain and only Brittany, Gascony, Flanders, and Burgundy lie outside it! The king of France—for this is his title now—directly or indirectly rules some 15 to 20 million people, and is the richest and strongest ruler in the whole of Europe. This does not mean that he had created a homogenous community or a common law as in England. Far from it. He and his predecessors had created a political system, but they had not homogenized the political communities. The various petty seigneuries and the great territorial principalities which contained them still remained diverse political and juridical units, but formed into a single system as by a multitude of radial *dyadic* ties which all centred upon the Crown. And those ties were ties of *feudal* law.

The turning-point in this development is the reign of Philip II (or Philippe-Auguste), 1179–1223. By this time the castellanies had been subjugated and the king was at last the full master of his domain. Furthermore, this had become much richer.[39]

One course his predecessors had unwaveringly pursued was to proclaim and, where possible, enforce the dignity and authority of kingship, and it is surprising how successfully they did this in view of their material weakness. Royal charters become more abundant. Kings show their person outside the domain, even in far Aquitaine and Languedoc, then expand the number of their *fideles* by decreeing that all prelates who still had no feudal lord and protector should come under the *garde* of the Crown, so that by 1180 half of the bishops in the kingdom were *fideles* of the Crown. They had succeeded in getting the great counts and dukes, finally, to do homage for their lands, even including Henry II of England, who did homage to an apparently insignificant king for all the territories of the Angevin empire.

'Apparently insignificant', because the king was not alone in consolidating his domain and asserting his feudal dominion over the feudatories, for the 'vassal' courts and the dukes were doing likewise and some were now powerful centralized principalities. So, the path to the creation of a unitary kingdom in France was bound to be different from the one taken in England. It had to work upon already established territorial units, and the French state never ceased, until the eighteenth century, to have a marked confederal character. Integrated by the monarchy, it was the most powerful state in Europe, but as soon as—for any reason—the monarchical grip was slackened, it fell apart into its original constituents. Between 1179 and 1337 the Crown won the centralization race against the principalities. In 1349–51 and intermittently till 1445 the process went into reverse.

[39] F. Lot and R. Fawtier, *Histoire des institutions françaises au moyen-âge*, 2 vols. (Presses Universitaires de France, Paris 1957–62), ii. 159 and Dunbabin, *France*, 297–8.

The reason the reign of Philippe-Auguste was so critical was that by successful war against the Anglo-French Angevin empire, and further campaigns in the south, he had in ten years trebled the area of his domain, doubled his ordinary revenue, and vastly multiplied the numbers of his feudal host. Towards the end of his reign his son, the future Louis VIII, was commanding one army of 800 knights, 2,000 cavalry sergeants, and 7,000 infantry while he himself commanded 1,200 knights, 3,000 mounted sergeants and 10,000 infantry. Armies of this size were not to be deployed again by French kings for another hundred years.[40] In short, the entire feudal balance in the kingdom had tipped decisively and overwhelmingly in favour of the king. Its superior resources plus his authority as *rex* enabled the monarch to expand the domain still further and, moreover, bring the remaining great fiefs into dependency.

The subsequent course of events was as follows: the domain was extended and extended; royal officials governed and exploited it, while central organs of government became more differentiated and professionalized; by judicial means the feudal jurisdiction of the tenants of the king's domain was brought into conformity with that of his own suzerain court and, by a parallel process, so were those of the four great principalities still outside his domain. The domain was expanded by a number of techniques: by marriages; by purchase for a lump sum or an annuity; by sharp legal practice which left its victim with the choice of submitting to a one-sided judgment or defying it and courting war. War was used only marginally, but it was the decisive factor; the law or diplomacy merely provided the pretext. By the end of the century *all* the kingdom except Gascony, Brittany, Flanders, and Burgundy was royal domain.

In the olden days, when the domain was small and rebellious, the Capetians had exploited it through officials called *prévôts*. These *prévôts* (provosts) were something like the earliest English sheriffs (i.e. shire-reeves) in that their task was to collect the royal revenues from manors, customs, tolls, and the like. By Philippe-Auguste's day they were little but hereditary tax-farmers. Philip introduced all-purpose supervisors to the *prévôts*, called *baillis* in the north and *seneschaux* in the Midi. These soon acquired fixed territories to administer. They were directly salaried and removable agents, drawn from the lesser nobility, and so dedicated to the royal cause that Louis IX (1226–70) had to send out 'investigators' to correct their numerous extortions and illegalities. As all-purpose administrators, those *baillis* and *seneschaux* themselves came to employ large paid staffs of road-agents, foresters, beadles, and the like. Here is the origin of what was to prove

---

[40] F. Lot, *L'Art Militaire et les armées au moyen âge*, 2 vols. (Payot, Paris, 1946), 223–35.

one of the most striking differences between the administrations of France and England until the late nineteenth century. France was administered by paid local officials in huge numbers, while in England the functions they performed were carried out by unpaid freemen of the shire court under the supervision of the similarly unpaid knights of the shire.

Compared with contemporary England, France's central institutions were retarded. Philippe-Auguste's *curia* was still undifferentiated and only the Chancery showed much appreciable advance on its early origins in the royal chapel. But by the time of Philip IV (1285–1314) an inner council was clearly distinguishable; also a distinct accounting office, the *Chambre des Comptes*, had emerged; and most significantly, so had a strictly judicial organ, the *parlement*. In the middle of the thirteenth century the *curia* had begun to hold specialized judicial sessions called *parlements*, a term which denoted the process, but now the term applied to a structure which itself was subdivided into a Chamber of Pleas, a Chamber of Requests, and a Chamber of Investigations. Here we find the source of another feature distinguishing the future evolution of France and England. In England the traditional Great Council of the realm was being replaced by those meetings which were being called parliaments. They were all-purpose assemblies. But a French *parlement* is nothing but a court of law, so that when Philip IV found it useful to convoke wide assemblies these have no judicial functions. Unlike the English Parliament, they were never the highest court in the land, and so lacked the very feature that made the English Parliament pre-eminent.

French constitutional development as discussed so far, then, displays three major characteristics which were to go on to shape the nature of the state in the future: the way the royal demesne is built up from disparate feudal units; administration by paid officials of the Crown; and the divergence between the 'Grand Councils' of the realm and the supreme judicial bodies, the *parlements*. Perhaps the most remarkable feature, however, is surely a fourth—the way feudal law was manipulated so as to bring the feudatories and vassals—even the rear vassals—into the ambit of the royal policy.

This came about by the development of the *appeal*. For, half-way through the thirteenth century, the cunning lawyers[41] of the *curia* got away with the view that if a seigneurial court failed to do justice and gave false judgment, appeal lay to the king. Few had cared to appeal to the remote count of Paris, but now the *bailli* or *seneschal* was near at hand. The plaintiff made appeal to him, whereupon the *bailli* placed him under the king's protection until he heard the case. Furthermore, subordinate officers of the *bailli* were to be

---

[41] Cf. Rabelais's mockery: 'Les Chats fourrés': furred (law) cats; i.e. fur-collared magistrates!

found in every *seigneurie*, their lords did not 'lose their courts' thereby, and so local seigneurial justice remained on a scale and with a scope that was virtually ended in England by 1300. But if the seigneur ordered a suitor to behave in a certain way, and the suitor chosen to appeal to the *bailli* and if necessary beyond him to the *curia*-now-turned-*parlement*, the latter could now substitute its own command for the local seigneur's and tell him to carry it out. Failing to do so put him in contempt.

This policy was rigorously—indeed over-rigorously—applied through-out the domain. But why should its logic not apply to all feudatories, outside as well as inside the domain? The area outside the domain is known as *le mouvance*, and one-third of the kingdom's population lived there in the four great fiefs of Brittany, Flanders, Aquitaine, and Burgundy. By the end of the century the kings of France were indeed applying the technique of the appeal to these great principalities. In this way, by the mid-fourteenth century the entire area of the *regnum* was brought into direct or indirect dependency on the king and his court. Thus was constructed the feudal kingdom of France. It is, obviously, a *very* different constitutional structure from England's.

It is one thing to have a legal right, but sometimes it is very imprudent to use it. By the middle of the fourteenth century the four great principalities had had enough and made common league in armed resistance. That is the true character of the 'Hundred Years War' between France and England. But this is to anticipate.

4.2. *The Kingdom of France under Philip IV 'Le Bel' (1285–1314)*

4.2.1. THE CENTRAL ADMINISTRATION

The kingdom at this time was, roughly speaking, confined to the west of the Meuse and the Rhône, two-thirds the area of modern France. It consisted of the royal domain, the royal apanages, and the *mouvance*. Apanages were parts of the royal domain administered by princes of the blood. The three apanages at this time were Poitou; the Marche; and Anjou, Maine, La Perche, and Alençon (being administered by Philip IV's brother, Charles of Valois). Apanages reverted to the Crown on the failure of the male line of its lord. The latter owed liege loyalty to the king, of course, but for the rest governed the apanage through his own court and his own *prévôts* and *baillis*, in his own way (subject always to the appeal procedure). In practice, the arrangements were replicas of the royal system of administration.

The king, who keeps a sumptuous court and maintains at his expense diplomatic missions from all Europe, is the richest king in Europe, with the most powerful army, the widest dominion, and the greatest number of subjects. Ever since Philippe-Auguste, the crown has become hereditary in the House of Capet. The king is anointed, then crowned at Rheims; his person is thus sacralized and his special relationship with the Church reaffirmed. Like his English counterpart, he is both *dominus* and *rex*. In the latter capacity he has the mission and hence the right to defend the kingdom, implying, *inter alia*, the right to the men and money to do so; to enforce the peace and protect the weakest (the former being far more prominent in this reign); to do justice, for he is the fountain of law— and in the light of this Philip will in fact, on occasion, go far beyond his strict rights as a *dominus*. Finally, he is the protector of the Church: he will 'defend' it in a curious way—taxing it in defiance of the Papacy, arraigning a pope, having him arrested, and so hastening his death.

Philippe de Beaumanoir was an authoritative codifier and commentator of the feudal *Customs of Beauvaisis*: but in this book nevertheless affirms that 'what has pleased the Prince has the force of law', the principle enunciated by Ulpian![42] The royal court now swarmed with lawyers versed in Roman law and these *légistes* were to press the royal prerogative against strict feudality; in particular, they would use (for instance) the notion of *utilitas*, the king's overriding duty and right to take any measures whatsoever in the cause of the 'public weal'. But (as we noted) the legists were equally skilled in turning feudal law itself against the feudatories, so that while the barons in England were successfully turning their feudal duties into rights against the Crown,[43] in France the king was turning his feudal rights into duties against his barons.

The central organs of government superficially seem to resemble those in England: an inner council, a set of specialized and semi-specialized departments, and assemblies with a fluid nomenclature which the king convenes *ad hoc*. But the differences are considerable.

The traditional grand officers and the ancient lineages are no longer at the heart of things, exception made for certain individuals chosen by the king. The king has filled his court with the equivalent of Edward's 'royal clerks'—both churchmen and laymen. They are variously called *palatini*, *curiales*, *familiares*, *amici regni*, and so forth, or else 'clerks and royal knights'. They are gentlefolk, not barons. Some indeed are of non-noble houses. Many are legists, schooled in feudal and in Roman law. They are the nursery for the king's accountants, judges, *baillis*, investigators, and diplomats. Under Louis IX and Philip III the clerical element preponderated. Now it is the

---

[42] Cf. Ullmann, *Principles of Governance*, 205. Cf. Bk. II, Ch. 7 ('The Roman Empire: the Principate'), at p. 544 above. [43] See pp. 905 and 911 above.

turn of lawyers, partly because the old Roman (and new Canon) law procedure we know as 'inquisitorial' had superseded the archaic feudal modes, partly because of the plethora of cases coming up through the new 'appeals' procedure.

The hub of Philip's government and administration is his council. This moves with the king. It is beginning to be called the *Grand* or the *Grander* Council, and it contains the ablest and most trusted of these 'royal knights': Normans like Pierre de Marigny, a *méridionale* like Guillaume de Nogaret or Pierre Flotte. Though of humble origin and no soldier, de Nogaret is a knight for all that, a *chevalier ès lois*. In the council there also sit some of the magnates, particularly the princes of the blood. There is nothing but enmity between these 'natural councillors' of the Crown and the upstarts, and in the uncertain years after Philip IV's death the nobility will exact revenge on their rivals.

This Grand Council is the king's policy-making body. The fact that it follows him on his royal progresses is now sealing it off from former parts of the royal *curia* which have been given a fixed domicile. One of these is the *Chambre des Comptes*, associated with the two treasurers. It reflects on the primitive and disorderly state of central and fiscal administration, especially in contrast to the English, that only now has it been laid down that no order of payment may issue except under the written command of either the king or a treasurer, that the Treasury shall periodically send its receipts for audit to the *Chambre*. This too is still rather inchoate. It has a small staff of eight *maîtres* and fourteen clerks, and just after the end of the reign its jurisdiction extends to all sources of revenue, from the royal domain and the judicial processes, and to expenditures in the Treasury, the *Hôtel du Roi*, the Chancery, and the provincial offices. Like the English Exchequer, it functioned as a court for revenue cases as well as an audit board and, as events turned out, it was far more interested in the former than in the boring routine of accountancy which it accordingly came to neglect. In practice this fiscal administration was rudimentary, a point we shall take up again later.

The second part of the old *curia* to split away was the *parlement*. This court has become sedentary, save on rarer and rarer occasions. It is now the clearly specialized judicial branch of the original *curia regis* with its own permanent paid staff of professional jurists. Various barons might be called in as assessors in cases where their presence was thought desirable, but from 1319 prelates no longer sit in it. Of its three sections (Pleas, *Enquêtes*, and Requests) the first, 'the Bench' proper, is the place where cases are tried. *Enquêtes* developed rapidly as royal justice took over the inquisitorial procedures of Church courts, based on written documentation. This section employs a number of *auditeurs* who go down to the scene of the action to collect information, which is then passed over to others who examine it and draw up a report which goes in the end to the trial judges. (In England petty juries of fact had to travel up to Westminster with this information unless the assizes had come down to them first, but in France the entire matter was centralized and bureaucratized.) Finally, the Requests division takes cognizance of petitions from subjects who seek the jurisdiction of the Crown. It sends the most important ones to the king himself and, for the rest, either handles the case itself or sends it to the local *bailli*. After 1306 it is divided into one section for the *langue d'oc* and another for *la langue française*.

The jurisdiction of this Court has now become wide and is growing wider all the time. The chief reason lies in the royal legists' invention of novel procedures to attract cases from the seigneurial courts; these—and their political effects—are described in connection with the local and provincial government below.

The *parlement* does not merely adjudicate. It has administrative and even legislative competence, for it checks administrative actions and imposes disciplines, fixes the limits of inferior jurisdictions, and helps to draw up royal ordinances. In these activities lie the seeds of its rights of *enregistration* and *remonstrance* that were to be of immense constitutional importance in the seventeenth and eighteenth centuries as the last surviving legal barrier to the absolutism of the monarchy.

As the *comptes* and the *parlement* become routine and sedentary, and the policy-making body resides in the Grand Council which follows the king, a new role and format opens for the primal *curia*—that 'outer' council— namely, the circle of magnates and great churchmen and indeed any others it is necessary to consult or conciliate. For instance, Philip IV multiplies the number of royal charters and makes ordinances of widely varying kinds, some of individual, some of general scope, some trivial and others important, and under all manner of different names. But the feudatories have their traditional rights in such matters, and, correspondingly, the king has a duty to consult them. Other issues may be so narrow—currency, for instance— that it is as natural for the king to do that as for our own governments to consult trade unions or employers' organizations on matters of administrative detail. But above all, in this period, there is so much naked military power lying about the kingdom and so much money that a feudal monarch simply has to win the support of their possessors.

Hence the need for grand assemblies. They have no fixed designation, but are called *curia*, or *concilium*, or *conventus*, or *colloquium*.[44] For the most part they consist of the so-called *proceres*—the 'great men'—the chief feudatories

---

[44] They are not *parliamentum*; that name has been pre-empted.

and churchmen, and these are summoned personally. There had always been some such kind of assembly at the three great feasts of Christmas, Easter, and Pentecost where business was no doubt discussed, but the assemblies we are concerned with are convened *ad hoc*, and irregularly, as the king sees fit. As they represent the original, the pristine *curia regis*, they are omnicompetent, but will not be called unless the king thinks it unsafe to proceed in council without their advice and support. When Church matters are in question it is mostly clerics who will come; for foreign or internal policy, the magnates will arrive as well. The kind of matters that have been discussed are war and peace, Crusades, royal marriages, the treatment of the Jews. Sometimes—in 1262, for instance, when the currency was under discussion—even burghers will be invited. In practice only the grandest magnates actually deliberate; the rest acclaim the decisions reached.

But in the latter years of his reign Philip cast his net wider. He was involved in a series of wars with England and Flanders and his need for money was desperate. This brought him into conflict with the pope, Boniface VIII, who united a belief in the supremacy of the Papacy over lay monarchy with a choleric tactlessness in how and when to press his policy. Boniface's Bull *Asculta fili* which, *inter alia*, proclaimed a Council at Rome for 1302, warned Philip that he was subordinate to the Papacy. Philip's retort was the public burning of the Bull and a summons of the widest assembly ever yet convened. This is usually regarded as the transition-point from the general assemblies of the past to the Estates-General of the future, because he not only convoked the Church and the lay magnates (each by way of personal summons) but also the 'Third Estate'. This consisted of procurators from the 'good towns' and of the entire kingdom (by general summons through the *baillis* and *seneschaux*). Each of the three orders duly addressed a letter to the pope asserting that the king held his kingdom from God alone. Boniface backed down.

Again, when Pope Clement (1308) tried to intervene in Philip's murderous trial of the Templars,[45] he again summoned the Three Estates to support his denunciation of both pope and Templars and once again was successful. Not so in 1314, the last year of his reign. He was in such financial straits that he convened the Estates to get them to agree in principle to extraordinary taxation. Now such general assemblies had not been the vehicle for such financial exercises, in this way sharply diverging from the English ones. The French practice had been to negotiate with individual localities, magnates, and corporations. By this date the country was seething with discontent and this meeting of the Estates broke up in confusion with nothing decided; but

---

[45] For a full account, M. Barber, *The Trial of the Templars* (CUP, Cambridge, 1978).

by now the precedent of convening not just an *ad hoc* general assembly but the Three Estates of the Realm had been firmly set, and the sequels will be set out in Chapter 8 below.

4.2.2. THE LOCALITIES

On his domain the king's main officials remain the *prévôts* and the *baillis* (called *seneschaux* in the Languedoc). The *prévôts* 'farm' from the king the handling of the revenues of his estates but are responsible to the *baillis*. These are appointed and removed by the king-in-council, paid regular salaries, and moved from one place to another every two or three years or so. They are whole-hearted dependants of the monarch, whose interests, moreover, they serve with inordinate zeal. They are so many petty viceroys: they transmit the royal orders, execute the *arrêts* of the *parlement*, see that the royal ordinances are obeyed, appoint and control their subaltern officials. They are the Crown's financial agents, who control the *prévôts'* 'farms', take over the revenues from them, and transmit the money to the Treasury along with their accounts. Usually knights themselves, it is they who issue the royal summons to the host. They are responsible for maintaining order and pursuing and arresting criminals. They have large staffs of subordinates: mayors in the villages, sergeants and beadles, foresters, toll- and customs-collectors, and such like. Their feared agents are the sergeants who, holding the *bâton* with the *fleur de lys* as symbol of their authority, execute their commands and are notorious for venality, corruption, and extortion.

The link between these local officials and the central organs of government is chiefly the juridical one, through the *parlement*, by way of the appeal procedure, but now via two new procedures, *prévention* and *cas royaux*. These operate to link the kingdom together. To understand how, we must remember, through all this talk of 'royal administration', 'administrator', and the like, that France is feudal, indeed classically so. Certainly there are numerous manors of which the king is the immediate lord, and these are administered directly by his agents, but by and large the domain, like all France, is a patchwork quilt of seigneuries, some great and others tiny, in which each seigneur holds court for his tenants and owes suit of court to his overlords and so forth, culminating in the king as his liege lord. For among their various legalistic devices to enhance the status of the king, the Crown legists have overcome the original problem in feudal law which allowed a vassal to serve many lords. The law now says that where a vassal owes duty to other lords besides the king, the king takes precedence. This, essentially, is what 'liege homage' means.

The Crown did not extinguish these seigneurial courts or even their functions, but one thing it did do was to try to take so-called *cas royaux* away from them into the royal courts (those of the *baillis* in first instance and the *parlement* as court of appeal from there). This creation—or extension—of the *cas royaux* is an example of the substitution of Roman law concepts for those of feudal law, and the exaltation of the king as *rex* as against his status as *dominus*. The *cas royaux*, like the English Pleas of the Crown, were never itemized, but defined generically as (according to Beaumanoir) 'matters touching the King', matters which belong *ad honorem regium, ad regiam dignitatem*, that is, 'to the office and dignity of the kingship'.[46] The royal legists derived the notion from the Roman emperors' law *de maiestate*, that is, high treason and *lèse-majesté* and the host of trumped-up offences that could be attached to these.[47] Under Philip IV the category extended to crimes like murder, homicide, rape, and counterfeiting, as well as to attempts on 'the king's dignity', violating the protection he offered to persons or property, and the like.[48]

The action called *prévention* also derived from a non-feudal attribute of the kingship, in this case *utilitas*—the common weal. Here the *bailli* could summon any party on any charge to answer in his court but the party had the right to claim judgment in the jurisdiction where he belonged. The rationale was that the *bailli* had to act to prevent some serious worsening of the situation, and that where this was threatened the king's justice came first.

Appeals could be lodged either from the *baillis'* court or the seigneurial court, but the appeal procedure subjected both to judicial control and its effect was similar in both cases. It diminished the independence of the *bailli* and served to control his malfeasances, but did the same to the seigneurial courts also, especially since an ordinance of 1278 forbade seigneurs to establish their own appeal courts, so that they immediately became courts of first instance only. But this judicial control was very much a political control, for the following reason. Once the suitor launched his appeal, the *bailli* put him and his goods under royal protection until the case was heard: at the best the seigneur was obstructed, at the worst his decision was overturned. The *baillis* were most zealous to bring their royal justice to bear—even in territories outside the domains—and used every possible pretext for intervening on behalf of this or another suitor. The political aspect of the appeal procedures is best seen if we turn from the petty seigneurial jurisdictions inside the domain to the great fiefdoms and apanages outside it.

Aquitaine is a striking illustration. This was the last major English possession in France. The king of England, as its duke, did homage for

---

[46] Luchaire, *Histoire des institutions*, 571.   [47] Above, Bk. II, Ch. 7.

[48] Luchaire, *Histoire des institutions*, 571.

it to the French Crown. Philip IV was determined to annex it but played the legal card. First the royal lawyers, or some *bailli* in an adjacent area, contested a jurisdiction, or some other such pretext was found, as a consequence of which the king-duke was cited to the court of his overlord the king of France. If the king-duke went, it was to a kangaroo court and, if he did not appear, that court declared his fief vacant for contempt. Either way, the last argument rested with force and Edward I was able to beat Philip off. After that the French approach was to apply the appeals procedure more and more strictly and vexatiously to the duchy. The French king applied his ordinances to Aquitaine, so that the king-duke had to legislate in similar manner and argue that his courts were enforcing his own law, not the French king's, or he had to come to a private arrangement, or in the last resort 'defy', that is, wage war. But in addition, any individual might appeal from his courts to the French king's and the moment he did so he was under the king's protection until the case was settled. So even if in the end the *parlement* upheld the king-duke, his administration had been paralysed, and if it found against him it destroyed it altogether. The legists used their law to force the counts and dukes of the great fiefdoms to hold their fiefs only on their king's conditions and become, so to speak, his surrogates, doing only those things his own royal administration was not yet ready to take over.[49] This, then, was the way the mosaic of feudal fiefs was articulated. Ideally all would be ancillaries to the central administration and its political direction; they would be subordinate jurisdictions, doing only what the king did not want his own officials to undertake.

The achievement is remarkable. There now existed a recognizable, viable governmental structure: the kingdom of France. Now it may be thought that our account, earlier, of the development of the French polity was, despite abbreviation, an author's self-indulgence. But without this the kingdom's terrible weaknesses pass all comprehension, for within a mere quarter-century of Philip IV's death the entire *regnum* was to fly apart again.[50] As Marc Bloch put it, France had not been unified but reassembled. The enormously various bits and pieces of this very large country, each with their legal customs, sometimes with their own language, and with local institutions and dynasties and historic traditions, were not fused together but welded. In retrospect, one sees that the reign of Philip IV marks the premature, indeed the precocious supremacy of the royal power, and invites comment on the structural weaknesses of the most important of all the

---

[49] Cf. J. Le Patourel, 'The Origin of the War', in K. Fowler (ed.), *The Hundred Years' War* (Macmillan, London, 1971), 28–50.

[50] And let us repeat: no matter what the vicissitudes, this *never* happened to England.

monarchies of this time and on the rule of 'the king who is an emperor in his kingdom'.

The first structural weakness was the developing incompatibility between feudatories, particularly the great ones, who were intent on running their fiefs with a free hand, and the Crown, which was equally intent on a free hand in running the kingdom as a whole. For one thing, the fiefs were unifying and centralizing their administration as fast and perhaps faster (because their territories were smaller) than the Crown was unifying the kingdom, and this is true for the apanages too. (Thus, in Berry in mid-fourteenth century 'the duke [who was, of course, a prince of the blood] is pretty nearly absolute master of his apanage. Everything is organized on the lines of the monarchy: Household, Council, Chancery, *Chambre des Comptes*, administration, justice.')[51] This was, *mutatis mutandis*, true of all the fiefs as well as the apanages. In the second place, the feudatories, great and small, took their great chance to reassert themselves in the period of dynastic weakness that followed Philip's death. One symptom was the revolt of the petty nobility who formed *ligues nobiliaires*. The feudatories of the domain resented the *baillis*, those outside it the centralizing activities of their over-lords, and all together demanded *and received* charters which restored their legal right to conduct private war, to maintain their seigneurial jurisdictions, and to avoid the inquisitorial procedure by once again having the right to trial by battle. In the great fiefs, and notably among the burghers of Flanders and at the court of the king-duke of Aquitaine, fury welled up against what they saw as endless provocations by the royal officers, and it was precisely a provocation of this kind which in 1338 prompted an Anglo-Flemish alliance and set off the Hundred Years War. This was a feudal revolt in which the two other great feudatories, the dukes of Brittany and of Burgundy, were to join. In this way the kingdom had burst apart along its historic seams.

Its second weakness was fiscal. Philip IV was spending far more than he received from his 'ordinary' expenditures: he was engaged in war with Flanders and England, he had to pay a large establishment of clerks and officials, and he had to maintain his extended family in the pomp befitting the French Crown. But the patchwork nature of 'unification' becomes apparent the moment one examines the Crown's ways of raising revenue. It had no finance office as central, methodical, and systematic as the English Exchequer and Wardrobe, and it had no central assembly or court from which general assent to extraordinary taxation could be obtained, like the English Parliament. A glance in Henneman's detailed study[52] shows a

---

[51] Lot and Fawtier, *Histoire des institutions*, ii. 134.

[52] J. B. Henneman, *Royal Taxation in Fourteenth-Century France* (Princeton UP, Princeton, 1971).

succession of makeshifts and expedients which have to be negotiated individually, with or without success, between the local agents of the king and a city here, delegates of a county there, and in some cases individual personages—and so on throughout the kingdom. Nothing better illustrates how hasty, piecemeal, and imperfect the unification of the Crown's domain lands had been and how much of it had been effected by a local bargain, a charter, or some such expedient. It reflects the sketchy nature of the state-building and explains, too, why the Crown could not mobilize the sums it required despite the vast potential of the kingdom.

The third weakness was due to the change in military techniques and the format of the army. This was now an aristocratic preserve. The proclamation of the *ban* and *arrière-ban* was a mere fiscal device, the infantry being either auxiliaries or skilled crossbowmen hired from Genoa. Though summoned as a feudal host, the limitations of feudal service were such that, as in England, the noble was summoned, paid if he served, and made a money commutation if he did not. For pay, many landless knights sought the king's service eagerly, but this only reinforced the mentality that saw the armoured knight as invulnerable and master of the battlefield. The cost of such a force of heavy cavalry with a mercenary infantry component, especially as plate-armour was replacing mail, was enormous. Thus the military developments reinforced the financial weakness of the Crown. In the meantime the great feudatories and the apanagists themselves (who were not necessarily loyal to the throne, aspiring as some did to setting up their own independent kingdom) were relatively wealthier, united, and militarily stronger. After the military calamities of Crécy and Poitiers, and the subsequent disaster at Agincourt, the pieces of which France were composed had to be put together in a different way.

5. THE DISTINTEGRATION OF THE KINGDOM OF GERMANY

In Germany the course of government ran counter to that in France. The latter started out with a feeble monarchy which grew strong enough to check the centrifugal tendencies in feudalism. It became the keystone of an integrated territorial structure and paved the way for the national state. Germany starts off with a strong monarchy which falls into ruin in the eleventh century and then, despite a vigorous revival in the next century, declines until it is virtually effaced, while the nobles establish independent territorial principalities. Its unity is destroyed for some 700 years. The original German monarchy, up to 1077, was non-feudal. After an anarchy of seventy-five years, the monarchy that emerged—the Hohenstaufen—was not a feudal one, but one where the feudal law gave the nobility advantages denied them in France and England. They pressed these relentlessly against the monarchy and were ultimately victorious. 'Germany' became the name of a people, place, a culture but not of a state. A large proportion of Germans did indeed live in that shadowy system called the Holy Roman Empire. It was hardly an empire. It was not even a state. And it was by no means, even, exclusively German. It became an anachronism, a figment, where the reality consisted of many hundred independent principalities, bishoprics, even kingdoms.

CHRONOLOGY

771–814	Charlemagne
800	Charlemagne crowned emperor by the pope in Rome
843	Treaty of Verdun. Louis the German king of the East Franks
900–11	Louis the Child
911	Extinction of the Carolingian line
911–18	Conrad, duke of Franconia, elected king
919	Election of Henry, duke of Saxony, as king
919–1024	Saxon (or Ottonian) dynasty
936–73	Otto I, the Great
962	Otto crowned emperor in Rome. Revival of the Empire
1024–1138	The Franconian (Salian) Dynasty
1056–1106	Henry IV
1075	Gregory VII's reform programme. The Investitures dispute
1122	Synod of Worms: conference on the Investitures issue
1138	The Hohenstaufen dynasty
1152–90	Frederick I, Barbarossa
1176	Battle of Legnano
1188	Peace of Constance gives autonomy to Lombard cities
1197–1212	Civil War—Welf (Guelph) v. Waiblingen (Ghibelline), i.e. the Hohenstaufen
1211–50	Frederick II
1250–73	The Great Interregnum
1250–68	Relentless persecution of the Hohenstaufen by the pope
1255	Manfred, illegitimate half-brother of Emperor Conrad IV, regent of Sicily
1257	Richard of Cornwall elected emperor
1266	Charles of Anjou defeats and kills Manfred at Benevento
1268	Conradin (son of Emperor Conrad IV) defeated at Tagliacozzo and executed. Extinction of the Hohenstaufen line
1273	Rudolf of Habsburg elected emperor
1356	The Golden Bull

The following account will differ from the form pursued in the French and English case-studies. The narrative sequences there were designed only to explain how the *regna* became consolidated, and the consolidated *regnum* as the *terminus ad quem* is a system of government which can, subsequently, be described. But in Germany the kingship and the kingdom start out as everything and end as nothing. The *terminus ad quem* is not a system of government but a non-system—a condition of disintegration. Consequently, the account is almost entirely narrative—how a united pre-feudal kingdom falls apart owing to the *disintegrative* potentialities of feudalism and the debility of elective monarchy.

The political history of 'Germany' began in 911, with the end of the line of 'Eastern' Carolingians. Thereafter, the Germans—by which anachronistic term I mean simply the German peoples of the eastern third of Charlemagne's empire—had their own native dynasties. The kingdom stretched from the Meuse to the Elbe. It was a wild and sparsely populated land of forests and of marsh, where tracks served as roads, and towns—save in the Romanized Rhineland—were few and insignificant. It was exposed to the Danes in the north, but its openness to the east posed the greatest threat, where the lands between Elbe and Oder were filling up with pagan Slavs; and in 862 an even more savage threat came when the Magyars began to raid right across the country from their bases in what is modern Hungary. Its inhabitants did not recognize themselves as 'German' but as Saxons, Franks, Swabians (*Alemanni*), and Bavarians. They were only now emerging from a tribal condition. Each had its own historical traditions, laws, and customs. They were above all military communities and it was as such that their individual consciousness survived. Society and government were almost unbelievably primitive. In the West, in Frisia, Lotharingia, and Franconia, a proto-feudalism was developing, but elsewhere the dominant economic characteristic was *allod*, that is, the freeholding. But the allodial class, though free, was dominated by some 300 families who in times gone by, and through processes still obscure to us, had come to own huge estates on which they had brought the peasants into dependency. This class, sometimes styled 'the old nobility', sometimes the 'dynasts', supplied all the superior governing posts—the 'dukes', the counts, the margraves, and the bishops—throughout their land. Their estates and their local influence owed *nothing at all to the monarchy*. It was prescriptive and wholly independent of the Crown.

As to government, this was primitive in machinery and almost non-existent in scope. As in England, justice was exercised through the traditional popular courts of the hundred (for petty offences) and of the county (for those affecting life and limb and others entailing capital punishment). Both types of court were presided by the Crown-appointed counts, whose territorial jurisdiction was defined simply by the aggregate of courts they presided over. The justice and the procedures in these popular courts owed nothing to royal capitularies. They dispensed the customary laws of the various communities according to the traditional German procedures of compurgations, ordeal, and *Wergild*. No itinerant justices controlled the exercise of such local power, but instead the central power moved around the kingdom, the king's own justice supplanting that of the local court wherever he might stay. It seems superfluous to add that royal taxation (save on royal domain lands) was totally absent. The king 'lived off his own' and progressed through places where his lands could feed and accommodate his household or preferably where he had rights to stay at his host's expense, notably (as we shall see) in abbeys and bishop's palaces.

Apart from its duty to protect the Church, the monarchy's overriding obligation was to protect the country. The Magyar raids, bolder on each campaign, made this paramount. The mighty warriors in the four great 'stems' took over the task. Only nominally the king's generals, they were the men who convened the 'stem' host and led it to the royal rendezvous. These dukes were the great rivals of the royal power, and used their enormous local military influence to nominate the counts and the bishops who were the traditional agents of the Crown, and wherever they could they took over the royal domain lands. So emerged the four 'stem' duchies. One of these dukes, Henry 'the Fowler', was presented by the Saxon and the Franconian notables to those of the other stem duchies. Accepting, they swore fealty to him, acting out the role of his household officers—chamberlain, butler, and so on—at his coronation as King Henry I (919). So arose this Saxon or 'Ottonian' line. When it died out in 1024 it was succeeded by a collateral branch, the Salians. Between 919 and 1077 the Saxon-Salian line built up the kingship to a dominating position. But it emphatically was *not* a feudal monarchy. Bloch calls it 'archaistic' by way of contrast to the contemporary feudal monarchies in England and France. It was in fact the collapse of this kind of monarchy that introduced feudalism into Germany. Before turning to that, it is therefore necessary to explain the peculiarity of this so-called 'Ottonian' or Salian system of governing.

5.1. *The Ottonian Kingdom, 919–1077*

The Saxon line rebuilt royal prestige and power by, first of all, delivering the country from the Magyars. Otto I, who succeeded despite ducal rebellion, surpassed his father Henry I at the Battle of the Lechfeld in 955, which was decisive: the Magyars were crushed. For this feat Otto was called 'the Great'.

Internally, the dukes had assumed semi-regal powers and the Crown's problem was to find the resources to match them. It is the device by which it did so that makes the system specifically 'Ottonian'. The device was to divert the enormous resources of the Church into the service of the Crown. In German tradition, the founder and endower of a church possessed the right to nominate its incumbent and enjoy the usufruct of his grants. Secondly, there still persisted the Carolingian tradition that the king was both *rex et sacerdos*: effectively a Byzantine tradition where the king was *isoapostolos*—equal to the apostles. The Ottonian practice was to endow abbeys and bishoprics with lands and to give them 'immunity' from the dukes and the royal courts alike. Superficially, it seems as if the king were simply giving regalian authority and resources away. In fact, it was the reverse. The immunity he granted them protected them from the local dukes and counts, by extending to them 'king's peace'—his *mundeburgium* or *tuitio*. Of course, at this time it was the king who nominated bishops and abbots. He now took to appointing, also, the lay administrators called advocates or *vogt*, who managed their estates. In return for his *mundeburgium* and endowments the king received the provision of food and shelter (on a vast scale, given the size of his court and retinue) when he was progressing through the kingdom, and likewise, military contingents when he called on them. Germany was renowned—or notorious—for its fighting bishops who led their troops into battle; failing them, the 'advocates' would lead. The churches provided the Crown with by far its main single source of soldiers: in Otto II's 981 campaign in Italy no less than 75 per cent of his army was provided by the Church.

Later kings extended the policy to all the royal abbeys and took under protection all the ancient bishoprics, and the new sees (like Magdeburg) which were set up east of the Elbe. The process, the formation of a *Reichskirche*, was complete by 1024. The bishops were given full rights of administration (*Justitiam*) in their lands and achieved a territorial jurisdiction. So arose the territorial administration of the archbishops of Mainz, Cologne, and Magdeburg, and the bishoprics of Speyer, Chur, Worms, Minden and Bamberg, and Wurzburg. Here lies the origin of the prince-bishops, territorial princes, who are such a distinctive feature in subsequent German history.

A correlate of royal control over the bishops and abbots in Germany was the control of the head of the Church, the Papacy. Now, the 'imperial' kingdom of Lotharingia–Burgundy–Lombardy had long since disintegrated and the imperial title and office had itself lapsed in 924. Otto I decided to revive the empire with himself as emperor. Otto conceived the relationship between the emperor and the pope in Carolingian terms. The emperor was the protector of the Papacy. He took it and its territory (the supposed 'donation of Constantine') into his *mundeburgium* virtually as an imperial dependency; he saw to it that popes were worthy and, when they manifestly were not, could and should convene a synod to replace them. After Otto had delivered Europe from the Magyars at the Lechfeld, the pope, John XII, young scion of the principal noble family of Rome (and a highly dubious character) was threatened by another great Italian house in the person of Berengar of Friuw (an old enemy of Otto's into the bargain). The situation was similar to that of 800 when the then-pope had called Charlemagne to expel the Lombards. In 961 Otto descended on Rome and in 962 he was crowned emperor. So was the Roman Empire reborn. But that was not the end of it. In 963, after having deposed one pope and imposed his own choice of successor, the latter had to agree that in future no pope could be consecrated until he had taken an oath of loyalty to the emperor. Caesaro-papism had triumphed. The Roman Empire of the West (styled *sacrum* only in 1157, but called by us the Holy Roman Empire) was again in being.

The direct Saxon line died out in 1024. The Crown was elective, not hereditary as in France and England; but in the usual way every attempt was made by the magnates (on whom, in practice, the choice depended) to select a candidate from within the ruling house. In this case the candidate who presented himself was Conrad, a descendant of the Emperor Otto I. A majority supported him and an attempt by his opponents to elect a counter-king was quickly abandoned. The subsequent Salian line pursued the same imperial and Church policy as the Saxon, but went further. By this time the royal domain was smaller than it had ever been since the distant days of the last Carolingian in 911, and the king's vicarious control of the Church's revenues for his own use had its limitations (e.g. once in office, prelates were hard to remove and often pursued their own ambitions). It is essential to realize that the power of the German ruler was entirely personal. There was no legally binding feudal contract on which he could insist. If personal loyalty failed the king had to have the power to overawe the aristocracy, and so the Salians began to rebuild a personal domain. This entailed adminis-tration via personal servants of the monarch, and since the aristocracy were wholly untrustworthy, the Salians turned to a class, unique to Germany, which was already being employed by many ecclesiastical foundations. This was the class of *ministeriales*. A *ministerialis* was a *serf*. The preceding Saxon dynasty had made use of this (highly superior) serf class as soldiers,[53] so that they were often called 'serf-knights'. The Salians began to use them, as

---

[53] J. W. Thompson, *Feudal Germany* (University of Chicago Press, Chicago, 1928), 330. Cf. the 'slave'-soldiers under the Caliphate, and the Mamluks of Egypt (Bk. III, Ch. 2 and Addendum A).

the clerics did, to administer their domain. It is the first sign of an emerging bureaucracy, which never emerged. The best the German monarchs could ever manage was a Chancery, and at this date it did not even make file-copies, and no judicial or financial departments ever developed. Thus, during the frequent minorities or contested elections or interregnums, there was no core of permanent officials to carry on even the most elementary routines of royal government.

While management of the royal estates (now much expanded) was given over to the *ministeriales*, resistance built up among the magnates. The stem-dukes had faded: over time many lineages had been removed, others had been forfeited through rebellion, and still others had died out; and the ancient communal solidarity of the stems had virtually disappeared also, except in Saxony. But behind the ancient dukes still stood the local 'dynasts' who were now brought face-to-face with the monarchy. Those local mag-nates wanted to enjoy over their own lands the same governmental powers that the counts had been wont to enjoy in their circumscription. Their lands, and usually their powers of jurisdiction, were freeholds, often imme-morial, for which they owed no feudal dues or obligations. Futhermore, they had immensely strengthened their economic and political position by founding new monasteries of which, as proprietors, they enjoyed the resources. Thus, for instance, in 973 there were 108 monasteries, nearly all of them attached to the Crown, while in 1073 there were more than 700, and nearly all the new ones were aristocratic. These aristocrats or 'dynasts' had every incentive to resist the monarch. They had an interest in preventing him taking over the Church foundations as part of the *Reichskirche*. They bitterly resented losing their traditional court position to the serf-knights, the vile *ministeriales*. They suffered when the forests and wastes were reclaimed for the Crown. It is unsurprising that the aristocracy and free peasants of Saxony rebelled in 1070, in 1073, and once again in 1075. They were defeated, but their grievances lived on. Then—at this moment—the Papacy in a revolutionary act of self-assertion totally destroyed the 'theory' of the Ottonian 'system' and threatened to bring the entire monarchical edifice crashing down. For we have already mentioned the policy of Pope Gregory VII to make the Church independent of all secular control. How could the German kings function without the Church's vast military and financial resources, and how could they enjoy these unless they themselves appointed the bishops and abbots?

Yet the reform party at Rome insisted that bishops and abbots be freely elected by their chapters without any royal interference; it desacralized kings as being merely laymen; and Gregory VII's *Dictatus Papae* (thoughts put down in his private letter book) maintained

The Pope can be judged by no one.
The Pope alone can use the Imperial insignia.
The Pope can depose Emperors.
The Pope can absolve subjects from their allegiance.
All princes should kiss his feet . . .[54]

The reform party stood Byzantine (and Ottonian) Caesaro-papism on its
head and demanded in its stead a *hierocracy*, of which the pope was the
supreme and uncontestable head. Furthermore—not one of the assertions
of the *Dictatus* was 'an idle boast . . . each one of them became a practical
force in European life within an astonishingly short space of time'.[55]

In England and France the kings and Papacy were able, after initial
friction, to work out acceptable compromises. This indeed was what was
to happen in Germany by the Concordat of Worms in 1122, forty-five years
after Gregory made his initial demand for an end to any lay involvement in
Church appointments.[56] But the end result was not as satisfactory to the
German monarchy and the initial friction was far more severe than in
England and in France. There the nomination to ecclesiastical office was
certainly significant to the monarch's authority, but they had feudal law and
their own domains as alternative sources of support. In Germany, by
contrast, the Crown's vicarious control of ecclesiastical resources was the
very bedrock of its power. The reforms sapped it irretrievably. Even worse:
when the Emperor Henry IV tried (like his forbears) to depose Gregory
VII, the latter excommunicated him and plunged Germany into civil war.
And so it was to continue in one way or another for seventy-five years, for
the popes could always find a papal party to support them in Germany. This
utter breakdown of central authority had the same effect as France had
experienced in the ninth century: Germany slid into feudalism.

5.2. *Feudal Germany*

By the end of the wars (1077–1135) the entire social landscape had changed.
There were private castles. The weakest peasants commended themselves to
the protection of the lords of the castle, and the feeblest of the latter did the
same to the strongest among them. At the same time, these themselves had
learned in the wars that the traditional peasant militias were useless against
the new shock cavalry who fought in the new French feudal manner, and
that their castles could not be guarded without professional castellans and

---

[54] Southern, *Western Society*, 102.   [55] Ibid. 102–3.
[56] Cf. the views of P. Classen as quoted in H. Fuhrmann, *Germany in the High Middle Ages, c.1050–1200*
(CUP, Cambridge, 1986), 97.

garrisons. Such professionals could be found only among the *ministeriales*, and king, lords, abbots, and bishops all turned to these serf-knights. To attract them, they were willing to allow freedom to change employer and contractual fiefs. No longer servile and fighting as *ritters*, the *ministeriales* were now accounted noble in order to distinguish them from the peasant rabble. Simultaneously—as one expects during times of war and uncertainty—ancient powerful families among the 'three hundred' dynasts sank to *ministeriales* level, while parvenus rose to supreme power, so that ultimately a graded hierarchy emerged, with the *ministeriales* at the base and a few most powerful warriors at the top. The latter began to be styled 'princes' (*Fürsten*). Bit by bit, they regularized the *de facto* dominance over their lesser nobles by feudal ties of vassaldom-fiefdom, and the great bishops were not behindhand in doing the same thing.

As a consequence, the political and constitutional landscape also altered. On the ruins of the former imperial counties arose a new mosaic of territorial units based on their private castles. Erected on the hereditary family estates, these dominated the area around and became the local centres of administration. This is where we came in, in ninth-century France! Government had devolved to a basic unit, a *castellany* (in German, the *Burgbezirk*). Their petty lords strove to legitimate their power to dispense justice, keep order, and to tax—in brief, to govern their territory—and herein lies the genesis of the residuary legatees of the once-united German kingdom: the territorial principalities.

And the Crown fell into the hands of the greatest of their princes. The prestige of the former Saxon and the Salian dynasties and a continuous succession had made the electivity of the kingship nominal. Hitherto the designation of the heir was met by acclamation. But papal intervention now turned election into a live practice, for it gave rebels just the opportunity they sought to challenge the Crown. The princes set aside the hereditary principle and intervened to elect, now a Welf, now a Hohenstaufen. But who *were* these electors? Already in the election of 1125 we find a small number of magnates exercising a claimed right of pre-election, that is, choosing the candidate and then presenting him to the rest for approval. Pope Innocent III (1198–1216) speaks of the 'princes in whom the election of the King of the Romans largely resides'.[57] By 1263 those princes were confined to seven: the archbishops of Mainz, Trèves, and Cologne; the count palatine of the Rhine; the duke of Saxony; and (marking the effect of German colonization of the Slav lands up to the Oder and the vast power accreting to those who ruled in those regions), the margrave of Brandenburg together with—very

[57] J. Bryce, *The Holy Roman Empire*, 4th edn. (Macmillan, London, 1889), 229, n. i.

odd—the king of Bohemia.[58] The significant point here, however, is that mere accession to the throne now lay in the disposition of a handful of magnates.

5.3. *The Systematization of Feudalism in Germany*

In the teeth of papal hostility the house of Hohenstaufen acceded in 1138, and its emperor, Frederick I (Barbarossa), set out to reconstitute the kingdom by means of feudal laws.[59] The policy and practice of Barbarossa and of his grandson Frederick II are vastly controversial. If, however, it is possible to infer conscious policy from incontrovertible actions, one could propose that Barbarossa saw his main domestic problems as the proliferation of the *Burgbezirken,* that he looked to the princes to bring these under their control, and that he decided to introduce feudal arrangements to attach them to himself while, all the time, rebuilding his domain for military backup. His many expeditions to Italy were not simply to reclaim his traditional imperial rights as king of the Lombards or to put pressure on the pope, but, just as much, to tap the resources of the Lombard cities which he reckoned would bring in 30,000 lbs of silver in revenue. In the event, this ended in total defeat at Legnano in 1176, and Frederick had to sign the Peace of Constance in 1183, by which these Lombard cities obtained self-government. By contrast, the building of a domain in Germany was highly successful. Barbarossa was a formidable warrior and this was one of his strengths in his feudal settlement with the princes. The other was his authority as emperor: for the nobles were uneasy at exercising power *de facto.* They wanted legal title. Nobody but the king-emperor could offer that. It was precisely on the basis of confirming (usurped) regalian rights in return for feudal homage and service that Barbarossa systematized the political structure of the kingdom.

About thirty years after Barbarossa's death a man called Eike von Repkow completed the *Sachsenspiegel.* This is a compilation of the public law as it then stood. From it we see quite clearly that Germany was now

---

[58] The bizarre circumstances by which this Slav king was finally recognized as an elector are briefly summarized in Bryce, *Holy Roman Empire,* 229–31. In the 11th cent. the number was increased to eight and in 1708 to nine—this one being the duke of Hanover who was, in 1714, also the king of Great Britain!

[59] Barraclough (whose work is regarded in England almost as canonical, cf. G. Barraclough, *Medieval Germany* (2 vols; Blackwell, Oxford, 1938), I), and *Factors in German History* (Blackwell, Oxford 1946) takes Barbarossa as his hero. He rubbishes the early works of J. W. Thompson (*Feudal Germany*) for whom Barbarossa was a reckless imperialist and centralizer who ruined the chances of a 'federal' Germany under the house of Welf and equally that of E. Kantorowicz, author (*Frederick the Second 1194–1250*) of the splendid biography of Frederick II, his idol.

fully feudalized.[60] The laws relate to fiefs, to the way in which the feudatories pay homage, to the symbols by which the king grants seisin (the sceptre to the ecclesiastics, the banner to the laymen), and the conditions of the military service they owe him in return. In all these respects, Germany is as clearly and unequivocally feudal as France or England.

But when we turn to the specifics, these show how that balance is strongly tilted in the feudatories' favour and against the monarchy, and this is quite apart from the electivity of the kingly office which provided the feudatories with an ever-present sanction. It is true that Frederick had ordained that a rear vassal must reserve, in every oath of fealty, the fealty he owed the king; and equally that the fiefs, once granted by him, could not be disposed of without his consent.[61] But in three ways the feudal laws reflect the weakness of the Crown and the entrenched position of the magnates.

The first is the Crown's recognition of a very restricted class of magnates—confined to his tenants-in-chief—as a special Estate at the apex of the lay hierarchy, as 'imperial princes'. Since this Estate alone could open its ranks to any newcomers, the monarch could not fill all high positions with persons of his own free choice. Furthermore, this Estate acted as a rank between the king and the counts: at any rate, it now became usual for a count to receive his office (which was supposedly a Crown office) from the imperial prince and not directly from the king. It was as though, for instance, an English sheriff were to receive his office from a count or duke, instead of directly from the monarch.

Secondly, there was established a graded hierarchy of similar ranks which was all but unalterable. The arrangement is called the *Heerschild*, literally the *shield of war*. The *Sachsenspiegel* declares the existence of six ranks of nobility. They are: the king; bishops and abbots; lay princes; 'free lords'; those capable of so becoming; and finally their vassals. The last are, in fact, the *ministeriales*, who thus are recognized as noblemen. No son could retain his father's rank if, by an act of homage, he had lowered that rank. He had to do homage only to equals or superiors to retain it. So the hierarchy became fixed except for the occasions when a king could raise the rank of a feudatory by granting him a banner fief. And that, the law said, was the only way he could rise.[62] In practice, what this all signified was that the 'dynasts' or free aristocracy who made the fourth rank had come up as far as they could and could never attain princely rank save by the consent of the princes themselves.

[60] Cf. Fuhrmann, *Germany*, p. 170, 'Feudal law became definitively the basis of royal government'.
[61] Boutruche, *Seigneurie et féodalité*, p. 190.   [62] Ibid. ii, p. 432.

The third principle underwrote this freezing of the feudal hierarchy in terms of property and by that act it also imposed a fatal limitation on the Crown's efforts to construct a domain.[63] For in France escheated estates became Crown property and something like this existed in England too. But in Germany it was customary that the king might not keep any banner fief vacant for more than a year and a day.[64] Instead, forfeited or vacant fiefs had to be recycled among the existing fief-holders. So though one member of the feudality might suffer at the hands of the king, the feudality as a whole did not. The Capetians could never have formed their domain and come to rule the *mouvance* through the power it gave them had a similar rule been in force.

A practical example of how the new system worked is what happened to Henry the Lion, the great duke of Saxony. As a result of a territorial dispute, Frederick summoned him to his court and, when he failed to appear, had him tried and condemned under feudal law as a contumacious vassal. The magnates of his court were those who delivered this verdict. They could well afford to do so because it was to them and not to the king that Henry's escheated lands were allocated.

5.4. *The Dismemberment of the German Kingdom*

Had matters run an uninterrupted course—had Barbarossa not died on Crusade, had his son Henry VI also not died prematurely, had a continuous succession of industrious kings concentrated on rebuilding a domain and utilizing such feudal rights as they had against their vassals—the kingdom of Germany might have developed just as, at precisely this moment, it was developing in France under Philippe-Auguste. It was, however, far more vulnerable because the throne was actively elective and the ruling dynasty faced an implacable foe in the Papacy which could and did intervene in any vacancy of the throne to raise internal opposition (a latent condition in any feudal state) against the Crown. Because the king of the German realm was king of the Romans and asserted his claim to the Iron Crown of Lombardy, but had to enter Rome to be crowned by a pope as emperor, he was ineluctably bound to have an Italian policy. Because the Papacy, in the fashion of the time, only felt secure if it exercised temporal power over its own domain (the 'Donation of Constantine', later called simply the Papal States, and which lay athwart the Italian peninsula to divide Lombardy from

[63] This *Leiheswang* was not a legal obligation but tenaciously customary. The domain lands were acquired in these ways: 1) by the exchange of property; 2) by exploitation of the right of escheat; and 3) by purchase.   [64] Boutruche, *Seigneurie et féodalité*, ii, p. 433.

the south and Sicily), the popes were equally constrained to look on any alteration in the local balance of power as a threat.

As we noted, Barbarossa's attempt to subjugate Lombardy (a component part of the empire) foundered against papal diplomacy. But the Italian entanglement emerged in a different shape when, by dynastic marriage, the Emperor Henry VI and his heir Frederick became kings of Sicily. Under its Norman dynasty this was both powerful and wealthy, so that the popes feared the imperial effort, thwarted in Lombardy, would now develop in the south: and this is exactly what happened when Frederick II, whom Innocent III had had to acknowledge and crown emperor in the end, broke his pledge not to unite the German and Sicilian crowns.

This extraordinary man, known to his contemporaries as *Stupor Mundi*— the 'wonder of the world'—deserves much more than so passing a reference, and were we dealing with political history and not the history of government he would assuredly receive it here. As it is, what has to be noted is that he made Sicily his base, leaving German government to his *ministeriales* and his son Henry. His motives are obscure but my personal view is that he thought his predecessors had tried to unite the empire from the wrong direction by descending from impoverished Germany into wealthy Italy instead of the other way round. In short, he planned to unite Italy from Sicily and then use its resources to reassert himself in Germany. I think it was to this end that he was prepared to make any concessions to the German princes until he was capable of settling their account from overwhelming strength. In the event he died prematurely, so that his Italian conquests had no lasting effects on government there, whereas in Germany his concessions proved permanent.

These concessions were, respectively, the Bull of Eger (1213), the *Confederatio cum principibus ecclesiasticis* (1220), and the *Statutum in favorem principum* (1231). The first two opened the path to independent ecclesiastical princedoms. By the Bull of Eger, Frederick renounced his *regalia*, gave up his right to play any part in elections to the bishoprics, and acknowledged the clergy's right to appeal to Rome, so putting an end to the Investitures dispute on the Papacy's terms. But the *Confederatio* of 1220 went much further and set the bishops on their long historic path as territorial princes. It accepted as established fact that the prince-bishops exercised the rights to exact tolls and coin currency. It sanctioned their building new castles and walling towns on their territories. It made it illegal for fugitive villeins from the Church estates to settle in towns. It promised not to acquire ecclesiastical fiefs. The king would levy no new taxes on ecclesiastical lands, nor build castles or cities there. The prince-bishops were confirmed in free disposition of the fiefs of their vassals. The consequence was that, in the course of time, the prince-bishops sealed off their territory from the king's writ.

But what of the lay princes? The *Statutum* applied every one of those provisions to the lay princes but went even further. It recognized (though in general terms) the princes' right to exercise supreme jurisdiction in their territories providing they abided by ancient custom (in this way precluding the extension of royal law throughout the kingdom). True, it did reserve the king's right to remove pleas from the princely court to his own, but in time the princes had that set aside by securing a *privilegia de non evocando et appellando*, which made their judgment final. And the *Statutum*, at the behest of the lay princes, struck at the emerging towns. Founding and fostering towns on the domain was a marked feature of the Hohenstaufens and was rewarded by the loyalty of their citizens. Now the *Statutum* terminated the policy and made it illegal for towns to expand their jurisdiction into the surrounding country-side or to form alliances. (In fact, as will be seen, the towns were able to disregard these restrictions, but the monarchy ceased to gain any resources or political advantage from that.)

The evidence strongly suggests that Frederick saw these concessions as temporary and limited and regarded the formation of territorial principa-lities with equanimity, as a mere preliminary consolidation which he would later knit together under his *curia*.[65] But his death precluded any such development and indeed made the concessions irreversible. His imperial house of Hohenstaufen was, in the most literal manner, extinguished in the Papacy's implacable vendetta, and from 1257 to 1273 the new emperor (who was not even a German, but the Englishman, Richard of Cornwall) was nominal only. Indeed, the period is known as the Great Interregnum. Subsequent elections, now in the hands of the Seven Electors, ushered in nothing but more foreign and papal interventions resulting in instant alternations of dynasty, disputed decisions, and often, civil wars. These circumstances were fostered by the Electors who had everything to gain from them, and the path of constitutional development veered further and further away from a monarch-centred kingdom towards the consolidation of the territorial principalities.

The Golden Bull of 1356 formalized the position and forms a convenient point to terminate the story of the rise and subsequent fragmentation of the German kingdom. The Bull confirmed the seven-man electoral college; established that the majority vote carried the day; and made provision for a regency in the event of a vacancy. (These provisions were designed to close the opportunities for the Papacy to pursue its own objects.) In another set

---

[65] H. Mitteis, *The State in the Middle Ages* (North Holland Publishing Co., Amsterdam, 1975).

of articles the Bull confirmed and extended the rights of the Seven Electors: they could build castles, mint currency, and impose tolls; there was no appeal from their courts; conspiracy or rebellion against them was high treason; each year they were to meet the ruler as a supreme advisory council; and the formation of city leagues against them was forbidden. The subsequent history of Germany revolves largely around the efforts of the other territorial units—including the cities—to obtain equivalent powers. It is, in short, a history of particularism. And this Bull was promulgated at the very moment when the kingdoms of England and France, embarked against each other in the Hundred Years War, were on the high road to becoming unified national states.

7

The Republican Alternative: Florence and Venice

*E*ver since the Roman Republic fell, the ideal and practice of government throughout the entire globe had been, without exception, monarchical. In Europe, in the eleventh century, that began to change. In the loose, feebly articulated feudal monarchies bodies of townsfolk began to thrust for independence. In this they behaved no differently from any other groups or individuals who had sufficient clout—vassals, knights, the Church. The Middle Ages are the scene of a perpetual struggle for rights, privileges, and immunities against the duly constituted authorities. Where these were strong enough, they limited the autonomy they conceded to towns: as in France and England and, to a degree, in the Low Countries. Where they were weak the towns became *de facto* self-governing, as in Germany. And where, as in Italy, the towns were at their strongest and most numerous and the central power at its most intermittent and fleeting, they became independent republics, behaving just as all the footloose feudatories of France and Germany were doing, that is, fighting one another incessantly. They brought first the countryside and then other towns under their sway, until a few cities ended up as the masters of virtually independent and medium-sized country-states.

Towns might be non-feudal or anti-feudal. The former were, so to speak, licensed by the feudal authority, and assimilated into the overarching feudal polity as a particular kind of 'immunity' or 'liberty' and then, in the fourteenth century, incorporated in the self-elaborating and self-transforming feudal monarchies and principalities of the late Middle Ages. Here they formed an indispensable component in the representative assemblies that sprang up all over Europe. This aspect of the rise of the towns is dealt with in the next chapter. The present one deals with the anti-feudal aspect. A number of the German cities, the *Reichstädte*, became *de facto* republics but were to be reincorporated into the confederal loose association which the Holy Roman Empire was to become. In Italy it was quite otherwise; they were never reincorporated in the monarchy. On the contrary, they took over and superseded the feudal-monarchical order altogether. With the exception of Venice none were *de jure* sovereign, it is true, but their non-sovereign status was purely nominal.

These cities became republics by the simple fact of shaking off their dependency. But some survived as republics, and in the course of time became increasingly conscious of their identity as such. Florence and Venice in particular became emblematic of a counter-feudal and counter-monarchical theory and practice of government—'Republicanism'. This revived not just the practice but the theory of a long-extinguished form. It is an example of *ideational* transmission of governmental forms.

To their contemporaries in the period 1100–1400 the republics were exceptional, not the rule, and were short-lived at that. Nor was their practice anything like as equitable and libertarian as their contemporary apologists and the liberal and nationalist historians of the nineteenth century affirmed. But they *were* different, and their difference had consequences, and that is the rationale for this chapter.

We cannot, however, begin with medieval Florence and Venice. Something has to be said about the emergence of towns in general and the form their polities took. From that it will be seen how much the Italian town shared common features with towns in other countries. Something must then be said about the Italian ambience, whence it will be evident that the towns in northern and central Italy shared a remarkably similar constitutional evolution. Only then can we describe the government of the Florentine and Venetian republics and only then situate their experience in the course of the history of government as a whole.

1. THE THRUST TO AUTONOMY

Such old Roman towns as survived were miserably shrunken by the tenth century, important mostly as the seats of prelates or as military headquarters. Few contained any sizeable nucleus of merchants or craftsmen. Towns revived from the tenth century with the reawakening of long-distance trade. From then onwards, as Europe suffered a population explosion and a steady intensification of agricultural yields, the towns were upborne with these and extensive urbanization occurred. Its first major sites were the areas where towns had had their most uninterrupted continuity: Italy, the French Midi, and the Rhine–Scheldt–Meuse areas, served by river and sea-coast. Not till the thirteenth century did towns multiply in Germany (it is said 3,000 were planted there in the fourteenth century, most of them what we would think of as mere hamlets, the average size being only 400 inhabitants).[1]

---

[1] F. Braudel, *Civilisation and Capitalism: Fifteenth–Eighteenth Century*, trans. Siàn Reynolds (Fontana, London, 1985), i. 482.

These towns were all tiny by our standards,[2] but the largest were astonishing to their contemporaries: in 1340 the biggest—Paris, Venice, Florence, and Genoa—neared 100,000 inhabitants each. But thousands had less than 2,000 inhabitants apiece, and even a famous city like Nuremberg had only 20,000.[3] Towns were *walled*, everywhere; and that wall was not just a defence, but a symbol which cut off the rural and feudal countryside with its lords and serfs. The common name for a town—*bourg* or *burgh* or *burg*—gave its inhabitants the appellation of *burgenses*, hence *bourgeois*. At the same time the word *civis* ceased to be used in its old Roman sense of an individual who participated in his government, and came to be used for someone who lived in a town rather than the countryside.[4] *Stadtluft macht frei*—anybody who had resided in a town for a year and a day was deemed free (because, it seems, in no country was there a *presumption* of serfdom).[5] Moreover, *burgenses*—free men—held property by a special tenure (*burgage, bourgage, Burgrecht, etc.*) which did not involve personal dependence and permitted free alienation, quite unlike feudal tenures. So, from the first the *burgensis* had John Locke's essential prerequisites for being an individual: he was master of his person and master of his possessions (Life, Liberty, and Property).

Thus the towns were non-feudal and some were even anti-feudal, and they began to do what any local body with authority was doing, trying to assert its autonomy. The interests and outlook of townsmen were antithetical to the feudal political and economic order. They resented the lord's tolls, the duty to bake in his ovens and grind in his mills, possibly, even, to serve as his soldiers. The formalistic, quasi-ritualistic procedures of feudal courts were worse than useless to adjudicate financial and contractual suits.[6] They wanted to frame their own municipal laws, their own taxation system, and administer them themselves. So much for their being 'non-feudal'. As for their clout: to begin with towns had *cash* whereas feudal lords had lands, that is, liquid capital as against fixed capital, in an age when any emergency, from wedding one's daughter to going on Crusade, made the marginal utility of ready money enormous. Secondly, they had armed force. The armoured

---

[2] Or by Asian standards. Marco Polo was totally disbelieved when he described the immense populations in the greater Chinese cities, and mocked as *Marco milione*. The Florentines' attitude brings to mind the passage in Montesquieu's *Lettres Persanes*, where one of the two Persians starts his letter home with the sentence: 'Paris is as big as Isfahan.'

[3] C. C. Cipolla, *Fontana Economic History of Europe*, vol. I., *The Middle Ages* (Fontana, Glasgow, 1972), 34–5.

[4] H. Sidgwick, *The Development of the European Polity* (Macmillan, London, 1903), 234–5.

[5] S. Reynolds, *Kingdoms and Communities in Western Europe, 900–1300* (Clarendon Press, Oxford, 1984), 164.

[6] Cf. H. Pirenne, *Medieval Cities* (Princeton UP, Princeton, 1925), 138–45. Cf. also—*malgré elle*—Reynolds, *Kingdoms and Communities*, 181, 168.

cavalry charge was no use in city streets, and storming a defended walled town was no easy matter.

From the middle of the eleventh century town after town either bought or fought its way to its privileges or immunities. What it demanded and how it obtained it depended on whom the townsfolk were confronting— prelates or laymen, seigneurs or king. Bishops, necessary residents in their city and theologically outraged by the challenge to hierarchy, were usually more resistant than lay lords, unless all their liquid revenue happened to come from one town situated in their lands, when they were more prepared to do a cash deal with the town and commute their dues for an annual income, the *firma burgi*. Kings reacted and conceded privileges where it seemed advantageous, and this largely depended on force to make an unequal bargain.

The widespread demand for municipal autonomy is known as 'the *communal* movement' and spread through Italy, southern and northern France, the Netherlands, and parts of Germany. (In England only London—and that but flickeringly—became a 'commune'.) 'Commune' was a vague term. In the late-eleventh and twelfth centuries it came to mean any local collectivity that possessed autonomy. By the thirteenth century it could mean either the entire local community *or* the ruling body of the community, *but* (and this will emerge very sharply when we turn to Italy) it also meant something much narrower: an association of individuals. Many of these, notably in Italy, were bound by a common oath: these were the *conjurationes*. But townsfolk could and often did band together as a commune without such oaths. Likewise, many 'communes' acquired their privileges by piecemeal dickering over a long period. But others, in Italy, Germany, and to some extent the Low Countries, were sworn associations who seized their autonomy by insurrection and maintained it by armed force.

The political institutions and the course of constitutional development in these communes followed a (broadly defined) common pattern throughout Europe. The fundamental institution was the open town assembly, and it remained so, though used more and more rarely as time went on. It did not include all the inhabitants by any means, but only the citizens, who formed a very small proportion as we shall see. The task of the assembly was to consent to grave policies—which they did by acclamation, not by debate; and to choose—or at least assent to—a list of magistrates. The latter, from the very beginning, were the rich and powerful, and indeed the first communes (in the sense of associations) were simply confederacies of the wealthiest citizens whose purpose was to take over the authority of the governing bishop, count, or seigneur. By the thirteenth century the plenary assemblies had been supplanted everywhere (except for rare emergencies) by small elected councils. Modes of election varied—sometimes by full assembly, more often by the city's wards (*quartiere, contrade, sestieri*) or by its guilds—and again they were sometimes direct, sometimes indirect, and sometimes by simple co-optation. But without exception, it was invariably the strong and wealthy who composed the council, which is why they are often called (by us, not by their contemporaries) the 'patriciate' or 'oligarchies'. Furthermore, from the thirteenth century these groups were beginning to close their ranks to newcomers.[7] But as they did so they came under pressure from the less wealthy or newly wealthy elements demanding a due share in office; the so-called 'democratic' movement. These elements, characteristically, used their guild organizations to channel their pressure, so that the struggle looks like craft-guilds trying to break the political monopoly of the wealthier and more prestigious merchant-guilds. In Italy, as will be seen, these excluded elements formed themselves into sworn associations and called themselves the 'People'—the *popolo*—and tried to assert their claims by revolt. But what happened in Italy is but the paradigm case of what was occurring in much of urbanized Europe as the thirteenth century began to close: resistance to the oligarchy, violence, even revolution. In Flanders towns were convulsed in 1225, there was rebellion in Liege in 1253, and a general rising in the Flanders towns in 1280, culminating in their smashing victory over the French knighthood at Courtrai in 1302. Similar risings took place in south-west Germany and in Cologne (1371, 1396). France and England were spared such convulsions because there the monarchs imposed their peace. It was in the areas where central authority was contested or weak or both, the Low Countries, Southern Germany, and Italy, that the conflicts raged.

Some brief examples from Germany may illustrate these general remarks, and, in view of this chapter's main preoccupation, serve as a comparison and contrast with what passed in the most intensively urban area, namely north and central Italy. But even here we must generalize widely. No German city ever became juridically independent. The 'imperial cities' (*Reichstädt*), ultimately numbering fifty-one, were the most autonomous. They acknowledged only the suzerainty of the emperor, an authority which became ever more shadowy after the Great Interregnum of 1250–73. As direct subjects of the emperor they were immune from the claims of the local princes, and the emperors found it to their advantage to let them alone, intervening rarely and even then mostly at a patriciate's invitation to fight off the lower classes'

---

[7] Cf. H. van Werveke, 'The Economic Policies of Governments: The Low Countries', *Cambridge Economic History of Europe* [hereafter referred to as *CEH*] (CUP, Cambridge, 1963), iii. 30. Reynolds makes some fussy remarks about the alleged anachronism of the term 'patriciate' and 'oligarchy' but grudgingly concedes the main point: Reynolds, *Kingdoms and Communities*, 204–6, 221.

demands for participation. But many of the towns on princely territory had won an equal degree of autonomy, and it was their permanent and fully justified suspicion of the local prince that preoccupied their governments and led them to form the defensive leagues.

Unlike the Italian cities, they did not try to conquer the countryside to any extent, their oligarchies contained no knightly element but were town families, a highly homogeneous group mostly and often wholly engaged in long-distance trade. With one or two exceptions—Nuremberg is the prime example—they engaged mercenaries rather than taking the field themselves. Their rivals for governmental power were usually of the same social status group—outsiders striving to become insiders, not social revolutionaries—and perhaps this is why, very unlike the Italian cities, the ruling groups were able to come to terms with their opponents after defeating them. Furthermore, even where they did break in, these opponents, often supported as they were by humbler strata, could not maintain their power for very long, nor were the conflicts anything like as protracted as in Italy. For this reason—but also because they could call in or be forced to receive the authority of the emperor or a prince—they offered neither inducement nor opportunity for the personal 'despotisms' that became the rule in Italy. Their form of government became and was to remain one of wealthy oligarchies punctuated by frequent, widespread, but ephemeral revolts and risings. Whereas the Italian city-states went through an evolving cycle of political forms, the German ones had only brief interludes of unrest. The Italian cities' experiences add something significant and universal to the study of political change, as witness Guicciardini, Machiavelli, and Botero. The German cities do not.

In their basic format the town constitutions differed only in particulars. Here, as elsewhere, the primeval institution was the *Volksammlung*, the general assembly of citizens, to which the *Schöffen* (magistrates) were accountable. Then in the twelfth century this was supplanted, except in emergencies, by a *Stadtrat* (council), presided over by one or many more *Bürgermeisters*, up to as many as twenty-four in some towns. Elsewhere the *Stadtrat* was very large to begin with and threw off an inner council of some half-a-dozen men who acted as a collegiate executive (e.g. Lübeck, and early-fourteenth-century Cologne). For a very long time these councils and magistrates continued to be drawn from very small and interconnected groups of rich merchant families, the so-called *Geschlechter* or 'unclehood'. This was so whether the mode of appointment was by co-optation or some form of election. One reason was the increasingly exclusive qualification for office-holding and another was the fact that few other citizens possessed the leisure to devote their time to arduous and protracted honorary activity, as well as having a necessary experience of negotiation and an understanding of the changing balance of political forces.

Unrest and demonstrations against this patrician rule were frequent and widespread, particularly towards the close of the fourteenth century. An incomplete catalogue alone shows that between 1300 and 1550 no less than 210 risings occurred in 105 towns.[8] Contemporary accounts make it seem as though these insurrections were launched by the craft-guilds to break the merchant's control of their activities. Recent research shows, to the contrary, that the leaders (who used the poor artisan class to further the attacks) were 'an amalgam of various social elements who either were or felt excluded from the top, hereditary management . . . The object of the rebellions was participation, not revolution, the breaking of family mono-polies, not the upsetting of a constitution or the inauguration of a new guild policy'.[9] Not that there was a lack of upward mobility into the old patriciate. On the contrary—this not only occurred but did so conform-ably to Pareto's model of the 'circulation of élites'—it creamed off the top echelon of the upwardly mobile from the craft-guilds and left the gap wider than before.[10] The plain fact is that there was no constitutional process by which the dissatisfied (usually on account of a new tax) could control policy. The taxpayers' only recourse was to riot in order to break into the policy-making circle. And so, even when they did manage to secure the right to elect their 'own' men on to the governing bodies, the persons they chose were not petty tradesmen or artisans but patricians. This is why, after the initial convulsion, the governing bodies returned in quite a short time to being an oligarchy as before.

Towns had to struggle to keep their independence, especially after the Great Interregnum, when central authority wilted and Germany became an anarchy of predators. The towns' great enemies were the local knights, above all the princes on the road to building territorial principalities. In reply, the cities banded themselves into the Rhineland and Swabian Leagues and the like of the fourteenth century. They were ephemeral, with two great exceptions. The Hanse (the confederacy of mostly Baltic merchant towns) lasted well into the sixteenth century, and was militarily strong enough to crush the by-no-means negligible Danish monarchy and secure its shipping the freedom of the Baltic. The Hanse is of major interest to economic historians as one of the dominant mercantile networks of its time, but for the historian of governmental forms it is negligible. Its political institutions were less than rudimentary. It was the loosest of fighting city associations,

---

[8] F. R. H. Du Boulay, *Germany in the Later Middle Ages* (Athlone Press, London, 1985), 146.
[9] Ibid. 146.   [10] S. E. Finer, *Pareto, Sociological Writings* (1966), e.g. 130–8.

much less structured than, say, the Aetolean League,[11] and its membership was continually changing.

Quite different was the fate of the second great exception, namely, the union of three 'forest' communes, shortly joined by a few cities in the district of Lake Lucerne. This was destined to become the Helvetic Confederation or, in everyday terms, 'Switzerland'. Since it was durable—no mean feat for any polity—and since some hail it as the 'first democratic country in Europe', it merits at least a brief notice here even if the principal subject of this chapter is the city republics of Italy.

The three valley communities of Uri, Schwyz, and Unterwalden, with a meagre population of 20,000–30,000 poor free peasantry, were dependencies of either the German king-emperor or the Habsburg-Austrian counts (a matter of dispute between them). They suddenly acquired capital strategic importance around 1220, when the notorious 'Devil's Bridge' was constructed opening up the St Gotthard Pass and so permitting direct passage from the Rhineland via Zurich to Milan and all Italy. The Swiss tradition of a revolt led by William Tell against the tyranny of the Habsburg's local steward was long dismissed as legendary, but now seems to be true, albeit with embellishments. At all events, in 1291 we find the three cantons signing a perpetual mutual-assistance treaty binding them also, inter alia, to arbitration in disputed matters, the prevention of violent crimes, and the substitution of judicial process for blood feud. It still acknowledged its feudal dependency but, caught up in a war for the imperial crown, met an Austrian army of heavily armoured knights at Morgarten (in circumstances remarkably similar to that of the Romans at Lake Trasimeno) and annihilated it in 1314. The 1291 treaty was reaffirmed with the further provision that no canton could unilaterally make peace or alliances with a third party. In 1351 Zurich (population 600) joined the League for domestic reasons. Berne joined in 1353 so as to promote its conquests in its hinterland, and by 1388 the rural areas of Zug and Glarus—hitherto protectorates—were allowed to join as full treaty members. In 1381 Lucerne threw off Habsburg overlordship and in 1386 Duke Leopold of Austria marched to crush it, but the three original cantons rallied to its defence and destroyed his army at Sempach. By the subsequent peace of 1389 the Habsburgs abandoned the entire western Alps and faced a threat to their dominions in the Aargau and Thurgau. Both fell to the now self-confidently aggressive Confederation in 1415.

Still, the political future of this League was not to be established until its grand victories over Charles the Bold of Burgundy at the battles of

---

[11] See p. 373 ff. above.

Morat and Grandison (1476); in 1415 it was contingent. It was highly incongruous: the forest cantons were peasantry, Lucerne was run by a rich oligarchy, Zurich underwent a *popolo* insurrection and fell into the hands of a local 'despot', and Berne was ruled by noblemen. It was also extremely aggressive. The cantons set out to conquer their countryside and then governed it harshly as overlords, in no way conceding citizenship to its inhabitants. Why did it stay together? At times it did slide into civil war and might well have disintegrated. There were few and feeble institutional links. There was no single federal pact, but no fewer than six interlocking treaties. The very notion of commonalty was absent. The cantons had allied together to protect their individuality, not to give it away. There was no provision for a general assembly. In brief, the Confederacy possessed no constitution, no regular representative assembly, no executive organs, no capital, no Chancery, no depository for documents, not even a seal of its own.[12]

At the most, there were pacts laying down a common policy on a limited range of matters, such as maintaining order on the Zurich St Gotthard Road, a common code for troops in the field, the principles by which the common, confederally acquired lands of the Aargau were to be administered; but even so there was no executive authority to enforce these principles. The chief reasons for the enduring units were principally that, unlike the German city leagues, the cantons linked up to form a contiguous territory; they had a common interest in holding the Transalpine routes; and, above all, they relished the sweet smell of continuous military success.

Nobody at that time thought of the Confederation as a state, or of 'Switzerland' as anything other than a geographical expression. It was simply a confederation of *de facto* republics and not sovereign until the Treaty of Westphalia (1648). As for being 'democratic', this was certainly not true of the urban cantons. They were the usual city oligarchies. The population of the subjected countryside were *Untertanen* (subjects) not citizens. But the forest cantons were different. These were direct democracies, where decisions lay in the *Landgemeinde*, the communal assembly. They were led by outstanding families, some of them indeed being noble; but for all that, the citizenry followed them of their own free will. In that sense, it is no way improper to regard them as democracies and hence unique in Europe.

---

[12] Quoted E. Bonjour, H. Offler, and G. R. Potter, *A Short History of Switzerland* (Clarendon Press, Oxford, 1952), 101.

2. *ITALIA INSANGUINATA*

The unity and peace of Italy ended when the Emperor Justinian decided in 535 to reconquer it from the heirs of Theodoric, king of the Ostrogoths, who had held it from the empire and given it wise and just rule. From then on it was a battlefield for waves of different invaders: Byzantines, Lombards, Arabs, Franks, Germans, and Normans who pulverized the country and never succeeded in imposing their rule on any but parts of it at any one time. Its complicated and fluid political geography was somewhat simplified after 1103, when Norman adventurers began to conquer the areas south of Rome, including Sicily. By the century's end they had founded powerful centralized feudal monarchies there. In these areas the towns were given no chance to assert autonomy. The Papal State (in Central Italy) was ruled by the 'Bishop of Rome', the pope, and northwards lay imperial territory, the kingdom of Lombardy. It is this area we are concerned with, for it is here that the towns became the residual legatees of a flickering and ultimately vacuous imperial authority.

In the aftermath of the Carolingian Empire, rival counts, margraves, and the like fought one another and bought support from the towns by granting privileges to their bishops, who obtained the right, *inter alia*, to fortify, to exact market dues and tolls, and, finally, to exemption from the count's jurisdiction. Both Spoleto (a duchy) and Tuscany (a margravate) were ruled by individuals strong enough to keep the cities in their own hands, but by the mid-tenth century the Lombard cities were ruled by bishops. Rule by bishops was congenial to the Emperor Otto I, as we saw.[13] The Ottonian bishop-based control of northern Italy was the first step towards ending the anarchy of the last century. Unfortunately, it was to prove the last. A number of factors now converged to cut away any continuous imperial control over the kingdom of Lombardy and to prevent any alternative central authority from replacing it. To begin with, as these north Italian towns began to flourish and expand greatly with the revival of long-distance trade, their great families coveted the authority the bishops exercised and determined to seize it for themselves. The struggle between the empire and the papacy completely undermined the emperor's control over his bishops and, finally, the imperial regime in Lombardy quite vanished when Frederick Barbarossa conceded autonomy to the cities in the Peace of Constance in 1183. Tuscany was different until shortly before this time, since it had been powerfully ruled by its great Countess Matilda. Only with her death in 1115 did the Tuscan cities begin to assert their independence.

[13] See p. 939 above.

Such is the essential historical background to the rise of the Italian city-republics. It shows that Italy was an even more extreme, perhaps the most extreme case of the disintegration of a polity witnessed in the Middle Ages.[14]

But this is not the only peculiarity of the north and central Italian scene. As will become ever more clear, the political process in these cities (Venice apart) follows a rhythm: magnates or *grandi* never cease contesting the control of the cities with *cives*, *popolo* or *popolani*, even *plebe*. The reason is simply that as the nature of the *grandi* changes, so does that of the *popolo*. Both changed over time. The nature of the Italian 'nobility' defies precise analysis for this very reason. From the beginning there was a noble, feudal, knightly class, but it did not necessarily despise commerce, while for their part the top echelons of the merchant and banker stratum aspired to live like the nobles of ancient family. There occurred something like Pareto's 'circulation of the élites', whereby the top layer of the *popolo* were recruited ceaselessly into the ways and mores of the *magnati*, so that the gap in social status between the *popolo* and the *magnati* never closed.

There is more to this yet. Why does Sidgwick, in his *European Polity*, say that the German cities represented the 'pure' type of city-state, in contrast to the Italian ones?[15] It is because the German city-oligarchies were purely mercantile families, sitting inside their walls and fighting off attacks from the castled knights of the countryside. In Italy, however, from the very beginning such knightly families lived *inside* the city as well as outside. Such families, moreover, tended to be the very ones who pooled their resources and rights *a comune*—in commonalty—to wrest control from the resident bishops. This led the townsmen into a never-to-be solved dilemma. They both needed these knightly families, for they provided the cities' cavalry, and found them intolerable because of their arrogance and violence. So they could never decide definitively whether to leave the nobles outside the city or compel them to come and live inside, under surveillance. If left outside they levied war on the city. If forced to live inside they simultaneously fought one another, and tried to take the government over.

The *magnati* or *grandi* are these noblemen united by intermarriage with the most powerful and wealthy merchant and banking families, and in such intermarriages lies another and perhaps the most significant difference between the Italian scene and other parts of Europe: the importance of *family* and the values this carried with it. Lineage ties, noble affinities, and family rivalries occur everywhere in Europe in these centuries but nowhere

---

[14] See pp. 855 and 953 above. And see further, p. 962 below.
[15] Sidgwick, *Development of the European Polity*, 244–5.

else with the intensity and passion of Italy, just as nowhere else was the attachment to one's native town, to the *patria*, so deeply felt, so committed. To match the latter one would have to go back all the way to the Greek *poleis*.[16] To glimpse the former, and it is a merest glimpse compared with the times we are discussing, one can turn to the familial culture of Sicily and Calabria today, where it still survives, with the notions of *omù*, *omertà*, and the *cosa nostra* and *mafia* networks.[17]

The medieval *casa* was a *parentado*, an extended network of relatives with the same surname descended from a common ancestor. An individual household comprised perhaps four persons, but the *casa* was an *albergo* or *consorteria* of many such. In the late fifteenth century, for example, we find in Genoa the Spinola family of eighty-one households, the Doria with fifty-nine, the Grimaldi with forty-one. In Florence, the Altoviti numbered sixty-six households, the Albizzi sixty-five, the Rucellai sixty, the Strozzi fifty-three.[18] Like the great Chinese clans of the late Ming and the Ch'ing dynasties, they governed themselves under a family statute with their own officials, *parlamenta*, police powers, and private codes. In the towns they lived side by side, erecting those tall stone towers one still sees in Bologna or Florence or San Gimigniano. These towers could be linked by bridges in case of assault, and one can still see the placements from which beams or chains could be thrown across the narrow street to block enemy inroads, especially cavalry, which could make no headway here. On all the members of the family rested the duty of *vendetta*: remorseless, merciless, unforgiving, and perpetual. To have recourse to the courts was regarded as despicable. The feuds were ferocious and, seemingly, never-ending and they kept the cities in turmoil. In *Romeo and Juliet* Shakespeare has given a vivid picture of how quarrels were picked and how large-scale feuding began. We do not have to deny the existence of class-hatred and status-envy in the Italian cities to acknowledge that what animated these and guided (and misguided them, too) were uncompromising ambition and the limitless *libido dominandi* of the great families.

Nineteenth-century historians interpreted these bloody struggles in terms of liberalism, democracy, and nationalism; many twentieth-century historians (e.g. Salvemini) saw them as class struggles. In this way the slogan and passions of the *trecento* and *quattrocento* have passed into the vocabulary of the most sanguinary civil battles of post-1918 Italy, with the major but

---

[16] See p. 330 ff. above.

[17] See, *inter alia*, J. Boissevain, 'Patronage in Sicily', *Man*, ns, 1: 1 (Mar. 1966), 18–33; Roger Vailland's splendid novel, *La Loi: roman* (Gallimard, Paris, 1957; repr. 1963); N. Lewis, *The Honoured Society: The Mafia Conspiracy Observed* (Collins, London, 1964).

[18] P. Burke, *Tradition and Innovation in Renaissance Italy* (Fontana, London, 1974), 297.

significant exception that the political party has taken the place once occupied by the family *consorteria*.[19] British protest movements almost never raise the cry of 'Liberty', or 'the People', 'our Rights': they would be foreign to the point of absurdity. But these words, borrowed from the communal struggles of the Middle Ages, are part of the living vocabulary of the Italian Left. Its campaign songs repeat them continually—*Riscossa*; *Libertà*; *popolo*; *sangue*; (counter-attack, liberty, the People, blood)—the words resound again and again.

The welter of castellanies in the distintegrated Regnum Francorum (950–1050) is, as the previous chapter reported, often regarded as the supreme example of political disintegration in Western Europe. But perhaps conditions in the kingdom of Lombardy between, say, 1000 and 1300 were even more anarchical. The great difference is that here the actors were not individual lords but towns, that is to say, corporate groups of individuals, and this made the anarchy much worse, for once the 'communes' took the place of the local bishop they were launched on a bottomless sea of violence. At one and the same time they were contending with either the emperor or the Papacy, with the nobles of the *contado* (which they aspired to conquer up to the limits of the episcopal diocese), with other cities in the *contado* who allied themselves with their enemies, and with themselves: *consortería* fought against *consortería*, *popolo* against *comune*, *popolo grosso* against *popolo minuto*, in a cycle of struggle, fighting, executions, and exile without end. It is reckoned that by *c*.1200 there were no less than some 200–300 autonomous communes in north and central Italy[20] with their own *consuls* and popular assemblies. The historian Ferrari calculated that in 1190–1250, 1,465 wars took place between rival communes, not counting their wars against very small places.[21] There is no conveniently compact statistic to give a similar impression of the scale and intensity of domestic struggle. Even the brief accounts of Milan and Florence which follow give but the faintest notion. But one can form some glimpse of an idea when one sees the tiny medieval city of San Gimigniano, whose present population of 7,000 is most unlikely ever to have been exceeded, and realizes that the thirteen noble families' enormous towers that are the town's most striking characteristic are all that remain of an original total of seventy-six! Or that the two towers in the centre of Bologna are the last of what were, at one time, 180!

---

[19] And cf. Gramsci's essay on 'The Modern Prince', in *The Modern Prince and Other Writings* (Lawrence & Wishart, London, 1957), where he maintains that the political party replaces the ancient prince, an echo of Machiavelli.

[20] P. Burke, 'City States', in J. A. Hall (ed.), *States in History* (Blackwell, Oxford, 1986).

[21] W. F. Butler, *The Lombard Communes: A History of the Republics of North Italy* (Fisher Unwin, London, 1906), 229.

3. THE CITY-REPUBLIC

As the Italian cities stumbled into a republican polity, they developed similar institutions and underwent similar political transformations at much the same time throughout the north and centre; Venice alone, in many respects, is the exception. The simultaneity and uniformity of the phases of their development is quite remarkable.

In the beginning leading families in the towns form an association, a 'commune', and appoint their officers, called *consuls*, to exercise over the townsfolk the powers they have stripped from the local imperial authority—bishop, margrave, or count as the case may be. This stage is the *Consular Commune, 1083–1183*. A troubled period ensues in which the ruling group splits into rival factions, while the wealthiest strata of the excluded citizens press for a share in the public office. To try to compose the subsequent violence and disorder and perversion of justice, the towns innovate by bringing in an outsider for law and order, the *podestà*. He does not replace the consuls and the Commune and its other institutions but is grafted on to them. The heyday of the *Podestarial Commune* runs from *c.*1220 to 1270, but it does not serve. From the very beginning of this period one town after another witnesses the sudden explosive emergence of a counter-association to the Commune. This is the *popolo*, with its own organization, military force, and magistrates. Everywhere the *popolo* ends up by sharing in the government with the Commune and *podestà* and then by replacing the Commune altogether. As it secures this position, it finds itself facing the kind of challenge from the middle-ranking guilds or even the minor ones (the *popolo minuto*) that it itself, as the *popolo grosso*, mounted against the *grandi* or *magnati*. The middle and last years of the fourteenth century are marked by frequent revolts against its authority. It is able to suppress them, but in the course of the turmoil exacerbated by famine, disease, and above all by the mounting costs and dramatic exigencies of war, most of the cities accept rule by a single individual, a *signore*. A minority continue as republics, but of a decidedly oligarchical kind. The evolved city-republics of the fourteenth century share a number of common characteristics:

1. The fundamental institutions comprised the *podestà* in charge of judicial business (the office survived within the Popular Commune); one or two great legislative councils, and numerous small councils with executive powers. The assembly of all the citizens persisted but was called out only in rare emergency.

2. The members of these councils held office on a very brief tenure, reckoned in months and at the most one year, and were ineligible for re-election until time had elapsed.

3. These councils were responsible for taxation, judicial matters, trade and industry, the subject territories, and the like, and in some cases could even mete out capital punishment.

4. The councils, especially when exercising emergency powers, allowed themselves to be guided by *ad hoc* groups of specialist advisers, and these developed great influence.

5. All the councils—legislative and executive—were appointed by direct or indirect election, or by sortition (casting lots). But the only citizens who could sit in them were those considered eligible after an official 'scrutiny', not dissimilar from the role of the censors in Republican Rome. The proportion of eligibles was very small. Martines calculates that it varied from 2 per cent of the total population in Venice to 12 per cent in Bologna.[22] The full citizen body was also a small fraction of the total population, but larger than the 'eligibles'. In Florence, for instance, it would have been some 4,000 to 5,000 men in the 1330s, which was about 5 per cent of the population.

6. Finally, the population of the subjugated countryside and subject towns were not granted citizenship of the metropolitan city. They were ruled by the *podestàs* it appointed there, though under the terms of the charter or treaty by which the original annexation was negotiated.

4. THE GOVERNMENT OF FLORENCE, *c.*1370

Florence exhibits all the characteristic features of the Italian city-republic, the good and the bad, but to a startling degree. She was one of the larger cities, with a population in excess of 100,000 just before the Black Death; very rich because of her textile industries and far-flung banking operations; the most powerful city in central Italy; a *capoluogo* and conquest centre that was soon to bring all Tuscany under its control. She was, famously, the focus of the most intense and influential cultural activity in the whole of Italy, the home, simultaneously, of its most distinguished and original painters, architects, sculptors, poets and prose writers, political theorists, and historians, so much so that the Tuscan dialect became the standard for the entire peninsula: *lingua Toscana in bocca Romana.* Her political evolution went through every one of the phases outlined above and epitomizes to the point of exaggeration the role of violence, family, and vendetta, the mut-

[22] L. Martines, *Power and Imagination* (Knopf, New York, 1979), 148.

ability of institutions, and the challenge of the mob. She was the very fountainhead of the republican ideology and home of its most eloquent and influential publicists. At the same time her history, if protracted only a few years beyond the period here under discussion, shows the inherent incoherence of the republican institutions unless a political party and/or a notable individual could orchestrate and then 'steer' them. And it shows, too, how if the splendid cultural panoply is thought away, the form (or forms) of government as practised rather than as publicized were singularly defective. The wonder is how the city managed to prosper, for one is bound to suspect, at least, if not to assert positively, that it did so despite and not because of its political institutions. So much was observed by Machiavelli, and a quotation from his *History of Florence* provides the best possible introduction to the 'style' of the Florentine republic. 'In Florence', he says:

at first the nobles were divided against each other, then the people against the nobles, and lastly the people against the populace; and it ofttimes happened that when one of these parties got the upper hand, it split into two. And from these divisions there resulted so many deaths, so many banishments, so many destructions of families, as never befell in any other city of which we have record. Verily, in my opinion, nothing manifests more clearly the power of our city than the result of these divisions, which would have been able to destroy every great and most potent city. Nevertheless ours seemed thereby to grow ever greater; such was the virtue of those citizens, and the power of their genius and disposition to make themselves and their country great, that those who remained free from their evils could exalt her with their virtue more than the malignity of those accidents, which had diminished them, had been able to cast her down.[23]

4.1. *The Early Florentine Republic*

CHRONOLOGY

1053	Matilda of Canossa succeeds to margravate of Tuscany. Florence a village under her rule. Matilda supports papacy against the emperor, thus initiating the Guelf tradition of Florence
1115	Death of Matilda. Control over townsfolk weakened
1138	First attestation of the *Comune*: 12 *consules* (the executive), 100 *buon'omines* (legislature), and a *parliamentum* of all citizens. Control firmly in hands of the *grandi*, mostly noble
1138–1202	Florentine raids into and conquest of the *contado*
1202–10	Introduction and institutionalization of the *podestà*. Foreigner, one-year appointment, Council led by 7 councillors and 7 rectors

---

[23] N. Machiavelli, *The Proemio* to the *Istorie Fiorentine*: 'nobles' is *nobili*, 'people' is *popolo*, and 'populace' is *plebe*.

1216	The townsfolk split into Guelfs (pro-Papacy) and Ghibellines (supporters of Hohenstaufen emperors): the family vendetta arising out of the murder of Buondelmonte taken as the conventional opening date for this development
1218–50	Florence becoming a commercial centre, three new bridges over the Arno. Battles between Guelfs and Ghibellines
1249	Emperor Frederick II sets up Ghibellines; exile of the Guelfs
1250	Guelfs defeat Ghibellines at Figlino. Exile of Ghibellines. PRIMO POPOLO: alongside the *podestà*, and the organs of the commune (above), new institutions, of the *capitano del popolo*, guided by 12 *anziani*, and commanding 20 armed companies of citizens
1260	Ghibelline exiles plus the Sienese crush Florentine Guelfs at Montaperti. Ghibellines in power, suppress the *popolo*.
1266	Papacy defeats Manfred of Hohenstaufen, installs duke of Anjou as Papal Vicar of Florence, definitive triumph of Guelfs. Exile of Ghibellines, who fade out as a political faction. Their properties confiscated and administered by the *Parte Guelfa*
1282	The Sicilian Vespers undermines Charles of Anjou; popular revolt, and the SECONDO POPOLO Government by 6 *priori*. Proscription of Ghibellines. Anti-magnate laws
1293	*The Ordinances of Justice*. Punitive anti-magnate laws: e.g. bonds for good behaviour, extraordinary criminal trial procedure, exclusion from highest office. To implement them, a *gonfaloniere della giustizia*, with large armed force at his command. The triumphant new Guelfs split into the Blacks (anti-Ordinances) and the pro-Ordinances Whites (including Dante Alighieri)
1302	Blacks victorious: 559 death sentences pronounced on Whites, others exiled
1340	Economic crisis following collapse of the Bardi and Peruzzi banks. Civil disorders
1342	The *Signoria* confers dictatorship ('Lordship of the City') on its military commander, Walter of Brienne. Brienne's reign of terror.
1343	Uprising. Brienne driven out, the constitution restored, but with changes in mode of selecting magistrates—not election, but by sortition or lot
1348–9	The Black Death. One-third to one-half of the city's inhabitants die. Population falls to some 50,000

4.2. The Policy Organs

The constitution bore all the marks of its long evolution: it still contained the organs of the original Commune; then of the Podestarial Commune; and of the Popular Commune.

The chief executive body, the *Signoria*, was a college of eight *Priori* (two from each of the *quartiere* into which the city was now divided) *plus* the *gonfaloniere della giustizia*. These men served a two-month term only, and were not immediately re-eligible.[24] They were assisted and advised by two colleges. One comprised the sixteen *gonfalonieri*, each from a *gonfalone*, which was the fourth part of a *quartiere*. These *gonfalonieri* (standard-bearers) marshalled the citizen-militia of their district and served in a domestic role, since the foreign campaigns of the city were now being fought by mercenary companies. The second advisory college was that of the twelve *buon' omini*, the successor to the one-time council of 100 *buon' omini*. The *gonfalonieri*, or the *Sedici* (the Sixteen) as they were called, served for three months, the *buon' omini*, or *Dodici*, served for four.

The *Signoria* and the two colleges (the *Tre Maggiori*) were in charge of a number of executive commissions, staffed by notaries, who were a large and growing profession and indeed formed a veritable town-hall clique. There were, *inter alia*, two commissions for grain supplies, another two in charge of the mercenary armies, another one responsible for the prisons, and quite a number of specialized fiscal offices.

The *Signoria* could initiate legislation on any matter whatsoever. It was responsible for foreign policy and for peace and war, and it saw its proposed laws through the legislative councils. It had the right to intervene and instruct the courts on whether prosecutions should be launched or not. It participated in the selection of most officials. It was often—as is common even with the most supreme executives—caught up in tricky questions of administrative detail. It and its colleges elected the legislative councils.

There were two of these, the *Council of the Commune* and the *Council of the People*; their size varied from one time to another, though not by much; at this time the former numbered 200, the latter 300, and each sat for six-month terms (after 1366, four-month terms). They did not have legislative initiative: their task was to discuss and vote, by two-thirds majority, on the bills presented by the *Signoria*. This body, for its part, frequently received draft bills from interested bodies of citizens in the form of petitions, as well as initiating legislation on its own account.

Justice, security, and order were, startlingly for us, not in the citizen's hands at all, but were dispensed by foreign officials appointed by and responsible to the *Signoria*. They were the familiar *podestà*, the *capitano del popolo*, and a third, the 'Executor of the Ordinances of Justice'.[25] They were also responsible for policing the city and executing its laws, and to these

---

[24] The bar on re-eligibility was called the *divieto*. See p. 969 below.
[25] Those passed (see Chronology) in 1293.

ends were assigned bodies of armed men. They had considerable staffs. The *podestà*'s numbered 100, the *capitano*'s seventy-five.[26]

There were two reasons for the short mandates of the magistrates and councils, and for the elaborate checks and balances in the system (e.g. two legislatures and not one, two advisory colleges to the *Signoria* and not one). One was the intention to prevent any individual or his family or *consorteria* obtaining absolute power. (We may remark, parenthetically, that this veritable passion to prevent such domination was largely responsible for the enormous numbers exiled from the Italian cities.) The other reason was the desire to give every qualified citizen the opportunity to hold a public office, that is, the 'rotation of office'. These two principles are constitutive of 'republicanism' as it was then understood. They reflect the conviction that all citizens are politically equal and that the essence of being a citizen is to be a participant in governing one's community. They are, therefore, identical with the classical world's conceptions of republic and citizenship and raise the question (to be addressed subsequently) as to whether they were a conscious imitation of the past or a re-invention.[27]

Who chose the members of these councils and by what method? Up to 1343 they had been elected, but from then they were chosen by lot.[28] The essential technique was very simple: there was a pouch (*borsa*) for every office, into which were placed the name-tags of the citizens eligible to fill it and then, on the duly calendared day, a name was pulled out, rather like pulling a prize from a lucky-dip. In practice it was very complex. On the one hand, not every citizen was eligible for every post: for instance, the eight priors had in some periods to include two citizens from the major *arti* and three apiece from the middle and minor *arti*; or again, each one of the 'Sixteen' (the *gonfalonieri*) had to come from one of the sixteen city *gonfalone*, so that sixteen pouches were required for this college alone. On the other hand, an individual citizen was simultaneously eligible for many different offices so that his name-tag appeared in dozens of different pouches. So jealous were the Florentines of the sortition that they took the most elaborate precaution to prevent tampering with the pouches. They were kept in a locked chest which was locked in another chest, and kept in Santa Croce. One key was held by that church's Franciscans and the other by the Dominicans of S. Maria Novella at the other end of town, so the chests could be opened only by the two sets of clerics, in the presence of the *podestà* and the *Signoria*.

[26] Brucker, *Florentine Politics*, 62, n. 28.   [27] See below, pp. 979–83.
[28] Some prefer the more technical term 'sortition'.

Schevill, observing that for all the pother the 'same old clique was still on top', wrote the entire exercise off as 'an enormous futility'.[29] In fact it was so hard to tamper with the pouches that from time to time the sortition did throw up unpleasant surprises for the ruling oligarchy of the day. But Schevill had missed the point. The system *was* rigged, but not by the sortition exercise. It was rigged *before* this took place, namely by the pre-selection, the screening of candidates. It was effected by means of a 'scrutiny' (*squittino*) a formal process which normally took place every three years. From preliminary lists of citizens put forward from the guilds, and the *Parte Guelpha*, a city-wide commission compiled a definitive list of eligibles. This commission was made up of the *Signoria* and its two colleges, various *ex officio* groups, and eighty co-opted members. It played the same role as the censors in Republican Rome in that it added certain names and (to a far greater extent) it eliminated others. For there were many conditions to fulfil to be an eligible candidate. A man must be 30 or over and pay taxes; he must not be a bankrupt or a Ghibelline: and for the highest executive posts he must not be a 'magnate' either. In addition, it is clear that the commission exercised a discretion over nominations for the most senior posts, excluding those it thought 'unsuitable'. The effect was to cut down the number of available candidates from the 3,000 or so on the original list to a mere 500 in 1361, or 750 (out of 5,000 names) in 1382. These were the 'active citizens' who alone could hold, in rotation, the approximately 2,500 posts which had to be filled in the course of the year, and included not just the *Signoria* and its colleges and the two legislative councils but the numerous executive commissions that served them. After the revised list was established, a still further paring-down occurred by reason of the *divieto*: that is to say, the time interval that had to elapse before an individual or member of his family might return to an office he had vacated. For instance, a prior had to wait three years before reappointment to that post and a member of his family had to wait one year before appointment. The *divieto* was applied as soon as the name had been drawn from the bag. It made the constitution of a *Signoria* a tediously long-drawn-out process.

Such were the regular organs of government: a number of short-term overlapping councils made up of 500 or 600 lay citizens, with ample powers to check and balance one another.

They worked haltingly even in the quietest of times, but the times were rarely quiet and the Republic was only able to surmount its frequent domestic and foreign crises because it had a set of *ad hoc* extraordinary institutions alongside the regular ones. For one thing, the *Signoria* was in the

[29] F. Schevill, *History of Florence* (F. Ungar, New York; repr. 1976), 209.

habit of forming *ad hoc* advisory bodies drawn from a wide range of interested and knowledgeable citizens—such a body was called a *Pratica*—and by using them the authorities not only made up for their lack of technical knowledge and experience but reached out to their public also. Rarely indeed were important decisions made against the advice of a *Pratica*.[30] Such consultation could take time. Yet the Republic had its own ways to counter tardiness and irresolution, and these were via the *Balía* and the *Parliamentum* (the primeval general assembly). The two often went together: the *Signoria* would convene the *Parliamentum* and ask it to approve the *Balía*. The *Parliamentum* consisted of every citizen aged over 14, not just the 'select men' described above. The *gonfalonieri* marshalled them in their district and marched them into the Piazza della Signoria, where they were called on to declare that two-thirds of the citizenry were present, in order to constitute a legal quorum. From the steps of the Palazzo Vecchio the *Signoria* would then make its proposals. A *Balía* meant simply an extraordinary commission to perform a certain function, such as altering the constitution or conducting some executive task. Sometimes it was given dictatorial powers, as in the case of the *Balía of Eight* set up to conduct the war against the Papacy in 1375. The *Parliamentum* could be and was utilized by demagogues, rather like plebiscites and referenda in contemporary Europe, to go over the heads of the multitudinous councils and appeal to the crowd. (This was how the scoundrelly Walter de Brienne was voted *signore* for life in 1342). It is significant that in the last years of the fourteenth century and the first part of the fifteenth, when the Republic was taking its first unconscious steps towards personal rule, the *Parliamentum* and *Balía* were used more frequently, and to effect dramatic political changes.

Yet one other governmental device helped preserve the Republic: its bureaucracy, which functioned regardless of political convulsions.

4.3. *Administration and Services*

Defence of the cult, a principal obsession in many polities, seems almost irrelevant here in Florence, where it was taken for granted. Florence was a Guelph, that is, pro-papal city *par excellence*, and the defence of the Church was a matter for the pope if for anyone; and in fact the general drift of Florentine policy was to curtail clerical privilege. Opinion in the city ranged from emotionally pietistic religious confraternities, including even flagellants, to the frankly anti-clerical cynicism one finds in, for instance, Bocca-

---

[30] See 76, n. 80, of G. A. Brucker, *Florentine Politics and Society, 1343–1378* (Princeton UP, Princeton, 1962), for an assortment of views on the compelling nature of the advice given.

cio's *Decameron*. Much more obsessive was the Florentine quest for riches and hence for commercial power. It accounts for its close monitoring of the city's economic institutions and the wars to dominate rivals like Siena and, above all, Pisa, which controlled the mouth of the Arno, Florence's artery to the sea. In brief, Florence was a merchant city, run by rich merchants for rich merchants.

A constant characteristic is the public authority's steadily increasing control over its constituent groups. Its struggle with the *Parte Guelfa* is a topic in itself, to be dealt with subsequently, but here one may note straight away the process of integrating the Church and the guilds. By 1382 churchmen could no longer plead benefit of clergy, the Church courts had been squeezed out of prosecutions for usury, the Church had to make regular payments to the fisc, the more powerful religious confraternities had to accept the imposition of commune-appointed captains and their assets were under direct fiscal supervision. As to the guilds, these were a constituent component of the city's government, represented as such in the *Signoria*, for example. Their role in economic policy was immense, since they regulated the production and sale of most commodities. The Commune threw its own authority behind the guild-masters in enforcing their internal discipline, but on the other hand forbade any guild to select its consuls without the *Signoria*'s express consent. Inter-guild disputes involved the *Signoria* and the settlement was enforceable by the Commune's law officers. Towards the lower guilds it presented an even more domineering front. Those guilds were predominantly manufacturers' and small artisans' organizations and they naturally wanted to have prices, wages, and production all fixed, whereas the great merchant guilds wanted free trade and cut-throat competition. The Commune came down heavily on the side of the latter. It expressly forbade combinations of any kind relating to buying and selling of commodities. Only in the last years of the trecento did both merchant guilds and the manufacturing guilds come to agree on the need for protection from foreign competition and not until then did the Commune change its earlier free-trade policy and enact the necessary legislation.

These regulatory activities necessitated more bureaucrats, but a more important cause of increase was the increasing centrality of tax and revenue matters, especially from the last decades of the 1300s, and this in turn was due to something common to every other state in Europe: the vastly increased cost of warfare. The 1362 campaign against Pisa was 'the last major war in which a substantial contingent of Florentine citizens participated in the fighting'.[31] The cost of hiring mercenary companies instead

[31] Brucker, *Florentine Politics*, 188.

became crushing. Between 1343 and 1378 Florence was engaged in four major wars—two with Milan, one with Pisa, and a fourth with the Papacy. Up to 1320 income and expenditure balanced and the public debt stood at about 50,000 florins; in 1404 it stood at 250,000.[32] The consequences were a remarkable set of novel devices to raise cash, and a very sharp increase indeed in the bureaucracy to administer them. The money was raised by direct taxes in the *contado* (taxation without representation, be it noted) and by *gabelles*, sales tax on goods (which hit the poor much more than the rich). Such taxes were not novel and the *catasto* (the direct income tax) was resolutely rejected by *Signoria* after *Signoria* until 1427. But what was novel (outside Italy) was Florence's system of funded loans, and its formation of a 'national' debt. These reached far beyond the capacities and indeed the imagination of the courts of England, France, or Burgundy.

In the early days of the Republic it was common for the rich to make loans to the Commune, and the returns were high,[33] but in the thirteenth century (to use Martines's ironic words), 'credit-minded early merchants, in an astonishing stroke, hit on the idea of the forced loan, which imposed[!] a profit on a select list of lenders'.[34] You had to be very wealthy to be obliged to lend but the interest was good: 10 to 15 per cent. The authorities, credit-minded to a man, regarded repayment as an absolute priority, except in a state of emergency. Not unnaturally, these 'forced loans' were therefore highly popular! From the sacrosanctity of repayment it was no step at all to a funded public debt. The receipts from the indirect taxes went into a central fund which serviced the interest on these forced loans. The Venetians had been the first to do this (as early as 1262), but Florence, as a late developer, did so in 1345 when it created the so-called *Monte*. The 'mount' was central to treasury strategy and as the charges on it became larger and larger, all hope of wiping out the debt disappeared. The treasury therefore sought for additional sources of cash and invented *special* forced loans at still higher rates of interest (*prestazioni*), contracts with pawnbrokers, and so forth. At the same time it exerted greater fiscal pressure on the *contado*. In the 1330s this had contributed only about 10 per cent of the Republic's tax-income. In the 1380s the proportion was 20 per cent. By 1402 it would reach 50 per cent.[35]

---

[32] P. Becker, 'The Florentine Territorial State and Civic Humanism in the Early Renaissance', in N. Rubinstein (ed.), *Florentine Studies* (London, 1968), 122–3.

[33] Martines, *Power and Imagination*, 177.   [34] Ibid.

[35] Becker, 'The Florentine Territorial State', 130–1. Matteo Villani (1338) listed no less than 30 different indirect taxes in his *Chronicles* and even then omitted to mention four others. New levies were invented subsequently. Up to c.1340 the *gabelles* were farmed out to private bidders. From then on the Commune began administering them through its own officials. For a thorough discussion see de la Roncière, 'Indirect Taxes or 'Gabelles' at Florence', in N. Rubinstein (ed.), *Florentine Studies: Anthology* (London, 1968), 140–2.

The result was a huge expansion of public officials in the fiscal services. Between 1343 and 1393 the number of treasury officials quintupled, and additional new fiscal posts were also created which took on new and intrusive duties: regulating the *gabelles*, licensing pawnbrokers, operating a credit bank for the mercenaries. Officers called *regulatores*, originally concerned with *gabelles*, were drawn into assessing rural quotas, making cadastral surveys, and collecting unpaid taxes from the great rural feudatories. Other new posts were created to manage public properties. The *gabelles* became too complex for a single crop of officers, so that specialized posts were created to administer the customs on wine, salt, and various tolls. A corps of 'castle officers' (*officiales castrorum*) administered the financing of the Republic's forts and strong-points.[36]

So Florence—like most other large Italian city-states at this time—created a public bureaucracy on a scale, compared to its population, far larger than in the kingdoms and principalities north of the Alps. And this bureaucracy had a significantly different character. The kingdoms of France and England were still to a considerable extent relying on Church dignitaries to head the very great departments of state and fill many of their senior posts. In contrast, the chancellors of Florence were the illustrious lawyers and rhetoricians. Coluccio Salutati, Leonardo Bruni, and the entire administration were laic to the core. For Florence was the most literate place in Europe, and ran her own communal education system on a wide scale in total independence of the Church. According to Villani (1338), 8,000–10,000 boys and girls (out of a total population of some 100,000) went to elementary schools to learn reading and writing; 1,000–1,200 boys (no girls) went to commercial schools to learn arithmetic and how to use the abacus;[37] and some 550–600 boys went to grammar schools to learn the traditional 'grammar and logic'.

4.4. *The Working Constitution*

In the representative democracies of today, policy direction over time is set by a political party which mobilizes electors behind it and is able to win control of the legislative and executive organs by this process. Where the party programmes are widely divergent, the system will produce major discontinuities as one party succeeds another in power and these can be large enough to disrupt and discredit the system.

---

[36] Becker, 'The Florentine Territorial State', 117–19.

[37] Known from Babylonian times, in universal use in the Middle Ages in Europe and the Middle and Far East, this instrument is not to be despised. It is currently in daily use throughout China where the commonest street-vendor could calculate faster than I could with my electronic calculator.

The Florentine constitution was emphatically not of this kind at all. It presupposed consensus and concord between the numerous governing councils, by reason of their constantly changing personnel, overlapping through time. The possibility that one view would consistently or simultaneously prevail in all of them was quite fortuitous since it depended on the luck of the draw from the electoral pouches (the *borse*). And yet there *was* no consensus. On the contrary, there was angry contestation between the old patrician families and the *nouveaux riches* (the *gente nuova*), the grandees (or magnates), and the craftsmen and petty shopkeepers, the partisans of one leading family (the patrician Albizzi) and the other (the parvenu Ricci and later the Medici). From around 1360 these social antagonisms began to acquire an ideological and political dimension and from around 1370 they became polarized almost to the point of civil war. Underlying the forms the struggles took and the swaying fortunes of the antagonists, there runs one basic theme: it is the endeavour to make a system presupposing consensus respond to the *libido dominandi* of one part of the *de facto* dissensus.

Let us start with the proponents. In Florence, one of them is highly exceptional. As in all other city-republics and certainly through Florence's entire history, the struggle revolves around rival family-led *consorterie*. These are often called 'parties', but we shall call them factions or blocs, for reasons soon to be apparent. Brucker has described them admirably. They were not formal organizations and they did not advance clearly defined policies. They were, he says,

'loosely-knit amorphous associations whose members were united by a variety of ties for a variety of purposes. Their personnel was constantly changing . . . Of the two parties [*sic*] the oligarchic group headed by the Albizzi had more stability . . . its leaders included men from the city's most illustrious houses . . . The opposing clique, formed around the Ricci, was more heterogeneous. It was less a coalition of family blocs than an association of individuals, who for diverse reasons opposed the personnel and the policies of the oligarchic faction. Many of its adherents came from the ranks of the gente nuova . . . It certainly contained patrician leaders but these represented small family blocs that feared the concentrated power of the great clans in the Albizzi party . . .[38]

But where Florence was unusual—to say the least—was that besides *consorterie* of this type and common to all Italian city-politics, she harboured an organization not dissimilar to a modern political party (it speedily became the politically organized vanguard of the Albizzi faction) and this was the *Parte Guelfa*. Between 1260 and the extinction of the Hohenstaufen (Ghibelline) dynasty in 1266, a so-called *Parte Guelfa* (first attested in 1267) succeeded

---

[38] Brucker, *Florentine Politics*, 202.

to the Ghibellines' expropriated properties, and was accorded a special political status and access to the organs of government. Now, a century later, Florence was a wholly Guelph city. Its constitutive myth was 'Guelph-ism', compounded of a consistent history, ever since the days of the Countess Matilda, of fighting against the empire and a devotion to the interests of the Holy See. With no tangible Ghibelline opposition in existence the *Parte* nowadays survived and indeed flourished as an organ of Guelph triumphalism. Its prestige was enormous simply because all Florentines shared in the vague ideology of anti-Ghibellinism although nobody was a Ghibelline any more.

Since it emerged at the time when the city contained a host of semi-autonomous associations such as guilds and religious fraternities, so, like them, the *Parte* possessed a highly autonomous status. It was regulated by its statute, and one clause in this declared that 'the Party, the People and the Commune shall be [*sic*]³⁹ one and the same'. Each new group of its captains was enjoined, when they were appointed for their two-month stint, to call on the *Signoria* and two colleges (the *Tre Maggiore*) and admonish them to do their duty, offering to lend them its authority to this end. The statute decreed also that the authorities must not act against the interests of the party but should, indeed, actively advance them. And it vested in the party the vital privilege of conferring Guelph status, vital because this status was a prerequisite of holding public office.

The *Parte* was organized in every respect like a miniature Commune. It too had its *Tre Maggiore*, where four (later six, then eight, then nine) captains, serving two-monthly terms, mimicked the *Signoria*. It had its own legislative council. As in the Commune, the personnel of these ruling bodies was drawn from the membership after a preliminary 'scrutiny'. That member-ship must have been extensive, since we know that in 1364 the *Parte* nominated 17,000 men for public office, somewhat more than half of the entire citizen body. The 'scrutiny' was administered by the captains, the two colleges, and persons nominated by both, so that in practice the captains nominated their successors, and part of the story that follows turns pre-cisely on the fact that the captains could commit the membership and not the other way round. The *Parte* was the official custodian of Guelph ideology. Not surprisingly its leaders tended to be much more fervent and extreme than other political leaders. All those were nominally Guelph, but the party leaders were the *Arciguelfi*, the arch-Guelphs. And for decades no Florentine was ever opposed to the *Parte* and conversely all were for the *Parte*, because it was, as the statute declared it ought to be, congruent with

---

³⁹ Could also be translated as 'ought to be'.

the outlook of the public authorities: *unus et idem*—one and the same. Its petitions (i.e. draft bills) were therefore sure to be well received by its many partisans in the *Signoria* and the legislative councils.

In the 1360s the Albizzi and Ricci factions found themselves on opposite sides in a series of matters affecting Church and Commune. The Albizzi opposed, the Ricci supported measures abolishing benefit of clergy and limiting Church courts. A similar gulf opened up over the city's foreign policy. The Albizzi—which by and large was the oligarchic bloc—took a complacent view of the papal efforts to control parts of the papal States adjoining Tuscany, notably Perugia and especially Bologna, and looked enthusiastically on being part of a great papal coalition of the traditional Guelf allies. The Ricci faction, representing the *gente nuova*, were pragmatic 'little Florentines': their horizon was confined to the defence of the Commune's independence and they opposed squandering its wealth for the aggrandizement of the Papacy.

As the struggle between the two blocs grew more polarized and embittered, it also became apparent that neither side could count on securing a decisive victory. For as we have said, the Commune's institutions were geared to *randomizing* bias, not to mobilizing it. It was the *Parte Guelfa* that hit on a way to do the latter. As the emblematic organization *par excellence* of traditional Guelfism, it was more shocked even than the Albizzi coalition by the 'popular' bloc's coolness towards the interests of the Holy See. Furthermore, its captains interlocked with the arch-Guelph families in the Albizzi-oligarchic coalition. The *Parte* leadership now threw its entire organizational strength behind the Albizzi faction, which reciprocated.

The point the *Parte Guelfa* suddenly grasped was that, although it was impossible to manipulate in any permanent way the names that popped *out* of the electoral *borse*, it was certainly possible to manipulate the names that went *into* them! The key to winning a permanent majority was to use the scrutiny to screen out all potential opponents, that is, to strike down their nominations. Now it was the *Parte* which possessed the legal privilege of determining Guelph status, and no non-Guelph could hold public office, so the *Parte* decided to revive the obsolescent anti-Ghibelline laws. Its first shot, in 1358, was to intimidate the *Tre Maggiore* into passing a statute under which anybody suspected of being a Ghibelline could be secretly denounced to the authorities, the only proof required being the testimony of six witnesses vouched for by the Guelph captains. The next year they dispensed with legal procedures altogether. On the vote of any four Guelph captains, any citizen could be warned (*ammonito*) that if he allowed his nomination to go forward he was liable to prosecution as a Ghibelline. Even more, the *Parte* was still so prestigious and influential that it got its right to warn written into legislation along with the provision that any citizen voicing opposition to the anti-Ghibelline laws automatically forfeited his rights to hold office.

The following years were ones of the *Parte*'s struggle to use its new powers and give itself legal immunity against its victims' efforts to counter them. The popular party's more effective retort was a mirror-image of the *Parte*'s. *Magnates* might hold no public offices except one-fifth of the places in the council of the Commune. So the popular faction revived the old magnate laws: any citizen who claimed maltreatment at the hands of another could denounce him to the *Tre Maggiore* plus representatives of the guilds, who, by a two-thirds majority could *designate* him as a magnate and so eliminate him from office!

The struggle waged by these alternative modes of manipulating candidacies reached a climax in 1378. The Commune had done something that challenged the very essence of Florentine Guelphism: it actually declared war on the Holy See! The pope's operations against Bologna and Milan had aroused the deep anxiety of the popular bloc, but the discovery of an alleged papal plot to stage an uprising aroused the entire population. The *Parte*, assisted by the religious confraternities and the oligarchic faction, inveighed against this irreligious war, preached pacifism, and organized maudlin peace marches (in a manner uncomfortably reminiscent of similar movements in twentieth-century Western Europe). It launched a barrage of 'warnings' on an unprecedented scale; every week seven or eight citizens of all walks of life were 'warned'. Then the *Parte* turned from mere candidates for office to those already serving, even 'warning' one of the eight-men War Commission. It went on to organize identically worded secret denunciations, along with lists of witnesses, which poured in—on one occasion, 100 within a week—to the *gonfaloniere della giustizia*. For every citizen 'warned', perhaps ten went in terror of being 'warned'. The citizenry was for a time, cowed with fear.

One day in 1378 the *Parte* forced through two 'warnings', which, however, were in direct contravention of the laws. It so happened that the *gonfaloniere della giustizia* of the day was (despite all the *Parte*'s efforts to disqualify him) the populist oligarch Salvestro dei Medici. Here was a direct confrontation between *Parte* captains and Communal *Signoria*. Although both drew back, not so the common people. An enraged mob, led on by the furrier's guild, burst into the streets and systematically went from one *quartiere* to another burning or tearing down the palaces of all the leading oligarchs. The *Signoria*, after quickly suppressing the riot, called a *Parliamentum* and got it to establish a temporary *Balía*, which strengthened the old anti-magnate laws and promptly designated all the leaders of the *Parte Guelfa* as magnates (hence ineligibles). Having thus eliminated its opponents, it rewarded its own supporters: it allowed citizens who had been classed as Ghibellines to appeal their designation to the *Signoria* and likewise all those who had been 'warned' as far back as 1357. Thus the popular faction triumphed over oligarchs and *Parte* alike.

The riot of 1378 was followed by another, the so-called revolt of the *ciompi* (the unorganized and poverty-stricken workers, mostly of the textile guilds). Concessions were made to them, only to be ended by a counter-revolution in 1382. But one measure of capital importance endured: the one forbidding the *Parte Guelfa* to make use of the 'warning'; and from this time on the *Parte Guelfa* sank to be little more than a social club.

The year 1382 marks a new period in the constitutional practice of the Commune, for it solved the problem of how to mobilize bias in a structure designed to randomize it and so secure stable and enduring majorities for the policies of a reigning faction. It did this by a combination of old and new contrivances. One of these, of increasing importance as the fifteenth century wore on, was the transfer of executive powers from the *Signoria* and its colleges to specially appointed commissions such as had been fore-shadowed indeed in the *Otto* (the Eight) which had conducted the war against the pope. For instance, a commission of the *Otto di Guardia* was responsible for internal security, the *Dieci di Balìa* for the conduct of war. And the practice of convening informal groups of specialist advisers, the *Pratiche*, became the rule, not the exception.

But the three most characteristic modes of securing a stable and perma-nent paramountcy in the short-lived, overlapping, and counter-checking councils of the Commune were all utilized together in 1387, repeated in 1393, and thereafter became common practice. The first was to break a deadlock by summoning a *Parliamentum* in the Piazza and getting it (by a variety of methods, not excluding intimidation by troops of armed men) to appoint a *Balìa* to take the action deemed necessary. The second was to induce it to permit an entirely new scrutiny—the old *borse* being destroyed—and seeing to it that only known supporters of the ruling group were included. The third was to tackle the nominations at the other end, when they emerged from the electoral pouches. To this end special little pouches—*borselline*—were introduced, containing particularly favoured names, and a proportion of the high offices, for example, two of the eight priors, was reserved to these alone.

The family that came to the leadership after 1382 was that of Maso degli Albizzi—an oligarch but in no way a fanatic. On the contrary, he was pragmatic and serious. He created a *consorteria* with other similar-minded pragmatic oligarchs. As usual they formed the core of all extensive coali-tions. This guaranteed itself the majority needed to steer the commune by the methods described. Under Maso degli Albizzi and his chosen successors (Gino Capponi and Nicolò da Uzzano), power moved away from the councils to private meetings. The republic was moving to the *signoria velata* which the Medici would perfect after 1434. The constitution was suborned, but in return it was enjoying stable and consistent policies under competent leadership for the first time.

4.5. *An Appraisal*

Since the Republic of Florence passed through the same developments as all the other northern and central Italian cities (Venice excepted) and ended up with very similar institutions, what is said hereafter about its originality or otherwise applies, *mutatis mutandis*, to these others as well. All conform to the basic characteristic of the republics of antiquity, be they Greek or Roman. Like the Greek city republics, their twin passions are *autonomia* and *eleutheria*—independence and freedom. 'Freedom' comprises a batch of characteristics. It includes citizenship, meaning the right and duty to participate in the government and administration of the city; the rotation of office among the said citizens; the grading of citizen rights and obligations according to established criteria; and the plural executive, bound by laws, as opposed to one-man rule which, even if it too is initially law-bound, is feared lest it subvert those laws and become an Aristotelian *tyranny*.

What is surprising is how closely the institutions of the Florentine Republic seem to parallel those of Athens in some respects, and Rome in many more. One is bound to wonder whether they were not conscious copies of the classical originals. There are good reasons, which appeal to me, to think they were not.

First, consider the striking parallels with Rome. Like the Roman Republic, the Florentine constitution is an unplanned sequence of newer institutions and practices piled on the old which, however, are left in being. Both are collegiate forms of government and the populations of both share a passionate antagonism to one-man rule, anathematized by the Romans as a *rex*, by the Florentines as a *tiranno*, a tyrant. In both cases, the executive is subject to multiplex power: of the tribunes in Rome and of the two legislative councils in Florence, as well as the independent status of its *podestà* and judges. Even more startling is the duplex form of the two constitutions—that they embrace, simultaneously, two equal-and-opposite sets of institutions: the tribunate and the *concilium plebis* in Rome, the *capitano del popolo* and the *consiglio del popolo* in Florence. Even the *raison d'être* of this dyarchy is the same—to defend the *plebs* or *popolo* against the exclusiveness of the patricians/nobles.

Again, the sociological and political dynamics are similar in the two republics. Both Florence and Rome were oligarchic and the modalities of achieving this outcome are functionally equivalent: the censors in Rome, the 'scrutiny' in Florence. In both, political activity is initiated and moulded by great families and the factions they form. And both develop a form of proto-parties.

But besides Roman institutions and practices, Florence—along with most other Communes—also possessed others that look like Greek ones. The most obvious is sortition: this Athenian practice was institutionalized in Florence in 1343. Allied to it is the rotation of offices, by way of very short tenures, much shorter than Roman ones which usually ran for one year. The two-monthly term of the *priori* of the *Signoria* in Florence is not unlike the monthly presidencies—the *prytany*—in Athens. Again, the Florentine *Parliamentum* of the citizens and its relationship to the *Signoria* and the two colleges parallels the Athenian *ekklesia* and its relationship to the *boulé*.

But these parallels should not carry us away into believing that the Florentine Republic was even nearly the same as the classical republics, let alone a conscious copy of them. In the first place, Florence and the other Italian republics possessed institutions that were unknown to antiquity and which give them a very different character. The *podestà* is a uniquely medieval Italian innovation. New also are the overlapping tenures between the *Signoria*, its colleges, and the legislative councils; equally the mode of determining the franchise, which in Florence is bound up with membership of a guild, but in Athens and other Greek cities by possession of a land-holding (*kleros*), while in Rome it is by wealth alone. Yet none of these alone or separately distinguish the Florentine and other Italian republics from the classical models in any but a marginal way. What does do so is the absence of any paid professional bureaucracy in the republics of antiquity—their reliance on unpaid, amateur, brief-tenured, everyday citizens for administration—whereas in Italy, more so than anywhere else throughout Europe, the city-states employ paid, long-tenured professionals to carry out an increasingly complex set of regulatory and extractive activities. Athens and the Roman Republic rely through and through on the ministrations of unpaid, part-time citizens, but Florence and the other Italian city-polities are layered into a class of unpaid, part-time policy-makers and the permanent professionals who carry the policies out. Here they foreshadow the future in Europe, and for that reason have been referred to as 'modern'. Perhaps that is an exaggeration, but this feature differentiates them from their classical precursors and makes them another species.

In the second place, even when Florence does possess an institution that closely resembles one in the classical republics, examination usually shows that it did not operate in the same way or with the same results. Take collegiality, for instance. The Roman consuls could veto one another, the tribune could veto the consuls, each praetor could veto his colleagues, and each tribune could veto him. But the Florentine *priors* and *gonfaloniere* who constituted the *Signoria* were housed in the *Palazzo Vecchio*, where they lived communally and acted as a single collective executive. Likewise with the 'dyarchy' in Rome. The tribunate and its associated organs was a genuine counter-institution which was not only capable of countermanding the magistrates but did so. Indeed, as we saw, the constitution of the Roman Republic left the *locus* of final decision undecided. Not so in Florence, where the conjoint action of the *Signoria* and the two legislative councils, or alternatively of the *Signoria* and the *Parliamentum* was final and paramount. Here the Florentine constitution resembles Athens, not Rome.

The *consorterie* in Florence, led as they were by great families supported by their dependants, bear a resemblance to the family alliances in Rome backed up by their *clientela*. This resemblance deepens as the Roman *populares* and *optimates* are paralleled by the Florentine 'oligarchic' and 'popular' factions we have described. But the *Parte Guelfa* was quite different from any Roman party. It was structured with a formal constitution, it had captains, a ward organization, and its own internal constitutional procedures. Also, unlike the Roman parties, it had a political ideology and programme. It resembles, indeed, the highly personalized but nevertheless ideological and structured parties found in some early- and mid-nineteenth-century Latin American Republics: the Federalist Party of Rosas, in Argentina, springs to mind.

Furthermore, time and circumstances would provide sufficient explanation for the emergence of typical institutions, without any recourse to conscious imitations of antiquity. Self-consciousness of being differently governed from the generality of places in monarchical Europe does not seem to have surfaced until Brunetto Latini and Ptolemy of Lucca in the thirteenth century.[40] A *societas*, even a sworn *societas* (*coniuratio*), was not exceptional but very common in the Middle Ages,[41] so that if such a body assumed the local overlord's rights and duties—as it did—the result could be none other than a group of equals exercising those rights through its own officers. Such an evolution adequately accounts for the plenary assembly of the *societas* as its sovereign body and the magistrates as the executive, even if they chose to call these *consules*. The term is antiquarian,

[40] N. Rubinstein, 'Marsilius of Padua and Italian Political Thought of his Time', in J. R. Hale, J. Highfield, and B. Smalley (eds.), *Europe in the Late Middle Ages* (Faber & Faber, London, 1965), 50–4; J. H. Mundy, *Europe in the High Middle Ages*, 1150–1309 (Longman, London, 1973), 424, 442–50.

[41] Cf. S. Reynolds, *Kingdoms and Communities in Western Europe, 900–1300* (Clarendon Press, Oxford, 1985), 172, 175.

certainly, and implies an acquaintance with Rome; but, to judge by Arnold of Brescia's 'renovation' of the Commune of Rome (1143), it was Imperial Rome and not the Republic—and in a very garbled form at that.[42] We are better informed about the rise of the *popolo* than about the earliest days of the Communes, and the additional detail makes it seem even more likely that the *popolo* and its 'counter-institutions' (the *capitano*, etc.) were a response to time and circumstances, not a conscious renewal of plebs versus patricians. The *popolo*, originally a secret society of *popolani*, that is, of those who were not magnates, was only one among many burgeoning groupings. Furthermore, its institutions were quickly brought into conformity with those of the Commune, so that to take Florence as the example, the *capitano*, along with the *podestà*, was subordinate to the *Signoria*—he had no power of *intercessio* like the Roman tribune.

There is a further reason for scepticism over the Florentine or other republics' constitutions being conscious revivals of the classical republics, and it turns on how much was known about these at that time. Here there is a sharp distinction between the knowledge of classical Greece and that of Rome. The three features of the Florentine constitution that might be thought to have derived from Athens and not Rome are the *Parliamentum* (cf. the *Ecclesia*), the short-term rotation of offices, and sortition. Now the only knowledge of Athens that the early Middle Ages could have had was in scattered references in Latin literature. They had no Greek sources until Aristotle's *Ethics* was rendered into Latin *c.*1240 and the *Politics c.*1255. Then and only then is it that this latter work begins to be widely cited, as in Aquinas, Ptolemy of Lucca, and Brunetto Latini; but even these works contain no sustained description of any individual Greek city-state. Yet the *Parliamentum* is coeval with the very emergence of the Communes a century *before* the translations. So too is the practice of rotating offices for very short terms. Sortition, admittedly, was introduced later (1343) than the translations; but Aristotle's *Politics* tends to mention it only parenthetically, never in detail. Thus sortition may just possibly (though I think it most unlikely) be an imitation of Athens; but the town assembly and the rapid rotation of office must be ruled out.

The case stands somewhat differently with the Roman Republic. Latin was the language of the *literati*, and a number of sources for the history of the Republic were available. And certainly in the thirteenth century Ptolemy of Lucca discusses Republican Rome, while early chroniclers and Villani (*c.*1330) traced the city's origins back to the city of Rome. But Villani, who

---

[42] R. L. Benson, 'Political *Renovatio*: Two Models from Roman Antiquity', in R. L. Benson and G. Constable (eds.), *Renaissance and Renewal in the Twelfth Century* (Clarendon Press, Oxford, 1977), 339–86.

claimed that its early government was founded on the Roman model, takes the latter as being a council of 100 senators and two consuls. This hardly betrays a knowledge of the Roman Republic, where the senator held a life appointment and the Senate itself was a permanency. Certainly the Florentines, and the Italians generally, used terms like consuls and plebs (*plebe*), but this need be no more than antiquarianism. It seems unlikely that the founding fathers of the Florentine Commune or popular Commune had enough detailed knowledge of the Roman Republic to make copies of its institutions. Alternatively, if that is what they did do, the copies bear little relation to their originals.

4.5.1. THE POLITICAL PROCESS

Athens and the heyday of Republican Rome were models of the viability of a republic compared with Florence. Its laws and institutions were chopped and changed with dizzying rapidity. Its internal revolutions were frequent. Its great families and their allies and dependants hunted and harried and persecuted one another without cease. Violence and riot were commonplace.

Unlike Athens, Florence was never a democracy, but it was not so narrow an oligarchy as scholars like Schevill or Brucker, for instance, so strongly believe. After the Black Death (1349), the population was only some 50,000. The citizen body was 3,000, a mere 6 per cent of the total. But it was some 12 per cent of the total *male* population, and about double that—say 25 per cent—of the male population aged over 14. (In the UK the electorate of 1900 formed some 22 per cent of the total population.) It is true that not many more than 750 of Florence's 3,000-odd citizens, at the best, were eligible for public office;[43] but in the pre–1900 UK the cumulative effect of the property qualification and the non-payment of MPs disqualified a far greater proportion of the electorate from standing for, let alone sitting in Parliament and attaining ministerial office. In terms of the fourteenth century, the Florentine franchise and access to office was beyond any comparison whatsoever with the still semi-feudal monarchies and principalities of Europe. Nor should our stress on the leadership of the great families and the hegemony of the rich mislead us into supposing that they alone held public office. On the contrary. The 'Minor Arts' tended to be better represented than the grandee families, and it was precisely the fact that they had to sit alongside and confer with and possibly submit to being voted down by butchers, armourers, and small shopkeepers that enraged the oligarchy.

[43] Brucker, *Florentine Politics*, 133–4.

The constitution was not so much unworkable as unwieldy. It compares unfavourably with the Athenian and the Roman polities at their best. In Florence the magistracies were too brief, too overlapping, and too diffused (via collegiality) to operate smoothly except in the most placid times when nothing was required but day-to-day administration, and such times were very rare. The Republic was always under threat from its magnates on the one hand and its hungry, disenfranchised masses on the other. It was usually threatened from outside as well: first by the exiled noblemen, then by exiled Guelph or Ghibelline parties, later by the Free Companies of mercenary troops. It was threatened by imperial irruptions then by papal ones, and was continually at war with its neighbours. At all times, too, its government had to have regard to economic conditions: to its world markets when threatened by papal interdict, to its banking houses caught by defaulting debtors as in the case of the Bardi and Peruzzi débâcle of 1340, to frequent famines and, in the mid-fourteenth century, to plague.

The constitution was strong in its 'lateral' dimension—the political equality of its citizenry—but weak in the vertical, the hierarchical one. This is true both of its administrative as well as its political style. As to the former, the striking feature of the administrative system—if that is what we must call it—was the lack of centralized control. It appears as a congeries of devices, each dealing with separate aspects of society inside the city limits. Defence, diplomacy, food supply, and justice had to be provided, but within a context in which nothing was more feared than the dominance of a single family.

Politically speaking, it did not focus leadership. In default the lead was taken by knots of powerful families but, given the culture of *casa nostra* and *vendetta*, these were always at violent odds, so that governance was always partisan and provisional. The Republic did not attain stability until it became more oligarchical and under manipulation of the 'godfather' figures, like Maso degli Albizzi and those who succeeded him after 1382. Cosimo de Medici, who succeeded them in the opposed, popular interest, was a surer, more self-effacing, and much more sophisticated 'godfather' of the same political style. He and his successors Piero and Lorenzo perfected the articulation of the city-wide faction of supporters and sympathizers which is the hallmark of the post-1382 era, as well as the careful redefinition and manipulation of the 'scrutiny', the sortitions, and the use of the extraordinary devices of *Parliamentum*, *Balía*, and *Pratiche*. It needed men of this stripe to make the disparate parts of the governmental structure work together harmoniously and speedily, and for all Machiavelli's denunciation of the 'veiled *Signoria*' (*la Signoria velata*) and his eloquent republicanism, I find it difficult not to believe that the Republic was never so well governed as under the Medici up to the death of Lorenzo. This is a paradox—that the Republic was best governed when it was ceasing to be Republican—but the paradox is explained by the faults of the original constitution which were such that the only way to cure them was to circumvent them; just as the original faults of the Roman Republican constitution were cured only by the convention of tacitly according supremacy to the (nominally advisory) Senate. The paradox might be expressed by what Giovanni Guarini said in 1599 of the Roman Principate, but here substituting Florence for his Rome. 'Roma non fu mai tanto libera quanto allora ch'era men' libera' ('Never was Rome more free than when she had lost her liberty').[44]

5. VENICE: *LA SERENISSIMA*

Unlike stormy, volatile Florence, Venice came to be called *La Serenissima*. Even the vain Florentines came finally to marvel at its success and sought its secret. When the other Italian city-republics were almost all extinguished and the kingdoms of Western Europe were on the high-road, it was Venice and not Florence that became emblematic of republicanism. For in addition to having an ancient and stable form of government, Venice was no mere city-state. The largest city in north Italy, she was an imperial republic, with a landward as well as seaward empire, immensely rich and powerful. Though her landward expansion was checked in 1509, she continued to guard the eastern Mediterranean against the mighty and aggressive Ottoman Empire. Not till the end of the eighteenth century did her power fall away, and only in 1797 did she succumb to an invader. By that year she had successfully preserved her independence for over 1,300 years and the identical constitution for the last 500.

5.1. *A Chronology*

The other republics ran a course from communal and oligarchic government to a *Signoria*. Venice did just the opposite. She progressed in an unbroken line from one-man government to oligarchy. And stayed there for half-a-millennium.

Every datum of geography and history conspired to make her development different from the others. Her site, to begin with, was a cluster of low-lying sand-spits in a shallow lagoon, so difficult of access that the city was never conquered. Originally a haven of fisher-folk, then of merchant adventurers, it lay on the rim of Italy on which it turned its back, looking neither

---

[44] Quoted in H. Baron, *The Crisis of the Italian Renaissance* (Princeton UP, Princeton, 1966), 71.

north to the emperors nor south to the Holy See, but rather eastwards and seawards to the Levant. It was part of the Byzantine Empire and its first *dux* (or doge) was almost certainly a Byzantine official or at least was accredited as such, although (and this is significant) the later chroniclers of Venice claimed the city was independent from her very origins. She parted company with Byzantium bit by bit after the ninth century, but was at all times autonomous, at the very least. None the less, as part of the Byzantine space (and not that of the Western 'Empire'), Venice never experienced feudalism, nor the dominion of either an imperial bishop or duke. So she did not experience, either, that collision between the old feudal warrior families and the wealthy merchant class that animated the early politics of the other cities. On the contrary, the patriciate of Venice were the merchant-adventurers and the merchant-adventurers were its patriciate. For a long time long-distance trade, not manufacture, was the source of the city's wealth; so that the artisanate—the *popolo minuto*—was weaker than in cities like Florence and Milan. Nor did the merchant-aristocracy have to court the artisanate for support against a territorial nobility. Family vendettas there were, but they remained as such; they were not expanded into a class or status faction as in Florence nor divided into Guelphs and Ghibellines. In brief, the social, religious, and political struggles that convulsed the other republics simply passed Venice by.

The origins of the city are obscure. It was populated by successive waves of refugees, who scattered themselves among the outer islands. Each island settlement elected its tribune. There were twelve such. Modern research suggest that the first doge-*dux* was an outcome of the Iconoclastic policy of Byzantium in 726, which drove many of that empire's Italian possessions to revolt. Venice was one, and its people thereupon chose their own local commander, a man called Orgo from Eraclea. They called him *dux*—in Venetian *doge*. The chroniclers' account tells it another way: that the twelve tribunes of the islands decided jointly to establish a single leader.

The insurrection against Byzantium was short-lived, and the community continued as a Byzantine possession. In 810 Charlemagne sent his son King Pepin of Italy to capture the islands. He failed, but the islanders, meanwhile, had learned a lesson. Their outlying islands—like today's Lido, Chioggia, and so on—were vulnerable to attack, as well as jealous of one another; whereas the sandbanks around the Rialto—what is in fact today's Venice—were almost impossible to approach without intimate knowledge of shoal and channel; and, uninhabited as they were, could provide the site for a politically neutral capital. So the site was ditched, drained, endyked, and finally built up, and the capital moved there. With this the constitutional history proper of Venice begins. It falls into four stages.

Its original form could hardly be more crude. The general assembly or *Arengo* elected a doge for life, with two tribunes to counsel and assist him. He had absolute executive power, subject to the *Arengo*'s approval of his major decisions. Enjoying quasi-regal authority, doges sought to perpetuate their authority by associating their sons or other relatives with them as co-doges. Doganal dynasties arose in this way only to fall 'by popular riot'. Between 804 and 1032 no less than six doges were driven out or assassinated. The ambitious family policy of a renowned line of doges—the Orseoli—raised justifiable suspicions that it was aiming at a hereditary monarchy. It was terminated in insurrection and exile. Laws were passed ostracizing the family and a new doge, Flabiniaco, was elected. Flabiniaco took the first of many successive steps to bridle the doganal power.

5.1.1. THE FLABINIACO CONSTITUTION, 1032

The new doge summoned an *Arengo* and, denouncing the history of the doges over the last three centuries, got this *Arengo* to abolish co-regency and succession in the same family. In addition to two counsellors to assist the doge, the latter was instructed, in matters of the gravest importance and urgency, to invite the more prominent citizens to his council. In this we have the origins of the Doganal ('Lesser') Council, and of the *Pregadi*—the 'bidden'—later to be the Senate. The choice of the doge was still by nomination and acclamation in the *Arengo*.

The year 1000 had seen the first 'marriage of the sea' by the doge. It symbolized Venice's mastery of the Adriatic. Buoyed by trade with the eastern Mediterranean, the city began to be populous, rich, and powerful, as she acquired trading counters in Constantinople. The First Crusade (1095) gave this trade a violent acceleration. By now, though, relationships with Constantinople were turning sour, while the revived Western Empire under Frederick Barbarossa posed a threat on the mainland. When the Lombard League was founded in 1167 Venice joined it and benefited from its victory over the emperor. But in 1171, as a consequence of a trade dispute in Constantinople, Venice learned that the Byzantine emperor had arrested all her merchants and confiscated their property. Riding a wave of popular indignation the Doge Michiel set sail with a splendid fleet. Alas for him! The wretched man returned in utter disaster and, to make matters even worse, his disembarked sailors spread the plague to the city. The frenzied populace rioted and Doge Michiel was cut down. This was the first time for any doge to meet a violent death in 200 years. The Venetian citizenry stood back to reflect. They realized that the 'safeguards' had proved useless: the two counsellors had been ignored, the *Pregadi* had not been summoned, and now the population was so large, the *Arengo* was no more than a vast licensed mob.

5.1.2. THE CONSTITUTION OF 1172

The consequential reforms strike the note that was henceforth to go on resounding through all Venice's subsequent constitutional development: to *narrow* the popular base and to *expand* the ruling apex. The *Arengo* lost its direct power to elect the doge and was allowed only to select an electoral college of eleven members instead. Later (1177) this electoral college lost even that power and simply elected four men who in their turn elected the electoral college, this time of forty members. The *Arengo* retained only the right to acclaim a duly nominated doge and to approve peace or war. For all other matters a very restricted body of 480 councillors was established. The first time round, the 480 was made up of eighty persons nominated in each of the six *sestieri* by two citizens elected there for that purpose. Thereafter, though, the outgoing council (which was renewed annually) itself appointed the electors in the *sestieri* who duly proceeded to nominate the new councillors. In practice, of course, they simply perpetuated the old. This was the *Consiglio Maggiore*, the Great Council. In addition the doge, at the apex, was now surrounded by six counsellors who were to attend him always. The doge and this 'lesser' council together formed the *Signoria*, the government as such, which presided over every subsidiary council and acted as the supreme executive.

It was with these institutions that Venice embarked on the great military drives that founded her overseas empire and established her as the most populous and wealthy of all Italy's city-states. In 1177 she played host to the reconciliation between Barbarossa and the Papacy and seized the occasion to proclaim that she was a sovereign independent entity subject to God alone. And in 1204, to her great infamy, she diverted the Fourth Crusade to the siege of Constantinople and, when that noble city fell, claimed and got from the penniless Crusaders a 'quarter and a half of a quarter' of the fallen empire's territories. The flag of St Mark now waved over cities and trading stations from Dalmatia and Corfu, through the Greek islands and the promontories of the Morea, as far as Crete.

The expansion of her population, the rapid increase in her trading activities, and the enormous accretion of wealth which multiplied the numbers of rich, sophisticated, and active citizens complicated the affairs of state and necessitated multiplex administrative tasks. The acquisition of empire generated a new cycle of wars: repressing the city's rebellious Greek subjects and sparring with her Genoese competitors in the Levant. The Constitution of 1172 was altered piecemeal to accommodate to the new conditions. The Great Council was too large, unskilled, and uninformed to act as a governing body, especially in judicial, financial, and currency matters. It is in 1179 that we have the first mention of 'the Forty', elected as a commission of the Great Council to deal with these matters from among those who had served as doges' counsellors, judges, and communal advocates. Although their mandate was for only one year, they were immediately re-eligible. Their chief business was judicial, as the Court of Appeal. (Later they became a judicial bench exclusively.) The Forty elected its own presidency, the Three *capi* (heads), and these three joined the doge and his six counsellors to form a *Signoria* of Ten. This *Signoria* presided over the sessions of the Forty.

Another body, of sixty men, was instituted in 1229 as the *Pregadi* or *Senate*. It was responsible for commerce and navigation and hence had an interest in foreign affairs, so that it also came to instruct ambassadors and review their missions. But its chief task came to be preparing the legislation that would be considered by the Great Council.

Thus the citizen-base of the Republic was being made more capable of legislating, judging, and supervising legislation. This in itself did not weaken the authority of a doge because, as head of the *Signoria* (and a life-tenure, unlike the ephemeral tenures of his colleagues), he presided over all councils throughout the governmental system. But the merchant citizen-nobility had taken fright at the way the aged Doge Dandolo had personally captained and led in battle the fleet that took Constantinople (1204). They feared such a combination of military and civil power. Of old it had been the custom that an incoming doge should swear a sort of coronation oath. So far these had been couched broadly, but the *promissione* which Doge Tiepolo was obliged to sign in 1229 was, by contrast, highly specific. He promised to renounce all claim on public revenue except his salary; to contribute to all public loans; to respect state secrets; and, more important than all these, never to communicate with a foreign power nor open correspondence from one, except with permission and in the presence of his counsellors. From this time on the *promissioni* became more and more restrictive until in the end the doge was to be reduced to little more than a figurehead. Furthermore, the Doge Tiepolo himself put teeth into the *promissioni* by instituting a board of five *correctors* to draft each new *promissione*, and a trio of *inquisitors* to examine the late doge's record and make appropriate recommendations to the Board of Correctors.

5.1.3. THE COMPLETION OF THE CONSTITUTION

In 1297 a revolutionary change was made to the constitution and proved definitive. It drew a line between the narrow stratum entitled to sit in the Great Council and the rest of the population. Effectively only those already sitting there, or who had sat there during the last four years, plus their descendants, were entitled to membership in future. There were to be no more elections to the Great Council. A member sat for life, and his male descendants also. A specially designated committee was, temporarily, permitted to add some additional names. To these, but subsequently, candidacies for membership would be decided only by a consultation of pedigrees followed by a vote. After the great popular defence of the city against the blockading Genoese in its most critical hours in 1380, when at the last moment the enemy were defeated *ante portas* never to rise again, thirty citizens who had distinguished themselves in the defence were admitted *ex gratia*. But save for this and a few other later exceptions the Great Council was closed—*serrata*—to all but the category mentioned, later to be inscribed family by family in the *Libro d'Oro*, the Golden Book, which attested aristocratic lineage. Henceforth—somewhat as in the Roman Republic—whoever—and only those—who sat in the Great Council were *nobilis*, and conversely a 'noble' was anybody entitled to sit in that Council.

The reasons for closing the Great Council are obscure. It had the effect of making the ancient *Arengo* completely redundant, and a few years later this body was extinguished; but it does not follow that this was the motive for the *serrata*. It might have been an aristocratic desire to keep undesirables and *nouveaux riches* out, but it did not in fact make the Great Council smaller; on the contrary, it doubled its size. Conversely, it may have been intended to bring in worthy men of good lineage where the co-optative process of the Great Council had hitherto excluded them, in which case it did not go very far, and prevented any further ascents into the governing class.

The constitutional effect was prodigious. We shall explore it in another place, but for the moment it is enough to say that it decisively shifted the point of balance in the government. With its size doubled to some 1,100–1,200 participants, the Great Council was far too large to govern. It remained the sovereign body but at the cost of shifting upwards to the *Quarantia* (the Forty) and the Senate the details of drafting bills and controlling administrative processes. And, as more and more *ex officio* members joined the Senate, so this came to be the pivotal organ in the state. But even the Senate itself was much too large for emergency action and the *Signoria* was too little trusted. In 1310 an aristocratic conspiracy was launched against the Republic. It was crushed with little difficulty but its ringleader and some of his followers remained at large in the vicinity of the city, conspiring against it. To deal with this danger, an emergency Council of Ten was set up for a few months only, but it quickly became a permanency. Elected annually by the Senate, the Ten became the Republic's

Central Intelligence Agency and Committee of Public Safety rolled into one. With the coming of the Ten the basic institutions of the Republic—those that were to rule Venice till 1797—were all in place.

5.2. *Venice, c.1420*

The city proper was large even after the Black Death had wiped out at least half of its population, but it was also the centre of a sea and land empire. The *Mar* was the string of islands and coastal bases stretching from Corfu to Crete and Cyprus. The *Terra Ferma*, mostly acquired between 1405 and 1427, was the Veneto which contained such towns as Padua, Verona, Brescia, and Bergamo. The city's population stood at some 100,000; the 'empire's' at another million-and-a-half. (England, in 1400, had a population of some 2.5 million.)

'Some 3,000 merchant ships carry out our trade', said the dying Doge Mocenigo in 1423, 'and they are protected by 43 major warships and 300 smaller ones, manned by a total of 19,000 seamen.'[45] But not only was Venice an international power, it was far wealthier than most of the others. The annual receipts of the city, *c.*1423, were 750,000–800,000 ducats;[46] but France (admittedly, in the throes of the Hundred Years War) could muster only 1,000,000, and England only a little more than Venice. But this is to speak only of the city of Venice. If we add in the revenues from the *Terra Ferma* (464,000 ducats) and the *Mar* (376,000 ducats), Venice's total is 1,615,000 ducats, *perhaps the largest state revenue in Europe*. Furthermore, the total population of Venice and the empire was, at 1.5 millions, only one-tenth of that of France, yet its income was 50 per cent higher![47]

The heights of Venetian society were occupied by twenty to thirty great Houses, prominent for centuries in prestige, political power, and wealth, and, next to them, another 100 families ranked as noble because they were entitled to sit in the Great Council. Altogether there were some 1,200 adult males in this noble group. This was not (or rather, not yet) an idle *rentier* class. To the contrary. The normal pattern would be for the nobleman to take to trade and the sea until rich enough in his middle age to enter on full-time legal and political activities for the Republic. For not only was this class alone entitled to fill all the government councils, judgeships, magistracies, top naval commands, and diplomatic missions, as well as the highest administrative posts of the polity; it was *compelled* to.

---

[45] Quoted in E. R. Chamberlin, *The World of the Italian Renaissance* (Book Club Associates, London, 1982), 120. [46] 1 ducat = 3.55 gm. pure gold, so at 1987 prices this is approx. $36,523,221. [47] Braudel, *Civilisation and Capitalism*, 118–23.

Not all these nobles were rich, any more than all non-nobles were poor. We have precise figures for 1379 giving the assessments of the worth of personal property, and these show that there were 117 persons valued at 10,000–15,000 ducats, of whom ninety-one were nobles and twenty-six commoners. If one takes the entire band of those worth more than 300 ducats, it numbers 2,128 persons—one-eighth of all households—and of these 1,211 were noble but as many as 917 were commoners.[48]

These non-noble rich were to be found among the next-lower class or rank of *cittadine*, divided into the *originarii* and the immigrants, the former having the higher status. Together these accounted for perhaps another 2,000 or 3,000 adults. The *originarii* supplied the Doganal Chancery, the notaries, and the superior administrative posts. Some engaged in international trade where they enjoyed the same rights as nobles, or managed industries such as, for instance, the glass manufacture on Burano. Immigrant citizens were those who had managed, often by marriage, to acquire residence and had held it for twenty-five years. (After the first ten years they could acquire a 'half-citizenship', which gave them the rights to trade *inside* the city.)

Below these two élite groups, which numbered perhaps 5 per cent of the total city population, there came the skilled workers (forming some two-thirds of the labour force), organized in their *arti*. The remainder, about one-quarter of the total population, were the free, that is, unregulated workers and their families.[49]

The most arresting, attractive, and significant feature of this society was its civic sense. It was far from lacking the predictable friction between the arrogance of young nobles and the resentment of the commoners, between rival families and the like. But as a whole the Venetian combined a tenacious patriotism with a deep respect for the law, and together these generated a sense of state and civic dedication, a gravity and realism in public affairs that existed nowhere else in Italy. The reasons for this will be canvassed at a later point. Here it suffices to say that Venice never suffered from the upheavals, civil wars, exile and expropriation of opponents, and mutations of the constitution that prevailed everywhere else. The closing of the Grand Council provoked no uprising. The two conspiracies against the constitution—the Querini-Tiepolo plot of 1310 and that of Doge Marin Falier in 1355—were affairs of desperate handfuls of men, out of tune with general sentiment and lacking any popular sympathy. The swift apprehension, trial, and execution of the doge-conspirator was, on the contrary, greeted with

[48] F. Lane, *Venice: A Maritime Republic* (Johns Hopkins UP, Baltimore, 1973), 151.
[49] Braudel, *Civilisation and Capitalism*, 133–5.

universal pride. The Venetians' sense of solidarity under the laws resembles the Romans when the Republic was at its best, in the days of Hannibal. No Venetian of any significance came from exile to bear arms against his native city, and in Venice as in Rome it was deemed only right and proper that no leader or politician should, even in the darkest hour, ever 'despair of the Republic'.

5.3. *The Structure of Government*

All the usual characteristics of the republic (understood in its classical and its medieval sense) are found in Venice. Those characteristics have been listed above and there is no need to repeat them here. The idiosyncracy of Venice was to make its citizenship, or rather its full or active citizenship, a hereditary class or, indeed, caste. In numbers or as a proportion of the total population, there was not a lot in it. Florence had had some 3,000 full citizens out of a pre-Black Death population of some 100,000, while Venice had some 1,200–1,500 noblemen out of a population of 100,000, representing some 5 or 6 per cent of the eligible male inhabitants (assuming these to form about a quarter of the total). Apart from that, Venice was everything a republic was expected to be: independent (*autonomia*) and ruled by collegiate bodies that checked and balanced each other, and through which the full citizens rotated in brief tenures.[50]

The details of the Venetian constitution are enormously complex, so that it is as well to begin with a few general observations. Venice was run— organized and administered, that is—by a cabinet of twenty-six persons, the *Collegio*, headed by the doge. The *Collegio* was in the last resort accountable to the Great Council of some 1,500 persons, which comprised the entire citizen body; but between *Collegio* and Great Council lay two elected bodies. These were the Council of Ten and the Senate (about 260 persons), and these now discharged most of the original functions of the Great Council. The interrelationship of these bodies is often represented as a pyramid (see Fig. 3.7.1).

But in another sense it is better represented as a set of concentric circles (see Fig. 3.7.2), because this underlines the important, indeed fundamental fact that the senators are elected by and *from* the great councillors, and that the members of the *Collegio* are elected by and *from* senators and/or great councillors, nearly always the former.

It is helpful, in grasping the practice of the system, to bear in mind six general features, some similar to other Italian city-republics, others diver-

---

[50] See pp. 968–9 above.

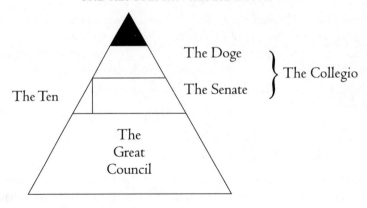

FIG. 3.7.1 *Venetian government ('pyramid' model)*

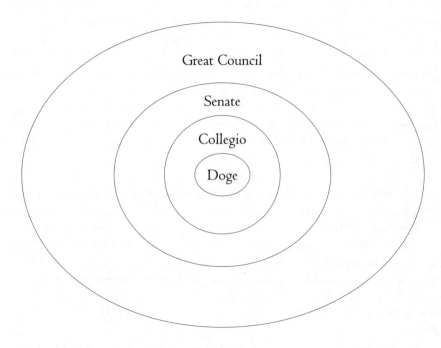

FIG. 3.7.2 *Venetian government ('circles' model)*

ging very significantly. One of the latter is that, unlike what we have learned about Florence, all posts and offices in Venice were filled by deliberate and highly calculated *election*, not randomly distributed by lot. The exception, of course, is the Great Council which is not elected or selected in any way, but consists of citizens sitting there hereditarily, by right. This suggests the second feature, again quite different from Florentine practice, that in Venice any and every full citizen has as valid and equal a right to be proposed for election as any other. There is no 'scrutiny' here by which a commission weeds out 'undesirables'. It will be remembered how Florentine politics revolved around the efforts of some groups to become eligible for office and magistracies and the efforts of others to keep them out. But in Venice, once its Great Council had been simultaneously enlarged and closed, no such contests took place. All great councillors were, like the Spartans, *homoii*, a band of privileged equals. This is the most important of all the reasons for the famous stability of the Venetian political system. This was further enhanced by a third feature, one which Venice shared with the other republics: the short mandates of most offices. They were never longer than one year and often ran for only four- or six-monthly terms, without immediate re-eligibility. This made more posts available and hence made the competition that much less fierce (though it was fierce enough, as will be seen).

But there were other features apart from the constitutional arrangements that promoted stability in Venice as against the turmoil of Florence. One is the relative unimportance of industry in Venice, whereas Florence was a great cloth-producer and was thus subject both to the internal pressures of the guilds and the fluctuations of prices on the European markets. Perhaps much more important is Venice's geographical security. Florence, as we have already observed, was exposed to predators on all sides. Venice, on the other hand, was all but impregnable among the shifting sandbanks of the lagoon. Indeed only once did the city stand in real fear of invasion and that was in 1380–1, when the Genoese fleet defeated the Venetians at Pola and Chioggia and installed a naval blockade. The way the Venetians turned the tables and in turn blockaded Doria's fleet in its channel until a relieving Venetian fleet arrived from the Levant is one of the great epic feats of the Republic. It was a blow, too, from which Genoa never recovered, giving Venice the mastery of the Levantine trade.[51]

Like all the other city-republics, the governmental structure consisted of a large number of councils so interlocked as to check and balance one another. But in its *Collegio* Venice had a supreme organ for co-ordinating and steering them. Thus the *Collegio* could initiate legislation and decrees but could not enact them, while the Senate could enact them it but had no powers of initiative. The Council of Ten could not act without the doge and his Inner Council. The doge could not act without his Inner Council, but for some purposes the latter could act in default of the doge. What kept

---

[51] This is well described in J. J. Norwich, *A History of Venice* (Penguin, Harmondsworth, 1983), 243–56.

these various components of the governmental structure together was the central role of the doge and his Council, which sat *ex officio* in every council of the Republic, and the structure and the role of the *Collegio*. The latter was in a sense representative of the most vital organs in the system, for it included the three heads (*capi*) of the Forty and counsellors (*savii*) elected by *and from* the Senate, as well as the doge and his Council (collectively known as the *Signoria*). It was therefore fully in touch with all these organs. It acted, therefore, as a pre-deliberative body, deciding what matters should go forward and to whom: to the Senate or—if it were a matter of speed, secrecy, and urgency—to the Ten. And the Senate's own composition could not fail to add to the stability of the entire system, for two reasons. In the first place, though elected by the Great Council, its members were immediately re-eligible and in the event tended to be re-elected, so that its composition remained much the same over time. Secondly, holders of all important posts and magistracies were *ex officio* senators, so that this body was informed by the best practical advice available in the city. Among these *ex officio* members were the Forty (the judicial bench) *in toto*.

Finally, the system successfully combined the principle of checks and balances with that of emergency action. The former spelt delays and debates where, so often, immediate action was urgent. In Florence they dealt with this extra-constitutionally.[52] They would call an assembly, set up a *Balía*, and entrust it with emergency powers. But in Venice they institutionalized secret, rapid executive action in the Council of Ten and it was for the *Collegio*, seized with the Republic's business, to decide whether to move it in the Senate or to hand it over to the Ten.

With these general features in mind, we can turn to the individual components of the governmental system, and first of all the Great Council.

The Great Council consisted of the males who had sat in that body during the four years preceding the *serrata* (1297) or could prove that a paternal ancestor had once sat, and who subsequently received a positive vote from a body to whom their candidatures stood referred. (This was the Republic's judicial body, the Forty.) Others were indeed added, but in very small numbers and on exceptional occasions. Overwhelmingly it was a hereditary body. Immediately after the *serrata* it numbered 1,100 members but its size steadily increased until in the seventeenth and eighteenth centuries it amounted to some 2,300 members.

For a time the Great Council coexisted with the *Arengo*, the general body of the citizens, in respect of which 'citizens' were defined by some quite different and less restrictive formulae. But the enlargement of the Great

---

[52] Not *unconstitutionally*, but outside the normal rules.

Council overshadowed the *Arengo* and, after losing one residual power after another, it formally expired in 1423.

In practice, the Council's great size made it unwieldy and over time it divested itself of most of its legislative authority to other bodies, notably to the Senate. Juridically, this was because it elected the Senate which was, technically, one of its sub-commissions. In fact the Great Council always retained the right of final decision on any proposal brought directly to it by certain high magistrates: the doganal councillors, the 'Three Heads' of the Forty, the *avogados* (state prosecutors). Thus, all these were legally entitled to raise matters.

These were powers of last resort, however. The principal power retained and exercised in full by the Great Council was not direct legislation at all but *appointment*. It elected the vast majority of the magistracies and other officers of authority, from the doge downward. The Council was endlessly engaged in cycles of elections.

In the normal way it met every Sunday. The agenda would have been published and circulated, and the doors of the Ducal Palace closed behind the members, of whom 600 constituted a quorum. There was no special order of seating, except for the places reserved for the magistracy. This disposed itself on either side of the doge, who presided (as he did all governmental councils).

The most important of all the elections was, obviously, that of the doge; but being a life appointment this was fairly infrequent. By contrast, the other elections were annual, with the result that there were rarely less than nine elections to be resolved at most weekly sessions of the Council.

The Venetian attitude to appointment was quite different from that of Florence: it was a deliberate and purposive activity to choose the best man, *not* a random allocation. The procedure, therefore, was designed to ensure that the election was as free as possible from any human distortion or pressure. Elaborate precautions were laid down to prevent bribery and corruption of electors, even to the extent of suppressing favourable publicity, let alone electoral campaigns. But the Venetians were wise enough to see that no election could be more 'free' than the process for nominating the candidates, and the greatest part of their effort was thus devoted to ensuring that everybody had a fair chance of at least being nominated. This is why their electoral procedure strikes us at first as being slightly insane.

The procedure for the actual election is quite straightforward. What seems so grotesque is the nomination process—until the procedure is seen for what it actually was: a device to prevent the conspiratorial reduction of choices open to the electors.

The most striking, because to our minds the most seemingly absurd, is the mode of electing the doge. This had been taken away from the *Arengo* and put in the hands of the Great Council who appointed eleven electors to choose the doge. Later these eleven (somehow) reduced themselves to four who then (somehow) expanded themselves to forty (later, forty-one) who proceeded to the actual election. The secret lies in the successive 'reductions' and 'expansions'. If the original eleven had elected the four who then elected the forty-one, this need not have stopped a determined clique and might, indeed, have made its task very easy. If it had six of the initial eleven, it could have had all four of the 'four' and hence all forty-one of the 'forty-one'! But this was precluded by the fact that these processes of 'reduction' and 'expansion' were ones of *sortition*, as well as election. Furthermore, the more protracted the number of stages of sortition and election, the less, *pro tanto*, the chances of an organized clique. In its completed form, in 1268, the procedure went like this. First, the Great Council was purged of all members under the age of 30. For every member remaining a little ball (originally wax, then a hollow ball of gold) was made ready, into thirty of which a parchment tag inscribed *Lector* was inserted. A boy, picked up at random off the streets, handed out these little balls to the councillors. The thirty who drew *Lector* remained; the others all left. Once again a ballot was prepared for each one of the thirty, of which only nine contained the word *Lector*. Once again these ballots were randomly distributed, so only nine remained, the others going away. But now the nine had to expand themselves to forty! They did this by successive nomination, retaining only those who received at least seven votes out of the possible total of nine. Then the forty went through the balloting process again till only twelve were left—and so forth. The full process went on and on like this:

From the Great Council	by lot	30
From the 30	by lot	9
From the 9	by election	40
From the 40	by lot	12
From the 12	by election	25
From the 25	by lot	9
From the 9	by election	45
From the 45	by lot	11
From the 11	by election	41

The forty-one proceeded by election to nominate the doge for approval by the assembly, which by the fifteenth century was purely formal.

When the Great Council elected to lesser posts, the same mixture of sortition-cum-election was applied to the nominations but in a much-modified framework. In the first place, the Great Council came increasingly to believe that there ought to be at least two candidates for any post, and in the end, by 1482, it was normal to have four, for example, when it came to electing senators from the body of the Great Council. Basically this was accomplished by establishing four nomination committees or, in Italian, *mani* (literally 'hands'). So there were three stages: the setting up of the 'Hands', nominations by the Hands, and the election of one of the candidates by the Great Council.

The first stage—establishing a Hand (usually of nine men)—was very complicated and ritualistic. First, certain ineligibilities were declared: for no Hand could contain more than one member of an individual family or household, and no two Hands might contain members of the same individual family either.

Thereupon the constitution of the Hands began. At the front of the Great *Sala del Maggiore Consiglio*, as we know it to this day in the Ducal Palace, three urns were positioned in a row. One and then another bench of councillors was called on by lot to proceed to the left- or right-hand urns. Each was filled with 800 silver and thirty gold balls. Each councillor in turn thrust his hand into the urn and withdrew a ball. If a silver one, he returned to his seat. If the ball was gold, he proceeded to the central urn. This contained only twenty-four silver and thirty-six gold balls. If he drew a silver he returned to his seat but if it was a gold one, lo! he was a member of the Hand and was immediately whisked away to a secluded chamber so that no councillors could influence him.

In this way four Hands were selected and the second, the *nomination* stage, began. Now, in the general way nine posts were up for election in every weekly session of the Great Council, some very important, some petty. Once again we have urns filled with little balls but this time each ball contained a number and that number corresponded to one or other of the nine posts. Each member of the Hand, in order of seniority, plucked out a ball, and by virtue of the number it contained became the nominator (*lezionario*) for the corresponding post. He was free to name a relative, or even himself, but one interesting qualification should be noted, for it is identical to a provision in more or less contemporary China under the Sung, when nominations were made there for posts in the Imperial Civil Service. From 1305 the Venetian nominator was deemed legally in bond for any and every tortious act committed against the state by his candidate, if the latter were appointed.

When the nominator pronounced the name, it was voted on by his eight fellow members and in order to stand had to receive six votes. If it did not, he would have to try with other names until an acceptable candidate was found. Then the secretary noted this name and earmarked it for its particular post. Then the nomination passed to the next councillor until, in the end, nine candidates for the nine posts were all registered.

While this was happening the other Hands (as we have said, by this time, four was the usual number) were doing exactly the same; so that at the end of the exercise there were four nominations for each of the nine posts that were to be filled.

All was now ready for the Council to go forward and elect. It sometimes happened that all four Hands had nominated the same candidate, in which case he was declared elected *de facto*. The exception was where the Council was left with only one candidate because, for some reason or another, his competitors were ineligible; in that case he could only be declared elected if at least two of the Hands had put his name forward. But the most likely event was a list of four candidates per post. Starting with the first post to be filled, urns were carried around the benches in the Great Hall, and the councillors dropped their choice inside in such a way that the secrecy of their ballot was inviolate. The ballots were then counted. To be elected required a 51 per cent majority at least. If this was not reached on the first ballot, the candidate with the least votes was eliminated and another ballot was held until finally the post was filled. The Council then proceeded with the next vacant post, and so on until at the end of the day all nine had been filled up. When we recall that posts were held for only one year or a lesser term, it becomes quite obvious why the main part of the Council's time was taken up with a never-ending cycle of elections.

In the course of time it became usual for some nominations to be received from outside the Great Council's own nominating committees, from 'on high', as the phrase went. These were for offices of greater than usual importance and the nominations would usually come from the Senate, but sometimes from a more specialized body, such as the *Signoria*. Such nominations were not received with resentment, as one might expect, but—to the contrary—with exceptional respect and consequently usually carried the day. By *c*.1500 the oligarchical consequences had become obvious and both the *Signoria* and the Senate agreed to renounce their privilege. But although this checked the oligarchical trend, it led to a rash of corrupt pressures in the Great Council, despite all the elaborate safeguards we have been describing. The times were very bad, because of the wars of the League of Cambrai (1508–10), and the Republic was desperately short of cash. Appeals were made for loans and gifts to the treasury. In itself this was nothing new, but now ambitious nobles began to announce their contributions just before the vote came up, though this did not always guarantee

election! Subsequent laws to prevent the influence of money proved ineffectual. All the same, it would be quite wrong to conclude that money had
now proved decisive. In this tight-knit society, where success or failure in a
position of authority was open to every nobleman's scrutiny and appraisal,
public service counted very heavily. The fact was that long-established
wealth, established public reputation, and certain great Houses often coincided, and these were what dominated the election of the highest posts in
the Republic. But, by the same token, it narrowed the circle of those with
great political authority and concentrated it in fewer hands and in smaller
bodies than the Great Council: in the Senate, but more than that in the
Collegio and the Council of Ten. But this by no means signified the role of
unqualified incompetents such as occurred in the West European monarchies. Just the reverse: the Republic was in capable hands and (as will be
noted later) did well for all its population, not just a favoured few.

The Senate was also known as the *Pregadi*—the 'invited' or 'the bidden
ones'—an echo of the earlier, shadowy group of advisors whom a doge was
supposed to call upon. The Senate's role changed after the enlargement of
the Great Council in 1297. As, by reason of its increased size, the latter lost
its deliberative role, so this was assumed by the Senate, whose current pre-
deliberative role was itself taken over by the *Collegio*. In short, the *serrata* led
to an upward shift in the previous distribution of responsibilities, with the
Senate playing the pivotal role.

By the early fifteenth century it numbered some 260 members and was to
rise, subsequently, to 300. But more than half of these were senators *ex officio*.
The core of the Senate consisted of the 120 elected members and these, in
turn, fell into two groups. The core group, of sixty, were elected in the
Great Council: from 1343 there had to be two candidates (nominated, as
described above, by two *mani*) and the elections, at the rate of six per
session, were completed in ten sessions starting in August. Unlike most
offices in the Republic, outgoing senators were eligible for immediate re-
election and in the event they were re-elected time after time. Over and
above this, the sixty outgoing electors themselves elected sixty *additional*
senators whose elections, however, had to be confirmed by the Great
Council. This group of senators was called the *Zonta* or 'Addition'.

The mere fact that the senate was a very permanent body and only one-
tenth of the size of the Great Council helps to explain its relative importance; but this was greatly accentuated by the incorporation of first one then
another group of important *ex officio* members. The doge and his six
councillors were naturally members, since they presided, but over time
others came to be added: the Forty (i.e. the Criminal Bench), the Council
of Ten, the six *savii grandi* (and later, in 1434 and 1442, the *savii* of the *Mar* and

the *savii* of the *Terra Ferma*), and all manner of superintending officials. The officers for tax-collection, fiscal investigation, audit, and control were among the first, followed (1312) by numerous less important officials such as superintendents of public works or state concessions. These *ex officio* senators multiplied through the fifteenth century.[53] A very important group of *ex officio* members was that of the three *avogadori del comune*. These were the state procurators, charged with ensuring the legality of its actions (as well as acting as state prosecutors), and they were therefore entitled to suspend bills in any councils if they breached legality.

It was for the Senate and not the Great Council to make some of the most important elections. Among these were the three boards of *savii* (described below), a high proportion of the ambassadors, and the commissioners of dependencies like Zante, Cephalonia, and Corfu. But its indirect role in filling offices was more important than the preceding for, as we have seen, it acquired the right to present its own official candidates to the Great Council for many offices and these stood a high chance of success. This is a good place to mention the Senate's procedure for election which was not necessarily the same as the Great Council's, because apart from nominating by the *mani* (as already described), in respect of the most important posts the Senate used a different procedure—the so-called 'ticket' (*polizza*). Here each senator wrote the name and particulars of his candidate on a card or *polizza*, signed it, and placed it in the urn. Election proceeded as in any multiple contest: ballotting went on, by eliminating the least favoured candidate at each round, until one candidate had secured 51 per cent of the votes.

The Senate's main function in the governmental system was, however, debate and legislation. By 1285 all the most secret and serious matters were discussed there and—it must be stressed—its sessions were always held in conditions of strict secrecy. At first, instructing ambassadors and handling international disputes were deputed to it. Then (in the fourteenth and fifteenth centuries) most other matters of international import; but from the fifteenth century onwards it became omnicompetent and by 1600 has been described as 'the delegate-general of the Great Council'. By then the Senate had acquired final plenipotentiary authority in making treaties, paying the *condottieri*, and arming the fleets; also, of taking decisions in currency matters, public health and hygiene, and Church–state relations. As time went on it established numerous administrative boards and commissions, until the entire administration apparatus of the Republic was directed and controlled by it.[54] And one can easily see why: not only was it the

---

[53] Cf. G. Maranini, *La costituzione di Venezia*, 2 vols. (La nuove Italia, Venice, 1927–31), ii. 153–9 for a list. [54] Ibid. 217.

elected élite of the Great Council, but it contained *ex officio* every officer of note in the Republic, so that its collective experience was complete—indeed, absolute. But this great reservoir of technical knowledge and talent had to be channelled before it could affect public policy, and this is why its procedure is of no mean importance. And here the utmost significance attaches to the role of the *Collegio*. Every deliberative body requires some organ to set its agenda, order its debates, and bring them to a conclusion: the Cabinet and the speaker in the British House of Commons, the speaker in the US House of Representatives, the *bureau* in European parliaments. This function was performed in Venice by the *Collegio*.

The Senate was convened by the *Collegio* and had to meet regularly on certain days of the week according to the season. Extraordinary meetings could be called at the command of numerous magistracies which had been granted this right, too. In the usual way, however, the Senate met twice or three times every week. There was no fixed order of seating apart from the magistrates benches. The *Collegio* chaired the debates. In these the senator had to mount the podium. He had complete freedom of expression short of sedition or illegality, but there were strict rules to ensure temperate language and no slander or demagoguery. The sessions, as we remarked before, were secret, and severe penalties attended any senator who divulged its proceedings.

The only commoners who attended were the Senate's twenty-four secretaries. Before the discussion began, the attendance was checked for all interested individuals, and these were thereupon excluded from the sitting. This exercise was directed with particular care against the Roman Curia. A similar exclusion was applied to all those who had benefited, or were likely to do so, from the hands of a foreign power.

Debate was regulated by the *Collegio*, whose place in the wider system is to be described next. What has to be said in this context is that the *Collegio* was the meeting-point of the holders of all the top political and administrative posts in the government who were also, however, *ex officio* senators. Therefore, it was *not* a separate body inserting or superposing itself on the Senate but an organic outgrowth of this body, rather like the way a British cabinet is part and parcel of the Houses of Parliament. As we saw,[55] the *Collegio* included the three boards of *savii* who controlled the administration, and it was the *savio grande* of the week who formulated the agenda. The procedure of debate followed a set pattern allowing free speech and argument to both sides; no closures, no abstentions; and an absolute majority was required. In a number of highly important matters a mere absolute majority did not

[55] See pp. 996 above.

suffice; larger majorities were requisite. Such matters included relationships with the Holy See, peace and war, and certain fiscal and economic items.

The Senate was an impressive body by any criterion. It was immensely knowledgeable. It was (apart from one or two notorious 'votes of no confidence', when its list of the *Zonta* was rejected by the Great Council) continuous. It was measured in debate. It was responsible. It was all these things because above all it consisted of everybody who was anybody in the Republic.

Just as today one can see the British Cabinet as the extension of the legislature, or the legislature as an extension of the Cabinet,[56] so the Venetian *Collegio* is part and parcel of the Senate. It is also the highest executive organ of the Republic. The comparison goes further. Like the British Cabinet it was the *Collegio* which, in the Senate, possessed (with trivial exceptions) the *initiative* in debate, legislation, and the order of business. This is its most significant attribute: it *led* the state.

The *Collegio* was in fact the residuary legatee of the initial autocracy of the doge. The doge was its prime mover, admittedly, since he presided over every council in the government. When his personal power had been limited by the six ducal councillors (the Ducal Council) he and they were referred to collectively as the *Signoria*, who presided over every council in the government. *Now*, to the Signoria were conjoined the three *capi* of the Forty (the legal officers), and the three groups of *savii*, making twenty-six in all.

The doge, as we know well, was a life appointment; the six ducal councillors sat for one-year terms, and were not immediately re-eligible; the *capi* of the Forty sat for two-monthly terms and the *saviis'* terms were for six months. Yet this rapid rotation of office, these very short tenures, did not impair the efficiency of the *Collegio* because, for the most part, the rotation was from one office (say the Forty) which sat in the *Collegio* to another such as, say, a ducal councillor! It is reckoned that the inner circle from which the *Collegio* and that of its high councils and magistracies were drawn consisted of not more than about 150 men, constantly revolved from one elected post to another.[57]

The *savii grandi* (or *savii di consiglio*) were hierarchically superior to the other two groups of *savii* and superintended their action. They acted as the *Collegio*'s inner steering committees; they prepared all the business to be laid before it. Each week one of the six *savii* took it in turn to discharge this task and for that period he (and not the doge) acted as chief minister. The doge presided but it was the *savio* who took the *Collegio* through the business and suggested what steps should be taken.

[56] Finer, *Comparative Government*, 173.   [57] Martines, *Power and Imagination*, 160.

Most of the *Collegio's* functions were of the pre-deliberative kind, but it had executive powers as well. As to the former, most of the proposals before the Senate came there with the authority of the *Collegio*, which tried as far as possible to act as a collective body. Sometimes, however, it found itself irrevocably divided and in such cases the members concerned were permitted to put their own proposals before the Senate. In law all magistrates had a similar right, but in practice the initiative had become reserved to the *Collegio* alone, and furthermore the Senate could not vote in favour of a proposal unless the *Collegio* itself approved it.

By the beginning of the fifteenth century, *c.*1420, the *Collegio* began to accumulate executive powers also. At first it acquired the right to give effect to the public decrees and ordinances, and then followed a host of specific lesser tasks: policing the city, the cleansing of the canals, the sale of meat, the production and the sale of oil, and matters of this kind. When the Senate was on vacation the *Collegio* was empowered to issue emergency decrees. It also had the power to suspend the operation of a law if it thought this desirable, but it had to justify this action at the very next session of the Senate.

At the apex of the governmental pyramid stood the doge. The pomp which surrounded him was as exotic as it was immense. He personified the Republic. In his name its treaties were made, its laws passed and carried out. He presided in every council of government. Yet, as we have pointed out, the entire thrust of Venice's constitutional history had been to circumscribe his power, first by putting it into commission by the appointment of the doganal councillors and then by transferring elsewhere the powers he had only exercised in person. Yet it would be quite wrong to regard him as a figurehead—during this period, at least. A powerful personality could make much of the office. No man was elected doge without a lifetime of experience in the most prominent and responsible offices of state, and doges were, in fact, generally elected at an age—from 60 onwards—when most persons would be thinking of retirement. Youthful doges like Gradenigo were very rare. These experienced statesmen, then, sat in every council of state, all the time—in a sense—watching the faces change around them as year followed on year. Though without authority to dictate, the doge was excellently placed to counsel, to warn, to manipulate, and even to inspire. The supreme example, Doge Francesco Foscari (1423–57), shows how decisive a doge could be. It was precisely because it was evident he would be able to get his way that his dying predecessors warned against him. He was able to carry out his controversial policy, although, at any time, the effective organs of the governmental system could have stopped him had they wished. In the end this is precisely what they did, but by that time the change in foreign policy Foscari had wrought was irreversible.

There were innumerable anomalies in the Venetian governmental system, such as the arbitrary division between what offices were elected by the Senate and what by the Great Council; or the ever-increasing number of separate executive boards and commissions appointed and responsible to the Senate. But through all these, the main lines are clear: it is a bicameral system in which the lower house has retained all its elective powers and still possesses residual legislative ones, while the legislative power has come to reside in the smaller and half-appointive upper house (the Senate) where the initiative for action and its execution once it has been duly approved resides in a Cabinet, which is at once part of the legislative and head of the executive. This description, however, omits two unusual and complicating features. One of these is the Council of Forty, or rather, the Councils of Forty which by this time have become benches of magistrates in criminal and civil actions, but these are best described later as part of the services provided by the Republic. The other is the *Council of Ten*.

The Ten was an extraordinary tribunal which was made permanent. When the *Collegio* wanted rapid and secret emergency action, it had the option of sending the business to the Ten rather than the Senate. It is useful to think of it as standing on a par with the Senate and below the *Collegio*, which sends business to the one or the other as it thinks fit. Made permanent in 1335, the Ten became financially autonomous, with its own treasury and audit, in 1382. It was accustomed to act with a *Zonta* of supernumeraries. This practice began in the suppression of the conspiracy of Doge Marino Falier, which resulted in mass trials and executions. The Ten themselves felt a need for moral and material support in handling the matter. Originally the *Zonta* was chosen by the Ten itself, but later it was elected by the Senate, in a four-candidate election from among its own members, and numbered twenty. But it was abolished by a vote of the Great Council in 1582.

The Ten were senators elected consecutively, in different sessions, by the Great Council in four-candidate elections. Service was obligatory and the members received neither pay nor benefits in kind. The office was annual and not immediately renewable. The Ten nominated three members as a presidency, each serving one month apiece so as to rotate the responsibility.

It was the supreme tribunal in political crimes. Espionage, forging, riot, commotion, conspiracy against the state: such were some of the gravest matters it would contemplate. It acted against promoters of rumours and false news which, from 1692, was a short step towards the censorship of publication. It came to regulate the affairs of the great philanthropic fraternities (the *scuole grande*) and thence became the supreme regulator of public morality. A large part of its work concerned 'corruption' in the most extended sense of this word, for instance, anything tending to impinge on the freedom of conscience in the councils of state: requests, intimidation, threats, bribes, and indeed even indirect modes of influence like electoral propaganda, congratulations to those elected, public praise, and the like. It kept watch on public and private assemblies, breaking them up where it found them threatening. It was responsible for public order, the control of arms, fire prevention, the laws against hired assassins. And among the most important of its duties was the protection of state secrets, and this brought it later into the conduct of foreign diplomacy.

The Ten acquired the most sinister of reputations. It was accused of secret arrests, imprisonments, stranglings, and poisonings. It was believed to immure its victims, *incommunicati*, in the *Piombi*, the torrid spaces underneath the leads, or else in the waterlogged cells fitted with instruments of torture—the so-called *Pozzi*—below the water-line. The Ten did indeed contemplate poisoning enemy statesmen from time to time.[58] It did sometimes carry out executions in secret, but usually to spare the feelings of a noble victim's family; and it did sometimes make quite tragic mistakes. It undoubtedly exceeded its powers in forcing the abdication of Francesco Foscari; it was tragically mistaken in condemning Foscarini and having him strangled (1621); and by that time it was certainly taking on powers never originally contemplated for it. But its evil reputation is a grotesque misrepresentation, especially for the period up to the fifteenth century. To begin with, the Ten did not try cases alone: it was always joined by the *Signoria*, that is, the doge and his six councillors, and an *avogadore* (procurator) was also present. Secret denunciations, especially the unsigned ones, that had been placed in the *Bocca del Leone* were subject to a careful procedure. The accused were interrogated in darkness, but five-sixths of the tribunal could agree to do so in the light. They could call witnesses. To be found guilty required an absolute majority of votes and that absolute majority was subjected to four re-ballots before being made final. The snag was that these trials were secret, so that there was no way of knowing and no way, for that matter, of contriving that these humane rules were observed. What the public observed were the results: secret sudden arrests, decapitations in the *Piazetta*, or strangled victims dangling between the two columns that stand there by the water edge. The Council of Ten struck terror; but it also broke conspiracies. It shattered the conspiracy of Doge Marino Falier and undid

[58] H. Brown, *Studies in the History of Venice*, 2 vols. (Murray, London, 1907), i. 216–54, just as in other states.

the Spanish conspiracy of 1618 (commemorated in Thomas Otway's *Venice Preserved*).

Venice was famous for the quality of its justice. Unlike all the other cities, which perforce drew their *podestà* and their judges from other places (which was, very often, Venice), this city not only called on its own native population, but upon that same nobility which staffed all other departments of the state. Few polities demonstrate better than Venice the distinction between the 'separation of powers' (into the judicial, executive, and legislative branches) and the notion of 'checks and balances'. The Venetian political system embodied the latter to an extremity that prevented any one organ from acting independently of at least one and usually more than one of the others. But the most important of these organs—Great Council, Senate, the Ten, the *Collegio*—all wielded in some degree elements of executive legislative and judicial authority. This is even true of the most specialized of such organs, the 'Ancient Forty', which was the criminal bench. For although it behaved exclusively like a court when it was hearing criminal actions, its members were *ex officio* senators, and in that capacity they participated in the activities of that body just like all the others. Not only that: as we have noted, the three *capi* or presidents of the Forty also sat as members of the *Collegio*.

This mingling of the executive and the judicial is observable in the lowest tier of courts, those of first instance, which are in one sense boards or commissions which have highly specialized jurisdictions for police and public order. These were the courts of the *Signori di Notte* and of the *Cinque alla Pace*. Cases concerning contracts went to the *Pievogo* court. There was a special court for public health and sanitation matters; another for Jews; another for foreigners. From these courts appeals went to one or another of four courts, the least significant being the *Collegio delle Biade*, consisting of twenty-two judges, which took civil cases where relatively small sums were in dispute. The major appeal courts for civil cases were two benches of forty judges, the 'Ancient Civil Forty' and 'the New Civil Forty'. Its members, having served on the latter for eight months, vacated office but went on to serve, for another eight months, on the 'Ancient Civil Forty', and when they had served that term they passed to the great criminal court, the original 'Forty' whose *capi* served (as we have noted) on the *Signoria*. Only when they had served on the 'Criminal Forty' for their eight months (so completing two years of judicial duties in all) did these nobles' duties lapse and they were ineligible for a further term for eight months.

Each of these three courts was served by three officials, who prepared the cases and explained them to the bench. Those in the 'Criminal Forty' were the three *avogadori di commun* and they were part of the highest governing circle in the city (amounting to no more than some forty people) for they were, as already noted, charged with securing the legality of proceedings in all and each of the Republic's councils, all of which they were entitled to attend. They were a kind of judge advocate-general or procurator, active against any illegality whether committed against the state or by it.

5.4. The Political Process

A simple comparison between the elaborate electoral procedures outlined above and their outcomes is enough to demonstrate that there was more in the electoral process than procedures alone. The greatest of all the electoral prizes was to be doge. Yet for all the fantastical elaborateness of the mode of electing one, the fact is that of the seventy-five doges elected in the 530 year period up to the extinction of the Republic in 1797, no less than thirty-five came from a mere *eight* families. The high magistracies rotated in a narrow circle also. In his *Oceana* James Harrington, writing in 1656, para-phrases Giannotti's *Libro de la Republica de Venitiani* (1564) as follows: 'if a gentleman comes once to be *Savio di terra ferma*, it seldom happens that he fails from thenceforward to be adorned with someone of the greater magistracies, as *Savi di mare, Savi di terra ferma, Savi Grandi*, counsellors, those of the decemvirate or dictatorian council, the *avrogatori*, or censors . . .' The fundamentals of Venetian political life rested upon election, which in turn rested upon *broglio* (graft), which in its turn rested on the family. But one might say much the same about Florence. What has to be explained is why these processes led to murderous feuds and uprisings in Florence, but stability in Venice.

We have already drawn attention to the frequency of elections, particu-larly in the Great Council, which did little else, thereby causing wry astonishment to Harrington as he saw rank on rank of the councillors advancing to and returning from the urns with never a word exchanged between them. 'For a Council and not a word spoken in it, is a contra-diction. But there is such a pudder with their marching and counter-marching as, though never a one of them drew a Sword, you would think they were training.' He describes the operations as a 'dumb-show'.[59]

By the end of the fifteenth century the Great Council was electing to 831 posts, 550 of them in the city itself. This is about one-third of the entire body of patricians, and about one-half of those who regularly attended the Great Council. For some, election to the Senate or to some high magistracy was a matter of prestige. For a full three-quarters of the nobles, those who

---

[59] J. Harrington, *The Commonwealth of Oceana* (1656; Routledge, London, 1887), 126.

were poor, it had become their source of livelihood. And the Great Council sometimes used its electoral powers to go further than simply filling individual posts, and used them instead to make a resounding political gesture. As has been remarked an outgoing Senate nominated a slate of sixty candidates—*Zonta*—to form half of the next Senate. And it was customary for the Council to vote this *en bloc*. But sometimes, when it felt that the affairs of the Republic had been mishandled, the Great Council expressed its fury by rejecting the *Zonta* slate; it was a mode of expressing 'no confidence' in the ruling group. Again, in Venice it was impossible for a nobleman to get on or even obtain a paid office unless he was elected, so that the Great Council could reward and it could punish. Individually, the power of a nobleman was slight indeed, but the fact that he was a free and equal member of this basic electoral college made him feel part and parcel of the regime.

Family was no less the very root of politics than in all other Italian cities. Now obviously, the larger the extended family or clan, the greater its chance of having one of its members on a nominating committee and, even more obviously, the greater its voting strength in the Great Council. In 1527 the total number of patricians was 2,700, composed of 134 clans; but the big clans averaged fifty-two members apiece, the middle clans only twenty-seven, while the small clans had only eleven or less. Thirty clans with some thirty or more members apiece accounted for 59 per cent of the nobility, and indeed a mere nineteen clans, with over forty members apiece, accounted for 45 per cent of their total number. In vain did the Council or Senate promulgate laws to prevent families voting as blocs or colluding with other families.[60] For one thing, great families intermarried. For another, one clan might assist another on a particular occasion and then be repaid in kind by that other clan many years later. This is the principal explanation of why, until the sixteenth century, the dogeship was confined, pretty well, to the ancient 'twenty-four families', that is, the purported founders of the city. Understandings of these kinds were reached—supposedly—as magnates strolled about, before a Council or Senate meeting, in the shade of the Doge's Palace, on that part of the *Piazetta* known as the *broglio*. By way of this association, the word *broglio* obtained its present-day connotation, in the Italian language, of electoral well-wishing or 'graft'. But as in the Tammany days of New York, a distinction could be and was drawn between what Boss Tweed would have called 'honest graft' and true graft. Intermarriage and mutual support were 'honest' graft. But bit by bit, by the sixteenth century, corruption became more blatant and shameless. Maranini, whose work we

---

[60] R. Finlay, *Politics in Renaissance Venice* (Benn, London, 1980), 83.

have had good reason to cite, took the anti-corruption laws of the Republic at their legal face value, but he was deluded. By the sixteenth century a great number of nobles were very poor. Their votes could be and were bought. The elaborate laws against rigging the balloting we described earlier could, surely, not have been circumvented? But they were! Golden ballot-balls were smuggled into the Great Council chamber. When the law was altered and slips of paper were put into the ballot boxes instead, the youngsters who carried the ballot boxes around found that by holding them to one side or another they could manipulate the number of votes cast for a particular candidate. And so forth. So family and fraud counted in Venice, as everywhere else. Yet this did not lead to instability.

The explanation is complex. To begin with, one wonders why this narrow group of less than 3,000 aristocrats should be able to control the great multitude of inhabitants without the use of troops and with very small police-forces. The principal reason lay in the aristocracy's consciousness of the potential dangers to their position. Not just elections and appointments were discussed in the *broglio*; the Great Council was acutely sensitive to public rumblings, to what was called its *mormorazione*, and adjusted measures accordingly. Next, for reasons already explained, the lesser and poorer nobility were reconciled to the hegemony of the higher few because, as electors, they had real power to reward and punish. Additionally, there were a number of important reasons why the great clans did not act as murderously rival factions. One of these was the undoubtedly mitigating effect of intermarriages. Another, wherein Venice differed from every other state in Europe, was the advanced age required for obtaining public office. Venice was a gerontocracy. The Venetian definition of 'old age' was similar to our own; it began in the mid-sixties, whereas everywhere else a man was thought to be beginning his old age when he was 40! Between 1400 and 1600 the average age of a doge at election was 72, and this is eighteen years older than the average age at which the popes were elected. Other high posts like that of ambassador, *podestà*, member of the *Collegio*, or *capo* of the Ten also went to the aged, that is, to persons of between 70 and 80 years of age. Even the generals and admirals were aged between 60 and 75, possibly the reason for Venice's subsequently poor military performance.[61] And not only did the Venetian nobleman have to wait much longer to obtain high office than elsewhere, he entered on citizenship at later age. For instance, in Florence a citizen began to exercise his rights (as a member of the *parlamento*) at the age of 14. In Venice he had to wait till he was 25 to enter the Great Council, 30 to enter the Senate and 40 before he could become a member of the Ten.

[61] R. Finlay, 120–30.

These rules strongly promoted stability. The *vecchi* shared the experiences of a lifetime of wheeling and dealing and negotiating with one another. Their thirst for office was mitigated by a sort of 'seniority rule' by which, other things being equal, a nobleman could expect high office as he grew older. By the time he was old enough to obtain high office, he had already served fifteen or twenty years' apprenticeship in the system after reaching the conventional 'old age' of 40, and by then he had learned to subordinate himself to the constitution.

Additionally, Venetians were famous everywhere for their almost antique Roman values. Whether these were the product of the gerontocratic nature of the political system is a matter for surmise. What can be said for certain is that they were consistent with it and they reinforced one another. The system deplored 'arrogance, ostentation and personal power'.[62] The nobles were brought up to work within a constitutional structure where the slightest task required them to accommodate and conciliate their peers. Those who governed knew that they could retain their office only by submitting to the electoral judgement of their peers. Hence Venetian politics provides one of the best historical examples of the apparent paradox that corruption and graft can actually be 'functional' (i.e. beneficent) to the political system.[63] They softened and made amenable the otherwise divisive potentialities of family rivalry in an order based on short mandates and incessant elections. In the sixteenth and seventeenth centuries the Republic's famed stability was attributed to its supposed 'mixed constitution', where the doge represented the monarchical element, the Senate the aristocratic, and the Great Council the democratic one. Not only was this a total misrepresentation of the actual constitutional arrangements; it also made the fundamental blunder of attributing to the constitution and its procedures much that was extra-constitutional and the product of its social structures and outlooks.

5.5. *The Activities of Government*

The immediate impression one receives is that the government did a great deal and did it pretty well. On reflection this seems somewhat surprising. The *Collegio* could do no more than co-ordinate and correct, but even here it was limited. The number of administrative boards elected by and directly accountable to the Senate was large, and in the course of the fifteenth and

---

[62] R. Finlay, 137.

[63] Cf. A. J. Heidenheimer (ed.), *Political Corruption* (Transaction Books, New Brunswick/London, 1989), esp. ch. 11.

sixteenth centuries expanded incessantly; and the doge and *Signoria* could neither appoint nor dismiss them as their salaried officials, so that there was no such thing as a unified and hierarchical civil service such as had existed in the late Roman Empire, in the Byzantine Empire, and had reached maturity in Ming China. The policy-making layer of the administration consisted in Venice of these numerous boards and commissions for highly specialized purposes, manned by noblemen for periods rarely exceeding a year at a time before they went off to serve on another board. The regular, full-time officials who ministered to these boards, the administrators proper, comprised secretaries, accountants, and notaries. They often knew the business better than their noble superiors. The highest positions in their administrative sector were held by the class of *cittadini-originarii*, and notably in the Chancery. The 'Grand Chancellor' took precedence over almost all other office-holders, noble or not, and indeed the dignity afforded this non-noble was symbolically important to the entire class of *cittadini-originarii*, whom it reconciled to the political monopoly of the nobility. Under the Grand Chancellor were ranged the groups of secretaries who handled the business for the Ten, the Senate, and the *Collegio*. They were trained in a special school. A decree of 1443 required the doge and *Signoria* to elect every year twelve scholars who were to be taught Latin, rhetoric, and philosophy. They passed out after examinations to enter a graded career, first as extraordinaries and ordinaries (the 'notaries ducal'), then secretaries to the Senate, and finally, secretaries to the Ten. Such men were in constant attendance in the councils. Sometimes they were sent on diplomatic missions.

The Chancery was the hub of all this activity and was divided into three. The *Cancelleria Inferiore* was staffed by the most junior grades, the 'notaries ducal'. Its work concerned the doge: his rights, his possessions, his *promissioni*, and the audits carried out on the life and work of each deceased doge. The second was the Ducal Chancellery: it compiled the collections of the statutes, handled elections in the Great Council, and staffed the offices of the *savii* responsible for the administration of the empire (the *Mar*) and the mainland possessions (the *Terra Ferma*). The third Chancellery was established only in 1402, to preserve the most secret documents, and came under the control of the Council of Ten.

Government had a hand in almost every activity and what it did not direct, it proximately controlled. This is most strikingly illustrated, for example, in the tight control it exercised over the Church, to the extent that one might be forgiven for imagining one saw an independent 'See of St Mark'. The magnificent church of San Marco was from its beginning the private chapel of the doge and it was, therefore, he who appointed its clergy.

The bishop played virtually no role in the civic life and government of the city, and his own church—S Pietro in Castello—lay in an outlying island. It was the government and not the clerical establishment which managed the custody of sacred relics (with which the Venetians do appear indeed to be veritably obsessed and for which they scoured the seas), regulated the content of sermons, and made provision for religious services when the clergy absented themselves. The bishops, from the patriarch down, were Venetians elected by the Senate, whom the pope would then usually confirm; the converse—papal nomination in the teeth of Venetian opposition—never occurred because the Republic retained control over the temporalities. Consequently, the hierarchy was first and foremost Venetian noblemen. As to the lower clergy, they were traditionally elected by the property-owners in the sixty-odd parishes where, as we shall see, they were a most important part of the mechanisms for local control. All clergy were deemed to be subject to the overriding laws of the Republic, though the methods of effectuating this differed. It was a long time, not till way beyond our period, in 1464, before the Republic consented to request papal consent to tax the clergy. Finally, the Republic simply refused to accept the Papacy's contention that heresy was a matter for it alone. On the contrary, it only admitted the Inquisition into its territory (1289) under conditions, and successfully insisted on having its own lay representatives participate in all its proceedings both in the city and on the *Terra Firma*. Venice was always reserved towards the Papacy and her relationships with the Holy See are punctuated by disputes. These sometimes earned her papal interdicts, to which her unwavering reaction was defiance. She had to yield in the case of the 1309–13 interdict over the war with Ferrara; was able to fend off a second (1482–4, also over Ferrara); buckled under the third, launched by the pope in support of his infamous League of Cambrai (1509); but defied and in the event totally nullified the fourth interdict of 1605—so dramatically that no pope ever, anywhere, launched one again.[64]

Government also intervened heavily in economic life, and indeed, one could interpret its entire foreign and domestic policy as simply the political dimension of a vast manufacturing and trading co-operative. 'The business of Venice is business', would be a prefectly appropriate comment. The regulation of standards and conditions of manufacture, labour relations, and the like were regulated indirectly, through the guilds or by free contract within the city's general laws.[65] But the government also acted directly and

[64] The above is based on the excellent account in W. Bouwsma, *Venice and the Defence of Republican Liberty* (University of California Press, Berkeley and Los Angeles, 1968), 71–83.
[65] See p. 954 above.

on a massive scale. One example is the state-owned and operated Arsenal. Founded in the first years of the twelfth century, so famous by 1300 that Dante describes it to give his impression of Hell, the Arsenal employed some 3,000 workmen to build and equip the Republic's great merchant galleys and warships. The government undertook long-term building pro-grammes to store up a mothball fleet as a reserve, and this Arsenal used assembly-line techniques in equipping the vessels. As a ship neared comple-tion it moved down a channel flanked by warehouses:

Out came a galley towed by a boat and from the windows [of the warehouses] they handed to the occupants from one cordage, from another the arms and from another the ballistas and mortars and so from all sides everything that was required, and when the galley had reached the end of the canal all the men required were on board and she was equipped from end to end.

This operation took two hours.[66]

A second example is provided by the public control and direction of the merchant fleets. Certainly the great bulk of merchant shipping was *naviga-zione libera*, but the most precious of the cargoes went to sea in state-built boats which were leased out at public auction, the freight rates having been debated and fixed in the Senate. These great galleys were made to sail in convoy at fixed times and on fixed routes, under the command of a *capitaneo*, who was nominated in the Senate and a salaried official. Sometimes the convoy was put on a war footing, and then even the individual ships' masters were salaried and became the Republic's agents for making sure that all their cargoes had paid freight and for defending their ships when attacked. By the end of the fourteenth century there were usually six such convoys, each of some 500 ships, per year.

As elsewhere in Italy, and for that matter throughout the European towns, the public authorities intervened actively in all important spheres of life, but in certain respects Venice was unusual, if not unique. Her arrangements for public assistance were farmed. The 'unregulated' labourers (with no guild to help them) became the responsibility of the great charitable foundations called the 'schools' (the *scuole*), quite apart from a dozen or so private charities also. Venice seems to have been the first city in the West to provide its population with a free medical service: in 1335 the state began paying salaries to twelve surgeon-doctors; in 1368 it established a School of Medicine and it was always lavishing invitations to attract doctors from other places. The feeding and provisioning of the city was a para-mount duty; there were 100,000 mouths to fill and everything except fish and

---

[66] Quoted in Chamberlin, *World of the Italian Renaissance*, 143.

fresh water had to be brought from outside. Here the authorities turned geography to their advantage, forcing all ships in the Adriatic to discharge at Venice, posting high prices for grain with guarantees against loss, and so attracting supplies from the mainland and overseas in such abundance that the city became the grain emporium for the entire region. Her merchant fleet reduced the incidence of famine to which inland cities like Florence were often subjected when the harvests failed, for in times of scarcity the Venetian vessels were sent to scour the entire eastern Mediterranean— sometimes even the Black Sea—in search of grain.

There were no armed forces in the city! The nearest it got to this was the honour guard for the doge, a small force drawn from men picked out of the labour force of the Arsenal, the *arsenalotti*. Yet the city was kept calm and peacable. Its *sestiere* were subdivided into so many *contrade*, some sixty or seventy in all. Each had its own priest who, as we noted earlier, was elected by the local great families. In addition the *Signoria* appointed a *capo de contrada*, a local nobleman of weight who was responsible, *inter alia*, for registering adult males and for tax-assessments. Co-operating with him were police- men—again, local inhabitants[67]—who, city-wide, formed a body of about 120 men under the control of the Board of the six *signori di notte*, the 'Lords of the Night'.

5.6. *The Best-Governed Place in the World?*

'In the fourteenth and fifteenth centuries', wrote Charles Diehl, 'the gov- ernment of Venice was probably one of the best in the world.'[68] The judgement is too modest. It *was* the best in the world and it would remain so till perhaps the eighteenth century. No matter what aspect of living is concerned, it was Venice that best provided for it. It never suffered the horrors of a medieval sack or occupation; the nearest the enemy ever came to its limits was in the war of Chioggia. It was never prey to civil war and even its civil disturbances were small beer, absolutely and relatively. They bear no comparison at all with the murderous feuds in Milan or Perugia or Siena or even in Florence, and as for the European monarchies, these do not even enter the picture at all, considering what was going on in the way of wars, *Jacqueries* or peasant revolts, civil wars, and the depositions and murders of crowned kings. Although the city was ruled by an aristocracy of perhaps only one-fortieth of the total population, that proportion of active citizens

---

[67] But though this was the regulation, many exceptions were made and most policeman seem to have been north Italians: S. Chojnacki, 'In Search of the Venetian Patriciate: Families and Factions in the Fourteenth Century', in J. R. Hale, *Renaissance Venice* (London, 1973), 204.

[68] Quoted in Norwich, *History of Venice*, 181.

was a far wider band of participants than was to be met with in the late-feudal monarchies and principalities. Its non-citizens were (except for a few domestic slaves) not serfs but freemen. And, the unique feature of Venice—the ruling minority—not only did not oppress their subjects but cared for them. Everything suggests that the constitution enjoyed popular support, for there were no troops in the city and just a handful of policemen in the *contrade*. And there were good reasons for their loyalty. As we saw, Venice was one of the richest localities in Europe, and although the gap was enormous between the richest and the poorest, even the latter were well fed compared with other places and suffered far less from famines owing to the work of the Grain Commission, one of the best-managed branches of the administration.

Though the mass of the people were denied active participation in government, they enjoyed passive civil rights—to association, occupation, mobility—all of them denied in the monarchies and hedged about in most other towns. Above all, they enjoyed a freedom of speech and a toleration for individual views that were a byword throughout Italy. 'The only evil prevailing [there]', wrote Petrarch, '[is] far too much freedom of speech.'[69] It was the same three centures later, since Sir Henry Wotton, the British ambassador, reported home that 'it is a state that whether it be in fear or otherwise, heareth all men speak willingly'.[70] But, more than any other thing, all inhabitants enjoyed a genuine equality before the law. The rules relating to criminal investigation, even those governing arrest, were scrupulous. Though only one witness was legally necessary to secure a conviction, the practice was to secure as many as possible, often at great expense. Prisoners too poor to have a lawyer were provided with one of the city's licensed lawyers, allocated by lot. Although torture was permissible to extract information (as in all Continental countries by then), it might be admitted only if all six *signori di notte* concurred, and could be applied only in the presence of two of these *signori*, two ducal councillors, one of the *capi* of the Forty, and an *avogado di commune*. And even then the information yielded had to be corroborated from other sources. An examination of the police and court records demonstrates that they were completely impartial in their treatment of nobles and commoners. The justice of Venice was famous throughout the whole of Europe. It was her impartial justice that made the population of the cities of the *Terra Ferma* stand by the Republic in her dark hours after the disaster of Agnadello in 1509. 'The guarantees of individual rights, protected in Venice—in so far as not incompatible with the life of the state [found] a form', wrote Maranini, 'whose energy and efficacy would

[69] Quoted in Bouwsma, *Venice and the Defence*, 93.   [70] Ibid. 94.

find nothing to envy in the system of modern Britain', and he draws attention to 'the collegiality of the tribunals, the absolute personal independence of the judges, the exasperating meticulousness of the procedures and the system of appeals'.[71]

The qualities that strike the observer when he contemplates the government of Venice are not the collegiate structure, the elaborate checks and balances, the rotation of office, and the like, for these are commonplace in medieval city-republics. Admittedly, Venice's structure was better designed than most in three respects: the impressive expert knowledge of its Senate, the directing and executive role of the *Collegio*, and the incorporation of an emerging mechanism, the Council of Ten. But if the active citizenry who manned the councils and rotated through the ever-more numerous boards and commissions had been even a fraction as contentious and violent as those in cities like Florence, the Venetian constitution would hardly have worked any better. It worked so splendidly because, in the last resort, the aristocracy that worked it—and for that matter the quasi-aristocracy of *cittadine originarii* with their names in their own 'Silver Book'—were imbued with a sense of responsibility for the Republic that transcended their rivalries. It is harder to explain this than to observe its many manifestations. It has been remarked frequently, for instance, that there are very few prominent names in Venetian history—the political actors are largely anonymous, or symbolize a few great families, perhaps—but they conform to a type. The rules of debate, especially in the Senate, which forbid insult and slander, reprove emotionalism and demagoguery, and seek—successfully in the event—to keep discussion low-key, practical, and consensual, are another manifestation of their attitudes. In their great crises this Venetian aristocracy behaved like Roman senators and magistrates in their golden days during the Hannibalic wars. They exhibited a respect for the *mos maiorum*, the laws of the Republic, and then exhibited what one can only call, really, a sense of state.

The Doge Francesco Foscari is one of the four names that stand out in Venetian history—the tragic hero of Byron's poem and Verdi's opera. Foscari was a great and energetic doge, the man who turned Venice towards the *Terra Ferma*. In his old age he was brought low by the crimes of his son Jacopo. What occurred when Jacopo, found guilty, was led into the doge's room with the marks of torture still on him would be melodrama were it not what actually happened; and what happened was an echo of the Roman Republic. The old man embraced the son who was going into exile. 'Father, father,' he is said to have cried, 'I beg you, procure me permission to return

---

[71] Maranini, *La costituzione*, ii. 221–2.

to my house.' But the heart-broken doge replied only: 'Jacopo, thou must obey the law of the land and struggle no more.'

This sense of state was acknowledged throughout Italy as the outstanding characteristic of the Venetian aristocracy. To some it was detestable, to others just the contrary. Pius II exemplifies the former: 'they are hypocrites. They wish to appear Christian before the world but in reality they never think of God and, except for the state, which they regard as a deity, they hold nothing sacred, nothing holy. To a Venetian that is just which is for the good of the state . . .' But the more common verdict, the one that was embodied in the celebrated 'Myth of Venice', is best expressed by Petrarch: 'Urbs . . . solidis fundata marmoribus, sed solidiore etiam fundamento civilis concordie stabilita': 'a city founded solidly on marble, but more solidly yet on an established foundation of civil concord'.[72]

6. THE LEGACY OF THE MEDIEVAL REPUBLICS

There would be republics after the medieval ones had passed away. Indeed, in the end there were to be almost nothing but republics throughout the entire globe. The only element they would have in common with the medieval kind was what Ullmann has called the 'ascending theory' of authority: 'that original power is located in the people, or in the community itself', as contrasted with the view that all magistrates were appointed from above, not elected by a popular assembly but deriving from the original power of God.[73] But the latter-day republics did not owe this characteristic 'ascending theory' to the medieval ones either ideationally or by force of the few surviving exemplars. On the contrary. Not only did they not recognize themselves in these predecessors, they shunned and abhorred them as the very antithesis of republics. For they could not discern in the oligarchic minorities who constituted the citizenry of Venice and Genoa, the Swiss towns, and the German *Reichstädte* anything other than privilege, and certainly nothing resembling the 'people or the community itself'. It may seem paradoxical that the 500-year-old Republic of Venice was brutally destroyed in 1797 by another republic in the name of republicanism. It becomes clear and simple once one realizes that the connotation of 'republic' had decisively changed in the interim. The medieval city-republics bear striking resemblances to certain features of the classical republics, which we have pointed out,[74] and not least is the very fact that they were *city*-republics,

---

[72] Quoted in F. Gilbert, 'The Venetian Constitution in Florentine Political Thought', in Rubinstein (ed.), *Florentine Studies*, 467, n. 3.   [73] Ullmann, *History of Political Thought*, 12–13.
[74] See p. 979 ff. above.

since it was only this that made the rotation of offices through the citizen body even thinkable. Their successors in time—the United Netherlands and the short-lived English Commonwealth—were, by contrast, territorial states, requiring a quite different application of the 'ascending theory' and, furthermore, their ideological inspiration owed nothing to Greece or Rome, but sprang from the Protestant Reformation and (in its most remote ancestry) from the ancient Jewish theocracy.

Susan Reynolds is right when she says that the medieval cities were at first 'republics but republics almost by accident'.[75] They did not rush into independence from a pre-established ideology. As we noted earlier, it is not till the mid-thirteenth century that any self-consciousness of their republicanism appears and it does not seem accidental that the publicists who wrote of it did so immediately after Aristotle's *Politics* became accessible in Latin (*c.*1250). Brunetto Latini (1220–94) distinguished republics from monarchies and despotisms as polities where the people selected their own *podestà* or *signori* and praised them as the best type of government. Bartolus noted (significantly in view of the overwhelming presumption that 'Rome' meant the Roman Empire) that the Romans had instituted a Republic after expelling their kings and founded it on the body of the people, and for his part, he opined that for small places like Perugia (where he lived for a long time) it was the best form of government, though it might be inappropriate for large countries. Bartolomeo (or Ptolemy) of Lucca, the man who completed Thomas Aquinas's (pro-monarchical) tract on 'The Rule of Princes', also thought the Roman Republic and not the Empire was Rome's great period, praising Cicero and Cato for their republican resistance to Julius Caesar, the great hero of the medieval world. For him despotism and monarchy were two sub-varieties of the same stripe, as contrasted with 'political' governments, where the major officers were elected for annual terms. And the same theme is expressed in the *Defensor Pacis* (1324) of Marsiglio of Padua (1275–1342). Herein we find brief delineations of some of the specific features of the (now evolved) city-republics: periodic elections, not hereditary succession; checks and balances via a *parliamentum*, a council, and the magistrates; and the last-named to be law-bound, with a minimum of personal discretion.

But the persuasive effect of these writings seems to have been minute if not negligible, to judge by the course of events, since in the larger territorial entities of Europe monarchy was consolidating itself, while in Italy itself the republics were giving way to *Signorie*. Republics were exceptional and, Venice apart, not regarded as of great international importance.

---

[75] Reynolds, *Kingdoms and Communities*, 215.

Republican self-consciousness and apologetic attained a new intensity and a new tone in Florence at the end of the fourteenth and first part of the fifteenth century in the work of Coluccio Salutati (1331–1406) and Leonardo Bruni (1369–1444). Bruni, in his 'Praise' (*Laudatio*) of Florence, launches an impassioned attack on the despotism of her deadly foe, the Visconti of Milan, and an equally eloquent eulogy of Florence's republican constitution whose essence—according to him—is that it 'makes it equally possible for everyone to take part in the affairs of the Republic'[76] (a lie, as we know), and that everybody was free to criticize the government and to control it. These authors, along with others such as Vergerio, have been styled 'civic humanists' by Baron,[77] who credits them, and particularly Bruni, with a revolutionary originality. It would not be too much to say that an entire cult has grown up around this group, a cult greatly assisted by some other historians of ideas, notably Pocock,[78] whose book, erudite to the point of pedantry, seeks (unsuccessfully, to my mind) to trace a direct filiation between these humanistic ideas, the English revolutions, and American political culture. In fact none of this group were significant political thinkers and it is the next century, in the death-throes of the Florentine Republic, that we meet the only republican theorist of historic stature in the person of Machiavelli.

One great misunderstanding was that Venice was a model and a signal proof of the success of what was deemed the 'mixed constitution'. The notion derived from Plato's *Laws* (not translated into Latin, until *c*.1481) and Aristotle's *Politics*, which of course, as we know, had been circulating in Latin translation since 1250. There is a difficulty in making this connection, though, because these authors reflect on a balance of social classes, not of organs of government. The latter is the doctrine of Polybius, in chapter 6 of his *History*.[79] That chapter was not translated into Latin till 1530, but would have been accessible to Giannotti, the Greek who described the Venetian Constitution to the Florentines in a 'Dialogue' circulating 1527–8, because Giannotti was a lecturer in Greek. In a project for a new constitution for Florence, Giannotti did actually mention Polybius' chapter 6, but proof that his conception of the Venetian constitution was modelled on Polybius is remarkably elusive. However, whatever his sources, Giannotti, picked up a notion already adumbrated at the end of the fourteenth century by Vergerio in 1394 and the Cretan George of Trebizond in 1481: that Venice combined in itself the principles of monarchy (the doge), aristocracy (the

---

[76] Quoted in Q. Skinner, *The Foundations of Modern Political Thought*, 2 vols. (CUP, Cambridge, 1978), i. 78. [77] Baron, *Crisis of the Italian Renaissance* (Princeton UP, Princeton, 1966).

[78] J. Pocock, *The Machiavellian Moment* (Princeton UP, Princeton, 1975).

[79] See Bk. II, Ch. 4, 'The Roman Republic', p. 396 above.

Senate), and democracy (the Great Council).[80] This view, together with a great admiration for Venice, found its way into Harrington's strange, original, and subsequently (in America) influential book *Oceana* (1656). Here is the last great work to identify 'Republic' with those found in classical antiquity: its great swan-song, for the 'swan in dying makes death sweet'.[81] In his book, basing himself on models from the ancient Jews, Athenians, Spartans, and now the Venetians, as well as his own ingenious imagination, Harrington constructs a Utopia where the principal features of classical republics—and of the medieval city-republics—are all to be found. It is a republic of citizen participation, of rotating short-term offices, of collegiate or conciliar magistracies, and a system of checks and balances between them.

But from then on this specific connotation of 'Republic' wasted away. True, new republics arose in Europe, to offset the fall of Florence—the United Netherlands, the Cromwellian Commonwealth in Britain—but emphatically, neither of these originated in a republican ideology of any variety whatsoever. The rebel Dutch provinces were so far from being republican ideologues that they initially offered a throne to the duc d'Anjou; the Commonwealth was a republic only in the sense that after the execution of Charles I in 1649 the country was ruled by an elective dictator instead of a hereditary king.

In the sixteenth and seventeenth centuries the term 'Republic' covered a diversity of meanings. In its widest sense it was the 'public concern', the 'common-wealth'. In a more restricted usage, often employed by poets, travellers, and historians, it might mean a state or a political community: thus, one wrote of 'the Republic of the Iroquois' in America. Bodin, in his *Six Books of the Republic* (1576), applies it to any sovereign state, whether a monarchy or an aristocracy. Rousseau took the same line: 'By Republic, I mean any state ruled by the laws, no matter what its form of administration.'[82] But Montesquieu held to the ancient connotation of a government where the people, in whole or in part, exercise the sovereign power.

In quite another sense, more in common with the medieval concept of the *Respublica Christiana*, the word might refer to some sort of collectivity: so Sully wrote of the 'most Christian republic of the fifteen nations' (of Europe), in contradistinction to the infidels; but it could also be used, analogously, to connote a 'Republic of Letters', the network of the European intellectuals.

---

[80] The filiation of ideas is very complicated and indecisive. See particularly, Gilbert, 'The Venetian Constitution', 468–9; Pocock, *The Machiavellian Moment*, ch. 9, pp. 272–330.

[81] 'Sic mea fata canendo solor, Ut nece proxima facit olor.'

[82] J. J. Rousseau, *Contrat Social* (Manchester UP, Manchester, 1918; repr. 1955), vol. ii. ch. 6, p. 32.

Some political theorists defined a republic as 'a popular state, or government' where the sovereign authority is in the hands of the people as a whole, or a part of them. Others thought of it rather as a state where sovereign power was held by the many; but then subdivided these into aristocracies (or oligarchies) and democracies, which all shared one thing in common—that the highest offices were all elective.[83]

What is notable in all these diverse definitions is that the term has quite lost its association with every hallmark of medieval—and classical—republicanism save one. They have retained the notion of the 'ascending theory' of sovereignty and its entailed characteristic of elective office. What they have shed would include collegiality, checks and balances, and the rotation of offices. Because of this, even the kingdom of Poland as an elective monarchy and all-powerful nobility could be described as a republic.

Then, in the eighteenth century, the 'ascending theory' becomes, increasingly, extended and deepened in a popular or a democratic direction. As the 'natural equality of man'—as found in John Locke, for instance—becomes the new political axiom as compared with the Middle Ages' 'hierarchy' and 'degree', so a new phase of republicanism is ushered in. It is elective government, where the popular constituency is wide; and it is indirect, or representative, government in contrast to direct democracy as practiced in classical antiquity. This new paradigm of 'Republic' is admirably caught by Madison in 1788. He asks, 'What are the distinctive characters of the republican form?', and his first response is that the term was now so widely applied as to have lost all specificity.[84] Holland is called a republic, yet there 'no particle of the supreme authority is derived from the people'. Poland is called a republic, but it is 'a mixture of aristocracy and of monarchy in their worst forms'. England has been similarly misnamed: its government 'has one republican branch only'. And finally: *La Serenissima*? This state, for so long the very exemplar of the republican form and its great glory, is now dismissed as a state wherein 'absolute power over the great body of the people is exercised in the most absolute manner by a small body of hereditary nobles'.

With this verdict, the way was open for a new paradigm, with revolutionary consequences; symbolized in 1797 by the destruction of the Venetian Republic by the French Republic in the name of republicanism's new meaning.

---

[83] The above is based on the excellent little survey of Y. Durand, *Les Républiques au temps des monarchies* (Collection SUP, Presses Universitaires de France, Paris, 1973), 7–11.

[84] J. Madison, *The Federalist Papers* (Penguin Classics, Harmondsworth, 1987), no. 39.

8

Representative Assemblies

1. THE GREAT POLITICAL INVENTION OF THE MIDDLE AGES

During the thirteenth and fourteenth centuries when the free cities and the Italian republics were moving into their heyday, a sea-change was occurring in the kingdoms and principalities. Beginning with Spain, next in England, France, and Italy, then spreading into Germany, Scandinavia, and even Poland and Hungary, there sprang up a multitude of conciliar bodies to give consent to but also—by the same token—to exert some control over their rulers. Some countries, like England, Ireland, Scotland, Sicily, the Papal States, and the great Kingdom of Naples called them parliaments or *parlamenti*. In the Iberian peninsula they were called *cortes* or *corts*. In France and the Lowlands they went under the name of Estates- or States-General. In Germany they were called *landtage*, in Denmark and Norway the assembly was the *Rigsdag*, in Sweden the *Riksdag*, and in Poland the *Sejm*. Their first common characteristic has been put thus: all of them were 'political assemblies composed of the representatives of the privileged order or orders of a country, who act in the name of these orders and of all the country, on the one hand to watch over the maintenance of the privileges of the orders, groups and individuals, and on the other to offer the prince the counterpart of the rights and privileges recognized and conceded by him'. Their second characteristic was that they were regular institutions, not *ad hoc* arrangements like the feudal *magna concilia* which had gone before.[1] In Lord's words, 'the power of the crown was . . . more or less extensively limited by those of assemblies, in part elective, whose members, though directly and immediately representing only the politically active classses, were also regarded as representing in a general way the whole population of the land'. And he states that this 'development of the representative system

---

[1] Emile Lousse, quoted in A. Marongiu, *Medieval Parliaments: A Comparative Study*, trans. and adapted by S. J. Woolf, foreword by H. Cam (Eyre & Spottiswoode, London, 1968) (originally published as *Parlamento in Italia nel mediævo e nell'erè moderna* (1949)), 51.

and of parliaments' was 'one of the greatest achievements of the Middle Ages'.[2] Lord was completely correct.

The central notion was that of the *pars pro toto*, the idea that a small group or even a single individual can—in senses I shall explore later—somehow *stand for* a larger collectivity, and be able and willing to commit it to a line of action. This is not a sufficient condition for what we would call 'representative government' today, but it is the necessary one. For today's representative government we must think not just of representation but also of the supremacy of the lower chamber, the system of competitive parties, a wide franchise, and the responsibility of the government's ministers towards the assembly. Not one of these was in force during the late Middle Ages, and, indeed, they all owe their present currency to the particular evolution of one particular assembly over time, the Parliament of England. But the simple point here is that all these developments were predicated on the principle of representation and this principle was entirely new. As we saw,[3] it was not used in the Greek leagues of the Hellenistic period, and the absence of something like it was what provoked the Social War in Italy under the Republic; and the curious solution the Romans adopted after their victory was based on an extension of direct citizenship, completely antithetical to the representative principle. The monarchies and empires of the Middle East and in China knew nothing of the principle either, but then they were all based on the principle of autocracy, as indeed was the Roman Empire.

But unlike the feudal systems of Western Europe and equally unlike its city-republics, the principle of representation was to prove durable. We studied feudalism because it was an innovation in the modes of governing, because it spanned a large area and population, because it was the foundation of much that was to come in Europe (including representation itself), and because it has its analogues in today's world. Then we looked at the city republics because they stumbled on to a notion of citizenship akin to that of the ancient *poleis* of Greece or early Rome. But neither of these two forms of government proved durable. We have shown how the medieval notion of a republic came to be looked at, four centuries later, as nothing but a corrupt oligarchy; and as for feudalism, it was its very decadence that sparked the emergence and rise of the representative assemblies.

The representative assembly stumbled into existence just as unselfconsciously as these other two forms. In some cases the *magnum concilium* of the

[2] R. H. Lord, 'The Parliaments of the Middle Ages and the Early Modern Period', *Catholic Historical Review*, 16 (1930), 125–8, quoted in P. Spufford, *The Origins of the English Parliament: Readings* (Longman, London, 1967), 21.   [3] See p. 380 above.

feudal magnates became conscious of itself as a collectivity and of its potentialities, and effectively usurped the monarch's powers, as in the example of Simon de Montfort and the barons of England, 1258–65. In other cases the ruler decided—sometimes out of weakness but sometimes because he was very strong—to treat the members of the assembly as proxies for their communities. He asked or demanded commitments from them on behalf of those who were absent. (It was this particular path that fore-shadowed what we mean by 'representation', a multiplex term which will be explored later on.) In yet a third set of instances political groups, organized into corporations or *universitates*, forced the ruler by threats or violence to accept them, when assembled, as participants in his major political deci-sions. And of course, there was always the fourth way, that of *mimesis*, imitation; once one assembly had come into being, it served as inspiration and model for others. Once these assemblies came to exercise defined prerogatives within the context of decision-making, they were on the threshold of representativeness—but a representativeness peculiar to the Middle Ages, not that of today. That is to say, it was unusual for them to exercise these representative functions on account of their having been elected (what Ullmann would call the 'ascending principle' of sovereignty[4]); they did so, most commonly, simply as a result of an explicit legal decision.

If this helps to explain how the representative assemblies came into existence, it does not tell us *why* they sprang up so suddenly and ubiqui-tously. The variety of reasons, each peculiar to a certain historical context, must not distract us from the one perennial, common factor: the kings and princes wanted to make war, the customary feudal dues to which they were entitled did not suffice, and—in brief—*they needed money*. But throughout Western Europe there existed the common conviction, expressed as *n'impose qui ne veut*. Therefore, if the king or prince wanted money beyond what was his customary due, he had to *ask* for it.

Sometimes the assemblies emerged because the throne was vacant or contested and the assembled magnates were the sole remaining pillar of continuity in the state. (This was the most important factor in the Polish case, discussed later.) Sometimes the sovereign would convene them not so much for their money as for political support, as Philip the Fair of France did in his struggle against the pretensions of Boniface VIII. But the most important and constant activity was the grant of money; as the Germans put it, *Landtage sind Geldtage*. Any new money had to come from a voluntary grant. It was clearly convenient for monarchs to deal with one meeting or assembly which had the authority to make such a grant rather than several. The

---

[4] Ullmann, *Principles of Governance, passim.*

exceptional case is the failure of the Estates-General in France, but it is the exception that proves the rule. The kings of France certainly had to ask their corporate subjects for extra monies, but they asked it of regional Estates and individual towns, not from the Estates-General as the representative of the entire community.

The representative assemblies emerge as feudalism perishes, between the thirteenth and the fifteenth century. We are very remote from the barbarous improvisations of the tormented tenth century. Two political developments in particular mark the end of the feudal period: the decline and disappearence of the military *raison d'être* of feudalism, and the formation of both territorial and also functional communities; in particular, the clergy, the nobility, the towns, and in rare instances, even the peasantry.

Feudalism was a makeshift arrangement for raising a military force in a natural economy based on the barter of goods and services. Land was held from the sovereign in return for the promise of knight-service. Hence vassalage and homage and the entire structure of political and social relationships were reared on the basis of the supremacy of the armoured and mounted knight. The feudal array was the clumsiest of military instruments. The knight customarily served for only forty days. Yet medieval campaigns were, on the whole, very slow, wasteful affairs of protracted sieges. To fight such campaigns the sovereign required long-term castellans to hold his fortresses and a long-term field force to invest those of his enemy. Unsurprisingly, from quite early times—in the twelfth century in England and France—kings turned, as far as their limited supplies of currency permitted, to mercenary troops who might well be knights of noble lineage but who served for pay. Thus arose the commutation of knight-service for cash—in England called a 'scutage'. England was some fifty to seventy years ahead of France in pursuing cash commutations but the drift was everywhere in the same direction and had similar consequences: cash payments replaced personal military service. True, the ruler would still turn towards his nobility to raise and lead his contingents, but they served at his pay. This had already occurred in England by the end of Edward I's reign (1307), and the last time the feudal levy as such was called out in that country was 1327. Thus the barons' obligation to perform feudal military service to the Crown came to an end. Instead the baron increasingly came to consider the land as his own property, subject to the payment to the Crown landlord of certain customary fees.

Unfortunately for the Crown, those fees had been fixed at a time when the cost of a knight's service was far lower than in the thirteenth and fourteenth centuries. The cost of waging war had risen sharply, partly because of the general price inflation which made castle-building and the like prodigiously dearer, but due also to the technical improvements in the equipment of a knight. Plate armour replaced mail, more remounts were required, and finally, even the horses themselves were protected by armour. So, although the cost of a knight rose threefold in the thirteenth century, the cash the king received to pay for his service remained at the original level.[5] The customary ex-feudal dues and commutations were completely inadequate. *N'impose qui ne veut* left only one way to get the additional finance (apart from expedients like pawning the crown jewels, borrowing from Lombard bankers, robbing the Templars, and pulling out the teeth of the Jews), and that was to *ask* for the money. Once a ruler had to do that, he came under the control of those he asked.

By the fourteenth century Western European societies had differentiated themselves out into a myriad of *universitates*, each with its own legal privileges, rights, and obligations: the magnates and the lesser nobility; the Church and, inside the Church, the regular as against the secular clergy, and among the former the multiplying orders of monks or mendicants; there were not only the chartered towns but the numerous guilds within them; there were the universities, and so on. These relatively defined bodies were thought of as parts of looser and wider categories. These have been called 'Estates' or 'Orders'. The German word for the latter is *stand*, and a powerful German school of historians have seen the fourteenth century as ushering in the *Standestaat*, that is to say, the state of Estates or Orders or corporations.

The most obvious of these was the Church; for it came under the control of one supreme pontiff and was regulated by its own highly methodized and complete legal code (the Canon law). The Church could, if asked, give amicable grants but was under orders to contest forced impositions. The nobility made another such Order. Its size and solidarity differed from one country to another. In England, for instance, the rule of primogeniture excluded the younger sons from the 'nobility', giving them the humbler status of 'gentles' or 'gentlemen'. In France, on the other hand, all the male offspring of a nobleman belonged to the noble Order. In any case, the greater nobles everywhere sought to distinguish themselves from the humbler ones. So in some cases, for instance in the Iberian lands, the nobles formed two distinct Estates and not one: the *nobles*, or noblemen and the *caballeros*, the lesser gentlemen.

In some countries the entire universe of non-clerical and non-noble groups was regarded as a composite Order of its own, a Third Estate.

---

[5] See, *inter multa alia*, S. Painter, *Studies in the History of the English Feudal Barony* (Johns Hopkins UP, Baltimore, 1943), 193–7, 44–5.

But in others, like Sweden, the richer peasantry were also distinguished as a separate Order. Certainly the most common form of organization was into the three Estates where the clergy formed the first Estate, the nobility the second, and the rest of society the third. England is a deviant case. Despite this, the German 'corporatist' school and its followers in other countries see the *standestaat* as a distinctive phase in the development of European political institutions, lasting for four centuries and unique to Western Europe. The dispute need not concern us here. The point to notice is that however we choose to view the development, it manifested the end of the man–man relationship of dependency which was the characteristic of feudalism, but did not replace it with the man–man relationship of equality that was the hallmark of liberalism. Instead it created dualism: a two-way relationship between corporation and the Crown, between the 'community of the realm' on the one side and the 'government' on the other.[6]

2. THE CLERICAL AND THE SECULAR LINEAGES OF REPRESENTATION

We have already[7] stressed that Church and state were not antithetical but symbiotic. The institutions of the one always intertwined with those of the other. The lineages of the assemblies derive from the feudal *concilia*—the secular lineage—but also from the clerical models, especially those of the newer religious Orders. (The Cistercians were founded in 1098, the Dominicans in 1206.)

The secular lineage need not detain us too long, for a great deal of what needs to be said has already been foreshadowed. Briefly, the representative assemblies of which we are talking are based on the narrower *concilia* of feudal magnates. They were the only politically significant class, and what they decided was decided for the whole realm. As military service was replaced by cash payments and the mounting cost of war had to be spread over wider sectors of the community, so those sectors had to be called in, alongside the magnates, to consent to these extraordinary exactions. The most conspicuous example was, of course, the towns. No matter where we turn in west and central Europe, we always find the towns as a component of the assemblies. In England another politically significant sector emerged, by no means common elsewhere: the counties or shires. These had become a

---

[6] The *standestaat* thesis is very vigorously promoted in G. Poggi, *The Development of the Modern State* (Hutchinson, London, 1978), ch. 3, and see the extensive and (mostly) German bibliography there cited at 157–9. See also A. R. Myers, *Parliaments and Estates in Europe* (Thames & Hudson, London, 1975); E. Lousse, *La Société d'ancien régime*, 2nd edn. (Editions Universitas, Louvain, 1952).

[7] See pp. 888–93 above.

genuine focus for a wide range of activities of the powerful and centralizing monarchy. All freemen were expected to attend the shire court, but it was natural that the numerous tasks undertaken—assessing and collecting taxes, for example—should become the preoccupation of a small knot of knights who were able and above all willing, even eager, to spend their time and energy on such matters. In England these people were called *buzones*. The shire court consisted of a knot of people who all knew one another very well, co-operated over long periods, and left day-to-day matters in the hands of these *buzones*. It was the most natural move in the world for kings who were short of money to invite this newly significant class to their assemblies. They were elected, but by what process we do not know. At all events they were regarded as 'standing for' the county community as a whole, by their colleagues on the one side and by the Crown on the other. In England, then, an important and for a long time more significant element than the burgesses consisted of the knights of the shire.

To sum up the entire process, irrespective of any particular country: in the thirteenth and fourteenth centuries the range of those who were to give aid, counsel, and consent to the Crown had widened from the circle of military magnates to 'proxies' of the new politically significant sectors.

It used to be not uncommon to attribute the extension of the assemblies' membership to the conscious application of the Roman law formula, which runs *Quod omnes tangit, ab omnibus approbetur* ('that which affects everyone should be approved by everyone'). This was a formula from Roman private law, but it was taken over into the Canon law of the Church and applied by the newer religious Orders. Some observers have traced a close parallelism between the patterns of representation in these Orders and in the state, and have concluded that the former was a conscious model for the latter.[8] However, it is more likely that the lay and the secular mutually influenced one another than that the representative principle in one was a simple counterfeit of the other.[9] What is certain is that a number of the elements of representative systems were given a sharper and more self-conscious definition in the Church and especially in the Cistercian and the Dominican Orders than was to be found in the earliest laic assemblies. The notion of election was pretty well coeval with the very origins of the Church hierarchy: the bishops were elected by their congregations. (St Ambrose of Milan, at the time a lay official in the Roman Empire was, it may be remembered, elected bishop on the insistent acclamation and pressure of the congrega-

---

[8] For England, Sir E. Barker, *The Dominican Order and Convocation* (OUP, Oxford, 1913). Generally, G. de Lagarde, 'Les Théories représentatives du XIV–XV siècle et l'église', 10th International Congress of the Historical Sciences, Études, XVIII (Louvain, 1958). For a radical criticism, see Marongiu, *Medieval Parliaments*, 33–41. [9] See ibid. 41.

tion.) After the Hildebrandine reforms, the electorate was confined to the clergy of the diocese (usually, however, a matter of nomination by the monarch or the pope). The pope himself, as Bishop of Rome, was elected by the chapter and the congregation of Rome, and it was precisely the presence of the lay electors that had allowed the great Italian feudal families to manipulate the proceedings. This is why in 1060 the laymen were expressly excluded and the popes were elected by the Chapter, later to be the College of Cardinals, through a strict procedure which in 1179 required a two-thirds majority. Note that this system of elections had been in being long before we have any idea at all of how the English knights of the shire were elected in the shire court.

But the most striking parallels (and antecedents for that matter) of the representative principle lie in two features of the Cistercian and the Dominican Orders, namely, a representative system from base to apex, and a range of criteria for arriving at decisions. For instance, the Dominicans were organized as follows: the friars of each convent elected their prior; a Chapter, consisting of the prior plus two other friars from each community, elected the provincial superior; and the superiors, plus two friars from each Provincial Chapter, made up the General Chapter. This structure, promulgated in 1220, was just a modified copy of the one brought into the Cistercian Order by its abbot general, St Stephen Harding, in 1109.

Since the entire internal stucture of such organizations was founded on election and deliberation, the members had to make specific rules about who were to be considered electors, and what kind of vote would be considered decisive. What seems to us the most obvious solution—majority decision—was long complicated by the Church belief that the decisive voice was to be that of the *maior et sanior pars*—'the greater and wiser part'—and all kinds of contested elections had to take place before the Church concluded that, by its very plurality of voices, the larger party was *ipso facto* the wiser one.[10] In the end four possible techniques could be followed. One of these was the *compromissum*—the compromise—but not quite in our sense. When and only when all the members of a chapter unanimously agreed to this method, they designated a number, which had to be uneven, of 'compromisers' and left the decision to them. The other three methods are self-explanatory. Moulin,[11] in Table 3.8.1, shows clearly how in every case, Church practice anteceded the secular.

The emergence and final shape of the assemblies derives, then, from the confluence of these two streams of development. At what date an assembly

---

[10] By Innocent IV (1245–54); see L. Moulin, 'Policy-making in the Religious Orders', *Government and Opposition*, 1: 1 (1965), 38.   [11] Ibid. 41.

TABLE 3.8.1 *Timing of first introduction of electoral decision-making formulae*

Techniques	In religious institutions	In civil institutions
Absolute majority	251	1143
Two-thirds majority	951	968
Secret ballot	1159	1217
'Compromise'	1049	1229

can be held to have become deliberative and determinative for the community, that is, a 'parliament', is moot, for all origins are obscure by their very nature. The regularity of the meetings fulfils one criterion; the fixing of the forms and modes of representation another; and their permanent insertion into the governmental structure as the intermediary between the government and the community fulfils a third. Also, there comes a point in time (differing from one country to another) when these assemblies become self-conscious of their role, and this forms a fourth criterion: their members act in a legally defined coherence, accept that they are politically responsible, and above all, that they embody the community as a whole, that is to say, they 'represent' it. Such an assembly or parliament is qualitatively different from the *ad hoc concilia* that had preceded it. It is a quite new institution; one which incorporates the elements of representation, collaboration, and consent.

3. THE MEANING OF 'REPRESENTATION'

Political scientists do not all agree on the meaning of 'representation'. I propose to select the most typical views and to ask how far each of these definitions of 'representation' is applicable to medieval parliaments (for the meanings of the term continued to proliferate long after the Middle Ages, and indeed, does so up to the present day).[12]

One view is that a representative is someone who is authorized to act for others who themselves are responsible for that action as though they had done it. One possible corollary to this view is that anybody performing functions for such others is their representative. This is the sense in which we can think of a military dictator as his country's representative; equally the emperor of China was the representative of the Chinese people. Clearly, this view of 'representation' does not require the representative to be elected; anyone performing a function on behalf of a group is a representative of

---

[12] In what follows I have relied almost entirely on the admirable analysis of Hannah Pitkin in her *The Concept of Representation* (University of California Press, Berkeley and Los Angeles, 1967).

that group. In this sense medieval parliaments were all representative. But the sense is fairly trivial.

Therefore another school requires that the representative must also have to answer to the group for what he has done ; this is the 'accountability' school. We shall see that this was true of some medieval parliamentary representatives but not true of others. The answer turns on whether they were regarded as delegates with restricted mandates from their constituents or not. We shall return to this important distinction.

Together both the 'authorization' and the 'accountability' schools can be regarded as 'formalistic'. They concentrate their definition on whether the representative acts *after* authorization, or whether he acts *before* being held to account, but neither tells us what a representative is like. Here enter what Pitkin calls the 'descriptive' schools. They are not concerned with the representative being a person or group that *acts* for others, so much as one that in some sense *stands for* them. What lurks here is the notion of some similarity between the representative and the represented. In certain respects—the ones that contemporaries consider to be the only important ones—the representative is held to be typical of, identical with, or at least similar to the represented. To the extent that this is believed, that person or (much more realistically) that group is regarded as a substitute for the entire relevant community. In our own day this view is linked up with ideas of democratic election, and attaining an isomorphism by this means. Outside the city-republics this view was not widely held in the Middle Ages. On the contrary, in so far as there was conscious theorizing about the nature and role of parliaments (and there was singularly little) these bodies were regarded as a substitute for the meeting-together of everyone in the country because the real thing was clearly impossible. There was absolutely no demand for an accurate correspondence between the assembly and the community as a whole nor (and here it differed from the political theory of citizenship in the city-republics) any demand that every individual must participate in the framing and execution of policies. It was not, in short, a democratic doctrine at all. But that the assembly or parliament was a microcosm of community of the realm is the most powerful view we encounter in the Middle Ages.[13] There is a further way in which the Middle Ages visualized these parliaments, which is somewhat akin to the preceding, and that is as a *symbol*; in this case as personifying the community of the realm.

The shortcoming of such views is that they see representation as some kind of mirroring of something else, but have no room for any concept of

---

[13] For a number of examples, in Spain and Italy, see Marongiu, *Medieval Parliaments*, 223–6.

representation as entailing in some degree the notion of *agency*; that is to say, acting so as to look after the interests of the represented. But once parliaments realized their power to withhold or modify the grant of tax, the members did indeed begin to carry their communities' petitions and grievances to the king for redress. This is a late development, not found till the later fourteenth century in England. The parliaments were, then, to a certain extent agencies; they acted for the community as a factor or actor acts for others. To a certain extent they were substitutes: vicars or deputies for the larger community. Equally they could be regarded as ambassadors of the local community. All these notions reflect contemporary ideas of the role and nature of these assemblies.

Such shades of meaning are reflected in the etymology and the changing usage of 'representation'. In classical Latin *repraesentare* meant to 'make present', or 'make manifest' some *inanimate* object, certainly never the *populus*. In the thirteenth and fourteenth centuries, however, the Church was writing that the pope and the cardinals 'represented' Christ and the Apostles; and they did not mean by this that they were the delegates or agents of Christ, but that somehow they embodied and personified them. From there it was a step to applying the verb to collectivities: a community was not a 'natural person' but it was a *persona*, and so it was possible to talk of a *persona repraesentata*. This was acknowledgedly fictive—not a real person but one by representation only—or, in the Latin, *persona non vera sed repraesentata*.[14] Then, from the end of the thirteenth century, the jurists started to use the word for a magistrate or attorney acting for his community and, though not widespread at first, this meaning gained currency throughout the fourteenth century.

In English, too, there is a steady broadening of meaning from the fourteenth to the seventeenth century that runs somewhat parallel to the Latin. The word 'represent' appears in the fourteenth century, when it can mean either to bring somebody into the presence of another, or to symbolize something other. In the next century it is found with the additional meaning of 'to portray or delineate', even 'to produce' a play. Here the word is used to convey the idea of an image, a likeness of something else. It is in the next century that the modern 'political' usage of the word begins to appear. The *OED* gives 1509 as the date when it could mean: 'to act or take the place of (another) in some respect or for some purpose; to be a substitute in some capacity for (a person or body); to act for (another) by a deputed right.' But not until 1595 does one find an instance of the word

---

[14] Pitkin, *Concept of Representation*, 242.

meaning specifically 'to act for someone as his authorized agent or deputy'.[15]

These etymologies and changing usages do not address certain distinctions which are vital to understanding the differences between the various parliaments in Western Europe. One of these is whether the representative, in the latest senses covered above, had to be elected or not. Some 'representative' assemblies consisted of members who were nominated rather than elected. We shall find other examples later, but for the moment it is enough to point to an English Writ of Summons to a shire court in 1231. It tells the sheriff of Yorkshire to *summon* the reeve and four responsible men from each vill and twelve responsible burgesses from each borough.[16] 'If in the early days, the king or the magnates occasionally nominated people to speak for their shires, the nominees would not necessarily seem to be any the less representative—unless of course conflict had already created distrust and polarized ideas of eligibility.'[17]

Another question is whether the parliaments' members were plenipotentiaries or delegates with a limited mandate. The practice throughout Europe varied widely.[18] Confining ourselves, then, to these, one important distinction between them is whether they were representative of the entire realm or, rather, of historic provinces or even individual towns. Kings found it hard to achieve the former. The English Parliament is taken as a prime example of an assembly which represented the entire realm, but it is worth noting that English kings did not insist on the representation of Wales, Cheshire, or Durham before the sixteenth century, while the representation of Ireland or the French possessions in the English Parliament was not even dreamed of. These omissions reflect the exigencies of distance, sparse communication, and the intense particularism of the times. These factors are an important reason for the ineffectuality of the French Estates-General. These same reasons help to explain why so many assemblies had only limited mandates, unlike the (highly exceptional) plenipotentiary mandate of the English Parliament.[19]

Again, the structure of the assemblies could differ greatly. The two chambers of the English Parliament were somewhat exceptional. More common was a meeting of three Estates, together or separately, but there were cases where the Estates numbered four or more (Sweden, for instance);

---

[15] Pitkin, 243–8.

[16] Spufford, *Origins of the English Parliament*, 34; Marongiu, *Medieval Parliaments*, 52, para. 2.

[17] Reynolds, *Kingdoms and Communities*, 310, 318.

[18] Marongiu, *Medieval Parliaments*, 228–32, gives many examples. Spufford, *Origins of the English Parliament*, 10. Myers, *Parliaments and Estates*, 36–46. [19] Myers, 147–8.

in Poland the towns were usually excluded and the entire body consisted eventually of noblemen.

The powers of these assemblies *vis-à-vis* the monarch also differed greatly, as well as fluctuating over time. Generally speaking, the weaker the monarch (either because his title was defective, or because he needed money badly, and so forth) the stronger the power of the assembly. Such was the situation of the German *Landtage*, and in Poland; whereas the very reverse was true in England until the Lancastrians. Also, the weaker the towns—as in Poland—the stronger the nobility; the reverse was true in Aragon, where the towns were at first much more powerful than the nobles.

4. THE CHARACTERISTICS OF ASSEMBLIES

Assemblies rarely resembled each other in all major respects. Among these were geographical jurisdiction; structure; limited or unlimited mandate; taxing power, legislative power, consultative power, judicial power. By reviewing these one after another for some ten assemblies, we can obtain an impression of the wide variety of assemblies in general.

4.1. *Geographical Jurisdiction*

In Leon-Castile the assembly represented the entire realm. Not so in neighbouring Aragon, where, very much to the contrary, there were three assemblies—for Aragon, for Catalonia, and for Valencia. France (reviewed in more detail below) had one Estate for the Langue d'öil and one for the Langue d'oc, and it also had a large number of Provincial Estates which were destined to be more important than the General Estates and to last longer. In the Holy Roman Empire there was indeed a weak and ephemeral Imperial Diet, but the effective representative bodies were those in the principalities, the *landtage*. The Parliament of England, famously representing the entire 'community of the realm', will be discussed below. Two relative latecomers to the list of assemblies were the Swedish *Riksdag* and the Polish *Sejm*. The former represented the entire country from 1435 onwards. In Poland the *Sejm* also represented the whole country, but this was covered also by a number of local *sejmiki*.

4.2. *Structure*

In Leon-Castile the assembly was composed of three Estates—the clergy, the nobles, and the towns. The same was true in Catalonia and Valencia but not in Aragon. There the noble class had split into the nobles and the *caballeros*, so that the assembly comprised four Estates. The French Estates, whether General or Provincial, all comprised the three Orders. The same was true of many of the German *Landtage*, but in some cases, for instance Friesland, the peasants also participated. The composition of England's two chambers, Lords and Commons, is highly peculiar. In Sweden the *Riksdag* contained four Estates—the peasants being the fourth—and at one time even the miners participated as a fifth. The Polish *Sejm* was for a long time made up of the three Estates of clergy, nobility, and a tiny few of the towns, but the *sejmiki* consisted only of the nobles. The evolution of the central *Sejm* into a body that consisted solely of noblemen is described below.

4.3. *Limited or Unlimited Mandates*

In the Iberian assemblies it was common form for the burgesses to be bound by specific, highly limited mandates. The same tended to be true of members of the Third Estate in the French Estates-General. Town influence and the nature of their mandates varied in the German *Landtage*, towns being weak in the north-east and strong in the south-west. In England, as we have seen, burgesses came with full authority to bind their communities.

4.4. *Powers*

4.4.1. EXTRAORDINARY TAXATION

All save one of the assemblies mentioned here had acquired control over extraordinary taxation and this was, of course, the source of their other acquired powers. The French Estates-General, however, are an exception. Their earliest efforts to control taxation (under Étienne Marcel in 1355–8) were short-lived, and in the second half of the fifteenth century the Crown managed to establish fiscal absolutism tempered by the need to negotiate specific sums with the Provincial Estates and the towns. Poland is exceptional in that the *Sejm* successfully insisted that its consent was necessary for taxation and for the raising of an army also; although some of the German *Landtage* were able to put a ceiling on the number of troops raised.

4.4.2. PETITIONING AND LEGISLATING

Pretty well any assembly that had acquired financial control could expect to be able to petition the Crown with some prospects of success and in some cases, like the English and the Polish, to prevent the government from legislating without its consent. Here again the great exception is the French Estates-General, which had lost any such powers it had ever possessed by the fifteenth century.

4.4.3. CONSULTATIVE POWERS

The French Estates-General was most frequently used to evoke shows of loyalty and support for the Crown in various emergencies, but by the end of the fifteenth century were distinctly subordinate to the Crown in peace, war, and administration in a way that the Iberian assemblies were most decidely not. These had acquired the last word on such matters. In Germany one important power acquired by the *Landtage* was ratifying changes in the dynasty, which were frequent. In Poland the *Sejm* actually elected the king, and it was the Swedish *Riksdag* which elected Vasa as king in 1523. The English Parliament was involved in two depositions of reigning monarchs in the fourteenth century; the Lancastrian dynasty held the throne by what in effect was a parliamentary title, and it was during this period that the Parliament was most effectual *vis-à-vis* the Crown, exerting a precocious influence.

4.4.4. JUDICIAL POWERS

Some assemblies were the highest courts in the land whereas others had no judicial powers. The English Parliament was the High Court of Parliament and had successfully asserted this status since the early fourteenth century. In France, just the opposite: the Estates, whether General or Provincial, had no judicial powers whatsoever. These were a matter for the specialized lawcourts known as the *parlements*. The Assembly of Leon–Castile had no judicial powers, while that of Aragon did. The Polish *Sejm* also acted as a high court.

4.5. *Some Characteristic Strengths or Weaknesses*

In all cases the power of the assemblies *vis-à-vis* the Crown tended to fluctuate over time—now stronger, now weaker—but in the longer term one can discern trends one way or the other. Thus in Leon–Castile the Cortes, so very dominant at first, became progressively weaker: its grant of taxation had never been made dependent on the redress of grievances, the powerful towns were disunited and in rivalry, their numbers were in any case declining, and the assembly met entirely at the royal pleasure. The French Estates-General also went into a decline. Since it was summoned most irregularly, at the royal pleasure, it never acquired significant powers for long. But the *Landtage* of Germany tended to become stronger because of the frequent changes of dynasty and the apparently perennial impoverishment of their princes. As for Poland, that was the strongest assembly of all and by the seventeenth century had reduced the power of the Crown to a mere cipher. The French, the English, and the Polish cases will illustrate some of these points.

5. THREE CONTRASTING REPRESENTATIVE ASSEMBLIES

5.1. *The Parliament of England*

Even before Parliament emerged, the political process had consisted of a tense dialogue between the Crown and its close advisers on the one side and a magnate opposition on the other, and it always retained this character. However, the 'outer circle', whether it consisted of the magnates or, later, more humble subjects, did not seek to weaken the powers of the Crown but to control them. What it wanted was a strong centralized administration, but under its own control and, roughly, this is what it got until the Tudors in 1485. This dialogue between the king and his subjects began to be called a *parliamentum* from about the middle of the thirteenth century.

These subjects, as we have already hinted above, expanded from the magnates of the realm to include humbler elements. The first attested *parliamentum* when burgesses were convened alongside the knights of the shire is de Montfort's Parliament of 1265; but it is not until the so-called 'Model' Parliament of 1295 that this became standard practice. Yet parliaments or dialogues with specialized groups, such as the baronage or the merchants, continued to be convened for many decades after this date. By the middle of the century, however, they had died out, leaving only Parliament.

This representative body—*the King-in-Parliament*—had by 1322 established itself as the supreme judicial and legislative body in the kingdom. It was the High Court of Parliament. As early as 1310 the 'Lords Ordainers'—the very title indicates their magnate status—had their reform measures confirmed in the Parliament (baronial consent to royal appointments, to declarations of war, to the departure of the king from his kingdom). When the king defeated his magnate enemies in 1322, it was to a Parliament that he turned to repeal the ordinances. When he was pulled down again by his adulterous wife and her lover, Mortimer, it was to Parliament that these two turned to demand the abdication of Edward II in favour of his son. Thus the Westminster Parliament of 1327 established the precedent that the Parliament could dispose of the succession. The stormy reign of Richard II (1377–99) paralleled the events of 1307–27. Opposing Richard's pretensions for personal rule, the magnates (called the 'Lords Appellant') in 1388 secured the impeachment (see below) and condemnation of five of the king's party. Some ten years later, in a Parliament packed by his own supporters, Richard secured the execution of three of the Lords Appellant. But the very next year the duke of Lancaster and his party of magnates captured Richard and made him abdicate. (He was murdered in prison shortly afterwards.) The act of abdication did not take place in the Parliament for this was constitutionally impossible—Parliament was the king's own court and it could not try him. What it could and did do was to ratify the act of abdication, confer royal powers on the future Henry IV, and later, recognize the right of his heirs to the throne. In short, by its majestic authority it had legalized the change of dynasty and the succession to the throne. In all these events the magnates had masterminded its actions, it is true. But they would not have bothered had not Parliament been recognized as the supreme legal authority in the kingdom.

In 1307 there was no way of knowing how the various component members of the Parliament would work together. The lines along which Parliament split into two Chambers were unique. Apart from the prelates, the clerical element disappeared. The prelates continued to come as barons, that is, lords spiritual, alongside the magnates, who were the lords temporal. All these were summoned by individual writ. In 1307 there was no fixed rule determining which of the Crown's tenants-in-chief were to receive these writs but in the next half-century certain families came to receive them as a matter of course. By mid-century the lords spiritual and temporal had attained a certain fixity and sat together.

The issue now was whether, in their capacity as nobles, the knights would sit alongside them. In fact they did not. As early as 1325 the knights and burgesses are found presenting common petitions, though this implies only co-operation, not joint sesssions. But in the Roll of 1366 we find the prelates and magnates assigned to the White Chamber and the knights and burgesses together, as the Commons, to the Painted Chamber. When in 1377 the Commons elected a speaker to present their views, we can consider the separation into the House of Lords and the House of Commons as accomplished.

The powers of this body went very wide—and might be summed up as the supreme determination of civil and criminal cases, the discussion of affairs of state, grants of taxation, the audience of petitions and this petitioning process, and the redress of grievances, often ending in new legislation. In matters of high policy the Lords were the body that decided; the Commons never dared, even had it ever wanted, to meddle with such affairs. The judicial powers, also mostly exercised by the Lords, were of the highest political importance because of the device of impeachment. Towards the close of the century this was a principal method of punishing unpopular ministers and, by the same token, controlling their successors. The Commons made great advances in the fourteenth and fifteenth centuries in respect to its own privileges against capricious pressures by the Crown, to its central role in assenting to taxes and to all that ensued from this; but throughout the entire period it could be and was utilized as a compliant tool by the magnates whenever high affairs of state, peace and war, the change of dynasty, or the reward and punishment of the kings' councillors were at stake.

In matters of taxation, however, the Lords allowed the Commons to make the running, acquiescing in the grants they had made. Nobody is quite sure as to their motives but one might guess that they thought it unlikely that the Commons would offer more than they themselves would tolerate and could be expected in fact to offer something much less. At all events, by the end of the century all taxes required a grant by Parliament, and this included imposts on wool, and tonnage and poundage, that is, indirect as well as the direct taxes. From time to time the Commons was even able to insist on the appropriation of the money for a named purpose and likewise it made (ineffectual) attempts to have the accounts audited. What was quite clear by the fifteenth century was that the Crown would get no money—apart from the shrinking customary feudal dues and the rentals from the royal demesne—unless it could persuade the knights and the burgesses. Sensing this, the Commons began to hold up the grant of money until the very end of the session to pressurize the Crown into granting redress for the grievances expounded in their petitions. In this way the Commons became involved in the business of legislation. Earlier in the century the power to legislate was not exclusive to Parliament; ordinances were not sharply differentiated from statutes and either could be enacted by a transaction between the Crown and the affected group. But as the century moved on the statutes were made more and more often as the response to the petitions, and by 1351 an ordinance could obtain permanent effect only by explicit recognition by Parliament.

The fifteenth century opened the rule of the Lancastrians and, as these owed their title to Parliament, Henry IV and Henry V convened it regularly. The apparent prominence of the Commons during this period and the acquisition of its privileges against harassment, intimidation, or arrest by the Crown used to lead historians to think of this as a golden age of parliamentary government. It has been better described as a 'premature constitutionalism', for the magnates always dictated high policy. As they became the over-mighty subjects of Henry VI, and divided into the Lancastrian and Yorkist factions that contested the throne, so the intervals between the Parliaments became longer. When the Yorkist Edward IV acquired the throne he held only seven Parliaments. Richard III held only one and Henry VII only seven. The country had entered the Tudor era, when, not in England alone but all over Europe (except perhaps in Poland and some of the German states), the Crown was immensely strengthening itself at the expense of the representative assemblies.

5.2. *The Estates-General in France*

As we saw earlier, representative assemblies of one sort or another were convened by Louis IX in the thirteenth century; but they were *ad hoc* bodies consisting of the king and his councillors on the one hand and the relevant corporate bodies on the other. Philip the Fair (1285–1314), however, had occasion to convene representatives of the entire Langue d'öil and these are often reckoned as the first general Estates of France. The assemblies met as three sections or Chambers: the clergy as the first Estate, the nobility as the second Estate, and the remainder of the political class, which ranged from royal officials to representatives of towns, as the Third Estate. This was the most common pattern in Europe. One such Estates met in 1302, another in 1307. These were truly great occasions and they were deliberately meant to be so, because their purpose was not to haggle about grants of taxation (this had hitherto been arranged bilaterally between the Crown and the affected communities) but to show that in his policy the king had the entire French community behind him. The first such Estates was designed to ensure popular support for the king's struggle against the pretensions of Pope Boniface VIII; the second in 1307–8 was designed, again with success, to back up the king's monstrous destruction of the Knights-Templars. A third Estates, convened in 1314, was designed specifically to secure a great financial grant and, significantly, it broke up in discord between the nobles and the Third Estate. From time to time, in many of the infrequent and irregular conventions of the Estates-General betweeen this time and the middle of the fifteenth century, the assembly attempted to assert control over taxation, or at least over direct taxation, the *taille*. Fighting the English invaders, Charles VII (1422–61) felt entitled to raise taxation as and when he pleased. In 1440 he put down a nobiliar revolt (the *Praguerie*) which had raised the slogan of abolishing the royal *taille*. In 1442, when the noble Estate remonstrated against his pretensions, the King replied that he had the legal right to raise the *taille*: 'Et n'est besoin d'assembler les trois etats pour mettre sus lesdites tailles.' From 1451 he began to levy the *tailles* and *aides* systematically, without further reference to the Estates. When Charles VIII came to the throne in 1484 he found it expedient to bolster his accession with a show of popular support and consequently summoned an Estates. This too affirmed that the *taille* could not be levied without its consent. But once it had gone home its protest was totally ignored and the monarchy had become fiscally absolute. There would be two or three more Estates-General up to 1615, and after that none until the fateful one of 1789.

Few things have so confused the discussion of why this should have occurred than the example—consciously or unconsciously entertained—of the Parliament of England. The French Estates-General (if indeed this is the correct term to apply to the assemblies up to the undoubted Estates-General of 1484) were from their origin and in their relatively short and irregular career a different animal from the English Parliament. Much more frequently than in England, these grand assemblies were great national councils convened to give the king moral support and spread his propaganda in aid of some great issue. Again, while the English Parliament was regarded as early as 1322 as the sovereign lawcourt of the kingdom, the French Estates was never this. The supreme court, the *parlement*, was a different organ altogether and was institutionalized as such in 1345. Furthermore, the composition of the Estates-General was irregular and did not attain any fixity until the meeting in 1484. It was usual for the burgesses to come without power to bind their communities: they were to listen and report back. The entire notion of representation as entailing some persons having plenipotentiary powers to bind the absent was unpopular. Additionally, the three Estates were not necessarily all present together at an Estates-General: the most notable example was in the revolutionary sessions of 1335–9 (consequent on the disasters of the war with England) in which neither the clergy nor the nobility participated.

Furthermore, in so far as the Estates-General were money-granting assemblies (as on many occasions they were), they were neither the only such bodies nor the most important and authoritative. On the contrary, the Provincial Estates, and even more localized assemblies—together known as the *États-Particuliers*—had been, were, and would continue to be the ones that ultimately agreed or refused the tax, allocated it, and supervised its collection. This remained true even when the Estates-General itself authorized a tax; this was an authorization in principle and in advance but it was for the *États-Particuliers* to agree, and assist the administration.

Finally, the meetings of the large Estates-General, that is, the Estates of Langue d'öil and of Langue d'oc, were spasmodic. Only during the revolutionary years of 1335–8 did they establish a 'control' over the monarchy; and they did so in those years with such excesses that it discredited the attempt, so that the future Charles V found no difficulty in annulling its measures. Yet only at this period—neither before nor after—was the Estates-General 'a representative body with definite and recognizable attributes, and a deliberative power more or less accepted by public law.'[20] 'In fact [asserts this same author] the history of the French Estates is not so much the history of an institution as of single episodes and moments of history.'[21]

When one asks, however, why the French Estates acquired such different characteristics from the English Parliament, the answers lie in the way the French kingdom was built up, that is, by quite recent and rapid aggregation of disparate provinces, and in its increasingly caste-like *noblesse*. As to the first, it must be remembered that at that time France was the largest kingdom in Europe and England one of the small ones. But it was not distance and linguistic variety that inhibited attendance at the Estates-General so much as a widespread and deep *reluctance* to attend, and the reason for this was the intense particularism in France. This was not due to its size but to the very *recency* of what has been described as 'a precarious authority' of the Crown over a realm divided by these geographical, ethnographic, and linguistic barriers. 'Regional economy, law, custom, politics and sentiment had had time to harden under regional rulers effectively independent of the Crown.'[22]

But just as the kingdom was divided 'vertically' so it was stratified 'horizontally'. By the end of the fifteenth century the French nobility had secured exemption from the most onerous of the taxes, and once this was so they were without the strong motive for resisting the Crown that obtained throughout all classes in English society. As to the Third Estate, it was completely overshadowed by the prestige and power of the nobility which, by this time, had frozen into a caste-like legal category unbridgeably separated from even the richest of the bourgeois. And in any event this Third Estate was itself only a small group of persons comprising well-to-do burgesses and numbers of royal officials, which was in no way recognized as 'representative' of the wider community.

So it was that the 1439 Estates was the last from which Charles VII demanded assent to the *taille*. Thenceforward he levied it on his own authority. True, the Estate of the nobles protested but the other two Estates did not. The Estates of Langue d'oc continued to be convened in the south, but covered so relatively small an area that it increasingly took on the form of a purely local assembly. In the great fiefs, however, the princes continued to convene their own Estates for they, like the Crown, needed gifts, *aides*, and other taxes for their own private purposes. As and when these fiefs fell in to the Crown—mostly during the reign of Louis XI—the king, in order to ease the transition, allowed them to retain their Estates. In this way

[20] Marongiu, *Medieval Parliaments*, 100.   [21] Ibid. 103.
[22] P. S. Lewis, *The Recovery of France in the Fifteenth Century* (Macmillan, London, 1971), 302, 303.

Dauphiné, Burgundy, Artois, Provence, and (later) Brittany became the so-called *pays d'état* which negotiated taxation with the king's representative (as did Normandy) while the Langue d'öil became the *pays d'élection*, that is, where the taxes were struck directly by the king's own officers, the *élus*.

5.3. *The Polish* Sejm

The *Sejm* forms a most striking contrast to its English and French counterparts. In England the system settled down into a dialogue and counterpoint between a centralizing executive and a representative assembly. In France the monarchy gobbled up the Estates-General. But in Poland precisely the reverse occurred. The *Sejm* gobbled up the monarchy.

Though consultation has a long history in Poland, a central representative *Sejm* did not meet until 1493. A number of basic characteristics help explain this. The first, perhaps, is the geography: a flat plain exposed on all sides to aggressive and formidable enemies, a land of vast distances, sparse communications, and comparatively feeble urbanization. The earliest Polish kingdoms of the eleventh century were a patchwork of tribal divisions and regional loyalties, run by their local magnates, so that it was on the basis of an intense particularism that consultation and ultimately representation arrived. This particularism was aggravated in early times by the practice of dividing the kingdom between the royal heirs, by the emergence of prince-bishops (like those of Germany), and later, by the efforts of the towns to acquire autonomy like those further west. Threatened by such developments, the magnate turned to the lesser gentry, the squireens, for support. By the fourteenth century they talk of a *communitas nobilium* embracing all noblemen, great and small; the *szlachta*. A central feature of Poland's subsequent history is the juridical equality of every member, however humble, of this noble class, and the constitutional history of Poland is, in effect, its biography.

Poland never knew feudalism (although knighthood, with its responsibilities, which was imported in the twelfth and thirteenth centuries certainly helped to cement the relationship between the Crown and the noblemen), and it was not from a feudal tradition that the practice of representation developed. When Vladislaw I and Casimir the Great had reunited the various provinces from 1320 onward, the organization of the kingdom was still primitive. The former Palatinates retained their identity as provinces. Each was in the hands of a *starosta*, a governor, which office was to be the most important branch of the executive for the next 470 years. Such posts were always held by the local potentate. Each province was in its turn divided into castellanies. The king ruled with the support and advice of his privy council. It consisted of his choice of the influential magnates, most of them his provincial governors, bishops, and castellans. Loyalty was a personal matter. It was somewhat strengthened when knighthood was introduced, but these nobles were intensely rebellious and the first of the famous Confederations of Nobles, which were so often destined to challenge the Crown, dates from 1325–6.

The development of the powers of the *Sejm* falls into three phases. The first is when the assembled nobles act as a *limitation* on the Crown; the second when they move into *partnership* with it; and the third where they take *control* of it.

The first phase began with the death of Casimir the Great in 1370. He was succeeded by his son-in-law, Louis of Anjou, the king of Hungary, who had no male heir. So, in return for a promise that the Crown should be entailed on his daughter, Louis granted the *szlachta* the Pact of Koszyci. This confirmed their privileges, limited their taxes to 2 groschen per hide of land, and restricted all offices to them. The monarchy was now a limited one: the king could and did act on his own initiative, but only if his actions did not infringe the liberties granted in the Pact.

The second stage, where the *szlachta* became active co-participants with the Crown, opened when Louis died. He left two daughters and the *szlachta* decided to take as their queen the younger one, Jadwiga, instead of the elder one, Maria of Hungary. This implicitly asserted that the monarchy was elective, albeit in one family. But the accession of Queen Jadwiga was even more momentous in that she was married off to the great (and still pagan) Duke Jagiello of Lithuania, a vast, sprawling, inchoate kingdom to Poland's east which stretched from the Baltic down into the Ukraine. The result was a personal union of the two lands, making them jointly a great power.

So began the great Jagiellon dynasty. It was during its span that the *szlachta* became the partners of the Crown. Whereas the uncertainty of the succession had proved to be the first weakness of the monarchy, the second was the familiar one of needing money to make war. For the traditional basis of the Polish war effort—the general *insurrectio*—was obsolete. Like its fellows throughout Europe, the Crown now needed paid soldiers. It was by exploiting both of these two weaknesses that the *szlachta* moved from a blocking role to that of partnership. Jagiello (as Vladislaw V of Poland) began regular meetings of an expanded council or *Sejm*: officials of noble birth (prelates, governors, and castellans), other nobility, representatives of the cathedral chapters, and—the only non-nobles there—some representatives of the towns. In 1404, in search of extra money, he deputed members of this council to meet with the *szlachta* of each of Poland's districts. These bodies slowly became more regular and permanent, as *sejmiki*—little *Sejms*, or, as some western historians call them, the Dietines. In 1454 the Charter of Cerekwice reaffirmed the privileges of the *szlachta* and undertook to raise no new taxes nor to call out military levies without the consent of these *sejmiki*, which were composed entirely of nobles and now became standing bodies.

In 1493 there existed a completely organized political structure. There was a central *Sejm*, consisting of the former royal council and a lower chamber made up of elected representatives of the *sejmiki*. The central *Sejm* worked towards the provincial *Sejms* and the even more local *sejmiki*. There were thirty-seven of these in Poland and twelve in Lithuania. They were not so much administrative as parliamentary; that is to say, their chief task was to elect. Pre-*Sejm* sessions were convened to elect paid representatives and to mandate them strictly on the items of the agenda (which had been ciriculated to them already). The representatives of the *sejmiki* assembled in the provincial *Sejms* (six in number) to concert their policy for the *Sejm* itself. Once this had disbanded, these same representatives reported back to their *sejmiki*, which then took all the necessary administrative steps, such as assenting to a tax and arranging its collection. Thus, the national *Sejm* itself (in fact there were two, one for Poland and one for Lithuania until the Union of Lublin, 1569) consisted of two Chambers. An Upper House, the Senate, was the direct descendant of the former privy council and made up of the Catholic prelates, the provincial governors, the castellans, the Crown marshall, the chancellor, vice-chancellor, and the treasurer. In 1529 all these numbered eighty-seven; in 1569, after the union of Lublin, 140. All were mighty magnates. The Lower House, the Chamber of Deputies, was also composed of noblemen, except for representatives of Cracow the then-capital and, after the Union, of Vilna too; but they had no vote. (It should not be inferred from this that the towns were voiceless. In matters of taxation the Crown consulted them separately.) In principle every one of the 150,000 noblemen, many of them as poor as some of their peasants, was entitled to attend this House; and indeed, it was because time and expense kept them away that the system of election was introduced. The size of the Chamber of Deputies grew steadily, from forty-five members in 1504 to 158 in 1570.

From this time on the power of the *szlachta* never ceased to increase. This now-ruling class was by no means small. Estimates of its ratio to the population range from 8 to 12 per cent, much higher than in England and France where only some 2 or 3 per cent of the population were reckoned noble. Indeed, they formed a ruling stratum about as wide as the active citizens of Florence and much wider than the noble class of Venice.[23]

[23] See pp. 983, 1016 above.

With its now-exclusive command of the legislature, the *szlachta* quickly proceeded to strangle the towns and enserf the peasantry. As to the former, by 1600 their representation in the *Sejm* had disappeared, they had lost their autonomy, and townsmen were (since 1496) forbidden to acquire land; so, outside the towns all proprietors were noblemen.

These measures made the *szlachta* enormously prosperous in the sixteenth century and this new-found wealth was the foundation for the brilliant Polish Renaissance. For the enserfment enabled the large landowners to go over to commercial farming and there was a vast market in the west for Poland's grain and other agricultural products. By now Poland was the second largest state in Europe and the wealthiest of all countries in Eastern Europe. She was enjoying her golden age. In 1505 the ordinance *Nihil Novi* confirmed all the privileges of the *szlachta* and established the principle that new laws could be made only in the *Sejm*. In 1538 Sigismund I promised never to infringe the existing laws nor issue new ones *sua sponte*. There was by now a conscious recognition that the government consisted of a condominium of the king, the Senate, and the Chamber of Deputies, both of these latter being exclusively noble. And indeed in the Union of Lublin of 1569, which created one single state out of Poland and Lithuania, this was formally styled the *Rzeczpospolita Polska*—the *Republic* of Poland! It should be remembered that at that moment the only great extant republic was Venice. The affinities between what the Polish nobility had achieved against their kings and what the Venetian nobility had achieved against their doges are compelling—whether or not they were so seen at that time.

In 1572 the Jagiellon dynasty died out. The throne was vacant. It had always been thought of as elective, albeit the elections had been confined to the dynasty. Now the elective principle came to its full flower: who was to succeed, and who elect, and how? This was the moment of truth for the *szlachta* and with it Poland passed into its third phase, the absolute dominion of the *Sejm*. Candidates came forward from many realms. In 1573 40,000 noblemen gathered together and elected Henry of Anjou as their new king. This wretched creature abandoned his new kingdom only a few months later to become the king of France as Henry III; but not before he had conceded to the *szlachta* the Henrician Articles which sealed the doom of the executive power. These Articles confirmed that the throne was elective, and henceforth every election became an auction from which the *szlachta* extracted new concessions. The Crown was forbidden to dismiss its officials—all noblemen, of course. It was not empowered to enlarge the diminutive army of 3,000 men. It had to convoke the *Sejm* every two years and the latter's consent was necessary for all important decisions. No native

Polish dynasty was ever to rule the kingdom again. Instead, it was presided over by a succession of kings drawn from all over Europe, even if occasionally from Poland itself. A king could not even rely on his own demesne as a counterpoise against the greater magnates; many of these possessed estates, notably in the Ukraine, that were as large as his and maintained private armies that equalled his in size. The kingdom had become, effectively, a nobiliar republic with a royal figurehead.

The middle of the seventeenth century saw a gradual decline in prosperity, and then a catastrophe when the country was simultaneously overrun by Russians, Swedes, Prussians, and Cossacks while the peasants rose in a *jacquerie* against their landlords. The devastation wiped out more than a third of the population. Yet it is precisely then, in 1652, that we hear of the *szlachta's* final act of politicide—the *liberum veto*. By an extension of the notion that all nobles were juridically equal, it was maintained that every single member of the *Sejm* must concur for any decision to be valid. In other words, one nobleman, by crying out 'I object', could not only veto the proposition before the legislature but, *ipso facto*, bring about its dissolution. From then onwards it was used frequently; and naturally, the power of one petty nobleman to paralyse the entire business of the state brought its own nemesis. The magnates were not going to have their carefully concocted plans disrupted in this way. They began to form clienteles among the gentry, so that soon the entire country was dominated by some thirty great magnate families. At the same time foreign powers realized how easy it had become to intervene in the election of a new king in Poland, or to alter its foreign policy. From now on vetoes were bought and sold.

Unsurprisingly, therefore, Poland was defenceless against her powerful neighbours: Russia to the east, Prussia to the west, Austria to the South. In 1772 they moved in concert and hacked three slices, one apiece, off the defenceless royal republic. At last the alarm sounded. The *Sejm* appointed a Council of Thirty-Six to advise the king but did little to restore a central executive power. In 1791—two years, be it noticed, after the French Revolution—a patriot party, along with the king, terrified of further invasion, persuaded the *Sejm* after long, long last to accept a hereditary monarchy, a strong executive vested in its hands, the renunciation of aristocratic privilege, and the end to the *liberum veto*. The interesting thing about this catalogue is that (apart from French aristocratic privileges) England and France had never lacked any one of these from their very beginnings.

6. THE FATE OF THE REPRESENTATIVE PRINCIPLE

Let us repeat that the discovery of the principle of representation in medieval Western Europe was only the necessary and in no way the sufficient condition for 'representative government' as we understand this today. Today the notion of a representative assembly is bound up with two, logically quite separate notions: one, that it be elected, and the other that the executive be responsible towards it. We have already seen that in the Middle Ages election was not a necessary concomitant of representative assemblies. With the exception of Poland, the executive was never responsible to them either. On the contrary, until the eighteenth century, in Great Britain and subsequently France, the prevalent pattern was one where a free-standing executive is *balanced* by the elected and representative legislature. This pattern is evident even in the American Constitution of 1787 in so far as the president is elected by an entirely different constituency from that of the Congress and cannot be removed by it except by impeachment.

Now the parliaments or Estates of many of the more important countries of Europe were extinguished in the seventeenth century, so that some Anglocentric historians have assumed that only the English, later British, parliament remained to carry forward the theme of representative government. But parliaments and Estates did in fact survive in many parts of Europe; we have seen how they did so in Poland and the same would be true of Hungary, of many of the German statelets (particularly in the south), and in Sweden also, as well as in England. What occurred in the eighteenth and early nineteenth centuries was a *general revival* of the representative assembly. But here, the Anglocentric vision does contain a certain truth. For it was not via Sweden or Bavaria or Wurtemburg or Poland (above all not via Poland) that the revival took place. It took place via the English example and was based, directly or indirectly, on its model. The English Parliament had challenged and then defeated the throne in the seventeenth century and by the eighteenth had established a balanced constitution in which the executive was held in check by an elected Parliament. The fact that the electoral system had become highly unrepresentative and could be corrupted by the Crown or its ministers is not to the point; the system was oligarchic, but it was not by any means wholly unrepresentative of the opinions of the politically significant classes.

The initial democratization and the enhanced representativeness of the assembly was due to the English constitution being transplanted to America and, by default, adapted to the new circumstances of the thirteen confederated colonies once their common link with the English Crown had been broken. The American franchise was not widely democratic till around the middle of the nineteenth century, but the constitutional structure was certainly elective from the outset. What is more, the Congress was bicameral. Although its Upper House was not composed on the same basis as the British House of Lords, it *was* bicameral and not tri- or quadricameral. And finally, the executive, even if not removable by the elected legislature, was accountable to and checked by it. This adaptation of the English constitution was highly idiosyncratic and not destined to export itself widely save in a corrupt and distorted form to Latin America.

In the rest of the world the development of the representative system of government took place via the contagion of England in the Continent of Europe and the subsequent contagion of Europe in the rest of the world. The first plausible imitation was the French 1789 constitution (though this rejected a second chamber, as most of its subsequent revolutionary constitutions did not). The next batch of imitations occurred after 1812 and then with the defeat of Napoleon, when Sweden, the Netherlands, France, and Spain adopted their own varieties of the constitution of victorious England. Thence the imitation spread through Italy, Central Europe, and the Balkans and from there into the wider world, so that today it is regarded as the very norm of the modern state. It is in this respect that the Anglocentrism which sees England as 'the Mother of Parliaments' has stated a great truth. But this grand future for English parliamentarism was not due to its superior techniques or wisdom in medieval times compared to very many of the *cortes*, or *parlamenti*, or the *Riksdag* and the like. Its peculiar formation, its survival and supremacy over the executive and then, by historical accident, its export to the thirteen American colonies were, none of them, foreordained. Very much the reverse. All that we can say here is that the very basis from which the development took place and was universalized was based on a notion exclusive to Western and Catholic Europe in the Middle Ages— the principle of representation.

Bibliography

ACTON, J. E. E., Lord, 'The History of Freedom in Antiquity', in *Essays in the Liberal Interpretation of History*, with an introduction by W. H. McNeill (University of Chicago Press, Chicago, 1967), 243–70.

ADAMS, G. B., 'Feudalism', *Encyclopaedia Britannica* (11th edn., 1910), x. 297–302.

ARBERRY, A. J., *The Koran Interpreted* (Oxford University Press, Oxford, 1964).

ARDANT, G., *Histoire de l'impôt* (Fayard, Paris, 1971).

ASHTOR, E., *A Social and Economic History of the Near East in the Middle Ages* (Collins, London, 1976).

AYALON, D., *Studies on the Mamluks of Egypt (1250–1517)* (Variorum Reprints, London, 1975).

BACKHOUSE, E., and BLAND, J. O. P., *Annals Memoirs of the Court of Peking* (Heinemann, London, 1914).

BARBER, M., *The Trial of the Templars* (CUP, Cambridge, 1978).

BARKER, Sir E., *The Dominican Order and Convocation* (OUP, Oxford, 1913).

BARON, H., *The Crisis of the Italian Renaissance* (Princeton UP, Princeton, 1966).

BARRACLOUGH, G., *Factors in German History* (Blackwell, Oxford, 1946).

—— (ed., trans., and Introduction), *Medieval Germany, 911–1250: Essays by German Historians*, 2 vols. (Blackwell, Oxford, 1948).

—— *The Origins of Modern Germany* (Blackwell, 2nd revised edn., reprinted 1972, Oxford).

BAYNES, N. H., *The Byzantine Empire* (OUP, Oxford, 1925).

BECKER, P., 'The Florentine Territorial State and Civic Humanism in the Early Renaissance', in N. Rubinstein (ed.), *Florentine Studies* (Faber, London, 1968), 109–39.

BELLAH, R. N., *Sociologists at Work: Essays on the Craft of Social Research* (Basic Books, New York, 1964).

BENSON, R. L., 'Political *Renovatio*: Two Models from Roman Antiquity', in R. L. Benson and G. Constable (eds.), *Renaissance and Renewal in the Twelfth Century* (Clarendon Press, Oxford, 1977), 339–86.

BLOCH, M., *Feudal Society*, trans. L. Manyon, 2 vols. (Routledge & Kegan Paul, London, 1962; paperback edn., 1965).

BOISSEVAIN, J., 'Patronage in Sicily', *Man*, NS 1: 1 (Mar. 1966), 18–33.

—— *Friends of Friends* (Blackwell, Oxford, 1974).

BONJOUR, E., OFFLER, H., and POTTER, G. R., *A Short History of Switzerland* (Clarendon Press, Oxford, 1952).

BOSWORTH, C. E., 'Recruitment, Muster and Review in Medieval Islamic Armies', in V. J. Parry and M. G. Yapp, *War, Technology, and Society in the Middle East Essays* (OUP, Oxford, 1975), 44–77.

BOUTRUCHE, R., *Seigneurie et féodalité*, 2 vols. (Auber, Paris, 1968–70).

BOUWSMA, W., *Venice and the Defence of Republican Liberty* (University of California Press, Berkeley and Los Angeles, 1968).

BRAUDEL, F., *Civilisation and Capitalism: Fifteenth–Eighteenth Century*, trans. of *Le Temps du Monde* (1979), by S. Reynolds (Collins, London, 1981–4).

BRÉHIER, L., *Les Institutions de l'empire byzantin* (Albin Michel, Paris, 1949).

BROWN, H., *Studies in the History of Venice*, 2 vols. (Murray, London, 1907).

BROWN, P., *Augustine and Hippocratus* (Fodor, London, 1967).

BRUCKER, G. A., *Florentine Politics and Society, 1343–1378* (Princeton UP, Princeton, 1962).

BRYCE, J., *The Holy Roman Empire*, 4th edn. (Macmillan, London, 1889).

BULLIET, R. W., *Conversion to Islam in the Medieval Period* (Harvard UP, Cambridge, Mass., 1979).

BURKE, P., *Tradition and Innovation in Renaissance Italy* (Fontana, London, 1974).

—— 'City States', in J. A. Hall (ed.), *States in History* (Blackwell, Oxford, 1986), 137–53.

BURY, J. B. 'Roman Empire, Later', *Encyclopaedia Britannica* (11th edn.; 1910–11, vol. xxiii, p. 519).

BUTLER, W. F., *The Lombard Communes: A History of the Republics of North Italy* (Fisher Unwin, London, 1906), 229.

CAHEN, C., 'L'Évolution de l'iqta du IXe au XIIIe siécle' (first published in *Annales* (1953), 25–69; repr. in *Les Peuples musulmanes* (Damascus, Syria, 1977), 232–69).

Cambridge History of Africa, eds. J. D. Fage and R. Oliver, 8 vols. (CUP, Cambridge, 1975–85): vol. 2 (500 BC–AD 1050), ed. J. D. Fage (1979); vol. 3 (1050–1600), ed. R. Oliver (1977).

Cambridge History of China, vol. 3, pt. 1 ('Sui and T'ang China 509–906', ed. J. K. Fairbank & D. Twitchett (CUP, Cambridge, 1979).

Cambridge Medieval History, ed. J. M. Hussey (CUP, Cambridge, 1966).

CARLYLE, R. W., and A. J., *The History of Medieval Political Theory in the West*, 6 vols., 5th edn. (Blackwood, Edinburgh, 1971).

CHAMBERLIN, E. R., *The World of the Italian Renaissance* (Book Club Associates, London, 1982).

CHAN, A., *The Glory and Fall of the Ming Dynasty* (University of Oklahoma Press, 1982).

CH'IEN, M., HSUEH, C.-T., and TOTTEN, G. O., *Traditional Government in Imperial China* (Chinese UP, Hong Kong, 1982).

CHOJNACKI, S., 'In Search of the Venetian Patriciate: Families and Factions in the Fourteenth Century', in J. R. Hale, *Renaissance Venice* (London, 1973), 47–90.

CIPOLLA, C. C., *Fontana Economic History of Europe*, vol. I., *The Middle Ages* (Fontana, Glasgow, 1972).

COMNENA, A., *The Alexiad*, trans. E. R. A. Sewter (Penguin, Harmondsworth, 1969).

CONTAMINE, P., *War in the Middle Ages*, trans. M. Jones (Blackwell, Oxford, 1984).

COULBORN, R., *Feudalism in History* (Princeton UP, Princeton, 1956).

COULSON, N. J., *A History of Islamic Law* (Edinburgh UP, Edinburgh, 1964).

CRAWFORD, R. B., 'Eunuch Power in the Ming Dynasty', *T'oung Pao*, 49 (1961–2), 115–48.

CRONE, P., *Slaves on Horses: The Evolution of the Islamic Polity* (CUP, Cambridge, 1980).

—— *Roman, Provincial and Islamic Law* (CUP, Cambridge, 1987).

—— and COOK, M., *Hagarism: The Making of the Islamic World* (CUP, Cambridge, 1977).

—— and HINDS, M., *God's Caliph: Religious Authority in the First Centuries of Islam* (CUP, Cambridge, 1986).

DARDESS, J. W., *Conquerors and Confucians: Aspects of Political Change in Late Yüan China* (Columbia UP, New York, 1973).

DAWOOD, N. J. (ed.), and ROSENTHAL, F. (trans.), Ibu Khaldun (1332–1406): *The Muqaddimah: An Introduction to History* (Dawood abridged edn., Routledge, London, 1967).

DE BARY, W. T., 'Chinese Despotism and the Confucian Ideal: A Seventeenth-Century View', in J. Fairbank (ed.), *Chinese Thought and Institutions*, 163–203.

DE GOEJE, M. J., 'The Caliphate', *Encyclopaedia Britannica* (11th edn., 1910), v. 23–54.

DE LAGARDE, G., 'Les Théories représentatives du XIV–XV siècle et l'église', 10th International Congress of the Historical Sciences, Études, XVIII (Louvain, 1958).

DE LA RONCIÈRE, C. M., 'Indirect Taxes or "Gabelles" at Florence', in N. Rubenstein (ed.), *Florentine Studies* (London, 1968), 140–92.

DES ROTOURS, R., *Traité des fonctionnaires et traité de l'armée*, 2 vols., trans. from the *New History of the Tang* (Hsiu Ou Yang, chs. 46–50) (E. J. Brill, Leiden, 1947).

DIEHL, C., *Byzantium: Greatness and Decline*, trans. N. N. J. Watford (2nd French edn., 1926; Rutgers UP, Rutgers, 1957).

DONNER, F. M., *The Early Islamic Conquests* (Princeton UP, Princeton, 1981).

DU BOULAY, F. R. H., *Germany in the Later Middle Ages* (Athlone Press, London, 1985).

DUGUIT, L., *Law in the Modern State* (Allen & Unwin, London, 1924).

DUNBABIN, J., *France in the Making, 843–1180* (OUP, Oxford, 1985).

DURAND, Y., *Les Républiques au temps des monarchies* (Collection SUP, Presses Universitaires de France, Paris, 1973).

EBERHARD, W., *A History of China*, 4th edn. (Routledge and Kegan Paul, London, 1977; 1st edn., 1930).

—— *Conquerors and Rulers: Social Forces in Medieval China* (Brill, Leiden, 1952).

ELVIN, M., *Pattern of the Chinese Past* (Eyre-Methuen, London, 1973).

FAIRBANK, J. K. (ed.), *Chinese Thought and Institutions* (University of Chicago Press, Chicago, 1957).

FINER, S. E. (selected and introduced), *Pareto, Sociological Writings* (Pall Mall Press, London, 1966).

—— *Comparative Government* (Penguin, Harmondsworth, 1974).

—— *The Man on Horseback: The Role of the Military in Politics* (2nd edn., Westview Press, Boulder, Colorado, 1988).

—— 'Patrons, Clients and the State in the Work of Pareto and at the Present Day', *Atti dei convegni Lincei*, (Accademia dei Lincei, Rome, 1973), 165–86.

FINLAY, G., *History of the Byzantine Empire, 716–1057* (1st pub. 1854; Everyman edn., Dent, London, 1906).

FINLAY, R., *Politics in Renaissance Venice* (Benn, London, 1980).

FITZGERALD, C. P., *The Empress Wu* (University of British Columbia Press, Vancouver, 1968).

FOWLER, K. (ed.), *The Hundred Years War* (Macmillan, London, 1971).

FROISSART, J., *Chronicles*, trans. and ed. G. Brereton (abridged edn., Penguin, Harmondsworth, 1978).

FUHRMANN, H., *Germany in the High Middle Ages, c.1050–1200* (CUP, Cambridge, 1986).

GABRIELI, F., *Muhammed and the Conquests of Islam* (Weidenfeld and Nicolson, London, 1968).

GANSHOF, F. L., *Qu'est-ce-que La Féodalité?*, 2nd edn. (de la Baconnière, Neuchâtel, 1947).

GELLNER, E., *Muslim Society* (CUP, Cambridge, 1981).

—— and WATERBURY, J. (eds.), *Patrons and Clients* (Duckworth, London, 1977).

GERNET, J., *A History of Chinese Civilization*, trans. R. J. Foster (CUP, Cambridge, 1982).

GIBB, H. A. R., 'Al Mawardi's Theory of the Khilafa', *Islamic Culture*, 9: 3 (1937), 291–302.

—— 'Constitutional Organisation', in M. Khadduri and H. J. Liebesny (eds.), *Law in the Middle East*, vol. 1 (Washington, 1955), 3–27.

—— and BOWEN, H., *Islamic Society and the West*, vol. 1, pts. 1 and 2 (Royal Institute of International Affairs, London, 1950).

GIBBON, E., *The Decline and Fall of the Roman Empire* (David Campbell, London, 1993–4).

GILBERT, F., 'The Venetian Constitution in Florentine Political Thought', in N. Rubinstein (ed.), *Florentine Studies*, 463–500.

GRAMSCI, A., *The Modern Prince and other Writings* (Lawrence & Wishart, London, 1957).

GRÜNEBAUM, E. E. von, 'The Sources of Islamic Civilisation' in P. M. Holt, A. K. S. Lambton, and B. Lewis (eds.) *Cambridge History of Islam*, vol. 2 (CUP, Cambridge, 1970), 469–510.

GUILLAND, R., 'Fonctions et dignités des Eunuques', *Études byzantines*, 2 (1944), 185–255, and 3 (1945), 179–210.

GUILLAUME, A., *Islam* (Penguin, Harmondsworth, 1954).

HALE, J. R., *Renaissance Venice* (Faber and Faber, London, 1973).

—— HIGHFIELD, J., and SMALLEY, B. (eds.), *Europe in the Late Middle Ages* (Faber and Faber, London, 1965).

HALL, J. A. (ed.), *States in History* (Blackwell, Oxford, 1986).

HALLAQ, W. B., 'Was the Gate of Ijtihad Closed?', *International Journal of Middle East Studies*, 16 (1984), 3–41.

HARRINGTON, J., *The Commonwealth of Oceana* (1656; Routledge, London, 1887).

HEIDENHEIMER, A. J. (ed.), *Political Corruption* (Transaction Books, New Brunswick/London, 1989).

HENNEMAN, J. B., *Royal Taxation in Fourteenth-Century France* (Princeton UP, Princeton, 1971).

HODGSON, M. G. S., *The Venture of Islam*, vol. I, *The Classical Age of Islam* (University of Chicago Press, Chicago, 1974).

HOURANI, A., *A History of the Arab Peoples* (Faber, London, 1991).

—— *Islam in European Thought* (CUP, Cambridge, 1991).

HSIEN HSIEN, *The Li Ki*, trans. S. Couvreur, 2 vols. (Imprimerie de la Mission Catholique, 1913).

HSU, I. C. Y., *Rise of Modern China*, 3rd edn. (OUP, Oxford, 1983).

HUANG, R., *Taxation and Governmental Finance in XVI-Century Ming China* (CUP, London, 1974).

—— *1587: A Year of No Significance* (Yale UP, New Haven, Conn., 1981).

HUCKER, C. O., 'The Tung-lin Movement of the Late Ming Period', in Fairbank (ed.), *Chinese Thought and Institutions*, 132–62.

—— 'Government and Organisation of the Ming Dynasty', *Harvard Journal of Asiatic Studies*, 21 (1958), 1–66.

—— *The Traditional Chinese State in the Ming Times (1368–1644)* (University of Arizona Press, Tucson, Texas, 1961).

—— *The Censorial System of Ming China* (Stanford UP, Stanford, 1966).

—— *Chinese Government in Ming Times: Seven Studies* (Columbia UP, New York, 1969).

JOHNSON, W., *The T'ang Code*, vol. 1, *General Principles* (Princeton UP, Princeton, 1979).

KANTOROWICZ, E. H., *Frederick the Second: 1194–1250* (Constable, London, 1931).

—— *The King's Two Bodies: A Study in Medieval Political Theology* (Princeton UP, Princeton, 1957; paperback edn., 1981).

KENNEDY, H., 'Central Government and Provincial Élites in the Early Abbasid Empire', *Bulletin of the School of African and Oriental Studies*, 44 (1981), 26–38.

KENNEDY, P., *The Rise and Fall of the Great Powers: Economic Change and Military Conflict, 1500–2000* (Fontana, London, 1988).

KHADDURI, M., and LIEBESNY, H. J. (eds.), *Law in the Middle East*, vol. 1 (The Middle East Institute, Washington DC, 1955).

KRACKE, E. A., *The Civil Service in Early Sung China, 960–1067* (Harvard UP, Cambridge, Mass., 1953).

LANE, F., *Venice: A Maritime Republic* (Johns Hopkins UP, Baltimore, 1973).

LANGER, W. L., *Encyclopaedia of World History: Ancient, Medieval and Modern*, 5th edn. (Harrap, London, 1972).

LAOUST, H., *Les Schismes dans l'Islam* (Payot, Paris, 1977).

LE PATOUREL, J., 'The Origin of the War', in K. Fowler (ed.), *The Hundred Years War* (Macmillan, London, 1971), 28–50.

LECKY, W. H., *History of the Rise and Influence of the Spirit of Rationalism in Europe* (1st edn., Longman, London, 1865; Green, 1910).

—— *The History of Morals from Constantine to Charlemagne* (Watt and Co., London, 1924).

LEVY, R., *The Social Structure of Islam*, 2nd edn. (CUP, Cambridge, 1957).

LEWIS, B. (ed.), *Islam: From the Prophet Muhammad to the Capture of Constantinople*, 2 vols., *Excerpts from Muslim Writers: The Documentary History of Western Civilization* (Macmillan, London, 1974).

LEWIS, N., *The Honoured Society: The Mafia Conspiracy Observed* (Collins, London, 1964).

LEWIS, P. S., *The Recovery of France in the Fifteenth Century* (Macmillan, London, 1971).

LO, J. P., 'Policy Formulation and Decision-Making', in C. O. Hucker, *Chinese Government in Ming Times*, 41–72.

LORD, R. H., 'The Parliaments of the Middle Ages and the Early Modern Period', *Catholic Historical Review*, 16 (1930), 125–8.

LOT, F., *L'Art militaire et les armées au moyen âge*, 2 vols. (Payot, Paris, 1946).

—— and FAWTIER, R., *Histoire des institutions françaises au moyen-âge*, 2 vols. (Presses Universitaires de France, Paris 1957–62).

LOUSSE, E., *La Société d'ancien régime*, 2nd edn. (Editions Universitas, Louvain, 1952).

LUCHAIRE, A., *Histoire des institutions monarchiques de la France sous les premiers Capétiens* (Paris, 1892).

LYONS, H. R., *Anglo-Saxon England and the Norman Conquest* (Longman, London, 1962).

MACHIAVELLI, N., *Istorie fiorentine* (Feltrinelli Editore, Milano, 1962).

McILWAIN, C. H., *The Growth of Political Thought in the West* (Macmillan, London, 1932).

—— *Constitutionalism, Ancient and Modern* (Cornell UP, Ithaca, 1940).

McKNIGHT, B. E., *Village and Bureaucracy in Southern Sung China* (Chicago UP, Chicago, 1971).

MADISON, J., HAMILTON, A., and Jay, J. *The Federalist Papers* (Penguin, Harmondsworth, 1987).

MAITLAND, F. W., *The Constitutional History of England* (CUP, Cambridge, 1908).

MAMMITZSCH, U. H.-R., 'Wei Chung-Hsien (1568–1628): A Reappraisal of the Eunuch and Factional Strife at the Late Ming Court', unpublished Ph.D. thesis, University of Hawaii, 1968.

MANGO, C., *Byzantium: The Empire of New Rome* (Weidenfeld and Nicolson, London, 1980).

MARANINI, G., *La Costituzione di Venezia*, 2 vols. (La nuove Italia, Venice, 1927–31).

MARGOLIOUTH, D., and AMEDROZ, H. (eds.), *The Eclipse of the Abbasid Caliphate (being the 'History' of Ibn-Maiskawayhi [930–1030])*, 6 vols. (Blackwells, Oxford, 1921).

MARONGIU, A., *Medieval Parliaments: A Comparative Study*, trans. and adapted by S. J. Woolf, foreword by H. Cam (Eyre & Spottiswoode, London, 1968). (Originally published as *Parlamento in Italia nel mediævo e nell'eré moderna*, 1949.)

MARTINES, L., *Power and Imagination: City States in Renaissance Italy* (Knopf, New York, 1979).

MASPERO, H., and BALAZS, E., *Histoire et institutions de la Chine ancienne* (revised edn., Demi-ville, Paris; Presses Universitaires de France, Paris, 1967).

MATHERS, E. P. (ed.), *A Thousand Nights and One Night*, English trans. from J. C. Mardrus's French trans. (Routledge, London, 1947).

MEZ, A., *The Renaissance of Islam*, trans. S. Baksh and D. Margoliouth (Jubilee Printing and Publishing House, Patna, India, 1937).

MITTEIS, H., *The State in the Middle Ages* (North Holland Publishing Co., Amsterdam, 1975).

MIYAZAKI, I., *The Administration of Justice During the Sung Dynasty: Essays on China's Legal Tradition*, eds. J. Cohen, R. Edwards, and F.-M. Cha (Princeton UP, Princeton, 1980).

MONTESQUIEU, *Lettres persanes*, preface de J. Starobinski (Gallimard, Paris, 1973).

MOTE, F. W., 'The Growth of Chinese Despotism: A Critique of Wittfogel's Theory of Oriental Despotism as Applied to China', *Oriens Extremus*, Year 8 (1961), 1–41.

MOULIN, L., 'Policy-making in the Religious Orders', *Government and Opposition*, 1: 1 (1965), 25–54.

MUIR, W., *The Caliphate: Its Rise, Decline and Fall* (Religious Tract Society, London, 1892).

MUNDY, J. H., *Europe in the High Middle Ages, 1150–1309* (Longman, London, 1973).

MYERS, A. R., *Parliaments and Estates in Europe* (Thames & Hudson, London, 1975).

NEILSON, N., 'The Early Pattern of the Common Law', *American Historical Review*, 49 (1944), 199–212.

NORWICH, J. J., *A History of Venice* (Penguin, Harmondsworth, 1983).

OBOLENSKY, D., *The Byzantine Commonwealth* (Cardinal edn., 1974; Weidenfeld & Nicolson, London, 1971).

OLDENBOURG, Z., *The World is Not Enough* (Gollancz, London, 1949).

—— *The Corner Stone* (Gollancz, London, 1954).

OSTROGORSKY, G., *History of the Byzantine State*, trans. J. Hussey (Blackwell, Oxford, 1956).

PAINTER, S., *Studies in the History of the English Feudal Barony* (Johns Hopkins UP, Baltimore, 1943).

PARETO, V., *A Treatise on General Sociology*, ed. A. Livingstone, trans. A. Bongiorno and A. Livingstone as 'The Mind and Society' (Cape, London, 1935).

PARRY, V. J., 'Warfare', *Cambridge History of Islam*, vol. 2. (CUP, Cambridge, 1970), 824–50.

—— and YAPP, M. G., *War Technology and Society in the Middle East: Essays* (OUP, Oxford, 1975).

PETERSON, C. A., 'The Restoration Completed: Emperor Hsian-tsung and the Provinces', in Wright and Twitchett, *Perspectives on the T'ang*, 151–191.

PETIT-DUTAILLIS, C., *La Monarchie féodale en France et en Angleterre, X–XII siècle* (Renaissance du Livre, Paris, 1933).

PIPES, D., *Slave Soldiers and Islam* (Yale UP, New Haven, Conn., 1981).

PIRENNE, H., *Medieval Cities* (Princeton UP, Princeton, 1925).

PITKIN, H., *The Concept of Representation* (University of California Press, Berkeley and Los Angeles, 1967).

POCOCK, J., *The Machiavellian Moment* (Princeton UP, Princeton, 1975).

POGGI, G., *The Development of the Modern State* (Hutchinson, London, 1978).

POWICKE, Sir M., *The Thirteenth Century, 1216–1307* (OUP, Oxford, 1962).

PRESTWICH, M., *War, Politics and Finance under Edward I* (Faber & Faber, London, 1972).

PSELLUS, Michael, *Fourteen Byzantine Rules (The Chronographia)*, trans. E. R. A. Sewter (Penguin, Harmondsworth, 1982).

PULLEYBLANK, E. G., *The Background of the Rebellion of An Lu-shan* (OUP, London, 1955).

REISCHAUER, E. O., *Ennin's Diary: The Record of a Pilgrimage to T'ang in Search of the Law* (Ronald Press, New York, 1955).

REYNOLDS, S., *Kingdoms and Communities in Western Europe, 900–1300* (Clarendon Press, Oxford, 1984).

RICCI, MATTEO, *Della entrata della Compagnia di Giesu e Christianita nella Cina*, 3 vols. (Vatican City, Rome, Fonte Ricciani, 1609).

RIDEOUT, J. K., 'The Rise of the Eunuchs During the T'ang Dynasty', Part I (618–705), *Asia Major*, 1 (1949), 53–72; Part II, *Asia Major*, 3 (1953), 42–58.

ROUSSEAU, J. J., *Contrat Social* (Manchester UP, Manchester, 1918; repr. 1955).

RUBINSTEIN, N., 'Marsilius of Padua and Italian Political Thought of his Time', in J. R. Hale, J. Highfield, and B. Smalley (eds.), *Europe in the Late Middle Ages* (Faber & Faber, London, 1965), 44–75.

—— (ed.), *Florentine Studies: Politics and Society in Renaissance Florence* (Faber & Faber, London, 1968).

RUNCIMAN, S., *The Emperor Romanos Lecapenus and his Reign* (CUP, Cambridge, 1963).

—— *A History of the Crusades*, 3 vols. (CUP, Cambridge, 1951; reissued Peregrine Books, Harmondsworth, 1978).

RUNCIMAN, W. G. (ed.), *Max Weber: Selection in Translation*, trans. E. Matthews (CUP, Cambridge, 1978).

RUTHVEN, M., *Islam in the World* (Penguin, Harmondsworth, 1984).

SAVORY, R. M., *Introduction to Islamic Civilization* (CUP, Cambridge, 1976).

SAYLES, G. O., *The Medieval Foundations of England*, 2nd edn. (Methuen, London, 1950).

SCHACHT, J., *The Origins of Muhammadan Jurisprudence* (OUP, Oxford, 1950).

—— *Introduction to Islamic Law* (OUP, Oxford, 1982).

SCHEVILL, F., *History of Florence* (F. Ungar, New York; repr. 1976).

SHIH, N., and LO, K.-C., *Outlaws of the Marsh*, trans. S. Shapiro (Foreign Language Press, Beijing, 1980).

SHOSHAN, B., 'Review of *The Politics of Notables in Medieval Islam*' (*Asian and African Studies*, Haifa, 1986).

SIDGWICK, H., *The Development of the European Polity* (Macmillan, London, 1903).

SKINNER, Q., *The Foundations of Modern Political Thought*, 2 vols. (CUP, Cambridge, 1978).

SOURDEL, D., *Le Vizirat abbasside de 749–936* (Damascus, Syria, 1959–60).

—— and J., *La Civilisation de l'Islam classique* (Artaud, Damascus, 1968).

SOUTHERN, R. W., *Western Society and the Church in the Middle Ages* (Penguin, Harmondsworth, 1970).

SPUFFORD, P., *The Origins of the English Parliament: Readings* (Longman, London, 1967).

STRAYER, J., and MUNRO, D., *The Middle Ages, 395–1500* (Appleton-Century, New York, 1942).

STUBBS, W., *The Constitutional History of England*, 3 vols. (OUP, Oxford, 1880).

—— *Select Charters*, 8th edn. (OUP, Oxford, 1900).

TABARI, *Chroniques: L'Age d'or des Abbasides*, trans. H. Zotenberg (Sinahad, Paris, 1983).

TEMPERLEY, H. (ed.), *Selected Essays of J. B. Bury* (CUP, Cambridge, 1930).

THOMPSON, J. W., *Feudal Germany* (University of Chicago Press, Chicago, 1928).

TSURUMI, N., 'Rural Control in the Ming Dynasty', in L. Groves and C. Daniels (eds.), *State and Society in China: Japanese Perspectives on Ming and Qing Social and Economic History* (University of Tokyo Press, Tokyo, 1984).

TWITCHETT, D. C., 'The T'ang Market System', *Asia Major*, 12: 2 (1966), 202–48.

—— 'Local Financial Administration in Early T'ang Times', *Asia Major*, 15 (1969), 82–143.

TYAN, E., *Histoire de l'organisation judiciaire en pays d'Islam* (Brill, Leiden, 1960).

ULLMANN, W., *Principles of Governance and Politics in the Middle Ages* (Methuen, London, 1961).

—— *A History of Political Thought in the Middle Ages* (Penguin, Harmondsworth, 1965).

VAILLAND, R., *La Loi: roman* (Gallimard, Paris, 1957; repr. 1963).

VAN GULIK, R., *The Chinese Lake Murders* (University Chicago Press, Chicago, 1977).

VAN WERVEKE, H., 'The Economic Policies of Governments: The Low Countries', *Cambridge Economic History of Europe*, vol. 3 (CUP, Cambridge, 1963).

VASILIEV, A. A., *History of the Byzantine Empire*, 2nd Eng. edn. (Blackwell, Oxford, 1952).

VATIKIOTIS, P. J., *Islam and the State* (Routledge, London, 1987).

VILLON, F., *Ballades* (Allan Wingate, London, 1946).

WAKEMAN, F., and GRANT, C. (eds.), *Conflict and Control in Late Imperial China: Essays* (University of California Press, Berkeley, 1978).

WALLACE-HADRILL, J. M., *Early Germanic Kingship in England and on the Continent* (Clarendon Press, Oxford, 1971).

WANG, G., *The Structure of Power in North China During the Five Dynasties* (Stanford UP, Stanford, 1963).

WARE, T., *The Orthodox Church* (Penguin, Harmondsworth, 1980).

WATT, W. M., *Islamic Political Thought* (Edinburgh UP, Edinburgh, 1964; paperback edn., 1980).

WEBER, M., *Economy and Society: An Outline of Interpretive Sociology*, vol. 2, eds. G. Roth and C. Wittich (University of California Press, Berkeley, 1978).

WECHSLER, H. J., *Mirror to the Son of Heaven: Wei-ching at the Court of T'ang Tai-tsung* (Yale UP, New Haven, Conn., 1974).

WELLHAUSEN, J., *The Arab Kingdom and its Fall* (= *Das Arabische Reich und sein Sturz*, Berlin 1902; repr. Calcutta, 1927).

WHITE, L., *Medieval Technology and Social Change* (OUP, Oxford, 1962).

WRIGHT, A. F., and TWITCHETT, D. C. (eds.), *Perspectives on the T'ang* (Yale UP, New Haven, Conn., 1973).

WU, C.-T., *The Scholars* (Foreign Languages Press, Beijing, 1973).